CRIME STATE RANKINGS
1994

Crime in the 50 United States

Kathleen O'Leary Morgan, Scott Morgan and Neal Quitno, Editors

Morgan Quitno Corporation
© Copyright 1994, All Rights Reserved

P.O. Box 1656, Lawrence, KS 66044
800-457-0742 or 913-841-3534

Crime State Rankings 1994 sells for $43.95 (we pay shipping). For those who prefer ranking information tailored to a particular state, we also offer _Crime State Perspectives_, state-specific reports for each of the 50 states. These individual guides provide information on a state's data and rank for each of the categories featured in the national _Crime State Rankings_ volume. Perspectives sell for $18.00, $9.00 if ordered with _Crime State Rankings_. If you are interested in a general view of the states, please ask about our annual _State Rankings_. If health care statistics are your interest, please ask about our annual _Health Care State Rankings_.

First Edition
Printed in the United States of America
January 1994

PREFACE

Few issues are as widely discussed as crime is today. With so many Americans agreeing that crime is among this country's most serious problems, we decided that it was time to consult the experts and gather the facts about crime in the 50 United States.

Crime State Rankings 1994 was developed to shed light on the dark world of crime with accessible, easily understood facts. Within its covers, readers will find an overwhelming amount of data on arrests, offenses, corrections, law enforcement personnel and finance, courts and, because of their close link to crime, drugs and alcohol. It is important to note that the vast majority of crimes are not reported to police. Based on a recent survey of crime victims, the U.S. Department of Justice (DOJ) estimates that overall 39% of crimes were reported to police in 1992. Specifically, DOJ estimates that 50% of violent crimes, 41% of household crimes and 30% of personal thefts were reported. (Interestingly, 92% of motor vehicle thefts, an insured loss, were reported to police.) Given these estimates, the true dimension of the crime problem in the United States is mind boggling.

Much of what makes this book useful has been taken from what we have learned in publishing our general *State Rankings* volume since 1990 and our *Health Care State Rankings* book beginning last year. Features such as table listings at the beginning of each chapter, a detailed index, a complete table of contents and a chapter "thumb index" in the back of the book make this a reference tool that enables researchers to search for answers rather than hunt for instructions on how to use the book.

Every table follows the same format. Each tells a very different story, but in similar language. As with previous editions, this book presents each category on one page displaying all fifty states (and usually the District of Columbia) in rank order, from highest to lowest. We leave it to you to decide if a particular category is "good" or "bad". Any ties among the states are listed alphabetically for a given ranking. National figures are shown at the top of each table and all sources and footnotes appear on the same page for quick reference. Should you require further information from a source, a roster of addresses and telephone numbers is provided.

In cases where a table shows a national total, not only is each state's total listed, but also its percentage of the national total. This percentage number appears in a column headed by a percent sign (%). For example, table 311 shows that 16.1% of the nation's robberies are in New York. This percentage figure is particularly interesting when compared with a state's share of the nation's population for the appropriate year.

Another feature we've continued in this edition is including all the necessary "zeroes" in state and national numbers. This way those of you with broken calculators don't have to figure out if a table is showing thousands, millions or whatever. While this is a small matter, it is indicative of the care we take to see that the book does not get in the way of the facts.

For those interested in focusing on crime information for just one state, we once again are offering our *State Perspective* series of publications. These 23-page, comb-bound reports feature data and ranking information for an individual state, pulled from *Crime State Rankings 1994.* (For example, *New York Crime in Perspective* contains crime information about the state of New York only.) When purchased by themselves, *State Perspectives* sell for $18. When bought with a copy of *Crime State Rankings 1994,* perspectives are just $9.

Our company also continues to offer two other publications, *State Rankings* and *Health Care State Rankings.* In its fifth edition in 1994, *State Rankings* provides a general view of the states by featuring state statistics in categories ranging from agriculture to transportation, taxes to education and social welfare to health. This book has received great acclaim for its ease of use and simple presentation of state data. Also receiving rave reviews is *Health Care State Rankings,* a series we began last year. Following the same format as the book you are holding, *Health Care State Rankings* simply focuses on state health issues instead of crime. Included in this volume are data on health care facilities, providers, insurance and finance, incidence of disease, mortality, physical fitness, natality and reproductive health. Both *State Rankings* and *Health Care State Rankings* sell for $43.95 each including shipping. *State Perspectives* are also available for each of these books, selling for $18 individually and $9 if purchased with their corresponding national volume. If you would like a brochure or further information, please call us at 1-800-457-0742.

Finally, many thanks to all of the hard working librarians and government workers who so willingly helped us in developing, designing and producing this book. As always, a special thanks to the very helpful librarians at the Kansas State Library. Most of all, thanks to you, our readers. We enjoy doing this and appreciate your feedback -- so please give us a call or write us with your suggestions by filling out the postage-paid card provided .

THE EDITORS

WHICH STATE IS THE MOST *DANGEROUS?*

It's fun. It's beautiful. It's a great place for jazz. But on the whole, Louisiana is 1994's "Most Dangerous State." The Bayou State has the dubious distinction of being the first to receive this designation. Conversely, Vermont registers as the safest.

Using 16 basic criteria (listed below) the Most Dangerous State was determined by comparing factors such as state crime rates, juvenile crime statistics, crime clearances, police protection and expenditures. These provide a sound statistical basis for comparing states' abilities to keep their streets safe for the average citizen.

Once the factors were determined, we averaged each state's ranking for all 16 categories. Based on these averages, states were then ranked from "most dangerous" (lowest average ranking) to "safest" (highest average rankings). States with no data available for a given category were assigned a zero for that category and ranked on the remaining factors. In our book, data are listed from highest to lowest. However, for the purposes of this calculation, we inverted the rankings for those factors we determined to be "positive." Thus, in the book, the state with the lowest percent of crimes cleared (ranking 50th) would be given a #1 ranking for this designation.

Morgan Quitno prides itself on presenting facts without bias and in an objective manner. A central theme of our books is that we present the data and leave the analysis to our readers. However, with each new series we take what we determine to be the most critical statistics, throw them into our computer and present an "award" based on the results. Annually since 1991 we have named the "Most Livable State" and in 1993, the "Healthiest State." With the debut of this third series of books, *Crime State Rankings*, we begin the "Most Dangerous State" designation.

We realize that those living in high ranking states may take offense at our characterization of their home states as "dangerous." However, our intent is not to anger, but rather to facilitate a productive discussion on a problem of great concern to us all.

THE EDITORS

1994 MOST DANGEROUS STATE

STATE	AVG	STATE	AVG
1. Louisiana	10.63	26. Washington	25.13
2. Maryland	12.81	27. Oregon	25.44
3. Texas	15.00	28. Hawaii	25.75
4. Illinois	15.31	29. Massachusetts	26.63
5. Florida	15.81	30. Arkansas	27.00
6. California	16.50	31. Connecticut	27.44
7. Nevada	16.75	32. Mississippi	27.94
8. New York	17.13	33. Wisconsin	28.06
9. Arizona	18.13	34. Minnesota	28.31
10. South Carolina	18.14	35. Utah	29.44
11. Georgia	18.75	36. Rhode Island	29.63
12. Michigan	18.81	37. Pennsylvania	30.38
13. New Mexico	18.88	38. Virginia	30.63
14. Missouri	19.88	39. Idaho	31.94
15. Kansas	20.19	40. Wyoming	32.69
16. Alabama	20.44	41. Montana	33.13
17. New Jersey	20.63	42. Kentucky	34.00
18. Oklahoma	20.88	43. South Dakota	34.31
19. Tennessee	21.69	44. Nebraska	34.50
20. Colorado	22.88	45. New Hampshire	35.81
21. Delaware	22.94	46. West Virginia	37.75
22. North Carolina	23.25	47. North Dakota	39.00
23. Ohio	23.38	48. Iowa	39.43
24. Alaska	24.00	49. Maine	43.06
25. Indiana	24.81	50. Vermont	45.81

NEGATIVE FACTORS CONSIDERED:
1. Crime Rate in 1992 (Table 277)
2. Violent Crime Rate in 1992 (Table 283)
3. Murder Rate in 1992 (Table 289)
4. Rape Rate in 1992 (Table 308)
5. Robbery Rate in 1992 (Table 314)
6. Aggravated Assault Rate in 1992 (Table 328)
7. Property Crime Rate in 1992 (Table 343)
8. Percent Change in Crime Rate: 1988 to 1992 (Table 413)
9. Percent Change in Violent Crime Rate: 1988 to 1992 (Table 417)
10. State Prisoner Incarceration Rate in 1992 (Table 73)

11. Reported Arrests of Youths 17 Years and Younger as a Percent of All Arrests in 1992 (Table 36)
12. Reported Arrests of Youths 17 Years and Younger for Violent Crime as a Percent of All Such Arrests in 1992 (Table 38)
13. State-Local Government Expenditures for Police Protection as a Percent of All Direct Expenditures in 1991 (Table 182)
14. Full-Time Sworn Officers in Law Enforcement Agencies per 10,000 Population in 1992 (Table 224)

POSITIVE FACTORS CONSIDERED:
15. Percent of Crimes Cleared in 1991 (Table 450)
16. Percent of Violent Crimes Cleared in 1991 (Table 451)

TABLE OF CONTENTS

I. Arrests

1	Reported Arrests in 1992
2	Reported Arrest Rate in 1992
3	Reported Arrests for Violent Crime in 1992
4	Reported Arrest Rate for Violent Crime in 1992
5	Reported Arrests for Murder in 1992
6	Reported Arrest Rate for Murder in 1992
7	Reported Arrests for Rape in 1992
8	Reported Arrest Rate for Rape in 1992
9	Reported Arrests for Robbery in 1992
10	Reported Arrest Rate for Robbery in 1992
11	Reported Arrests for Aggravated Assault in 1992
12	Reported Arrest Rate for Aggravated Assault in 1992
13	Reported Arrests for Property Crime in 1992
14	Reported Arrest Rate for Property Crime in 1992
15	Reported Arrests for Burglary in 1992
16	Reported Arrest Rate for Burglary in 1992
17	Reported Arrests for Larceny and Theft in 1992
18	Reported Arrest Rate for Larceny and Theft in 1992
19	Reported Arrests for Motor Vehicle Theft in 1992
20	Reported Arrest Rate for Motor Vehicle Theft in 1992
21	Reported Arrests for Arson in 1992
22	Reported Arrest Rate for Arson in 1992
23	Reported Arrests for Weapons Violations in 1992
24	Reported Arrest Rate for Weapons Violations in 1992
25	Reported Arrests for Driving Under the Influence in 1992

26   Reported Arrest Rate for Driving Under the Influence in 1992

27   Reported Arrests for Drug Abuse Violations in 1992

28   Reported Arrest Rate for Drug Abuse Violations in 1992

29   Reported Arrests for Sex Offenses in 1992

30   Reported Arrest Rate for Sex Offenses in 1992

31   Reported Arrests for Prostitution and Commercialized Vice in 1992

32   Reported Arrest Rate for Prostitution and Commercialized Vice in 1992

33   Reported Arrests for Offenses Against Families and Children in 1992

34   Reported Arrest Rate for Offenses Against Families and Children in 1992

Juvenile Arrests

35   Reported Arrests of Youths 17 Years and Younger in 1992

36   Reported Arrests of Youths 17 Years and Younger as a Percent of All Arrests in 1992

37   Reported Arrests of Youths 17 Years and Younger for Violent Crime in 1992

38   Reported Arrests of Youths 17 Years and Younger for Violent Crime as a Percent of All Such Arrests in 1992

39   Reported Arrests of Youths 17 Years and Younger for Murder in 1992

40   Reported Arrests of Youths 17 Years and Younger for Murder as a Percent of All Such Arrests in 1992

41   Reported Arrests of Youths 17 Years and Younger for Rape in 1992

42   Reported Arrests of Youths 17 Years and Younger for Rape as a Percent of All Such Arrests in 1992

43   Reported Arrests of Youths 17 Years and Younger for Robbery in 1992

44   Reported Arrests of Youths 17 Years and Younger for Robbery as a Percent of All Such Arrests in 1992

45   Reported Arrests of Youths 17 Years and Younger for Aggravated Assault in 1992

46   Reported Arrests of Youths 17 Years & Younger for Aggravated Assault as a Percent of All Such Arrests 1992

47   Reported Arrests of Youths 17 Years and Younger for Property Crimes in 1992

48   Reported Arrests of Youths 17 Years & Younger for Property Crime as a Percent of All Such Arrests in 1992

49   Reported Arrests of Youths 17 Years and Younger for Burglary in 1992

50   Reported Arrests of Youths 17 Years and Younger for Burglary as a Percent of All Such Arrests in 1992

51   Reported Arrests of Youths 17 Years and Younger for Larceny and Theft in 1992

52   Reported Arrests of Youths 17 Years and Younger for Larceny & Theft as a Percent of All Such Arrests: 1992

53   Reported Arrests of Youths 17 Years and Younger for Motor Vehicle Theft in 1992

54 Reported Arrests of Youths 17 Years and Younger for Motor Vehicle Theft as a Percent of All Such Arrests in 1992
55 Reported Arrests of Youths 17 Years and Younger for Arson in 1992
56 Reported Arrests of Youths 17 Years and Younger for Arson as a Percent of All Such Arrests in 1992
57 Reported Arrests of Youths 17 Years and Younger for Weapons Violations in 1992
58 Reported Arrests of Youths 17 Years and Younger for Weapons Violations as a Percent of All Such Arrests in 1992
59 Reported Arrests of Youths 17 Years and Younger for Driving Under the Influence in 1992
60 Reported Arrests of Youths 17 & Younger for Driving Under the Influence as a Percent of All Such Arrests in 1992
61 Reported Arrests of Youths 17 Years and Younger for Drug Abuse Violations in 1992
62 Reported Arrests of Youths 17 & Younger for Drug Abuse Violations as a Percent of All Such Arrests: 1992
63 Reported Arrests of Youths 17 Years and Younger for Sex Offenses in 1992
64 Reported Arrests of Youths 17 Years & Younger for Sex Offenses as a Percent of All Such Arrests: 1992
65 Reported Arrests of Youths 17 and Younger for Prostitution & Commercialized Vice in 1992
66 Reported Arrests of Youths 17 & Younger for Prostitution & Commercialized Vice as a % of All Such Arrests: 1992
67 Reported Arrests of Youths 17 and Younger for Offenses Against Families and Children in 1992
68 Reported Arrests of Youths 17 & Younger for Offenses Against Families & Children as a % of All Such Arrests: 1992

II. Corrections

69 Prisoners in State Correctional Institutions in 1992
70 Prisoners in State Correctional Institutions in 1991
71 Percent Change in Number of State Prisoners: 1991 to 1992
72 State Prisoners Sentenced to More than One Year in 1992
73 State Prisoner Incarceration Rate in 1992
74 State Prison Population as a Percent of Highest Capacity in 1992
75 Female Prisoners in State Correctional Institutions in 1992
76 Female Prisoners in State Correctional Institutions as a Percent of All Prisoners: 1992
77 Percent Change in Female Prisoner Population: 1991 to 1992
78 White Prisoners in State Correctional Institutions in 1991
79 Black Prisoners in State Correctional Institutions in 1991

80 Average Annual Operating Expenditures per Inmate in 1990
81 State Prison Inmates Serving Life Sentences in 1992
82 Percent of State Prison Inmates Serving Life Sentences in 1992
83 Prisoners Under Sentence of Death in 1991
84 Male Prisoners Under Sentence of Death in 1991
85 Female Prisoners Under Sentence of Death in 1991
86 Percent of Prisoners Under Sentence of Death Who Are Female: 1991
87 White Prisoners Under Sentence of Death in 1991
88 Percent of Prisoners Under Sentence of Death Who Are White: 1991
89 Black Prisoners Under Sentence of Death in 1991
90 Percent of Prisoners Under Sentence of Death Who Are Black: 1991
91 Prisoners Executed: 1930 to 1991
92 Prisoners Executed: 1977 to 1991
93 Prisoners Sentenced to Death: 1973 to 1991
94 Death Sentences Overturned or Commuted: 1973–91
95 Percent of Death Penalty Sentences Overturned or Commuted: 1973–91
96 Sentenced Prisoners Admitted to State Correctional Institutions in 1991
97 New State Prisoners Admitted Through New Court Commitments in 1991
98 Parole Violators Returned to State Prison in 1991
99 Escapees Returned to State Prison in 1991
100 Prisoners Released from State Correctional Institutions in 1991
101 State Prisoners Released with Conditions in 1991
102 State Prisoners Released Conditionally as a Percent of All Releases in 1991
103 State Prisoners Released on Parole in 1991
104 State Prisoners Released on Probation in 1991
105 State Prisoners Released on Supervised Mandatory Release in 1991
106 State Prisoners Released Unconditionally in 1991
107 State Prisoners Released Unconditionally as a Percent of All Releases in 1991
108 State Prisoners Released on Appeal or Bond in 1991

109 State Prisoners Escaped in 1991

110 State Prisoner Deaths in 1991

111 State Prisoner Deaths by Illness or Other Natural Causes in 1991

112 State Prisoner Deaths by Illness or Other Natural Causes as a Percent of All Prison Deaths in 1991

113 Deaths of State Prisoners by AIDS in 1991

114 Deaths of State Prisoners by AIDS as a Percent of All Prison Deaths in 1991

115 State Prisoners Known to be Positive for HIV Infection/AIDS in 1991

116 State Prisoners Known to be Positive for HIV Infection/AIDS as a Percent of Total Prison Population in 1991

117 State Prisoner Deaths by Suicide in 1991

118 Deaths of State Prisoners by Suicide as a Percent of All Prison Deaths in 1991

119 Adults on State Probation in 1990

120 Percent of Adult Population on State Probation in 1990

121 Adults Under State Parole Supervision in 1990

122 State and Local Corrections Employees at Correctional Institutions in 1990

123 Percent of State and Local Corrections Employees Serving at Correctional Institutions in 1990

124 State and Local Corrections Employees in Probation, Pardon or Parole Work in 1990

125 Percent of State and Local Corrections Employees in Probation, Pardon or Parole Work in 1990

126 Employees in State Correctional Facilities in 1990

127 State Correctional Officers in Adult Systems in 1992

128 Male Correctional Officers in Adult Systems in 1992

129 Female Correctional Officers in Adult Systems in 1992

130 State Prisoners per Correctional Officer in 1992

131 Turnover Rate of Correctional Officers in Adult Systems in 1992

132 Average Annual Salary of State Corrections Officers in 1992

133 Inmates in Local Jails in 1988

134 Male Inmates in Local Jails in 1988

135 Female Inmates in Local Jails in 1988

136 White Inmates in Local Jails in 1988

137 White Inmates in Local Jails as a Percent of All Inmates in 1988

138   Black Inmates in Local Jails in 1988

139   Black Inmates in Local Jails as a Percent of All Inmates in 1988

140   Hispanic Inmates in Local Jails in 1988

141   Hispanic Inmates in Local Jails as a Percent of All Inmates in 1988

142   Juveniles Held in Public Juvenile Facilities in 1991

143   Juvenile Custody Rate in 1991

144   Juveniles Admitted to Public Juvenile Facilities in 1990

145   Juveniles Discharged from Public Juvenile Facilities in 1990

146   Public Juvenile Facilities Administered by State and Local Governments in 1991

147   Prison Boot Camp Participants in 1992

III. Drugs and Alcohol

148   Marijuana Seized by the Federal Drug Enforcement Administration in 1992

149   Cocaine Removed by the Federal Drug Enforcement Agency in 1993

150   Clients in State-Supported Drug & Alcoholism Treatment Units in 1991

151   Cost per Client in State-Supported Drug & Alcoholism Treatment Units in 1991

152   Male Clients in State-Supported Drug & Alcoholism Treatment Units in 1992

153   Male Clients in State-Supported Drug & Alcoholism Treatment Units as a Percent of All Clients: 1991

154   Female Clients in State-Supported Drug & Alcoholism Treatment Units in 1991

155   Female Clients in State-Supported Drug & Alcoholism Treatment Units as a Percent of All Clients: 1991

156   White Clients in State-Supported Drug & Alcoholism Treatment Units in 1991

157   White Clients in State-Supported Drug & Alcoholism Treatment Units as a Percent of All Clients: 1991

158   Black Clients in State-Supported Drug & Alcoholism Treatment Units in 1991

159   Black Clients in State-Supported Drug & Alcoholism Treatment Units as a Percent of All Clients: 1991

160   Hispanic Clients in State-Supported Drug & Alcoholism Treatment Units in 1991

161   Hispanic Clients in State-Supported Drug & Alcoholism Treatment Units as a Percent of All Clients in 1991

162   Juveniles in State-Supported Drug & Alcoholism Treatment Units in 1991

163   Juveniles in State-Supported Drug & Alcoholism Treatment Units as a Percent of All Clients in 1991

164   Expenditures for State-Supported Alcohol and Drug Abuse Services in 1991

165   Per Capita Expenditures for State–Supported Alcohol and Drug Abuse Services in 1991

166   Expenditures for State–Supported Alcohol and Drug Abuse Treatment Programs in 1991

167   Per Capita Expenditures for State–Supported Alcohol and Drug Abuse Treatment Programs in 1991

168   Expenditures for State–Supported Alcohol and Drug Abuse Prevention Programs in 1991

169   Per Capita Expenditures for State–Supported Alcohol and Drug Abuse Prevention Programs in 1991

170   Drug and Alcoholism Treatment and Prevention Units in 1992

IV. Finance

171   State and Local Government Expenditures for Justice Activities in 1991

172   Per Capita State and Local Government Expenditures for Justice Activities in 1991

173   State–Local Government Expenditures for Justice Activities as a Percent of All Direct Expenditures: 1991

174   State Government Expenditures for Justice Activities in 1991

175   Per Capita State Government Expenditures for Justice Activities in 1991

176   State Government Expenditures for Judicial Activities as a Percent of All Direct Expenditures in 1991

177   Local Government Expenditures for Justice Activities in 1991

178   Per Capita Local Government Expenditures for Justice Activities in 1991

179   Local Government Expenditures for Justice Activities as a Percent of All Direct Expenditures in 1991

180   State and Local Government Expenditures for Police Protection in 1991

181   Per Capita State and Local Government Expenditures for Police Protection in 1991

182   State–Local Government Expenditures for Police Protection as a Percent of All Direct Expenditures in 1991

183   State Government Expenditures for Police Protection in 1991

184   Per Capita State Government Expenditures for Police Protection in 1991

185   State Government Expenditures for Police Protection as a Percent of All Direct Expenditures in 1991

186   Local Government Expenditures for Police Protection in 1991

187   Per Capita Local Government Expenditures for Police Protection in 1991

188   Local Government Expenditures for Police Protection as a Percent of All Direct Expenditures in 1991

189   State and Local Government Expenditures for Corrections in 1991

190   Per Capita State and Local Government Expenditures for Corrections in 1991

191   State and Local Government Expenditures for Corrections as a Percent of All Direct Expenditures in 1991

192   State Government Expenditures for Corrections in 1991

193   Per Capita State Government Expenditures for Corrections in 1991

194   State Government Expenditures for Corrections as a Percent of All Direct Expenditures in 1991

195   Local Government Expenditures for Corrections in 1991

196   Per Capita Local Government Expenditures for Corrections in 1991

197   Local Government Expenditures for Corrections as a Percent of All Direct Expenditures in 1991

198   State and Local Government Expenditures for Judicial and Legal Services in 1991

199   Per Capita State and Local Government Expenditures for Judicial and Legal Services in 1991

200   State & Local Government Expenditures for Judicial & Legal Services as a Percent of All Direct Expenditures in 1991

201   State Government Expenditures for Judicial and Legal Services in 1991

202   Per Capita State Government Expenditures for Judicial and Legal Services in 1991

203   State Government Expenditures for Judicial and Legal Services as a Percent of All Direct Expenditures: 1991

204   Local Government Expenditures for Judicial and Legal Services in 1991

205   Per Capita Local Government Expenditures for Judicial and Legal Services in 1991

206   Local Government Expenditures for Judicial and Legal Services as a Percent of All Direct Expenditures: 1991

207   Base Salary for Justices of States' Highest Courts in 1993

208   Base Salary of Judges of Intermediate Appellate Courts in 1993

209   Base Salaries of Judges of General Trial Courts in 1993

210   State and Local Government Justice System Payroll in 1990

211   State and Local Government Payroll for Police Protection in 1990

212   State and Local Government Payroll for Corrections in 1990

213   State and Local Government Payroll for Courts in 1990

214   State and Local Government Payroll for Prosecution and Legal Services in 1990

215   State and Local Government Payroll for Public Defense in 1990

216   State Victim Compensation Claims Filed in 1989

217   State Victim Compensation Benefits Paid in 1989

218   Average State Victim Compensation Benefit Paid in 1989

V. Law Enforcement

219   Law Enforcement Agencies in 1992

220   Population per Law Enforcement Agency in 1992

221   Law Enforcement Agencies per 1,000 Square Miles in 1992

222   Full-Time Sworn Officers in Law Enforcement Agencies in 1992

223   Percent of Full-Time Law Enforcement Agency Employees Who Are Sworn Officers: 1992

224   Full-Time Sworn Officers in Law Enforcement Agencies per 10,000 Population in 1992

225   Full-Time Sworn Law Enforcement Officers per 1,000 Square Miles in 1992

226   Full-Time Employees in Law Enforcement Agencies in 1992

227   Full-Time Employees in Law Enforcement Agencies per 10,000 Population in 1992

228   Full-Time Sworn Officers in State Police Departments in 1992

229   Percent of Full-Time State Police Department Employees Who Are Sworn Officers: 1992

230   Rate of Full-Time Sworn Officers in State Police Departments in 1992

231   Male Officers in State Police Departments in 1990

232   Female Officers in State Police Departments in 1990

233   Female Officers as a Percent of All Officers in State Police Departments in 1990

234   White Officers in State Police Departments in 1990

235   White Officers as a Percent of All Officers in State Police Departments in 1990

236   Black Officers in State Police Departments in 1990

237   Black Officers as a Percent of All Officers in State Police Departments in 1990

238   Hispanic Officers in State Police Departments in 1990

239   Hispanic Officers as a Percent of All Officers in State Police Departments in 1990

240   Full-Time Employees in State Police Departments in 1992

241   Local Police Departments in 1992

242   Full-Time Sworn Officers in Local Police Departments in 1992

243   Percent of Full-Time Local Police Department Employees Who Are Sworn Officers: 1992

244   Rate of Full-Time Sworn Officers in Local Police Departments in 1992

245   Full-Time Employees in Local Police Departments in 1992

246 Sheriffs' Departments in 1992

247 Full–Time Sworn Officers in Sheriffs' Departments in 1992

248 Percent of Full–Time Sheriffs' Departments Employees Who Are Sworn Officers: 1992

249 Rate of Full–Time Sworn Officers in Sheriffs' Departments in 1992

250 Full–Time Employees in Sheriffs' Departments in 1992

251 Special Police Agencies in 1992

252 Full–Time Sworn Officers in Special Police Departments in 1992

253 Percent of Full–Time Special Police Department Employees Who Are Sworn Officers: 1992

254 Rate of Full–Time Sworn Officers in Special Police Departments in 1992

255 Full–Time Employees in Special Police Departments in 1992

256 Law Enforcement Officers Feloniously Killed in 1992

257 Law Enforcement Officers Feloniously Killed: 1983 to 1992

258 U.S. District Court Judgeships in 1992

259 Criminal Cases Filed in U.S. District Court in 1992

260 Criminal Cases Completed in U.S. District Court in 1992

261 Median Length of Federal Criminal Cases in 1992

262 Federal Prosecutions of Corrupt Public Officials: 1976 to 1990

263 State and Local Justice System Employment in 1990

264 Rate of State and Local Justice System Employment in 1990

265 State Judges of General Jurisdiction in 1990

266 Rate of State Judges of General Jurisdiction in 1990

267 State and Local Courts Employment in 1990

268 State and Local Prosecution Employment in 1990

269 Full–Time State Prosecuting Attorneys in 1990

270 State and Local Public Defense Employment in 1990

271 Public Defenders in 1990

272 Authorized Wiretaps: 1991 and 1992

VI. Offenses

273   Crimes in 1992

274   Average Time Between Crimes in 1992

275   Crimes per Square Mile in 1992

276   Percent Change in Number of Crimes: 1991 to 1992

277   Crime Rate in 1992

278   Percent Change in Crime Rate: 1991 to 1992

279   Violent Crimes in 1992

280   Average Time Between Violent Crimes in 1992

281   Violent Crimes per Square Mile in 1992

282   Percent Change in Number of Violent Crimes: 1991 to 1992

283   Violent Crime Rate in 1992

284   Percent Change in Violent Crime Rate: 1991 to 1992

285   Violent Crime Rate with Firearms in 1992

286   Murders in 1992

287   Average Time Between Murders in 1992

288   Percent Change in Number of Murders: 1991 to 1992

289   Murder Rate in 1992

290   Percent Change in Murder Rate: 1991 to 1992

291   Murders with Firearms in 1992

292   Murder Rate with Firearms in 1992

293   Percent of Murders Involving Firearms in 1992

294   Murders with Handguns in 1992

295   Murder Rate with Handguns in 1992

296   Percent of Murders Involving Handguns in 1992

297   Murders with Rifles in 1992

298   Percent of Murders Involving Rifles in 1992

299   Murders with Shotguns in 1992

300   Percent of Murders Involving Shotguns in 1992

301   Murders with Knives or Cutting Instruments in 1992

302   Percent of Murders Involving Knives or Cutting Instruments in 1992

303   Murders by Hands, Fists or Feet in 1992

304   Percent of Murders Involving Hands, Fists or Feet in 1992

305   Rapes in 1992

306   Average Time Between Rapes in 1992

307   Percent Change in Number of Rapes: 1991 to 1992

308   Rape Rate in 1992

309   Percent Change in Rape Rate: 1991 to 1992

310   Rape Rate per 100,000 Female Population in 1992

311   Robberies in 1992

312   Average Time Between Robberies in 1992

313   Percent Change in Number of Robberies: 1991 to 1992

314   Robbery Rate in 1992

315   Percent Change in Robbery Rate: 1991 to 1992

316   Robberies with Firearms in 1992

317   Robbery Rate with Firearms in 1992

318   Percent of Robberies Involving Firearms in 1992

319   Robberies with Knives or Cutting Instruments in 1992

320   Percent of Robberies Involving Knives or Cutting Instruments in 1992

321   Robberies with Blunt Objects and Other Dangerous Weapons in 1992

322   Percent of Robberies Involving Blunt Objects and Other Dangerous Objects in 1992

323   Robberies Using Hands, Fists or Feet in 1992

324   Percent of Robberies Using Hands, Fists or Feet in 1992

325   Aggravated Assaults in 1992

326   Average Time Between Aggravated Assaults in 1992

327   Percent Change in Number of Aggravated Assaults: 1991 to 1992

328   Aggravated Assault Rate in 1992

329   Percent Change in Rate of Aggravated Assaults: 1991 to 1992

330   Aggravated Assaults with Firearms in 1992

331   Aggravated Assault Rate with Firearms in 1992

332   Percent of Aggravated Assaults Involving Firearms in 1992

333   Aggravated Assaults with Knives or Cutting Instruments in 1992

334   Percent of Aggravated Assaults Involving Knives or Cutting Instruments in 1992

335   Aggravated Assaults with Blunt Objects and Other Dangerous Weapons in 1992

336   Percent of Aggravated Assaults Involving Blunt Objects and Other Dangerous Objects in 1992

337   Aggravated Assaults Using Hands, Fists or Feet in 1992

338   Percent of Aggravated Assaults Involving Hands, Fists or Feet in 1992

339   Property Crimes in 1992

340   Average Time Between Property Crimes in 1992

341   Property Crimes per Square Mile in 1992

342   Percent Change in Number of Property Crimes: 1991 to 1992

343   Property Crime Rate in 1992

344   Percent Change in Rate of Property Crime: 1991 to 1992

345   Burglaries in 1992

346   Average Time Between Burglaries in 1992

347   Percent Change in Number of Burglaries: 1991 to 1992

348   Burglary Rate in 1992

349   Percent Change in Rate of Burglaries: 1991 to 1992

350   Larceny and Theft in 1992

351   Average Time Between Larcenies–Thefts in 1992

352   Percent Change in Number of Larcenies and Thefts: 1991 to 1992

353   Larceny and Theft Rate in 1992

354   Percent Change in Rate of Larceny and Theft: 1991 to 1992

355   Motor Vehicle Thefts in 1992

356   Average Time Between Motor Vehicle Thefts in 1992

357   Percent Change in Number of Motor Vehicle Thefts: 1991 to 1992

358   Motor Vehicle Theft Rate in 1992
359   Percent Change in Rate of Motor Vehicle Thefts: 1991 to 1992

Urban/Rural Crime

360   Crime in Urban Areas in 1992
361   Urban Crime Rate in 1992
362   Percent of Crime Occurring in Urban Areas in 1992
363   Crime in Rural Areas in 1992
364   Rural Crime Rate in 1992
365   Percent of Crime Occurring in Rural Areas in 1992
366   Violent Crime in Urban Areas in 1992
367   Percent of Violent Crime Occurring in Urban Areas in 1992
368   Violent Crime in Rural Areas in 1992
369   Percent of Violent Crime Occurring in Rural Areas in 1992
370   Murder in Urban Areas in 1992
371   Percent of Murders Occurring in Urban Areas in 1992
372   Murder in Rural Areas in 1992
373   Percent of Murders Occurring in Rural Areas in 1992
374   Rape in Urban Areas in 1992
375   Percent of Rapes Occurring in Urban Areas in 1992
376   Rape in Rural Areas in 1992
377   Percent of Rapes Occurring in Rural Areas in 1992
378   Robbery in Urban Areas in 1992
379   Percent of Robberies Occurring in Urban Areas in 1992
380   Robbery in Rural Areas in 1992
381   Percent of Robberies Occurring in Rural Areas in 1992
382   Aggravated Assault in Urban Areas in 1992
383   Percent of Aggravated Assaults Occurring in Urban Areas in 1992
384   Aggravated Assault in Rural Areas in 1992
385   Percent of Aggravated Assaults Occurring in Rural Areas in 1992

386   Property Crime in Urban Areas in 1992

387   Percent of Property Crime Occurring in Urban Areas in 1992

388   Property Crime in Rural Areas in 1992

389   Percent of Property Crime Occurring in Rural Areas in 1992

390   Burglary in Urban Areas in 1992

391   Percent of Burglaries Occurring in Urban Areas in 1992

392   Burglary in Rural Areas in 1992

393   Percent of Burglaries Occurring in Rural Areas in 1992

394   Larceny and Theft in Urban Areas in 1992

395   Percent of Larcenies and Thefts Occurring in Urban Areas in 1992

396   Larceny and Theft in Rural Areas in 1992

397   Percent of Larcenies and Thefts Occurring in Rural Areas in 1992

398   Motor Vehicle Theft in Urban Areas in 1992

399   Percent of Motor Vehicle Thefts Occurring in Urban Areas in 1992

400   Motor Vehicle Thefts in Rural Areas in 1992

401   Percent of Motor Vehicle Thefts Occurring in Rural Areas in 1992

402   Crimes Reported at Universities and Colleges in 1992

403   Crimes Reported at Universities and Colleges as a Percent of All Crimes in 1992

404   Violent Crimes Reported at Universities and Colleges in 1992

405   Violent Crimes Reported at Universities and Colleges as a Percent of All Violent Crimes in 1992

406   Property Crimes Reported at Universities and Colleges in 1992

407   Property Crimes Reported at Universities and Colleges as a Percent of All Property Crimes in 1992

408   Bank Robberies in 1992

409   Bombings in 1992

1988 Crimes

410   Crimes in 1988

411   Crime Rate in 1988

412   Percent Change in Number of Crimes: 1988 to 1992

413   Percent Change in Crime Rate: 1988 to 1992

414   Violent Crimes in 1988

415   Violent Crime Rate in 1988

416   Percent Change in Number of Violent Crimes: 1988 to 1992

417   Percent Change in Violent Crime Rate: 1988 to 1992

418   Murders in 1988

419   Murder Rate in 1988

420   Percent Change in Number of Murders: 1988 to 1992

421   Percent Change in Murder Rate: 1988 to 1992

422   Rapes in 1988

423   Rape Rate in 1988

424   Percent Change in Number of Rapes: 1988 to 1992

425   Percent Change in Rape Rate: 1988 to 1992

426   Aggravated Assaults in 1988

427   Aggravated Assault Rate in 1988

428   Percent Change in Number of Aggravated Assaults: 1988 to 1992

429   Percent Change in Rate of Aggravated Assaults: 1988 to 1992

430   Robberies in 1988

431   Robbery Rate in 1988

432   Percent Change in Number of Robberies: 1988 to 1992

433   Percent Change in Robbery Rate: 1988 to 1992

434   Property Crimes in 1988

435   Property Crime Rate in 1988

436   Percent Change in Number of Property Crimes: 1988 to 1992

437   Percent Change in Rate of Property Crime: 1988 to 1992

438   Burglaries in 1988

439   Burglary Rate in 1988

440   Percent Change in Number of Burglaries: 1988 to 1992

441   Percent Change in Rate of Burglaries: 1988 to 1992

442   Larceny and Theft in 1988

443   Larceny and Theft Rate in 1988
444   Percent Change in Number of Larcenies and Thefts: 1988 to 1992
445   Percent Change in Rate of Larcenies and Thefts: 1988 to 1992
446   Motor Vehicle Thefts in 1988
447   Motor Vehicle Theft Rate in 1988
448   Percent Change in Number of Motor Vehicle Thefts: 1988 to 1992
449   Percent Change in Rate of Motor Vehicle Thefts: 1988 to 1992
450   Percent of Crimes Cleared in 1991
451   Percent of Violent Crimes Cleared in 1991
452   Percent of Murders Cleared in 1991
453   Percent of Rapes Cleared in 1991
454   Percent of Robberies Cleared in 1991
455   Percent of Aggravated Assaults Cleared in 1991
456   Percent of Property Crimes Cleared in 1991
457   Percent of Burglaries Cleared in 1991
458   Percent of Larcenies and Thefts Cleared in 1991
459   Percent of Motor Vehicle Thefts Cleared in 1991

VII. Appendix

A-1   Resident State Population in 1992
A-2   Resident State Population in 1991
A-3   Resident State Population in 1990
A-4   Urban Population in 1990
A-5   Rural Population in 1990

VIII. Sources

IX. Index

I. ARRESTS

Table	Title
1	Reported Arrests in 1992
2	Reported Arrest Rate in 1992
3	Reported Arrests for Violent Crime in 1992
4	Reported Arrest Rate for Violent Crime in 1992
5	Reported Arrests for Murder in 1992
6	Reported Arrest Rate for Murder in 1992
7	Reported Arrests for Rape in 1992
8	Reported Arrest Rate for Rape in 1992
9	Reported Arrests for Robbery in 1992
10	Reported Arrest Rate for Robbery in 1992
11	Reported Arrests for Aggravated Assault in 1992
12	Reported Arrest Rate for Aggravated Assault in 1992
13	Reported Arrests for Property Crime in 1992
14	Reported Arrest Rate for Property Crime in 1992
15	Reported Arrests for Burglary in 1992
16	Reported Arrest Rate for Burglary in 1992
17	Reported Arrests for Larceny and Theft in 1992
18	Reported Arrest Rate for Larceny and Theft in 1992
19	Reported Arrests for Motor Vehicle Theft in 1992
20	Reported Arrest Rate for Motor Vehicle Theft in 1992
21	Reported Arrests for Arson in 1992
22	Reported Arrest Rate for Arson in 1992
23	Reported Arrests for Weapons Violations in 1992
24	Reported Arrest Rate for Weapons Violations in 1992
25	Reported Arrests for Driving Under the Influence in 1992
26	Reported Arrest Rate for Driving Under the Influence in 1992
27	Reported Arrests for Drug Abuse Violations in 1992
28	Reported Arrest Rate for Drug Abuse Violations in 1992
29	Reported Arrests for Sex Offenses in 1992
30	Reported Arrest Rate for Sex Offenses in 1992
31	Reported Arrests for Prostitution and Commercialized Vice in 1992
32	Reported Arrest Rate for Prostitution and Commercialized Vice in 1992
33	Reported Arrests for Offenses Against Families and Children in 1992
34	Reported Arrest Rate for Offenses Against Families and Children in 1992

I. ARRESTS (continued)

Table	Title
35	Reported Arrests of Youths 17 Years and Younger in 1992
36	Reported Arrests of Youths 17 Years and Younger as a Percent of All Arrests in 1992
37	Reported Arrests of Youths 17 Years and Younger for Violent Crime in 1992
38	Reported Arrests of Youths 17 Years and Younger for Violent Crime as a Percent of All Such Arrests in 1992
39	Reported Arrests of Youths 17 Years and Younger for Murder in 1992
40	Reported Arrests of Youths 17 Years and Younger for Murder as a Percent of All Such Arrests in 1992
41	Reported Arrests of Youths 17 Years and Younger for Rape in 1992
42	Reported Arrests of Youths 17 Years and Younger for Rape as a Percent of All Such Arrests in 1992
43	Reported Arrests of Youths 17 Years and Younger for Robbery in 1992
44	Reported Arrests of Youths 17 Years and Younger for Robbery as a Percent of All Such Arrests in 1992
45	Reported Arrests of Youths 17 Years and Younger for Aggravated Assault in 1992
46	Reported Arrests of Youths 17 Years & Younger for Aggravated Assault as a Percent of All Such Arrests 1992
47	Reported Arrests of Youths 17 Years and Younger for Property Crimes in 1992
48	Reported Arrests of Youths 17 Years & Younger for Property Crime as a Percent of All Such Arrests in 1992
49	Reported Arrests of Youths 17 Years and Younger for Burglary in 1992
50	Reported Arrests of Youths 17 Years and Younger for Burglary as a Percent of All Such Arrests in 1992
51	Reported Arrests of Youths 17 Years and Younger for Larceny and Theft in 1992
52	Reported Arrests of Youths 17 Years and Younger for Larceny & Theft as a Percent of All Such Arrests: 1992
53	Reported Arrests of Youths 17 Years and Younger for Motor Vehicle Theft in 1992
54	Reported Arrests of Youths 17 Years and Younger for Motor Vehicle Theft as a Percent of All Such Arrests in 1992
55	Reported Arrests of Youths 17 Years and Younger for Arson in 1992
56	Reported Arrests of Youths 17 Years and Younger for Arson as a Percent of All Such Arrests in 1992
57	Reported Arrests of Youths 17 Years and Younger for Weapons Violations in 1992
58	Reported Arrests of Youths 17 Years and Younger for Weapons Violations as a Percent of All Such Arrests in 1992
59	Reported Arrests of Youths 17 Years and Younger for Driving Under the Influence in 1992
60	Reported Arrests of Youths 17 & Younger for Driving Under the Influence as a Percent of All Such Arrests in 1992
61	Reported Arrests of Youths 17 Years and Younger for Drug Abuse Violations in 1992
62	Reported Arrests of Youths 17 & Younger for Drug Abuse Violations as a Percent of All Such Arrests: 1992
63	Reported Arrests of Youths 17 Years and Younger for Sex Offenses in 1992
64	Reported Arrests of Youths 17 Years & Younger for Sex Offenses as a Percent of All Such Arrests: 1992
65	Reported Arrests of Youths 17 and Younger for Prostitution & Commercialized Vice in 1992
66	Reported Arrests of Youths 17 & Younger for Prostitution & Commercialized Vice as a % of All Such Arrests: 1992
67	Reported Arrests of Youths 17 and Younger for Offenses Against Families and Children in 1992
68	Reported Arrests of Youths 17 & Younger for Offenses Against Families & Children as a % of All Such Arrests: 1992

Reported Arrests in 1992

National Total = 11,877,802 Reported Arrests*

RANK	STATE	ARRESTS	%	RANK	STATE	ARRESTS	%
1	California	1,659,184	13.97%	26	Oklahoma	142,495	1.20%
2	New York	1,159,763	9.76%	27	Massachusetts	136,787	1.15%
3	Texas	1,037,745	8.74%	28	Kansas	130,654	1.10%
4	Florida	633,595	5.33%	29	Missouri	130,031	1.09%
5	North Carolina	483,580	4.07%	30	Indiana	124,407	1.05%
6	Virginia	394,502	3.32%	31	South Carolina	124,308	1.05%
7	Wisconsin	383,179	3.23%	32	Utah	86,159	0.73%
8	Pennsylvania	381,247	3.21%	33	Nevada	81,340	0.68%
9	Michigan	379,638	3.20%	34	New Mexico	65,409	0.55%
10	Ohio	378,024	3.18%	35	Hawaii	64,991	0.55%
11	New Jersey	372,969	3.14%	36	West Virginia	63,054	0.53%
12	Georgia	288,583	2.43%	37	Mississippi	59,275	0.50%
13	Kentucky	283,180	2.38%	38	Iowa	59,119	0.50%
14	Maryland	264,647	2.23%	39	Nebraska	55,034	0.46%
15	Washington	240,717	2.03%	40	Idaho	54,331	0.46%
16	Colorado	240,050	2.02%	41	Maine	46,195	0.39%
17	Arizona	239,330	2.01%	42	Rhode Island	42,998	0.36%
18	Illinois	224,100	1.89%	43	Alaska	34,226	0.29%
19	Alabama	182,413	1.54%	44	South Dakota	30,643	0.26%
20	Arkansas	173,106	1.46%	45	New Hampshire	29,941	0.25%
21	Connecticut	172,183	1.45%	46	Montana	28,859	0.24%
22	Louisiana	167,445	1.41%	47	Wyoming	25,859	0.22%
23	Tennessee	162,671	1.37%	48	North Dakota	17,967	0.15%
24	Oregon	148,581	1.25%	49	Delaware	10,298	0.09%
25	Minnesota	143,703	1.21%	50	Vermont	4,723	0.04%
					District of Columbia	50,388	0.42%

Source: U.S. Department of Justice, Federal Bureau of Investigation
"Crime in the United States 1992" (Uniform Crime Reports, October 3, 1993)
*By law enforcement agencies submitting complete reports to the F.B.I. for 12 months in 1992. The F.B.I. estimates 14,075,100 reported and unreported arrests occurred in 1992.

Reported Arrest Rate in 1992

National Rate = 5,574 Reported Arrests per 100,000 Population*

RANK	STATE	RATE	RANK	STATE	RATE
1	Kentucky	7,860	26	California	5,412
2	Wisconsin	7,790	27	Maryland	5,392
3	Nevada	7,717	28	Oregon	5,267
4	New York	7,553	29	Ohio	5,166
5	Colorado	7,523	30	Florida	5,087
6	New Mexico	7,416	31	New Jersey	4,935
7	North Carolina	7,280	32	Alabama	4,742
8	Arkansas	7,243	33	Nebraska	4,724
9	Kansas	6,711	34	Illinois	4,577
10	Arizona	6,624	35	Oklahoma	4,554
11	Tennessee	6,618	36	Maine	4,538
12	Louisiana	6,556	37	Michigan	4,482
13	Mississippi	6,521	38	Indiana	4,320
14	Utah	6,478	39	Rhode Island	4,278
15	Connecticut	6,410	40	Montana	3,889
16	Alaska	6,200	41	Pennsylvania	3,796
17	Virginia	6,190	42	North Dakota	3,671
18	South Dakota	6,068	43	South Carolina	3,597
19	Georgia	5,928	44	West Virginia	3,484
20	Texas	5,889	45	Massachusetts	3,451
21	Wyoming	5,850	46	New Hampshire	3,312
22	Washington	5,837	47	Iowa	3,308
23	Missouri	5,834	48	Minnesota	3,225
24	Idaho	5,798	49	Delaware	2,768
25	Hawaii	5,603	50	Vermont	1,564

District of Columbia   8,555

Source: Morgan Quitno Corporation using data from U.S. Department of Justice, Federal Bureau of Investigation
"Crime in the United States 1992" (Uniform Crime Reports, October 3, 1993)
*By law enforcement agencies submitting complete reports to the F.B.I. for 12 months in 1992. These rates based on population estimates for areas under the jurisdiction of those agencies reporting. Arrest rate based on the F.B.I. estimate of total arrests is 5,518 reported and unreported arrests per 100,000 population.

Reported Arrests for Violent Crime in 1992

National Total = 641,250 Reported Arrests*

RANK	STATE	ARRESTS	%	RANK	STATE	ARRESTS	%
1	California	146,709	22.88%	26	Oklahoma	5,871	0.92%
2	New York	65,040	10.14%	27	South Carolina	5,164	0.81%
3	Florida	53,849	8.40%	28	Arkansas	4,917	0.77%
4	Texas	40,877	6.37%	29	Oregon	4,452	0.69%
5	North Carolina	26,254	4.09%	30	Kansas	4,011	0.63%
6	Pennsylvania	22,929	3.58%	31	Minnesota	3,714	0.58%
7	Michigan	22,903	3.57%	32	Rhode Island	2,952	0.46%
8	New Jersey	21,497	3.35%	33	Nevada	2,658	0.41%
9	Kentucky	16,977	2.65%	34	New Mexico	2,400	0.37%
10	Ohio	14,881	2.32%	35	Utah	2,088	0.33%
11	Massachusetts	14,177	2.21%	36	Iowa	2,049	0.32%
12	Maryland	14,014	2.19%	37	Mississippi	1,926	0.30%
13	Georgia	12,023	1.87%	38	West Virginia	1,670	0.26%
14	Alabama	11,796	1.84%	39	Idaho	1,517	0.24%
15	Virginia	11,475	1.79%	40	Hawaii	1,352	0.21%
16	Illinois	11,034	1.72%	41	Maine	1,165	0.18%
17	Louisiana	10,820	1.69%	42	Alaska	1,060	0.17%
18	Connecticut	9,652	1.51%	43	Nebraska	808	0.13%
19	Arizona	9,286	1.45%	44	New Hampshire	614	0.10%
20	Colorado	8,802	1.37%	45	Delaware	582	0.09%
21	Tennessee	8,311	1.30%	46	Montana	579	0.09%
22	Wisconsin	8,032	1.25%	47	Wyoming	570	0.09%
23	Missouri	7,773	1.21%	48	South Dakota	497	0.08%
24	Washington	7,229	1.13%	49	North Dakota	155	0.02%
25	Indiana	6,776	1.06%	50	Vermont	103	0.02%
					District of Columbia	5,259	0.82%

Source: U.S. Department of Justice, Federal Bureau of Investigation
    "Crime in the United States 1992" (Uniform Crime Reports, October 3, 1993)
*By law enforcement agencies submitting complete reports to the F.B.I. for 12 months in 1992. The F.B.I estimates 742,130 reported and unreported arrests for violent crimes occurred in 1992. Violent crimes are offenses of murder, forcible rape, robbery and aggravated assault.

Reported Arrest Rate for Violent Crime in 1992

National Rate = 310 Reported Arrests per 100,000 Population*

RANK	STATE	RATE		RANK	STATE	RATE
1	California	479		26	Arkansas	206
2	Kentucky	471		26	Kansas	206
3	Florida	432		28	Ohio	203
4	Louisiana	424		29	Alaska	192
4	New York	424		30	Oklahoma	188
6	North Carolina	395		31	Virginia	180
7	Connecticut	359		32	Washington	175
8	Massachusetts	358		33	Wisconsin	163
9	Missouri	349		34	Idaho	162
10	Tennessee	338		35	Oregon	158
11	Alabama	307		36	Utah	157
12	Rhode Island	294		37	Delaware	156
13	Maryland	286		38	South Carolina	149
14	New Jersey	284		39	Wyoming	129
15	Colorado	276		40	Hawaii	117
16	New Mexico	272		41	Iowa	115
17	Michigan	270		42	Maine	114
18	Arizona	257		43	South Dakota	98
19	Nevada	252		44	West Virginia	92
20	Georgia	247		45	Minnesota	83
21	Indiana	235		46	Montana	78
22	Texas	232		47	Nebraska	69
23	Pennsylvania	228		48	New Hampshire	68
24	Illinois	225		49	Vermont	34
25	Mississippi	212		50	North Dakota	32

District of Columbia 893

Source: Morgan Quitno Corporation using data from U.S. Department of Justice, Federal Bureau of Investigation
"Crime in the United States 1992" (Uniform Crime Reports, October 3, 1993)
*By law enforcement agencies submitting complete reports to the F.B.I. for 12 months in 1992. These rates based on population estimates for areas under the jurisdiction of those agencies reporting. Arrest rate based on the F.B.I. estimate of reported and unreported arrests for violent crimes is 291 arrests per 100,000 population. Violent crimes are offenses of murder, forcible rape, robbery and aggravated assault.

Reported Arrests for Murder in 1992

National Total = 19,491 Reported Arrests*

RANK	STATE	ARRESTS	%	RANK	STATE	ARRESTS	%
1	California	3,421	17.55%	26	Nevada	157	0.81%
2	Texas	1,930	9.90%	27	Washington	156	0.80%
3	Michigan	1,850	9.49%	28	Mississippi	145	0.74%
4	New York	1,545	7.93%	29	Connecticut	143	0.73%
5	Florida	1,166	5.98%	30	Massachusetts	140	0.72%
6	North Carolina	813	4.17%	31	Oregon	135	0.69%
7	Pennsylvania	698	3.58%	32	Kansas	114	0.58%
8	Maryland	520	2.67%	33	Minnesota	110	0.56%
9	Virginia	508	2.61%	34	West Virginia	106	0.54%
10	Ohio	495	2.54%	35	New Mexico	46	0.24%
11	Louisiana	453	2.32%	36	Hawaii	39	0.20%
12	Wisconsin	445	2.28%	37	Utah	35	0.18%
13	Georgia	436	2.24%	38	Idaho	28	0.14%
14	Alabama	429	2.20%	39	Montana	27	0.14%
15	Tennessee	384	1.97%	39	Nebraska	27	0.14%
16	New Jersey	349	1.79%	41	Alaska	24	0.12%
17	Illinois	335	1.72%	41	Rhode Island	24	0.12%
18	Missouri	310	1.59%	43	Iowa	16	0.08%
19	Kentucky	293	1.50%	44	New Hampshire	15	0.08%
20	Arkansas	276	1.42%	44	Wyoming	15	0.08%
21	Arizona	229	1.17%	46	Maine	12	0.06%
22	South Carolina	215	1.10%	47	Delaware	10	0.05%
23	Colorado	209	1.07%	48	North Dakota	7	0.04%
24	Indiana	196	1.01%	49	Vermont	4	0.02%
25	Oklahoma	194	1.00%	50	South Dakota	3	0.02%
					District of Columbia	254	1.30%

Source: U.S. Department of Justice, Federal Bureau of Investigation
"Crime in the United States 1992" (Uniform Crime Reports, October 3, 1993)
By law enforcement agencies submitting complete reports to the F.B.I. for 12 months in 1992. The F.B.I. estimates 22,510 reported and unreported murder arrests occurred in 1992. Includes nonnegligent manslaughter.

Reported Arrest Rate for Murder in 1992

National Rate = 9.13 Reported Arrests per 100,000 Population*

RANK	STATE	RATE	RANK	STATE	RATE
1	Michigan	21.84	26	Oklahoma	6.20
2	Louisiana	17.74	27	Kansas	5.86
3	Mississippi	15.95	27	West Virginia	5.86
4	Tennessee	15.62	29	Connecticut	5.32
5	Nevada	14.90	30	New Mexico	5.22
6	Missouri	13.91	31	Oregon	4.79
7	North Carolina	12.24	32	New Jersey	4.62
8	Arkansas	11.55	33	Alaska	4.35
9	California	11.16	34	Washington	3.78
10	Alabama	11.15	35	Montana	3.64
11	Texas	10.95	36	Massachusetts	3.53
12	Maryland	10.59	37	Wyoming	3.39
13	New York	10.06	38	Hawaii	3.36
14	Florida	9.36	39	Idaho	2.99
15	Wisconsin	9.05	40	Delaware	2.69
16	Georgia	8.96	41	Utah	2.63
17	Kentucky	8.13	42	Minnesota	2.47
18	Virginia	7.97	43	Rhode Island	2.39
19	Pennsylvania	6.95	44	Nebraska	2.32
20	Illinois	6.84	45	New Hampshire	1.66
21	Indiana	6.81	46	North Dakota	1.43
22	Ohio	6.77	47	Vermont	1.32
23	Colorado	6.55	48	Maine	1.18
24	Arizona	6.34	49	Iowa	0.90
25	South Carolina	6.22	50	South Dakota	0.59

District of Columbia   43.12

Source: Morgan Quitno Corporation using data from U.S. Department of Justice, Federal Bureau of Investigation
     "Crime in the United States 1992" (Uniform Crime Reports, October 3, 1993)
*By law enforcement agencies submitting complete reports to the F.B.I. for 12 months in 1992. These rates based on population estimates for areas under the jurisdiction of those agencies reporting. Arrest rate based on the F.B.I. estimate of reported and unreported arrests for murder is 8.82 arrests per 100,000 population. Includes nonnegligent manslaughter.

Reported Arrests for Rape in 1992

National Total = 33,385 Reported Arrests*

RANK	STATE	ARRESTS	%	RANK	STATE	ARRESTS	%
1	California	4,028	12.07%	26	Arkansas	431	1.29%
2	Texas	2,761	8.27%	27	Missouri	420	1.26%
3	Michigan	2,287	6.85%	28	Arizona	346	1.04%
4	Florida	2,262	6.78%	29	Minnesota	319	0.96%
5	New York	1,945	5.83%	30	Nevada	255	0.76%
6	Pennsylvania	1,591	4.77%	31	Kansas	241	0.72%
7	Ohio	1,445	4.33%	32	Mississippi	207	0.62%
8	New Jersey	1,257	3.77%	33	West Virginia	203	0.61%
9	Illinois	1,047	3.14%	34	Indiana	201	0.60%
10	Maryland	1,011	3.03%	35	Utah	176	0.53%
11	Virginia	997	2.99%	36	Hawaii	173	0.52%
12	Washington	921	2.76%	37	Rhode Island	137	0.41%
13	North Carolina	817	2.45%	38	Nebraska	115	0.34%
14	Georgia	744	2.23%	39	New Mexico	109	0.33%
15	Massachusetts	701	2.10%	40	Idaho	99	0.30%
16	Wisconsin	684	2.05%	41	Montana	92	0.28%
17	Kentucky	648	1.94%	41	South Dakota	92	0.28%
18	Alabama	545	1.63%	43	Alaska	91	0.27%
19	Colorado	539	1.61%	44	Maine	86	0.26%
20	Louisiana	517	1.55%	45	Delaware	83	0.25%
21	Oklahoma	503	1.51%	46	Iowa	80	0.24%
22	Tennessee	486	1.46%	47	New Hampshire	77	0.23%
23	Oregon	482	1.44%	48	Wyoming	40	0.12%
24	South Carolina	471	1.41%	49	North Dakota	35	0.10%
25	Connecticut	454	1.36%	50	Vermont	19	0.06%

District of Columbia 115 0.34%

Source: U.S. Department of Justice, Federal Bureau of Investigation
"Crime in the United States 1992" (Uniform Crime Reports, October 3, 1993)

*By law enforcement agencies submitting complete reports to the F.B.I. for 12 months in 1992. The F.B.I. estimates 39,100 reported and unreported arrests for forcible rape occurred in 1992. Forcible rape is the carnal knowledge of a female forcibly and against her will. Assaults or attempts to commit rape by force or threat of force are included. However, statutory rape without force and other sex offenses are excluded.

Reported Arrest Rate for Rape in 1992

National Rate = 15.65 Reported Arrests per 100,000 Population*

RANK	STATE	RATE	RANK	STATE	RATE
1	Michigan	27.00	26	Georgia	15.28
2	Nevada	24.19	26	Hawaii	14.91
3	Mississippi	22.77	28	Alabama	14.17
4	Washington	22.33	29	Wisconsin	13.91
4	Delaware	22.31	30	Rhode Island	13.63
6	Illinois	21.38	31	South Carolina	13.63
7	Maryland	20.60	32	Utah	13.23
8	Louisiana	20.24	33	California	13.14
9	Tennessee	19.77	34	New York	12.67
10	Ohio	19.75	35	Montana	12.40
11	Missouri	18.84	36	Kansas	12.38
12	South Dakota	18.22	37	New Mexico	12.36
13	Florida	18.16	38	North Carolina	12.30
14	Arkansas	18.03	39	West Virginia	11.22
15	Kentucky	17.99	40	Idaho	10.57
16	Massachusetts	17.68	41	Nebraska	9.87
17	Oregon	17.09	42	Arizona	9.58
18	Connecticut	16.90	43	Wyoming	9.05
19	Colorado	16.89	44	New Hampshire	8.52
20	New Jersey	16.63	45	Maine	8.45
21	Alaska	16.49	46	Minnesota	7.16
22	Oklahoma	16.08	47	North Dakota	7.15
23	Pennsylvania	15.84	48	Indiana	6.98
24	Texas	15.67	49	Vermont	6.29
25	Virginia	15.64	50	Iowa	4.48

District of Columbia   19.52

Source: Morgan Quitno Corporation using data from U.S. Department of Justice, Federal Bureau of Investigation
    "Crime in the United States 1992" (Uniform Crime Reports, October 3, 1993)

*By law enforcement agencies submitting complete reports to the F.B.I. for 12 months in 1992. These rates based on population estimates for areas under the jurisdiction of those agencies reporting. Arrest rate based on the F.B.I. estimate of reported and unreported arrests for forcible rape is 15.33 arrests per 100,000 population. Forcible rape is the carnal knowledge of a female forcibly and against her will. Assaults or attempts to commit rape are included.

8

Reported Arrests for Robbery in 1992

National Total = 153,456 Reported Arrests*

RANK	STATE	ARRESTS	%	RANK	STATE	ARRESTS	%
1	California	31,080	20.25%	26	Colorado	1,034	0.67%
2	New York	29,979	19.54%	27	Nevada	967	0.63%
3	Florida	11,587	7.55%	28	Arkansas	904	0.59%
4	Texas	9,734	6.34%	29	Indiana	832	0.54%
5	Pennsylvania	8,056	5.25%	30	South Carolina	721	0.47%
6	New Jersey	5,850	3.81%	31	Kansas	660	0.43%
7	Michigan	4,878	3.18%	32	Mississippi	509	0.33%
8	Ohio	4,854	3.16%	33	Hawaii	496	0.32%
9	Maryland	4,540	2.96%	34	Minnesota	397	0.26%
10	North Carolina	3,629	2.36%	35	Utah	315	0.21%
11	Virginia	2,718	1.77%	36	Rhode Island	279	0.18%
12	Massachusetts	2,459	1.60%	37	West Virginia	271	0.18%
13	Wisconsin	2,408	1.57%	38	New Mexico	259	0.17%
14	Georgia	2,346	1.53%	39	Iowa	217	0.14%
15	Illinois	2,153	1.40%	40	Maine	135	0.09%
16	Alabama	2,141	1.40%	41	Nebraska	128	0.08%
17	Louisiana	2,130	1.39%	42	Alaska	114	0.07%
18	Missouri	1,993	1.30%	42	New Hampshire	114	0.07%
19	Connecticut	1,978	1.29%	44	Montana	92	0.06%
20	Tennessee	1,950	1.27%	45	Idaho	82	0.05%
21	Arizona	1,590	1.04%	46	Delaware	71	0.05%
22	Kentucky	1,467	0.96%	47	South Dakota	36	0.02%
23	Washington	1,433	0.93%	48	North Dakota	29	0.02%
24	Oregon	1,431	0.93%	49	Wyoming	28	0.02%
25	Oklahoma	1,069	0.70%	50	Vermont	9	0.01%
					District of Columbia	1,304	0.85%

Source: U.S. Department of Justice, Federal Bureau of Investigation

"Crime in the United States 1992" (Uniform Crime Reports, October 3, 1993)

*By law enforcement agencies submitting complete reports to the F.B.I. for 12 months in 1992. The F.B.I. estimates 173,310 reported and unreported arrests for robbery occurred in 1992. Robbery is the taking of anything of value by force or threat of force. Attempts are included.

Reported Arrest Rate for Robbery in 1992

National Rate = 71.91 Reported Arrests per 100,000 Population*

RANK	STATE	RATE		RANK	STATE	RATE
1	New York	195.24		26	Kentucky	40.72
2	California	101.37		26	Arkansas	37.82
3	Florida	93.04		28	Washington	34.75
4	Maryland	92.50		29	Oklahoma	34.16
4	Nevada	91.75		30	Kansas	33.90
6	Missouri	89.41		31	Colorado	32.40
7	Louisiana	83.40		32	New Mexico	29.37
8	Pennsylvania	80.21		33	Indiana	28.89
9	Tennessee	79.33		34	Rhode Island	27.76
10	New Jersey	77.41		35	Utah	23.68
11	Connecticut	73.64		36	South Carolina	20.86
12	Ohio	66.34		37	Alaska	20.65
13	Massachusetts	62.03		38	Delaware	19.09
14	Michigan	57.59		39	West Virginia	14.97
15	Mississippi	56.00		40	Maine	13.26
16	Alabama	55.65		41	New Hampshire	12.61
17	Texas	55.23		42	Montana	12.40
18	North Carolina	54.63		43	Iowa	12.14
19	Oregon	50.73		44	Nebraska	10.99
20	Wisconsin	48.95		45	Minnesota	8.91
21	Georgia	48.19		46	Idaho	8.75
22	Arizona	44.01		47	South Dakota	7.13
23	Illinois	43.97		48	Wyoming	6.33
24	Hawaii	42.76		49	North Dakota	5.93
25	Virginia	42.65		50	Vermont	2.98

District of Columbia 221.39

Source: Morgan Quitno Corporation using data from U.S. Department of Justice, Federal Bureau of Investigation
"Crime in the United States 1992" (Uniform Crime Reports, October 3, 1993)
*By law enforcement agencies submitting complete reports to the F.B.I. for 12 months in 1992. These rates based on population estimates for areas under the jurisdiction of those agencies reporting. Arrest rate based on the F.B.I. estimate of reported and unreported arrests for robbery is 67.94 arrests per 100,000 population. Robbery is the taking of anything of value by force or threat of force. Attempts are included.

Reported Arrests for Aggravated Assault in 1992

National Total = 434,918 Reported Arrests*

RANK	STATE	ARRESTS	%	RANK	STATE	ARRESTS	%
1	California	108,180	24.87%	26	Oklahoma	4,105	0.94%
2	Florida	38,834	8.93%	27	South Carolina	3,757	0.86%
3	New York	31,571	7.26%	28	Arkansas	3,306	0.76%
4	Texas	26,452	6.08%	29	Kansas	2,996	0.69%
5	North Carolina	20,995	4.83%	30	Minnesota	2,888	0.66%
6	Kentucky	14,569	3.35%	31	Rhode Island	2,512	0.58%
7	New Jersey	14,041	3.23%	32	Oregon	2,404	0.55%
8	Michigan	13,888	3.19%	33	New Mexico	1,986	0.46%
9	Pennsylvania	12,584	2.89%	34	Iowa	1,736	0.40%
10	Massachusetts	10,877	2.50%	35	Utah	1,562	0.36%
11	Alabama	8,681	2.00%	36	Idaho	1,308	0.30%
12	Georgia	8,497	1.95%	37	Nevada	1,279	0.29%
13	Ohio	8,087	1.86%	38	West Virginia	1,090	0.25%
14	Maryland	7,943	1.83%	39	Mississippi	1,065	0.24%
15	Louisiana	7,720	1.78%	40	Maine	932	0.21%
16	Illinois	7,499	1.72%	41	Alaska	831	0.19%
17	Virginia	7,252	1.67%	42	Hawaii	644	0.15%
18	Arizona	7,121	1.64%	43	Nebraska	538	0.12%
19	Connecticut	7,077	1.63%	44	Wyoming	487	0.11%
20	Colorado	7,020	1.61%	45	Delaware	418	0.10%
21	Indiana	5,547	1.28%	46	New Hampshire	408	0.09%
22	Tennessee	5,491	1.26%	47	Montana	368	0.08%
23	Missouri	5,050	1.16%	48	South Dakota	366	0.08%
24	Washington	4,719	1.09%	49	North Dakota	84	0.02%
25	Wisconsin	4,495	1.03%	50	Vermont	71	0.02%
					District of Columbia	3,586	0.82%

Source: U.S. Department of Justice, Federal Bureau of Investigation
    "Crime in the United States 1992" (Uniform Crime Reports, October 3, 1993)
*By law enforcement agencies submitting complete reports to the F.B.I. for 12 months in 1992. The F.B.I. estimates 507,210 reported and unreported arrests for aggravated assault occurred in 1992. Aggravated assault is an attack for the purpose of inflicting severe bodily injury.

Reported Arrest Rate for Aggravated Assault in 1992

National Rate = 204 Reported Arrests per 100,000 Population*

RANK	STATE	RATE		RANK	STATE	RATE
1	Kentucky	404		26	Arkansas	138
2	California	353		26	Oklahoma	131
3	North Carolina	316		28	Pennsylvania	125
4	Florida	312		29	Nevada	121
4	Louisiana	302		30	Mississippi	117
6	Massachusetts	274		31	Utah	117
7	Connecticut	263		32	Virginia	114
8	Rhode Island	250		33	Washington	114
9	Missouri	227		34	Delaware	112
10	Alabama	226		35	Ohio	111
11	New Mexico	225		36	Wyoming	110
12	Tennessee	223		37	South Carolina	109
13	Colorado	220		38	Iowa	97
14	New York	206		39	Maine	92
15	Arizona	197		40	Wisconsin	91
16	Indiana	193		41	Oregon	85
17	New Jersey	186		42	South Dakota	72
18	Georgia	175		43	Minnesota	65
19	Michigan	164		44	West Virginia	60
20	Maryland	162		45	Hawaii	56
21	Kansas	154		46	Montana	50
22	Illinois	153		47	Nebraska	46
23	Alaska	151		48	New Hampshire	45
24	Texas	150		49	Vermont	24
25	Idaho	140		50	North Dakota	17

District of Columbia   609

Source: Morgan Quitno Corporation using data from U.S. Department of Justice, Federal Bureau of Investigation
"Crime in the United States 1992" (Uniform Crime Reports, October 3, 1993)

*By law enforcement agencies submitting complete reports to the F.B.I. for 12 months in 1992. These rates based on population estimates for areas under the jurisdiction of those agencies reporting. Arrest rate based on the F.B.I. estimate of reported and unreported arrests for aggravated assault is 199 arrests per 100,000 population. Aggravated assault is an attack for the purpose of inflicting severe bodily injury.

Reported Arrests for Property Crime in 1992

National Total = 1,839,274 Reported Arrests*

RANK	STATE	ARRESTS	%	RANK	STATE	ARRESTS	%
1	California	289,402	15.73%	26	Oklahoma	22,180	1.21%
2	Texas	161,156	8.76%	27	Massachusetts	20,833	1.13%
3	Florida	122,918	6.68%	28	Indiana	20,634	1.12%
4	New York	110,443	6.00%	29	Utah	20,621	1.12%
5	Pennsylvania	63,962	3.48%	30	Kansas	19,538	1.06%
6	North Carolina	61,490	3.34%	31	Arkansas	18,930	1.03%
7	Wisconsin	58,111	3.16%	32	Nevada	13,114	0.71%
8	New Jersey	56,363	3.06%	33	Hawaii	11,364	0.62%
9	Michigan	55,168	3.00%	34	New Mexico	11,198	0.61%
10	Virginia	54,516	2.96%	35	Mississippi	10,310	0.56%
11	Maryland	50,247	2.73%	36	South Carolina	10,269	0.56%
12	Ohio	49,922	2.71%	37	Idaho	9,713	0.53%
13	Washington	47,862	2.60%	38	Maine	9,057	0.49%
14	Illinois	45,127	2.45%	39	West Virginia	8,983	0.49%
15	Arizona	44,786	2.43%	40	Iowa	8,721	0.47%
16	Georgia	40,911	2.22%	41	Nebraska	7,476	0.41%
17	Colorado	38,189	2.08%	42	Rhode Island	6,706	0.36%
18	Oregon	33,848	1.84%	43	Montana	6,437	0.35%
19	Connecticut	32,943	1.79%	44	Alaska	6,074	0.33%
20	Minnesota	29,354	1.60%	45	New Hampshire	4,460	0.24%
21	Louisiana	27,280	1.48%	46	South Dakota	4,421	0.24%
22	Tennessee	26,146	1.42%	47	North Dakota	3,573	0.19%
23	Kentucky	25,417	1.38%	48	Wyoming	3,078	0.17%
24	Missouri	23,886	1.30%	49	Delaware	1,641	0.09%
25	Alabama	23,271	1.27%	50	Vermont	854	0.05%
					District of Columbia	6,370	0.35%

Source: U.S. Department of Justice, Federal Bureau of Investigation
"Crime in the United States 1992" (Uniform Crime Reports, October 3, 1993)
By law enforcement agencies submitting complete reports to the F.B.I. for 12 months in 1992. The F.B.I. estimates 2,146,000 reported and unreported arrests for property crimes occurred in 1992. Property crimes are offenses of burglary, larceny-theft, motor vehicle theft and arson.

Reported Arrest Rate for Property Crime in 1992

National Rate = 862 Reported Arrests per 100,000 Population*

RANK	STATE	RATE	RANK	STATE	RATE
1	Utah	1,550	26	Montana	868
2	New Mexico	1,270	26	Virginia	855
3	Nevada	1,244	28	Georgia	840
4	Arizona	1,240	29	Arkansas	792
1	Connecticut	1,226	26	New Jersey	746
2	Oregon	1,200	26	North Dakota	730
3	Colorado	1,197	28	New York	719
4	Wisconsin	1,181	29	Indiana	716
4	Washington	1,161	30	Oklahoma	709
6	Mississippi	1,134	31	Kentucky	705
7	Alaska	1,100	32	Wyoming	696
8	Missouri	1,072	33	Ohio	682
9	Louisiana	1,068	34	Rhode Island	667
10	Tennessee	1,064	35	Minnesota	659
11	Idaho	1,037	36	Michigan	651
12	Maryland	1,024	37	Nebraska	642
13	Kansas	1,003	38	Pennsylvania	637
14	Florida	987	39	Alabama	605
15	Hawaii	980	40	Massachusetts	526
16	California	944	41	West Virginia	496
17	North Carolina	926	42	New Hampshire	493
18	Illinois	922	43	Iowa	488
19	Texas	914	44	Delaware	441
20	Maine	890	45	South Carolina	297
21	South Dakota	875	46	Vermont	283

District of Columbia   1,081

Source: Morgan Quitno Corporation using data from U.S. Department of Justice, Federal Bureau of Investigation
"Crime in the United States 1992" (Uniform Crime Reports, October 3, 1993)
By law enforcement agencies submitting complete reports to the F.B.I. for 12 months in 1992. These rates based on population estimates for areas under the jurisdiction of those agencies reporting. Arrest rate based on the F.B.I. estimate of reported and unreported arrests for property crimes is 841 arrests per 100,000 population. Property crimes are offenses of burglary, larceny-theft, motor vehicle theft and arson.

Reported Arrests for Burglary in 1992

National Total = 359,699 Reported Arrests*

RANK	STATE	ARRESTS	%	RANK	STATE	ARRESTS	%
1	California	80,090	22.27%	26	Alabama	3,871	1.08%
2	Texas	29,319	8.15%	27	Minnesota	3,808	1.06%
3	Florida	28,438	7.91%	28	Kansas	3,635	1.01%
4	New York	19,916	5.54%	29	Arkansas	3,609	1.00%
5	North Carolina	17,024	4.73%	30	Indiana	2,886	0.80%
6	Pennsylvania	12,330	3.43%	31	Nevada	2,734	0.76%
7	Maryland	10,899	3.03%	32	Utah	2,232	0.62%
8	New Jersey	10,586	2.94%	33	South Carolina	2,219	0.62%
9	Michigan	9,839	2.74%	34	Mississippi	2,061	0.57%
10	Ohio	8,908	2.48%	35	Hawaii	1,867	0.52%
11	Virginia	8,206	2.28%	36	Maine	1,797	0.50%
12	Arizona	7,426	2.06%	37	West Virginia	1,610	0.45%
13	Georgia	7,410	2.06%	38	Idaho	1,609	0.45%
14	Wisconsin	6,969	1.94%	39	Rhode Island	1,450	0.40%
15	Washington	6,733	1.87%	40	New Mexico	1,228	0.34%
16	Illinois	6,659	1.85%	41	Nebraska	1,144	0.32%
17	Connecticut	6,315	1.76%	42	Iowa	1,019	0.28%
18	Louisiana	6,098	1.70%	43	Alaska	744	0.21%
19	Kentucky	5,563	1.55%	44	Montana	636	0.18%
20	Massachusetts	5,351	1.49%	45	New Hampshire	630	0.18%
21	Oregon	4,736	1.32%	46	South Dakota	514	0.14%
22	Missouri	4,476	1.24%	47	North Dakota	407	0.11%
23	Tennessee	4,256	1.18%	48	Delaware	393	0.11%
24	Oklahoma	4,243	1.18%	49	Wyoming	379	0.11%
25	Colorado	4,033	1.12%	50	Vermont	321	0.09%
					District of Columbia	1,073	0.30%

Source: U.S. Department of Justice, Federal Bureau of Investigation
"Crime in the United States 1992" (Uniform Crime Reports, October 3, 1993)
*By law enforcement agencies submitting complete reports to the F.B.I. for 12 months in 1992. The F.B.I. estimates 424,000 reported and unreported arrests for burglary occurred in 1992. Burglary is the unlawful entry of a structure to commit a felony or theft. Attempts are included.

Reported Arrest Rate for Burglary in 1992

National Rate = 168.56 Reported Arrests per 100,000 Population*

RANK	STATE	RATE	RANK	STATE	RATE
1	California	261.22	26	New Mexico	139.23
2	Nevada	259.39	27	Illinois	136.01
3	North Carolina	256.27	28	Oklahoma	135.60
4	Louisiana	238.76	29	Massachusetts	134.99
5	Connecticut	235.11	30	Alaska	134.78
6	Florida	228.34	31	New York	129.70
7	Mississippi	226.73	32	Virginia	128.76
8	Maryland	222.07	33	Colorado	126.39
9	Arizona	205.54	34	Pennsylvania	122.76
10	Missouri	200.81	35	Ohio	121.74
11	Kansas	186.70	36	Michigan	116.16
12	Maine	176.52	37	Vermont	106.28
13	Tennessee	173.15	38	Delaware	105.65
14	Idaho	171.72	39	South Dakota	101.78
15	Oregon	167.88	40	Alabama	100.62
16	Utah	167.82	41	Indiana	100.21
17	Texas	166.37	42	Nebraska	98.20
18	Washington	163.26	43	West Virginia	88.95
19	Hawaii	160.95	44	Wyoming	85.75
20	Kentucky	154.40	45	Montana	85.71
21	Georgia	152.22	46	Minnesota	85.46
22	Arkansas	151.00	47	North Dakota	83.16
23	Rhode Island	144.28	48	New Hampshire	69.69
24	Wisconsin	141.68	49	South Carolina	64.21
25	New Jersey	140.08	50	Iowa	57.02

District of Columbia   182.17

Source: Morgan Quitno Corporation using data from U.S. Department of Justice, Federal Bureau of Investigation
"Crime in the United States 1992" (Uniform Crime Reports, October 3, 1993)

*By law enforcement agencies submitting complete reports to the F.B.I. for 12 months in 1992. These rates based on population estimates for areas under the jurisdiction of those agencies reporting. Arrest rate based on the F.B.I. estimate of total arrests for burglary is 166.22 reported and unreported arrests per 100,000 population. Burglary is the unlawful entry of a structure to commit a felony or theft. Attempts are included.

Reported Arrests for Larceny and Theft in 1992

National Total = 1,291,984 Reported Arrests*

RANK	STATE	ARRESTS	%	RANK	STATE	ARRESTS	%
1	California	160,454	12.42%	26	Utah	16,743	1.30%
2	Texas	114,469	8.86%	27	Indiana	15,738	1.22%
3	Florida	81,510	6.31%	28	Oklahoma	15,343	1.19%
4	New York	76,630	5.93%	29	Kansas	14,949	1.16%
5	Wisconsin	45,802	3.55%	30	Arkansas	14,424	1.12%
6	Pennsylvania	43,040	3.33%	31	Massachusetts	12,955	1.00%
7	New Jersey	42,313	3.28%	32	Nevada	9,702	0.75%
8	Virginia	42,170	3.26%	33	New Mexico	9,563	0.74%
9	North Carolina	41,608	3.22%	34	Hawaii	7,957	0.62%
10	Michigan	40,907	3.17%	35	Idaho	7,662	0.59%
11	Washington	38,070	2.95%	36	Mississippi	7,465	0.58%
12	Illinois	36,519	2.83%	37	South Carolina	7,370	0.57%
13	Ohio	36,371	2.82%	38	Iowa	7,264	0.56%
14	Arizona	33,674	2.61%	39	Maine	6,740	0.52%
15	Maryland	31,681	2.45%	40	West Virginia	6,725	0.52%
16	Colorado	31,541	2.44%	41	Nebraska	5,896	0.46%
17	Georgia	30,849	2.39%	42	Montana	5,308	0.41%
18	Oregon	25,542	1.98%	43	Alaska	4,896	0.38%
19	Connecticut	23,841	1.85%	44	Rhode Island	4,447	0.34%
20	Minnesota	23,159	1.79%	45	South Dakota	3,701	0.29%
21	Tennessee	20,611	1.60%	46	New Hampshire	3,615	0.28%
22	Louisiana	19,568	1.51%	47	North Dakota	2,903	0.22%
23	Kentucky	17,848	1.38%	48	Wyoming	2,529	0.20%
24	Alabama	17,819	1.38%	49	Delaware	1,169	0.09%
25	Missouri	17,278	1.34%	50	Vermont	504	0.04%
					District of Columbia	3,142	0.24%

Source: U.S. Department of Justice, Federal Bureau of Investigation
    "Crime in the United States 1992" (Uniform Crime Reports, October 3, 1993)
*By law enforcement agencies submitting complete reports to the F.B.I. for 12 months in 1992. The F.B.I. estimates 1,504,500 reported and unreported arrests for larceny and theft occurred in 1992. Larceny and theft is the unlawful taking of property. Attempts are included.

Reported Arrest Rate for Larceny and Theft in 1992

National Rate = 605 Reported Arrests per 100,000 Population*

RANK	STATE	RATE	RANK	STATE	RATE
1	Utah	1,259	26	Georgia	634
2	New Mexico	1,084	27	North Carolina	626
3	Colorado	988	28	Arkansas	604
4	Arizona	932	29	North Dakota	593
5	Wisconsin	931	30	Wyoming	572
6	Washington	923	31	New Jersey	560
7	Nevada	920	32	Indiana	546
8	Oregon	905	33	California	523
9	Connecticut	888	34	Minnesota	520
10	Alaska	887	35	Nebraska	506
11	Tennessee	839	36	New York	499
12	Mississippi	821	37	Ohio	497
13	Idaho	818	38	Kentucky	495
14	Missouri	775	39	Oklahoma	490
15	Kansas	768	40	Michigan	483
16	Louisiana	766	41	Alabama	463
17	Illinois	746	42	Rhode Island	442
18	South Dakota	733	43	Pennsylvania	429
19	Montana	715	44	Iowa	406
20	Hawaii	686	45	New Hampshire	400
21	Maine	662	46	West Virginia	372
21	Virginia	662	47	Massachusetts	327
23	Florida	654	48	Delaware	314
24	Texas	650	49	South Carolina	213
25	Maryland	645	50	Vermont	167

District of Columbia   533

Source: Morgan Quitno Corporation using data from U.S. Department of Justice, Federal Bureau of Investigation
    "Crime in the United States 1992" (Uniform Crime Reports, October 3, 1993)
*By law enforcement agencies submitting complete reports to the F.B.I. for 12 months in 1992. These rates based on population estimates for areas under the jurisdiction of those agencies reporting. Arrest rate based on the F.B.I. estimate of reported and unreported arrests for larceny and theft is 590 arrests per 100,000 population. Larceny and theft is the unlawful taking of property. Attempts are included.

Reported Arrests for Motor Vehicle Theft in 1992

National Total = 171,269 Reported Arrests*

RANK	STATE	ARRESTS	%	RANK	STATE	ARRESTS	%
1	California	46,444	27.12%	26	Hawaii	1,484	0.87%
2	Texas	16,291	9.51%	27	Alabama	1,452	0.85%
3	New York	12,984	7.58%	28	Utah	1,423	0.83%
4	Florida	12,398	7.24%	29	Louisiana	1,373	0.80%
5	Pennsylvania	7,781	4.54%	30	Tennessee	1,072	0.63%
6	Maryland	7,177	4.19%	31	Arkansas	747	0.44%
7	Wisconsin	4,823	2.82%	32	Kansas	743	0.43%
8	Ohio	3,982	2.32%	33	Mississippi	711	0.42%
9	Michigan	3,691	2.16%	34	Rhode Island	684	0.40%
10	Virginia	3,690	2.15%	35	Nevada	617	0.36%
11	Arizona	3,366	1.97%	36	South Carolina	601	0.35%
12	Oregon	3,072	1.79%	37	West Virginia	509	0.30%
13	New Jersey	2,900	1.69%	38	Montana	438	0.26%
14	Washington	2,723	1.59%	39	Alaska	418	0.24%
15	Connecticut	2,531	1.48%	40	Maine	408	0.24%
16	Georgia	2,334	1.36%	41	New Mexico	372	0.22%
17	Massachusetts	2,334	1.36%	42	Idaho	345	0.20%
18	North Carolina	2,273	1.33%	43	Iowa	342	0.20%
19	Colorado	2,269	1.32%	44	Nebraska	326	0.19%
20	Oklahoma	2,207	1.29%	45	North Dakota	246	0.14%
21	Minnesota	2,146	1.25%	46	New Hampshire	162	0.09%
22	Missouri	1,835	1.07%	47	South Dakota	159	0.09%
23	Indiana	1,832	1.07%	48	Wyoming	137	0.08%
24	Kentucky	1,707	1.00%	49	Delaware	60	0.04%
25	Illinois	1,528	0.89%	50	Vermont	16	0.01%
					District of Columbia	2,105	1.23%

Source: U.S. Department of Justice, Federal Bureau of Investigation
"Crime in the United States 1992" (Uniform Crime Reports, October 3, 1993)
*By law enforcement agencies submitting complete reports to the F.B.I. for 12 months in 1992. The F.B.I. estimates 197,600 reported and unreported arrests for motor vehicle theft occurred in 1992. The theft or attempted theft of a self-propelled vehicle. Excludes motorboats, construction equipment, airplanes, and farming equipment.

Reported Arrest Rate for Motor Vehicle Theft in 1992

National Rate = 80.26 Reported Arrests per 100,000 Population*

RANK	STATE	RATE	RANK	STATE	RATE
1	California	151.48	26	Louisiana	53.76
2	Maryland	146.23	27	North Dakota	50.27
3	Hawaii	127.93	28	Minnesota	48.16
4	Oregon	108.90	29	Georgia	47.95
5	Utah	106.99	30	Kentucky	47.38
6	Florida	99.55	31	Tennessee	43.61
7	Wisconsin	98.05	32	Michigan	43.58
8	Connecticut	94.23	33	New Mexico	42.18
9	Arizona	93.16	34	Maine	40.08
10	Texas	92.44	35	New Jersey	38.38
11	New York	84.56	36	Kansas	38.16
12	Missouri	82.32	37	Alabama	37.74
13	Mississippi	78.22	38	Idaho	36.82
14	Pennsylvania	77.47	39	North Carolina	34.22
15	Alaska	75.72	40	South Dakota	31.49
16	Colorado	71.11	41	Arkansas	31.26
17	Oklahoma	70.53	42	Illinois	31.21
18	Rhode Island	68.06	43	Wyoming	31.00
19	Washington	66.03	44	West Virginia	28.12
20	Indiana	63.61	45	Nebraska	27.98
21	Montana	59.03	46	Iowa	19.14
22	Massachusetts	58.88	47	New Hampshire	17.92
23	Nevada	58.54	48	South Carolina	17.39
24	Virginia	57.90	49	Delaware	16.13
25	Ohio	54.42	50	Vermont	5.30

District of Columbia   357.39

Source: Morgan Quitno Corporation using data from U.S. Department of Justice, Federal Bureau of Investigation
   "Crime in the United States 1992" (Uniform Crime Reports, October 3, 1993)
*By law enforcement agencies submitting complete reports to the F.B.I. for 12 months in 1992. These rates based on population estimates for areas under the jurisdiction of those agencies reporting. Arrest rate based on the F.B.I. estimate of reported and unreported arrests for motor vehicle theft is 77.47 arrests per 100,000 population. The theft or attempted theft of a self-propelled vehicle. Excludes motorboats, construction equipment, airplanes, and farming equipment.

Reported Arrests for Arson in 1992

National Total = 16,322 Reported Arrests*

RANK	STATE	ARRESTS	%	RANK	STATE	ARRESTS	%
1	California	2,414	14.79%	26	Kansas	211	1.29%
2	Texas	1,077	6.60%	27	Tennessee	207	1.27%
3	New York	913	5.59%	28	Massachusetts	193	1.18%
4	Pennsylvania	811	4.97%	29	Indiana	178	1.09%
5	Michigan	731	4.48%	30	Arkansas	150	0.92%
6	Ohio	661	4.05%	31	West Virginia	139	0.85%
7	North Carolina	585	3.58%	32	Alabama	129	0.79%
8	Florida	572	3.50%	33	Rhode Island	125	0.77%
9	New Jersey	564	3.46%	34	Maine	112	0.69%
10	Wisconsin	517	3.17%	35	Nebraska	110	0.67%
11	Oregon	498	3.05%	36	Idaho	97	0.59%
12	Maryland	490	3.00%	37	Iowa	96	0.59%
13	Virginia	450	2.76%	38	South Carolina	79	0.48%
14	Illinois	421	2.58%	39	Mississippi	73	0.45%
15	Oklahoma	387	2.37%	40	Nevada	61	0.37%
16	Colorado	346	2.12%	41	Hawaii	56	0.34%
17	Washington	336	2.06%	42	Montana	55	0.34%
18	Arizona	320	1.96%	43	New Hampshire	53	0.32%
19	Georgia	318	1.95%	44	South Dakota	47	0.29%
20	Kentucky	299	1.83%	45	New Mexico	35	0.21%
21	Missouri	297	1.82%	46	Wyoming	33	0.20%
22	Connecticut	256	1.57%	47	Delaware	19	0.12%
23	Louisiana	241	1.48%	48	North Dakota	17	0.10%
23	Minnesota	241	1.48%	49	Alaska	16	0.10%
25	Utah	223	1.37%	50	Vermont	13	0.08%
					District of Columbia	50	0.31%

Source: U.S. Department of Justice, Federal Bureau of Investigation
    "Crime in the United States 1992" (Uniform Crime Reports, October 3, 1993)
*By law enforcement agencies submitting complete reports to the F.B.I. for 12 months in 1992. The F.B.I. estimates 19,900 reported and unreported arrests for arson occurred in 1992.

Reported Arrest Rate for Arson in 1992

National Rate = 7.65 Reported Arrests per 100,000 Population*

RANK	STATE	RATE	RANK	STATE	RATE
1	Oregon	17.65	26	California	7.87
2	Utah	16.77	27	West Virginia	7.68
3	Missouri	13.32	28	Wyoming	7.47
4	Rhode Island	12.44	29	New Jersey	7.46
5	Oklahoma	12.37	30	Montana	7.41
6	Maine	11.00	31	Virginia	7.06
7	Colorado	10.84	32	Georgia	6.53
7	Kansas	10.84	33	Arkansas	6.28
9	Wisconsin	10.51	34	Indiana	6.18
10	Idaho	10.35	35	Texas	6.11
11	Maryland	9.98	36	New York	5.95
12	Connecticut	9.53	37	New Hampshire	5.86
13	Louisiana	9.44	38	Nevada	5.79
13	Nebraska	9.44	39	Minnesota	5.41
15	South Dakota	9.31	40	Iowa	5.37
16	Ohio	9.03	41	Delaware	5.11
17	Arizona	8.86	42	Massachusetts	4.87
18	North Carolina	8.81	43	Hawaii	4.83
19	Michigan	8.63	44	Florida	4.59
20	Illinois	8.60	45	Vermont	4.30
21	Tennessee	8.42	46	New Mexico	3.97
22	Kentucky	8.30	47	North Dakota	3.47
23	Washington	8.15	48	Alabama	3.35
24	Pennsylvania	8.07	49	Alaska	2.90
25	Mississippi	8.03	50	South Carolina	2.29

District of Columbia   8.49

Source: Morgan Quitno Corporation using data from U.S. Department of Justice, Federal Bureau of Investigation "Crime in the United States 1992" (Uniform Crime Reports, October 3, 1993)

By law enforcement agencies submitting complete reports to the F.B.I. for 12 months in 1992. These rates based on population estimates for areas under the jurisdiction of those agencies reporting. Arrest rate based on the F.B.I. estimate of reported and unreported arrests is 7.80 arrests for arson per 100,000 population.

Reported Arrests for Weapons Violations in 1992

National Total = 204,116 Reported Arrests*

RANK	STATE	ARRESTS	%	RANK	STATE	ARRESTS	%
1	California	36,457	17.86%	26	Kansas	2,254	1.10%
2	Texas	25,096	12.29%	27	Oregon	2,253	1.10%
3	New York	15,314	7.50%	28	South Carolina	1,657	0.81%
4	Michigan	8,722	4.27%	29	Indiana	1,464	0.72%
5	Florida	8,637	4.23%	30	West Virginia	1,391	0.68%
6	North Carolina	7,969	3.90%	31	Massachusetts	1,360	0.67%
7	Virginia	7,763	3.80%	32	Minnesota	1,330	0.65%
8	Wisconsin	7,442	3.65%	33	Nevada	1,223	0.60%
9	Ohio	7,097	3.48%	34	Mississippi	1,075	0.53%
10	New Jersey	6,963	3.41%	35	Utah	961	0.47%
11	Maryland	5,124	2.51%	36	Hawaii	924	0.45%
12	Illinois	4,271	2.09%	37	New Mexico	639	0.31%
13	Georgia	4,190	2.05%	38	Rhode Island	491	0.24%
14	Colorado	4,011	1.97%	39	Alaska	487	0.24%
15	Pennsylvania	3,955	1.94%	40	Nebraska	481	0.24%
16	Tennessee	3,641	1.78%	41	Iowa	426	0.21%
17	Kentucky	3,487	1.71%	42	Idaho	384	0.19%
18	Missouri	3,405	1.67%	43	Maine	321	0.16%
19	Arizona	3,002	1.47%	44	South Dakota	185	0.09%
20	Louisiana	2,950	1.45%	45	Montana	123	0.06%
21	Arkansas	2,937	1.44%	46	Wyoming	122	0.06%
22	Connecticut	2,874	1.41%	47	New Hampshire	104	0.05%
23	Washington	2,599	1.27%	48	Delaware	96	0.05%
24	Oklahoma	2,598	1.27%	49	North Dakota	93	0.05%
25	Alabama	2,273	1.11%	50	Vermont	0	0.00%
					District of Columbia	1,495	0.73%

Source: U.S. Department of Justice, Federal Bureau of Investigation
"Crime in the United States 1992" (Uniform Crime Reports, October 3, 1993)
*By law enforcement agencies submitting complete reports to the F.B.I. for 12 months in 1992. The F.B.I. estimates 239,300 reported and unreported arrests for weapons violations occurred in 1992. Weapons violations include illegal carrying and possession.

Reported Arrest Rate for Weapons Violations in 1992

National Rate = 95.65 Reported Arrests per 100,000 Population*

RANK	STATE	RATE	RANK	STATE	RATE
1	Missouri	152.76	26	Oregon	79.87
2	Wisconsin	151.29	27	Hawaii	79.66
3	Tennessee	148.13	28	West Virginia	76.85
4	Texas	142.40	29	New Mexico	72.45
5	Colorado	125.70	30	Utah	72.26
6	Arkansas	122.89	31	Florida	69.35
7	Virginia	121.81	32	Washington	63.02
8	North Carolina	119.96	33	Alabama	59.09
9	California	118.91	34	Indiana	50.83
10	Mississippi	118.26	35	Rhode Island	48.86
11	Nevada	116.03	36	South Carolina	47.95
12	Kansas	115.77	37	Nebraska	41.29
13	Louisiana	115.51	38	Idaho	40.98
14	Connecticut	107.00	39	Pennsylvania	39.38
15	Maryland	104.40	40	South Dakota	36.63
16	Michigan	102.98	41	Massachusetts	34.31
17	New York	99.73	42	Maine	31.53
18	Ohio	96.99	43	Minnesota	29.85
19	Kentucky	96.78	44	Wyoming	27.60
20	New Jersey	92.14	45	Delaware	25.81
21	Alaska	88.22	46	Iowa	23.84
22	Illinois	87.23	47	North Dakota	19.00
23	Georgia	86.07	48	Montana	16.58
24	Arizona	83.09	49	New Hampshire	11.50
25	Oklahoma	83.03	50	Vermont	0.00

District of Columbia   253.82

Source: Morgan Quitno Corporation using data from U.S. Department of Justice, Federal Bureau of Investigation
     "Crime in the United States 1992" (Uniform Crime Reports, October 3, 1993)
*By law enforcement agencies submitting complete reports to the F.B.I. for 12 months in 1992. These rates based on population estimates for areas
under the jurisdiction of those agencies reporting. Arrest rate based on the F.B.I. estimate of reported and unreported arrests for weapons violations is
93.81 arrests per 100,000 population. Weapons violations include illegal carrying and possession.

Reported Arrests for Driving Under the Influence in 1992

National Total = 1,319,583 Reported Arrests*

RANK	STATE	ARRESTS	%	RANK	STATE	ARRESTS	%
1	California	255,856	19.39%	26	Indiana	14,926	1.13%
2	Texas	109,956	8.33%	27	Missouri	14,821	1.12%
3	North Carolina	72,889	5.52%	28	South Carolina	14,553	1.10%
4	Michigan	49,957	3.79%	29	Massachusetts	13,752	1.04%
5	Georgia	47,578	3.61%	30	New Mexico	11,995	0.91%
6	Kentucky	40,875	3.10%	31	Louisiana	11,065	0.84%
7	Virginia	40,097	3.04%	32	Idaho	10,774	0.82%
8	Florida	40,079	3.04%	33	Connecticut	10,425	0.79%
9	Washington	39,654	3.01%	34	Nebraska	10,304	0.78%
10	New York	37,869	2.87%	35	Iowa	10,048	0.76%
11	Wisconsin	35,085	2.66%	36	West Virginia	9,089	0.69%
12	Ohio	33,978	2.57%	37	Maine	7,857	0.60%
13	Pennsylvania	32,478	2.46%	38	Mississippi	7,071	0.54%
14	Colorado	29,389	2.23%	39	Nevada	6,222	0.47%
15	Arizona	28,458	2.16%	40	Utah	5,824	0.44%
16	New Jersey	26,580	2.01%	41	New Hampshire	5,792	0.44%
17	Minnesota	26,036	1.97%	42	Hawaii	5,559	0.42%
18	Maryland	25,583	1.94%	43	Montana	5,557	0.42%
19	Oregon	23,653	1.79%	44	South Dakota	5,320	0.40%
20	Oklahoma	22,384	1.70%	45	Alaska	5,088	0.39%
21	Illinois	21,237	1.61%	46	Wyoming	4,966	0.38%
22	Arkansas	20,424	1.55%	47	Rhode Island	2,585	0.20%
23	Alabama	19,736	1.50%	48	North Dakota	2,284	0.17%
24	Kansas	19,696	1.49%	49	Vermont	1,625	0.12%
25	Tennessee	19,391	1.47%	50	Delaware	1	0.00%
					District of Columbia	3,162	0.24%

Source: U.S. Department of Justice, Federal Bureau of Investigation
"Crime in the United States 1992" (Uniform Crime Reports, October 3, 1993)
*By law enforcement agencies submitting complete reports to the F.B.I. for 12 months in 1992. The F.B.I. estimates 1,624,500 reported and unreported arrests for driving under the influence in 1992. Includes driving or operating any vehicle or common carrier while drunk or under the influence of liquor or narcotics.

Reported Arrest Rate for Driving Under the Influence in 1992

National Rate = 618 Reported Arrests per 100,000 Population*

RANK	STATE	RATE	RANK	STATE	RATE
1	New Mexico	1,360	26	Texas	624
2	Idaho	1,150	27	Michigan	590
3	Kentucky	1,134	27	Nevada	590
4	Wyoming	1,124	29	Minnesota	584
5	North Carolina	1,097	30	Iowa	562
6	South Dakota	1,053	31	Vermont	538
7	Kansas	1,012	32	Maryland	521
8	Georgia	977	33	Indiana	518
9	Washington	962	34	Alabama	513
10	Alaska	922	35	West Virginia	502
11	Colorado	921	36	Hawaii	479
12	Nebraska	884	37	North Dakota	467
13	Arkansas	855	38	Ohio	464
14	Oregon	838	39	Utah	438
15	California	834	40	Illinois	434
16	Tennessee	789	41	Louisiana	433
17	Arizona	788	42	South Carolina	421
18	Mississippi	778	43	Connecticut	388
19	Maine	772	44	New Jersey	352
20	Montana	749	45	Massachusetts	347
21	Oklahoma	715	46	Pennsylvania	323
22	Wisconsin	713	47	Florida	322
23	Missouri	665	48	Rhode Island	257
24	New Hampshire	641	49	New York	247
25	Virginia	629	50	Delaware	0

District of Columbia   537

Source: Morgan Quitno Corporation using data from U.S. Department of Justice, Federal Bureau of Investigation
       "Crime in the United States 1992" (Uniform Crime Reports, October 3, 1993)

*By law enforcement agencies submitting complete reports to the F.B.I. for 12 months in 1992. These rates based on population estimates for areas under the jurisdiction of those agencies reporting. Arrest rate based on the F.B.I. estimate of reported and unreported arrests for driving under the influence is 637 arrests per 100,000 population. Includes driving or operating any vehicle or common carrier while drunk or under the influence of liquor or narcotics.

Reported Arrests for Drug Abuse Violations in 1992

National Total = 920,424 Reported Arrests*

RANK	STATE	ARRESTS	%
1	California	227,784	24.75%
2	New York	101,348	11.01%
3	Texas	69,835	7.59%
4	Florida	60,598	6.58%
5	New Jersey	41,182	4.47%
6	Maryland	29,103	3.16%
7	North Carolina	29,034	3.15%
8	Pennsylvania	28,288	3.07%
9	Michigan	27,355	2.97%
10	Ohio	26,293	2.86%
11	Kentucky	20,434	2.22%
12	Georgia	20,409	2.22%
13	Virginia	19,404	2.11%
14	Massachusetts	17,041	1.85%
15	Connecticut	15,533	1.69%
16	Arizona	15,398	1.67%
17	Louisiana	13,417	1.46%
18	Wisconsin	11,320	1.23%
19	Tennessee	11,218	1.22%
20	Illinois	11,133	1.21%
21	Washington	10,633	1.16%
22	Oregon	10,355	1.13%
23	Oklahoma	9,010	0.98%
24	Alabama	8,766	0.95%
25	Colorado	8,275	0.90%

RANK	STATE	ARRESTS	%
26	Missouri	7,566	0.82%
27	Arkansas	7,216	0.78%
28	Kansas	6,655	0.72%
29	Nevada	5,919	0.64%
30	Indiana	5,152	0.56%
31	Minnesota	5,120	0.56%
32	Mississippi	4,489	0.49%
33	Hawaii	3,758	0.41%
34	Rhode Island	3,142	0.34%
35	Utah	3,097	0.34%
36	Nebraska	2,637	0.29%
37	New Mexico	2,116	0.23%
38	New Hampshire	1,993	0.22%
39	West Virginia	1,976	0.21%
40	Maine	1,799	0.20%
41	Idaho	1,305	0.14%
41	South Carolina	1,223	0.13%
43	Iowa	840	0.09%
44	Alaska	837	0.09%
45	South Dakota	675	0.07%
46	Wyoming	566	0.06%
47	Delaware	525	0.06%
48	Montana	403	0.04%
49	North Dakota	282	0.03%
50	Vermont	214	0.02%

| | District of Columbia | 7,753 | 0.84% |

Source: U.S. Department of Justice, Federal Bureau of Investigation
"Crime in the United States 1992" (Uniform Crime Reports, October 3, 1993)
*By law enforcement agencies submitting complete reports to the F.B.I. for 12 months in 1992. The F.B.I. estimates 1,066,400 reported and unreported arrests for drug abuse violations occurred in 1992. Includes offenses relating to possession, sale, use, growing and manufacturing of narcotic drugs.

Reported Arrest Rate for Drug Abuse Violations in 1992

National Rate = 431 Reported Arrests per 100,000 Population*

RANK	STATE	RATE		RANK	STATE	RATE
1	California	743		26	Oklahoma	288
2	New York	660		27	Pennsylvania	282
3	Maryland	593		28	Colorado	259
4	Connecticut	578		29	Washington	258
5	Kentucky	567		30	New Mexico	240
6	Nevada	562		31	Utah	233
7	New Jersey	545		32	Wisconsin	230
8	Louisiana	525		33	Alabama	228
9	Mississippi	494		34	Illinois	227
10	Florida	487		35	Nebraska	226
11	Tennessee	456		36	New Hampshire	220
12	North Carolina	437		37	Indiana	179
13	Massachusetts	430		38	Maine	177
14	Arizona	426		39	Alaska	152
15	Georgia	419		40	Delaware	141
16	Texas	396		41	Idaho	139
17	Oregon	367		42	South Dakota	134
18	Ohio	359		43	Wyoming	128
19	Kansas	342		44	Minnesota	115
20	Missouri	339		45	West Virginia	109
21	Hawaii	324		46	Vermont	71
22	Michigan	323		47	North Dakota	58
23	Rhode Island	313		48	Montana	54
24	Virginia	304		49	Iowa	47
25	Arkansas	302		50	South Carolina	35

District of Columbia 1,316

Source: Morgan Quitno Corporation using data from U.S. Department of Justice, Federal Bureau of Investigation

"Crime in the United States 1992" (Uniform Crime Reports, October 3, 1993)

*By law enforcement agencies submitting complete reports to the F.B.I. for 12 months in 1992. These rates based on population estimates for areas under the jurisdiction of those agencies reporting. Arrest rate based on the F.B.I. estimate of reported and unreported arrests for drug abuse violations is 418 arrests per 100,000 population. Includes offenses relating to possession, sale, use, growing and manufacturing of narcotic drugs.

Reported Arrests for Sex Offenses in 1992

National Total = 91,560 Reported Arrests*

RANK	STATE	ARRESTS	%	RANK	STATE	ARRESTS	%
1	California	18,021	19.68%	26	Connecticut	931	1.02%
2	Texas	7,106	7.76%	27	Kansas	922	1.01%
3	New York	5,962	6.51%	28	Massachusetts	906	0.99%
4	Florida	4,983	5.44%	29	Hawaii	686	0.75%
5	Wisconsin	4,122	4.50%	30	Nevada	629	0.69%
6	Kentucky	3,357	3.67%	31	Tennessee	497	0.54%
7	Virginia	3,098	3.38%	32	Arkansas	485	0.53%
8	Michigan	2,920	3.19%	33	Nebraska	465	0.51%
9	Pennsylvania	2,837	3.10%	34	Rhode Island	449	0.49%
10	North Carolina	2,727	2.98%	35	Alabama	436	0.48%
11	Ohio	2,658	2.90%	36	South Carolina	358	0.39%
12	Washington	2,597	2.84%	37	West Virginia	352	0.38%
13	New Jersey	2,300	2.51%	38	Maine	334	0.36%
14	Arizona	2,296	2.51%	39	New Hampshire	290	0.32%
15	Colorado	2,296	2.51%	40	Montana	287	0.31%
16	Georgia	1,943	2.12%	41	Alaska	275	0.30%
17	Maryland	1,828	2.00%	41	New Mexico	268	0.29%
18	Oregon	1,738	1.90%	43	Idaho	265	0.29%
19	Illinois	1,547	1.69%	44	Mississippi	227	0.25%
20	Minnesota	1,281	1.40%	45	Iowa	219	0.24%
21	Indiana	1,250	1.37%	46	South Dakota	162	0.18%
22	Missouri	1,210	1.32%	47	Wyoming	140	0.15%
23	Louisiana	1,190	1.30%	48	Vermont	115	0.13%
24	Utah	1,169	1.28%	49	Delaware	80	0.09%
25	Oklahoma	1,142	1.25%	50	North Dakota	65	0.07%
					District of Columbia	163	0.18%

Source: U.S. Department of Justice, Federal Bureau of Investigation

"Crime in the United States 1992" (Uniform Crime Reports, October 3, 1993)

*By law enforcement agencies submitting complete reports to the F.B.I. for 12 months in 1992. The F.B.I. estimates 108,400 reported and unreported arrests for sex offenses occurred in 1992. Excludes forcible rape, prostitution and commercialized vice. Includes statutory rape and offenses against chastity, common decency, morals and the like. Attempts are included.

Reported Arrest Rate for Sex Offenses in 1992

National Rate = 42.91 Reported Arrests per 100,000 Population*

RANK	STATE	RATE		RANK	STATE	RATE
1	Kentucky	93.17		26	Maryland	37.25
2	Utah	87.89		27	Oklahoma	36.50
3	Wisconsin	83.80		28	Ohio	36.33
4	Colorado	71.95		29	Connecticut	34.66
5	Arizona	63.55		30	Michigan	34.47
6	Washington	62.97		31	Maine	32.81
7	Oregon	61.61		32	New Hampshire	32.08
8	Nevada	59.68		32	South Dakota	32.08
9	Hawaii	59.14		34	Wyoming	31.67
10	California	58.78		35	Illinois	31.60
11	Missouri	54.28		36	New Jersey	30.44
12	Alaska	49.82		37	New Mexico	30.39
13	Virginia	48.61		38	Minnesota	28.75
14	Kansas	47.35		39	Idaho	28.28
15	Louisiana	46.59		40	Pennsylvania	28.25
16	Rhode Island	44.68		41	Mississippi	24.97
17	Indiana	43.40		42	Massachusetts	22.86
18	North Carolina	41.05		43	Delaware	21.51
19	Texas	40.32		44	Arkansas	20.29
20	Florida	40.01		45	Tennessee	20.22
21	Georgia	39.91		46	West Virginia	19.45
21	Nebraska	39.91		47	North Dakota	13.28
23	New York	38.83		48	Iowa	12.26
24	Montana	38.68		49	Alabama	11.33
25	Vermont	38.08		50	South Carolina	10.36

District of Columbia   27.67

Source: Morgan Quitno Corporation using data from U.S. Department of Justice, Federal Bureau of Investigation
"Crime in the United States 1992" (Uniform Crime Reports, October 3, 1993)

*By law enforcement agencies submitting complete reports to the F.B.I. for 12 months in 1992. These rates based on population estimates for areas under the jurisdiction of those agencies reporting. Arrest rate based on the F.B.I. estimate of reported and unreported arrests for sex offenses is 42.50 arrests per 100,000 population. Excludes forcible rape, prostitution and commercialized vice. Includes statutory rape and of chastity, common decency, morals and the like. Attempts are included.

Reported Arrests for Prostitution and Commercialized Vice in 1992

National Total = 86,988 Reported Arrests*

RANK	STATE	ARRESTS	%	RANK	STATE	ARRESTS	%
1	California	18,534	21.31%	26	Oklahoma	603	0.69%
2	New York	12,438	14.30%	27	Hawaii	583	0.67%
3	Texas	7,676	8.82%	28	New Mexico	571	0.66%
4	Florida	6,508	7.48%	29	Kentucky	524	0.60%
5	Ohio	4,196	4.82%	30	Louisiana	440	0.51%
6	Massachusetts	3,335	3.83%	31	Georgia	419	0.48%
7	Michigan	3,050	3.51%	32	Rhode Island	358	0.41%
8	New Jersey	2,514	2.89%	33	Arkansas	348	0.40%
9	Nevada	2,303	2.65%	34	South Carolina	288	0.33%
10	Arizona	2,053	2.36%	35	Iowa	244	0.28%
11	Pennsylvania	2,042	2.35%	36	Alabama	184	0.21%
12	Tennessee	1,579	1.82%	37	Maine	109	0.13%
13	Virginia	1,535	1.76%	38	West Virginia	69	0.08%
14	Maryland	1,359	1.56%	39	Mississippi	57	0.07%
15	North Carolina	1,285	1.48%	40	Alaska	53	0.06%
16	Illinois	1,265	1.45%	41	Minnesota	42	0.05%
17	Colorado	1,246	1.43%	42	Montana	39	0.04%
18	Wisconsin	1,230	1.41%	43	New Hampshire	33	0.04%
19	Washington	1,191	1.37%	44	Idaho	11	0.01%
20	Connecticut	1,039	1.19%	45	Delaware	6	0.01%
21	Oregon	1,007	1.16%	46	South Dakota	3	0.00%
22	Missouri	938	1.08%	46	Wyoming	3	0.00%
23	Utah	893	1.03%	48	Nebraska	2	0.00%
24	Indiana	852	0.98%	49	North Dakota	1	0.00%
25	Kansas	683	0.79%	49	Vermont	1	0.00%
					District of Columbia	1,257	1.45%

Source: U.S. Department of Justice, Federal Bureau of Investigation
   "Crime in the United States 1992" (Uniform Crime Reports, October 3, 1993)
*By law enforcement agencies submitting complete reports to the F.B.I. for 12 months in 1992. The F.B.I. estimates 96,200 reported and unreported prostitution and commercialized vice arrests occurred in 1992. Includes keeping a bawdy house, procuring or transporting women for immoral purposes. Attempts are included.

31

Reported Arrest Rate for Prostitution and Commercialized Vice in 1992

National Rate = 40.77 Reported Arrests per 100,000 Population*

RANK	STATE	RATE	RANK	STATE	RATE
1	Nevada	218.50	26	Virginia	24.09
2	Massachusetts	84.13	27	Pennsylvania	20.33
3	New York	81.00	28	North Carolina	19.34
4	Utah	67.14	29	Oklahoma	19.27
5	New Mexico	64.74	30	Louisiana	17.23
6	Tennessee	64.24	31	Arkansas	14.56
7	California	60.45	32	Kentucky	14.54
8	Ohio	57.35	33	Iowa	13.65
9	Arizona	56.82	34	Maine	10.71
10	Florida	52.26	35	Alaska	9.60
11	Hawaii	50.26	36	Georgia	8.61
12	Texas	43.56	37	South Carolina	8.33
13	Missouri	42.08	38	Mississippi	6.27
14	Colorado	39.05	39	Montana	5.26
15	Connecticut	38.68	40	Alabama	4.78
16	Michigan	36.01	41	West Virginia	3.81
17	Oregon	35.70	42	New Hampshire	3.65
18	Rhode Island	35.62	43	Delaware	1.61
19	Kansas	35.08	44	Idaho	1.17
20	New Jersey	33.27	45	Minnesota	0.94
21	Indiana	29.58	46	Wyoming	0.68
22	Washington	28.88	47	South Dakota	0.59
23	Maryland	27.69	48	Vermont	0.33
24	Illinois	25.84	49	North Dakota	0.20
25	Wisconsin	25.01	50	Nebraska	0.17

District of Columbia   213.41

Source: Morgan Quitno Corporation using data from U.S. Department of Justice, Federal Bureau of Investigation
"Crime in the United States 1992" (Uniform Crime Reports, October 3, 1993)

*By law enforcement agencies submitting complete reports to the F.B.I. for 12 months in 1992. These rates based on population estimates for areas under the jurisdiction of those agencies reporting. Arrest rate based on the F.B.I. estimate of reported and unreported arrests for prostitution and commercialized vice is 37.71 arrests per 100,000 population. Includes keeping a bawdy house, procuring or transporting women for immoral purposes. Attempts are included.

32

Reported Arrests for Offenses Against Families and Children in 1992

National Total = 84,328 Reported Arrests*

RANK	STATE	ARRESTS	%	RANK	STATE	ARRESTS	%
1	New Jersey	15,042	17.84%	26	New Mexico	708	0.84%
2	Ohio	10,342	12.26%	27	California	596	0.71%
3	Texas	6,813	8.08%	28	Washington	559	0.66%
4	North Carolina	6,228	7.39%	29	Indiana	540	0.64%
5	Wisconsin	4,993	5.92%	30	Oklahoma	514	0.61%
6	Kentucky	4,192	4.97%	31	Nevada	469	0.56%
7	New York	3,176	3.77%	32	Rhode Island	467	0.55%
8	Hawaii	3,021	3.58%	33	Mississippi	443	0.53%
9	Georgia	2,791	3.31%	34	Kansas	414	0.49%
10	Massachusetts	2,497	2.96%	35	Minnesota	375	0.44%
11	Arizona	1,828	2.17%	36	Utah	367	0.44%
12	Colorado	1,672	1.98%	37	Oregon	294	0.35%
13	Connecticut	1,604	1.90%	38	Maine	247	0.29%
14	Missouri	1,475	1.75%	39	Wyoming	240	0.28%
15	Virginia	1,461	1.73%	40	West Virginia	223	0.26%
16	Michigan	1,449	1.72%	41	North Dakota	191	0.23%
17	Maryland	1,241	1.47%	42	Idaho	142	0.17%
18	Pennsylvania	1,014	1.20%	43	South Dakota	140	0.17%
19	Louisiana	1,012	1.20%	44	Montana	117	0.14%
20	Tennessee	955	1.13%	45	Alaska	112	0.13%
21	Alabama	896	1.06%	46	Vermont	104	0.12%
22	Illinois	858	1.02%	47	Iowa	71	0.08%
23	Nebraska	803	0.95%	48	Delaware	50	0.06%
24	Arkansas	771	0.91%	49	New Hampshire	47	0.06%
25	South Carolina	721	0.85%	50	Florida	16	0.02%
					District of Columbia	27	0.03%

Source: U.S. Department of Justice, Federal Bureau of Investigation
"Crime in the United States 1992" (Uniform Crime Reports, October 3, 1993)
*By law enforcement agencies submitting complete reports to the F.B.I. for 12 months in 1992. The F.B.I. estimates 109,200 reported and unreported arrests for offenses against families and children occurred in 1992. Includes nonsupport, neglect, desertion or abuse of family and children.

Reported Arrest Rate for Offenses Against Families and Children in 1992

National Rate = 39.52 Reported Arrests per 100,000 Population*

RANK	STATE	RATE	RANK	STATE	RATE
1	Hawaii	260.43	26	Utah	27.59
2	New Jersey	199.05	27	Maryland	25.29
3	Ohio	141.34	28	Maine	24.26
4	Kentucky	116.35	29	Alabama	23.29
5	Wisconsin	101.50	30	Virginia	22.92
6	North Carolina	93.75	31	Kansas	21.26
7	New Mexico	80.27	32	South Carolina	20.86
8	Nebraska	68.93	33	New York	20.68
9	Missouri	66.17	34	Alaska	20.29
10	Massachusetts	62.99	35	Indiana	18.75
11	Connecticut	59.72	36	Illinois	17.52
12	Georgia	57.33	37	Michigan	17.11
13	Wyoming	54.30	38	Oklahoma	16.43
14	Colorado	52.40	39	Montana	15.77
15	Arizona	50.60	40	Idaho	15.15
16	Mississippi	48.73	41	Washington	13.55
17	Rhode Island	46.47	41	Delaware	13.44
18	Nevada	44.50	43	West Virginia	12.32
19	Louisiana	39.62	44	Oregon	10.42
20	North Dakota	39.03	45	Pennsylvania	10.10
21	Tennessee	38.85	46	Minnesota	8.42
22	Texas	38.66	47	New Hampshire	5.20
23	Vermont	34.43	48	Iowa	3.97
24	Arkansas	32.26	49	California	1.94
25	South Dakota	27.72	49	Florida	0.13

District of Columbia 4.58

Source: Morgan Quitno Corporation using data from U.S. Department of Justice, Federal Bureau of Investigation
     "Crime in the United States 1992" (Uniform Crime Reports, October 3, 1993)
*By law enforcement agencies submitting complete reports to the F.B.I. for 12 months in 1992. These rates based on population estimates for areas under the jurisdiction of those agencies reporting. Arrest rate based on the F.B.I. estimate of reported and unreported arrests for offenses against families and children is 42.81 arrests per 100,000 population. Includes nonsupport, neglect, desertion or abuse of family and children.

Reported Arrests of Youths 17 Years and Younger in 1992

National Total = 1,943,138 Reported Arrests*

RANK	STATE	ARRESTS	%	RANK	STATE	ARRESTS	%
1	California	246,332	12.68%	26	Missouri	22,573	1.16%
2	Texas	175,075	9.01%	27	Kansas	21,587	1.11%
3	New York	151,694	7.81%	28	Kentucky	20,977	1.08%
4	Wisconsin	111,311	5.73%	29	Hawaii	18,841	0.97%
5	New Jersey	86,735	4.46%	30	Idaho	17,323	0.89%
6	Pennsylvania	84,133	4.33%	31	Arkansas	16,576	0.85%
7	Florida	82,150	4.23%	32	Massachusetts	16,204	0.83%
8	Ohio	71,656	3.69%	33	Alabama	13,263	0.68%
9	Illinois	54,481	2.80%	34	Nevada	12,530	0.64%
10	Michigan	53,290	2.74%	35	Nebraska	11,482	0.59%
11	Colorado	52,073	2.68%	36	New Mexico	11,061	0.57%
12	Arizona	51,000	2.62%	37	Iowa	9,796	0.50%
13	Washington	46,746	2.41%	38	South Carolina	9,669	0.50%
14	Virginia	46,298	2.38%	39	Rhode Island	9,139	0.47%
15	North Carolina	41,484	2.13%	40	Maine	8,920	0.46%
16	Maryland	41,260	2.12%	41	Montana	8,460	0.44%
17	Minnesota	39,923	2.05%	42	South Dakota	7,773	0.40%
18	Oregon	39,132	2.01%	43	Mississippi	7,052	0.36%
19	Utah	31,023	1.60%	44	West Virginia	6,547	0.34%
20	Indiana	30,085	1.55%	45	Wyoming	6,023	0.31%
21	Georgia	29,531	1.52%	46	North Dakota	5,854	0.30%
22	Oklahoma	25,672	1.32%	47	New Hampshire	5,626	0.29%
23	Connecticut	25,348	1.30%	48	Alaska	4,904	0.25%
24	Louisiana	24,823	1.28%	49	Delaware	2,014	0.10%
25	Tennessee	23,955	1.23%	50	Vermont	466	0.02%

District of Columbia 3,741 0.19%

Source: U.S. Department of Justice, Federal Bureau of Investigation
"Crime in the United States 1992" (Uniform Crime Reports, October 3, 1993)
*By law enforcement agencies submitting complete reports to the F.B.I. for 12 months in 1992.

Reported Arrests of Youths 17 Years and Younger as a Percent of All Arrests in 1992

National Percent = 16.36% of All Reported Arrests*

RANK	STATE	PERCENT	RANK	STATE	PERCENT
1	Utah	36.01	26	New Mexico	16.91
2	North Dakota	32.58	27	Texas	16.87
3	Idaho	31.88	28	Iowa	16.57
4	Montana	29.31	29	Kansas	16.52
5	Wisconsin	29.05	30	Maryland	15.59
6	Hawaii	28.99	31	Nevada	15.40
7	Minnesota	27.78	32	California	14.85
8	Oregon	26.34	33	Louisiana	14.82
9	South Dakota	25.37	34	Tennessee	14.73
10	Illinois	24.31	35	Connecticut	14.72
11	Indiana	24.18	36	Alaska	14.33
12	Wyoming	23.29	37	Michigan	14.04
13	New Jersey	23.26	38	New York	13.08
14	Pennsylvania	22.07	39	Florida	12.97
15	Colorado	21.69	40	Mississippi	11.90
16	Arizona	21.31	41	Massachusetts	11.85
17	Rhode Island	21.25	42	Virginia	11.74
18	Nebraska	20.86	43	West Virginia	10.38
19	Delaware	19.56	44	Georgia	10.23
20	Washington	19.42	45	Vermont	9.87
21	Maine	19.31	46	Arkansas	9.58
22	Ohio	18.96	47	North Carolina	8.58
23	New Hampshire	18.79	48	South Carolina	7.78
24	Oklahoma	18.02	49	Kentucky	7.41
25	Missouri	17.36	50	Alabama	7.27

District of Columbia   7.42

Source: Morgan Quitno Corporation using data from U.S. Department of Justice, Federal Bureau of Investigation
"Crime in the United States 1992" (Uniform Crime Reports, October 3, 1993)
*By law enforcement agencies submitting complete reports to the F.B.I. for 12 months in 1992.

Reported Arrests of Youths 17 Years and Younger for Violent Crime in 1992

National Total = 112,408 Reported Arrests*

RANK	STATE	ARRESTS	%	RANK	STATE	ARRESTS	%
1	California	20,930	18.62%	26	Alabama	1,001	0.89%
2	New York	15,608	13.89%	27	Minnesota	932	0.83%
3	Florida	8,812	7.84%	28	Kansas	865	0.77%
4	Texas	8,216	7.31%	29	Utah	861	0.77%
5	New Jersey	5,243	4.66%	30	Tennessee	807	0.72%
6	Pennsylvania	4,791	4.26%	31	South Carolina	798	0.71%
7	Michigan	3,794	3.38%	32	Arkansas	758	0.67%
8	Maryland	3,202	2.85%	33	Rhode Island	595	0.53%
9	Ohio	3,077	2.74%	34	New Mexico	433	0.39%
10	North Carolina	2,772	2.47%	35	Nevada	426	0.38%
11	Illinois	2,527	2.25%	36	Idaho	417	0.37%
12	Wisconsin	2,184	1.94%	37	Iowa	340	0.30%
13	Arizona	2,128	1.89%	38	Hawaii	334	0.30%
14	Massachusetts	2,029	1.81%	39	Mississippi	267	0.24%
15	Louisiana	1,873	1.67%	40	West Virginia	167	0.15%
16	Colorado	1,794	1.60%	41	Nebraska	148	0.13%
17	Washington	1,790	1.59%	42	Maine	144	0.13%
18	Indiana	1,629	1.45%	43	Alaska	142	0.13%
19	Virginia	1,502	1.34%	44	Delaware	131	0.12%
20	Missouri	1,458	1.30%	45	New Hampshire	96	0.09%
21	Kentucky	1,419	1.26%	46	Montana	88	0.08%
22	Georgia	1,408	1.25%	47	South Dakota	78	0.07%
23	Oklahoma	1,326	1.18%	48	Wyoming	50	0.04%
24	Connecticut	1,292	1.15%	49	North Dakota	35	0.03%
25	Oregon	1,093	0.97%	50	Vermont	12	0.01%
					District of Columbia	586	0.52%

Source: U.S. Department of Justice, Federal Bureau of Investigation
"Crime in the United States 1992" (Uniform Crime Reports, October 3, 1993)
*By law enforcement agencies submitting complete reports to the F.B.I. for 12 months in 1992. Violent crimes are offenses of murder, forcible rape, robbery and aggravated assault.

Reported Arrests of Youths 17 Years and Younger for Violent Crime as a Percent of All Such Arrests in 1992

National Rate = 17.53% of Reported Arrests for Violent Crime*

RANK	STATE	PERCENT	RANK	STATE	PERCENT
1	Utah	41.24	26	Louisiana	17.31
2	Idaho	27.49	27	Iowa	16.59
3	Wisconsin	27.19	28	Michigan	16.57
4	Minnesota	25.09	29	Florida	16.36
5	Washington	24.76	30	Nevada	16.03
6	Hawaii	24.70	31	South Dakota	15.69
7	Oregon	24.55	32	New Hampshire	15.64
8	New Jersey	24.39	33	South Carolina	15.45
9	Indiana	24.04	34	Arkansas	15.42
10	New York	24.00	35	Montana	15.20
11	Arizona	22.92	36	Massachusetts	14.31
12	Illinois	22.90	37	California	14.27
13	Maryland	22.85	38	Mississippi	13.86
14	Oklahoma	22.59	39	Alaska	13.40
15	North Dakota	22.58	40	Connecticut	13.39
16	Delaware	22.51	41	Virginia	13.09
17	Kansas	21.57	42	Maine	12.36
18	Pennsylvania	20.89	43	Georgia	11.71
19	Ohio	20.68	44	Vermont	11.65
20	Colorado	20.38	45	North Carolina	10.56
21	Rhode Island	20.16	46	West Virginia	10.00
22	Texas	20.10	47	Tennessee	9.71
23	Missouri	18.76	48	Wyoming	8.77
24	Nebraska	18.32	49	Alabama	8.49
25	New Mexico	18.04	50	Kentucky	8.36
				District of Columbia	11.14

Source: Morgan Quitno Corporation using data from U.S. Department of Justice, Federal Bureau of Investigation
    "Crime in the United States 1992" (Uniform Crime Reports, October 3, 1993)
*By law enforcement agencies submitting complete reports to the F.B.I. for 12 months in 1992. Violent crimes are offenses of murder, forcible rape, robbery and aggravated assault.

Reported Arrests of Youths 17 Years and Younger for Murder in 1992

National Total = 2,829 Reported Arrests*

RANK	STATE	ARRESTS	%	RANK	STATE	ARRESTS	%
1	California	649	22.94%	26	Colorado	21	0.74%
2	Texas	367	12.97%	27	Massachusetts	20	0.71%
3	New York	235	8.31%	28	Connecticut	19	0.67%
4	Michigan	193	6.82%	29	Mississippi	18	0.64%
5	Florida	147	5.20%	30	Indiana	15	0.53%
6	Maryland	103	3.64%	30	Oregon	15	0.53%
7	North Carolina	95	3.36%	32	Minnesota	14	0.49%
8	Wisconsin	94	3.32%	33	Kansas	9	0.32%
9	Pennsylvania	90	3.18%	34	West Virginia	7	0.25%
10	Louisiana	75	2.65%	35	New Mexico	5	0.18%
11	Virginia	72	2.55%	35	Utah	5	0.18%
12	Ohio	61	2.16%	37	Rhode Island	4	0.14%
13	New Jersey	51	1.80%	38	Hawaii	3	0.11%
14	Alabama	49	1.73%	39	Idaho	2	0.07%
15	Arizona	45	1.59%	39	Maine	2	0.07%
15	Missouri	45	1.59%	41	Alaska	1	0.04%
17	Arkansas	39	1.38%	41	Delaware	1	0.04%
18	Georgia	35	1.24%	41	Montana	1	0.04%
19	Tennessee	34	1.20%	41	Nebraska	1	0.04%
20	Oklahoma	30	1.06%	41	South Dakota	1	0.04%
21	Illinois	28	0.99%	41	Vermont	1	0.04%
22	Nevada	27	0.95%	41	Wyoming	1	0.04%
23	South Carolina	25	0.88%	48	Iowa	0	0.00%
24	Washington	23	0.81%	48	New Hampshire	0	0.00%
25	Kentucky	22	0.78%	48	North Dakota	0	0.00%
					District of Columbia	29	1.03%

Source: U.S. Department of Justice, Federal Bureau of Investigation
"Crime in the United States 1992" (Uniform Crime Reports, October 3, 1993)
*By law enforcement agencies submitting complete reports to the F.B.I. for 12 months in 1992. Includes nonnegligent manslaughter.

Reported Arrests of Youths 17 Years and Younger for Murder as a Percent of All Such Arrests in 1992

National Rate = 14.51% of Reported Arrests for Murder*

RANK	STATE	PERCENT	RANK	STATE	PERCENT
1	South Dakota	33.33	26	Ohio	12.32
2	Vermont	25.00	27	North Carolina	11.69
3	Wisconsin	21.12	28	South Carolina	11.63
4	Maryland	19.81	29	Alabama	11.42
5	Arizona	19.65	30	Oregon	11.11
6	Texas	19.02	31	New Mexico	10.87
7	California	18.97	32	Michigan	10.43
8	Nevada	17.20	33	Colorado	10.05
9	Maine	16.67	34	Delaware	10.00
9	Rhode Island	16.67	35	Tennessee	8.85
11	Louisiana	16.56	36	Illinois	8.36
12	Oklahoma	15.46	37	Georgia	8.03
13	New York	15.21	38	Kansas	7.89
14	Washington	14.74	39	Hawaii	7.69
15	New Jersey	14.61	40	Indiana	7.65
16	Missouri	14.52	41	Kentucky	7.51
17	Massachusetts	14.29	42	Idaho	7.14
17	Utah	14.29	43	Wyoming	6.67
19	Virginia	14.17	44	West Virginia	6.60
20	Arkansas	14.13	45	Alaska	4.17
21	Connecticut	13.29	46	Montana	3.70
22	Pennsylvania	12.89	46	Nebraska	3.70
23	Minnesota	12.73	48	Iowa	0.00
24	Florida	12.61	48	New Hampshire	0.00
25	Mississippi	12.41	48	North Dakota	0.00

District of Columbia   11.42

Source: Morgan Quitno Corporation using data from U.S. Department of Justice, Federal Bureau of Investigation
    "Crime in the United States 1992" (Uniform Crime Reports, October 3, 1993)
*By law enforcement agencies submitting complete reports to the F.B.I. for 12 months in 1992. Includes nonnegligent manslaughter.

Reported Arrests of Youths 17 Years and Younger for Rape in 1992

National Total = 5,369 Reported Arrests*

RANK	STATE	ARRESTS	%	RANK	STATE	ARRESTS	%
1	California	565	10.52%	26	Minnesota	62	1.15%
2	Michigan	429	7.99%	27	Missouri	58	1.08%
3	Texas	378	7.04%	28	Utah	57	1.06%
4	Ohio	342	6.37%	29	Kentucky	52	0.97%
5	Florida	341	6.35%	30	Alabama	43	0.80%
6	Illinois	282	5.25%	31	Nevada	42	0.78%
7	New York	269	5.01%	32	Indiana	38	0.71%
8	Pennsylvania	264	4.92%	33	Mississippi	37	0.69%
9	New Jersey	230	4.28%	34	Rhode Island	32	0.60%
10	Washington	223	4.15%	35	Hawaii	31	0.58%
11	Maryland	176	3.28%	36	Kansas	26	0.48%
12	Virginia	133	2.48%	37	Delaware	21	0.39%
13	Wisconsin	121	2.25%	37	Maine	21	0.39%
14	Oklahoma	91	1.69%	39	West Virginia	20	0.37%
15	North Carolina	88	1.64%	40	Iowa	19	0.35%
16	Oregon	87	1.62%	41	Nebraska	18	0.34%
17	Louisiana	85	1.58%	42	New Mexico	17	0.32%
18	Georgia	79	1.47%	43	Alaska	16	0.30%
19	South Carolina	78	1.45%	44	Montana	15	0.28%
20	Colorado	73	1.36%	44	South Dakota	15	0.28%
21	Massachusetts	71	1.32%	46	New Hampshire	14	0.26%
22	Arizona	67	1.25%	47	Idaho	12	0.22%
23	Arkansas	64	1.19%	48	North Dakota	9	0.17%
24	Connecticut	63	1.17%	49	Wyoming	6	0.11%
24	Tennessee	63	1.17%	50	Vermont	3	0.06%
					District of Columbia	23	0.43%

Source: U.S. Department of Justice, Federal Bureau of Investigation
   "Crime in the United States 1992" (Uniform Crime Reports, October 3, 1993)
*By law enforcement agencies submitting complete reports to the F.B.I. for 12 months in 1992. Forcible rape is the carnal knowledge of a female forcibly and against her will. Assaults or attempts to commit rape by force or threat of force are included. However, statutory rape without force and other sex offenses are excluded.

Reported Arrests of Youths 17 Years and Younger for Rape as a Percent of All Such Arrests in 1992

National Percent = 16.08% of Arrests*

RANK	STATE	PERCENT		RANK	STATE	PERCENT
1	Utah	32.39		26	Louisiana	16.44
2	Illinois	26.93		27	Montana	16.30
3	North Dakota	25.71		27	South Dakota	16.30
4	Delaware	25.30		29	Vermont	15.79
5	Maine	24.42		30	Nebraska	15.65
6	Washington	24.21		31	New Mexico	15.60
7	Iowa	23.75		32	Florida	15.08
8	Ohio	23.67		33	Wyoming	15.00
9	Rhode Island	23.36		34	Arkansas	14.85
10	Minnesota	19.44		35	California	14.03
11	Arizona	19.36		36	Connecticut	13.88
12	Indiana	18.91		37	New York	13.83
13	Michigan	18.76		38	Missouri	13.81
14	New Jersey	18.30		39	Texas	13.69
15	New Hampshire	18.18		40	Colorado	13.54
16	Oklahoma	18.09		41	Virginia	13.34
17	Oregon	18.05		42	Tennessee	12.96
18	Hawaii	17.92		43	Idaho	12.12
19	Mississippi	17.87		44	Kansas	10.79
20	Wisconsin	17.69		45	North Carolina	10.77
21	Alaska	17.58		46	Georgia	10.62
22	Maryland	17.41		47	Massachusetts	10.13
23	Pennsylvania	16.59		48	West Virginia	9.85
24	South Carolina	16.56		49	Kentucky	8.02
25	Nevada	16.47		50	Alabama	7.89

District of Columbia   20.00

Source: Morgan Quitno Corporation using data from U.S. Department of Justice, Federal Bureau of Investigation
   "Crime in the United States 1992" (Uniform Crime Reports, October 3, 1993)
*By law enforcement agencies submitting complete reports to the F.B.I. for 12 months in 1992. Forcible rape is the carnal knowledge of a female forcibly and against her will. Assaults or attempts to commit rape by force or threat of force are included. However, statutory rape without force and other sex offenses are excluded.

Reported Arrests of Youths 17 Years and Younger for Robbery in 1992

National Total = 40,434 Reported Arrests*

RANK	STATE	ARRESTS	%	RANK	STATE	ARRESTS	%
1	New York	10,062	24.88%	26	Tennessee	272	0.67%
2	California	8,130	20.11%	27	Indiana	202	0.50%
3	Florida	2,951	7.30%	28	Hawaii	180	0.45%
4	Texas	2,839	7.02%	29	Kansas	177	0.44%
5	Pennsylvania	1,918	4.74%	30	Arkansas	173	0.43%
6	New Jersey	1,917	4.74%	31	Nevada	157	0.39%
7	Ohio	1,285	3.18%	32	Minnesota	150	0.37%
8	Maryland	990	2.45%	33	Utah	124	0.31%
9	Michigan	989	2.45%	34	South Carolina	110	0.27%
10	Wisconsin	867	2.14%	35	Mississippi	87	0.22%
11	Virginia	604	1.49%	36	Rhode Island	80	0.20%
12	Illinois	553	1.37%	37	New Mexico	62	0.15%
13	Massachusetts	510	1.26%	38	West Virginia	52	0.13%
14	North Carolina	502	1.24%	39	Nebraska	45	0.11%
15	Washington	493	1.22%	40	Iowa	36	0.09%
16	Arizona	468	1.16%	41	Maine	31	0.08%
17	Louisiana	425	1.05%	42	Alaska	26	0.06%
18	Oregon	420	1.04%	43	Delaware	24	0.06%
19	Missouri	394	0.97%	43	New Hampshire	24	0.06%
20	Georgia	349	0.86%	45	Idaho	21	0.05%
21	Oklahoma	339	0.84%	46	Montana	18	0.04%
22	Connecticut	323	0.80%	47	North Dakota	8	0.02%
23	Colorado	302	0.75%	48	South Dakota	5	0.01%
24	Alabama	278	0.69%	49	Wyoming	3	0.01%
25	Kentucky	273	0.68%	50	Vermont	1	0.00%
					District of Columbia	185	0.46%

Source: U.S. Department of Justice, Federal Bureau of Investigation

"Crime in the United States 1992" (Uniform Crime Reports, October 3, 1993)

*By law enforcement agencies submitting complete reports to the F.B.I. for 12 months in 1992. Robbery is the taking of anything of value by force or threat of force. Attempts are included.

Reported Arrests of Youths 17 Years and Younger for Robbery as a Percent of All Such Arrests in 1992

National Rate = 26.35% of Reported Arrests for Robbery*

RANK	STATE	PERCENT	RANK	STATE	PERCENT
1	Utah	39.37	26	Maine	22.96
2	Minnesota	37.78	27	Alaska	22.81
3	Hawaii	36.29	28	Virginia	22.22
4	Wisconsin	36.00	29	Maryland	21.81
5	Nebraska	35.16	30	New Hampshire	21.05
6	Washington	34.40	31	Massachusetts	20.74
7	Delaware	33.80	32	Michigan	20.27
8	New York	33.56	33	Louisiana	19.95
9	New Jersey	32.77	34	Missouri	19.77
10	Oklahoma	31.71	35	Montana	19.57
11	Arizona	29.43	36	West Virginia	19.19
12	Oregon	29.35	37	Arkansas	19.14
13	Colorado	29.21	38	Kentucky	18.61
14	Texas	29.17	39	Mississippi	17.09
15	Rhode Island	28.67	40	Iowa	16.59
16	North Dakota	27.59	41	Connecticut	16.33
17	Kansas	26.82	42	Nevada	16.24
18	Ohio	26.47	43	South Carolina	15.26
19	California	26.16	44	Georgia	14.88
20	Illinois	25.69	45	Tennessee	13.95
21	Idaho	25.61	46	South Dakota	13.89
22	Florida	25.47	47	North Carolina	13.83
23	Indiana	24.28	48	Alabama	12.98
24	New Mexico	23.94	49	Vermont	11.11
25	Pennsylvania	23.81	50	Wyoming	10.71

District of Columbia   14.19

Source: Morgan Quitno Corporation using data from U.S. Department of Justice, Federal Bureau of Investigation
"Crime in the United States 1992" (Uniform Crime Reports, October 3, 1993)
*By law enforcement agencies submitting complete reports to the F.B.I. for 12 months in 1992. Robbery is the taking of anything of value by force or threat of force. Attempts are included.

Reported Arrests of Youths 17 Years and Younger for Aggravated Assault in 1992

National Total = 63,776 Reported Arrests*

RANK	STATE	ARRESTS	%	RANK	STATE	ARRESTS	%
1	California	11,586	18.17%	26	Utah	675	1.06%
2	Florida	5,373	8.42%	27	Kansas	653	1.02%
3	New York	5,042	7.91%	28	Alabama	631	0.99%
4	Texas	4,632	7.26%	29	South Carolina	585	0.92%
5	New Jersey	3,045	4.77%	30	Oregon	571	0.90%
6	Pennsylvania	2,519	3.95%	31	Arkansas	482	0.76%
7	Michigan	2,183	3.42%	32	Rhode Island	479	0.75%
8	North Carolina	2,087	3.27%	33	Tennessee	438	0.69%
9	Maryland	1,933	3.03%	34	Idaho	382	0.60%
10	Illinois	1,664	2.61%	35	New Mexico	349	0.55%
11	Arizona	1,548	2.43%	36	Iowa	285	0.45%
12	Massachusetts	1,428	2.24%	37	Nevada	200	0.31%
13	Colorado	1,398	2.19%	38	Mississippi	125	0.20%
14	Ohio	1,389	2.18%	39	Hawaii	120	0.19%
15	Indiana	1,374	2.15%	40	Alaska	99	0.16%
16	Louisiana	1,288	2.02%	41	Maine	90	0.14%
17	Wisconsin	1,102	1.73%	42	West Virginia	88	0.14%
18	Kentucky	1,072	1.68%	43	Delaware	85	0.13%
19	Washington	1,051	1.65%	44	Nebraska	84	0.13%
20	Missouri	961	1.51%	45	New Hampshire	58	0.09%
21	Georgia	945	1.48%	46	South Dakota	57	0.09%
22	Connecticut	887	1.39%	47	Montana	54	0.08%
23	Oklahoma	866	1.36%	48	Wyoming	40	0.06%
24	Minnesota	706	1.11%	49	North Dakota	18	0.03%
25	Virginia	693	1.09%	50	Vermont	7	0.01%
					District of Columbia	349	0.55%

Source: U.S. Department of Justice, Federal Bureau of Investigation
   "Crime in the United States 1992" (Uniform Crime Reports, October 3, 1993)
*By law enforcement agencies submitting complete reports to the F.B.I. for 12 months in 1992. Aggravated assault is an attack for the purpose of inflicting severe bodily injury.

Reported Arrests of Youths 17 Years & Younger for Aggravated Assault as a Percent of All Such Arrests 1992

National Rate = 14.66% of Reported Arrests for Aggravated Assault*

RANK	STATE	PERCENT		RANK	STATE	PERCENT
1	Utah	43.21		26	New York	15.97
2	Idaho	29.20		27	Michigan	15.72
3	Indiana	24.77		28	Nevada	15.64
4	Wisconsin	24.52		29	Nebraska	15.61
5	Minnesota	24.45		30	South Carolina	15.57
6	Maryland	24.34		30	South Dakota	15.57
7	Oregon	23.75		32	Montana	14.67
8	Washington	22.27		33	Arkansas	14.58
9	Illinois	22.19		34	New Hampshire	14.22
10	Kansas	21.80		35	Florida	13.84
11	Arizona	21.74		36	Massachusetts	13.13
12	New Jersey	21.69		37	Connecticut	12.53
13	North Dakota	21.43		38	Alaska	11.91
14	Oklahoma	21.10		39	Mississippi	11.74
15	Delaware	20.33		40	Georgia	11.12
16	Pennsylvania	20.02		41	California	10.71
17	Colorado	19.91		42	North Carolina	9.94
18	Rhode Island	19.07		43	Vermont	9.86
19	Missouri	19.03		44	Maine	9.66
20	Hawaii	18.63		45	Virginia	9.56
21	New Mexico	17.57		46	Wyoming	8.21
22	Texas	17.51		47	West Virginia	8.07
23	Ohio	17.18		48	Tennessee	7.98
24	Louisiana	16.68		49	Kentucky	7.36
25	Iowa	16.42		50	Alabama	7.27

District of Columbia   9.73

Source: Morgan Quitno Corporation using data from U.S. Department of Justice, Federal Bureau of Investigation
    "Crime in the United States 1992" (Uniform Crime Reports, October 3, 1993)
*By law enforcement agencies submitting complete reports to the F.B.I. for 12 months in 1992. Aggravated assault is an attack for the purpose of inflicting severe bodily injury.

Reported Arrests of Youths 17 Years and Younger for Property Crimes in 1992

National Total = 680,400 Reported Arrests*

RANK	STATE	ARRESTS	%	RANK	STATE	ARRESTS	%
1	California	89,753	14.75%	26	Kansas	7,334	1.21%
2	Texas	53,290	8.76%	27	Tennessee	6,318	1.04%
3	Florida	39,482	6.49%	28	Missouri	6,269	1.03%
4	Wisconsin	28,952	4.76%	29	Idaho	5,754	0.95%
5	New York	27,072	4.45%	30	Arkansas	5,421	0.89%
6	Washington	21,108	3.47%	31	Alabama	4,857	0.80%
7	New Jersey	19,892	3.27%	32	Hawaii	4,724	0.78%
8	Pennsylvania	19,442	3.20%	33	Massachusetts	4,422	0.73%
9	Michigan	19,068	3.13%	34	New Mexico	4,321	0.71%
10	Ohio	18,168	2.99%	35	Maine	3,898	0.64%
11	Illinois	17,291	2.84%	36	Nevada	3,690	0.61%
12	Arizona	16,622	2.73%	37	Nebraska	3,557	0.58%
13	Colorado	15,604	2.56%	38	Montana	3,070	0.50%
14	Maryland	15,235	2.50%	39	Iowa	2,698	0.44%
15	Minnesota	14,741	2.42%	40	Mississippi	2,674	0.44%
16	Virginia	13,918	2.29%	41	Rhode Island	2,561	0.42%
17	Oregon	13,842	2.28%	42	South Carolina	2,474	0.41%
18	North Carolina	13,056	2.15%	43	Alaska	2,467	0.41%
19	Utah	12,355	2.03%	44	West Virginia	2,376	0.39%
20	Oklahoma	9,968	1.64%	45	South Dakota	2,297	0.38%
21	Georgia	9,038	1.49%	46	North Dakota	2,077	0.34%
22	Indiana	8,743	1.44%	47	New Hampshire	1,700	0.28%
23	Connecticut	8,115	1.33%	48	Wyoming	1,563	0.26%
24	Louisiana	7,847	1.29%	49	Delaware	684	0.11%
25	Kentucky	7,538	1.24%	50	Vermont	228	0.04%
					District of Columbia	826	0.14%

Source: U.S. Department of Justice, Federal Bureau of Investigation
   "Crime in the United States 1992" (Uniform Crime Reports, October 3, 1993)
*By law enforcement agencies submitting complete reports to the F.B.I. for 12 months in 1992. Property crimes are offenses of burglary, larceny-theft, motor vehicle theft and arson. Attempts are included.

Reported Arrests of Youths 17 Years & Younger for Property Crime as a Percent of All Such Arrests in 1992

National Rate = 36.99% of Reported Arrests for Property Crimes*

RANK	STATE	PERCENT	RANK	STATE	PERCENT
1	Utah	59.91	26	New Jersey	35.29
2	Idaho	59.24	27	Michigan	34.56
3	North Dakota	58.13	28	Texas	33.07
4	South Dakota	51.96	29	Florida	32.12
5	Wyoming	50.78	30	California	31.01
6	Minnesota	50.22	31	Iowa	30.94
7	Wisconsin	49.82	32	Pennsylvania	30.40
8	Montana	47.69	33	Maryland	30.32
9	Nebraska	47.58	34	Kentucky	29.66
10	Oklahoma	44.94	35	Louisiana	28.76
11	Washington	44.10	36	Arkansas	28.64
12	Maine	43.04	37	Nevada	28.14
13	Indiana	42.37	38	Vermont	26.70
14	Delaware	41.68	39	West Virginia	26.45
15	Hawaii	41.57	40	Missouri	26.25
16	Oregon	40.89	41	Mississippi	25.94
17	Colorado	40.86	42	Virginia	25.53
18	Alaska	40.62	43	Connecticut	24.63
19	New Mexico	38.59	44	New York	24.51
20	Illinois	38.32	45	Tennessee	24.16
21	Rhode Island	38.19	46	South Carolina	24.09
22	New Hampshire	38.12	47	Georgia	22.09
23	Kansas	37.54	48	Massachusetts	21.23
24	Arizona	37.11	48	North Carolina	21.23
25	Ohio	36.39	50	Alabama	20.87
				District of Columbia	12.97

Source: Morgan Quitno Corporation using data from U.S. Department of Justice, Federal Bureau of Investigation

"Crime in the United States 1992" (Uniform Crime Reports, October 3, 1993)

*By law enforcement agencies submitting complete reports to the F.B.I. for 12 months in 1992. Property crimes are offenses of burglary, larceny-theft, motor vehicle theft and arson. Attempts are included.

Reported Arrests of Youths 17 Years and Younger for Burglary in 1992

National Total = 122,567 Reported Arrests*

RANK	STATE	ARRESTS	%	RANK	STATE	ARRESTS	%
1	California	24,966	20.37%	26	Massachusetts	1,357	1.11%
2	Texas	11,598	9.46%	27	Arkansas	1,331	1.09%
3	Florida	10,365	8.46%	28	Indiana	1,178	0.96%
4	New York	5,138	4.19%	29	Missouri	1,134	0.93%
5	New Jersey	4,038	3.29%	30	Tennessee	993	0.81%
6	Pennsylvania	3,854	3.14%	31	Idaho	980	0.80%
7	North Carolina	3,810	3.11%	32	Hawaii	926	0.76%
8	Wisconsin	3,686	3.01%	33	Alabama	859	0.70%
9	Arizona	3,480	2.84%	34	Maine	793	0.65%
10	Ohio	3,375	2.75%	35	Nevada	743	0.61%
11	Washington	3,365	2.75%	36	Mississippi	602	0.49%
12	Michigan	3,226	2.63%	37	South Carolina	583	0.48%
13	Maryland	2,751	2.24%	38	Rhode Island	562	0.46%
14	Illinois	2,710	2.21%	39	Nebraska	536	0.44%
15	Virginia	2,421	1.98%	40	New Mexico	535	0.44%
16	Oregon	2,147	1.75%	41	West Virginia	518	0.42%
17	Oklahoma	2,008	1.64%	42	Iowa	380	0.31%
18	Georgia	1,973	1.61%	43	Alaska	367	0.30%
19	Colorado	1,898	1.55%	44	New Hampshire	270	0.22%
20	Minnesota	1,818	1.48%	45	South Dakota	232	0.19%
21	Louisiana	1,770	1.44%	46	Montana	229	0.19%
22	Connecticut	1,687	1.38%	47	North Dakota	218	0.18%
22	Kentucky	1,687	1.38%	48	Delaware	184	0.15%
24	Kansas	1,519	1.24%	49	Wyoming	147	0.12%
25	Utah	1,452	1.18%	50	Vermont	106	0.09%
					District of Columbia	62	0.05%

Source: U.S. Department of Justice, Federal Bureau of Investigation
    "Crime in the United States 1992" (Uniform Crime Reports, October 3, 1993)
*By law enforcement agencies submitting complete reports to the F.B.I. for 12 months in 1992. Burglary is the unlawful entry of a structure to commit a felony or theft. Attempts are included.

49

Reported Arrests of Youths 17 Years and Younger for Burglary as a Percent of All Such Arrests in 1992

National Rate = 34.07% of Reported Burglary Arrests*

RANK	STATE	PERCENT	RANK	STATE	PERCENT
1	Utah	65.05	26	Ohio	37.89
2	Idaho	60.91	27	Iowa	37.29
3	North Dakota	53.56	28	Arkansas	36.88
4	Wisconsin	52.89	29	Florida	36.45
5	Washington	49.98	30	Montana	36.01
6	Hawaii	49.60	31	Vermont	33.02
7	Alaska	49.33	32	Michigan	32.79
8	Minnesota	47.74	33	West Virginia	32.17
9	Oklahoma	47.33	34	Pennsylvania	31.26
10	Colorado	47.06	35	California	31.17
11	Arizona	46.86	36	Kentucky	30.33
12	Nebraska	46.85	37	Virginia	29.50
13	Delaware	46.82	38	Mississippi	29.21
14	Oregon	45.33	39	Louisiana	29.03
15	South Dakota	45.14	40	Nevada	27.18
16	Maine	44.13	41	Connecticut	26.71
17	New Mexico	43.57	42	Georgia	26.63
18	New Hampshire	42.86	43	South Carolina	26.27
19	Kansas	41.79	44	New York	25.80
20	Indiana	40.82	45	Massachusetts	25.36
21	Illinois	40.70	46	Missouri	25.34
22	Texas	39.56	47	Maryland	25.24
23	Wyoming	38.79	48	Tennessee	23.33
24	Rhode Island	38.76	49	North Carolina	22.38
25	New Jersey	38.14	50	Alabama	22.19

District of Columbia   5.78

Source: Morgan Quitno Corporation using data from U.S. Department of Justice, Federal Bureau of Investigation

"Crime in the United States 1992" (Uniform Crime Reports, October 3, 1993)

*By law enforcement agencies submitting complete reports to the F.B.I. for 12 months in 1992. Burglary is the unlawful entry of a structure to commit a felony or theft. Attempts are included.

Reported Arrests of Youths 17 Years and Younger for Larceny and Theft in 1992

National Total = 402,066 Reported Arrests*

RANK	STATE	ARRESTS	%	RANK	STATE	ARRESTS	%
1	California	45,464	11.31%	26	Connecticut	5,064	1.26%
2	Texas	33,926	8.44%	27	Tennessee	4,892	1.22%
3	Florida	23,208	5.77%	28	Idaho	4,431	1.10%
4	Wisconsin	21,630	5.38%	29	Missouri	4,400	1.09%
5	New York	17,996	4.48%	30	Arkansas	3,702	0.92%
6	Washington	15,739	3.91%	31	Alabama	3,607	0.90%
7	New Jersey	13,833	3.44%	32	New Mexico	3,600	0.90%
8	Michigan	13,759	3.42%	33	Hawaii	3,037	0.76%
9	Illinois	13,454	3.35%	34	Maine	2,862	0.71%
10	Colorado	12,406	3.09%	35	Nebraska	2,802	0.70%
11	Ohio	12,133	3.02%	36	Nevada	2,705	0.67%
12	Pennsylvania	11,864	2.95%	37	Montana	2,529	0.63%
13	Minnesota	11,435	2.84%	38	Massachusetts	2,217	0.55%
14	Arizona	10,976	2.73%	39	Iowa	2,106	0.52%
15	Oregon	9,952	2.48%	40	South Dakota	1,925	0.48%
16	Utah	9,694	2.41%	41	Alaska	1,887	0.47%
17	Virginia	9,571	2.38%	42	Mississippi	1,725	0.43%
18	Maryland	8,445	2.10%	43	North Dakota	1,679	0.42%
19	North Carolina	8,288	2.06%	44	South Carolina	1,613	0.40%
20	Indiana	6,565	1.63%	45	Rhode Island	1,602	0.40%
21	Oklahoma	6,529	1.62%	46	West Virginia	1,599	0.40%
22	Georgia	6,137	1.53%	47	New Hampshire	1,324	0.33%
23	Kansas	5,363	1.33%	48	Wyoming	1,319	0.33%
24	Louisiana	5,304	1.32%	49	Delaware	459	0.11%
25	Kentucky	5,069	1.26%	50	Vermont	112	0.03%
					District of Columbia	128	0.03%

Source: U.S. Department of Justice, Federal Bureau of Investigation
    "Crime in the United States 1992" (Uniform Crime Reports, October 3, 1993)
*By law enforcement agencies submitting complete reports to the F.B.I. for 12 months in 1992. Larceny and theft is the unlawful taking of property.
Attempts are included.

Reported Arrests of Youths 17 Years and Younger for Larceny & Theft as a Percent of All Such Arrests: 1992

National Rate = 31.12% of Reported Larceny and Theft Arrests*

RANK	STATE	PERCENT	RANK	STATE	PERCENT
1	Utah	57.90	26	New Jersey	32.69
2	North Dakota	57.84	27	Arizona	32.59
3	Idaho	57.83	28	Texas	29.64
4	Wyoming	52.16	29	Iowa	28.99
5	South Dakota	52.01	30	Florida	28.47
6	Minnesota	49.38	31	Kentucky	28.40
7	Montana	47.65	32	California	28.33
8	Nebraska	47.52	33	Nevada	27.88
9	Wisconsin	47.23	34	Pennsylvania	27.57
10	Oklahoma	42.55	35	Louisiana	27.11
11	Maine	42.46	36	Maryland	26.66
12	Indiana	41.71	37	Arkansas	25.67
13	Washington	41.34	38	Missouri	25.47
14	Colorado	39.33	39	West Virginia	23.78
15	Delaware	39.26	40	Tennessee	23.73
16	Oregon	38.96	41	New York	23.48
17	Alaska	38.54	42	Mississippi	23.11
18	Hawaii	38.17	43	Virginia	22.70
19	New Mexico	37.65	44	Vermont	22.22
20	Illinois	36.84	45	South Carolina	21.89
21	New Hampshire	36.63	46	Connecticut	21.24
22	Rhode Island	36.02	47	Alabama	20.24
23	Kansas	35.88	48	North Carolina	19.92
24	Michigan	33.63	49	Georgia	19.89
25	Ohio	33.36	50	Massachusetts	17.11

District of Columbia   4.07

Source: Morgan Quitno Corporation using data from U.S. Department of Justice, Federal Bureau of Investigation
    "Crime in the United States 1992" (Uniform Crime Reports, October 3, 1993)

*By law enforcement agencies submitting complete reports to the F.B.I. for 12 months in 1992. Larceny and theft is the unlawful taking of property. Attempts are included.

Reported Arrests of Youths 17 Years and Younger for Motor Vehicle Theft in 1992

National Total = 75,799 Reported Arrests*

RANK	STATE	ARRESTS	%	RANK	STATE	ARRESTS	%
1	California	18,030	23.79%	26	Kentucky	687	0.91%
2	Texas	7,376	9.73%	27	Louisiana	670	0.88%
3	Florida	5,720	7.55%	28	Missouri	618	0.82%
4	Maryland	3,760	4.96%	29	Tennessee	385	0.51%
5	New York	3,512	4.63%	30	Alabama	363	0.48%
6	Pennsylvania	3,357	4.43%	31	Kansas	362	0.48%
7	Wisconsin	3,285	4.33%	32	Arkansas	339	0.45%
8	Ohio	2,317	3.06%	33	Mississippi	332	0.44%
9	Arizona	1,967	2.60%	34	Rhode Island	312	0.41%
10	Washington	1,803	2.38%	35	Montana	274	0.36%
11	Michigan	1,772	2.34%	36	Idaho	267	0.35%
12	Virginia	1,763	2.33%	37	South Carolina	257	0.34%
13	New Jersey	1,684	2.22%	38	Nevada	210	0.28%
14	Oregon	1,452	1.92%	38	West Virginia	210	0.28%
15	Minnesota	1,342	1.77%	40	Alaska	207	0.27%
16	Connecticut	1,239	1.63%	41	Maine	179	0.24%
17	Oklahoma	1,197	1.58%	42	New Mexico	172	0.23%
18	Colorado	1,074	1.42%	43	North Dakota	165	0.22%
19	Utah	1,032	1.36%	44	Iowa	161	0.21%
20	Indiana	906	1.20%	45	Nebraska	143	0.19%
21	Illinois	881	1.16%	46	South Dakota	103	0.14%
22	Georgia	839	1.11%	47	Wyoming	80	0.11%
23	Massachusetts	795	1.05%	48	New Hampshire	69	0.09%
24	North Carolina	745	0.98%	49	Delaware	27	0.04%
25	Hawaii	727	0.96%	50	Vermont	8	0.01%
					District of Columbia	624	0.82%

Source: U.S. Department of Justice, Federal Bureau of Investigation

"Crime in the United States 1992" (Uniform Crime Reports, October 3, 1993)

*By law enforcement agencies submitting complete reports to the F.B.I. for 12 months in 1992. Includes the theft or attempted theft of a self-propelled vehicle. Excludes motorboats, construction equipment, airplanes, and farming equipment.

Reported Arrests of Youths 17 Years and Younger for Motor Vehicle Theft
As a Percent of All Such Arrests in 1992
National Rate = 44.26% of Reported Motor Vehicle Theft Arrests*

RANK	STATE	PERCENT	RANK	STATE	PERCENT
1	Idaho	77.39	26	Oregon	47.27
2	Utah	72.52	27	Iowa	47.08
3	Wisconsin	68.11	28	Mississippi	46.69
4	North Dakota	67.07	29	New Mexico	46.24
5	Washington	66.21	30	Florida	46.14
6	South Dakota	64.78	31	Rhode Island	45.61
7	Montana	62.56	32	Arkansas	45.38
8	Minnesota	62.53	33	Texas	45.28
9	Arizona	58.44	34	Delaware	45.00
10	Wyoming	58.39	35	Maine	43.87
11	Ohio	58.19	35	Nebraska	43.87
12	New Jersey	58.07	37	Pennsylvania	43.14
13	Illinois	57.66	38	South Carolina	42.76
14	Oklahoma	54.24	39	New Hampshire	42.59
15	Maryland	52.39	40	West Virginia	41.26
16	Vermont	50.00	41	Kentucky	40.25
17	Alaska	49.52	42	California	38.82
18	Indiana	49.45	43	Georgia	35.95
19	Hawaii	48.99	44	Tennessee	35.91
20	Connecticut	48.95	45	Massachusetts	34.06
21	Louisiana	48.80	46	Nevada	34.04
22	Kansas	48.72	47	Missouri	33.68
23	Michigan	48.01	48	North Carolina	32.78
24	Virginia	47.78	49	New York	27.05
25	Colorado	47.33	50	Alabama	25.00

District of Columbia   29.64

Source: Morgan Quitno Corporation using data from U.S. Department of Justice, Federal Bureau of Investigation
  "Crime in the United States 1992" (Uniform Crime Reports, October 3, 1993)
*By law enforcement agencies submitting complete reports to the F.B.I. for 12 months in 1992. Includes the theft or attempted theft of a self-propelled vehicle. Excludes motorboats, construction equipment, airplanes, and farming equipment.

Reported Arrests of Youths 17 Years and Younger for Arson in 1992

National Total = 7,968 Reported Arrests*

RANK	STATE	ARRESTS	%	RANK	STATE	ARRESTS	%
1	California	1,293	16.23%	26	Kansas	90	1.13%
2	New York	426	5.35%	27	Georgia	89	1.12%
3	Texas	390	4.89%	28	Rhode Island	85	1.07%
4	Pennsylvania	367	4.61%	29	Idaho	76	0.95%
5	Wisconsin	351	4.41%	29	Nebraska	76	0.95%
6	Ohio	343	4.30%	31	Maine	64	0.80%
7	New Jersey	337	4.23%	32	Massachusetts	53	0.67%
8	Michigan	311	3.90%	33	Iowa	51	0.64%
9	Oregon	291	3.65%	34	Arkansas	49	0.61%
10	Maryland	279	3.50%	34	West Virginia	49	0.61%
11	Illinois	246	3.09%	36	Tennessee	48	0.60%
12	Oklahoma	234	2.94%	37	Montana	38	0.48%
13	Colorado	226	2.84%	38	New Hampshire	37	0.46%
14	North Carolina	213	2.67%	38	South Dakota	37	0.46%
15	Washington	201	2.52%	40	Hawaii	34	0.43%
16	Arizona	199	2.50%	41	Nevada	32	0.40%
17	Florida	189	2.37%	42	Alabama	28	0.35%
18	Utah	177	2.22%	43	South Carolina	21	0.26%
19	Virginia	163	2.05%	44	Wyoming	17	0.21%
20	Minnesota	146	1.83%	45	Mississippi	15	0.19%
21	Connecticut	125	1.57%	45	North Dakota	15	0.19%
22	Missouri	117	1.47%	47	Delaware	14	0.18%
23	Louisiana	103	1.29%	47	New Mexico	14	0.18%
24	Kentucky	95	1.19%	49	Alaska	6	0.08%
25	Indiana	94	1.18%	50	Vermont	2	0.03%
					District of Columbia	12	0.15%

Source: U.S. Department of Justice, Federal Bureau of Investigation
"Crime in the United States 1992" (Uniform Crime Reports, October 3, 1993)
*By law enforcement agencies submitting complete reports to the F.B.I. for 12 months in 1992.

Reported Arrests of Youths 17 Years and Younger for Arson as a Percent of All Such Arrests in 1992

National Rate = 48.82% of Reported Arson Arrests*

RANK	STATE	PERCENT	RANK	STATE	PERCENT
1	North Dakota	88.24	26	Ohio	51.89
2	Utah	79.37	27	Wyoming	51.52
3	South Dakota	78.72	28	Connecticut	48.83
4	Idaho	78.35	29	New York	46.66
5	Delaware	73.68	30	Pennsylvania	45.25
6	New Hampshire	69.81	31	Louisiana	42.74
7	Montana	69.09	32	Kansas	42.65
7	Nebraska	69.09	33	Michigan	42.54
9	Rhode Island	68.00	34	New Mexico	40.00
10	Wisconsin	67.89	35	Missouri	39.39
11	Colorado	65.32	36	Alaska	37.50
12	Arizona	62.19	37	North Carolina	36.41
13	Hawaii	60.71	38	Virginia	36.22
14	Minnesota	60.58	39	Texas	36.21
15	Oklahoma	60.47	40	West Virginia	35.25
16	Washington	59.82	41	Florida	33.04
17	New Jersey	59.75	42	Arkansas	32.67
18	Illinois	58.43	43	Kentucky	31.77
18	Oregon	58.43	44	Georgia	27.99
20	Maine	57.14	45	Massachusetts	27.46
21	Maryland	56.94	46	South Carolina	26.58
22	California	53.56	47	Tennessee	23.19
23	Iowa	53.13	48	Alabama	21.71
24	Indiana	52.81	49	Mississippi	20.55
25	Nevada	52.46	50	Vermont	15.38
				District of Columbia	24.00

Source: Morgan Quitno Corporation using data from U.S. Department of Justice, Federal Bureau of Investigation
"Crime in the United States 1992" (Uniform Crime Reports, October 3, 1993)
*By law enforcement agencies submitting complete reports to the F.B.I. for 12 months in 1992.

Reported Arrests of Youths 17 Years and Younger for Weapons Violations in 1992

National Total = 46,256 Reported Arrests*

RANK	STATE	ARRESTS	%	RANK	STATE	ARRESTS	%
1	California	9,284	20.07%	26	Utah	498	1.08%
2	Texas	5,081	10.98%	27	Arkansas	496	1.07%
3	New York	3,256	7.04%	28	Alabama	427	0.92%
4	New Jersey	2,487	5.38%	29	Massachusetts	311	0.67%
5	Wisconsin	2,401	5.19%	30	Indiana	290	0.63%
6	Michigan	1,752	3.79%	30	South Carolina	290	0.63%
7	Florida	1,739	3.76%	32	Kentucky	277	0.60%
8	Virginia	1,449	3.13%	33	Nevada	271	0.59%
9	Ohio	1,316	2.85%	34	Mississippi	187	0.40%
10	Maryland	1,202	2.60%	34	New Mexico	187	0.40%
11	Colorado	1,135	2.45%	36	Nebraska	141	0.30%
12	North Carolina	1,105	2.39%	37	Idaho	133	0.29%
13	Pennsylvania	1,081	2.34%	38	West Virginia	130	0.28%
14	Illinois	1,062	2.30%	39	Rhode Island	116	0.25%
15	Washington	832	1.80%	40	Hawaii	97	0.21%
16	Connecticut	776	1.68%	41	Alaska	93	0.20%
17	Arizona	757	1.64%	42	Iowa	88	0.19%
18	Georgia	744	1.61%	43	South Dakota	69	0.15%
19	Tennessee	722	1.56%	44	Maine	66	0.14%
20	Missouri	687	1.49%	45	Montana	49	0.11%
21	Louisiana	643	1.39%	46	North Dakota	47	0.10%
22	Minnesota	589	1.27%	47	Wyoming	41	0.09%
23	Kansas	547	1.18%	48	New Hampshire	28	0.06%
24	Oklahoma	538	1.16%	49	Delaware	18	0.04%
25	Oregon	526	1.14%	50	Vermont	0	0.00%
					District of Columbia	195	0.42%

Source: U.S. Department of Justice, Federal Bureau of Investigation
    "Crime in the United States 1992" (Uniform Crime Reports, October 3, 1993)
*By law enforcement agencies submitting complete reports to the F.B.I. for 12 months in 1992. Weapons violations include illegal carrying and possession.

Reported Arrests of Youths 17 Years and Younger for Weapons Violations
As a Percent of All Such Arrests in 1992
National Rate = 22.66% of Reported Weapons Violation Arrests*

RANK	STATE	PERCENT	RANK	STATE	PERCENT
1	Utah	51.82	26	Louisiana	21.80
2	North Dakota	50.54	27	New York	21.26
3	Minnesota	44.29	28	Oklahoma	20.71
4	Montana	39.84	29	Iowa	20.66
5	South Dakota	37.30	30	Maine	20.56
6	New Jersey	35.72	31	Texas	20.25
7	Idaho	34.64	32	Missouri	20.18
8	Wyoming	33.61	33	Florida	20.13
9	Wisconsin	32.26	34	Michigan	20.09
10	Washington	32.01	35	Tennessee	19.83
11	Nebraska	29.31	36	Indiana	19.81
12	New Mexico	29.26	37	Alaska	19.10
13	Colorado	28.30	38	Alabama	18.79
14	Pennsylvania	27.33	39	Delaware	18.75
15	Connecticut	27.00	40	Virginia	18.67
16	New Hampshire	26.92	41	Ohio	18.54
17	California	25.47	42	Georgia	17.76
18	Arizona	25.22	43	South Carolina	17.50
19	Illinois	24.87	44	Mississippi	17.40
20	Kansas	24.27	45	Arkansas	16.89
21	Rhode Island	23.63	46	North Carolina	13.87
22	Maryland	23.46	47	Hawaii	10.50
23	Oregon	23.35	48	West Virginia	9.35
24	Massachusetts	22.87	49	Kentucky	7.94
25	Nevada	22.16	50	Vermont	0.00

District of Columbia   13.04

Source: U.S. Department of Justice, Federal Bureau of Investigation
"Crime in the United States 1992" (Uniform Crime Reports, October 3, 1993)
*By law enforcement agencies submitting complete reports to the F.B.I. for 12 months in 1992. Weapons violations include illegal carrying and possession.

Reported Arrests of Youths 17 Years and Younger for Driving Under the Influence in 1992

National Total = 11,956 Reported Arrests*

RANK	STATE	ARRESTS	%	RANK	STATE	ARRESTS	%
1	California	1,839	15.38%	26	Florida	160	1.34%
2	North Carolina	945	7.90%	27	New Jersey	158	1.32%
3	Texas	923	7.72%	28	Missouri	155	1.30%
4	Kentucky	568	4.75%	29	South Carolina	134	1.12%
5	Michigan	504	4.22%	30	Iowa	133	1.11%
6	Georgia	419	3.50%	31	Utah	104	0.87%
7	Minnesota	394	3.30%	32	Tennessee	100	0.84%
8	Wisconsin	389	3.25%	33	Louisiana	99	0.83%
9	Ohio	372	3.11%	34	Maine	96	0.80%
10	Colorado	341	2.85%	35	Idaho	94	0.79%
11	Washington	296	2.48%	36	South Dakota	86	0.72%
12	Oklahoma	261	2.18%	37	Indiana	82	0.69%
13	Oregon	250	2.09%	38	Wyoming	81	0.68%
14	Kansas	246	2.06%	39	Massachusetts	79	0.66%
15	Virginia	240	2.01%	40	Connecticut	75	0.63%
16	New York	231	1.93%	41	West Virginia	72	0.60%
17	Arizona	200	1.67%	42	Alaska	66	0.55%
18	Maryland	198	1.66%	43	Mississippi	60	0.50%
19	Pennsylvania	197	1.65%	44	New Hampshire	57	0.48%
20	Arkansas	192	1.61%	45	North Dakota	46	0.38%
21	Alabama	187	1.56%	46	Hawaii	38	0.32%
22	Nebraska	186	1.56%	46	Nevada	38	0.32%
23	New Mexico	185	1.55%	48	Rhode Island	27	0.23%
24	Montana	168	1.41%	49	Vermont	20	0.17%
25	Illinois	165	1.38%	50	Delaware	0	0.00%
					District of Columbia	0	0.00%

Source: U.S. Department of Justice, Federal Bureau of Investigation
      "Crime in the United States 1992" (Uniform Crime Reports, October 3, 1993)
*By law enforcement agencies submitting complete reports to the F.B.I. for 12 months in 1992. Includes driving or operating any vehicle or common carrier while drunk or under the influence of liquor or narcotics.

Reported Arrests of Youths 17 Years and Younger for Driving Under the Influence
As a Percent of All Such Arrests in 1992
National Rate = 0.91% of Reported Arrests for Driving Under the Influence*

RANK	STATE	PERCENT	RANK	STATE	PERCENT
1	Montana	3.02	26	Arkansas	0.94
2	North Dakota	2.01	27	South Carolina	0.92
3	Nebraska	1.81	28	Louisiana	0.89
4	Utah	1.79	29	Georgia	0.88
5	Wyoming	1.63	30	Idaho	0.87
6	South Dakota	1.62	31	Mississippi	0.85
7	New Mexico	1.54	32	Texas	0.84
8	Minnesota	1.51	33	West Virginia	0.79
9	Kentucky	1.39	34	Illinois	0.78
10	Iowa	1.32	35	Maryland	0.77
11	Alaska	1.30	36	Washington	0.75
11	North Carolina	1.30	37	California	0.72
13	Kansas	1.25	37	Connecticut	0.72
14	Vermont	1.23	39	Arizona	0.70
15	Maine	1.22	40	Hawaii	0.68
16	Oklahoma	1.17	41	Nevada	0.61
17	Colorado	1.16	41	New York	0.61
18	Wisconsin	1.11	41	Pennsylvania	0.61
19	Ohio	1.09	44	Virginia	0.60
20	Oregon	1.06	45	New Jersey	0.59
21	Missouri	1.05	46	Massachusetts	0.57
22	Rhode Island	1.04	47	Indiana	0.55
23	Michigan	1.01	48	Tennessee	0.52
24	New Hampshire	0.98	49	Florida	0.40
25	Alabama	0.95	50	Delaware	0.00

District of Columbia   0.00

Source: Morgan Quitno Corporation using data from U.S. Department of Justice, Federal Bureau of Investigation
   "Crime in the United States 1992" (Uniform Crime Reports, October 3, 1993)
*By law enforcement agencies submitting complete reports to the F.B.I. for 12 months in 1992. Includes driving or operating any vehicle or common carrier while drunk or under the influence of liquor or narcotics.

Reported Arrests of Youths 17 Years and Younger for Drug Abuse Violations in 1992

National Total = 73,981 Reported Arrests*

RANK	STATE	ARRESTS	%	RANK	STATE	ARRESTS	%
1	California	14,529	19.64%	26	Alabama	534	0.72%
2	New York	8,301	11.22%	27	Utah	510	0.69%
3	Texas	6,306	8.52%	28	Kansas	494	0.67%
4	New Jersey	4,810	6.50%	29	Indiana	492	0.67%
5	Florida	3,915	5.29%	30	Minnesota	481	0.65%
6	Maryland	3,231	4.37%	31	Arkansas	441	0.60%
7	Pennsylvania	2,828	3.82%	32	Hawaii	419	0.57%
8	Ohio	2,584	3.49%	33	Mississippi	366	0.49%
9	Michigan	2,341	3.16%	34	New Mexico	304	0.41%
10	North Carolina	2,014	2.72%	35	Nevada	303	0.41%
11	Arizona	1,765	2.39%	36	Rhode Island	271	0.37%
12	Connecticut	1,655	2.24%	37	Nebraska	160	0.22%
13	Virginia	1,465	1.98%	38	Maine	153	0.21%
14	Illinois	1,452	1.96%	39	New Hampshire	141	0.19%
15	Massachusetts	1,302	1.76%	40	Idaho	137	0.19%
16	Wisconsin	1,155	1.56%	40	West Virginia	137	0.19%
17	Georgia	1,146	1.55%	42	Alaska	109	0.15%
18	Louisiana	1,059	1.43%	43	South Carolina	95	0.13%
19	Tennessee	963	1.30%	44	Wyoming	71	0.10%
20	Washington	939	1.27%	45	Delaware	63	0.09%
21	Colorado	873	1.18%	46	Montana	46	0.06%
22	Missouri	868	1.17%	46	South Dakota	46	0.06%
23	Kentucky	818	1.11%	48	Iowa	36	0.05%
24	Oregon	770	1.04%	49	North Dakota	15	0.02%
25	Oklahoma	602	0.81%	49	Vermont	15	0.02%

	District of Columbia	451	0.61%

Source: U.S. Department of Justice, Federal Bureau of Investigation

"Crime in the United States 1992" (Uniform Crime Reports, October 3, 1993)

*By law enforcement agencies submitting complete reports to the F.B.I. for 12 months in 1992. Includes offenses relating to possession, sale, use, growing and manufacturing of narcotic drugs.

Reported Arrests of Youths 17 & Younger for Drug Abuse Violations as a Percent of All Such Arrests: 1992

National Rate = 8.04% of Reported Drug Abuse Violation Arrests*

RANK	STATE	PERCENT		RANK	STATE	PERCENT
1	Utah	16.47		26	Maine	8.50
2	New Mexico	14.37		27	New York	8.19
3	Illinois	13.04		28	Mississippi	8.15
4	Alaska	13.02		29	Louisiana	7.89
5	Wyoming	12.54		30	South Carolina	7.77
6	Delaware	12.00		31	Massachusetts	7.64
7	New Jersey	11.68		32	Virginia	7.55
8	Missouri	11.47		33	Oregon	7.44
9	Arizona	11.46		34	Kansas	7.42
10	Montana	11.41		35	New Hampshire	7.07
11	Hawaii	11.15		36	Vermont	7.01
12	Maryland	11.10		37	North Carolina	6.94
13	Connecticut	10.65		38	West Virginia	6.93
14	Colorado	10.55		39	South Dakota	6.81
15	Idaho	10.50		40	Oklahoma	6.68
16	Wisconsin	10.20		41	Florida	6.46
17	Pennsylvania	10.00		42	California	6.38
18	Ohio	9.83		43	Arkansas	6.11
19	Indiana	9.55		44	Alabama	6.09
20	Minnesota	9.39		45	Nebraska	6.07
21	Texas	9.03		46	Georgia	5.62
22	Washington	8.83		47	North Dakota	5.32
23	Rhode Island	8.63		48	Nevada	5.12
24	Tennessee	8.58		49	Iowa	4.29
25	Michigan	8.56		50	Kentucky	4.00

District of Columbia   5.82

Source: Morgan Quitno Corporation using data from U.S. Department of Justice, Federal Bureau of Investigation
    "Crime in the United States 1992" (Uniform Crime Reports, October 3, 1993)
*By law enforcement agencies submitting complete reports to the F.B.I. for 12 months in 1992. Includes offenses relating to possession, sale, use, growing and manufacturing of narcotic drugs.

Reported Arrests of Youths 17 Years and Younger for Sex Offenses in 1992

National Total = 16,656 Reported Arrests*

RANK	STATE	ARRESTS	%	RANK	STATE	ARRESTS	%
1	California	2,903	17.43%	26	Louisiana	175	1.05%
2	Wisconsin	1,689	10.14%	27	Hawaii	167	1.00%
3	New York	1,290	7.74%	28	Oklahoma	106	0.64%
4	Texas	1,121	6.73%	29	Maine	97	0.58%
5	Pennsylvania	683	4.10%	30	Nebraska	89	0.53%
6	Michigan	540	3.24%	31	Idaho	83	0.50%
7	Maryland	503	3.02%	32	South Carolina	82	0.49%
8	Washington	494	2.97%	33	Montana	80	0.48%
9	Ohio	482	2.89%	34	Massachusetts	78	0.47%
10	Florida	470	2.82%	35	Alaska	63	0.38%
11	New Jersey	468	2.81%	36	Arkansas	59	0.35%
12	Virginia	446	2.68%	37	Tennessee	48	0.29%
13	Arizona	425	2.55%	38	Rhode Island	44	0.26%
14	Oregon	422	2.53%	38	South Dakota	44	0.26%
15	Utah	421	2.53%	40	New Hampshire	43	0.26%
16	Colorado	413	2.48%	41	Nevada	42	0.25%
17	Minnesota	398	2.39%	42	New Mexico	41	0.25%
18	Illinois	331	1.99%	43	Iowa	33	0.20%
19	Missouri	274	1.65%	44	Mississippi	31	0.19%
20	Kentucky	243	1.46%	45	West Virginia	26	0.16%
21	North Carolina	242	1.45%	46	Alabama	24	0.14%
22	Georgia	241	1.45%	47	North Dakota	23	0.14%
23	Indiana	223	1.34%	48	Wyoming	22	0.13%
24	Connecticut	195	1.17%	49	Vermont	16	0.10%
25	Kansas	187	1.12%	50	Delaware	12	0.07%
					District of Columbia	24	0.14%

Source: U.S. Department of Justice, Federal Bureau of Investigation

"Crime in the United States 1992" (Uniform Crime Reports, October 3, 1993)

*By law enforcement agencies submitting complete reports to the F.B.I. for 12 months in 1992. Excludes forcible rape, prostitution and commercialized vice. Includes statutory rape and offenses against chastity, common decency, morals and the like. Attempts are included.

Reported Arrests of Youths 17 Years & Younger for Sex Offenses as a Percent of All Such Arrests: 1992

National Rate = 18.19% of Reported Sex Offense Arrests*

RANK	STATE	PERCENT	RANK	STATE	PERCENT
1	Wisconsin	40.98	26	Colorado	17.99
2	Utah	36.01	27	Indiana	17.84
3	North Dakota	35.38	28	California	16.11
4	Idaho	31.32	29	Texas	15.78
5	Minnesota	31.07	30	Wyoming	15.71
6	Maine	29.04	31	New Mexico	15.30
7	Montana	27.87	32	Iowa	15.07
8	Maryland	27.52	33	Delaware	15.00
9	South Dakota	27.16	34	New Hampshire	14.83
10	Hawaii	24.34	35	Louisiana	14.71
11	Oregon	24.28	36	Virginia	14.40
12	Pennsylvania	24.07	37	Vermont	13.91
13	Alaska	22.91	38	Mississippi	13.66
13	South Carolina	22.91	39	Georgia	12.40
15	Missouri	22.64	40	Arkansas	12.16
16	New York	21.64	41	Rhode Island	9.80
17	Illinois	21.40	42	Tennessee	9.66
18	Connecticut	20.95	43	Florida	9.43
19	New Jersey	20.35	44	Oklahoma	9.28
20	Kansas	20.28	45	North Carolina	8.87
21	Nebraska	19.14	46	Massachusetts	8.61
22	Washington	19.02	47	West Virginia	7.39
23	Arizona	18.51	48	Kentucky	7.24
24	Michigan	18.49	49	Nevada	6.68
25	Ohio	18.13	50	Alabama	5.50

District of Columbia   14.72

Source: Morgan Quitno Corporation using data from U.S. Department of Justice, Federal Bureau of Investigation
    "Crime in the United States 1992" (Uniform Crime Reports, October 3, 1993)
*By law enforcement agencies submitting complete reports to the F.B.I. for 12 months in 1992. Excludes forcible rape, prostitution and commercialized vice. Includes statutory rape and offenses against chastity, common decency, morals and the like. Attempts are included.

Reported Arrests of Youths 17 and Younger for Prostitution and Commercialized Vice in 1992

National Total = 1,106 Reported Arrests*

RANK	STATE	ARRESTS	%	RANK	STATE	ARRESTS	%
1	California	210	18.99%	26	Arkansas	11	0.99%
2	Texas	137	12.39%	26	Colorado	11	0.99%
3	Florida	81	7.32%	26	Virginia	11	0.99%
4	New York	78	7.05%	29	Nevada	9	0.81%
5	Ohio	47	4.25%	30	Louisiana	8	0.72%
6	Michigan	39	3.53%	31	Kentucky	7	0.63%
6	North Carolina	39	3.53%	32	Kansas	6	0.54%
8	Oregon	37	3.35%	33	South Carolina	4	0.36%
9	Pennsylvania	34	3.07%	34	Hawaii	3	0.27%
10	Washington	30	2.71%	34	Maine	3	0.27%
11	Massachusetts	26	2.35%	34	Minnesota	3	0.27%
12	Utah	25	2.26%	34	Rhode Island	3	0.27%
13	Maryland	24	2.17%	34	West Virginia	3	0.27%
14	New Jersey	21	1.90%	39	Alaska	2	0.18%
15	Connecticut	20	1.81%	39	Montana	2	0.18%
16	Arizona	19	1.72%	41	Delaware	1	0.09%
16	Wisconsin	19	1.72%	41	New Hampshire	1	0.09%
18	Georgia	17	1.54%	43	Idaho	0	0.00%
18	Indiana	17	1.54%	43	Iowa	0	0.00%
18	Oklahoma	17	1.54%	43	Mississippi	0	0.00%
21	Illinois	16	1.45%	43	Nebraska	0	0.00%
22	New Mexico	15	1.36%	43	North Dakota	0	0.00%
23	Tennessee	14	1.27%	43	South Dakota	0	0.00%
24	Missouri	13	1.18%	43	Vermont	0	0.00%
25	Alabama	12	1.08%	43	Wyoming	0	0.00%
					District of Columbia	11	0.99%

Source: U.S. Department of Justice, Federal Bureau of Investigation

"Crime in the United States 1992" (Uniform Crime Reports, October 3, 1993)

*By law enforcement agencies submitting complete reports to the F.B.I. for 12 months in 1992. Includes keeping a bawdy house, procuring or transporting women for immoral purposes. Attempts are included.

Reported Arrests of Youths 17 Years and Younger for Prostitution & Commercialized Vice
As a Percent of All Such Arrests in 1992
National Rate = 1.27% of Reported Prostitution & Commercialized Vice Arrests*

RANK	STATE	PERCENT	RANK	STATE	PERCENT
1	Delaware	16.67	26	Kentucky	1.34
2	Minnesota	7.14	27	Michigan	1.28
3	Alabama	6.52	28	Illinois	1.26
4	Montana	5.13	29	Florida	1.24
5	West Virginia	4.35	30	California	1.13
6	Georgia	4.06	31	Ohio	1.12
7	Alaska	3.77	32	Arizona	0.93
8	Oregon	3.67	33	Tennessee	0.89
9	Arkansas	3.16	34	Colorado	0.88
10	North Carolina	3.04	34	Kansas	0.88
11	New Hampshire	3.03	36	New Jersey	0.84
12	Oklahoma	2.82	36	Rhode Island	0.84
13	Utah	2.80	38	Massachusetts	0.78
14	Maine	2.75	39	Virginia	0.72
15	New Mexico	2.63	40	New York	0.63
16	Washington	2.52	41	Hawaii	0.51
17	Indiana	2.00	42	Nevada	0.39
18	Connecticut	1.92	43	Idaho	0.00
19	Louisiana	1.82	43	Iowa	0.00
20	Texas	1.78	43	Mississippi	0.00
21	Maryland	1.77	43	Nebraska	0.00
22	Pennsylvania	1.67	43	North Dakota	0.00
23	Wisconsin	1.54	43	South Dakota	0.00
24	Missouri	1.39	43	Vermont	0.00
24	South Carolina	1.39	43	Wyoming	0.00

District of Columbia   0.88

Source: Morgan Quitno Corporation using data from U.S. Department of Justice, Federal Bureau of Investigation
"Crime in the United States 1992" (Uniform Crime Reports, October 3, 1993)
*By law enforcement agencies submitting complete reports to the F.B.I. for 12 months in 1992. Includes keeping a bawdy house, procuring or transporting women for immoral purposes. Attempts are included.

Reported Arrests of Youths 17 Years & Younger for Offenses Against Families and Children in 1992

National Total = 3,940 Reported Arrests*

RANK	STATE	ARRESTS	%	RANK	STATE	ARRESTS	%
1	Ohio	941	23.88%	26	Utah	19	0.48%
2	Wisconsin	624	15.84%	27	Maryland	16	0.41%
3	Texas	566	14.37%	27	Minnesota	16	0.41%
4	New York	229	5.81%	29	Idaho	15	0.38%
5	Georgia	189	4.80%	30	Arkansas	14	0.36%
6	Louisiana	138	3.50%	30	Maine	14	0.36%
7	Hawaii	133	3.38%	32	Wyoming	13	0.33%
8	Massachusetts	105	2.66%	33	Oregon	12	0.30%
9	Rhode Island	102	2.59%	33	Virginia	12	0.30%
10	Connecticut	99	2.51%	35	Tennessee	11	0.28%
11	South Carolina	71	1.80%	36	Washington	9	0.23%
12	North Carolina	64	1.62%	37	Montana	7	0.18%
13	Missouri	61	1.55%	38	Nebraska	6	0.15%
14	Pennsylvania	59	1.50%	39	Alabama	5	0.13%
15	Kansas	49	1.24%	40	West Virginia	4	0.10%
16	Oklahoma	44	1.12%	41	Alaska	3	0.08%
17	Colorado	43	1.09%	41	Iowa	3	0.08%
18	North Dakota	42	1.07%	43	Mississippi	1	0.03%
19	Indiana	38	0.96%	44	Arizona	0	0.00%
20	New Jersey	37	0.94%	44	Delaware	0	0.00%
21	Nevada	33	0.84%	44	Florida	0	0.00%
22	Kentucky	26	0.66%	44	Michigan	0	0.00%
23	Illinois	23	0.58%	44	New Hampshire	0	0.00%
23	New Mexico	23	0.58%	44	South Dakota	0	0.00%
25	California	21	0.53%	44	Vermont	0	0.00%
					District of Columbia	0	0.00%

Source: U.S. Department of Justice, Federal Bureau of Investigation
    "Crime in the United States 1992" (Uniform Crime Reports, October 3, 1993)
*By law enforcement agencies submitting complete reports to the F.B.I. for 12 months in 1992. Includes nonsupport, neglect, desertion or abuse of family and children.

Reported Arrests of Youths 17 Years and Younger for Offenses Against Families and Children
As a Percent of All Such Arrests in 1992
National Rate = 4.67% of Reported Offenses Against Families and Children Arrests*

RANK	STATE	PERCENT	RANK	STATE	PERCENT
1	North Dakota	21.99	26	Oregon	4.08
2	Rhode Island	21.84	27	California	3.52
3	Louisiana	13.64	28	New Mexico	3.25
4	Wisconsin	12.50	29	Alaska	2.68
5	Kansas	11.84	29	Illinois	2.68
6	Idaho	10.56	31	Colorado	2.57
7	South Carolina	9.85	32	Arkansas	1.82
8	Ohio	9.10	33	West Virginia	1.79
9	Oklahoma	8.56	34	Washington	1.61
10	Texas	8.31	35	Maryland	1.29
11	New York	7.21	36	Tennessee	1.15
12	Indiana	7.04	37	North Carolina	1.03
12	Nevada	7.04	38	Virginia	0.82
14	Georgia	6.77	39	Nebraska	0.75
15	Connecticut	6.17	40	Kentucky	0.62
16	Montana	5.98	41	Alabama	0.56
17	Pennsylvania	5.82	42	New Jersey	0.25
18	Maine	5.67	43	Mississippi	0.23
19	Wyoming	5.42	44	Arizona	0.00
20	Utah	5.18	44	Delaware	0.00
21	Hawaii	4.40	44	Florida	0.00
22	Minnesota	4.27	44	Michigan	0.00
23	Iowa	4.23	44	New Hampshire	0.00
24	Massachusetts	4.21	44	South Dakota	0.00
25	Missouri	4.14	44	Vermont	0.00

District of Columbia   0.00

Source: Morgan Quitno Corporation using data from U.S. Department of Justice, Federal Bureau of Investigation

"Crime in the United States 1992" (Uniform Crime Reports, October 3, 1993)

By law enforcement agencies submitting complete reports to the F.B.I. for 12 months in 1992. Includes nonsupport, neglect, desertion or abuse of family and children.

II. CORRECTIONS

Table   **Title**

69   Prisoners in State Correctional Institutions in 1992

70   Prisoners in State Correctional Institutions in 1991

71   Percent Change in Number of State Prisoners: 1991 to 1992

72   State Prisoners Sentenced to More than One Year in 1992

73   State Prisoner Incarceration Rate in 1992

74   State Prison Population as a Percent of Highest Capacity in 1992

75   Female Prisoners in State Correctional Institutions in 1992

76   Female Prisoners in State Correctional Institutions as a Percent of All Prisoners: 1992

77   Percent Change in Female Prisoner Population: 1991 to 1992

78   White Prisoners in State Correctional Institutions in 1991

79   Black Prisoners in State Correctional Institutions in 1991

80   Average Annual Operating Expenditures per Inmate in 1990

81   State Prison Inmates Serving Life Sentences in 1992

82   Percent of State Prison Inmates Serving Life Sentences in 1992

83   Prisoners Under Sentence of Death in 1991

84   Male Prisoners Under Sentence of Death in 1991

85   Female Prisoners Under Sentence of Death in 1991

86   Percent of Prisoners Under Sentence of Death Who Are Female: 1991

87   White Prisoners Under Sentence of Death in 1991

88   Percent of Prisoners Under Sentence of Death Who Are White: 1991

89   Black Prisoners Under Sentence of Death in 1991

90   Percent of Prisoners Under Sentence of Death Who Are Black: 1991

91   Prisoners Executed: 1930 to 1991

92   Prisoners Executed: 1977 to 1991

93   Prisoners Sentenced to Death: 1973 to 1991

94   Death Sentences Overturned or Commuted: 1973-91

95   Percent of Death Penalty Sentences Overturned or Commuted: 1973-91

96   Sentenced Prisoners Admitted to State Correctional Institutions in 1991

97   New State Prisoners Admitted Through New Court Commitments in 1991

98   Parole Violators Returned to State Prison in 1991

99   Escapees Returned to State Prison in 1991

100   Prisoners Released from State Correctional Institutions in 1991

101   State Prisoners Released with Conditions in 1991

II. CORRECTIONS (continued)

Table	Title
102	State Prisoners Released Conditionally as a Percent of All Releases in 1991
103	State Prisoners Released on Parole in 1991
104	State Prisoners Released on Probation in 1991
105	State Prisoners Released on Supervised Mandatory Release in 1991
106	State Prisoners Released Unconditionally in 1991
107	State Prisoners Released Unconditionally as a Percent of All Releases in 1991
108	State Prisoners Released on Appeal or Bond in 1991
109	State Prisoners Escaped in 1991
110	State Prisoner Deaths in 1991
111	State Prisoner Deaths by Illness or Other Natural Causes in 1991
112	State Prisoner Deaths by Illness or Other Natural Causes as a Percent of All Prison Deaths in 1991
113	Deaths of State Prisoners by AIDS in 1991
114	Deaths of State Prisoners by AIDS as a Percent of All Prison Deaths in 1991
115	State Prisoners Known to be Positive for HIV Infection/AIDS in 1991
116	State Prisoners Known to be Positive for HIV Infection/AIDS as a Percent of Total Prison Population in 1991
117	State Prisoner Deaths by Suicide in 1991
118	Deaths of State Prisoners by Suicide as a Percent of All Prison Deaths in 1991
119	Adults on State Probation in 1990
120	Percent of Adult Population on State Probation in 1990
121	Adults Under State Parole Supervision in 1990
122	State and Local Corrections Employees at Correctional Institutions in 1990
123	Percent of State and Local Corrections Employees Serving at Correctional Institutions in 1990
124	State and Local Corrections Employees in Probation, Pardon or Parole Work in 1990
125	Percent of State and Local Corrections Employees in Probation, Pardon or Parole Work in 1990
126	Employees in State Correctional Facilities in 1990
127	State Correctional Officers in Adult Systems in 1992
128	Male Correctional Officers in Adult Systems in 1992
129	Female Correctional Officers in Adult Systems in 1992
130	State Prisoners per Correctional Officer in 1992
131	Turnover Rate of Correctional Officers in Adult Systems in 1992
132	Average Annual Salary of State Corrections Officers in 1992
133	Inmates in Local Jails in 1988

II. CORRECTIONS (continued)

Table	Title
134	Male Inmates in Local Jails in 1988
135	Female Inmates in Local Jails in 1988
136	White Inmates in Local Jails in 1988
137	White Inmates in Local Jails as a Percent of All Inmates in 1988
138	Black Inmates in Local Jails in 1988
139	Black Inmates in Local Jails as a Percent of All Inmates in 1988
140	Hispanic Inmates in Local Jails in 1988
141	Hispanic Inmates in Local Jails as a Percent of All Inmates in 1988
142	Juveniles Held in Public Juvenile Facilities in 1991
143	Juvenile Custody Rate in 1991
144	Juveniles Admitted to Public Juvenile Facilities in 1990
145	Juveniles Discharged from Public Juvenile Facilities in 1990
146	Public Juvenile Facilities Administered by State and Local Governments in 1991
147	Prison Boot Camp Participants in 1992

Prisoners in State Correctional Institutions in 1992

National Total = 803,334 State Prisoners*

RANK	STATE	PRISONERS	%	RANK	STATE	PRISONERS	%
1	California	109,496	13.63%	26	Mississippi	9,083	1.13%
2	New York	61,736	7.68%	27	Wisconsin	9,054	1.13%
3	Texas	61,178	7.62%	28	Colorado	8,997	1.12%
4	Florida	48,302	6.01%	29	Arkansas	8,433	1.05%
5	Michigan	39,019	4.86%	30	Oregon	6,596	0.82%
6	Ohio	38,378	4.78%	31	Nevada	6,049	0.75%
7	Illinois	31,640	3.94%	32	Kansas	6,028	0.75%
8	Georgia	25,290	3.15%	33	Iowa	4,518	0.56%
9	Pennsylvania	24,974	3.11%	34	Delaware	3,977	0.50%
10	New Jersey	22,653	2.82%	35	Minnesota	3,822	0.48%
11	Virginia	21,199	2.64%	36	New Mexico	3,271	0.41%
12	Louisiana	20,810	2.59%	37	Hawaii	2,926	0.36%
13	North Carolina	20,455	2.55%	38	Alaska	2,865	0.36%
14	Maryland	19,977	2.49%	39	Rhode Island	2,775	0.35%
15	South Carolina	18,643	2.32%	40	Utah	2,699	0.34%
16	Alabama	17,453	2.17%	41	Nebraska	2,565	0.32%
17	Arizona	16,477	2.05%	42	Idaho	2,475	0.31%
18	Missouri	16,198	2.02%	43	New Hampshire	1,777	0.22%
19	Oklahoma	14,821	1.84%	44	West Virginia	1,745	0.22%
20	Indiana	13,166	1.64%	45	Montana	1,553	0.19%
21	Tennessee	11,849	1.47%	46	Maine	1,515	0.19%
22	Connecticut	11,403	1.42%	47	South Dakota	1,487	0.19%
23	Kentucky	10,364	1.29%	48	Vermont	1,267	0.16%
24	Massachusetts	10,056	1.25%	49	Wyoming	1,022	0.13%
25	Washington	9,959	1.24%	50	North Dakota	464	0.06%

District of Columbia   10,875   1.35%

Source: U.S. Department of Justice, Bureau of Justice Statistics

"Prisoners in 1992" (Bulletin, May 1993, NCJ-141874)

*Advance figures. Totals reflect all prisoners, including those sentenced to a year or less and those unsentenced. Does not include 80,259 prisoners under federal jurisdiction. State and federal prisoners combined total 883,593.

Prisoners in State Correctional Institutions in 1991

National Total = 752,525 State Prisoners*

RANK	STATE	PRISONERS	%		RANK	STATE	PRISONERS	%
1	California	101,808	13.53%		26	Mississippi	8,904	1.18%
2	New York	57,862	7.69%		27	Colorado	8,392	1.12%
3	Texas	51,677	6.87%		28	Wisconsin	7,849	1.04%
4	Florida	46,533	6.18%		29	Arkansas	7,766	1.03%
5	Michigan	36,423	4.84%		30	Oregon	6,732	0.89%
6	Ohio	35,744	4.75%		31	Kansas	5,903	0.78%
7	Illinois	29,115	3.87%		32	Nevada	5,503	0.73%
8	Georgia	23,644	3.14%		33	Iowa	4,145	0.55%
9	New Jersey	23,483	3.12%		34	Delaware	3,717	0.49%
10	Pennsylvania	23,388	3.11%		35	Minnesota	3,472	0.46%
11	Louisiana	20,003	2.66%		36	New Mexico	3,119	0.41%
12	Virginia	19,829	2.63%		37	Rhode Island	2,771	0.37%
13	Maryland	19,291	2.56%		38	Alaska	2,706	0.36%
14	North Carolina	18,903	2.51%		39	Hawaii	2,700	0.36%
15	South Carolina	18,269	2.43%		40	Utah	2,625	0.35%
16	Alabama	16,760	2.23%		41	Nebraska	2,495	0.33%
17	Missouri	15,897	2.11%		42	Idaho	2,143	0.28%
18	Arizona	15,415	2.05%		43	Maine	1,579	0.21%
19	Oklahoma	13,340	1.77%		44	New Hampshire	1,533	0.20%
20	Indiana	13,008	1.73%		45	West Virginia	1,502	0.20%
21	Tennessee	11,474	1.52%		46	Montana	1,478	0.20%
22	Connecticut	10,977	1.46%		47	South Dakota	1,374	0.18%
23	Kentucky	9,799	1.30%		48	Vermont	1,118	0.15%
24	Washington	9,156	1.22%		49	Wyoming	1,099	0.15%
25	Massachusetts	9,155	1.22%		50	North Dakota	492	0.07%

District of Columbia	10,455	1.39%

Source: U.S. Department of Justice, Bureau of Justice Statistics

    "Prisoners in 1992" (Bulletin, May 1993, NCJ-141874)

*Final figures. Does not include 71,608 prisoners under federal jurisdiction. State and federal prisoners combined total 824,133.

Percent Change in Number of State Prisoners: 1991 to 1992

National Percent Change = 6.75% Increase*

RANK	STATE	PERCENT CHANGE	RANK	STATE	PERCENT CHANGE
1	Texas	18.39	26	Pennsylvania	6.78
2	West Virginia	16.18	27	New York	6.70
3	New Hampshire	15.92	28	Alaska	5.88
4	Idaho	15.49	29	Kentucky	5.77
5	Wisconsin	15.35	30	Montana	5.07
6	Vermont	13.33	31	New Mexico	4.87
7	Oklahoma	11.10	32	Alabama	4.13
8	Minnesota	10.08	33	Louisiana	4.03
9	Nevada	9.92	34	Connecticut	3.88
10	Massachusetts	9.84	35	Florida	3.80
11	Iowa	9.00	36	Maryland	3.56
12	Washington	8.77	37	Tennessee	3.27
13	Illinois	8.67	38	Utah	2.82
14	Arkansas	8.59	39	Nebraska	2.81
15	Hawaii	8.37	40	Kansas	2.12
16	South Dakota	8.22	41	South Carolina	2.05
17	North Carolina	8.21	42	Mississippi	2.01
18	California	7.55	43	Missouri	1.89
19	Ohio	7.37	44	Indiana	1.21
20	Colorado	7.21	45	Rhode Island	0.14
21	Michigan	7.13	46	Oregon	(2.02)
22	Delaware	6.99	47	New Jersey	(3.53)
23	Georgia	6.96	48	Maine	(4.05)
24	Virginia	6.91	49	North Dakota	(5.69)
25	Arizona	6.89	50	Wyoming	(7.01)

District of Columbia   4.02

Source: U.S. Department of Justice, Bureau of Justice Statistics

"Prisoners in 1992" (Bulletin, May 1993, NCJ-141874)

*Compares 1991 final figures to 1992 advance figures. The percent change in number of prisoners under federal jurisdiction during same period was a 12.08% increase. The combined state and federal increase was 7.21%.

State Prisoners Sentenced to More than One Year in 1992

National Total = 780,989 Prisoners*

RANK	STATE	PRISONERS	%	RANK	STATE	PRISONERS	%
1	California	105,467	13.50%	26	Colorado	8,997	1.15%
2	New York	61,736	7.90%	27	Mississippi	8,877	1.14%
3	Texas	61,178	7.83%	28	Connecticut	8,794	1.13%
4	Florida	48,302	6.18%	29	Arkansas	8,129	1.04%
5	Michigan	39,019	5.00%	30	Nevada	6,049	0.77%
6	Ohio	38,378	4.91%	31	Kansas	6,028	0.77%
7	Illinois	31,640	4.05%	32	Oregon	5,216	0.67%
8	Pennsylvania	24,966	3.20%	33	Iowa	4,518	0.58%
9	Georgia	24,848	3.18%	34	Minnesota	3,822	0.49%
10	New Jersey	22,653	2.90%	35	New Mexico	3,154	0.40%
11	Virginia	20,989	2.69%	36	Utah	2,687	0.34%
12	Louisiana	20,603	2.64%	37	Delaware	2,665	0.34%
13	North Carolina	20,024	2.56%	38	Nebraska	2,492	0.32%
14	Maryland	18,808	2.41%	39	Idaho	2,475	0.32%
15	South Carolina	17,612	2.26%	40	Alaska	1,944	0.25%
16	Alabama	16,938	2.17%	41	Hawaii	1,922	0.25%
17	Missouri	16,198	2.07%	42	New Hampshire	1,777	0.23%
18	Arizona	15,850	2.03%	43	West Virginia	1,745	0.22%
19	Oklahoma	14,821	1.90%	44	Rhode Island	1,709	0.22%
20	Indiana	13,012	1.67%	45	Montana	1,553	0.20%
21	Tennessee	11,849	1.52%	46	Maine	1,488	0.19%
22	Kentucky	10,364	1.33%	47	South Dakota	1,487	0.19%
23	Washington	9,959	1.28%	48	Wyoming	1,022	0.13%
24	Massachusetts	9,382	1.20%	49	Vermont	867	0.11%
25	Wisconsin	9,033	1.16%	50	North Dakota	415	0.05%
					District of Columbia	7,528	0.96%

Source: U.S. Department of Justice, Bureau of Justice Statistics

"Prisoners in 1992" (Bulletin, May 1993, NCJ-141874)

Advance figures. Does not include 65,706 prisoners under federal jurisdiction sentenced to more than one year. State and federal prisoners sentenced to more than one year total 846,695.

State Prisoner Incarceration Rate in 1992

National Rate = 303 Prisoners per 100,000 Population*

RANK	STATE	RATE	RANK	STATE	RATE
1	Louisiana	478	26	Colorado	266
2	South Carolina	477	27	Idaho	234
3	Oklahoma	463	27	Kansas	234
4	Nevada	461	29	Tennessee	232
5	Arizona	415	30	Indiana	227
6	Michigan	414	31	Wyoming	223
7	Alabama	404	32	South Dakota	206
8	Maryland	380	33	Pennsylvania	204
9	Delaware	371	34	New Mexico	197
10	Georgia	366	35	Washington	193
11	Alaska	363	36	Montana	192
12	Florida	348	37	Wisconsin	180
12	Texas	348	38	Oregon	173
14	Ohio	346	39	Rhode Island	168
15	New York	340	40	Hawaii	164
16	Mississippi	337	41	Iowa	157
17	Arkansas	332	42	Massachusetts	156
17	California	332	43	Nebraska	152
19	Virginia	327	43	Utah	152
20	Missouri	309	45	New Hampshire	150
21	North Carolina	291	46	Vermont	144
22	New Jersey	289	47	Maine	116
23	Kentucky	277	48	West Virginia	97
24	Connecticut	269	49	Minnesota	84
25	Illinois	267	50	North Dakota	65

District of Columbia   1,312

Source: U.S. Department of Justice, Bureau of Justice Statistics

"Prisoners in 1992" (Bulletin, May 1993, NCJ-141874)

*Advance figures for prisoners sentenced to more than one year. Does not include federal incarceration rate of 26 prisoners per 100,000 population. State and federal combined incarceration rate is 329 prisoners per 100,000 population.

State Prison Population as a Percent of Highest Capacity in 1992

National Percent = 118% of Highest Capacity*

RANK	STATE	PERCENT	RANK	STATE	PERCENT
1	California	191	24	Montana	106
2	Ohio	177	24	Texas	106
3	Nebraska	150	28	Nevada	105
4	Pennsylvania	149	28	Wyoming	105
5	Vermont	147	30	Arkansas	104
6	Massachusetts	144	30	Minnesota	104
6	Michigan	144	32	Connecticut	103
8	Virginia	139	32	New York	103
8	Wisconsin	139	34	Maryland	101
10	Iowa	138	34	Oregon	101
11	New Jersey	131	36	Georgia	100
12	Illinois	129	36	Missouri	100
13	Washington	128	36	West Virginia	100
14	South Dakota	125	39	Delaware	99
15	Hawaii	123	40	North Carolina	98
16	Oklahoma	119	41	Indiana	95
17	Alaska	116	41	Louisiana	95
18	Colorado	113	41	New Mexico	95
18	New Hampshire	113	44	Tennessee	94
20	Maine	112	45	Kansas	91
20	South Carolina	112	46	Mississippi	89
22	Alabama	111	47	Florida	88
23	Kentucky	107	48	Rhode Island	84
24	Arizona	106	49	North Dakota	81
24	Idaho	106	49	Utah	81

District of Columbia — 95

Source: U.S. Department of Justice, Bureau of Justice Statistics
   "Prisoners in 1992" (Bulletin, May 1993, NCJ-141874)

*As of December 31, 1992. Federal prison population is at 137% of highest capacity.

Female Prisoners in State Correctional Institutions in 1992

National Total = 44,010 Female Prisoners*

RANK	STATE	PRISONERS	%	RANK	STATE	PRISONERS	%
1	California	6,747	15.33%	26	Colorado	527	1.20%
2	New York	3,499	7.95%	–	Alaska**	N/A	N/A
3	Florida	2,599	5.91%	–	Arkansas**	N/A	N/A
4	Texas	2,487	5.65%	–	Delaware**	N/A	N/A
5	Ohio	2,419	5.50%	–	Hawaii**	N/A	N/A
6	Michigan	1,859	4.22%	–	Idaho**	N/A	N/A
7	Illinois	1,456	3.31%	–	Iowa**	N/A	N/A
8	Georgia	1,455	3.31%	–	Kansas**	N/A	N/A
9	Oklahoma	1,400	3.18%	–	Maine**	N/A	N/A
10	Virginia	1,163	2.64%	–	Minnesota**	N/A	N/A
11	South Carolina	1,127	2.56%	–	Montana**	N/A	N/A
12	Pennsylvania	1,106	2.51%	–	Nebraska**	N/A	N/A
13	Alabama	1,101	2.50%	–	Nevada**	N/A	N/A
14	New Jersey	1,095	2.49%	–	New Hampshire**	N/A	N/A
15	Louisiana	1,020	2.32%	–	New Mexico**	N/A	N/A
16	Arizona	1,001	2.27%	–	North Dakota**	N/A	N/A
17	Maryland	954	2.17%	–	Oregon**	N/A	N/A
18	North Carolina	951	2.16%	–	Rhode Island**	N/A	N/A
19	Missouri	858	1.95%	–	South Dakota**	N/A	N/A
20	Indiana	720	1.64%	–	Tennessee**	N/A	N/A
21	Connecticut	710	1.61%	–	Utah**	N/A	N/A
22	Washington	618	1.40%	–	Vermont**	N/A	N/A
23	Massachusetts	567	1.29%	–	West Virginia**	N/A	N/A
24	Mississippi	562	1.28%	–	Wisconsin**	N/A	N/A
25	Kentucky	545	1.24%	–	Wyoming**	N/A	N/A

District of Columbia   720   1.64%

Source: U.S. Department of Justice, Bureau of Justice Statistics
    "Prisoners in 1992" (Bulletin, May 1993, NCJ-141874)

*As of December 31, 1992. States shown have at least 500 female inmates. Total includes 4,744 female inmates in states not shown separately.
Total does not include 6,399 federal female inmates.

**Not available, fewer than 500 female inmates.

Female Prisoners in State Correctional Institutions as a Percent of All Prisoners: 1992

National Rate = 5.5% of Prisoners are Female*

RANK	STATE	PERCENT	RANK	STATE	PERCENT
1	Oklahoma	9.5	26	Texas	4.1
2	Alabama	6.3	–	Alaska**	N/A
2	Ohio	6.3	–	Arkansas**	N/A
4	California	6.2	–	Delaware**	N/A
4	Connecticut	6.2	–	Hawaii**	N/A
4	Mississippi	6.2	–	Idaho**	N/A
4	Washington	6.2	–	Iowa**	N/A
8	Arizona	6.1	–	Kansas**	N/A
8	South Carolina	6.1	–	Maine**	N/A
10	Colorado	5.9	–	Minnesota**	N/A
11	Georgia	5.8	–	Montana**	N/A
12	New York	5.7	–	Nebraska**	N/A
13	Massachusetts	5.6	–	Nevada**	N/A
14	Indiana	5.5	–	New Hampshire**	N/A
14	Virginia	5.5	–	New Mexico**	N/A
16	Florida	5.4	–	North Dakota**	N/A
17	Kentucky	5.3	–	Oregon**	N/A
17	Missouri	5.3	–	Rhode Island**	N/A
19	Louisiana	4.9	–	South Dakota**	N/A
20	Maryland	4.8	–	Tennessee**	N/A
20	Michigan	4.8	–	Utah**	N/A
20	New Jersey	4.8	–	Vermont**	N/A
23	North Carolina	4.7	–	West Virginia**	N/A
24	Illinois	4.6	–	Wisconsin**	N/A
25	Pennsylvania	4.4	–	Wyoming**	N/A

District of Columbia   6.6

Source: U.S. Department of Justice, Bureau of Justice Statistics
"Prisoners in 1992" (Bulletin, May 1993, NCJ-141874)

*As of December 31, 1992. States shown have at least 500 female inmates. National rate reflects 4,744 female inmates in states not shown separately. Total does not include federal female inmates. Federal female inmates constitute 8.0% of federal inmates. The federal/state combined rate is 5.7%.

**Not available, fewer than 500 female inmates.

Percent Change in Female Prisoner Population: 1991 to 1992

National Percent Change = 5.0% Increase*

RANK	STATE	PERCENT CHANGE	RANK	STATE	PERCENT CHANGE
1	Colorado	16.3	26	Massachusetts	(10.0)
2	Illinois	15.8	–	Alaska**	N/A
3	Washington	14.7	–	Arkansas**	N/A
4	Oklahoma	13.3	–	Delaware**	N/A
5	Louisiana	12.0	–	Hawaii**	N/A
6	Virginia	11.8	–	Idaho**	N/A
7	Mississippi	10.6	–	Iowa**	N/A
8	South Carolina	7.8	–	Kansas**	N/A
9	Connecticut	7.6	–	Maine**	N/A
10	Michigan	7.2	–	Minnesota**	N/A
11	California	7.1	–	Montana**	N/A
12	Arizona	6.6	–	Nebraska**	N/A
13	Kentucky	6.2	–	Nevada**	N/A
14	Ohio	5.5	–	New Hampshire**	N/A
15	Georgia	4.6	–	New Mexico**	N/A
16	Missouri	4.5	–	North Dakota**	N/A
17	Alabama	4.4	–	Oregon**	N/A
18	New York	3.9	–	Rhode Island**	N/A
19	Maryland	2.5	–	South Dakota**	N/A
20	Indiana	2.0	–	Tennessee**	N/A
21	Pennsylvania	1.6	–	Utah**	N/A
22	Texas	(0.2)	–	Vermont**	N/A
23	New Jersey	(1.1)	–	West Virginia**	N/A
24	Florida	(1.5)	–	Wisconsin**	N/A
25	North Carolina	(6.9)	–	Wyoming**	N/A

District of Columbia   (4.5)

Source: U.S. Department of Justice, Bureau of Justice Statistics

   "Prisoners in 1992" (Bulletin, May 1993, NCJ–141874)

*As of December 31, 1992. States shown have at least 500 female inmates. National rate reflects 4,744 female inmates in states not shown separately. Total does not include federal female inmates. Federal female inmate population increased by 13.2%. The combined federal/state female inmate population grew by 5.9%.

**Not available, fewer than 500 female inmates.

White Prisoners in State Correctional Institutions in 1991

National Total = 338,479 White Prisoners*

RANK	STATE	PRISONERS	%	RANK	STATE	PRISONERS	%
1	California	61,594	18.20%	26	Massachusetts	4,410	1.30%
2	New York	28,181	8.33%	27	Wisconsin	4,275	1.26%
3	Florida	18,383	5.43%	28	Kansas	3,329	0.98%
4	Ohio	16,433	4.85%	29	Arkansas	3,302	0.98%
5	Texas	15,013	4.44%	30	Nevada	3,141	0.93%
6	Michigan	14,586	4.31%	31	Iowa	3,089	0.91%
7	Arizona	12,271	3.63%	32	Connecticut	3,053	0.90%
8	Missouri	8,547	2.53%	33	New Mexico	2,680	0.79%
9	Pennsylvania	8,470	2.50%	34	Mississippi	2,437	0.72%
10	Illinois	8,055	2.38%	35	Utah	2,264	0.67%
11	Indiana	8,000	2.36%	36	Idaho	1,997	0.59%
12	Georgia	7,613	2.25%	37	Minnesota	1,960	0.58%
13	Oklahoma	7,522	2.22%	38	Rhode Island	1,856	0.55%
14	Virginia	6,942	2.05%	39	Nebraska	1,564	0.46%
15	New Jersey	6,762	2.00%	40	Maine	1,522	0.45%
16	North Carolina	6,747	1.99%	41	Alaska	1,488	0.44%
17	Kentucky	6,672	1.97%	42	New Hampshire	1,443	0.43%
18	Washington	6,345	1.87%	43	West Virginia	1,282	0.38%
19	South Carolina	6,099	1.80%	44	Montana	1,189	0.35%
20	Colorado	5,990	1.77%	45	Delaware	1,175	0.35%
21	Alabama	5,958	1.76%	46	Vermont	1,118	0.33%
22	Tennessee	5,857	1.73%	47	South Dakota	992	0.29%
23	Louisiana	5,168	1.53%	48	Wyoming	873	0.26%
24	Oregon	4,994	1.48%	49	Hawaii	642	0.19%
25	Maryland	4,581	1.35%	50	North Dakota	397	0.12%
					District of Columbia	218	0.06%

Source: U.S. Department of Justice, Bureau of Justice Statistics
   "Correctional Populations in the United States, 1991" (August 1993, NCJ-142729)
*As of December 31, 1991. Excludes 46,868 white federal prisoners.

Black Prisoners in State Correctional Institutions in 1991

National Total = 372,518 Black Prisoners*

RANK	STATE	PRISONERS	%	RANK	STATE	PRISONERS	%
1	California	35,205	9.45%	26	Massachusetts	3,036	0.81%
2	New York	29,151	7.83%	27	Arizona	2,633	0.71%
3	Florida	27,185	7.30%	28	Delaware	2,449	0.66%
4	Texas	24,520	6.58%	29	Kansas	2,145	0.58%
5	Michigan	20,985	5.63%	30	Washington	1,966	0.53%
6	Ohio	19,311	5.18%	31	Colorado	1,937	0.52%
7	Illinois	18,306	4.91%	32	Nevada	1,719	0.46%
8	Georgia	15,931	4.28%	33	Minnesota	1,051	0.28%
9	New Jersey	15,005	4.03%	34	Iowa	940	0.25%
10	Louisiana	14,834	3.98%	35	Oregon	923	0.25%
11	Maryland	14,638	3.93%	36	Rhode Island	899	0.24%
12	Pennsylvania	13,090	3.51%	37	Nebraska	830	0.22%
13	Virginia	12,769	3.43%	38	Alaska	339	0.09%
14	South Carolina	12,120	3.25%	39	New Mexico	316	0.08%
15	North Carolina	11,522	3.09%	40	Utah	222	0.06%
16	Alabama	10,793	2.90%	41	West Virginia	218	0.06%
17	Missouri	7,317	1.96%	42	Hawaii	155	0.04%
18	Mississippi	6,410	1.72%	43	New Hampshire	80	0.02%
19	Tennessee	5,503	1.48%	44	Wyoming	51	0.01%
20	Connecticut	5,144	1.38%	45	Maine	37	0.01%
21	Indiana	4,971	1.33%	46	Idaho	32	0.01%
22	Oklahoma	4,652	1.25%	46	South Dakota	32	0.01%
23	Arkansas	4,437	1.19%	48	Montana	20	0.01%
24	Wisconsin	3,325	0.89%	49	North Dakota	4	0.00%
25	Kentucky	3,123	0.84%	–	Vermont**	N/A	N/A

District of Columbia   10,237   2.75%

Source: U.S. Department of Justice, Bureau of Justice Statistics

"Correctional Populations in the United States, 1991" (August 1993, NCJ-142729)

*As of December 31, 1991. Excludes 22,727 black federal prisoners.

**Not reported.

Average Annual Operating Expenditures per Inmate in 1990

National Average = $15,586 per Inmate*

RANK	STATE	AVERAGE EXPENDITURE	RANK	STATE	AVERAGE EXPENDITURE
1	Alaska	$28,214	26	Kansas	$14,670
2	Minnesota	26,661	27	Montana	14,590
3	Maine	22,656	28	North Dakota	14,581
4	California	21,816	29	Colorado	14,180
5	New Jersey	20,703	30	Florida	13,902
6	Tennessee	20,048	31	Nebraska	13,012
7	Washington	19,742	32	Texas	12,988
8	Hawaii	19,542	33	Georgia	12,930
9	Wisconsin	18,965	34	Wyoming	12,151
10	New York	18,670	35	West Virginia	11,699
11	North Carolina	18,486	36	Oregon	11,516
12	Iowa	18,304	37	Delaware	11,208
13	Maryland	17,214	38	Kentucky	11,118
14	New Hampshire	17,208	39	Ohio	11,028
15	Connecticut	17,002	40	South Dakota	10,859
16	New Mexico	16,711	41	Arizona	10,311
17	Michigan	16,649	42	South Carolina	10,268
18	Rhode Island	16,497	43	Oklahoma	9,919
19	Virginia	16,145	44	Missouri	9,766
20	Illinois	15,980	45	Idaho	9,450
21	Vermont	15,905	46	Louisiana	9,337
22	Pennsylvania	15,438	47	Mississippi	9,133
23	Utah	15,251	48	Alabama	8,718
24	Massachusetts	15,152	49	Nevada	8,630
25	Indiana	14,822	50	Arkansas	7,557

District of Columbia   13,894

Source: U.S. Department of Justice, Bureau of Justice Statistics

   "Census of State and Federal Correctional Facilities, 1990" (1992, NCJ–137003)

For fiscal year 1990. Determined by dividing the amount spent on salaries, wages, supplies, utilities, transportation, contractual services and other current operating items by the average daily inmate population. Federal average is $14,456, combined federal/state average is $15,496.

State Prison Inmates Serving Life Sentences in 1992

National Total = 66,585 Inmates*

RANK	STATE	INMATES	%	RANK	STATE	INMATES	%
1	California	11,767	17.67%	26	Kansas	507	0.76%
2	New York	9,477	14.23%	27	Arkansas	494	0.74%
3	Florida	4,912	7.38%	28	Oregon	462	0.69%
4	Texas	4,237	6.36%	29	Delaware	403	0.61%
5	Georgia	3,381	5.08%	30	Iowa	391	0.59%
6	Michigan	3,193	4.80%	31	West Virginia	260	0.39%
7	Ohio	3,078	4.62%	32	Idaho	195	0.29%
8	Alabama	2,606	3.91%	33	New Mexico	165	0.25%
9	Pennsylvania	2,417	3.63%	34	Minnesota	160	0.24%
10	North Carolina	2,237	3.36%	35	Connecticut	152	0.23%
11	Louisiana	2,230	3.35%	36	Wyoming	111	0.17%
12	South Carolina	1,357	2.04%	37	South Dakota	102	0.15%
13	Tennessee	1,290	1.94%	38	Nebraska	84	0.13%
14	Virginia	1,273	1.91%	39	Rhode Island	83	0.12%
15	Missouri	1,218	1.83%	40	Mississippi	49	0.07%
16	Oklahoma	991	1.49%	41	Maine	44	0.07%
17	Massachusetts	949	1.43%	42	Utah	41	0.06%
18	Nevada	934	1.40%	43	New Hampshire	28	0.04%
19	New Jersey	910	1.37%	44	Montana	27	0.04%
20	Arizona	763	1.15%	45	Vermont	14	0.02%
21	Washington	608	0.91%	46	North Dakota	13	0.02%
22	Kentucky	586	0.88%	47	Hawaii	3	0.00%
23	Illinois	565	0.85%	–	Alaska**	N/A	N/A
24	Wisconsin	523	0.79%	–	Indiana**	N/A	N/A
25	Colorado	512	0.77%	–	Maryland**	N/A	N/A

District of Columbia 784 1.18%

Source: "Corrections Compendium" (Lincoln, NE) (January 1993)

As of September 30, 1992. Total does not include states without data.

**Not available.*

Percent of State Prison Inmates Serving Life Sentences in 1992

National Rate = 8.29% of Inmates*

RANK	STATE	PERCENT	RANK	STATE	PERCENT
1	Nevada	15.44	26	Washington	6.11
2	New York	15.35	27	Virginia	6.01
3	Alabama	14.93	28	Arkansas	5.86
4	West Virginia	14.90	29	Wisconsin	5.78
5	Georgia	13.37	30	Colorado	5.69
6	North Carolina	10.94	31	Kentucky	5.65
7	Tennessee	10.89	32	New Mexico	5.04
8	Wyoming	10.86	33	Arizona	4.63
9	California	10.75	34	Minnesota	4.19
10	Louisiana	10.72	35	New Jersey	4.02
11	Florida	10.17	36	Nebraska	3.27
12	Delaware	10.13	37	Rhode Island	2.99
13	Pennsylvania	9.68	38	Maine	2.90
14	Massachusetts	9.44	39	North Dakota	2.80
15	Iowa	8.65	40	Illinois	1.79
16	Kansas	8.41	41	Montana	1.74
17	Michigan	8.18	42	New Hampshire	1.58
18	Ohio	8.02	43	Utah	1.52
19	Idaho	7.88	44	Connecticut	1.33
20	Missouri	7.52	45	Vermont	1.10
21	South Carolina	7.28	46	Mississippi	0.54
22	Oregon	7.00	47	Hawaii	0.10
23	Texas	6.93	–	Alaska**	N/A
24	South Dakota	6.86	–	Indiana**	N/A
25	Oklahoma	6.69	–	Maryland**	N/A

District of Columbia 7.21

Source: Morgan Quitno Corporation using data from U.S. Department of Justice, Bureau of Justice Statistics

"Prisoners in 1992" (Bulletin, May 1993, NCJ-141874) and

"Corrections Compendium" (Lincoln, NE) (January 1993)

*National percent does not include states without data.

**Not available.

Prisoners Under Sentence of Death in 1991

National Total = 2,482 Prisoners*

RANK	STATE	PRISONERS	%	RANK	STATE	PRISONERS	%
1	Texas	340	13.70%	26	Washington	10	0.40%
2	Florida	311	12.53%	27	Oregon	9	0.36%
3	California	301	12.13%	28	Delaware	7	0.28%
4	Pennsylvania	137	5.52%	29	Montana	6	0.24%
5	Illinois	132	5.32%	30	Connecticut	4	0.16%
6	Oklahoma	125	5.04%	30	New Jersey	4	0.16%
7	Alabama	119	4.79%	32	Colorado	3	0.12%
8	Ohio	111	4.47%	33	New Mexico	1	0.04%
9	Georgia	101	4.07%	33	Wyoming	1	0.04%
10	Arizona	97	3.91%	35	New Hampshire	0	0.00%
10	Tennessee	97	3.91%	35	South Dakota	0	0.00%
12	Missouri	77	3.10%	–	Alaska**	N/A	N/A
13	North Carolina	74	2.98%	–	Hawaii**	N/A	N/A
14	Nevada	60	2.42%	–	Iowa**	N/A	N/A
15	Mississippi	51	2.05%	–	Kansas**	N/A	N/A
16	Indiana	49	1.97%	–	Maine**	N/A	N/A
17	Virginia	47	1.89%	–	Massachusetts**	N/A	N/A
18	South Carolina	45	1.81%	–	Michigan**	N/A	N/A
19	Louisiana	37	1.49%	–	Minnesota**	N/A	N/A
20	Arkansas	34	1.37%	–	New York**	N/A	N/A
21	Kentucky	30	1.21%	–	North Dakota**	N/A	N/A
22	Idaho	21	0.85%	–	Rhode Island**	N/A	N/A
23	Maryland	16	0.64%	–	Vermont**	N/A	N/A
24	Nebraska	12	0.48%	–	West Virginia**	N/A	N/A
24	Utah	12	0.48%	–	Wisconsin**	N/A	N/A
					District of Columbia**	N/A	N/A

Source: U.S. Department of Justice, Bureau of Justice Statistics
   "Capital Punishment 1991" (Bulletin, October 1992, NCJ-136946)
*As of December 31, 1991. Includes one federal prisoner under sentence of death. There were 14 executions in 1991.
**No death penalty.

Male Prisoners Under Sentence of Death in 1991

National Total = 2,448 Male Prisoners*

RANK	STATE	PRISONERS	%	RANK	STATE	PRISONERS	%
1	Texas	337	13.77%	26	Washington	10	0.41%
2	Florida	309	12.62%	27	Oregon	9	0.37%
3	California	300	12.25%	28	Delaware	7	0.29%
4	Pennsylvania	136	5.56%	29	Montana	6	0.25%
5	Illinois	132	5.39%	30	Connecticut	4	0.16%
6	Oklahoma	121	4.94%	30	New Jersey	4	0.16%
7	Alabama	114	4.66%	32	Colorado	3	0.12%
8	Ohio	108	4.41%	33	New Mexico	1	0.04%
9	Georgia	101	4.13%	33	Wyoming	1	0.04%
10	Arizona	96	3.92%	35	New Hampshire	0	0.00%
10	Tennessee	96	3.92%	35	South Dakota	0	0.00%
12	Missouri	75	3.06%	–	Alaska**	N/A	N/A
13	North Carolina	68	2.78%	–	Hawaii**	N/A	N/A
14	Nevada	59	2.41%	–	Iowa**	N/A	N/A
15	Indiana	49	2.00%	–	Kansas**	N/A	N/A
15	Mississippi	49	2.00%	–	Maine**	N/A	N/A
17	Virginia	47	1.92%	–	Massachusetts**	N/A	N/A
18	South Carolina	44	1.80%	–	Michigan**	N/A	N/A
19	Louisiana	37	1.51%	–	Minnesota**	N/A	N/A
20	Arkansas	34	1.39%	–	New York**	N/A	N/A
21	Kentucky	29	1.18%	–	North Dakota**	N/A	N/A
22	Idaho	21	0.86%	–	Rhode Island**	N/A	N/A
23	Maryland	16	0.65%	–	Vermont**	N/A	N/A
24	Nebraska	12	0.49%	–	West Virginia**	N/A	N/A
24	Utah	12	0.49%	–	Wisconsin**	N/A	N/A
					District of Columbia**	N/A	N/A

Source: Morgan Quitno Corporation using data from U.S. Department of Justice, Bureau of Justice Statistics
   "Capital Punishment 1991" (Bulletin, October 1992, NCJ-136946)

*As of December 31, 1991. Includes one federal prisoner under sentence of death. There were 14 executions in 1991.

**No death penalty.

Female Prisoners Under Sentence of Death in 1991

National Total = 34 Female Prisoners*

RANK	STATE	PRISONERS	%	RANK	STATE	PRISONERS	%
1	North Carolina	6	17.65%	16	Montana	0	0.00%
2	Alabama	5	14.71%	16	Nebraska	0	0.00%
3	Oklahoma	4	11.76%	16	New Hampshire	0	0.00%
4	Ohio	3	8.82%	16	New Jersey	0	0.00%
4	Texas	3	8.82%	16	New Mexico	0	0.00%
6	Florida	2	5.88%	16	Oregon	0	0.00%
6	Mississippi	2	5.88%	16	South Dakota	0	0.00%
6	Missouri	2	5.88%	16	Utah	0	0.00%
9	Arizona	1	2.94%	16	Virginia	0	0.00%
9	California	1	2.94%	16	Washington	0	0.00%
9	Kentucky	1	2.94%	16	Wyoming	0	0.00%
9	Nevada	1	2.94%	–	Alaska**	N/A	N/A
9	Pennsylvania	1	2.94%	–	Hawaii**	N/A	N/A
9	South Carolina	1	2.94%	–	Iowa**	N/A	N/A
9	Tennessee	1	2.94%	–	Kansas**	N/A	N/A
16	Arkansas	0	0.00%	–	Maine**	N/A	N/A
16	Colorado	0	0.00%	–	Massachusetts**	N/A	N/A
16	Connecticut	0	0.00%	–	Michigan**	N/A	N/A
16	Delaware	0	0.00%	–	Minnesota**	N/A	N/A
16	Georgia	0	0.00%	–	New York**	N/A	N/A
16	Idaho	0	0.00%	–	North Dakota**	N/A	N/A
16	Illinois	0	0.00%	–	Rhode Island**	N/A	N/A
16	Indiana	0	0.00%	–	Vermont**	N/A	N/A
16	Louisiana	0	0.00%	–	West Virginia**	N/A	N/A
16	Maryland	0	0.00%	–	Wisconsin**	N/A	N/A
					District of Columbia**	N/A	N/A

Source: U.S. Department of Justice, Bureau of Justice Statistics
"Capital Punishment 1991" (Bulletin, October 1992, NCJ-136946)

*As of December 31, 1991. There were 14 executions in 1991. No women were executed. Since 1977 one woman has been executed.

**No death penalty.

Percent of Prisoners Under Sentence of Death Who Are Female: 1991

National Rate = 1.37% of Prisoners*

RANK	STATE	PERCENT	RANK	STATE	PERCENT
1	North Carolina	8.11	16	Montana	0.00
2	Alabama	4.20	16	Nebraska	0.00
3	Mississippi	3.92	16	New Hampshire	0.00
4	Kentucky	3.33	16	New Jersey	0.00
5	Oklahoma	3.20	16	New Mexico	0.00
6	Ohio	2.70	16	Oregon	0.00
7	Missouri	2.60	16	South Dakota	0.00
8	South Carolina	2.22	16	Utah	0.00
9	Nevada	1.67	16	Virginia	0.00
10	Arizona	1.03	16	Washington	0.00
10	Tennessee	1.03	16	Wyoming	0.00
12	Texas	0.88	–	Alaska**	N/A
13	Pennsylvania	0.73	–	Hawaii**	N/A
14	Florida	0.64	–	Iowa**	N/A
15	California	0.33	–	Kansas**	N/A
16	Arkansas	0.00	–	Maine**	N/A
16	Colorado	0.00	–	Massachusetts**	N/A
16	Connecticut	0.00	–	Michigan**	N/A
16	Delaware	0.00	–	Minnesota**	N/A
16	Georgia	0.00	–	New York**	N/A
16	Idaho	0.00	–	North Dakota**	N/A
16	Illinois	0.00	–	Rhode Island**	N/A
16	Indiana	0.00	–	Vermont**	N/A
16	Louisiana	0.00	–	West Virginia**	N/A
16	Maryland	0.00	–	Wisconsin**	N/A

District of Columbia**   N/A

Source: Morgan Quitno Corporation using data from U.S. Department of Justice, Bureau of Justice Statistics
    "Capital Punishment 1991" (Bulletin, October 1992, NCJ-136946)
*As of December 31, 1991. There were 14 executions in 1991. No women were executed. Since 1977 one woman has been executed.
**No death penalty.

White Prisoners Under Sentence of Death in 1991

National Total = 1,464 White Prisoners*

RANK	STATE	PRISONERS	%	RANK	STATE	PRISONERS	%
1	Texas	214	14.62%	24	Washington	8	0.55%
2	Florida	204	13.93%	27	Montana	4	0.27%
3	California	182	12.43%	28	Colorado	3	0.20%
4	Arizona	85	5.81%	28	Delaware	3	0.20%
5	Oklahoma	83	5.67%	30	Connecticut	2	0.14%
6	Tennessee	67	4.58%	30	New Jersey	2	0.14%
7	Alabama	60	4.10%	32	Maryland	1	0.07%
8	Georgia	54	3.69%	32	New Mexico	1	0.07%
9	Pennsylvania	53	3.62%	32	Wyoming	1	0.07%
10	Ohio	51	3.48%	35	New Hampshire	0	0.00%
11	Illinois	48	3.28%	35	South Dakota	0	0.00%
12	Missouri	45	3.07%	–	Alaska**	N/A	N/A
13	Nevada	41	2.80%	–	Hawaii**	N/A	N/A
13	North Carolina	41	2.80%	–	Iowa**	N/A	N/A
15	Indiana	33	2.25%	–	Kansas**	N/A	N/A
16	Virginia	26	1.78%	–	Maine**	N/A	N/A
17	Kentucky	24	1.64%	–	Massachusetts**	N/A	N/A
18	Arkansas	22	1.50%	–	Michigan**	N/A	N/A
19	Idaho	21	1.43%	–	Minnesota**	N/A	N/A
19	Mississippi	21	1.43%	–	New York**	N/A	N/A
19	South Carolina	21	1.43%	–	North Dakota**	N/A	N/A
22	Louisiana	17	1.16%	–	Rhode Island**	N/A	N/A
23	Utah	9	0.61%	–	Vermont**	N/A	N/A
24	Nebraska	8	0.55%	–	West Virginia**	N/A	N/A
24	Oregon	8	0.55%	–	Wisconsin**	N/A	N/A
					District of Columbia**	N/A	N/A

Source: U.S. Department of Justice, Bureau of Justice Statistics
   "Capital Punishment 1991" (Bulletin, October 1992, NCJ-136946)
*As of December 31, 1991. Includes one white federal prisoner under sentence of death. There were 14 executions in 1991, seven of whom were white prisoners.
**No death penalty.

Percent of Prisoners Under Sentence of Death Who Are White: 1991

National Rate = 58.98% of Prisoners*

RANK	STATE	PERCENT		RANK	STATE	PERCENT
1	Colorado	100.00		25	New Jersey	50.00
1	Idaho	100.00		27	South Carolina	46.67
1	New Mexico	100.00		28	Louisiana	45.95
1	Wyoming	100.00		28	Ohio	45.95
5	Oregon	88.89		30	Delaware	42.86
6	Arizona	87.63		31	Mississippi	41.18
7	Kentucky	80.00		32	Pennsylvania	38.69
7	Washington	80.00		33	Illinois	36.36
9	Utah	75.00		34	Maryland	6.25
10	Tennessee	69.07		35	New Hampshire	0.00
11	Nevada	68.33		35	South Dakota	0.00
12	Indiana	67.35		–	Alaska**	N/A
13	Montana	66.67		–	Hawaii**	N/A
13	Nebraska	66.67		–	Iowa**	N/A
15	Oklahoma	66.40		–	Kansas**	N/A
16	Florida	65.59		–	Maine**	N/A
17	Arkansas	64.71		–	Massachusetts**	N/A
18	Texas	62.94		–	Michigan**	N/A
19	California	60.47		–	Minnesota**	N/A
20	Missouri	58.44		–	New York**	N/A
21	North Carolina	55.41		–	North Dakota**	N/A
22	Virginia	55.32		–	Rhode Island**	N/A
23	Georgia	53.47		–	Vermont**	N/A
24	Alabama	50.42		–	West Virginia**	N/A
25	Connecticut	50.00		–	Wisconsin**	N/A

District of Columbia**   N/A

Source: Morgan Quitno Corporation using data from U.S. Department of Justice, Bureau of Justice Statistics
   "Capital Punishment 1991" (Bulletin, October 1992, NCJ-136946)
*As of December 31, 1991. Includes one white federal prisoner under sentence of death. There were 14 executions in 1991, seven of whom were white prisoners.
**No death penalty.

Black Prisoners Under Sentence of Death in 1991

National Total = 982 Black Prisoners*

RANK	STATE	PRISONERS	%	RANK	STATE	PRISONERS	%
1	Texas	121	12.32%	26	Connecticut	2	0.20%
2	California	112	11.41%	26	New Jersey	2	0.20%
3	Florida	107	10.90%	26	Washington	2	0.20%
4	Illinois	84	8.55%	29	Oregon	1	0.10%
5	Pennsylvania	82	8.35%	30	Colorado	0	0.00%
6	Ohio	59	6.01%	30	Idaho	0	0.00%
7	Alabama	58	5.91%	30	Montana	0	0.00%
8	Georgia	47	4.79%	30	New Hampshire	0	0.00%
9	Missouri	32	3.26%	30	New Mexico	0	0.00%
9	Oklahoma	32	3.26%	30	South Dakota	0	0.00%
11	North Carolina	31	3.16%	30	Wyoming	0	0.00%
12	Mississippi	30	3.05%	–	Alaska**	N/A	N/A
13	Tennessee	28	2.85%	–	Hawaii**	N/A	N/A
14	South Carolina	24	2.44%	–	Iowa**	N/A	N/A
15	Virginia	21	2.14%	–	Kansas**	N/A	N/A
16	Louisiana	20	2.04%	–	Maine**	N/A	N/A
17	Nevada	19	1.93%	–	Massachusetts**	N/A	N/A
18	Indiana	16	1.63%	–	Michigan**	N/A	N/A
19	Maryland	15	1.53%	–	Minnesota**	N/A	N/A
20	Arkansas	12	1.22%	–	New York**	N/A	N/A
21	Arizona	9	0.92%	–	North Dakota**	N/A	N/A
22	Kentucky	6	0.61%	–	Rhode Island**	N/A	N/A
23	Delaware	4	0.41%	–	Vermont**	N/A	N/A
24	Nebraska	3	0.31%	–	West Virginia**	N/A	N/A
24	Utah	3	0.31%	–	Wisconsin**	N/A	N/A
					District of Columbia**	N/A	N/A

Source: U.S. Department of Justice, Bureau of Justice Statistics
"Capital Punishment 1991" (Bulletin, October 1992, NCJ-136946)

*As of December 31, 1991. There were 14 executions in 1991, seven of whom were black prisoners.

**No death penalty.

Percent of Prisoners Under Sentence of Death Who Are Black: 1991

National Rate = 39.56% of Prisoners*

RANK	STATE	PERCENT		RANK	STATE	PERCENT
1	Maryland	93.75		26	Kentucky	20.00
2	Illinois	63.64		26	Washington	20.00
3	Pennsylvania	59.85		28	Oregon	11.11
4	Mississippi	58.82		29	Arizona	9.28
5	Delaware	57.14		30	Colorado	0.00
6	Louisiana	54.05		30	Idaho	0.00
7	South Carolina	53.33		30	Montana	0.00
8	Ohio	53.15		30	New Hampshire	0.00
9	Connecticut	50.00		30	New Mexico	0.00
9	New Jersey	50.00		30	South Dakota	0.00
11	Alabama	48.74		30	Wyoming	0.00
12	Georgia	46.53		–	Alaska**	N/A
13	Virginia	44.68		–	Hawaii**	N/A
14	North Carolina	41.89		–	Iowa**	N/A
15	Missouri	41.56		–	Kansas**	N/A
16	California	37.21		–	Maine**	N/A
17	Texas	35.59		–	Massachusetts**	N/A
18	Arkansas	35.29		–	Michigan**	N/A
19	Florida	34.41		–	Minnesota**	N/A
20	Indiana	32.65		–	New York**	N/A
21	Nevada	31.67		–	North Dakota**	N/A
22	Tennessee	28.87		–	Rhode Island**	N/A
23	Oklahoma	25.60		–	Vermont**	N/A
24	Nebraska	25.00		–	West Virginia**	N/A
24	Utah	25.00		–	Wisconsin**	N/A
					District of Columbia**	N/A

Source: Morgan Quitno Corporation using data from U.S. Department of Justice, Bureau of Justice Statistics
    "Capital Punishment 1991" (Bulletin, October 1992, NCJ-136946)

*As of December 31, 1991. There were 14 executions in 1991, seven of whom were black prisoners.

**No death penalty.

Prisoners Executed: 1930 to 1991

National Total = 4,016 Prisoners*

RANK	STATE	EXECUTIONS	%	RANK	STATE	EXECUTIONS	%
1	Georgia	381	9.49%	26	Arizona	38	0.95%
2	Texas	339	8.44%	27	Nevada	34	0.85%
3	New York	329	8.19%	28	Massachusetts	27	0.67%
4	California	292	7.27%	29	Connecticut	21	0.52%
5	North Carolina	267	6.65%	30	Oregon	19	0.47%
6	Florida	197	4.91%	31	Iowa	18	0.45%
7	Ohio	172	4.28%	32	Utah	16	0.40%
8	South Carolina	166	4.13%	33	Kansas	15	0.37%
9	Mississippi	158	3.93%	34	Delaware	12	0.30%
10	Louisiana	153	3.81%	35	New Mexico	8	0.20%
11	Pennsylvania	152	3.78%	36	Wyoming	7	0.17%
12	Alabama	143	3.56%	37	Montana	6	0.15%
13	Arkansas	120	2.99%	38	Nebraska	4	0.10%
14	Virginia	105	2.61%	38	Vermont	4	0.10%
15	Kentucky	103	2.56%	40	Idaho	3	0.07%
16	Tennessee	93	2.32%	41	New Hampshire	1	0.02%
17	Illinois	91	2.27%	41	South Dakota	1	0.02%
18	New Jersey	74	1.84%	43	Alaska	0	0.00%
19	Maryland	68	1.69%	43	Hawaii	0	0.00%
19	Missouri	68	1.69%	43	Maine	0	0.00%
21	Oklahoma	61	1.52%	43	Michigan	0	0.00%
22	Colorado	47	1.17%	43	Minnesota	0	0.00%
22	Washington	47	1.17%	43	North Dakota	0	0.00%
24	Indiana	43	1.07%	43	Rhode Island	0	0.00%
25	West Virginia	40	1.00%	43	Wisconsin	0	0.00%
					District of Columbia	40	1.00%

Source: U.S. Department of Justice, Bureau of Justice Statistics

"Capital Punishment 1991" (Bulletin, October 1992, NCJ-136946)

*Includes 33 executions by the federal government. Does not include 160 executions carried out under military authority. There were no executions from 1968 to 1976. Of the total, 3,491 were executed for murder, 455 for rape and 70 for other offenses (armed robbery (25), kidnapping (20), burglary (11), sabotage (6), aggravated assault (6) and espionage (2)).

Prisoners Executed: 1977 to 1991

National Total = 157 Prisoners*

RANK	STATE	EXECUTIONS	%		RANK	STATE	EXECUTIONS	%
1	Texas	42	26.75%		17	Kansas	0	0.00%
2	Florida	27	17.20%		17	Kentucky	0	0.00%
3	Louisiana	20	12.74%		17	Maine	0	0.00%
4	Georgia	15	9.55%		17	Maryland	0	0.00%
5	Virginia	13	8.28%		17	Massachusetts	0	0.00%
6	Alabama	8	5.10%		17	Michigan	0	0.00%
7	Missouri	6	3.82%		17	Minnesota	0	0.00%
8	Nevada	5	3.18%		17	Montana	0	0.00%
9	Mississippi	4	2.55%		17	Nebraska	0	0.00%
9	North Carolina	4	2.55%		17	New Hampshire	0	0.00%
9	South Carolina	4	2.55%		17	New Jersey	0	0.00%
12	Utah	3	1.91%		17	New Mexico	0	0.00%
13	Arkansas	2	1.27%		17	New York	0	0.00%
13	Indiana	2	1.27%		17	North Dakota	0	0.00%
15	Illinois	1	0.64%		17	Ohio	0	0.00%
15	Oklahoma	1	0.64%		17	Oregon	0	0.00%
17	Alaska	0	0.00%		17	Pennsylvania	0	0.00%
17	Arizona	0	0.00%		17	Rhode Island	0	0.00%
17	California	0	0.00%		17	South Dakota	0	0.00%
17	Colorado	0	0.00%		17	Tennessee	0	0.00%
17	Connecticut	0	0.00%		17	Vermont	0	0.00%
17	Delaware	0	0.00%		17	Washington	0	0.00%
17	Hawaii	0	0.00%		17	West Virginia	0	0.00%
17	Idaho	0	0.00%		17	Wisconsin	0	0.00%
17	Iowa	0	0.00%		17	Wyoming	0	0.00%

District of Columbia   0   0.00%

Source: U.S. Department of Justice, Bureau of Justice Statistics
    "Capital Punishment 1991" (Bulletin, October 1992, NCJ-136946)
*All executions since 1977 have been for murder.

Prisoners Sentenced to Death: 1973 to 1991

National Total = 4,442 Death Sentences*

RANK	STATE	SENTENCED	%	RANK	STATE	SENTENCED	%
1	Florida	600	13.51%	26	New Mexico	22	0.50%
2	Texas	508	11.44%	26	Utah	22	0.50%
3	California	439	9.88%	28	Delaware	20	0.45%
4	North Carolina	299	6.73%	28	Nebraska	20	0.45%
5	Ohio	239	5.38%	28	Washington	20	0.45%
6	Georgia	225	5.07%	31	Colorado	14	0.32%
7	Oklahoma	212	4.77%	32	Montana	11	0.25%
8	Pennsylvania	190	4.28%	33	Wyoming	9	0.20%
9	Alabama	185	4.16%	34	Connecticut	4	0.09%
9	Illinois	185	4.16%	34	Massachusetts	4	0.09%
11	Arizona	155	3.49%	36	New York	3	0.07%
12	Tennessee	149	3.35%	37	Rhode Island	2	0.05%
13	Louisiana	124	2.79%	38	Alaska	0	0.00%
14	South Carolina	113	2.54%	38	Hawaii	0	0.00%
15	Mississippi	112	2.52%	38	Iowa	0	0.00%
16	Missouri	98	2.21%	38	Kansas	0	0.00%
17	Nevada	82	1.85%	38	Maine	0	0.00%
18	Virginia	73	1.64%	38	Michigan	0	0.00%
19	Indiana	72	1.62%	38	Minnesota	0	0.00%
20	Arkansas	59	1.33%	38	New Hampshire	0	0.00%
21	Kentucky	50	1.13%	38	North Dakota	0	0.00%
22	Maryland	34	0.77%	38	South Dakota	0	0.00%
22	New Jersey	34	0.77%	38	Vermont	0	0.00%
24	Idaho	28	0.63%	38	West Virginia	0	0.00%
25	Oregon	26	0.59%	38	Wisconsin	0	0.00%
					District of Columbia	0	0.00%

Source: U.S. Department of Justice, Bureau of Justice Statistics
    "Capital Punishment 1991" (Bulletin, October 1992, NCJ-136946)
*Does not include two federal prisoners sentenced to death.

Death Sentences Overturned or Commuted: 1973–91

National Total = 1,686 Sentences*

RANK	STATE	SENTENCES	%	RANK	STATE	SENTENCES	%
1	Florida	248	14.71%	26	Colorado	10	0.59%
2	North Carolina	217	12.87%	26	Virginia	10	0.59%
3	Ohio	125	7.41%	28	Washington	9	0.53%
4	California	123	7.30%	29	Utah	7	0.42%
5	Texas	116	6.88%	29	Wyoming	7	0.42%
6	Georgia	103	6.11%	31	Idaho	6	0.36%
7	Oklahoma	84	4.98%	31	Nebraska	6	0.36%
8	Louisiana	63	3.74%	33	Montana	5	0.30%
9	South Carolina	61	3.62%	34	Massachusetts	4	0.24%
10	Alabama	56	3.32%	35	New York	3	0.18%
11	Arizona	55	3.26%	36	Rhode Island	2	0.12%
12	Mississippi	53	3.14%	37	Alaska	0	0.00%
13	Pennsylvania	48	2.85%	37	Connecticut	0	0.00%
14	Tennessee	47	2.79%	37	Hawaii	0	0.00%
15	Illinois	42	2.49%	37	Iowa	0	0.00%
16	Arkansas	22	1.30%	37	Kansas	0	0.00%
17	New Jersey	21	1.25%	37	Maine	0	0.00%
17	New Mexico	21	1.25%	37	Michigan	0	0.00%
19	Indiana	20	1.19%	37	Minnesota	0	0.00%
20	Kentucky	19	1.13%	37	New Hampshire	0	0.00%
21	Maryland	17	1.01%	37	North Dakota	0	0.00%
21	Oregon	17	1.01%	37	South Dakota	0	0.00%
23	Nevada	14	0.83%	37	Vermont	0	0.00%
24	Delaware	13	0.77%	37	West Virginia	0	0.00%
25	Missouri	12	0.71%	37	Wisconsin	0	0.00%

District of Columbia   0   0.00%

Source: U.S. Department of Justice, Bureau of Justice Statistics
"Capital Punishment 1991" (Bulletin, October 1992, NCJ-136946)
Does not include one federal prisoner whose sentence was overturned.

Percent of Death Penalty Sentences Overturned or Commuted: 1973–91

National Percent = 37.96% of Sentences*

RANK	STATE	PERCENT	RANK	STATE	PERCENT
1	Massachusetts	100.00	26	Alabama	30.27
1	New York	100.00	27	Nebraska	30.00
1	Rhode Island	100.00	28	California	28.02
4	New Mexico	95.45	29	Indiana	27.78
5	Wyoming	77.78	30	Pennsylvania	25.26
6	North Carolina	72.58	31	Texas	22.83
7	Colorado	71.43	32	Illinois	22.70
8	Oregon	65.38	33	Idaho	21.43
9	Delaware	65.00	34	Nevada	17.07
10	New Jersey	61.76	35	Virginia	13.70
11	South Carolina	53.98	36	Missouri	12.24
12	Ohio	52.30	37	Alaska	0.00
13	Louisiana	50.81	37	Connecticut	0.00
14	Maryland	50.00	37	Hawaii	0.00
15	Mississippi	47.32	37	Iowa	0.00
16	Georgia	45.78	37	Kansas	0.00
17	Montana	45.45	37	Maine	0.00
18	Washington	45.00	37	Michigan	0.00
19	Florida	41.33	37	Minnesota	0.00
20	Oklahoma	39.62	37	New Hampshire	0.00
21	Kentucky	38.00	37	North Dakota	0.00
22	Arkansas	37.29	37	South Dakota	0.00
23	Arizona	35.48	37	Vermont	0.00
24	Utah	31.82	37	West Virginia	0.00
25	Tennessee	31.54	37	Wisconsin	0.00
				District of Columbia	0.00

Source: Morgan Quitno Corporation using data from U.S. Department of Justice, Bureau of Justice Statistics
"Capital Punishment 1991" (Bulletin, October 1992, NCJ-136946)
*Does not include one federal prisoner whose sentence was overturned.

Sentenced Prisoners Admitted to State Correctional Institutions in 1991

National Total = 480,046 Prisoners Admitted*

RANK	STATE	ADMISSIONS	%	RANK	STATE	ADMISSIONS	%
1	California	96,865	20.18%	26	Washington	4,905	1.02%
2	Texas	37,820	7.88%	27	Arkansas	4,574	0.95%
3	Florida	37,440	7.80%	28	Colorado	4,037	0.84%
4	New York	29,743	6.20%	29	Wisconsin	3,968	0.83%
5	Ohio	22,138	4.61%	30	Mississippi	3,910	0.81%
6	North Carolina	21,696	4.52%	31	Kansas	3,477	0.72%
7	Illinois	18,880	3.93%	32	Nevada	3,163	0.66%
8	Georgia	15,812	3.29%	33	Iowa	2,985	0.62%
9	Michigan	13,453	2.80%	34	Minnesota	2,568	0.53%
10	Virginia	12,513	2.61%	35	Hawaii	1,750	0.36%
11	New Jersey	12,134	2.53%	36	New Mexico	1,632	0.34%
12	Connecticut	11,832	2.46%	37	Utah	1,623	0.34%
13	Pennsylvania	9,611	2.00%	38	Nebraska	1,404	0.29%
14	Missouri	8,756	1.82%	39	Idaho	1,402	0.29%
15	Maryland	8,561	1.78%	40	Alaska	1,341	0.28%
16	Louisiana	8,381	1.75%	41	Delaware	1,206	0.25%
17	Alabama	7,908	1.65%	42	Maine	909	0.19%
18	Arizona	7,790	1.62%	43	Rhode Island	840	0.17%
19	South Carolina	7,009	1.46%	44	New Hampshire	828	0.17%
20	Tennessee	6,350	1.32%	45	South Dakota	764	0.16%
21	Oregon	6,247	1.30%	46	West Virginia	690	0.14%
22	Oklahoma	6,243	1.30%	47	Montana	643	0.13%
23	Indiana	5,927	1.23%	48	Vermont	470	0.10%
24	Massachusetts	5,485	1.14%	49	Wyoming	432	0.09%
25	Kentucky	5,116	1.07%	50	North Dakota	340	0.07%
					District of Columbia	6,475	1.35%

Source: U.S. Department of Justice, Bureau of Justice Statistics
  "Correctional Populations in the United States, 1991" (August 1993, NCJ-142729)
*As of December 31, 1991. Includes sentenced prisoners admitted because of new court commitments, parole violators returned, escapees returned and others.

New State Prisoners Admitted Through New Court Commitments in 1991

National Total = 317,237 New Prisoners*

RANK	STATE	PRISONERS	%	RANK	STATE	PRISONERS	%
1	California	38,253	12.06%	26	Mississippi	3,294	1.04%
2	Florida	33,094	10.43%	27	Wisconsin	3,208	1.01%
3	New York	24,119	7.60%	28	Arkansas	3,181	1.00%
4	Texas	21,417	6.75%	29	Colorado	2,887	0.91%
5	Ohio	18,377	5.79%	30	Massachusetts	2,705	0.85%
6	North Carolina	18,056	5.69%	31	Nevada	2,421	0.76%
7	Illinois	14,650	4.62%	32	Kansas	2,118	0.67%
8	Georgia	12,189	3.84%	33	Minnesota	1,905	0.60%
9	Virginia	9,716	3.06%	34	Iowa	1,818	0.57%
10	Michigan	9,054	2.85%	35	New Mexico	1,152	0.36%
11	New Jersey	8,665	2.73%	36	Idaho	1,101	0.35%
12	Maryland	7,008	2.21%	37	Nebraska	1,064	0.34%
13	Pennsylvania	6,435	2.03%	38	Alaska	1,021	0.32%
14	Connecticut	6,401	2.02%	39	Hawaii	846	0.27%
15	Missouri	6,164	1.94%	40	Delaware	794	0.25%
16	Arizona	6,144	1.94%	41	Utah	720	0.23%
17	Alabama	5,721	1.80%	42	New Hampshire	677	0.21%
18	Oklahoma	5,718	1.80%	43	Maine	672	0.21%
19	Indiana	5,503	1.73%	44	Rhode Island	589	0.19%
20	South Carolina	5,342	1.68%	45	West Virginia	584	0.18%
21	Louisiana	4,200	1.32%	46	South Dakota	583	0.18%
22	Washington	4,070	1.28%	47	Montana	489	0.15%
23	Tennessee	4,026	1.27%	48	Wyoming	394	0.12%
24	Kentucky	3,720	1.17%	49	Vermont	310	0.10%
25	Oregon	3,308	1.04%	50	North Dakota	293	0.09%
					District of Columbia	1,061	0.33%

Source: U.S. Department of Justice, Bureau of Justice Statistics
"Correctional Populations in the United States, 1991" (August 1993, NCJ-142729)
*As of December 31, 1991.

Parole Violators Returned to State Prison in 1991

National Total = 142,100 Prisoners*

RANK	STATE	PRISONERS	%	RANK	STATE	PRISONERS	%
1	California	57,737	40.63%	26	Hawaii	901	0.63%
2	Texas	16,378	11.53%	27	Utah	875	0.62%
3	Connecticut	4,711	3.32%	28	Iowa	796	0.56%
4	Illinois	3,995	2.81%	29	Wisconsin	748	0.53%
5	Georgia	3,531	2.48%	30	Colorado	699	0.49%
6	Ohio	3,476	2.45%	30	Nevada	699	0.49%
7	Michigan	3,381	2.38%	32	Minnesota	646	0.45%
8	North Carolina	3,320	2.34%	33	Washington	606	0.43%
9	New York	3,284	2.31%	34	Mississippi	474	0.33%
10	Louisiana	3,174	2.23%	35	New Mexico	444	0.31%
11	Florida	2,981	2.10%	36	Indiana	409	0.29%
12	Oregon	2,694	1.90%	37	Nebraska	328	0.23%
13	New Jersey	2,410	1.70%	38	Alaska	316	0.22%
14	Missouri	2,278	1.60%	39	Idaho	280	0.20%
15	Tennessee	2,209	1.55%	40	Oklahoma	229	0.16%
16	Alabama	1,734	1.22%	41	Maine	215	0.15%
17	Pennsylvania	1,690	1.19%	42	Rhode Island	187	0.13%
18	Virginia	1,649	1.16%	43	South Dakota	166	0.12%
19	Massachusetts	1,536	1.08%	44	New Hampshire	136	0.10%
20	South Carolina	1,518	1.07%	45	Montana	120	0.08%
21	Maryland	1,422	1.00%	46	West Virginia	101	0.07%
22	Kansas	1,305	0.92%	47	Vermont	77	0.05%
23	Kentucky	1,289	0.91%	48	North Dakota	43	0.03%
24	Arizona	1,283	0.90%	49	Delaware	34	0.02%
25	Arkansas	1,218	0.86%	50	Wyoming	31	0.02%
					District of Columbia	2,337	1.64%

Source: U.S. Department of Justice, Bureau of Justice Statistics

"Correctional Populations in the United States, 1991" (August 1993, NCJ-142729)

*As of December 31, 1991. Includes other conditional release violators.

Escapees Returned to State Prison in 1991

National Total = 9,586 Prisoners*

RANK	STATE	PRISONERS	%	RANK	STATE	PRISONERS	%
1	New York	1,276	13.31%	26	Pennsylvania	54	0.56%
2	Michigan	748	7.80%	27	Kansas	48	0.50%
3	Connecticut	713	7.44%	28	Rhode Island	45	0.47%
4	California	494	5.15%	29	Nevada	43	0.45%
5	Colorado	361	3.77%	30	Montana	33	0.34%
6	Florida	352	3.67%	31	Texas	25	0.26%
7	Arizona	321	3.35%	31	Utah	25	0.26%
8	New Jersey	307	3.20%	33	New Mexico	23	0.24%
9	Oklahoma	294	3.07%	34	Virginia	19	0.20%
10	North Carolina	280	2.92%	35	Minnesota	17	0.18%
11	Iowa	208	2.17%	36	Arkansas	15	0.16%
12	Illinois	180	1.88%	36	New Hampshire	15	0.16%
13	Alabama	174	1.82%	38	Nebraska	12	0.13%
14	Oregon	156	1.63%	39	Idaho	9	0.09%
15	Washington	147	1.53%	39	South Dakota	9	0.09%
16	Massachusetts	131	1.37%	41	Ohio	8	0.08%
17	Maryland	128	1.34%	42	Indiana	7	0.07%
18	South Carolina	126	1.31%	43	Maine	6	0.06%
19	Louisiana	100	1.04%	44	West Virginia	5	0.05%
20	Georgia	92	0.96%	45	North Dakota	4	0.04%
21	Kentucky	90	0.94%	46	Hawaii	3	0.03%
22	Tennessee	88	0.92%	46	Wyoming	3	0.03%
23	Delaware	84	0.88%	48	Alaska	0	0.00%
24	Mississippi	56	0.58%	–	Missouri**	N/A	N/A
25	Vermont	55	0.57%	–	Wisconsin**	N/A	N/A

	District of Columbia	2,197	22.92%

Source: U.S. Department of Justice, Bureau of Justice Statistics
"Correctional Populations in the United States, 1991" (August 1993, NCJ-142729)
*As of December 31, 1991. Includes AWOLs returned.
**Not available.

Prisoners Released from State Correctional Institutions in 1991

National Total = 436,991 Prisoners*

RANK	STATE	PRISONERS	%	RANK	STATE	PRISONERS	%
1	California	92,472	21.16%	26	Arkansas	4,126	0.94%
2	Texas	36,185	8.28%	27	Washington	3,744	0.86%
3	Florida	35,289	8.08%	28	Wisconsin	3,587	0.82%
4	New York	26,776	6.13%	29	Kansas	3,349	0.77%
5	North Carolina	21,188	4.85%	30	Colorado	3,316	0.76%
6	Ohio	18,216	4.17%	31	Mississippi	3,312	0.76%
7	Illinois	17,281	3.95%	32	Nevada	2,982	0.68%
8	Georgia	14,573	3.33%	33	Iowa	2,807	0.64%
9	Michigan	11,297	2.59%	34	Minnesota	2,272	0.52%
10	Connecticut	11,018	2.52%	35	Hawaii	1,692	0.39%
11	Virginia	10,271	2.35%	36	New Mexico	1,683	0.39%
12	New Jersey	9,779	2.24%	37	Utah	1,492	0.34%
13	Pennsylvania	8,506	1.95%	38	Alaska	1,352	0.31%
14	Missouri	7,802	1.79%	39	Nebraska	1,315	0.30%
15	Maryland	7,471	1.71%	40	Idaho	1,220	0.28%
16	Louisiana	6,977	1.60%	41	Delaware	1,017	0.23%
17	Alabama	6,873	1.57%	42	Maine	850	0.19%
18	Arizona	6,728	1.54%	43	West Virginia	753	0.17%
19	South Carolina	6,009	1.38%	44	South Dakota	731	0.17%
20	Oregon	6,007	1.37%	45	Rhode Island	677	0.15%
21	Indiana	5,677	1.30%	46	New Hampshire	637	0.15%
22	Tennessee	5,264	1.20%	47	Montana	590	0.14%
23	Oklahoma	5,188	1.19%	48	Wyoming	443	0.10%
24	Massachusetts	4,938	1.13%	49	Vermont	418	0.10%
25	Kentucky	4,340	0.99%	50	North Dakota	334	0.08%

District of Columbia   6,167   1.41%

Source: U.S. Department of Justice, Bureau of Justice Statistics

"Correctional Populations in the United States, 1991" (August 1993, NCJ-142729)

*As of December 31, 1991. Includes conditional releases, unconditional releases, escapees, out on appeal, deaths and other releases.

State Prisoners Released with Conditions in 1991

National Total = 353,774 Prisoners*

RANK	STATE	PRISONERS	%	RANK	STATE	PRISONERS	%
1	California	85,682	24.22%	26	Arkansas	3,165	0.89%
2	Texas	35,319	9.98%	27	Kentucky	2,624	0.74%
3	New York	22,643	6.40%	28	Iowa	2,520	0.71%
4	Florida	21,347	6.03%	29	Mississippi	2,261	0.64%
5	North Carolina	20,503	5.80%	30	Minnesota	2,092	0.59%
6	Illinois	15,877	4.49%	31	Colorado	2,083	0.59%
7	Georgia	12,849	3.63%	32	Washington	1,998	0.56%
8	Virginia	9,294	2.63%	33	Massachusetts	1,576	0.45%
9	Michigan	9,248	2.61%	34	Nevada	1,569	0.44%
10	Ohio	8,345	2.36%	35	Utah	1,324	0.37%
11	Connecticut	8,136	2.30%	36	New Mexico	1,171	0.33%
12	New Jersey	7,961	2.25%	37	Hawaii	1,133	0.32%
13	Maryland	6,558	1.85%	38	Idaho	1,018	0.29%
14	Missouri	6,528	1.85%	39	Nebraska	876	0.25%
15	Pennsylvania	6,394	1.81%	40	Alaska	757	0.21%
16	Arizona	5,678	1.60%	41	West Virginia	633	0.18%
17	Louisiana	5,651	1.60%	42	Rhode Island	605	0.17%
18	Oregon	5,629	1.59%	43	Delaware	540	0.15%
19	Indiana	5,246	1.48%	44	Maine	484	0.14%
20	Alabama	4,477	1.27%	45	South Dakota	483	0.14%
21	Tennessee	4,342	1.23%	46	Montana	467	0.13%
22	South Carolina	3,477	0.98%	47	New Hampshire	427	0.12%
23	Wisconsin	3,432	0.97%	48	Wyoming	268	0.08%
24	Oklahoma	3,282	0.93%	49	Vermont	251	0.07%
25	Kansas	3,176	0.90%	50	North Dakota	239	0.07%
					District of Columbia	2,136	0.60%

Source: U.S. Department of Justice, Bureau of Justice Statistics
"Correctional Populations in the United States, 1991" (August 1993, NCJ-142729)
*As of December 31, 1991. Released on parole, probation, supervised mandatory releases or other conditions.

State Prisoners Released Conditionally as a Percent of All Releases in 1991

National Percent = 80.96% of Prisoners Released*

RANK	STATE	PERCENT	RANK	STATE	PERCENT
1	Texas	97.61	26	Arkansas	76.71
2	North Carolina	96.77	27	Pennsylvania	75.17
3	Wisconsin	95.68	28	Connecticut	73.84
4	Kansas	94.83	29	North Dakota	71.56
5	Oregon	93.71	30	New Mexico	69.58
6	California	92.66	31	Mississippi	68.27
7	Indiana	92.41	32	New Hampshire	67.03
8	Minnesota	92.08	33	Hawaii	66.96
9	Illinois	91.88	34	Nebraska	66.62
10	Virginia	90.49	35	South Dakota	66.07
11	Iowa	89.78	36	Alabama	65.14
12	Rhode Island	89.36	37	Oklahoma	63.26
13	Utah	88.74	38	Colorado	62.82
14	Georgia	88.17	39	Wyoming	60.50
15	Maryland	87.78	40	Florida	60.49
16	New York	84.56	41	Kentucky	60.46
17	Arizona	84.39	42	Vermont	60.05
18	West Virginia	84.06	43	South Carolina	57.86
19	Missouri	83.67	44	Maine	56.94
20	Idaho	83.44	45	Alaska	55.99
21	Tennessee	82.48	46	Washington	53.37
22	Michigan	81.86	47	Delaware	53.10
23	New Jersey	81.41	48	Nevada	52.62
24	Louisiana	80.99	49	Ohio	45.81
25	Montana	79.15	50	Massachusetts	31.92

District of Columbia   34.64

Source: Morgan Quitno Corporation using data from U.S. Department of Justice, Bureau of Justice Statistics
   "Correctional Populations in the United States, 1991" (August 1993, NCJ-142729)
*As of December 31, 1991. Released on parole, probation, supervised mandatory release or other conditions.

State Prisoners Released on Parole in 1991

National Total = 167,487 Prisoners*

RANK	STATE	PRISONERS	%	RANK	STATE	PRISONERS	%
1	Texas	31,714	18.94%	26	Utah	1,324	0.79%
2	North Carolina	20,475	12.22%	27	Arizona	1,269	0.76%
3	New York	19,393	11.58%	28	Louisiana	1,254	0.75%
4	Michigan	9,248	5.52%	29	New Mexico	1,020	0.61%
5	New Jersey	7,716	4.61%	30	Nebraska	876	0.52%
6	Georgia	7,178	4.29%	31	Hawaii	468	0.28%
7	Pennsylvania	6,394	3.82%	32	South Dakota	453	0.27%
8	Virginia	6,301	3.76%	33	Idaho	403	0.24%
9	Missouri	5,704	3.41%	34	West Virginia	399	0.24%
10	Oregon	5,629	3.36%	35	Montana	359	0.21%
11	Ohio	5,249	3.13%	36	New Hampshire	343	0.20%
12	Maryland	3,740	2.23%	37	Florida	321	0.19%
13	Tennessee	2,962	1.77%	38	Washington	288	0.17%
14	Alabama	2,618	1.56%	39	Rhode Island	232	0.14%
15	Arkansas	2,448	1.46%	40	Vermont	220	0.13%
16	Wisconsin	2,286	1.36%	41	Wyoming	184	0.11%
17	Kansas	2,264	1.35%	42	Connecticut	175	0.10%
18	South Carolina	2,223	1.33%	43	Delaware	168	0.10%
19	Kentucky	2,064	1.23%	44	Alaska	151	0.09%
20	Colorado	1,965	1.17%	45	North Dakota	120	0.07%
21	Oklahoma	1,725	1.03%	46	Illinois	70	0.04%
22	Iowa	1,655	0.99%	47	Minnesota	37	0.02%
23	Massachusetts	1,576	0.94%	48	Indiana	3	0.00%
24	Nevada	1,569	0.94%	49	Maine	2	0.00%
25	Mississippi	1,357	0.81%	–	California**	N/A	N/A
					District of Columbia	1,895	1.13%

Source: U.S. Department of Justice, Bureau of Justice Statistics
     "Correctional Populations in the United States, 1991" (August 1993, NCJ-142729)
*As of December 31, 1991.
**Not available.

State Prisoners Released on Probation in 1991

National Total = 20,200 Prisoners*

RANK	STATE	PRISONERS	%	RANK	STATE	PRISONERS	%
1	Ohio	3,096	15.33%	26	Georgia	36	0.18%
2	Florida	2,043	10.11%	27	Arizona	32	0.16%
3	Alabama	1,859	9.20%	28	Vermont	31	0.15%
4	Texas	1,614	7.99%	29	South Dakota	30	0.15%
5	Oklahoma	1,382	6.84%	30	North Carolina	28	0.14%
6	Indiana	1,337	6.62%	31	Arkansas	0	0.00%
7	South Carolina	1,205	5.97%	31	California	0	0.00%
8	Tennessee	1,194	5.91%	31	Illinois	0	0.00%
9	Mississippi	901	4.46%	31	Maryland	0	0.00%
10	Missouri	824	4.08%	31	Michigan	0	0.00%
11	Idaho	615	3.04%	31	Minnesota	0	0.00%
12	Hawaii	604	2.99%	31	Nebraska	0	0.00%
13	Kansas	591	2.93%	31	Nevada	0	0.00%
14	Kentucky	560	2.77%	31	New Jersey	0	0.00%
15	Maine	462	2.29%	31	New Mexico	0	0.00%
16	Alaska	386	1.91%	31	New York	0	0.00%
17	Rhode Island	372	1.84%	31	Oregon	0	0.00%
18	West Virginia	202	1.00%	31	Pennsylvania	0	0.00%
19	Iowa	198	0.98%	31	Utah	0	0.00%
20	Colorado	118	0.58%	31	Virginia	0	0.00%
21	Montana	108	0.53%	31	Washington	0	0.00%
21	North Dakota	108	0.53%	31	Wisconsin	0	0.00%
23	Louisiana	100	0.50%	–	Connecticut**	N/A	N/A
24	New Hampshire	84	0.42%	–	Delaware**	N/A	N/A
25	Wyoming	80	0.40%	–	Massachusetts**	N/A	N/A
					District of Columbia**	N/A	N/A

Source: U.S. Department of Justice, Bureau of Justice Statistics
    "Correctional Populations in the United States, 1991" (August 1993, NCJ-142729)

*As of December 31, 1991.

**Not available.

State Prisoners Released on Supervised Mandatory Release in 1991

National Total = 126,271 Prisoners*

RANK	STATE	PRISONERS	%	RANK	STATE	PRISONERS	%
1	California	85,682	67.86%	15	Maine	0	0.00%
2	Illinois	15,807	12.52%	15	Massachusetts	0	0.00%
3	Louisiana	4,297	3.40%	15	Michigan	0	0.00%
4	Indiana	3,906	3.09%	15	Mississippi	0	0.00%
5	New York	3,250	2.57%	15	Missouri	0	0.00%
6	Virginia	2,993	2.37%	15	Montana	0	0.00%
7	Maryland	2,818	2.23%	15	Nebraska	0	0.00%
8	Texas	1,991	1.58%	15	Nevada	0	0.00%
9	Washington	1,710	1.35%	15	New Hampshire	0	0.00%
10	Minnesota	1,606	1.27%	15	New Jersey	0	0.00%
11	Wisconsin	1,139	0.90%	15	New Mexico	0	0.00%
12	Delaware	372	0.29%	15	North Dakota	0	0.00%
13	Arizona	239	0.19%	15	Ohio	0	0.00%
14	Alaska	220	0.17%	15	Oklahoma	0	0.00%
15	Alabama	0	0.00%	15	Oregon	0	0.00%
15	Arkansas	0	0.00%	15	Pennsylvania	0	0.00%
15	Colorado	0	0.00%	15	Rhode Island	0	0.00%
15	Connecticut	0	0.00%	15	South Carolina	0	0.00%
15	Florida	0	0.00%	15	South Dakota	0	0.00%
15	Georgia	0	0.00%	15	Utah	0	0.00%
15	Hawaii	0	0.00%	15	Vermont	0	0.00%
15	Idaho	0	0.00%	15	West Virginia	0	0.00%
15	Iowa	0	0.00%	15	Wyoming	0	0.00%
15	Kansas	0	0.00%	–	North Carolina**	N/A	N/A
15	Kentucky	0	0.00%	–	Tennessee**	N/A	N/A
					District of Columbia	241	0.19%

Source: U.S. Department of Justice, Bureau of Justice Statistics

"Correctional Populations in the United States, 1991" (August 1993, NCJ-142729)

*As of December 31, 1991.

**Not available.

State Prisoners Released Unconditionally in 1991

National Total = 55,579 Prisoners*

RANK	STATE	PRISONERS	%	RANK	STATE	PRISONERS	%
1	Florida	13,468	24.23%	26	Alaska	541	0.97%
2	Ohio	9,517	17.12%	27	New Mexico	486	0.87%
3	South Carolina	2,316	4.17%	28	Arizona	420	0.76%
4	Alabama	1,978	3.56%	29	Nebraska	419	0.75%
5	Washington	1,564	2.81%	30	Indiana	395	0.71%
6	Oklahoma	1,519	2.73%	31	North Carolina	378	0.68%
7	Kentucky	1,505	2.71%	32	Maine	320	0.58%
8	New Jersey	1,376	2.48%	33	Hawaii	316	0.57%
9	California	1,365	2.46%	34	Delaware	244	0.44%
10	Connecticut	1,355	2.44%	35	South Dakota	227	0.41%
11	Massachusetts	1,354	2.44%	36	Texas	206	0.37%
12	Nevada	1,350	2.43%	37	Iowa	187	0.34%
13	Illinois	1,090	1.96%	38	Idaho	168	0.30%
14	Louisiana	1,024	1.84%	39	Oregon	161	0.29%
15	Mississippi	968	1.74%	40	Minnesota	149	0.27%
16	Georgia	940	1.69%	41	Wyoming	135	0.24%
17	Virginia	851	1.53%	42	Utah	122	0.22%
18	Colorado	792	1.42%	42	Wisconsin	122	0.22%
19	New York	777	1.40%	44	Vermont	109	0.20%
20	Maryland	762	1.37%	45	New Hampshire	105	0.19%
21	Arkansas	750	1.35%	46	Kansas	104	0.19%
22	Tennessee	741	1.33%	47	North Dakota	91	0.16%
23	Pennsylvania	666	1.20%	48	Montana	85	0.15%
24	Michigan	632	1.14%	49	West Virginia	83	0.15%
25	Missouri	587	1.06%	50	Rhode Island	8	0.01%
					District of Columbia	751	1.35%

Source: U.S. Department of Justice, Bureau of Justice Statistics

"Correctional Populations in the United States, 1991" (August 1993, NCJ-142729)

*As of December 31, 1991.

State Prisoners Released Unconditionally as a Percent of All Releases in 1991

National Percent = 12.72% of Released Prisoners*

RANK	STATE	PERCENT	RANK	STATE	PERCENT
1	Ohio	52.25	26	Tennessee	14.08
2	Nevada	45.27	27	New Jersey	14.07
3	Washington	41.77	28	Idaho	13.77
4	Alaska	40.01	29	Connecticut	12.30
5	South Carolina	38.54	30	West Virginia	11.02
6	Florida	38.16	31	Maryland	10.20
7	Maine	37.65	32	Virginia	8.29
8	Kentucky	34.68	33	Utah	8.18
9	Nebraska	31.86	34	Pennsylvania	7.83
10	South Dakota	31.05	35	Missouri	7.52
11	Wyoming	30.47	36	Indiana	6.96
12	Oklahoma	29.28	37	Iowa	6.66
13	Mississippi	29.23	38	Minnesota	6.56
14	New Mexico	28.88	39	Georgia	6.45
15	Alabama	28.78	40	Illinois	6.31
16	Massachusetts	27.42	41	Arizona	6.24
17	North Dakota	27.25	42	Michigan	5.59
18	Vermont	26.08	43	Wisconsin	3.40
19	Delaware	23.99	44	Kansas	3.11
20	Colorado	23.88	45	New York	2.90
21	Hawaii	18.68	46	Oregon	2.68
22	Arkansas	18.18	47	North Carolina	1.78
23	New Hampshire	16.48	48	California	1.48
24	Louisiana	14.68	49	Rhode Island	1.18
25	Montana	14.41	50	Texas	0.57

District of Columbia   12.18

Source: Morgan Quitno Corporation using data from U.S. Department of Justice, Bureau of Justice Statistics
"Correctional Populations in the United States, 1991" (August 1993, NCJ-142729)
*As of December 31, 1991.

State Prisoners Released on Appeal or Bond in 1991

National Total = 2,208 Prisoners*

RANK	STATE	PRISONERS	%	RANK	STATE	PRISONERS	%
1	Connecticut	1,027	46.51%	25	Montana	4	0.18%
2	Hawaii	186	8.42%	25	Oregon	4	0.18%
3	New York	171	7.74%	28	Nevada	3	0.14%
4	Arkansas	148	6.70%	29	South Dakota	2	0.09%
5	Michigan	101	4.57%	29	Wyoming	2	0.09%
6	New Jersey	76	3.44%	31	Arizona	0	0.00%
7	Alabama	71	3.22%	31	Delaware	0	0.00%
8	Tennessee	50	2.26%	31	Louisiana	0	0.00%
9	Pennsylvania	48	2.17%	31	Minnesota	0	0.00%
10	Missouri	44	1.99%	31	North Carolina	0	0.00%
11	Ohio	39	1.77%	31	North Dakota	0	0.00%
12	South Carolina	31	1.40%	31	Oklahoma	0	0.00%
13	Alaska	30	1.36%	31	West Virginia	0	0.00%
13	Illinois	30	1.36%	–	California**	N/A	N/A
15	Washington	22	1.00%	–	Florida**	N/A	N/A
16	Iowa	21	0.95%	–	Georgia**	N/A	N/A
16	Utah	21	0.95%	–	Indiana**	N/A	N/A
18	Colorado	17	0.77%	–	Kentucky**	N/A	N/A
19	Kansas	12	0.54%	–	Maryland**	N/A	N/A
19	Rhode Island	12	0.54%	–	Massachusetts**	N/A	N/A
21	Virginia	10	0.45%	–	Mississippi**	N/A	N/A
22	New Mexico	9	0.41%	–	Nebraska**	N/A	N/A
23	New Hampshire	7	0.32%	–	Texas**	N/A	N/A
24	Maine	6	0.27%	–	Vermont**	N/A	N/A
25	Idaho	4	0.18%	–	Wisconsin**	N/A	N/A
					District of Columbia**	N/A	N/A

Source: U.S. Department of Justice, Bureau of Justice Statistics
"Correctional Populations in the United States, 1991" (August 1993, NCJ-142729)

*As of December 31, 1991.

**Not available.

State Prisoners Escaped in 1991

National Total = 9,921 Prisoners*

RANK	STATE	PRISONERS	%	RANK	STATE	PRISONERS	%
1	New York	1,952	19.68%	26	Kansas	47	0.47%
2	Michigan	1,161	11.70%	27	Texas	46	0.46%
3	California	932	9.39%	28	Rhode Island	35	0.35%
4	Arizona	406	4.09%	29	West Virginia	33	0.33%
5	Connecticut	371	3.74%	30	Mississippi	29	0.29%
6	Oklahoma	310	3.12%	31	Montana	26	0.26%
7	Colorado	296	2.98%	32	Minnesota	21	0.21%
8	New Jersey	270	2.72%	32	Utah	21	0.21%
9	Florida	261	2.63%	34	Nebraska	15	0.15%
9	North Carolina	261	2.63%	34	New Hampshire	15	0.15%
11	Alabama	150	1.51%	36	Iowa	13	0.13%
12	Washington	148	1.49%	36	Wyoming	13	0.13%
13	Illinois	142	1.43%	38	New Mexico	12	0.12%
14	South Carolina	136	1.37%	39	Indiana	9	0.09%
15	Massachusetts	118	1.19%	39	Ohio	9	0.09%
16	Georgia	111	1.12%	41	Arkansas	7	0.07%
17	Delaware	108	1.09%	41	Maine	7	0.07%
18	Maryland	102	1.03%	41	South Dakota	7	0.07%
19	Oregon	95	0.96%	44	Idaho	6	0.06%
20	Kentucky	94	0.95%	45	Alaska	4	0.04%
20	Tennessee	94	0.95%	45	North Dakota	4	0.04%
22	Louisiana	76	0.77%	47	Hawaii	3	0.03%
23	Vermont	54	0.54%	47	Virginia	3	0.03%
24	Nevada	51	0.51%	–	Missouri**	N/A	N/A
25	Pennsylvania	49	0.49%	–	Wisconsin**	N/A	N/A
					District of Columbia	1,788	18.02%

Source: U.S. Department of Justice, Bureau of Justice Statistics
"Correctional Populations in the United States, 1991" (August 1993, NCJ-142729)
*As of December 31, 1991. Includes AWOLs.
**Not available.

State Prisoner Deaths in 1991

National Total = 1,856 Prisoners*

RANK	STATE	PRISONERS	%	RANK	STATE	PRISONERS	%
1	New York	318	17.13%	26	Mississippi	16	0.86%
2	California	135	7.27%	27	Oregon	15	0.81%
3	Florida	126	6.79%	28	Colorado	10	0.54%
4	Texas	111	5.98%	28	Kansas	10	0.54%
5	Virginia	106	5.71%	28	Minnesota	10	0.54%
6	New Jersey	96	5.17%	31	Nevada	9	0.48%
7	Pennsylvania	83	4.47%	31	Washington	9	0.48%
8	Connecticut	75	4.04%	33	Montana	8	0.43%
9	Georgia	62	3.34%	34	Idaho	7	0.38%
10	Michigan	56	3.02%	34	South Dakota	7	0.38%
11	Illinois	55	2.96%	36	Delaware	6	0.32%
12	Alabama	52	2.80%	36	New Hampshire	6	0.32%
13	South Carolina	49	2.64%	38	New Mexico	5	0.27%
14	North Carolina	46	2.48%	38	Wisconsin	5	0.27%
15	Maryland	42	2.26%	40	Maine	4	0.22%
16	Ohio	41	2.21%	40	Utah	4	0.22%
17	Tennessee	37	1.99%	40	West Virginia	4	0.22%
18	Louisiana	35	1.89%	43	Iowa	3	0.16%
19	Arizona	34	1.83%	43	Rhode Island	3	0.16%
20	Oklahoma	32	1.72%	45	Hawaii	2	0.11%
21	Indiana	27	1.45%	45	Nebraska	2	0.11%
21	Massachusetts	27	1.45%	47	Alaska	1	0.05%
23	Arkansas	22	1.19%	47	Wyoming	1	0.05%
23	Kentucky	22	1.19%	49	North Dakota	0	0.00%
25	Missouri	20	1.08%	49	Vermont	0	0.00%
					District of Columbia**	N/A	N/A

Source: U.S. Department of Justice, Bureau of Justice Statistics
    "Correctional Populations in the United States, 1991" (August 1993, NCJ-142729)
*As of December 31, 1991.
**Not available.

State Prisoner Deaths by Illness or Other Natural Causes in 1991

National Total = 813 Deaths*

RANK	STATE	DEATHS	%	RANK	STATE	DEATHS	%
1	New York	83	10.21%	26	Minnesota	6	0.74%
2	California	78	9.59%	26	Nevada	6	0.74%
3	Florida	63	7.75%	28	Delaware	4	0.49%
4	Pennsylvania	55	6.77%	28	Idaho	4	0.49%
5	Michigan	50	6.15%	28	New Hampshire	4	0.49%
6	Georgia	41	5.04%	28	West Virginia	4	0.49%
7	Ohio	36	4.43%	28	Wisconsin	4	0.49%
8	Illinois	35	4.31%	33	Colorado	3	0.37%
9	Virginia	32	3.94%	33	Maine	3	0.37%
10	New Jersey	29	3.57%	35	Kansas	2	0.25%
10	Tennessee	29	3.57%	35	Montana	2	0.25%
12	South Carolina	28	3.44%	37	Hawaii	1	0.12%
13	North Carolina	25	3.08%	37	Iowa	1	0.12%
14	Maryland	23	2.83%	37	Nebraska	1	0.12%
14	Oklahoma	23	2.83%	37	Rhode Island	1	0.12%
16	Indiana	20	2.46%	37	Utah	1	0.12%
17	Arizona	18	2.21%	37	Wyoming	1	0.12%
18	Arkansas	16	1.97%	43	Alabama	0	0.00%
18	Kentucky	16	1.97%	43	Alaska	0	0.00%
20	Massachusetts	14	1.72%	43	North Dakota	0	0.00%
20	Missouri	14	1.72%	43	Vermont	0	0.00%
22	Oregon	12	1.48%	–	Connecticut**	N/A	N/A
23	Mississippi	11	1.35%	–	Louisiana**	N/A	N/A
24	South Dakota	7	0.86%	–	New Mexico**	N/A	N/A
24	Washington	7	0.86%	–	Texas**	N/A	N/A

District of Columbia**   N/A   N/A

Source: U.S. Department of Justice, Bureau of Justice Statistics

"Correctional Populations in the United States, 1991" (August 1993, NCJ-142729)

*As of December 31, 1991. Excludes AIDS.

**Not available.

State Prisoner Deaths by Illness or Other Natural Causes as a Percent of All Prison Deaths in 1991

National Percent = 43.8% of Deaths*

RANK	STATE	PERCENT	RANK	STATE	PERCENT
1	South Dakota	100.00	25	South Carolina	57.14
1	West Virginia	100.00	27	Maryland	54.76
1	Wyoming	100.00	28	North Carolina	54.35
4	Michigan	89.29	29	Arizona	52.94
5	Ohio	87.80	30	Massachusetts	51.85
6	Oregon	80.00	31	Florida	50.00
6	Wisconsin	80.00	31	Hawaii	50.00
8	Tennessee	78.38	31	Nebraska	50.00
9	Washington	77.78	34	Iowa	33.33
10	Maine	75.00	34	Rhode Island	33.33
11	Indiana	74.07	36	New Jersey	30.21
12	Arkansas	72.73	37	Virginia	30.19
12	Kentucky	72.73	38	Colorado	30.00
14	Oklahoma	71.88	39	New York	26.10
15	Missouri	70.00	40	Montana	25.00
16	Mississippi	68.75	40	Utah	25.00
17	Delaware	66.67	42	Kansas	20.00
17	Nevada	66.67	43	Alabama	0.00
17	New Hampshire	66.67	43	Alaska	0.00
20	Pennsylvania	66.27	43	North Dakota	0.00
21	Georgia	66.13	43	Vermont	0.00
22	Illinois	63.64	–	Connecticut**	N/A
23	Minnesota	60.00	–	Louisiana**	N/A
24	California	57.78	–	New Mexico**	N/A
25	Idaho	57.14	–	Texas**	N/A
				District of Columbia**	N/A

Source: Morgan Quitno Corporation using data from U.S. Department of Justice, Bureau of Justice Statistics
   "Correctional Populations in the United States, 1991" (August 1993, NCJ-142729)

*As of December 31, 1991. Excludes AIDS.

**Not available.

Deaths of State Prisoners by AIDS in 1991

National Total = 528 Deaths

RANK	STATE	DEATHS	%	RANK	STATE	DEATHS	%
1	New York	210	39.77%	22	Mississippi	1	0.19%
2	New Jersey	66	12.50%	22	Rhode Island	1	0.19%
3	Florida	59	11.17%	22	Tennessee	1	0.19%
4	California	38	7.20%	22	Wisconsin	1	0.19%
5	Pennsylvania	19	3.60%	30	Alabama	0	0.00%
6	Texas	18	3.41%	30	Alaska	0	0.00%
7	Maryland	14	2.65%	30	Iowa	0	0.00%
7	North Carolina	14	2.65%	30	Louisiana	0	0.00%
9	Georgia	13	2.46%	30	Maine	0	0.00%
10	South Carolina	12	2.27%	30	Minnesota	0	0.00%
11	Connecticut	11	2.08%	30	Missouri	0	0.00%
12	Illinois	10	1.89%	30	Montana	0	0.00%
13	Massachusetts	8	1.52%	30	Nebraska	0	0.00%
13	Virginia	8	1.52%	30	Nevada	0	0.00%
15	Indiana	5	0.95%	30	New Hampshire	0	0.00%
16	Arizona	4	0.76%	30	New Mexico	0	0.00%
17	Oklahoma	3	0.57%	30	North Dakota	0	0.00%
18	Delaware	2	0.38%	30	Oregon	0	0.00%
18	Kansas	2	0.38%	30	South Dakota	0	0.00%
18	Kentucky	2	0.38%	30	Utah	0	0.00%
18	Ohio	2	0.38%	30	Vermont	0	0.00%
22	Arkansas	1	0.19%	30	Washington	0	0.00%
22	Colorado	1	0.19%	30	West Virginia	0	0.00%
22	Hawaii	1	0.19%	30	Wyoming	0	0.00%
22	Idaho	1	0.19%	–	Michigan*	N/A	N/A
					District of Columbia*	N/A	N/A

Source: U.S. Department of Justice, Bureau of Justice Statistics

"HIV in U.S. Prisons and Jails" (Special Report, September 1993, NCJ-143292)

*Not available.

Deaths of State Prisoners by AIDS as a Percent of All Prison Deaths in 1991

National Percent = 28.38% of Deaths*

RANK	STATE	PERCENT	RANK	STATE	PERCENT
1	New Jersey	68.75	26	Mississippi	6.25
2	New York	66.04	27	Ohio	4.88
3	Hawaii	50.00	28	Arkansas	4.55
4	Florida	44.36	29	Tennessee	2.70
5	Delaware	33.33	30	Alabama	0.00
5	Maryland	33.33	30	Alaska	0.00
5	Rhode Island	33.33	30	Iowa	0.00
8	North Carolina	30.43	30	Louisiana	0.00
9	Massachusetts	29.63	30	Maine	0.00
10	California	28.15	30	Minnesota	0.00
11	South Carolina	24.49	30	Missouri	0.00
12	Pennsylvania	22.89	30	Montana	0.00
13	Georgia	20.97	30	Nebraska	0.00
14	Kansas	20.00	30	Nevada	0.00
14	Wisconsin	20.00	30	New Hampshire	0.00
16	Indiana	18.52	30	New Mexico	0.00
17	Illinois	18.18	30	North Dakota	0.00
18	Texas	16.22	30	Oregon	0.00
19	Connecticut	14.67	30	South Dakota	0.00
20	Idaho	14.29	30	Utah	0.00
21	Arizona	11.76	30	Vermont	0.00
22	Colorado	10.00	30	Washington	0.00
23	Oklahoma	9.38	30	West Virginia	0.00
24	Kentucky	9.09	30	Wyoming	0.00
25	Virginia	7.55	–	Michigan*	N/A
				District of Columbia*	N/A

Source: Morgan Quitno Corporation using data from U.S. Department of Justice, Bureau of Justice Statistics
   "HIV in U.S. Prisons and Jails" (Special Report, September 1993, NCJ-143292)
*Not available.

State Prisoners Known to be Positive for HIV Infection/AIDS in 1991

National Total = 16,849 Inmates*

RANK	STATE	INMATES	%	RANK	STATE	INMATES	%
1	New York	8,000	47.48%	26	Oklahoma	74	0.44%
2	Florida	1,105	6.56%	27	Arkansas	68	0.40%
3	Georgia	807	4.79%	28	Indiana	62	0.37%
4	New Jersey	756	4.49%	29	Washington	42	0.25%
5	California	714	4.24%	30	Wisconsin	40	0.24%
6	Texas	615	3.65%	31	Utah	35	0.21%
7	Connecticut	574	3.41%	32	Tennessee	28	0.17%
8	Massachusetts	484	2.87%	33	Kentucky	27	0.16%
9	Maryland	478	2.84%	34	Oregon	24	0.14%
10	Michigan	390	2.31%	35	Hawaii	19	0.11%
11	South Carolina	316	1.88%	35	Iowa	19	0.11%
12	Pennsylvania	313	1.86%	37	New Hampshire	18	0.11%
13	Illinois	299	1.77%	38	Minnesota	14	0.08%
14	Alabama	178	1.06%	39	Kansas	13	0.08%
15	North Carolina	170	1.01%	40	Nebraska	11	0.07%
16	Ohio	152	0.90%	41	Idaho	10	0.06%
16	Virginia	152	0.90%	41	New Mexico	10	0.06%
18	Missouri	127	0.75%	43	Alaska	9	0.05%
19	Nevada	117	0.69%	44	Montana	7	0.04%
20	Mississippi	106	0.63%	44	Wyoming	7	0.04%
21	Louisiana	100	0.59%	46	West Virginia	5	0.03%
22	Rhode Island	98	0.58%	47	Vermont	3	0.02%
23	Delaware	85	0.50%	48	Maine	1	0.01%
24	Arizona	84	0.50%	48	North Dakota	1	0.01%
25	Colorado	82	0.49%	–	South Dakota**	N/A	N/A
					District of Columbia**	N/A	N/A

Source: U.S. Department of Justice, Bureau of Justice Statistics

"HIV in U.S. Prisons and Jails" (Special Report, September 1993, NCJ-143292)

*Does not include 630 federal inmates.

**Not available.

State Prisoners Known to be Positive for HIV Infection/AIDS
As a Percent of Total Prison Population in 1991
National Percent = 2.3% of State Prisoners*

RANK	STATE	PERCENT
1	New York	13.8
2	Connecticut	5.4
3	Massachusetts	5.3
4	New Jersey	4.0
5	Rhode Island	3.5
6	Georgia	3.4
7	Delaware	2.6
8	Maryland	2.5
9	Florida	2.4
10	Nevada	2.0
10	South Carolina	2.0
12	Mississippi	1.3
12	Pennsylvania	1.3
12	Utah	1.3
15	New Hampshire	1.2
15	Texas	1.2
17	Alabama	1.1
17	Michigan	1.1
19	Colorado	1.0
19	Illinois	1.0
21	Arkansas	0.9
21	North Carolina	0.9
21	Virginia	0.9
24	Hawaii	0.8
24	Missouri	0.8

RANK	STATE	PERCENT
26	California	0.7
26	Louisiana	0.7
26	Oklahoma	0.7
29	Wyoming	0.6
30	Arizona	0.5
30	Idaho	0.5
30	Indiana	0.5
30	Iowa	0.5
30	Montana	0.5
30	Washington	0.5
30	Wisconsin	0.5
37	Alaska	0.4
37	Minnesota	0.4
37	Nebraska	0.4
37	Ohio	0.4
37	Oregon	0.4
42	Kentucky	0.3
42	New Mexico	0.3
42	Tennessee	0.3
42	Vermont	0.3
42	West Virginia	0.3
47	Kansas	0.2
47	North Dakota	0.2
49	Maine	0.1
–	South Dakota**	N/A

District of Columbia**   N/A

Source: U.S. Department of Justice, Bureau of Justice Statistics

"HIV in U.S. Prisons and Jails" (Special Report, September 1993, NCJ-143292)

*Federal rate is 1.0%, combined state and federal rate is 2.2%.

**Not available.

State Prisoner Deaths by Suicide in 1991

National Total = 90 Suicides*

RANK	STATE	SUICIDES	%		RANK	STATE	SUICIDES	%
1	California	15	16.67%		15	Washington	2	2.22%
2	New York	6	6.67%		27	Alaska	1	1.11%
3	Colorado	4	4.44%		27	Mississippi	1	1.11%
3	Tennessee	4	4.44%		27	Montana	1	1.11%
5	Arizona	3	3.33%		27	Nebraska	1	1.11%
5	Florida	3	3.33%		27	New Jersey	1	1.11%
5	Kansas	3	3.33%		27	Virginia	1	1.11%
5	Maryland	3	3.33%		33	Alabama	0	0.00%
5	Massachusetts	3	3.33%		33	Delaware	0	0.00%
5	Michigan	3	3.33%		33	Hawaii	0	0.00%
5	Missouri	3	3.33%		33	Iowa	0	0.00%
5	Ohio	3	3.33%		33	Maine	0	0.00%
5	Oklahoma	3	3.33%		33	New Hampshire	0	0.00%
5	Pennsylvania	3	3.33%		33	North Dakota	0	0.00%
15	Arkansas	2	2.22%		33	Rhode Island	0	0.00%
15	Georgia	2	2.22%		33	South Dakota	0	0.00%
15	Idaho	2	2.22%		33	Utah	0	0.00%
15	Illinois	2	2.22%		33	Vermont	0	0.00%
15	Indiana	2	2.22%		33	West Virginia	0	0.00%
15	Kentucky	2	2.22%		33	Wisconsin	0	0.00%
15	Minnesota	2	2.22%		33	Wyoming	0	0.00%
15	Nevada	2	2.22%		–	Connecticut**	N/A	N/A
15	North Carolina	2	2.22%		–	Louisiana**	N/A	N/A
15	Oregon	2	2.22%		–	New Mexico**	N/A	N/A
15	South Carolina	2	2.22%		–	Texas**	N/A	N/A
						District of Columbia**	N/A	N/A

Source: U.S. Department of Justice, Bureau of Justice Statistics
   "Correctional Populations in the United States, 1991" (August 1993, NCJ-142729)
*As of December 31, 1991.
**Not available.

Deaths of State Prisoners by Suicide as a Percent of All Prison Deaths in 1991

National Percent = 4.85% of Deaths*

RANK	STATE	PERCENT	RANK	STATE	PERCENT
1	Alaska	100.00	26	Illinois	3.64
2	Nebraska	50.00	27	Pennsylvania	3.61
3	Colorado	40.00	28	Georgia	3.23
4	Kansas	30.00	29	Florida	2.38
5	Idaho	28.57	30	New York	1.89
6	Nevada	22.22	31	New Jersey	1.04
6	Washington	22.22	32	Virginia	0.94
8	Minnesota	20.00	33	Alabama	0.00
9	Missouri	15.00	33	Delaware	0.00
10	Oregon	13.33	33	Hawaii	0.00
11	Montana	12.50	33	Iowa	0.00
12	California	11.11	33	Maine	0.00
12	Massachusetts	11.11	33	New Hampshire	0.00
14	Tennessee	10.81	33	North Dakota	0.00
15	Oklahoma	9.38	33	Rhode Island	0.00
16	Arkansas	9.09	33	South Dakota	0.00
16	Kentucky	9.09	33	Utah	0.00
18	Arizona	8.82	33	Vermont	0.00
19	Indiana	7.41	33	West Virginia	0.00
20	Ohio	7.32	33	Wisconsin	0.00
21	Maryland	7.14	33	Wyoming	0.00
22	Mississippi	6.25	–	Connecticut**	N/A
23	Michigan	5.36	–	Louisiana**	N/A
24	North Carolina	4.35	–	New Mexico**	N/A
25	South Carolina	4.08	–	Texas**	N/A

District of Columbia**   N/A

Source: Morgan Quitno Corporation using data from U.S. Department of Justice, Bureau of Justice Statistics
    "Correctional Populations in the United States, 1991" (August 1993, NCJ-142729)
*As of December 31, 1991.
**Not available.

Adults on State Probation in 1990

National Total = 2,612,012 Adults*

RANK	STATE	ADULTS	%	RANK	STATE	ADULTS	%
1	Texas	308,357	11.81%	26	Alabama	27,686	1.06%
2	California	305,700	11.70%	27	Oklahoma	24,411	0.93%
3	Florida	210,781	8.07%	28	Kansas	22,183	0.85%
4	New York	145,266	5.56%	29	Virginia	21,303	0.82%
5	Georgia	134,840	5.16%	30	Arkansas	15,983	0.61%
6	Michigan	133,439	5.11%	31	Rhode Island	15,366	0.59%
7	Pennsylvania	97,327	3.73%	32	Nebraska	14,654	0.56%
8	Illinois	95,699	3.66%	33	Iowa	13,895	0.53%
9	Washington	84,817	3.25%	34	Delaware	12,223	0.47%
10	Ohio	83,380	3.19%	35	Hawaii	11,667	0.45%
11	Maryland	82,898	3.17%	36	Mississippi	8,221	0.31%
12	North Carolina	77,829	2.98%	37	Nevada	7,700	0.29%
13	Massachusetts	72,459	2.77%	38	Maine	7,549	0.29%
14	New Jersey	72,341	2.77%	39	Kentucky	7,482	0.29%
15	Indiana	68,683	2.63%	40	New Mexico	6,294	0.24%
16	Minnesota	59,323	2.27%	41	Vermont	5,912	0.23%
17	Connecticut	46,640	1.79%	42	Utah	5,830	0.22%
18	Missouri	42,322	1.62%	43	West Virginia	5,059	0.19%
19	Oregon	37,631	1.44%	44	Idaho	4,377	0.17%
20	Tennessee	32,719	1.25%	45	Montana	4,052	0.16%
21	South Carolina	32,287	1.24%	46	Alaska	3,599	0.14%
22	Colorado	31,111	1.19%	47	South Dakota	3,160	0.12%
23	Arizona	30,397	1.16%	48	New Hampshire	3,146	0.12%
24	Louisiana	30,191	1.16%	49	Wyoming	2,980	0.11%
25	Wisconsin	29,370	1.12%	50	North Dakota	1,731	0.07%
					District of Columbia	9,742	0.37%

Source: U.S. Department of Justice, Bureau of Justice Statistics
    "Correctional Populations in the United States, 1990" (July 1992, NCJ-134946)
*Excludes 58,222 adults on federal probation.

Percent of Adult Population on State Probation in 1990

National Rate = 1.41% of Adult Population*

RANK	STATE	PERCENT	RANK	STATE	PERCENT
1	Georgia	2.84	26	Pennsylvania	1.07
2	Texas	2.54	27	New York	1.06
3	Delaware	2.43	27	Oklahoma	1.06
4	Washington	2.35	29	Ohio	1.04
5	Maryland	2.29	30	Louisiana	1.01
6	Florida	2.09	31	Alaska	0.95
7	Rhode Island	1.98	32	Wyoming	0.94
8	Michigan	1.95	33	Alabama	0.93
9	Minnesota	1.85	34	Arkansas	0.92
10	Connecticut	1.84	35	Tennessee	0.89
11	Oregon	1.78	36	Nevada	0.85
12	Indiana	1.68	37	Maine	0.82
13	Massachusetts	1.55	37	Wisconsin	0.82
13	North Carolina	1.55	39	Montana	0.70
15	Hawaii	1.41	40	Iowa	0.68
15	Vermont	1.41	41	South Dakota	0.64
17	California	1.39	42	Idaho	0.63
18	Colorado	1.28	43	New Mexico	0.59
19	Nebraska	1.27	44	Utah	0.53
20	South Carolina	1.26	45	Mississippi	0.45
21	Kansas	1.22	45	Virginia	0.45
21	New Jersey	1.22	47	New Hampshire	0.38
23	Arizona	1.13	48	North Dakota	0.37
23	Illinois	1.13	48	West Virginia	0.37
25	Missouri	1.11	50	Kentucky	0.27

District of Columbia   1.99

Source: Morgan Quitno Corporation using data from U.S. Department of Justice, Bureau of Justice Statistics
   "Correctional Populations in the United States, 1990" (July 1992, NCJ-134946)
*Population 18 years old and older. National rate excludes 58,222 adults on federal probation.

Adults Under State Parole Supervision in 1990

National Total = 509,714 Parolees*

RANK	STATE	PAROLEES	%	RANK	STATE	PAROLEES	%
1	Texas	109,726	21.53%	26	Oklahoma	3,236	0.63%
2	California	67,562	13.25%	27	Kentucky	3,183	0.62%
3	Pennsylvania	56,657	11.12%	28	Nevada	2,850	0.56%
4	New York	42,837	8.40%	29	Arizona	2,711	0.53%
5	New Jersey	23,298	4.57%	30	Colorado	2,396	0.47%
6	Georgia	22,646	4.44%	31	Iowa	2,111	0.41%
7	Illinois	17,671	3.47%	32	Florida	2,064	0.40%
8	Michigan	11,901	2.33%	33	Minnesota	1,873	0.37%
9	Tennessee	11,327	2.22%	34	Utah	1,561	0.31%
10	Maryland	11,192	2.20%	35	Hawaii	1,425	0.28%
11	North Carolina	9,883	1.94%	36	Delaware	1,283	0.25%
12	Washington	9,615	1.89%	37	New Mexico	1,224	0.24%
13	Missouri	9,196	1.80%	38	West Virginia	1,000	0.20%
14	Virginia	9,048	1.78%	39	Montana	811	0.16%
15	Louisiana	8,877	1.74%	40	Nebraska	632	0.12%
16	Oregon	8,023	1.57%	41	South Dakota	620	0.12%
17	Ohio	7,945	1.56%	42	Alaska	568	0.11%
18	Alabama	5,970	1.17%	43	New Hampshire	522	0.10%
19	Kansas	5,751	1.13%	44	Rhode Island	321	0.06%
20	Massachusetts	4,720	0.93%	45	Wyoming	313	0.06%
21	Wisconsin	4,099	0.80%	46	Vermont	300	0.06%
22	Arkansas	3,971	0.78%	47	Connecticut	291	0.06%
23	Indiana	3,778	0.74%	48	Idaho	243	0.05%
24	South Carolina	3,543	0.70%	49	North Dakota	116	0.02%
25	Mississippi	3,478	0.68%	50	Maine	0	0.00%

District of Columbia 5,346 1.05%

Source: U.S. Department of Justice, Bureau of Justice Statistics
"Probation and Parole 1990" (Bulletin, November 1991, NCJ-133285)
*Excludes 21,693 adults under federal parole.

State and Local Corrections Employees at Correctional Institutions in 1990

National Total = 436,774 Employees*

RANK	STATE	EMPLOYEES	%	RANK	STATE	EMPLOYEES	%
1	New York	56,312	12.89%	26	Oklahoma	4,812	1.10%
2	California	52,038	11.91%	27	Connecticut	4,318	0.99%
3	Florida	31,939	7.31%	28	Kansas	4,175	0.96%
4	Texas	30,352	6.95%	29	Oregon	4,119	0.94%
5	Michigan	17,525	4.01%	30	Minnesota	3,649	0.84%
6	Illinois	15,400	3.53%	31	Mississippi	3,483	0.80%
7	Ohio	14,552	3.33%	32	New Mexico	2,971	0.68%
8	Georgia	14,459	3.31%	33	Arkansas	2,951	0.68%
9	Pennsylvania	14,014	3.21%	34	Iowa	2,928	0.67%
10	New Jersey	13,981	3.20%	35	Nevada	2,873	0.66%
11	Virginia	13,348	3.06%	36	Nebraska	2,502	0.57%
12	North Carolina	11,670	2.67%	37	Utah	1,950	0.45%
13	Maryland	9,820	2.25%	38	Maine	1,613	0.37%
14	Louisiana	9,151	2.10%	39	Rhode Island	1,383	0.32%
15	Tennessee	8,142	1.86%	40	Hawaii	1,374	0.31%
16	Arizona	8,023	1.84%	41	Alaska	1,321	0.30%
17	Indiana	7,907	1.81%	42	West Virginia	1,303	0.30%
18	Massachusetts	7,895	1.81%	43	Idaho	1,158	0.27%
19	Missouri	7,341	1.68%	44	New Hampshire	1,116	0.26%
20	South Carolina	7,149	1.64%	45	Delaware	1,108	0.25%
21	Washington	6,843	1.57%	46	Montana	988	0.23%
22	Alabama	5,150	1.18%	47	Wyoming	799	0.18%
23	Kentucky	5,056	1.16%	48	South Dakota	704	0.16%
24	Colorado	4,881	1.12%	49	Vermont	511	0.12%
25	Wisconsin	4,847	1.11%	50	North Dakota	489	0.11%
					District of Columbia	4,381	1.00%

Source: U.S. Department of Justice, Bureau of Justice Statistics
"Justice Expenditures and Employment in the U.S., 1990" (1993, NCJ-137754, forthcoming)
*Full-time equivalent.

Percent of State and Local Corrections Employees Serving at Correctional Institutions in 1990

National Rate = 83.19% of Corrections Employees*

RANK	STATE	PERCENT		RANK	STATE	PERCENT
1	Maine	90.92		26	Alaska	83.13
2	New Hampshire	90.81		26	North Carolina	83.13
3	Louisiana	89.69		28	Washington	83.03
4	Mississippi	89.61		29	Maryland	83.02
5	Virginia	89.21		30	Nebraska	82.82
6	Wyoming	88.78		31	South Dakota	82.34
7	North Dakota	88.75		32	Massachusetts	81.71
8	Michigan	88.52		33	Nevada	81.23
9	New York	88.37		34	Pennsylvania	81.20
10	Indiana	88.34		35	West Virginia	80.63
11	Arkansas	87.46		36	Hawaii	79.74
12	Kansas	87.31		37	Arizona	79.69
13	Kentucky	85.94		38	Utah	79.56
14	New Mexico	85.45		39	Texas	79.53
15	Ohio	85.09		40	Georgia	79.50
16	Illinois	84.84		41	California	78.99
17	Tennessee	84.56		42	Rhode Island	78.67
18	Florida	84.50		43	Oklahoma	78.17
19	Colorado	84.49		44	New Jersey	76.77
20	Alabama	84.12		45	Oregon	76.69
21	Connecticut	84.02		46	Delaware	75.02
22	Montana	83.94		47	Wisconsin	74.98
23	South Carolina	83.81		48	Iowa	73.96
24	Missouri	83.53		49	Minnesota	73.84
25	Idaho	83.37		50	Vermont	68.13

District of Columbia   92.68

Source: Morgan Quitno Corporation using data from U.S. Department of Justice, Bureau of Justice Statistics
    "Justice Expenditures and Employment in the U.S., 1990" (1993, NCJ-137754, forthcoming)
*Full-time equivalent.

State and Local Corrections Employees in Probation, Pardon or Parole Work in 1990

National Total = 72,040 Employees*

RANK	STATE	EMPLOYEES	%	RANK	STATE	EMPLOYEES	%
1	California	11,904	16.52%	26	Louisiana	829	1.15%
2	New York	6,451	8.95%	27	Kentucky	698	0.97%
3	Texas	6,355	8.82%	28	Colorado	682	0.95%
4	Florida	5,154	7.15%	29	Connecticut	659	0.91%
5	New Jersey	3,387	4.70%	30	Alabama	621	0.86%
6	Pennsylvania	3,065	4.25%	31	Nevada	564	0.78%
7	Georgia	2,342	3.25%	32	Kansas	535	0.74%
8	Illinois	2,332	3.24%	33	Utah	408	0.57%
9	Ohio	2,048	2.84%	34	New Mexico	400	0.56%
10	Michigan	2,042	2.83%	35	Nebraska	294	0.41%
11	North Carolina	1,847	2.56%	36	Hawaii	270	0.37%
12	Arizona	1,776	2.47%	37	Mississippi	251	0.35%
13	Maryland	1,608	2.23%	38	Arkansas	233	0.32%
14	Massachusetts	1,562	2.17%	39	West Virginia	214	0.30%
15	Tennessee	1,203	1.67%	40	Alaska	192	0.27%
16	Washington	1,201	1.67%	41	Montana	186	0.26%
17	Virginia	1,185	1.64%	42	Vermont	179	0.25%
18	Missouri	1,145	1.59%	43	Idaho	146	0.20%
19	Minnesota	1,143	1.59%	44	Rhode Island	144	0.20%
20	South Carolina	1,029	1.43%	45	Maine	132	0.18%
21	Oklahoma	1,025	1.42%	46	South Dakota	130	0.18%
22	Iowa	986	1.37%	47	Delaware	106	0.15%
23	Oregon	947	1.31%	48	Wyoming	91	0.13%
24	Wisconsin	931	1.29%	49	New Hampshire	82	0.11%
25	Indiana	923	1.28%	50	North Dakota	57	0.08%
					District of Columbia	346	0.48%

Source: U.S. Department of Justice, Bureau of Justice Statistics
   "Justice Expenditures and Employment in the U.S., 1990" (1993, NCJ-137754, forthcoming)
*Full-time equivalent.

Percent of State and Local Corrections Employees in Probation, Pardon or Parole Work in 1990

National Rate = 13.72% of Corrections Employees*

RANK	STATE	PERCENT		RANK	STATE	PERCENT
1	Iowa	24.91		26	Connecticut	12.82
2	Vermont	23.87		27	Tennessee	12.49
3	Minnesota	23.13		28	Alaska	12.08
4	New Jersey	18.60		29	South Carolina	12.06
5	California	18.07		30	Ohio	11.98
6	Pennsylvania	17.76		31	Kentucky	11.86
7	Arizona	17.64		32	Colorado	11.81
8	Oregon	17.63		33	New Mexico	11.50
9	Oklahoma	16.65		34	Kansas	11.19
9	Texas	16.65		35	Idaho	10.51
9	Utah	16.65		36	North Dakota	10.34
12	Massachusetts	16.17		37	Indiana	10.31
13	Nevada	15.95		37	Michigan	10.31
14	Montana	15.80		39	Alabama	10.14
15	Hawaii	15.67		40	New York	10.12
16	South Dakota	15.20		41	Wyoming	10.11
17	Washington	14.57		42	Nebraska	9.73
18	Wisconsin	14.40		43	Rhode Island	8.19
19	Florida	13.64		44	Louisiana	8.13
20	Maryland	13.59		45	Virginia	7.92
21	West Virginia	13.24		46	Maine	7.44
22	North Carolina	13.16		47	Delaware	7.18
23	Missouri	13.03		48	Arkansas	6.91
24	Georgia	12.88		49	New Hampshire	6.67
25	Illinois	12.85		50	Mississippi	6.46

	District of Columbia	7.32

Source: Morgan Quitno Corporation using data from U.S. Department of Justice, Bureau of Justice Statistics
"Justice Expenditures and Employment in the U.S., 1990" (1993, NCJ-137754, forthcoming)
*Full-time equivalent.

Employees in State Correctional Facilities in 1990

National Total = 245,750 Employees*

RANK	STATE	EMPLOYEES	%	RANK	STATE	EMPLOYEES	%
1	New York	30,257	12.31%	26	Kansas	2,694	1.10%
2	California	25,453	10.36%	27	Kentucky	2,571	1.05%
3	Texas	18,561	7.55%	28	Mississippi	2,314	0.94%
4	Florida	14,262	5.80%	29	Iowa	2,098	0.85%
5	Michigan	12,522	5.10%	30	Colorado	1,942	0.79%
6	Illinois	10,267	4.18%	31	Minnesota	1,847	0.75%
7	North Carolina	8,439	3.43%	32	Arkansas	1,834	0.75%
8	Ohio	7,918	3.22%	33	New Mexico	1,691	0.69%
9	New Jersey	7,426	3.02%	34	Oregon	1,578	0.64%
10	Georgia	7,037	2.86%	35	Utah	1,423	0.58%
11	Virginia	6,900	2.81%	36	Nevada	1,413	0.57%
12	Pennsylvania	6,707	2.73%	37	Hawaii	1,349	0.55%
13	Maryland	5,996	2.44%	38	Rhode Island	1,341	0.55%
14	South Carolina	5,269	2.14%	39	Alaska	1,163	0.47%
15	Indiana	5,204	2.12%	40	Delaware	1,157	0.47%
16	Arizona	4,776	1.94%	41	Nebraska	1,130	0.46%
17	Louisiana	4,643	1.89%	42	Maine	859	0.35%
18	Tennessee	4,580	1.86%	43	West Virginia	650	0.26%
19	Missouri	4,563	1.86%	44	Idaho	572	0.23%
20	Massachusetts	3,796	1.54%	45	New Hampshire	553	0.23%
21	Washington	3,767	1.53%	46	Montana	521	0.21%
22	Connecticut	3,702	1.51%	47	Vermont	504	0.21%
23	Oklahoma	3,168	1.29%	48	South Dakota	401	0.16%
24	Alabama	2,979	1.21%	49	Wyoming	387	0.16%
25	Wisconsin	2,910	1.18%	50	North Dakota	213	0.09%
					District of Columbia	2,443	0.99%

Source: U.S. Department of Justice, Bureau of Justice Statistics
   "Census of Correctional Facilities, 1990" (1992, NCJ-137003)

*Excludes 18,451 federal employees. Includes all full-time, part-time, payroll, nonpayroll and contract staff.

State Correctional Officers in Adult Systems in 1992

National Total = 169,725 Officers*

RANK	STATE	OFFICERS	%	RANK	STATE	OFFICERS	%
1	New York	17,748	10.46%	26	Colorado	1,733	1.02%
2	California	15,681	9.24%	27	Oklahoma	1,709	1.01%
3	Texas	12,891	7.60%	28	Mississippi	1,656	0.98%
4	Florida	11,551	6.81%	29	Arkansas	1,596	0.94%
5	Michigan	7,714	4.54%	30	Kentucky	1,351	0.80%
6	North Carolina	7,289	4.29%	31	Minnesota	1,241	0.73%
7	Illinois	6,745	3.97%	32	New Mexico	1,189	0.70%
8	New Jersey	5,804	3.42%	33	Oregon	1,126	0.66%
9	Georgia	5,736	3.38%	34	Iowa	1,125	0.66%
10	Virginia	4,956	2.92%	35	Rhode Island	1,054	0.62%
11	Ohio	4,942	2.91%	36	Hawaii	985	0.58%
12	Pennsylvania	4,556	2.68%	37	Utah	901	0.53%
13	Maryland	4,222	2.49%	38	Delaware	841	0.50%
14	Arizona	3,801	2.24%	39	Alaska	779	0.46%
15	Louisiana	3,622	2.13%	40	Nevada	712	0.42%
16	South Carolina	3,588	2.11%	41	Maine	577	0.34%
17	Massachusetts	3,439	2.03%	42	Nebraska	567	0.33%
18	Indiana	3,367	1.98%	43	West Virginia	492	0.29%
19	Tennessee	2,955	1.74%	44	Idaho	450	0.27%
20	Connecticut	2,938	1.73%	45	New Hampshire	392	0.23%
21	Washington	2,694	1.59%	46	Vermont	371	0.22%
22	Missouri	2,671	1.57%	47	South Dakota	322	0.19%
23	Alabama	2,244	1.32%	48	Wyoming	239	0.14%
24	Wisconsin	2,181	1.29%	49	Montana	231	0.14%
25	Kansas	1,828	1.08%	50	North Dakota	131	0.08%

	District of Columbia	2,792	1.65%

Source: American Correctional Association (Laurel, MD)

"1993 Directory of Juvenile and Adult Correctional Departments, Institutions, Agencies and Paroling Authorities" (1993)

*As of June 30, 1992. Total does not include 9,094 federal correctional officers.

Male Correctional Officers in Adult Systems in 1992

National Total = 139,751 Male Officers*

RANK	STATE	OFFICERS	%	RANK	STATE	OFFICERS	%
1	New York	16,307	11.67%	26	Kansas	1,503	1.08%
2	California	12,809	9.17%	27	Colorado	1,425	1.02%
3	Texas	9,920	7.10%	28	Arkansas	1,373	0.98%
4	Florida	8,893	6.36%	29	Kentucky	1,103	0.79%
5	North Carolina	6,566	4.70%	30	New Mexico	1,078	0.77%
6	Michigan	6,216	4.45%	31	Mississippi	984	0.70%
7	Illinois	5,921	4.24%	32	Minnesota	982	0.70%
8	New Jersey	5,114	3.66%	33	Iowa	976	0.70%
9	Georgia	4,746	3.40%	34	Rhode Island	970	0.69%
10	Pennsylvania	4,152	2.97%	35	Oregon	934	0.67%
11	Ohio	4,082	2.92%	36	Hawaii	867	0.62%
12	Virginia	4,018	2.88%	37	Utah	740	0.53%
13	Maryland	3,301	2.36%	38	Delaware	718	0.51%
14	Arizona	3,051	2.18%	39	Alaska	632	0.45%
14	Massachusetts	3,051	2.18%	40	Nevada	584	0.42%
16	Louisiana	2,837	2.03%	41	Maine	535	0.38%
17	Indiana	2,634	1.88%	42	Nebraska	462	0.33%
18	South Carolina	2,599	1.86%	43	West Virginia	433	0.31%
19	Connecticut	2,535	1.81%	44	New Hampshire	354	0.25%
20	Tennessee	2,397	1.72%	45	South Dakota	232	0.17%
21	Missouri	2,271	1.63%	46	Wyoming	194	0.14%
22	Washington	2,150	1.54%	47	Montana	175	0.13%
23	Wisconsin	1,832	1.31%	48	North Dakota	111	0.08%
24	Alabama	1,779	1.27%	–	Idaho**	N/A	N/A
25	Oklahoma	1,518	1.09%	–	Vermont**	N/A	N/A

	District of Columbia	1,969	1.41%

Source: American Correctional Association (Laurel, MD)

"1993 Directory of Juvenile and Adult Correctional Departments, Institutions, Agencies and Paroling Authorities" (1993)

*As of June 30, 1992. Total does not include 8,074 male federal correctional officers.

**Sex of officers not available.

Female Correctional Officers in Adult Systems in 1992

National Total = 28,874 Female Officers*

RANK	STATE	OFFICERS	%	RANK	STATE	OFFICERS	%
1	Texas	2,971	10.29%	26	Kansas	325	1.13%
2	California	2,872	9.95%	27	Colorado	308	1.07%
3	Florida	2,658	9.21%	28	Minnesota	259	0.90%
4	Michigan	1,498	5.19%	29	Kentucky	248	0.86%
5	New York	1,441	4.99%	30	Arkansas	223	0.77%
6	Georgia	990	3.43%	31	Oregon	192	0.66%
7	South Carolina	989	3.43%	32	Oklahoma	191	0.66%
8	Virginia	938	3.25%	33	Utah	161	0.56%
9	Maryland	921	3.19%	34	Iowa	149	0.52%
10	Ohio	860	2.98%	35	Alaska	147	0.51%
11	Illinois	824	2.85%	36	Nevada	128	0.44%
12	Louisiana	785	2.72%	37	Delaware	123	0.43%
13	Arizona	750	2.60%	38	Hawaii	118	0.41%
14	Indiana	733	2.54%	39	New Mexico	111	0.38%
15	North Carolina	723	2.50%	40	Nebraska	105	0.36%
16	New Jersey	690	2.39%	41	South Dakota	90	0.31%
17	Mississippi	672	2.33%	42	Rhode Island	84	0.29%
18	Tennessee	558	1.93%	43	West Virginia	59	0.20%
19	Washington	544	1.88%	44	Montana	56	0.19%
20	Alabama	465	1.61%	45	Wyoming	45	0.16%
21	Pennsylvania	404	1.40%	46	Maine	42	0.15%
22	Connecticut	403	1.40%	47	New Hampshire	38	0.13%
23	Missouri	400	1.39%	48	North Dakota	20	0.07%
24	Massachusetts	388	1.34%	–	Idaho**	N/A	N/A
25	Wisconsin	349	1.21%	–	Vermont**	N/A	N/A
					District of Columbia	823	2.85%

Source: American Correctional Association (Laurel, MD)

"1993 Directory of Juvenile and Adult Correctional Departments, Institutions, Agencies and Paroling Authorities" (1993)

*As of June 30, 1992. Total does not include 1,020 female federal correctional officers.

**Sex of officers not available.

State Prisoners per Correctional Officer in 1992

National Rate = 4.73 Prisoners per Officer*

RANK	STATE	RATE		RANK	STATE	RATE
1	Oklahoma	8.67		26	Arizona	4.33
2	Nevada	8.50		27	Virginia	4.28
3	Alabama	7.78		27	Wyoming	4.28
4	Ohio	7.77		29	Florida	4.18
5	Kentucky	7.67		30	Wisconsin	4.15
6	California	6.98		31	Iowa	4.02
7	Montana	6.72		32	Tennessee	4.01
8	Missouri	6.06		33	Indiana	3.91
9	Oregon	5.86		34	New Jersey	3.90
10	Louisiana	5.75		35	Connecticut	3.88
11	Idaho	5.50		36	Washington	3.70
12	Mississippi	5.48		37	Alaska	3.68
12	Pennsylvania	5.48		38	West Virginia	3.55
14	Arkansas	5.28		39	North Dakota	3.54
15	South Carolina	5.20		40	New York	3.48
16	Colorado	5.19		41	Vermont	3.42
17	Michigan	5.06		42	Kansas	3.30
18	Texas	4.75		43	Minnesota	3.08
19	Delaware	4.73		44	Utah	3.00
19	Maryland	4.73		45	Hawaii	2.97
21	Illinois	4.69		46	Massachusetts	2.92
22	South Dakota	4.62		47	North Carolina	2.81
23	New Hampshire	4.53		48	New Mexico	2.75
24	Nebraska	4.52		49	Maine	2.63
25	Georgia	4.41		49	Rhode Island	2.63

District of Columbia   3.90

Source: Morgan Quitno Corporation using data from U.S. Department of Justice, Bureau of Justice Statistics
    "Prisoners in 1992" (Bulletin, May 1993, NCJ-141874) and
    American Correctional Association (Laurel, MD)
    "1993 Directory of Juvenile and Adult Correctional Departments, Institutions, Agencies and Paroling Authorities" (1993)

Turnover Rate of Correctional Officers in Adult Systems in 1992

National Rate = 12.00%*

RANK	STATE	TURNOVER RATE
1	Kansas	32.00
2	Louisiana	26.16
3	Arkansas	22.00
4	Georgia	20.00
4	South Carolina	20.00
6	Wyoming	19.00
7	Nevada	18.80
8	Maryland	18.00
9	Montana	17.90
10	Arizona	17.00
11	Indiana	16.30
12	South Dakota	16.00
13	Tennessee	15.90
14	Nebraska	15.52
15	Maine	15.00
15	New Mexico	15.00
15	West Virginia	15.00
18	Wisconsin	14.89
19	Idaho	14.41
20	Missouri	14.00
21	Alabama	13.50
22	Virginia	13.30
23	Alaska	13.00
24	Texas	12.00
25	Massachusetts	10.00

RANK	STATE	TURNOVER RATE
25	North Dakota	10.00
25	Rhode Island	10.00
28	Oregon	9.00
29	Florida	8.57
30	New Jersey	8.50
30	North Carolina	8.50
30	Utah	8.50
33	Hawaii	8.00
33	Ohio	8.00
35	Washington	7.64
36	Oklahoma	7.60
37	Illinois	7.50
38	Iowa	7.43
39	Minnesota	6.17
40	New Hampshire	6.00
41	California	5.50
42	Mississippi	5.40
42	Pennsylvania	5.40
44	Vermont	5.00
45	Colorado	4.50
46	Michigan	3.50
47	Delaware	3.20
48	New York	2.50
49	Connecticut	1.50
–	Kentucky**	N/A

District of Columbia   6.30

Source: American Correctional Association (Laurel, MD)

"1993 Directory of Juvenile and Adult Correctional Departments, Institutions, Agencies and Paroling Authorities" (1993)

*As of June 30, 1992. Federal officer rate is 7.50%.

**Not available.

Average Annual Salary of State Corrections Officers in 1992

National Average = $24,239*

RANK	STATE	SALARY	RANK	STATE	SALARY
1	Alaska	$41,215	26	Arizona	$20,250
2	California	38,604	27	Louisiana	20,184
3	New Jersey	34,984	28	Georgia	20,171
4	New York	29,128	29	Wisconsin	20,006
5	Connecticut	29,000	30	Nebraska	19,902
6	Oregon	28,944	31	Maine	19,427
7	Michigan	28,870	32	North Carolina	19,236
8	Pennsylvania	28,479	33	Oklahoma	19,038
9	Nevada	27,622	34	Florida	18,987
10	Minnesota	27,000	35	Delaware	18,902
11	Colorado	26,220	36	Missouri	18,015
12	Iowa	25,800	37	Mississippi	18,000
13	Illinois	25,440	37	Tennessee	18,000
14	Alabama	25,240	37	West Virginia	18,000
15	Washington	25,098	40	Kentucky	17,796
16	Massachusetts	25,000	41	Montana	17,506
17	Hawaii	24,701	42	New Mexico	17,325
18	Kansas	24,144	43	Wyoming	17,249
19	Rhode Island	24,136	44	South Carolina	16,498
20	New Hampshire	23,897	45	Arkansas	16,458
21	Texas	23,385	46	North Dakota	16,000
22	Ohio	23,046	47	South Dakota	15,548
23	Vermont	21,653	–	Indiana**	N/A
24	Virginia	21,534	–	Maryland**	N/A
25	Idaho	20,363	–	Utah**	N/A

District of Columbia   35,027

Source: Corrections Compendium (Lincoln, NE) (October 1992)

The national average was calculated by Morgan Quitno by using a weighted average of the 48 state averages.

**Not available.*

Inmates in Local Jails in 1988

National Total = 343,569 Inmates*

RANK	STATE	INMATES	%	RANK	STATE	INMATES	%
1	California	64,216	18.69%	26	South Carolina	3,497	1.02%
2	Texas	29,439	8.57%	27	Minnesota	3,227	0.94%
3	Florida	28,236	8.22%	28	Oregon	2,819	0.82%
4	New York	25,928	7.55%	29	Oklahoma	2,595	0.76%
5	Georgia	17,482	5.09%	30	Nevada	2,343	0.68%
6	Pennsylvania	13,649	3.97%	31	New Mexico	2,188	0.64%
7	Louisiana	11,222	3.27%	32	Arkansas	1,994	0.58%
8	New Jersey	11,124	3.24%	33	Kansas	1,906	0.55%
9	Tennessee	10,858	3.16%	34	West Virginia	1,393	0.41%
10	Illinois	9,891	2.88%	35	Utah	1,261	0.37%
11	Michigan	9,404	2.74%	36	Nebraska	1,156	0.34%
12	Virginia	9,372	2.73%	37	Iowa	1,036	0.30%
13	Ohio	9,160	2.67%	38	Idaho	810	0.24%
14	Maryland	7,486	2.18%	39	New Hampshire	789	0.23%
15	Arizona	6,006	1.75%	40	Maine	669	0.19%
16	Washington	5,934	1.73%	41	Montana	616	0.18%
17	North Carolina	5,469	1.59%	42	South Dakota	522	0.15%
18	Massachusetts	5,454	1.59%	43	Wyoming	457	0.13%
19	Indiana	5,235	1.52%	44	North Dakota	288	0.08%
20	Colorado	4,882	1.42%	45	Alaska	27	0.01%
21	Alabama	4,819	1.40%	–	Connecticut**	N/A	N/A
22	Kentucky	4,695	1.37%	–	Delaware**	N/A	N/A
23	Wisconsin	4,667	1.36%	–	Hawaii**	N/A	N/A
24	Missouri	4,154	1.21%	–	Rhode Island**	N/A	N/A
25	Mississippi	3,501	1.02%	–	Vermont**	N/A	N/A

District of Columbia   1,693   0.49%

Source: U.S. Department of Justice, Bureau of Justice Statistics
  "Census of Local Jails, 1988" (1991, NCJ-127992)
*As of June 30, 1988. National total does not include data from states not reporting.
**Not reported.

Male Inmates in Local Jails in 1988

National Total = 313,158 Male Inmates*

RANK	STATE	MALE INMATES	%	RANK	STATE	MALE INMATES	%
1	California	56,570	18.06%	26	South Carolina	3,259	1.04%
2	Texas	26,753	8.54%	27	Minnesota	3,034	0.97%
3	Florida	25,460	8.13%	28	Oregon	2,590	0.83%
4	New York	23,240	7.42%	29	Oklahoma	2,318	0.74%
5	Georgia	16,364	5.23%	30	Nevada	2,078	0.66%
6	Pennsylvania	12,663	4.04%	31	New Mexico	2,015	0.64%
7	Louisiana	10,397	3.32%	32	Arkansas	1,861	0.59%
8	Tennessee	10,244	3.27%	33	Kansas	1,772	0.57%
9	New Jersey	10,241	3.27%	34	West Virginia	1,310	0.42%
10	Illinois	9,333	2.98%	35	Utah	1,165	0.37%
11	Michigan	8,687	2.77%	36	Nebraska	1,044	0.33%
12	Virginia	8,544	2.73%	37	Iowa	958	0.31%
13	Ohio	8,355	2.67%	38	Idaho	766	0.24%
14	Maryland	6,897	2.20%	39	New Hampshire	749	0.24%
15	Arizona	5,496	1.76%	40	Maine	642	0.21%
16	Massachusetts	5,430	1.73%	41	Montana	547	0.17%
17	Washington	5,423	1.73%	42	South Dakota	478	0.15%
18	North Carolina	5,063	1.62%	43	Wyoming	402	0.13%
19	Indiana	4,870	1.56%	44	North Dakota	262	0.08%
20	Alabama	4,469	1.43%	45	Alaska	25	0.01%
21	Colorado	4,439	1.42%	–	Connecticut**	N/A	N/A
22	Kentucky	4,304	1.37%	–	Delaware**	N/A	N/A
23	Wisconsin	4,289	1.37%	–	Hawaii**	N/A	N/A
24	Missouri	3,845	1.23%	–	Rhode Island**	N/A	N/A
25	Mississippi	3,298	1.05%	–	Vermont**	N/A	N/A

District of Columbia   1,209   0.39%

Source: U.S. Department of Justice, Bureau of Justice Statistics
   "Census of Local Jails, 1988" (1991, NCJ-127992)

*As of June 30, 1988. National total does not include data from states not reporting.

**Not reported.

Female Inmates in Local Jails in 1988

National Total = 30,411 Female Inmates

RANK	STATE	FEMALE INMATES	%	RANK	STATE	FEMALE INMATES	%
1	California	7,646	25.14%	26	South Carolina	238	0.78%
2	Florida	2,776	9.13%	27	Oregon	229	0.75%
3	New York	2,688	8.84%	28	Mississippi	203	0.67%
4	Texas	2,686	8.83%	29	Minnesota	193	0.63%
5	Georgia	1,118	3.68%	30	New Mexico	173	0.57%
6	Pennsylvania	986	3.24%	31	Kansas	134	0.44%
7	New Jersey	883	2.90%	32	Arkansas	133	0.44%
8	Virginia	828	2.72%	33	Nebraska	112	0.37%
9	Louisiana	825	2.71%	34	Utah	96	0.32%
10	Ohio	805	2.65%	35	West Virginia	83	0.27%
11	Michigan	717	2.36%	36	Iowa	78	0.26%
12	Tennessee	614	2.02%	37	Montana	69	0.23%
13	Maryland	589	1.94%	38	Wyoming	55	0.18%
14	Illinois	558	1.83%	39	Idaho	44	0.14%
15	Washington	511	1.68%	39	South Dakota	44	0.14%
16	Arizona	510	1.68%	41	New Hampshire	40	0.13%
17	Colorado	443	1.46%	42	Maine	27	0.09%
18	North Carolina	406	1.34%	43	North Dakota	26	0.09%
19	Kentucky	391	1.29%	44	Massachusetts	24	0.08%
20	Wisconsin	378	1.24%	45	Alaska	2	0.01%
21	Indiana	365	1.20%	–	Connecticut**	N/A	N/A
22	Alabama	350	1.15%	–	Delaware**	N/A	N/A
23	Missouri	309	1.02%	–	Hawaii**	N/A	N/A
24	Oklahoma	277	0.91%	–	Rhode Island**	N/A	N/A
25	Nevada	265	0.87%	–	Vermont**	N/A	N/A
					District of Columbia	484	1.59%

Source: U.S. Department of Justice, Bureau of Justice Statistics
"Census of Local Jails, 1988" (1991, NCJ-127992)

As of June 30, 1988. National total does not include data from states not reporting.

**Not reported.*

White Inmates in Local Jails in 1988

National Total = 148,893 White Inmates*

RANK	STATE	WHITE INMATES	%	RANK	STATE	WHITE INMATES	%
1	California	22,992	15.44%	26	Oregon	2,240	1.50%
2	Florida	11,547	7.76%	27	Nevada	1,529	1.03%
3	Texas	10,513	7.06%	28	Oklahoma	1,522	1.02%
4	Georgia	7,022	4.72%	29	South Carolina	1,337	0.90%
5	Pennsylvania	6,978	4.69%	30	Kansas	1,298	0.87%
6	New York	6,821	4.58%	31	West Virginia	1,198	0.80%
7	Michigan	5,660	3.80%	32	Arkansas	1,136	0.76%
8	Tennessee	5,589	3.75%	33	Utah	1,061	0.71%
9	Ohio	5,267	3.54%	34	Mississippi	1,006	0.68%
10	Washington	3,819	2.56%	35	Iowa	816	0.55%
11	Virginia	3,806	2.56%	35	Nebraska	816	0.55%
12	Kentucky	3,511	2.36%	37	New Hampshire	734	0.49%
13	Arizona	3,391	2.28%	38	Maine	647	0.43%
14	Indiana	3,387	2.27%	39	New Mexico	635	0.43%
15	Illinois	3,272	2.20%	40	Idaho	622	0.42%
16	Louisiana	3,254	2.19%	41	Montana	447	0.30%
17	Massachusetts	3,075	2.07%	42	Wyoming	360	0.24%
18	New Jersey	3,069	2.06%	43	South Dakota	358	0.24%
19	Wisconsin	3,001	2.02%	44	North Dakota	194	0.13%
20	Colorado	2,773	1.86%	45	Alaska	14	0.01%
21	Maryland	2,699	1.81%	–	Connecticut**	N/A	N/A
22	Minnesota	2,385	1.60%	–	Delaware**	N/A	N/A
23	Missouri	2,339	1.57%	–	Hawaii**	N/A	N/A
24	Alabama	2,312	1.55%	–	Rhode Island**	N/A	N/A
25	North Carolina	2,271	1.53%	–	Vermont**	N/A	N/A
					District of Columbia	170	0.11%

Source: Morgan Quitno Corporation using data from U.S. Department of Justice, Bureau of Justice Statistics
    "Census of Local Jails, 1988" (1991, NCJ-127992)

*As of June 30, 1988. National total does not include data from states not reporting.

**Not reported.

White Inmates in Local Jails as a Percent of All Inmates in 1988

National Rate = 43.34% of Inmates*

RANK	STATE	PERCENT	RANK	STATE	PERCENT
1	Maine	96.71	26	Massachusetts	56.38
2	New Hampshire	93.03	27	Missouri	56.31
3	West Virginia	86.00	28	Alaska	51.85
4	Utah	84.14	29	Tennessee	51.47
5	Oregon	79.46	30	Pennsylvania	51.12
6	Wyoming	78.77	31	Alabama	47.98
7	Iowa	78.76	32	North Carolina	41.52
8	Idaho	76.79	33	Florida	40.89
9	Kentucky	74.78	34	Virginia	40.61
10	Minnesota	73.91	35	Georgia	40.17
11	Montana	72.56	36	South Carolina	38.23
12	Nebraska	70.59	37	Maryland	36.05
13	South Dakota	68.58	38	California	35.80
14	Kansas	68.10	39	Texas	35.71
15	North Dakota	67.36	40	Illinois	33.08
16	Nevada	65.26	41	New Mexico	29.02
17	Indiana	64.70	42	Louisiana	29.00
18	Washington	64.36	43	Mississippi	28.73
19	Wisconsin	64.30	44	New Jersey	27.59
20	Michigan	60.19	45	New York	26.31
21	Oklahoma	58.65	–	Connecticut**	N/A
22	Ohio	57.50	–	Delaware**	N/A
23	Arkansas	56.97	–	Hawaii**	N/A
24	Colorado	56.80	–	Rhode Island**	N/A
25	Arizona	56.46	–	Vermont**	N/A

District of Columbia   10.04

Source: Morgan Quitno Corporation using data from U.S. Department of Justice, Bureau of Justice Statistics
    "Census of Local Jails, 1988" (1991, NCJ-127992)
*As of June 30, 1988. National rate does not include data from states not reporting.
**Not reported.

Black Inmates in Local Jails in 1988

National Total = 139,289 Black Inmates*

RANK	STATE	BLACK INMATES	%	RANK	STATE	BLACK INMATES	%
1	California	17,495	12.56%	26	Arizona	850	0.61%
2	Florida	14,324	10.28%	27	Arkansas	808	0.58%
3	New York	12,755	9.16%	28	Oklahoma	757	0.54%
4	Texas	10,740	7.71%	29	Nevada	707	0.51%
5	Georgia	10,277	7.38%	30	Minnesota	551	0.40%
6	Louisiana	7,509	5.39%	31	Kansas	480	0.34%
7	New Jersey	5,980	4.29%	32	Oregon	294	0.21%
8	Illinois	5,810	4.17%	33	Nebraska	231	0.17%
9	Pennsylvania	5,642	4.05%	34	West Virginia	185	0.13%
10	Virginia	5,422	3.89%	35	Iowa	169	0.12%
11	Tennessee	5,178	3.72%	36	New Mexico	157	0.11%
12	Maryland	4,649	3.34%	37	Utah	61	0.04%
13	Ohio	3,713	2.67%	38	New Hampshire	37	0.03%
14	Michigan	3,433	2.46%	39	Maine	16	0.01%
15	North Carolina	3,105	2.23%	39	Montana	16	0.01%
16	Alabama	2,489	1.79%	41	Idaho	12	0.01%
17	Mississippi	2,433	1.75%	42	South Dakota	10	0.01%
18	South Carolina	2,129	1.53%	42	Wyoming	10	0.01%
19	Indiana	1,819	1.31%	44	North Dakota	5	0.00%
20	Missouri	1,747	1.25%	45	Alaska	1	0.00%
21	Wisconsin	1,342	0.96%	–	Connecticut**	N/A	N/A
22	Massachusetts	1,233	0.89%	–	Delaware**	N/A	N/A
23	Kentucky	1,158	0.83%	–	Hawaii**	N/A	N/A
24	Washington	1,098	0.79%	–	Rhode Island**	N/A	N/A
25	Colorado	929	0.67%	–	Vermont**	N/A	N/A

District of Columbia   1,523   1.09%

Source: Morgan Quitno Corporation using data from U.S. Department of Justice, Bureau of Justice Statistics
"Census of Local Jails, 1988" (1991, NCJ-127992)

*As of June 30, 1988. National total does not include data from states not reporting.

**Not reported.

Black Inmates in Local Jails as a Percent of All Inmates in 1988

National Rate = 40.54% of Inmates*

RANK	STATE	PERCENT		RANK	STATE	PERCENT
1	Mississippi	69.49		26	Kentucky	24.66
2	Louisiana	66.91		27	Massachusetts	22.61
3	Maryland	62.10		28	Nebraska	19.98
4	South Carolina	60.88		29	Colorado	19.03
5	Georgia	58.79		30	Washington	18.50
6	Illinois	58.74		31	Minnesota	17.07
7	Virginia	57.85		32	Iowa	16.31
8	North Carolina	56.77		33	Arizona	14.15
9	New Jersey	53.76		34	West Virginia	13.28
10	Alabama	51.65		35	Oregon	10.43
11	Florida	50.73		36	New Mexico	7.18
12	New York	49.19		37	Utah	4.84
13	Tennessee	47.69		38	New Hampshire	4.69
14	Missouri	42.06		39	Alaska	3.70
15	Pennsylvania	41.34		40	Montana	2.60
16	Ohio	40.53		41	Maine	2.39
17	Arkansas	40.52		42	Wyoming	2.19
18	Michigan	36.51		43	South Dakota	1.92
19	Texas	36.48		44	North Dakota	1.74
20	Indiana	34.75		45	Idaho	1.48
21	Nevada	30.17		–	Connecticut**	N/A
22	Oklahoma	29.17		–	Delaware**	N/A
23	Wisconsin	28.76		–	Hawaii**	N/A
24	California	27.24		–	Rhode Island**	N/A
25	Kansas	25.18		–	Vermont**	N/A

District of Columbia 89.96

Source: Morgan Quitno Corporation using data from U.S. Department of Justice, Bureau of Justice Statistics
"Census of Local Jails, 1988" (1991, NCJ-127992)

*As of June 30, 1988. National rate does not include data from states not reporting.

**Not reported.

Hispanic Inmates in Local Jails in 1988

National Total = 51,455 Hispanic Inmates*

RANK	STATE	HISPANIC INMATES	%	RANK	STATE	HISPANIC INMATES	%
1	California	22,400	43.53%	26	Nevada	70	0.14%
2	Texas	8,151	15.84%	27	Wyoming	64	0.12%
3	New York	6,213	12.07%	28	Mississippi	60	0.12%
4	Florida	2,320	4.51%	28	Missouri	60	0.12%
5	New Jersey	2,055	3.99%	30	North Carolina	57	0.11%
6	Arizona	1,502	2.92%	31	Nebraska	54	0.10%
7	New Mexico	1,182	2.30%	32	Arkansas	44	0.09%
8	Colorado	1,130	2.20%	33	Iowa	30	0.06%
9	Massachusetts	1,115	2.17%	33	South Carolina	30	0.06%
10	Pennsylvania	985	1.91%	33	Tennessee	30	0.06%
11	Illinois	788	1.53%	36	Indiana	26	0.05%
12	Washington	720	1.40%	36	Kentucky	26	0.05%
13	Louisiana	424	0.82%	38	Montana	20	0.04%
14	Michigan	266	0.52%	39	New Hampshire	18	0.03%
15	Oregon	214	0.42%	40	Alabama	16	0.03%
15	Wisconsin	214	0.42%	41	West Virginia	9	0.02%
17	Georgia	178	0.35%	42	North Dakota	6	0.01%
18	Ohio	153	0.30%	43	South Dakota	4	0.01%
19	Idaho	139	0.27%	44	Maine	2	0.00%
20	Virginia	137	0.27%	45	Alaska	1	0.00%
21	Oklahoma	125	0.24%	–	Connecticut**	N/A	N/A
22	Kansas	114	0.22%	–	Delaware**	N/A	N/A
23	Utah	111	0.22%	–	Hawaii**	N/A	N/A
24	Maryland	107	0.21%	–	Rhode Island**	N/A	N/A
25	Minnesota	85	0.17%	–	Vermont**	N/A	N/A

District of Columbia   0   0.00%

Source: Morgan Quitno Corporation using data from U.S. Department of Justice, Bureau of Justice Statistics
"Census of Local Jails, 1988" (1991, NCJ-127992)

*As of June 30, 1988. National total does not include data from states not reporting.

**Not reported.

Hispanic Inmates in Local Jails as a Percent of All Inmates in 1988

National Rate = 14.98% of Inmates*

RANK	STATE	PERCENT	RANK	STATE	PERCENT
1	New Mexico	54.02	26	Michigan	2.83
2	California	34.88	27	Minnesota	2.63
3	Texas	27.69	28	New Hampshire	2.28
4	Arizona	25.01	29	Arkansas	2.21
5	New York	23.96	30	North Dakota	2.08
6	Colorado	23.15	31	Mississippi	1.71
7	Massachusetts	20.44	32	Ohio	1.67
8	New Jersey	18.47	33	Virginia	1.46
9	Idaho	17.16	34	Missouri	1.44
10	Wyoming	14.00	35	Maryland	1.43
11	Washington	12.13	36	North Carolina	1.04
12	Utah	8.80	37	Georgia	1.02
13	Florida	8.22	38	South Carolina	0.86
14	Illinois	7.97	39	South Dakota	0.77
15	Oregon	7.59	40	West Virginia	0.65
16	Pennsylvania	7.22	41	Kentucky	0.55
17	Kansas	5.98	42	Indiana	0.50
18	Oklahoma	4.82	43	Alabama	0.33
19	Nebraska	4.67	44	Maine	0.30
20	Wisconsin	4.59	45	Tennessee	0.28
21	Louisiana	3.78	–	Connecticut**	N/A
22	Alaska	3.70	–	Delaware**	N/A
23	Montana	3.25	–	Hawaii**	N/A
24	Nevada	2.99	–	Rhode Island**	N/A
25	Iowa	2.90	–	Vermont**	N/A

District of Columbia   0.00

Source: Morgan Quitno Corporation using data from U.S. Department of Justice, Bureau of Justice Statistics
 "Census of Local Jails, 1988" (1991, NCJ-127992)

*As of June 30, 1988. National rate does not include data from states not reporting.

**Not reported.

Juveniles Held in Public Juvenile Facilities in 1991

National Total = 57,542 Juveniles*

RANK	STATE	JUVENILES	%	RANK	STATE	JUVENILES	%
1	California	15,904	27.64%	26	Kentucky	666	1.16%
2	Ohio	3,696	6.42%	27	Minnesota	645	1.12%
3	Texas	2,661	4.62%	28	Nevada	555	0.96%
4	New York	2,648	4.60%	29	New Mexico	527	0.92%
5	Illinois	2,029	3.53%	30	Iowa	418	0.73%
6	Florida	2,008	3.49%	30	Mississippi	418	0.73%
7	Michigan	1,968	3.42%	32	Oklahoma	336	0.58%
8	New Jersey	1,719	2.99%	33	Nebraska	293	0.51%
9	Virginia	1,712	2.98%	34	Connecticut	290	0.50%
10	Georgia	1,566	2.72%	35	Arkansas	285	0.50%
11	Washington	1,418	2.46%	36	Utah	273	0.47%
12	Indiana	1,395	2.42%	37	Maine	249	0.43%
13	Pennsylvania	1,289	2.24%	38	Montana	230	0.40%
14	Louisiana	1,122	1.95%	39	Alaska	217	0.38%
15	Missouri	1,060	1.84%	39	South Dakota	217	0.38%
16	Arizona	947	1.65%	41	Massachusetts	180	0.31%
17	South Carolina	926	1.61%	42	West Virginia	166	0.29%
18	Wisconsin	896	1.56%	43	Rhode Island	161	0.28%
19	North Carolina	893	1.55%	44	Idaho	143	0.25%
20	Alabama	846	1.47%	45	Delaware	130	0.23%
21	Maryland	831	1.44%	46	Wyoming	113	0.20%
22	Tennessee	755	1.31%	47	New Hampshire	108	0.19%
23	Oregon	723	1.26%	48	Hawaii	84	0.15%
24	Colorado	687	1.19%	49	North Dakota	75	0.13%
25	Kansas	667	1.16%	50	Vermont	17	0.03%
					District of Columbia	380	0.66%

Source: U.S. Department of Justice, Bureau of Justice Statistics

"Sourcebook of Criminal Justice Statistics 1992" (September 1993, NCJ–143496)

*One day count reflecting number of juveniles in custody on February 15, 1991.

Juvenile Custody Rate in 1991

National Rate = 221 Juveniles per 100,000 Juveniles*

RANK	STATE	RATE	RANK	STATE	RATE
1	California	492	26	Maryland	172
2	Nevada	427	27	North Carolina	168
3	Alaska	312	27	Rhode Island	168
4	Ohio	300	29	Wyoming	164
5	New Mexico	268	30	Florida	161
6	Virginia	264	31	Wisconsin	157
7	South Carolina	257	32	Nebraska	155
8	Washington	256	33	Kentucky	151
9	Louisiana	251	34	Texas	144
10	South Dakota	246	35	Tennessee	138
11	Georgia	235	36	Iowa	128
12	Kansas	232	36	Minnesota	128
13	Montana	230	38	Connecticut	123
14	Arizona	226	38	Mississippi	123
15	New Jersey	222	40	Pennsylvania	106
16	Oregon	220	41	Arkansas	100
17	Indiana	214	42	North Dakota	99
18	Michigan	209	43	Idaho	98
19	Missouri	206	44	New Hampshire	95
20	New York	192	44	Utah	95
21	Delaware	187	46	Oklahoma	90
22	Colorado	186	47	West Virginia	77
23	Maine	185	48	Hawaii	71
24	Illinois	181	49	Massachusetts	37
25	Alabama	174	50	Vermont	28

District of Columbia   826

Source: U.S. Department of Justice, Bureau of Justice Statistics
   "Sourcebook of Criminal Justice Statistics 1992" (September 1993, NCJ-143496)
*One day count reflecting number of juveniles in custody on February 15, 1991.

Juveniles Admitted to Public Juvenile Facilities in 1990

National Total = 683,636 Juveniles

RANK	STATE	JUVENILES	%	RANK	STATE	JUVENILES	%
1	California	170,462	24.93%	26	North Carolina	6,977	1.02%
2	Ohio	48,035	7.03%	27	Louisiana	6,307	0.92%
3	Florida	40,276	5.89%	28	Mississippi	6,190	0.91%
4	Texas	38,398	5.62%	29	Oklahoma	5,963	0.87%
5	Washington	23,166	3.39%	30	Kansas	5,921	0.87%
6	Illinois	22,412	3.28%	31	Kentucky	5,526	0.81%
7	Tennessee	21,349	3.12%	32	South Carolina	4,742	0.69%
8	Nevada	19,665	2.88%	33	Arkansas	4,555	0.67%
9	Michigan	17,816	2.61%	34	Iowa	3,861	0.56%
10	Virginia	17,411	2.55%	35	Massachusetts	3,254	0.48%
11	Georgia	17,343	2.54%	36	Connecticut	2,960	0.43%
12	Indiana	16,363	2.39%	37	Nebraska	2,911	0.43%
13	Arizona	15,857	2.32%	38	South Dakota	2,837	0.41%
14	Pennsylvania	15,249	2.23%	39	West Virginia	1,611	0.24%
15	New Jersey	15,130	2.21%	40	Hawaii	1,555	0.23%
16	New York	15,109	2.21%	41	Alaska	1,482	0.22%
17	Colorado	13,691	2.00%	42	Delaware	1,424	0.21%
18	Missouri	10,945	1.60%	43	Idaho	1,235	0.18%
19	Minnesota	10,878	1.59%	44	Montana	1,084	0.16%
20	Oregon	10,354	1.51%	45	North Dakota	664	0.10%
21	Alabama	10,217	1.49%	46	Rhode Island	589	0.09%
22	Maryland	9,482	1.39%	47	Maine	572	0.08%
23	Wisconsin	9,269	1.36%	48	New Hampshire	516	0.08%
24	Utah	8,559	1.25%	49	Wyoming	353	0.05%
25	New Mexico	7,115	1.04%	50	Vermont	308	0.05%
					District of Columbia	5,688	0.83%

Source: U.S. Department of Justice, Bureau of Justice Statistics
"Sourcebook of Criminal Justice Statistics 1992" (September 1993, NCJ-143496)

Juveniles Discharged from Public Juvenile Facilities in 1990

National Total = 674,597 Juveniles

RANK	STATE	JUVENILES	%	RANK	STATE	JUVENILES	%
1	California	168,252	24.94%	26	North Carolina	6,736	1.00%
2	Ohio	47,264	7.01%	27	Mississippi	6,206	0.92%
3	Florida	40,133	5.95%	28	Oklahoma	5,943	0.88%
4	Texas	37,816	5.61%	29	Kansas	5,851	0.87%
5	Washington	22,683	3.36%	30	Louisiana	5,814	0.86%
6	Illinois	22,443	3.33%	31	Kentucky	5,445	0.81%
7	Tennessee	21,447	3.18%	32	South Carolina	4,543	0.67%
8	Nevada	19,585	2.90%	33	Arkansas	4,521	0.67%
9	Michigan	17,550	2.60%	34	Iowa	3,872	0.57%
10	Georgia	17,382	2.58%	35	Massachusetts	3,229	0.48%
11	Virginia	16,894	2.50%	36	Connecticut	2,948	0.44%
12	Indiana	15,933	2.36%	37	Nebraska	2,937	0.44%
13	Arizona	15,520	2.30%	38	South Dakota	2,842	0.42%
14	Pennsylvania	14,909	2.21%	39	West Virginia	1,597	0.24%
15	New York	14,791	2.19%	40	Hawaii	1,562	0.23%
16	New Jersey	14,611	2.17%	41	Alaska	1,472	0.22%
17	Colorado	13,593	2.01%	42	Delaware	1,432	0.21%
18	Minnesota	10,814	1.60%	43	Idaho	1,221	0.18%
19	Missouri	10,779	1.60%	44	Montana	966	0.14%
20	Alabama	10,322	1.53%	45	Rhode Island	607	0.09%
21	Oregon	10,204	1.51%	46	North Dakota	580	0.09%
22	Maryland	9,494	1.41%	47	New Hampshire	562	0.08%
23	Wisconsin	9,124	1.35%	48	Maine	386	0.06%
24	Utah	8,402	1.25%	49	Wyoming	344	0.05%
25	New Mexico	6,984	1.04%	50	Vermont	308	0.05%
					District of Columbia	5,744	0.85%

Source: U.S. Department of Justice, Bureau of Justice Statistics
"Sourcebook of Criminal Justice Statistics 1992" (September 1993, NCJ–143496)

Public Juvenile Facilities Administered by State and Local Governments in 1991

National Total = 1,076 Facilities

RANK	STATE	FACILITIES	%	RANK	STATE	FACILITIES	%
1	California	106	9.85%	26	New Mexico	14	1.30%
2	New York	78	7.25%	27	Iowa	12	1.12%
3	Ohio	64	5.95%	27	Kansas	12	1.12%
4	Virginia	61	5.67%	29	South Carolina	11	1.02%
5	Texas	56	5.20%	29	Wisconsin	11	1.02%
6	New Jersey	53	4.93%	31	Arkansas	10	0.93%
7	Florida	51	4.74%	32	Colorado	9	0.84%
8	Michigan	46	4.28%	32	Massachusetts	9	0.84%
9	Missouri	42	3.90%	32	Nevada	9	0.84%
10	Pennsylvania	35	3.25%	35	Mississippi	8	0.74%
11	Kentucky	34	3.16%	36	South Dakota	6	0.56%
12	Indiana	33	3.07%	36	West Virginia	6	0.56%
13	Washington	30	2.79%	38	Alaska	5	0.46%
14	Georgia	28	2.60%	38	Montana	5	0.46%
15	North Carolina	24	2.23%	40	Connecticut	4	0.37%
16	Alabama	22	2.04%	40	Nebraska	4	0.37%
16	Tennessee	22	2.04%	42	Delaware	3	0.28%
18	Illinois	20	1.86%	42	Idaho	3	0.28%
19	Minnesota	19	1.77%	42	North Dakota	3	0.28%
20	Utah	17	1.58%	45	Hawaii	2	0.19%
21	Arizona	16	1.49%	45	New Hampshire	2	0.19%
21	Oklahoma	16	1.49%	45	Rhode Island	2	0.19%
23	Louisiana	15	1.39%	45	Wyoming	2	0.19%
23	Maryland	15	1.39%	49	Maine	1	0.09%
23	Oregon	15	1.39%	49	Vermont	1	0.09%
					District of Columbia	4	0.37%

Source: U.S. Department of Justice, Bureau of Justice Statistics
    "Sourcebook of Criminal Justice Statistics 1992" (September 1993, NCJ-143496)

Prison Boot Camp Participants in 1992

National Total = 5,822 Participants*

RANK	STATE	PARTICIPANTS	%	RANK	STATE	PARTICIPANTS	%
1	New York	1,500	25.76%	26	Wisconsin	40	0.69%
2	Georgia	800	13.74%	27	New Hampshire	32	0.55%
3	Oklahoma	415	7.13%	28	Wyoming	23	0.40%
4	Maryland	332	5.70%	29	Minnesota	12	0.21%
5	Texas	329	5.65%	30	Alaska**	0	0.00%
6	Idaho	236	4.05%	30	Connecticut**	0	0.00%
7	Mississippi	223	3.83%	30	Delaware**	0	0.00%
8	Illinois	215	3.69%	30	Hawaii**	0	0.00%
9	South Carolina	198	3.40%	30	Indiana**	0	0.00%
10	Michigan	160	2.75%	30	Iowa**	0	0.00%
11	Arkansas	150	2.58%	30	Kentucky**	0	0.00%
12	Alabama	140	2.40%	30	Maine**	0	0.00%
13	Colorado	114	1.96%	30	Missouri**	0	0.00%
14	Tennessee	103	1.77%	30	Montana**	0	0.00%
15	Massachusetts	95	1.63%	30	Nebraska**	0	0.00%
16	Florida	93	1.60%	30	New Jersey**	0	0.00%
17	Arizona	92	1.58%	30	New Mexico**	0	0.00%
18	North Carolina	82	1.41%	30	North Dakota**	0	0.00%
19	Virginia	79	1.36%	30	Oregon**	0	0.00%
20	Ohio	76	1.31%	30	Rhode Island**	0	0.00%
21	Kansas	66	1.13%	30	South Dakota**	0	0.00%
22	Louisiana	64	1.10%	30	Utah**	0	0.00%
23	Nevada	60	1.03%	30	Vermont**	0	0.00%
24	California	48	0.82%	30	Washington**	0	0.00%
25	Pennsylvania	45	0.77%	30	West Virginia**	0	0.00%
					District of Columbia**	0	0.00%

Source: U.S. Department of Justice, Office of Justice Programs

   "National Institute of Justice Journal" (November 1993)

Prison boot camps for adults. Does not include 192 male federal participants and 119 female federal participants. Average stay is 121 days.

**No program.*

III. DRUGS AND ALCOHOL

Table	Title
148	Marijuana Seized by the Federal Drug Enforcement Administration in 1992
149	Cocaine Removed by the Federal Drug Enforcement Agency in 1993
150	Clients in State–Supported Drug & Alcoholism Treatment Units in 1991
151	Cost per Client in State–Supported Drug & Alcoholism Treatment Units in 1991
152	Male Clients in State–Supported Drug & Alcoholism Treatment Units in 1992
153	Male Clients in State–Supported Drug & Alcoholism Treatment Units as a Percent of All Clients: 1991
154	Female Clients in State–Supported Drug & Alcoholism Treatment Units in 1991
155	Female Clients in State–Supported Drug & Alcoholism Treatment Units as a Percent of All Clients: 1991
156	White Clients in State–Supported Drug & Alcoholism Treatment Units in 1991
157	White Clients in State–Supported Drug & Alcoholism Treatment Units as a Percent of All Clients: 1991
158	Black Clients in State–Supported Drug & Alcoholism Treatment Units in 1991
159	Black Clients in State–Supported Drug & Alcoholism Treatment Units as a Percent of All Clients: 1991
160	Hispanic Clients in State–Supported Drug & Alcoholism Treatment Units in 1991
161	Hispanic Clients in State–Supported Drug & Alcoholism Treatment Units as a Percent of All Clients in 1991
162	Juveniles in State–Supported Drug & Alcoholism Treatment Units in 1991
163	Juveniles in State–Supported Drug & Alcoholism Treatment Units as a Percent of All Clients in 1991
164	Expenditures for State–Supported Alcohol and Drug Abuse Services in 1991
165	Per Capita Expenditures for State–Supported Alcohol and Drug Abuse Services in 1991
166	Expenditures for State–Supported Alcohol and Drug Abuse Treatment Programs in 1991
167	Per Capita Expenditures for State–Supported Alcohol and Drug Abuse Treatment Programs in 1991
168	Expenditures for State–Supported Alcohol and Drug Abuse Prevention Programs in 1991
169	Per Capita Expenditures for State–Supported Alcohol and Drug Abuse Prevention Programs in 1991
170	Drug and Alcoholism Treatment and Prevention Units in 1992

Marijuana Seized by the Federal Drug Enforcement Administration in 1992

National Total = 156,598.6 Kilograms*

RANK	STATE	KILOGRAMS	%	RANK	STATE	KILOGRAMS	%
1	Texas	74,328.6	47.46%	26	Nevada	15.7	0.01%
2	New Mexico	29,201.7	18.65%	27	Minnesota	15.6	0.01%
3	California	19,602.2	12.52%	28	Hawaii	15.4	0.01%
4	Arizona	14,679.3	9.37%	29	Oklahoma	12.2	0.01%
5	Florida	3,234.0	2.07%	30	Maryland	12.0	0.01%
6	Michigan	2,563.6	1.64%	31	Montana	11.7	0.01%
7	Alabama	2,499.8	1.60%	32	Colorado	11.4	0.01%
8	Illinois	852.2	0.54%	33	Alaska	11.3	0.01%
9	Louisiana	689.0	0.44%	34	Connecticut	11.0	0.01%
10	Georgia	654.3	0.42%	35	Massachusetts	7.3	0.00%
11	Ohio	299.1	0.19%	36	Rhode Island	2.0	0.00%
12	Missouri	265.0	0.17%	37	Iowa	1.8	0.00%
13	Kentucky	224.2	0.14%	38	Wyoming	1.2	0.00%
14	Kansas	190.8	0.12%	39	Utah	0.9	0.00%
15	North Carolina	172.8	0.11%	40	Arkansas	0.6	0.00%
16	New York	138.5	0.09%	40	Vermont	0.6	0.00%
17	South Carolina	132.2	0.08%	42	Mississippi	0.5	0.00%
18	Pennsylvania	122.1	0.08%	42	North Dakota	0.5	0.00%
19	Virginia	66.3	0.04%	44	West Virginia	0.3	0.00%
20	Tennessee	59.6	0.04%	45	New Jersey	0.2	0.00%
21	Nebraska	58.5	0.04%	46	Delaware	0.0	0.00%
22	Indiana	55.4	0.04%	46	Idaho	0.0	0.00%
23	Wisconsin	44.7	0.03%	46	Maine	0.0	0.00%
24	Washington	21.1	0.01%	46	New Hampshire	0.0	0.00%
25	Oregon	15.9	0.01%	46	South Dakota	0.0	0.00%
					District of Columbia	4.9	0.00%

Source: U.S. Department of Justice, Drug Enforcement Administration
   unpublished data

*Preliminary for fiscal year 1993. National total does not include 6,291 kilograms removed by the DEA in U.S. territories or elsewhere. A kilogram is approximately 2.2 pounds.

Cocaine Removed by the Federal Drug Enforcement Agency in 1993

National Total = 51,991.4 Kilograms*

RANK	STATE	KILOGRAMS	%	RANK	STATE	KILOGRAMS	%
1	Florida	19,553.2	37.61%	26	Wisconsin	52.7	0.10%
2	California	13,258.6	25.50%	27	Hawaii	52.0	0.10%
3	Texas	9,786.4	18.82%	28	Michigan	49.6	0.10%
4	New York	2,067.9	3.98%	29	South Carolina	49.3	0.09%
5	Tennessee	1,104.6	2.12%	30	Virginia	26.9	0.05%
6	Utah	1,028.7	1.98%	31	Kansas	18.3	0.04%
7	Arizona	868.2	1.67%	32	Massachusetts	14.4	0.03%
8	Nebraska	777.2	1.49%	33	North Carolina	10.7	0.02%
9	New Jersey	477.4	0.92%	34	Kentucky	8.5	0.02%
10	Ohio	415.1	0.80%	35	Delaware	7.4	0.01%
11	Oregon	332.3	0.64%	36	Colorado	6.6	0.01%
12	Missouri	322.0	0.62%	37	Connecticut	6.4	0.01%
13	New Mexico	228.7	0.44%	38	Alaska	5.9	0.01%
14	Illinois	226.2	0.44%	39	Indiana	5.1	0.01%
15	Maryland	220.1	0.42%	40	South Dakota	3.8	0.01%
16	Nevada	187.6	0.36%	41	Montana	2.4	0.00%
17	Alabama	131.6	0.25%	42	Arkansas	2.3	0.00%
18	Georgia	107.9	0.21%	43	Minnesota	2.1	0.00%
19	Mississippi	102.7	0.20%	44	Rhode Island	1.0	0.00%
20	Pennsylvania	96.3	0.19%	45	North Dakota	0.4	0.00%
21	Oklahoma	94.3	0.18%	45	West Virginia	0.4	0.00%
22	Louisiana	71.8	0.14%	47	Maine	0.1	0.00%
23	Vermont	61.7	0.12%	47	New Hampshire	0.1	0.00%
24	Iowa	60.1	0.12%	47	Wyoming	0.1	0.00%
25	Washington	58.6	0.11%	50	Idaho	0.0	0.00%

District of Columbia 25.7 0.05%

Source: U.S. Department of Justice, Drug Enforcement Agency
    unpublished data

*Preliminary for fiscal year 1993. National total does not include 3,354 kilograms removed by the DEA in U.S. territories or elsewhere. A kilogram is approximately 2.2 pounds.

Clients in State-Supported Drug & Alcoholism Treatment Units in 1991

National Total = 763,115 Clients*

RANK	STATE	CLIENTS	%	RANK	STATE	CLIENTS	%
1	California	163,237	21.39%	26	Nebraska	5,294	0.69%
2	New York	94,440	12.38%	27	Tennessee	5,247	0.69%
3	Michigan	40,133	5.26%	28	Oklahoma	4,816	0.63%
4	Texas	29,400	3.85%	29	Rhode Island	4,780	0.63%
5	Florida	28,359	3.72%	30	Kansas	4,658	0.61%
6	Ohio	28,325	3.71%	31	Iowa	4,613	0.60%
7	Illinois	26,673	3.50%	32	Utah	4,308	0.56%
8	Pennsylvania	22,637	2.97%	33	Mississippi	4,123	0.54%
9	Washington	22,345	2.93%	34	Minnesota	4,055	0.53%
10	New Jersey	21,724	2.85%	35	New Mexico	3,616	0.47%
11	Maryland	21,627	2.83%	36	Alabama	3,334	0.44%
12	Massachusetts	19,578	2.57%	37	Arkansas	3,042	0.40%
13	North Carolina	17,406	2.28%	38	West Virginia	2,844	0.37%
14	Virginia	16,595	2.17%	39	Maine	2,160	0.28%
15	Colorado	16,523	2.17%	40	Delaware	2,100	0.28%
16	Oregon	15,787	2.07%	41	Nevada	1,809	0.24%
17	Wisconsin	14,631	1.92%	42	Idaho	1,799	0.24%
18	Louisiana	13,468	1.76%	43	Vermont	1,743	0.23%
19	Indiana	12,801	1.68%	44	Wyoming	1,703	0.22%
20	Arizona	11,629	1.52%	45	Montana	1,480	0.19%
21	South Carolina	11,239	1.47%	46	Alaska	1,381	0.18%
22	Connecticut	9,709	1.27%	47	South Dakota	1,277	0.17%
23	Missouri	9,329	1.22%	48	North Dakota	1,095	0.14%
24	Kentucky	8,910	1.17%	49	New Hampshire	1,016	0.13%
25	Georgia	7,369	0.97%	50	Hawaii	938	0.12%
					District of Columbia	6,010	0.79%

Source: U.S. Department of Health and Human Services, Substance Abuse and Mental Health Services Administration

"National Drug and Alcoholism Treatment Unit Survey 1991, Main Findings Report" (1993)

*Does not include 31,071 clients in federal units or 17,633 in U.S. territories.

Cost per Client in State–Supported Drug & Alcoholism Treatment Units in 1991

National Rate = $3,156 per Client*

RANK	STATE	COST	RANK	STATE	COST
1	Alaska	$18,041	26	West Virginia	$3,157
2	Minnesota	13,914	27	Rhode Island	3,144
3	Hawaii	9,694	28	Kansas	3,116
4	Montana	8,588	29	Missouri	3,080
5	Connecticut	7,218	30	Utah	2,854
6	Georgia	6,193	31	Delaware	2,850
7	Wisconsin	6,065	32	New Jersey	2,815
8	New York	5,275	33	Arkansas	2,676
9	Iowa	4,619	34	Indiana	2,644
10	Pennsylvania	4,433	35	Ohio	2,616
11	Florida	4,372	36	Arizona	2,593
12	Alabama	4,223	37	Washington	2,318
13	Illinois	4,025	38	South Carolina	2,272
14	Massachusetts	3,949	39	North Carolina	2,137
15	Maine	3,580	40	Idaho	2,039
16	North Dakota	3,576	41	Kentucky	1,868
17	Vermont	3,524	42	Nebraska	1,849
18	Oklahoma	3,515	43	Mississippi	1,825
19	Tennessee	3,476	44	Colorado	1,762
20	Virginia	3,457	45	California	1,720
21	Maryland	3,453	46	Texas	1,717
22	New Hampshire	3,388	47	Louisiana	1,612
23	New Mexico	3,382	48	Michigan	1,602
24	South Dakota	3,332	49	Oregon	1,381
25	Nevada	3,250	–	Wyoming**	N/A

District of Columbia   5,741

Source: Morgan Quitno Corporation using data from U.S. Department of Health & Human Services, Substance Abuse & Mental Health Services Admin.
"National Drug and Alcoholism Treatment Unit Survey 1991, Main Findings Report" (1993) and
"State Resources and Services Related to Alcohol and Other Drug Abuse Problems, Fiscal Year 1991" (1992)
*Does not include clients and expenditures in federal and territorial clinics.
**Not available.

Male Clients in State-Supported Drug & Alcoholism Treatment Units in 1992

National Total = 523,046 Male Clients*

RANK	STATE	CLIENTS	%	RANK	STATE	CLIENTS	%
1	California	119,377	22.82%	26	Tennessee	3,496	0.67%
2	New York	62,106	11.87%	27	Nebraska	3,486	0.67%
3	Michigan	25,459	4.87%	28	Kansas	3,421	0.65%
4	Texas	22,199	4.24%	29	Iowa	3,209	0.61%
5	Ohio	19,222	3.68%	30	Oklahoma	3,079	0.59%
6	Florida	18,511	3.54%	31	Utah	3,018	0.58%
7	Illinois	16,605	3.17%	32	Rhode Island	2,920	0.56%
8	Maryland	16,013	3.06%	33	Minnesota	2,807	0.54%
9	Washington	15,370	2.94%	34	Alabama	2,547	0.49%
10	Pennsylvania	14,236	2.72%	35	Mississippi	2,541	0.49%
11	New Jersey	13,336	2.55%	36	New Mexico	2,388	0.46%
12	North Carolina	12,918	2.47%	37	Arkansas	2,246	0.43%
13	Massachusetts	11,993	2.29%	38	West Virginia	2,119	0.41%
14	Louisiana	11,530	2.20%	39	Delaware	1,454	0.28%
15	Colorado	11,342	2.17%	40	Maine	1,385	0.26%
16	Virginia	10,833	2.07%	41	Nevada	1,247	0.24%
17	Oregon	10,515	2.01%	42	Vermont	1,192	0.23%
18	Wisconsin	9,380	1.79%	43	Wyoming	1,099	0.21%
19	Indiana	9,192	1.76%	44	Montana	1,058	0.20%
20	South Carolina	8,633	1.65%	45	Idaho	1,028	0.20%
21	Arizona	7,573	1.45%	46	South Dakota	873	0.17%
22	Connecticut	6,916	1.32%	47	Alaska	826	0.16%
23	Missouri	6,592	1.26%	48	North Dakota	738	0.14%
24	Kentucky	6,286	1.20%	49	New Hampshire	714	0.14%
25	Georgia	3,923	0.75%	50	Hawaii	652	0.12%
					District of Columbia	3,443	0.66%

Source: U.S. Department of Health and Human Services, Substance Abuse and Mental Health Services Administration
"National Drug and Alcoholism Treatment Unit Survey 1991, Main Findings Report" (1993)
*Does not include 22,849 clients in federal units or 16,493 clients in U.S. territories.

Male Clients in State–Supported Drug & Alcoholism Treatment Units as a Percent of All Clients: 1991

National Percent = 68.54% Males*

RANK	STATE	PERCENT		RANK	STATE	PERCENT
1	Louisiana	85.61		26	South Dakota	68.36
2	South Carolina	76.81		27	Ohio	67.86
3	Alabama	76.39		28	North Dakota	67.40
4	Texas	75.51		29	Tennessee	66.63
5	West Virginia	74.51		30	Oregon	66.61
6	North Carolina	74.22		31	New Mexico	66.04
7	Maryland	74.04		32	Nebraska	65.85
8	Arkansas	73.83		33	New York	65.76
9	Kansas	73.44		34	Virginia	65.28
10	California	73.13		35	Florida	65.27
11	Indiana	71.81		36	Arizona	65.12
12	Montana	71.49		37	Wyoming	64.53
13	Connecticut	71.23		38	Maine	64.12
14	Missouri	70.66		39	Wisconsin	64.11
15	Kentucky	70.55		40	Oklahoma	63.93
16	New Hampshire	70.28		41	Michigan	63.44
17	Utah	70.06		42	Pennsylvania	62.89
18	Iowa	69.56		43	Illinois	62.25
19	Hawaii	69.51		44	Mississippi	61.63
20	Delaware	69.24		45	New Jersey	61.39
21	Minnesota	69.22		46	Massachusetts	61.26
22	Nevada	68.93		47	Rhode Island	61.09
23	Washington	68.78		48	Alaska	59.81
24	Colorado	68.64		49	Idaho	57.14
25	Vermont	68.39		50	Georgia	53.24

District of Columbia   57.29

Source: Morgan Quitno Corporation using data from U.S. Department of Health & Human Services, Substance Abuse & Mental Health Services Admin.
"National Drug and Alcoholism Treatment Unit Survey 1991, Main Findings Report" (1993)
*Does not include clients whose sex was not reported or clients in federal and territorial clinics.

Female Clients in State–Supported Drug & Alcoholism Treatment Units in 1991

National Total = 209,662 Female Clients*

RANK	STATE	CLIENTS	%	RANK	STATE	CLIENTS	%
1	California	40,954	19.53%	26	Nebraska	1,677	0.80%
2	New York	30,726	14.66%	27	Georgia	1,671	0.80%
3	Michigan	11,098	5.29%	28	Tennessee	1,667	0.80%
4	Ohio	8,846	4.22%	29	Oklahoma	1,502	0.72%
5	Illinois	8,466	4.04%	30	Iowa	1,286	0.61%
6	Florida	8,176	3.90%	31	Utah	1,278	0.61%
7	Massachusetts	7,161	3.42%	32	Kansas	1,148	0.55%
8	Washington	6,717	3.20%	32	Minnesota	1,148	0.55%
9	New Jersey	6,571	3.13%	34	New Mexico	859	0.41%
10	Pennsylvania	6,362	3.03%	35	Mississippi	834	0.40%
11	Texas	5,919	2.82%	36	Alabama	787	0.38%
12	Maryland	5,490	2.62%	37	Arkansas	775	0.37%
13	Oregon	4,684	2.23%	38	West Virginia	682	0.33%
14	Virginia	4,315	2.06%	39	Wyoming	604	0.29%
15	North Carolina	4,130	1.97%	40	Nevada	556	0.27%
16	Wisconsin	4,048	1.93%	41	Maine	547	0.26%
17	Arizona	3,723	1.78%	42	Delaware	540	0.26%
18	Indiana	3,578	1.71%	43	Vermont	507	0.24%
19	Colorado	3,374	1.61%	44	Montana	422	0.20%
20	Missouri	2,708	1.29%	45	Idaho	410	0.20%
21	Connecticut	2,646	1.26%	46	South Dakota	384	0.18%
22	South Carolina	2,504	1.19%	47	North Dakota	346	0.17%
23	Louisiana	1,938	0.92%	48	Alaska	344	0.16%
24	Rhode Island	1,846	0.88%	49	New Hampshire	301	0.14%
25	Kentucky	1,807	0.86%	50	Hawaii	286	0.14%
					District of Columbia	1,314	0.63%

Source: U.S. Department of Health and Human Services, Substance Abuse and Mental Health Services Administration
"National Drug and Alcoholism Treatment Unit Survey 1991, Main Findings Report" (1993)
*Does not include 2,958 clients in federal units or 1,061 clients in U.S. territories.

Female Clients in State–Supported Drug & Alcoholism Treatment Units as a Percent of All Clients: 1991

National Percent = 27.47% Female*

RANK	STATE	PERCENT		RANK	STATE	PERCENT
1	Rhode Island	38.62		26	Indiana	27.95
2	Massachusetts	36.58		27	Iowa	27.88
3	Wyoming	35.47		28	Wisconsin	27.67
4	New York	32.53		29	Michigan	27.65
5	Arizona	32.01		30	Connecticut	27.25
6	Tennessee	31.77		31	Virginia	26.00
7	Illinois	31.74		32	Delaware	25.71
8	Nebraska	31.68		33	Arkansas	25.48
9	North Dakota	31.60		34	Maryland	25.38
10	Ohio	31.23		35	Maine	25.32
11	Oklahoma	31.19		36	California	25.09
12	Nevada	30.74		37	Alaska	24.91
13	Hawaii	30.49		38	Kansas	24.65
14	New Jersey	30.25		39	West Virginia	23.98
15	South Dakota	30.07		40	New Mexico	23.76
16	Washington	30.06		41	North Carolina	23.73
17	Oregon	29.67		42	Alabama	23.61
17	Utah	29.67		43	Idaho	22.79
19	New Hampshire	29.63		44	Georgia	22.68
20	Vermont	29.09		45	South Carolina	22.28
21	Missouri	29.03		46	Colorado	20.42
22	Florida	28.83		47	Kentucky	20.28
23	Montana	28.51		48	Mississippi	20.23
24	Minnesota	28.31		49	Texas	20.13
25	Pennsylvania	28.10		50	Louisiana	14.39

District of Columbia   21.86

Source: Morgan Quitno Corporation using data from U.S. Department of Health & Human Services, Substance Abuse & Mental Health Services Admin.
"National Drug and Alcoholism Treatment Unit Survey 1991, Main Findings Report" (1993)
*Does not include clients whose sex was not reported or clients in federal and territorial clinics.

White Clients in State–Supported Drug & Alcoholism Treatment Units in 1991

National Total = 442,289 White Clients*

RANK	STATE	CLIENTS	%	RANK	STATE	CLIENTS	%
1	California	83,972	18.99%	26	Iowa	4,052	0.92%
2	New York	46,909	10.61%	27	Utah	3,560	0.80%
3	Michigan	24,244	5.48%	28	Rhode Island	3,497	0.79%
4	Ohio	20,160	4.56%	29	Oklahoma	3,495	0.79%
5	Washington	17,689	4.00%	30	Kansas	3,353	0.76%
6	Florida	17,032	3.85%	31	Minnesota	3,291	0.74%
7	Illinois	15,233	3.44%	32	Georgia	2,942	0.67%
8	Massachusetts	13,658	3.09%	33	Louisiana	2,673	0.60%
9	Pennsylvania	13,376	3.02%	34	West Virginia	2,592	0.59%
10	Maryland	13,259	3.00%	35	Alabama	2,104	0.48%
11	Oregon	12,959	2.93%	36	Maine	1,876	0.42%
12	New Jersey	11,565	2.61%	37	Arkansas	1,871	0.42%
13	Wisconsin	10,702	2.42%	38	Vermont	1,598	0.36%
14	Indiana	10,315	2.33%	39	Wyoming	1,473	0.33%
15	North Carolina	10,194	2.30%	40	Nevada	1,382	0.31%
16	Texas	9,605	2.17%	41	Mississippi	1,307	0.30%
17	Colorado	9,456	2.14%	42	Idaho	1,293	0.29%
18	Virginia	9,277	2.10%	43	Montana	1,275	0.29%
19	Arizona	7,508	1.70%	44	New Mexico	1,140	0.26%
20	Kentucky	7,282	1.65%	45	New Hampshire	948	0.21%
21	South Carolina	7,168	1.62%	46	South Dakota	905	0.20%
22	Missouri	6,806	1.54%	47	North Dakota	874	0.20%
23	Connecticut	5,740	1.30%	48	Delaware	719	0.16%
24	Nebraska	4,361	0.99%	49	Alaska	704	0.16%
25	Tennessee	4,093	0.93%	50	Hawaii	382	0.09%
					District of Columbia	420	0.09%

Source: U.S. Department of Health and Human Services, Substance Abuse and Mental Health Services Administration
"National Drug and Alcoholism Treatment Unit Survey 1991, Main Findings Report" (1993)
*Does not include 9,666 clients in federal units or 216 clients in U.S. territories.

White Clients in State–Supported Drug & Alcoholism Treatment Units as a Percent of All Clients: 1991

National Percent = 57.96% White*

RANK	STATE	PERCENT
1	New Hampshire	93.31
2	Vermont	91.68
3	West Virginia	91.14
4	Iowa	87.84
5	Maine	86.85
6	Wyoming	86.49
7	Montana	86.15
8	Utah	82.64
9	Nebraska	82.38
10	Oregon	82.09
11	Kentucky	81.73
12	Minnesota	81.16
13	Indiana	80.58
14	North Dakota	79.82
15	Washington	79.16
16	Tennessee	78.01
17	Nevada	76.40
18	Rhode Island	73.16
19	Wisconsin	73.15
20	Missouri	72.96
21	Oklahoma	72.57
22	Kansas	71.98
23	Idaho	71.87
24	Ohio	71.17
25	South Dakota	70.87

RANK	STATE	PERCENT
26	Massachusetts	69.76
27	Arizona	64.56
28	South Carolina	63.78
29	Alabama	63.11
30	Arkansas	61.51
31	Maryland	61.31
32	Michigan	60.41
33	Florida	60.06
34	Connecticut	59.12
35	Pennsylvania	59.09
36	North Carolina	58.57
37	Colorado	57.23
38	Illinois	57.11
39	Virginia	55.90
40	New Jersey	53.24
41	California	51.44
42	Alaska	50.98
43	New York	49.67
44	Hawaii	40.72
45	Georgia	39.92
46	Delaware	34.24
47	Texas	32.67
48	Mississippi	31.70
49	New Mexico	31.53
50	Louisiana	19.85

District of Columbia 6.99

Source: Morgan Quitno Corporation using data from U.S. Department of Health & Human Services, Substance Abuse & Mental Health Services Admin.
"National Drug and Alcoholism Treatment Unit Survey 1991, Main Findings Report" (1993)
*Does not include clients whose race was not reported or clients in federal and territorial clinics.

Black Clients in State-Supported Drug & Alcoholism Treatment Units in 1991

National Total = 150,301 Black Clients*

RANK	STATE	CLIENTS	%	RANK	STATE	CLIENTS	%
1	New York	26,327	17.52%	26	Tennessee	965	0.64%
2	California	20,015	13.32%	27	Kentucky	836	0.56%
3	Michigan	9,963	6.63%	28	Oregon	729	0.49%
4	Illinois	8,048	5.35%	29	Arizona	696	0.46%
5	Maryland	7,756	5.16%	30	Kansas	646	0.43%
6	Florida	7,063	4.70%	31	Oklahoma	559	0.37%
7	Ohio	6,591	4.39%	32	Rhode Island	537	0.36%
8	North Carolina	6,212	4.13%	33	Delaware	435	0.29%
9	New Jersey	5,568	3.70%	34	Nebraska	398	0.26%
10	Pennsylvania	5,243	3.49%	35	Minnesota	350	0.23%
11	Virginia	5,239	3.49%	36	Iowa	285	0.19%
12	South Carolina	3,879	2.58%	37	Nevada	190	0.13%
13	Texas	3,694	2.46%	38	West Virginia	178	0.12%
14	Louisiana	2,921	1.94%	39	Utah	123	0.08%
15	Massachusetts	2,544	1.69%	40	New Mexico	72	0.05%
16	Georgia	2,539	1.69%	41	Alaska	33	0.02%
17	Connecticut	2,306	1.53%	42	Hawaii	28	0.02%
18	Missouri	2,295	1.53%	42	New Hampshire	28	0.02%
19	Indiana	2,172	1.45%	44	Vermont	24	0.02%
20	Wisconsin	1,961	1.30%	45	Wyoming	19	0.01%
21	Washington	1,661	1.11%	46	Maine	15	0.01%
22	Mississippi	1,609	1.07%	47	Montana	5	0.00%
23	Colorado	1,362	0.91%	47	South Dakota	5	0.00%
24	Alabama	1,208	0.80%	49	Idaho	4	0.00%
25	Arkansas	1,112	0.74%	49	North Dakota	4	0.00%
					District of Columbia	3,849	2.56%

Source: U.S. Department of Health and Human Services, Substance Abuse and Mental Health Services Administration

"National Drug and Alcoholism Treatment Unit Survey 1991, Main Findings Report" (1993)

*Does not include 5,560 clients in federal units or 153 clients in U.S. territories.

Black Clients in State-Supported Drug & Alcoholism Treatment Units as a Percent of All Clients: 1991

National Percent = 19.70% Black*

RANK	STATE	PERCENT	RANK	STATE	PERCENT
1	Mississippi	39.02	26	California	12.26
2	Arkansas	36.55	27	Oklahoma	11.61
3	Alabama	36.23	28	Rhode Island	11.23
4	Maryland	35.86	29	Nevada	10.50
5	North Carolina	35.69	30	Kentucky	9.38
6	South Carolina	34.51	31	Minnesota	8.63
7	Georgia	34.46	32	Colorado	8.24
8	Virginia	31.57	33	Nebraska	7.52
9	Illinois	30.17	34	Washington	7.43
10	New York	27.88	35	West Virginia	6.26
11	New Jersey	25.63	36	Iowa	6.18
12	Florida	24.91	37	Arizona	5.99
13	Michigan	24.82	38	Oregon	4.62
14	Missouri	24.60	39	Hawaii	2.99
15	Connecticut	23.75	40	Utah	2.86
16	Ohio	23.27	41	New Hampshire	2.76
17	Pennsylvania	23.16	42	Alaska	2.39
18	Louisiana	21.69	43	New Mexico	1.99
19	Delaware	20.71	44	Vermont	1.38
20	Tennessee	18.39	45	Wyoming	1.12
21	Indiana	16.97	46	Maine	0.69
22	Kansas	13.87	47	South Dakota	0.39
23	Wisconsin	13.40	48	North Dakota	0.37
24	Massachusetts	12.99	49	Montana	0.34
25	Texas	12.56	50	Idaho	0.22

District of Columbia   64.04

Source: Morgan Quitno Corporation using data from U.S. Department of Health & Human Services, Substance Abuse & Mental Health Services Admin.
"National Drug and Alcoholism Treatment Unit Survey 1991, Main Findings Report" (1993)
*Does not include clients whose race was not reported or clients in federal and territorial clinics.

Hispanic Clients in State–Supported Drug & Alcoholism Treatment Units in 1991

National Total = 97,728 Hispanic Clients*

RANK	STATE	CLIENTS	%	RANK	STATE	CLIENTS	%
1	California	47,609	48.94%	26	Nevada	139	0.14%
2	New York	18,490	19.01%	27	Missouri	127	0.13%
3	Texas	5,078	5.22%	28	North Carolina	107	0.11%
4	Colorado	4,153	4.27%	29	Idaho	89	0.09%
5	Arizona	2,420	2.49%	30	Iowa	68	0.07%
6	Florida	2,248	2.31%	30	Minnesota	68	0.07%
7	New Jersey	2,093	2.15%	32	Louisiana	67	0.07%
8	Massachusetts	1,850	1.90%	33	Hawaii	37	0.04%
9	Illinois	1,722	1.77%	33	South Carolina	37	0.04%
10	New Mexico	1,517	1.56%	35	Alaska	23	0.02%
11	Connecticut	1,406	1.45%	35	Georgia	23	0.02%
12	Oregon	1,054	1.08%	35	Oklahoma	23	0.02%
13	Michigan	1,026	1.05%	38	Arkansas	21	0.02%
14	Washington	930	0.96%	39	Montana	19	0.02%
15	Pennsylvania	816	0.84%	40	Delaware	18	0.02%
16	Ohio	634	0.65%	41	New Hampshire	17	0.02%
17	Wisconsin	435	0.45%	42	Kentucky	16	0.02%
18	Maryland	415	0.43%	43	Vermont	12	0.01%
19	Utah	398	0.41%	44	Alabama	11	0.01%
20	Virginia	359	0.37%	44	Tennessee	11	0.01%
21	Kansas	355	0.36%	46	West Virginia	9	0.01%
22	Rhode Island	301	0.31%	47	Maine	5	0.01%
23	Nebraska	234	0.24%	47	Mississippi	5	0.01%
24	Indiana	197	0.20%	47	North Dakota	5	0.01%
25	Wyoming	148	0.15%	50	South Dakota	4	0.00%
					District of Columbia	429	0.44%

Source: U.S. Department of Health and Human Services, Substance Abuse and Mental Health Services Administration
"National Drug and Alcoholism Treatment Unit Survey 1991, Main Findings Report" (1993)
*Does not include 1,576 clients in federal units or 5,130 clients in U.S. territories.

Hispanic Clients in State–Supported Drug & Alcoholism Treatment Units as a Percent of All Clients in 1991

National Percent = 12.81% Hispanic

RANK	STATE	PERCENT	RANK	STATE	PERCENT
1	New Mexico	41.95	26	Virginia	2.16
2	California	29.17	27	Maryland	1.92
3	Colorado	25.13	28	Minnesota	1.68
4	Arizona	20.81	29	Alaska	1.67
5	New York	19.58	29	New Hampshire	1.67
6	Texas	17.27	31	Indiana	1.54
7	Connecticut	14.48	32	Iowa	1.47
8	New Jersey	9.63	33	Missouri	1.36
9	Massachusetts	9.45	34	Montana	1.28
10	Utah	9.24	35	Delaware	0.86
11	Wyoming	8.69	36	Arkansas	0.69
12	Florida	7.93	36	Vermont	0.69
13	Nevada	7.68	38	North Carolina	0.61
14	Kansas	7.62	39	Louisiana	0.50
15	Oregon	6.68	40	Oklahoma	0.48
16	Illinois	6.46	41	North Dakota	0.46
17	Rhode Island	6.30	42	Alabama	0.33
18	Idaho	4.95	42	South Carolina	0.33
19	Nebraska	4.42	44	West Virginia	0.32
20	Washington	4.16	45	Georgia	0.31
21	Hawaii	3.94	45	South Dakota	0.31
22	Pennsylvania	3.60	47	Maine	0.23
23	Wisconsin	2.97	48	Tennessee	0.21
24	Michigan	2.56	49	Kentucky	0.18
25	Ohio	2.24	50	Mississippi	0.12

District of Columbia   7.14

Source: Morgan Quitno Corporation using data from U.S. Department of Health & Human Services, Substance Abuse & Mental Health Services Admin. "National Drug and Alcoholism Treatment Unit Survey 1991, Main Findings Report" (1993)
*Does not include clients whose race was not reported or clients in federal and territorial clinics.

Juveniles in State–Supported Drug & Alcoholism Treatment Units in 1991

National Total = 41,709 Juvenile Clients*

RANK	STATE	CLIENTS	%	RANK	STATE	CLIENTS	%
1	California	6,414	15.38%	26	Missouri	396	0.95%
2	New York	3,150	7.55%	27	Kansas	370	0.89%
3	Ohio	3,056	7.33%	28	Minnesota	362	0.87%
4	Illinois	2,403	5.76%	29	Louisiana	353	0.85%
5	Florida	2,050	4.92%	30	New Mexico	346	0.83%
6	Michigan	1,791	4.29%	31	Rhode Island	289	0.69%
7	Texas	1,778	4.26%	32	Georgia	276	0.66%
8	Pennsylvania	1,317	3.16%	33	Oklahoma	270	0.65%
9	Oregon	1,258	3.02%	34	West Virginia	260	0.62%
10	New Jersey	1,198	2.87%	35	Connecticut	244	0.59%
11	Washington	1,179	2.83%	36	South Dakota	242	0.58%
12	Maryland	1,142	2.74%	37	Wyoming	229	0.55%
13	Virginia	982	2.35%	38	Idaho	227	0.54%
14	Wisconsin	933	2.24%	39	Arkansas	209	0.50%
15	Arizona	883	2.12%	40	Nevada	203	0.49%
16	Colorado	811	1.94%	41	Alabama	173	0.41%
17	North Carolina	779	1.87%	42	New Hampshire	161	0.39%
18	Indiana	739	1.77%	43	Montana	149	0.36%
19	Massachusetts	701	1.68%	44	Mississippi	130	0.31%
20	Nebraska	652	1.56%	45	Hawaii	129	0.31%
21	Utah	646	1.55%	46	North Dakota	122	0.29%
22	South Carolina	609	1.46%	47	Alaska	103	0.25%
23	Kentucky	604	1.45%	48	Delaware	101	0.24%
24	Tennessee	512	1.23%	49	Maine	97	0.23%
25	Iowa	492	1.18%	50	Vermont	75	0.18%
					District of Columbia	114	0.27%

Source: U.S. Department of Health and Human Services, Substance Abuse and Mental Health Services Administration
    "National Drug and Alcoholism Treatment Unit Survey 1991, Main Findings Report" (1993)
*Youths 17 years and younger. Does not include 716 clients in federal units or 1,273 in U.S. territories.

Juveniles in State–Supported Drug & Alcoholism Treatment Units as a Percent of All Clients in 1991

National Rate = 5.47%

RANK	STATE	PERCENT	RANK	STATE	PERCENT
1	South Dakota	18.95	26	Rhode Island	6.05
2	New Hampshire	15.85	26	Texas	6.05
3	Utah	15.00	28	Virginia	5.92
4	Hawaii	13.75	29	Pennsylvania	5.82
5	Wyoming	13.45	30	Indiana	5.77
6	Idaho	12.62	31	Oklahoma	5.61
7	Nebraska	12.32	32	New Jersey	5.51
8	Nevada	11.22	33	South Carolina	5.42
9	North Dakota	11.14	34	Maryland	5.28
10	Ohio	10.79	34	Washington	5.28
11	Iowa	10.67	36	Alabama	5.19
12	Montana	10.07	37	Colorado	4.91
13	Tennessee	9.76	38	Delaware	4.81
14	New Mexico	9.57	39	Maine	4.49
15	West Virginia	9.14	40	North Carolina	4.48
16	Illinois	9.01	41	Michigan	4.46
17	Minnesota	8.93	42	Vermont	4.30
18	Oregon	7.97	43	Missouri	4.24
19	Kansas	7.94	44	California	3.93
20	Arizona	7.59	45	Georgia	3.75
21	Alaska	7.46	46	Massachusetts	3.58
22	Florida	7.23	47	New York	3.34
23	Arkansas	6.87	48	Mississippi	3.15
24	Kentucky	6.78	49	Louisiana	2.62
25	Wisconsin	6.38	50	Connecticut	2.51

	District of Columbia	1.90

Source: Morgan Quitno Corporation using data from U.S. Department of Health & Human Services, Substance Abuse & Mental Health Services Admin.
    "National Drug and Alcoholism Treatment Unit Survey 1991, Main Findings Report" (1993)
*Youths 17 years and younger. Does not include clients in federal units or in U.S. territories.

Expenditures for State-Supported Alcohol and Drug Abuse Services in 1991

National Total= $3,214,410,870*

RANK	STATE	EXPENDITURES	%	RANK	STATE	EXPENDITURES	%
1	New York	$659,047,664	20.50%	26	Tennessee	$27,024,300	0.84%
2	California	410,507,929	12.77%	27	Iowa	26,944,682	0.84%
3	Pennsylvania	141,852,490	4.41%	28	Alabama	25,644,899	0.80%
4	Florida	141,227,749	4.39%	29	Louisiana	24,304,510	0.76%
5	Illinois	137,775,529	4.29%	30	Kentucky	21,755,963	0.68%
6	Wisconsin	133,255,600	4.15%	31	Utah	21,399,197	0.67%
7	Ohio	117,157,450	3.64%	32	Oklahoma	20,688,985	0.64%
8	Michigan	94,243,121	2.93%	33	Rhode Island	20,626,354	0.64%
9	Maryland	90,431,983	2.81%	34	Kansas	18,940,800	0.59%
10	Massachusetts	87,652,000	2.73%	35	New Mexico	16,453,936	0.51%
11	Texas	86,933,921	2.70%	36	Montana	15,421,058	0.48%
12	New Jersey	85,316,000	2.65%	37	Nebraska	12,470,370	0.39%
13	Connecticut	81,547,898	2.54%	38	West Virginia	11,596,400	0.36%
14	Virginia	68,468,244	2.13%	39	Hawaii	11,562,115	0.36%
15	Washington	63,139,969	1.96%	40	Mississippi	10,394,474	0.32%
16	Minnesota	62,793,433	1.95%	41	Maine	10,346,730	0.32%
17	Georgia	51,682,152	1.61%	42	Arkansas	9,861,550	0.31%
18	North Carolina	48,786,750	1.52%	43	Nevada	8,674,209	0.27%
19	Oregon	42,002,961	1.31%	44	Vermont	8,153,422	0.25%
20	Indiana	41,666,860	1.30%	45	Delaware	6,903,274	0.21%
21	South Carolina	40,202,159	1.25%	46	South Dakota	6,246,726	0.19%
22	Colorado	39,045,786	1.21%	47	Idaho	5,179,122	0.16%
23	Missouri	35,249,096	1.10%	48	New Hampshire	5,154,525	0.16%
24	Arizona	34,156,831	1.06%	49	North Dakota	4,923,567	0.15%
25	Alaska	29,413,909	0.92%	–	Wyoming**	N/A	N/A

| | District of Columbia | 40,252,218 | 1.25% |

Source: U.S. Department of Health and Human Services, Substance Abuse and Mental Health Services Administration and
National Association of State Alcohol and Drug Abuse Directors, Inc.
"State Resources and Services Related to Alcohol and Other Drug Abuse Problems, Fiscal Year 1991" (1992)
*Funds for treatment and prevention programs as well as "other" costs (administration, research capital costs, etc.) Total does not include
$31,183,313 in Puerto Rico and $739,765 in Guam.
**Not available.

Per Capita Expenditures for State–Supported Alcohol and Drug Abuse Services in 1991

National Per Capita = $12.75*

RANK	STATE	PER CAPITA	RANK	STATE	PER CAPITA
1	Alaska	$51.60	26	Michigan	$10.06
2	New York	36.50	27	Iowa	9.64
3	Wisconsin	26.89	28	Arizona	9.11
4	Connecticut	24.78	29	South Dakota	8.89
5	Rhode Island	20.54	30	Maine	8.38
6	Montana	19.09	31	Nebraska	7.83
7	Maryland	18.61	32	Georgia	7.80
8	Massachusetts	14.62	33	North Dakota	7.75
9	Vermont	14.38	34	Kansas	7.59
10	Oregon	14.37	35	Indiana	7.43
11	Minnesota	14.17	36	North Carolina	7.24
12	California	13.51	37	Missouri	6.83
13	Washington	12.58	38	Nevada	6.76
14	Utah	12.09	39	Oklahoma	6.52
15	Illinois	11.94	40	West Virginia	6.44
16	Pennsylvania	11.86	41	Alabama	6.27
17	Colorado	11.56	42	Kentucky	5.86
18	South Carolina	11.29	43	Louisiana	5.72
19	New Jersey	10.99	44	Tennessee	5.46
20	Virginia	10.89	45	Texas	5.01
21	Ohio	10.71	46	Idaho	4.98
22	Florida	10.64	47	New Hampshire	4.66
23	New Mexico	10.63	48	Arkansas	4.16
24	Hawaii	10.19	49	Mississippi	4.01
25	Delaware	10.15	–	Wyoming**	N/A

District of Columbia   67.31

Source: Morgan Quitno Corp using data from U.S. Department of Health & Human Services, Substance Abuse & Mental Health Services Admin and National Association of State Alcohol and Drug Abuse Directors, Inc.
"State Resources and Services Related to Alcohol and Other Drug Abuse Problems, Fiscal Year 1991" (1992)
*Funds for treatment and prevention programs as well as "other" costs (administration, research capital costs, etc.) National per capita does not include expenditures in Puerto Rico and Guam.
**Not available.

Expenditures for State–Supported Alcohol and Drug Abuse Treatment Programs in 1991

National Total = $2,408,706,059*

RANK	STATE	EXPENDITURES	%	RANK	STATE	EXPENDITURES	%
1	New York	$498,201,309	20.68%	26	Louisiana	$21,710,464	0.90%
2	California	280,784,435	11.66%	27	Iowa	21,305,399	0.88%
3	Florida	123,997,671	5.15%	28	Tennessee	18,236,600	0.76%
4	Illinois	107,359,819	4.46%	29	Oklahoma	16,927,584	0.70%
5	Pennsylvania	100,359,829	4.17%	30	Kentucky	16,644,214	0.69%
6	Wisconsin	88,738,677	3.68%	31	Rhode Island	15,029,352	0.62%
7	Massachusetts	77,315,300	3.21%	32	Kansas	14,514,302	0.60%
8	Maryland	74,673,002	3.10%	33	Alabama	14,077,848	0.58%
9	Ohio	74,094,304	3.08%	34	Montana	12,709,558	0.53%
10	Connecticut	70,075,276	2.91%	35	Utah	12,295,803	0.51%
11	Michigan	64,275,948	2.67%	36	New Mexico	12,229,545	0.51%
12	New Jersey	61,148,000	2.54%	37	Nebraska	9,790,266	0.41%
13	Virginia	57,377,056	2.38%	38	Hawaii	9,092,545	0.38%
14	Minnesota	56,421,594	2.34%	39	West Virginia	8,978,089	0.37%
15	Washington	51,805,110	2.15%	40	Arkansas	8,140,276	0.34%
16	Texas	50,478,640	2.10%	41	Maine	7,732,761	0.32%
17	Georgia	45,634,792	1.89%	42	Mississippi	7,525,515	0.31%
18	North Carolina	37,194,021	1.54%	43	Vermont	6,142,932	0.26%
19	Indiana	33,842,544	1.41%	44	Delaware	5,985,062	0.25%
20	Arizona	30,156,537	1.25%	45	Nevada	5,878,726	0.24%
21	Colorado	29,121,341	1.21%	46	South Dakota	4,254,869	0.18%
22	Missouri	28,732,087	1.19%	47	North Dakota	3,915,711	0.16%
23	South Carolina	25,535,295	1.06%	48	Idaho	3,668,865	0.15%
24	Alaska	24,914,551	1.03%	49	New Hampshire	3,441,787	0.14%
25	Oregon	21,808,176	0.91%	–	Wyoming**	N/A	N/A

District of Columbia   34,502,672   1.43%

Source: U.S. Department of Health and Human Services, Substance Abuse and Mental Health Services Administration

   National Association of State Alcohol and Drug Abuse Directors, Inc.

    "State Resources and Services Related to Alcohol and Other Drug Abuse Problems, Fiscal Year 1991" (1992)

*Total does not include $25,660,516 in Puerto Rico and $594,807 in Guam.

**Not available.

Per Capita Expenditures for State-Supported Alcohol and Drug Abuse Treatment Programs in 1991

National Per Capita = $9.55*

RANK	STATE	PER CAPITA	RANK	STATE	PER CAPITA
1	Alaska	$43.71	26	Utah	$6.95
2	New York	27.59	27	Georgia	6.89
3	Connecticut	21.29	28	Michigan	6.86
4	Wisconsin	17.91	29	Ohio	6.77
5	Montana	15.73	30	Maine	6.26
6	Maryland	15.36	31	North Dakota	6.17
7	Rhode Island	14.97	32	Nebraska	6.15
8	Massachusetts	12.89	33	South Dakota	6.05
9	Minnesota	12.73	34	Indiana	6.03
10	Vermont	10.83	35	Kansas	5.82
11	Washington	10.32	36	Missouri	5.57
12	Florida	9.34	37	North Carolina	5.52
13	Illinois	9.30	38	Oklahoma	5.33
14	California	9.24	39	Louisiana	5.11
15	Virginia	9.13	40	West Virginia	4.99
16	Delaware	8.80	41	Nevada	4.58
17	Colorado	8.62	42	Kentucky	4.48
18	Pennsylvania	8.39	43	Tennessee	3.68
19	Arizona	8.04	44	Idaho	3.53
20	Hawaii	8.01	45	Alabama	3.44
21	New Mexico	7.90	46	Arkansas	3.43
22	New Jersey	7.88	47	New Hampshire	3.11
23	Iowa	7.62	48	Texas	2.91
24	Oregon	7.46	49	Mississippi	2.90
25	South Carolina	7.17	–	Wyoming**	N/A

District of Columbia   57.70

Source: Morgan Quitno Corporation using data from U.S. Department of Health & Human Services, Substance Abuse & Mental Health Services Admin.
National Association of State Alcohol and Drug Abuse Directors, Inc.
"State Resources and Services Related to Alcohol and Other Drug Abuse Problems, Fiscal Year 1991" (1992)

*National per capita does not include expenditures in Puerto Rico and Guam.

**Not available.

Expenditures for State–Supported Alcohol and Drug Abuse Prevention Programs in 1991

National Total = $523,786,263*

RANK	STATE	EXPENDITURES	%	RANK	STATE	EXPENDITURES	%
1	New York	$103,905,441	19.84%	26	Washington	$4,389,088	0.84%
2	California	65,689,911	12.54%	27	Missouri	4,315,786	0.82%
3	Texas	28,844,319	5.51%	28	Minnesota	4,177,278	0.80%
4	Ohio	28,013,490	5.35%	29	Kentucky	4,100,108	0.78%
5	Wisconsin	25,922,023	4.95%	30	Arizona	3,466,855	0.66%
6	Pennsylvania	25,770,247	4.92%	31	Kansas	3,156,669	0.60%
7	Oregon	20,194,785	3.86%	32	Oklahoma	2,971,377	0.57%
8	Michigan	18,911,177	3.61%	33	Alaska	2,290,558	0.44%
9	New Jersey	17,846,000	3.41%	34	Nebraska	2,280,022	0.44%
10	Illinois	17,696,084	3.38%	35	Montana	2,276,083	0.43%
11	South Carolina	13,795,774	2.63%	36	Hawaii	2,137,839	0.41%
12	Florida	13,135,805	2.51%	37	Nevada	1,721,091	0.33%
13	Alabama	10,706,241	2.04%	38	Louisiana	1,675,431	0.32%
14	Virginia	10,442,771	1.99%	39	Maine	1,608,922	0.31%
15	Maryland	8,643,189	1.65%	40	Vermont	1,560,597	0.30%
16	Colorado	7,400,152	1.41%	41	South Dakota	1,462,585	0.28%
17	Utah	7,093,464	1.35%	42	West Virginia	1,307,053	0.25%
18	Indiana	6,673,903	1.27%	43	New Mexico	1,182,156	0.23%
19	Tennessee	6,193,800	1.18%	44	Arkansas	1,055,566	0.20%
20	Massachusetts	6,144,800	1.17%	45	New Hampshire	995,265	0.19%
21	Connecticut	5,711,039	1.09%	46	Idaho	911,362	0.17%
22	North Carolina	5,409,464	1.03%	47	Mississippi	910,107	0.17%
23	Rhode Island	5,308,102	1.01%	48	North Dakota	777,837	0.15%
24	Iowa	4,856,384	0.93%	49	Delaware	610,832	0.12%
25	Georgia	4,645,431	0.89%	–	Wyoming**	N/A	N/A

| | | | | | District of Columbia | 3,492,000 | 0.67% |

Source: U.S. Department of Health and Human Services, Substance Abuse and Mental Health Services Administration

National Association of State Alcohol and Drug Abuse Directors, Inc.

"State Resources and Services Related to Alcohol and Other Drug Abuse Problems, Fiscal Year 1991" (1992)

Total does not include $5,522,797 in Puerto Rico and $69,420 in Guam.

**Not available.*

Per Capita Expenditures for State-Supported Alcohol and Drug Abuse Prevention Programs in 1991

National Per Capita = $2.08*

RANK	STATE	PER CAPITA	RANK	STATE	PER CAPITA
1	Oregon	$6.91	26	Nevada	$1.34
2	New York	5.75	27	Maine	1.30
3	Rhode Island	5.29	28	Kansas	1.27
4	Wisconsin	5.23	29	Tennessee	1.25
5	Alaska	4.02	30	North Dakota	1.22
6	Utah	4.01	31	Indiana	1.19
7	South Carolina	3.88	32	Kentucky	1.10
8	Montana	2.82	33	Massachusetts	1.02
9	Vermont	2.75	34	Florida	0.99
10	Alabama	2.62	35	Minnesota	0.94
11	Ohio	2.56	35	Oklahoma	0.94
12	New Jersey	2.30	37	Arizona	0.92
13	Colorado	2.19	38	Delaware	0.90
14	California	2.16	38	New Hampshire	0.90
15	Pennsylvania	2.15	40	Idaho	0.88
16	South Dakota	2.08	41	Washington	0.87
17	Michigan	2.02	42	Missouri	0.84
18	Hawaii	1.88	43	North Carolina	0.80
19	Maryland	1.78	44	New Mexico	0.76
20	Connecticut	1.74	45	West Virginia	0.73
20	Iowa	1.74	46	Georgia	0.70
22	Texas	1.66	47	Arkansas	0.45
22	Virginia	1.66	48	Louisiana	0.39
24	Illinois	1.53	49	Mississippi	0.35
25	Nebraska	1.43	–	Wyoming**	N/A

District of Columbia   5.84

Source: Morgan Quitno Corporation using data from U.S. Department of Health & Human Services, Substance Abuse & Mental Health Services Admin.
National Association of State Alcohol and Drug Abuse Directors, Inc.
"State Resources and Services Related to Alcohol and Other Drug Abuse Problems, Fiscal Year 1991" (1992)

*National per capita does not include expenditures in Puerto Rico and Guam.
**Not available.

Drug and Alcoholism Treatment and Prevention Units in 1992

National Total = 10,738 Units*

RANK	STATE	UNITS	%	RANK	STATE	UNITS	%
1	California	1,447	13.48%	26	Oklahoma	97	0.90%
2	New York	1,280	11.92%	27	Rhode Island	89	0.83%
3	Michigan	725	6.75%	28	Iowa	86	0.80%
4	Florida	713	6.64%	29	Georgia	77	0.72%
5	Ohio	601	5.60%	29	Louisiana	77	0.72%
6	Texas	506	4.71%	31	Maine	75	0.70%
7	Illinois	472	4.40%	32	Tennessee	66	0.61%
8	Pennsylvania	432	4.02%	33	Hawaii	65	0.61%
9	Wisconsin	293	2.73%	34	Mississippi	58	0.54%
10	Massachusetts	271	2.52%	35	Nevada	57	0.53%
11	New Jersey	270	2.51%	36	South Dakota	56	0.52%
12	Maryland	264	2.46%	37	South Carolina	53	0.49%
13	Indiana	215	2.00%	38	Alabama	52	0.48%
14	Minnesota	214	1.99%	39	Utah	45	0.42%
15	Connecticut	193	1.80%	40	Arkansas	43	0.40%
16	Colorado	174	1.62%	41	New Hampshire	41	0.38%
17	Arizona	173	1.61%	42	New Mexico	40	0.37%
18	Washington	171	1.59%	43	Wyoming	39	0.36%
19	Kentucky	162	1.51%	44	Alaska	37	0.34%
20	Oregon	155	1.44%	45	West Virginia	35	0.33%
21	Nebraska	133	1.24%	46	Delaware	34	0.32%
22	Missouri	128	1.19%	47	North Dakota	32	0.30%
23	Kansas	126	1.17%	48	Montana	31	0.29%
24	North Carolina	124	1.15%	49	Vermont	22	0.20%
25	Virginia	109	1.02%	50	Idaho	18	0.17%
					District of Columbia	62	0.58%

Source: U.S. Department of Health and Human Services, Substance Abuse and Mental Health Services Administration

"National Drug and Alcoholism Treatment Unit Survey 1991, Main Findings Report" (1993)

*Does not include 360 federal units or 179 units in U.S. territories.

IV. FINANCE

Table	Title
171	State and Local Government Expenditures for Justice Activities in 1991
172	Per Capita State and Local Government Expenditures for Justice Activities in 1991
173	State-Local Government Expenditures for Justice Activities as a Percent of All Direct Expenditures: 1991
174	State Government Expenditures for Justice Activities in 1991
175	Per Capita State Government Expenditures for Justice Activities in 1991
176	State Government Expenditures for Judicial Activities as a Percent of All Direct Expenditures in 1991
177	Local Government Expenditures for Justice Activities in 1991
178	Per Capita Local Government Expenditures for Justice Activities in 1991
179	Local Government Expenditures for Justice Activities as a Percent of All Direct Expenditures in 1991
180	State and Local Government Expenditures for Police Protection in 1991
181	Per Capita State and Local Government Expenditures for Police Protection in 1991
182	State-Local Government Expenditures for Police Protection as a Percent of All Direct Expenditures in 1991
183	State Government Expenditures for Police Protection in 1991
184	Per Capita State Government Expenditures for Police Protection in 1991
185	State Government Expenditures for Police Protection as a Percent of All Direct Expenditures in 1991
186	Local Government Expenditures for Police Protection in 1991
187	Per Capita Local Government Expenditures for Police Protection in 1991
188	Local Government Expenditures for Police Protection as a Percent of All Direct Expenditures in 1991
189	State and Local Government Expenditures for Corrections in 1991
190	Per Capita State and Local Government Expenditures for Corrections in 1991
191	State and Local Government Expenditures for Corrections as a Percent of All Direct Expenditures in 1991
192	State Government Expenditures for Corrections in 1991
193	Per Capita State Government Expenditures for Corrections in 1991
194	State Government Expenditures for Corrections as a Percent of All Direct Expenditures in 1991
195	Local Government Expenditures for Corrections in 1991
196	Per Capita Local Government Expenditures for Corrections in 1991
197	Local Government Expenditures for Corrections as a Percent of All Direct Expenditures in 1991
198	State and Local Government Expenditures for Judicial and Legal Services in 1991
199	Per Capita State and Local Government Expenditures for Judicial and Legal Services in 1991
200	State & Local Government Expenditures for Judicial & Legal Services as a Percent of All Direct Expenditures in 1991
201	State Government Expenditures for Judicial and Legal Services in 1991
202	Per Capita State Government Expenditures for Judicial and Legal Services in 1991
203	State Government Expenditures for Judicial and Legal Services as a Percent of All Direct Expenditures: 1991

IV. FINANCE (continued)

Table	Title
204	Local Government Expenditures for Judicial and Legal Services in 1991
205	Per Capita Local Government Expenditures for Judicial and Legal Services in 1991
206	Local Government Expenditures for Judicial and Legal Services as a Percent of All Direct Expenditures: 1991
207	Base Salary for Justices of States' Highest Courts in 1993
208	Base Salary of Judges of Intermediate Appellate Courts in 1993
209	Base Salaries of Judges of General Trial Courts in 1993
210	State and Local Government Justice System Payroll in 1990
211	State and Local Government Payroll for Police Protection in 1990
212	State and Local Government Payroll for Corrections in 1990
213	State and Local Government Payroll for Courts in 1990
214	State and Local Government Payroll for Prosecution and Legal Services in 1990
215	State and Local Government Payroll for Public Defense in 1990
216	State Victim Compensation Claims Filed in 1989
217	State Victim Compensation Benefits Paid in 1989
218	Average State Victim Compensation Benefit Paid in 1989

State and Local Government Expenditures for Justice Activities in 1991

National Total = $75,505,859,000*

RANK	STATE	EXPENDITURES	%	RANK	STATE	EXPENDITURES	%
1	California	$13,121,521,000	17.38%	26	South Carolina	$797,178,000	1.06%
2	New York	9,012,720,000	11.94%	27	Alabama	756,082,000	1.00%
3	Florida	4,695,969,000	6.22%	28	Kentucky	703,709,000	0.93%
4	Texas	4,113,789,000	5.45%	29	Oklahoma	618,932,000	0.82%
5	Illinois	3,068,250,000	4.06%	30	Kansas	596,401,000	0.79%
6	Michigan	2,837,913,000	3.76%	31	Nevada	536,028,000	0.71%
7	Pennsylvania	2,738,278,000	3.63%	32	Iowa	532,940,000	0.71%
8	Ohio	2,729,199,000	3.61%	33	New Mexico	439,331,000	0.58%
9	New Jersey	2,711,583,000	3.59%	34	Utah	389,581,000	0.52%
10	Massachusetts	1,881,306,000	2.49%	35	Hawaii	363,506,000	0.48%
11	Georgia	1,763,222,000	2.34%	36	Mississippi	347,806,000	0.46%
12	Maryland	1,742,123,000	2.31%	37	Alaska	342,644,000	0.45%
13	Virginia	1,635,704,000	2.17%	38	Arkansas	336,367,000	0.45%
14	North Carolina	1,559,062,000	2.06%	39	Nebraska	292,224,000	0.39%
15	Arizona	1,394,025,000	1.85%	40	Rhode Island	288,027,000	0.38%
16	Wisconsin	1,327,673,000	1.76%	41	New Hampshire	257,371,000	0.34%
17	Washington	1,309,668,000	1.73%	42	Maine	234,188,000	0.31%
18	Connecticut	1,139,413,000	1.51%	43	Delaware	222,965,000	0.30%
19	Tennessee	1,094,180,000	1.45%	44	West Virginia	211,991,000	0.28%
20	Louisiana	1,024,652,000	1.36%	45	Idaho	204,484,000	0.27%
21	Minnesota	1,009,274,000	1.34%	46	Montana	158,585,000	0.21%
22	Colorado	978,320,000	1.30%	47	Wyoming	137,960,000	0.18%
23	Missouri	975,114,000	1.29%	48	South Dakota	113,220,000	0.15%
24	Indiana	970,191,000	1.28%	49	Vermont	105,925,000	0.14%
25	Oregon	841,139,000	1.11%	50	North Dakota	89,979,000	0.12%

District of Columbia   754,147,000   1.00%

Source: Morgan Quitno Corporation using data from U.S. Bureau of the Census
"Government Finances: 1990-1991 (Preliminary Report)" (March 1993)
*Direct expenditures. Preliminary data. Includes Police Protection, Corrections and Judicial and Legal Services.

Per Capita State and Local Government Expenditures for Justice Activities in 1991

National Per Capita = $299.42*

RANK	STATE	PER CAPITA		RANK	STATE	PER CAPITA
1	Alaska	$601.13		26	Kansas	$239.04
2	New York	499.10		27	Texas	237.12
3	California	431.91		28	New Hampshire	232.91
4	Nevada	417.47		29	North Carolina	231.42
5	Arizona	371.74		30	Pennsylvania	228.93
6	Maryland	358.46		31	Minnesota	227.72
7	Florida	353.69		32	South Carolina	223.93
8	New Jersey	349.43		33	Tennessee	220.91
9	Connecticut	346.22		34	Utah	220.10
10	Delaware	327.89		35	Idaho	196.81
11	Hawaii	320.27		36	Montana	196.27
12	Massachusetts	313.76		37	Oklahoma	194.94
13	Michigan	302.94		38	Iowa	190.68
14	Wyoming	299.91		39	Maine	189.63
15	Colorado	289.70		40	Kentucky	189.53
16	Oregon	287.86		41	Missouri	189.05
17	Rhode Island	286.88		42	Vermont	186.82
18	New Mexico	283.81		43	Alabama	184.91
19	Wisconsin	267.95		44	Nebraska	183.44
20	Georgia	266.23		45	Indiana	172.94
21	Illinois	265.81		46	South Dakota	161.05
22	Washington	260.99		47	Arkansas	141.81
23	Virginia	260.21		48	North Dakota	141.70
24	Ohio	249.49		49	Mississippi	134.18
25	Louisiana	240.98		50	West Virginia	117.71

District of Columbia   1,261.12

Source: Morgan Quitno Corporation using data from U.S. Bureau of the Census
"Government Finances: 1990-1991 (Preliminary Report)" (March 1993)

*Direct expenditures. Preliminary data. Includes Police Protection, Corrections and Judicial and Legal Services.

State–Local Government Expenditures for Justice Activities as a Percent of All Direct Expenditures: 1991

National Percent = 7.12% of Direct Expenditures*

RANK	STATE	PERCENT	RANK	STATE	PERCENT
1	Nevada	9.18	26	Massachusetts	6.27
2	Florida	9.08	27	Missouri	6.24
3	California	8.97	28	Idaho	6.20
4	Arizona	8.88	29	Pennsylvania	6.12
5	Maryland	8.51	30	Tennessee	6.02
6	New York	7.68	31	South Carolina	6.00
7	New Jersey	7.50	32	Oklahoma	5.82
8	New Mexico	7.44	33	Kentucky	5.68
9	Delaware	7.30	34	Utah	5.67
10	Michigan	7.24	35	Alaska	5.45
11	Colorado	7.16	36	Wyoming	5.36
12	Virginia	7.15	37	Alabama	5.34
13	Georgia	7.12	38	Washington	5.27
14	Texas	7.08	39	Indiana	5.23
15	Illinois	7.02	40	Arkansas	5.22
16	Connecticut	6.94	41	Iowa	5.07
17	Oregon	6.83	42	Montana	4.96
18	New Hampshire	6.74	43	South Dakota	4.95
19	Wisconsin	6.64	44	Minnesota	4.77
20	Kansas	6.62	45	Maine	4.70
21	Ohio	6.48	46	Mississippi	4.42
22	Louisiana	6.44	47	Vermont	4.35
22	North Carolina	6.44	48	Nebraska	4.20
24	Rhode Island	6.38	49	North Dakota	3.68
25	Hawaii	6.30	50	West Virginia	3.50

District of Columbia   13.25

Source: Morgan Quitno Corporation using data from U.S. Bureau of the Census
    "Government Finances: 1990-1991 (Preliminary Report)" (March 1993)
*Preliminary data. Includes Courts, Prosecution and Legal Services and Public Defense.

State Government Expenditures for Justice Activities in 1991

National Total = $28,511,510,000*

RANK	STATE	EXPENDITURES	%	RANK	STATE	EXPENDITURES	%
1	California	$3,732,656,000	13.09%	26	Missouri	$360,260,000	1.26%
2	New York	3,333,963,000	11.69%	27	Alabama	347,935,000	1.22%
3	Florida	1,581,112,000	5.55%	28	Kansas	310,655,000	1.09%
4	Texas	1,300,432,000	4.56%	29	Oklahoma	306,120,000	1.07%
5	Michigan	1,138,829,000	3.99%	30	Minnesota	281,483,000	0.99%
6	Illinois	1,025,129,000	3.60%	31	Iowa	259,166,000	0.91%
7	Massachusetts	1,022,951,000	3.59%	32	Alaska	253,496,000	0.89%
8	New Jersey	995,163,000	3.49%	33	New Mexico	242,691,000	0.85%
9	Pennsylvania	957,553,000	3.36%	34	Hawaii	190,732,000	0.67%
10	North Carolina	872,096,000	3.06%	35	Utah	176,599,000	0.62%
11	Maryland	844,798,000	2.96%	36	Nevada	176,140,000	0.62%
12	Ohio	841,429,000	2.95%	37	Rhode Island	171,819,000	0.60%
13	Georgia	775,190,000	2.72%	38	Delaware	161,528,000	0.57%
14	Connecticut	736,095,000	2.58%	39	Arkansas	158,758,000	0.56%
15	Virginia	680,866,000	2.39%	40	Mississippi	149,053,000	0.52%
16	Arizona	485,816,000	1.70%	41	Maine	133,953,000	0.47%
17	Tennessee	471,257,000	1.65%	42	New Hampshire	123,009,000	0.43%
18	Washington	460,067,000	1.61%	43	Nebraska	120,434,000	0.42%
19	South Carolina	429,490,000	1.51%	44	West Virginia	106,851,000	0.37%
20	Wisconsin	416,472,000	1.46%	45	Idaho	94,644,000	0.33%
21	Indiana	415,268,000	1.46%	46	Vermont	78,244,000	0.27%
22	Kentucky	396,799,000	1.39%	47	Montana	69,853,000	0.24%
23	Colorado	396,668,000	1.39%	48	South Dakota	55,018,000	0.19%
24	Louisiana	394,022,000	1.38%	49	Wyoming	54,204,000	0.19%
25	Oregon	387,165,000	1.36%	50	North Dakota	37,579,000	0.13%
					District of Columbia**	N/A	N/A

Source: Morgan Quitno Corporation using data from U.S. Bureau of the Census
   "Government Finances: 1990-1991 (Preliminary Report)" (March 1993)
*Direct expenditures. Preliminary data. Includes Police Protection, Corrections and Judicial and Legal Services.
**Not applicable

Per Capita State Government Expenditures for Justice Activities in 1991

National Per Capita = $113.06*

RANK	STATE	PER CAPITA	RANK	STATE	PER CAPITA
1	Alaska	$444.73	26	Virginia	$108.31
2	Delaware	237.54	27	Kentucky	106.87
3	Connecticut	223.67	28	Utah	99.77
4	New York	184.63	29	Oklahoma	96.42
5	Maryland	173.83	30	Tennessee	95.15
6	Rhode Island	171.13	31	Iowa	92.72
7	Massachusetts	170.61	32	Louisiana	92.67
8	Hawaii	168.05	33	Washington	91.68
9	New Mexico	156.78	34	Idaho	91.09
10	Vermont	138.00	35	Illinois	88.81
11	Nevada	137.18	36	Montana	86.45
12	Oregon	132.50	37	Alabama	85.09
13	Arizona	129.55	38	Wisconsin	84.05
14	North Carolina	129.45	39	Pennsylvania	80.06
15	New Jersey	128.24	40	South Dakota	78.26
16	Kansas	124.51	41	Ohio	76.92
17	California	122.87	42	Nebraska	75.60
18	Michigan	121.57	43	Texas	74.96
19	South Carolina	120.64	44	Indiana	74.02
20	Florida	119.09	45	Missouri	69.84
21	Wyoming	117.83	46	Arkansas	66.93
22	Colorado	117.46	47	Minnesota	63.51
23	Georgia	117.05	48	West Virginia	59.33
24	New Hampshire	111.32	49	North Dakota	59.18
25	Maine	108.46	50	Mississippi	57.51

District of Columbia**   N/A

Source: Morgan Quitno Corporation using data from U.S. Bureau of the Census
"Government Finances: 1990-1991 (Preliminary Report)" (March 1993)
*Direct expenditures. Preliminary data. Includes Police Protection, Corrections and Judicial and Legal Services.
**Not applicable

State Government Expenditures for Judicial Activities as a Percent of All Direct Expenditures in 1991

National Percent = 6.45% of Direct Expenditures*

RANK	STATE	PERCENT	RANK	STATE	PERCENT
1	Florida	9.37	26	Utah	5.79
2	North Carolina	9.10	27	Idaho	5.77
3	Arizona	8.89	28	Oklahoma	5.74
4	Maryland	8.54	29	Illinois	5.66
5	Delaware	8.35	30	Iowa	5.51
5	Kansas	8.35	31	Missouri	5.47
7	New Mexico	8.16	32	Vermont	5.44
8	Georgia	8.14	33	Wisconsin	5.31
9	Connecticut	8.07	34	Indiana	5.22
10	Colorado	7.88	35	Alabama	5.11
11	New York	7.62	36	Nebraska	5.07
12	California	7.58	37	Louisiana	4.88
13	Nevada	7.34	38	Pennsylvania	4.83
14	Tennessee	6.95	39	South Dakota	4.80
15	Virginia	6.91	40	Maine	4.76
16	Oregon	6.85	41	Arkansas	4.68
17	New Hampshire	6.55	42	Wyoming	4.50
18	Michigan	6.53	43	Hawaii	4.33
19	Massachusetts	6.45	44	Mississippi	4.21
20	Alaska	6.32	45	Ohio	4.20
21	South Carolina	6.17	46	Washington	4.03
22	Texas	6.12	47	Montana	3.89
23	Rhode Island	6.05	48	Minnesota	3.59
24	New Jersey	5.82	49	West Virginia	2.97
25	Kentucky	5.81	50	North Dakota	2.68

District of Columbia**   N/A

Source: Morgan Quitno Corporation using data from U.S. Bureau of the Census
    "Government Finances: 1990-1991 (Preliminary Report)" (March 1993)
*Preliminary data. Includes Police Protection, Corrections and Judicial and Legal Services.
**Not applicable

Local Government Expenditures for Justice Activities in 1991

National Total = $46,994,349,000*

RANK	STATE	EXPENDITURES	%	RANK	STATE	EXPENDITURES	%
1	California	$9,388,865,000	19.98%	26	Connecticut	$403,318,000	0.86%
2	New York	5,678,757,000	12.08%	27	South Carolina	367,688,000	0.78%
3	Florida	3,114,857,000	6.63%	28	Nevada	359,888,000	0.77%
4	Texas	2,813,357,000	5.99%	29	Oklahoma	312,812,000	0.67%
5	Illinois	2,043,121,000	4.35%	30	Kentucky	306,910,000	0.65%
6	Ohio	1,887,770,000	4.02%	31	Kansas	285,746,000	0.61%
7	Pennsylvania	1,780,725,000	3.79%	32	Iowa	273,774,000	0.58%
8	New Jersey	1,716,420,000	3.65%	33	Utah	212,982,000	0.45%
9	Michigan	1,699,084,000	3.62%	34	Mississippi	198,753,000	0.42%
10	Georgia	988,032,000	2.10%	35	New Mexico	196,640,000	0.42%
11	Virginia	954,838,000	2.03%	36	Arkansas	177,609,000	0.38%
12	Wisconsin	911,201,000	1.94%	37	Hawaii	172,774,000	0.37%
13	Arizona	908,209,000	1.93%	38	Nebraska	171,790,000	0.37%
14	Maryland	897,325,000	1.91%	39	New Hampshire	134,362,000	0.29%
15	Massachusetts	858,355,000	1.83%	40	Rhode Island	116,208,000	0.25%
16	Washington	849,601,000	1.81%	41	Idaho	109,840,000	0.23%
17	Minnesota	727,791,000	1.55%	42	West Virginia	105,140,000	0.22%
18	North Carolina	686,966,000	1.46%	43	Maine	100,235,000	0.21%
19	Louisiana	630,630,000	1.34%	44	Alaska	89,148,000	0.19%
20	Tennessee	622,923,000	1.33%	45	Montana	88,732,000	0.19%
21	Missouri	614,854,000	1.31%	46	Wyoming	83,756,000	0.18%
22	Colorado	581,652,000	1.24%	47	Delaware	61,437,000	0.13%
23	Indiana	554,923,000	1.18%	48	South Dakota	58,202,000	0.12%
24	Oregon	453,974,000	0.97%	49	North Dakota	52,400,000	0.11%
25	Alabama	408,147,000	0.87%	50	Vermont	27,681,000	0.06%

District of Columbia 754,147,000 1.60%

Source: Morgan Quitno Corporation using data from U.S. Bureau of the Census
"Government Finances: 1990–1991 (Preliminary Report)" (March 1993)
*Direct expenditures. Preliminary data. Includes Police Protection, Corrections and Judicial and Legal Services.

Per Capita Local Government Expenditures for Justice Activities in 1991

National Per Capita = $186.35*

RANK	STATE	PER CAPITA		RANK	STATE	PER CAPITA
1	New York	$314.47		26	Tennessee	$125.77
2	California	309.05		27	Connecticut	122.55
3	Nevada	280.29		28	New Hampshire	121.59
4	Arizona	242.19		29	Utah	120.33
5	Florida	234.61		30	Missouri	119.20
6	New Jersey	221.19		31	Rhode Island	115.75
7	Maryland	184.63		32	Kansas	114.53
8	Wisconsin	183.90		33	Montana	109.82
9	Wyoming	182.08		34	Nebraska	107.84
10	Michigan	181.37		35	Idaho	105.72
11	Illinois	177.00		36	South Carolina	103.28
12	Ohio	172.57		37	North Carolina	101.97
13	Colorado	172.24		38	Alabama	99.82
14	Washington	169.31		39	Indiana	98.92
15	Minnesota	164.21		40	Oklahoma	98.52
16	Texas	162.16		41	Iowa	97.95
17	Alaska	156.40		42	Delaware	90.35
18	Oregon	155.36		43	South Dakota	82.79
19	Hawaii	152.22		44	Kentucky	82.66
20	Virginia	151.90		45	North Dakota	82.52
21	Georgia	149.18		46	Maine	81.16
22	Pennsylvania	148.88		47	Mississippi	76.68
23	Louisiana	148.31		48	Arkansas	74.88
24	Massachusetts	143.15		49	West Virginia	58.38
25	New Mexico	127.03		50	Vermont	48.82

District of Columbia   1,261.12

Source: Morgan Quitno Corporation using data from U.S. Bureau of the Census
"Government Finances: 1990–1991 (Preliminary Report)" (March 1993)
*Direct expenditures. Preliminary data. Includes Police Protection, Corrections and Judicial and Legal Services.

Local Government Expenditures for Justice Activities as a Percent of All Direct Expenditures in 1991

National Percent = 7.60% of Direct Expenditures*

RANK	STATE	PERCENT		RANK	STATE	PERCENT
1	Hawaii	12.64		25	Washington	6.33
2	Nevada	10.46		27	Wyoming	6.12
3	California	9.68		28	Massachusetts	6.07
4	New Jersey	9.01		29	Oklahoma	5.90
5	Florida	8.94		30	Arkansas	5.82
6	Arizona	8.88		30	South Carolina	5.82
7	Ohio	8.55		32	Utah	5.58
8	Maryland	8.48		33	Alabama	5.56
9	Louisiana	8.05		34	Connecticut	5.53
10	Illinois	7.97		35	Kentucky	5.51
11	Michigan	7.82		36	Delaware	5.47
12	New York	7.71		37	Minnesota	5.46
13	Texas	7.63		37	Tennessee	5.46
14	Wisconsin	7.49		39	Kansas	5.41
15	Virginia	7.34		40	Indiana	5.23
16	Pennsylvania	7.15		41	South Dakota	5.10
17	New Hampshire	6.92		42	North Dakota	5.05
17	Rhode Island	6.92		43	Iowa	4.71
19	Oregon	6.81		44	North Carolina	4.70
20	Missouri	6.80		45	Maine	4.61
21	Colorado	6.74		46	Mississippi	4.59
22	New Mexico	6.70		47	West Virginia	4.26
23	Idaho	6.63		48	Alaska	3.92
24	Georgia	6.48		49	Nebraska	3.74
25	Montana	6.33		50	Vermont	2.78

District of Columbia   13.25

Source: Morgan Quitno Corporation using data from U.S. Bureau of the Census
   "Government Finances: 1990-1991 (Preliminary Report)" (March 1993)
*Preliminary data. Includes Police Protection, Corrections and Judicial and Legal Services.

State and Local Government Expenditures for Police Protection in 1991

National Total = $32,771,685,000*

RANK	STATE	EXPENDITURES	%	RANK	STATE	EXPENDITURES	%
1	California	$5,401,716,000	16.48%	26	Oregon	$333,906,000	1.02%
2	New York	3,560,760,000	10.87%	27	South Carolina	316,154,000	0.96%
3	Florida	2,161,692,000	6.60%	28	Kentucky	301,575,000	0.92%
4	Texas	1,839,665,000	5.61%	29	Oklahoma	277,175,000	0.85%
5	Illinois	1,604,966,000	4.90%	30	Iowa	251,299,000	0.77%
6	New Jersey	1,241,142,000	3.79%	31	Kansas	245,198,000	0.75%
7	Ohio	1,233,467,000	3.76%	32	Nevada	219,843,000	0.67%
8	Michigan	1,231,561,000	3.76%	33	New Mexico	196,587,000	0.60%
9	Pennsylvania	1,163,045,000	3.55%	34	Mississippi	172,225,000	0.53%
10	Massachusetts	793,780,000	2.42%	35	Utah	161,796,000	0.49%
11	Maryland	757,473,000	2.31%	36	Arkansas	155,790,000	0.48%
12	Virginia	713,589,000	2.18%	37	Hawaii	148,415,000	0.45%
13	Georgia	695,002,000	2.12%	38	Nebraska	138,440,000	0.42%
14	North Carolina	685,582,000	2.09%	39	Rhode Island	129,622,000	0.40%
15	Wisconsin	654,390,000	2.00%	40	New Hampshire	126,470,000	0.39%
16	Arizona	595,196,000	1.82%	41	Alaska	115,294,000	0.35%
17	Washington	563,799,000	1.72%	42	Idaho	100,530,000	0.31%
18	Louisiana	514,990,000	1.57%	43	Maine	100,493,000	0.31%
19	Missouri	514,673,000	1.57%	44	West Virginia	91,029,000	0.28%
20	Minnesota	485,285,000	1.48%	45	Delaware	89,341,000	0.27%
21	Connecticut	481,233,000	1.47%	46	Montana	70,443,000	0.21%
22	Tennessee	437,179,000	1.33%	47	Wyoming	68,877,000	0.21%
23	Colorado	435,017,000	1.33%	48	South Dakota	53,470,000	0.16%
24	Indiana	423,829,000	1.29%	49	Vermont	49,127,000	0.15%
25	Alabama	361,725,000	1.10%	50	North Dakota	40,755,000	0.12%
					District of Columbia	267,075,000	0.81%

Source: U.S. Bureau of the Census

"Government Finances: 1990-1991 (Preliminary Report)" (March 1993)

*Direct expenditures. Preliminary data.

Per Capita State and Local Government Expenditures for Police Protection in 1991

National Per Capita = $129.96*

RANK	STATE	PER CAPITA		RANK	STATE	PER CAPITA
1	Alaska	$202.27		26	Minnesota	$109.50
2	New York	197.18		27	Texas	106.04
3	California	177.81		28	Georgia	104.94
4	Nevada	171.22		29	North Carolina	101.76
5	Florida	162.81		30	Missouri	99.78
6	New Jersey	159.94		31	Kansas	98.28
7	Arizona	158.72		32	Pennsylvania	97.24
8	Maryland	155.86		33	Idaho	96.76
9	Wyoming	149.73		34	Utah	91.41
10	Connecticut	146.23		35	Iowa	89.91
11	Illinois	139.04		36	South Carolina	88.81
12	Massachusetts	132.38		37	Alabama	88.46
13	Wisconsin	132.07		38	Tennessee	88.27
14	Michigan	131.46		39	Oklahoma	87.30
15	Delaware	131.38		40	Montana	87.18
16	Hawaii	130.76		41	Nebraska	86.91
17	Rhode Island	129.11		42	Vermont	86.64
18	Colorado	128.82		43	Maine	81.37
19	New Mexico	126.99		44	Kentucky	81.22
20	Louisiana	121.12		45	South Dakota	76.06
21	New Hampshire	114.45		46	Indiana	75.55
22	Oregon	114.27		47	Mississippi	66.44
23	Virginia	113.52		48	Arkansas	65.68
24	Ohio	112.76		49	North Dakota	64.18
25	Washington	112.36		50	West Virginia	50.54

District of Columbia   446.61

Source: Morgan Quitno Corporation using data from U.S. Bureau of the Census
"Government Finances: 1990–1991 (Preliminary Report)" (March 1993)
*Direct expenditures. Preliminary data.

State–Local Government Expenditures for Police Protection as a Percent of All Direct Expenditures in 1991

National Percent = 3.09% of Direct Expenditures*

RANK	STATE	PERCENT	RANK	STATE	PERCENT
1	Florida	4.18	26	Oregon	2.71
2	Arizona	3.79	27	Wyoming	2.68
3	Nevada	3.77	28	Massachusetts	2.65
4	Maryland	3.70	29	Oklahoma	2.61
5	California	3.69	30	Pennsylvania	2.60
6	Illinois	3.67	31	Hawaii	2.57
7	New Jersey	3.43	32	Alabama	2.55
8	New Mexico	3.33	33	Kentucky	2.43
9	New Hampshire	3.31	34	Arkansas	2.42
10	Missouri	3.29	35	Tennessee	2.41
11	Wisconsin	3.27	36	Iowa	2.39
12	Louisiana	3.24	37	South Carolina	2.38
13	Colorado	3.18	38	Utah	2.36
14	Texas	3.17	39	South Dakota	2.34
15	Michigan	3.14	40	Minnesota	2.29
16	Virginia	3.12	41	Indiana	2.28
17	Idaho	3.05	42	Washington	2.27
18	New York	3.03	43	Montana	2.20
19	Connecticut	2.93	44	Mississippi	2.19
19	Ohio	2.93	45	Maine	2.02
21	Delaware	2.92	45	Vermont	2.02
22	Rhode Island	2.87	47	Nebraska	1.99
23	North Carolina	2.83	48	Alaska	1.83
24	Georgia	2.81	49	North Dakota	1.67
25	Kansas	2.72	50	West Virginia	1.50

District of Columbia   4.69

Source: Morgan Quitno Corporation using data from U.S. Bureau of the Census
   "Government Finances: 1990–1991 (Preliminary Report)" (March 1993)
*Preliminary data.

State Government Expenditures for Police Protection in 1991

National Total = $4,785,299,000*

RANK	STATE	EXPENDITURES	%	RANK	STATE	EXPENDITURES	%
1	California	$680,375,000	14.22%	26	Minnesota	$57,226,000	1.20%
2	New York	306,281,000	6.40%	27	Iowa	45,245,000	0.95%
3	Pennsylvania	287,917,000	6.02%	28	New Mexico	43,507,000	0.91%
4	Florida	238,593,000	4.99%	29	Oklahoma	41,473,000	0.87%
5	Illinois	220,354,000	4.60%	30	Colorado	40,136,000	0.84%
6	New Jersey	207,948,000	4.35%	31	Wisconsin	39,863,000	0.83%
7	Texas	206,626,000	4.32%	32	Alaska	36,713,000	0.77%
8	Michigan	186,912,000	3.91%	33	Arkansas	35,284,000	0.74%
9	Maryland	181,701,000	3.80%	34	Delaware	34,661,000	0.72%
10	North Carolina	142,198,000	2.97%	35	Mississippi	31,951,000	0.67%
11	Ohio	140,681,000	2.94%	36	Kansas	30,147,000	0.63%
12	Virginia	133,942,000	2.80%	37	Maine	29,788,000	0.62%
13	Massachusetts	111,115,000	2.32%	38	Nebraska	29,007,000	0.61%
14	Georgia	108,214,000	2.26%	39	Utah	28,352,000	0.59%
15	Arizona	101,045,000	2.11%	40	West Virginia	25,095,000	0.52%
16	Washington	100,827,000	2.11%	41	Idaho	23,864,000	0.50%
17	Connecticut	99,256,000	2.07%	42	Nevada	23,747,000	0.50%
18	Louisiana	92,319,000	1.93%	43	Vermont	22,933,000	0.48%
19	Kentucky	91,598,000	1.91%	44	New Hampshire	22,854,000	0.48%
20	Indiana	88,589,000	1.85%	45	Rhode Island	20,583,000	0.43%
21	South Carolina	83,691,000	1.75%	46	Montana	15,300,000	0.32%
22	Missouri	72,456,000	1.51%	47	Wyoming	14,599,000	0.31%
23	Alabama	65,550,000	1.37%	48	South Dakota	13,277,000	0.28%
24	Oregon	63,280,000	1.32%	49	North Dakota	6,908,000	0.14%
25	Tennessee	57,474,000	1.20%	50	Hawaii	3,844,000	0.08%

District of Columbia**   N/A   N/A

Source: U.S. Bureau of the Census

"Government Finances: 1990-1991 (Preliminary Report)" (March 1993)

Direct expenditures. Preliminary data.

**Not applicable*

Per Capita State Government Expenditures for Police Protection in 1991

National Per Capita = $18.98*

RANK	STATE	PER CAPITA	RANK	STATE	PER CAPITA
1	Alaska	$64.41	26	South Dakota	$18.89
2	Delaware	50.97	27	Massachusetts	18.53
3	Vermont	40.45	28	Nevada	18.49
4	Maryland	37.39	29	Nebraska	18.21
5	Wyoming	31.74	30	Florida	17.97
6	Connecticut	30.16	31	New York	16.96
7	New Mexico	28.11	32	Georgia	16.34
8	Arizona	26.95	33	Iowa	16.19
9	New Jersey	26.80	34	Alabama	16.03
10	Kentucky	24.67	35	Utah	16.02
11	Maine	24.12	36	Indiana	15.79
12	Pennsylvania	24.07	37	Arkansas	14.88
13	South Carolina	23.51	38	Missouri	14.05
14	Idaho	22.97	39	West Virginia	13.93
15	California	22.40	40	Oklahoma	13.06
16	Louisiana	21.71	41	Minnesota	12.91
17	Oregon	21.66	42	Ohio	12.86
18	Virginia	21.31	43	Mississippi	12.33
19	North Carolina	21.11	44	Kansas	12.08
20	New Hampshire	20.68	45	Texas	11.91
21	Rhode Island	20.50	46	Colorado	11.89
22	Washington	20.09	47	Tennessee	11.60
23	Michigan	19.95	48	North Dakota	10.88
24	Illinois	19.09	49	Wisconsin	8.05
25	Montana	18.94	50	Hawaii	3.39

District of Columbia**   N/A

Source: Morgan Quitno Corporation using data from U.S. Bureau of the Census
    "Government Finances: 1990-1991 (Preliminary Report)" (March 1993)
*Direct expenditures. Preliminary data.
**Not applicable

State Government Expenditures for Police Protection as a Percent of All Direct Expenditures in 1991

National Percent = 1.08% of Direct Expenditures*

RANK	STATE	PERCENT	RANK	STATE	PERCENT
1	Arizona	1.85	26	Michigan	1.07
2	Maryland	1.84	27	Maine	1.06
3	Delaware	1.79	28	Arkansas	1.04
4	Vermont	1.59	29	Nevada	0.99
5	North Carolina	1.48	30	Texas	0.97
6	Idaho	1.46	31	Alabama	0.96
6	New Mexico	1.46	31	Iowa	0.96
8	Pennsylvania	1.45	33	Utah	0.93
9	Florida	1.41	34	Alaska	0.92
10	California	1.38	35	Mississippi	0.90
11	Virginia	1.36	36	Washington	0.88
12	Kentucky	1.34	37	Montana	0.85
13	Illinois	1.22	37	Tennessee	0.85
13	Nebraska	1.22	39	Kansas	0.81
13	New Hampshire	1.22	40	Colorado	0.80
13	New Jersey	1.22	41	Oklahoma	0.78
17	Wyoming	1.21	42	Minnesota	0.73
18	South Carolina	1.20	43	Rhode Island	0.72
19	South Dakota	1.16	44	Massachusetts	0.70
20	Georgia	1.14	44	New York	0.70
20	Louisiana	1.14	44	Ohio	0.70
22	Oregon	1.12	44	West Virginia	0.70
23	Indiana	1.11	48	Wisconsin	0.51
24	Missouri	1.10	49	North Dakota	0.49
25	Connecticut	1.09	50	Hawaii	0.09

District of Columbia**   N/A

Source: Morgan Quitno Corporation using data from U.S. Bureau of the Census
   "Government Finances: 1990–1991 (Preliminary Report)" (March 1993)
*Preliminary data.
**Not applicable

Local Government Expenditures for Police Protection in 1991

National Total = $27,986,386,000*

RANK	STATE	EXPENDITURES	%	RANK	STATE	EXPENDITURES	%
1	California	$4,721,341,000	16.87%	26	Oregon	$270,626,000	0.97%
2	New York	3,254,479,000	11.63%	27	Oklahoma	235,702,000	0.84%
3	Florida	1,923,099,000	6.87%	28	South Carolina	232,463,000	0.83%
4	Texas	1,633,039,000	5.84%	29	Kansas	215,051,000	0.77%
5	Illinois	1,384,612,000	4.95%	30	Kentucky	209,977,000	0.75%
6	Ohio	1,092,786,000	3.90%	31	Iowa	206,054,000	0.74%
7	Michigan	1,044,649,000	3.73%	32	Nevada	196,096,000	0.70%
8	New Jersey	1,033,194,000	3.69%	33	New Mexico	153,080,000	0.55%
9	Pennsylvania	875,128,000	3.13%	34	Hawaii	144,571,000	0.52%
10	Massachusetts	682,665,000	2.44%	35	Mississippi	140,274,000	0.50%
11	Wisconsin	614,527,000	2.20%	36	Utah	133,444,000	0.48%
12	Georgia	586,788,000	2.10%	37	Arkansas	120,506,000	0.43%
13	Virginia	579,647,000	2.07%	38	Nebraska	109,433,000	0.39%
14	Maryland	575,772,000	2.06%	39	Rhode Island	109,039,000	0.39%
15	North Carolina	543,384,000	1.94%	40	New Hampshire	103,616,000	0.37%
16	Arizona	494,151,000	1.77%	41	Alaska	78,581,000	0.28%
17	Washington	462,972,000	1.65%	42	Idaho	76,666,000	0.27%
18	Missouri	442,217,000	1.58%	43	Maine	70,705,000	0.25%
19	Minnesota	428,059,000	1.53%	44	West Virginia	65,934,000	0.24%
20	Louisiana	422,671,000	1.51%	45	Montana	55,143,000	0.20%
21	Colorado	394,881,000	1.41%	46	Delaware	54,680,000	0.20%
22	Connecticut	381,977,000	1.36%	47	Wyoming	54,278,000	0.19%
23	Tennessee	379,705,000	1.36%	48	South Dakota	40,193,000	0.14%
24	Indiana	335,240,000	1.20%	49	North Dakota	33,847,000	0.12%
25	Alabama	296,175,000	1.06%	50	Vermont	26,194,000	0.09%
					District of Columbia	267,075,000	0.95%

Source: U.S. Bureau of the Census

"Government Finances: 1990–1991 (Preliminary Report)" (March 1993)

*Direct expenditures. Preliminary data.

Per Capita Local Government Expenditures for Police Protection in 1991

National Per Capita = $110.98*

RANK	STATE	PER CAPITA	RANK	STATE	PER CAPITA
1	New York	$180.22	26	Virginia	$92.21
2	California	155.41	27	Georgia	88.60
3	Nevada	152.72	28	Kansas	86.19
4	Florida	144.84	29	Missouri	85.73
5	Alaska	137.86	30	North Carolina	80.66
6	New Jersey	133.14	31	Delaware	80.41
7	Arizona	131.77	32	Tennessee	76.66
8	Hawaii	127.38	33	Utah	75.39
9	Wisconsin	124.02	34	Oklahoma	74.24
10	Illinois	119.95	35	Idaho	73.79
11	Maryland	118.47	36	Iowa	73.72
12	Wyoming	118.00	37	Pennsylvania	73.17
13	Colorado	116.93	38	Alabama	72.43
14	Connecticut	116.07	39	Nebraska	68.70
15	Massachusetts	113.85	40	Montana	68.25
16	Michigan	111.51	41	South Carolina	65.30
17	Rhode Island	108.60	42	Indiana	59.76
18	Ohio	99.90	43	Maine	57.25
19	Louisiana	99.41	44	South Dakota	57.17
20	New Mexico	98.89	45	Kentucky	56.55
21	Minnesota	96.58	46	Mississippi	54.12
22	Texas	94.13	47	North Dakota	53.30
23	New Hampshire	93.77	48	Arkansas	50.80
24	Oregon	92.62	49	Vermont	46.20
25	Washington	92.26	50	West Virginia	36.61

District of Columbia   446.61

Source: Morgan Quitno Corporation using data from U.S. Bureau of the Census
    "Government Finances: 1990-1991 (Preliminary Report)" (March 1993)
*Direct expenditures. Preliminary data.

Local Government Expenditures for Police Protection as a Percent of All Direct Expenditures in 1991

National Percent = 4.53% of Direct Expenditures*

RANK	STATE	PERCENT	RANK	STATE	PERCENT
1	Hawaii	10.58	26	Kansas	4.07
2	Rhode Island	6.50	27	Oregon	4.06
3	Nevada	5.70	28	Alabama	4.03
4	Florida	5.52	29	Wyoming	3.96
5	Maryland	5.44	30	Arkansas	3.95
6	New Jersey	5.42	31	Montana	3.94
7	Illinois	5.40	32	Georgia	3.85
7	Louisiana	5.40	33	Kentucky	3.77
9	New Hampshire	5.33	34	North Carolina	3.72
10	Connecticut	5.24	35	South Carolina	3.68
11	New Mexico	5.22	36	Iowa	3.54
12	Wisconsin	5.05	37	South Dakota	3.52
13	Ohio	4.95	38	Pennsylvania	3.51
14	Missouri	4.89	39	Utah	3.49
15	California	4.87	40	Alaska	3.46
15	Delaware	4.87	41	Washington	3.45
17	Arizona	4.83	42	Tennessee	3.33
17	Massachusetts	4.83	43	North Dakota	3.26
19	Michigan	4.81	44	Maine	3.25
20	Idaho	4.63	45	Mississippi	3.24
21	Colorado	4.57	46	Minnesota	3.21
22	Oklahoma	4.45	47	Indiana	3.16
22	Virginia	4.45	48	West Virginia	2.67
24	Texas	4.43	49	Vermont	2.63
25	New York	4.42	50	Nebraska	2.38

District of Columbia   4.69

Source: Morgan Quitno Corporation using data from U.S. Bureau of the Census
      "Government Finances: 1990–1991 (Preliminary Report)" (March 1993)
*Preliminary data.

State and Local Government Expenditures for Corrections in 1991

National Total = $27,356,376,000*

RANK	STATE	EXPENDITURES	%		RANK	STATE	EXPENDITURES	%
1	California	$4,681,365,000	17.11%		26	Minnesota	$267,768,000	0.98%
2	New York	3,688,193,000	13.48%		27	Kentucky	250,118,000	0.91%
3	Florida	1,635,699,000	5.98%		28	Oklahoma	237,733,000	0.87%
4	Texas	1,533,982,000	5.61%		29	Alabama	231,886,000	0.85%
5	Michigan	1,038,912,000	3.80%		30	Kansas	225,897,000	0.83%
6	Pennsylvania	956,070,000	3.49%		31	Nevada	199,759,000	0.73%
7	Illinois	901,148,000	3.29%		32	New Mexico	156,935,000	0.57%
8	New Jersey	886,876,000	3.24%		33	Utah	141,247,000	0.52%
9	Ohio	851,111,000	3.11%		34	Iowa	136,403,000	0.50%
10	Georgia	808,082,000	2.95%		35	Alaska	126,879,000	0.46%
11	Massachusetts	727,500,000	2.66%		36	Arkansas	119,074,000	0.44%
12	Maryland	679,294,000	2.48%		37	Mississippi	105,857,000	0.39%
13	Virginia	635,120,000	2.32%		38	Nebraska	96,174,000	0.35%
14	North Carolina	633,251,000	2.31%		39	Rhode Island	92,086,000	0.34%
15	Arizona	492,093,000	1.80%		40	Hawaii	91,866,000	0.34%
16	Washington	469,715,000	1.72%		41	Maine	90,355,000	0.33%
17	Tennessee	464,623,000	1.70%		42	Delaware	82,707,000	0.30%
18	Connecticut	459,799,000	1.68%		43	New Hampshire	63,653,000	0.23%
19	Wisconsin	408,223,000	1.49%		44	Idaho	59,097,000	0.22%
20	South Carolina	371,496,000	1.36%		45	West Virginia	59,096,000	0.22%
21	Indiana	363,276,000	1.33%		46	Montana	53,852,000	0.20%
22	Colorado	354,188,000	1.29%		47	Wyoming	40,121,000	0.15%
23	Oregon	335,715,000	1.23%		48	South Dakota	36,506,000	0.13%
24	Louisiana	322,230,000	1.18%		49	Vermont	30,362,000	0.11%
25	Missouri	279,193,000	1.02%		50	North Dakota	21,658,000	0.08%
						District of Columbia	362,133,000	1.32%

Source: U.S. Bureau of the Census
   "Government Finances: 1990-1991 (Preliminary Report)" (March 1993)
*Direct expenditures. Preliminary data.

Per Capita State and Local Government Expenditures for Corrections in 1991

National Per Capita = $108.48*

RANK	STATE	PER CAPITA		RANK	STATE	PER CAPITA
1	Alaska	$222.59		26	Wisconsin	$82.39
2	New York	204.24		27	Hawaii	80.94
3	Nevada	155.58		28	Pennsylvania	79.93
4	California	154.09		29	Utah	79.80
5	Maryland	139.77		30	Illinois	78.07
6	Connecticut	139.71		31	Ohio	77.81
7	Arizona	131.22		32	Louisiana	75.78
8	Florida	123.20		33	Oklahoma	74.88
9	Georgia	122.01		34	Maine	73.16
10	Delaware	121.63		35	Kentucky	67.36
11	Massachusetts	121.33		36	Montana	66.65
12	Oregon	114.89		37	Indiana	64.76
13	New Jersey	114.29		38	Minnesota	60.42
14	Michigan	110.90		39	Nebraska	60.37
15	Colorado	104.88		40	New Hampshire	57.60
16	South Carolina	104.35		41	Idaho	56.88
17	New Mexico	101.38		42	Alabama	56.71
18	Virginia	101.04		43	Missouri	54.13
19	North Carolina	94.00		44	Vermont	53.55
20	Tennessee	93.81		45	South Dakota	51.93
21	Washington	93.61		46	Arkansas	50.20
22	Rhode Island	91.72		47	Iowa	48.80
23	Kansas	90.54		48	Mississippi	40.84
24	Texas	88.42		49	North Dakota	34.11
25	Wyoming	87.22		50	West Virginia	32.81

District of Columbia   605.57

Source: Morgan Quitno Corporation using data from U.S. Bureau of the Census
 "Government Finances: 1990–1991 (Preliminary Report)" (March 1993)
*Direct expenditures. Preliminary data.

State and Local Government Expenditures for Corrections as a Percent of All Direct Expenditures in 1991

National Percent = 2.58% of Direct Expenditures*

RANK	STATE	PERCENT		RANK	STATE	PERCENT
1	Nevada	3.42		26	Rhode Island	2.04
2	Maryland	3.32		26	Wisconsin	2.04
3	Georgia	3.26		28	Louisiana	2.03
4	California	3.20		29	Alaska	2.02
5	Florida	3.16		29	Kentucky	2.02
6	New York	3.14		29	Ohio	2.02
7	Arizona	3.13		32	Indiana	1.96
8	Connecticut	2.80		33	Washington	1.89
8	South Carolina	2.80		34	Arkansas	1.85
10	Virginia	2.78		35	Maine	1.81
11	Oregon	2.73		36	Idaho	1.79
12	Delaware	2.71		36	Missouri	1.79
13	New Mexico	2.66		38	Montana	1.68
14	Michigan	2.65		39	New Hampshire	1.67
15	Texas	2.64		40	Alabama	1.64
16	North Carolina	2.62		41	South Dakota	1.60
17	Colorado	2.59		42	Hawaii	1.59
18	Tennessee	2.56		43	Wyoming	1.56
19	Kansas	2.51		44	Nebraska	1.38
20	New Jersey	2.45		45	Mississippi	1.34
21	Massachusetts	2.43		46	Iowa	1.30
22	Oklahoma	2.24		47	Minnesota	1.26
23	Pennsylvania	2.14		48	Vermont	1.25
24	Illinois	2.06		49	West Virginia	0.98
24	Utah	2.06		50	North Dakota	0.89

District of Columbia   6.36

Source: Morgan Quitno Corporation using data from U.S. Bureau of the Census
"Government Finances: 1990-1991 (Preliminary Report)" (March 1993)
*Preliminary data.

State Government Expenditures for Corrections in 1991

National Total = $17,806,641,000*

RANK	STATE	EXPENDITURES	%		RANK	STATE	EXPENDITURES	%
1	California	$2,755,859,000	15.48%		26	Oklahoma	$197,187,000	1.11%
2	New York	1,980,621,000	11.12%		27	Missouri	196,080,000	1.10%
3	Florida	924,210,000	5.19%		28	Kentucky	179,786,000	1.01%
4	Texas	915,980,000	5.14%		29	Alabama	172,937,000	0.97%
5	Michigan	807,904,000	4.54%		30	Minnesota	144,178,000	0.81%
6	Illinois	629,393,000	3.53%		31	Alaska	125,678,000	0.71%
7	Georgia	610,645,000	3.43%		32	Nevada	124,558,000	0.70%
8	Ohio	598,219,000	3.36%		33	New Mexico	123,341,000	0.69%
9	Massachusetts	594,730,000	3.34%		34	Iowa	108,534,000	0.61%
10	New Jersey	559,118,000	3.14%		35	Arkansas	98,373,000	0.55%
11	Pennsylvania	521,676,000	2.93%		36	Rhode Island	92,086,000	0.52%
12	North Carolina	516,709,000	2.90%		37	Hawaii	91,866,000	0.52%
13	Maryland	493,204,000	2.77%		38	Utah	91,610,000	0.51%
14	Connecticut	459,799,000	2.58%		39	Mississippi	87,518,000	0.49%
15	Virginia	404,117,000	2.27%		40	Delaware	82,707,000	0.46%
16	Tennessee	337,396,000	1.89%		41	Maine	68,009,000	0.38%
17	Arizona	318,038,000	1.79%		42	Nebraska	66,098,000	0.37%
18	South Carolina	314,469,000	1.77%		43	Idaho	48,645,000	0.27%
19	Washington	309,198,000	1.74%		44	Montana	45,601,000	0.26%
20	Indiana	278,454,000	1.56%		45	New Hampshire	43,016,000	0.24%
21	Wisconsin	262,304,000	1.47%		46	West Virginia	40,470,000	0.23%
22	Colorado	253,437,000	1.42%		47	Vermont	30,309,000	0.17%
23	Louisiana	224,919,000	1.26%		48	South Dakota	28,220,000	0.16%
24	Oregon	212,999,000	1.20%		49	Wyoming	23,248,000	0.13%
25	Kansas	198,007,000	1.11%		50	North Dakota	15,181,000	0.09%

District of Columbia** N/A N/A

Source: U.S. Bureau of the Census

   "Government Finances: 1990–1991 (Preliminary Report)" (March 1993)

*Direct expenditures. Preliminary data.

**Not applicable

Per Capita State Government Expenditures for Corrections in 1991

National Per Capita = $70.61*

RANK	STATE	PER CAPITA	RANK	STATE	PER CAPITA
1	Alaska	$220.49	26	Montana	$56.44
2	Connecticut	139.71	27	Maine	55.07
3	Delaware	121.63	28	Ohio	54.69
4	New York	109.68	29	Illinois	54.53
5	Maryland	101.48	30	Vermont	53.46
6	Massachusetts	99.19	31	Wisconsin	52.94
7	Nevada	97.01	32	Louisiana	52.90
8	Georgia	92.20	33	Texas	52.80
9	Rhode Island	91.72	34	Utah	51.76
10	California	90.71	35	Wyoming	50.54
11	South Carolina	88.33	36	Indiana	49.64
12	Michigan	86.24	37	Kentucky	48.42
13	Arizona	84.81	38	Idaho	46.82
14	Hawaii	80.94	39	Pennsylvania	43.61
15	New Mexico	79.68	40	Alabama	42.29
16	Kansas	79.36	41	Nebraska	41.49
17	North Carolina	76.70	42	Arkansas	41.47
18	Colorado	75.05	43	South Dakota	40.14
19	Oregon	72.89	44	New Hampshire	38.93
20	New Jersey	72.05	45	Iowa	38.83
21	Florida	69.61	46	Missouri	38.01
22	Tennessee	68.12	47	Mississippi	33.76
23	Virginia	64.29	48	Minnesota	32.53
24	Oklahoma	62.11	49	North Dakota	23.91
25	Washington	61.62	50	West Virginia	22.47

District of Columbia**   N/A

Source: Morgan Quitno Corporation using data from U.S. Bureau of the Census
    "Government Finances: 1990-1991 (Preliminary Report)" (March 1993)

*Direct expenditures. Preliminary data.

**Not applicable

State Government Expenditures for Corrections as a Percent of All Direct Expenditures in 1991

National Percent = 4.03% of Direct Expenditures*

RANK	STATE	PERCENT		RANK	STATE	PERCENT
1	Georgia	6.41		26	Rhode Island	3.24
2	Arizona	5.82		27	Alaska	3.13
3	California	5.60		28	Utah	3.01
4	Florida	5.48		29	Ohio	2.99
5	North Carolina	5.39		30	Missouri	2.98
6	Kansas	5.32		31	Idaho	2.97
7	Nevada	5.19		32	Arkansas	2.90
8	Connecticut	5.04		33	Louisiana	2.79
9	Colorado	5.03		34	Nebraska	2.78
10	Maryland	4.98		35	Washington	2.71
10	Tennessee	4.98		36	Kentucky	2.63
12	Michigan	4.63		36	Pennsylvania	2.63
13	New York	4.53		38	Alabama	2.54
14	South Carolina	4.52		38	Montana	2.54
15	Texas	4.31		40	Mississippi	2.47
16	Delaware	4.28		41	South Dakota	2.46
17	New Mexico	4.15		42	Maine	2.42
18	Virginia	4.10		43	Iowa	2.31
19	Oregon	3.77		44	New Hampshire	2.29
20	Massachusetts	3.75		45	Vermont	2.11
21	Oklahoma	3.70		46	Hawaii	2.09
22	Indiana	3.50		47	Wyoming	1.93
23	Illinois	3.48		48	Minnesota	1.84
24	Wisconsin	3.34		49	West Virginia	1.13
25	New Jersey	3.27		50	North Dakota	1.08

District of Columbia**   N/A

Source: Morgan Quitno Corporation using data from U.S. Bureau of the Census
   "Government Finances: 1990-1991 (Preliminary Report)" (March 1993)
*Preliminary data.
**Not applicable

Local Government Expenditures for Corrections in 1991

National Total = $9,549,735,000*

RANK	STATE	EXPENDITURES	%		RANK	STATE	EXPENDITURES	%
1	California	$1,925,506,000	20.16%		26	Kentucky	$70,332,000	0.74%
2	New York	1,707,572,000	17.88%		27	Alabama	58,949,000	0.62%
3	Florida	711,489,000	7.45%		28	South Carolina	57,027,000	0.60%
4	Texas	618,002,000	6.47%		29	Utah	49,637,000	0.52%
5	Pennsylvania	434,394,000	4.55%		30	Oklahoma	40,546,000	0.42%
6	New Jersey	327,758,000	3.43%		31	New Mexico	33,594,000	0.35%
7	Illinois	271,755,000	2.85%		32	Nebraska	30,076,000	0.31%
8	Ohio	252,892,000	2.65%		33	Kansas	27,890,000	0.29%
9	Michigan	231,008,000	2.42%		34	Iowa	27,869,000	0.29%
10	Virginia	231,003,000	2.42%		35	Maine	22,346,000	0.23%
11	Georgia	197,437,000	2.07%		36	Arkansas	20,701,000	0.22%
12	Maryland	186,090,000	1.95%		37	New Hampshire	20,637,000	0.22%
13	Arizona	174,055,000	1.82%		38	West Virginia	18,626,000	0.20%
14	Washington	160,517,000	1.68%		39	Mississippi	18,339,000	0.19%
15	Wisconsin	145,919,000	1.53%		40	Wyoming	16,873,000	0.18%
16	Massachusetts	132,770,000	1.39%		41	Idaho	10,452,000	0.11%
17	Tennessee	127,227,000	1.33%		42	South Dakota	8,286,000	0.09%
18	Minnesota	123,590,000	1.29%		43	Montana	8,251,000	0.09%
19	Oregon	122,716,000	1.29%		44	North Dakota	6,477,000	0.07%
20	North Carolina	116,542,000	1.22%		45	Alaska	1,201,000	0.01%
21	Colorado	100,751,000	1.06%		46	Vermont	53,000	0.00%
22	Louisiana	97,311,000	1.02%		47	Connecticut	0	0.00%
23	Indiana	84,822,000	0.89%		47	Delaware	0	0.00%
24	Missouri	83,113,000	0.87%		47	Hawaii	0	0.00%
25	Nevada	75,201,000	0.79%		47	Rhode Island	0	0.00%
						District of Columbia	362,133,000	3.79%

Source: U.S. Bureau of the Census

"Government Finances: 1990-1991 (Preliminary Report)" (March 1993)

*Direct expenditures. Preliminary data.

Per Capita Local Government Expenditures for Corrections in 1991

National Per Capita = $37.87*

RANK	STATE	PER CAPITA		RANK	STATE	PER CAPITA
1	New York	$94.56		26	Kentucky	$18.94
2	California	63.38		27	Nebraska	18.88
3	Nevada	58.57		28	New Hampshire	18.68
4	Florida	53.59		29	Maine	18.09
5	Arizona	46.41		30	North Carolina	17.30
6	New Jersey	42.24		31	Missouri	16.11
7	Oregon	42.00		32	South Carolina	16.02
8	Maryland	38.29		33	Indiana	15.12
9	Virginia	36.75		34	Alabama	14.42
10	Wyoming	36.68		35	Oklahoma	12.77
11	Pennsylvania	36.32		36	South Dakota	11.79
12	Texas	35.62		37	Kansas	11.18
13	Washington	31.99		38	West Virginia	10.34
14	Colorado	29.83		39	Montana	10.21
15	Georgia	29.81		40	North Dakota	10.20
16	Wisconsin	29.45		41	Idaho	10.06
17	Utah	28.04		42	Iowa	9.97
18	Minnesota	27.89		43	Arkansas	8.73
19	Tennessee	25.69		44	Mississippi	7.08
20	Michigan	24.66		45	Alaska	2.11
21	Illinois	23.54		46	Vermont	0.09
22	Ohio	23.12		47	Connecticut	0.00
23	Louisiana	22.89		47	Delaware	0.00
24	Massachusetts	22.14		47	Hawaii	0.00
25	New Mexico	21.70		47	Rhode Island	0.00

District of Columbia   605.57

Source: Morgan Quitno Corporation using data from U.S. Bureau of the Census
   "Government Finances: 1990-1991 (Preliminary Report)" (March 1993)
*Direct expenditures. Preliminary data.

Local Government Expenditures for Corrections as a Percent of All Direct Expenditures in 1991

National Percent = 1.55% of Direct Expenditures*

RANK	STATE	PERCENT	RANK	STATE	PERCENT
1	New York	2.32	26	Maine	1.03
2	Nevada	2.19	27	Massachusetts	0.94
3	Florida	2.04	28	Minnesota	0.93
4	California	1.99	29	Missouri	0.92
5	Oregon	1.84	30	South Carolina	0.90
6	Virginia	1.77	31	Alabama	0.80
7	Maryland	1.76	31	Indiana	0.80
8	Pennsylvania	1.74	31	North Carolina	0.80
9	New Jersey	1.72	34	Oklahoma	0.77
10	Arizona	1.70	35	West Virginia	0.75
11	Texas	1.68	36	South Dakota	0.73
12	Georgia	1.30	37	Arkansas	0.68
12	Utah	1.30	38	Nebraska	0.66
14	Kentucky	1.26	39	Idaho	0.63
15	Louisiana	1.24	40	North Dakota	0.62
16	Wyoming	1.23	41	Montana	0.59
17	Washington	1.20	42	Kansas	0.53
17	Wisconsin	1.20	43	Iowa	0.48
19	Colorado	1.17	44	Mississippi	0.42
20	New Mexico	1.15	45	Alaska	0.05
20	Ohio	1.15	46	Vermont	0.01
22	Tennessee	1.12	47	Connecticut	0.00
23	Illinois	1.06	47	Delaware	0.00
23	Michigan	1.06	47	Hawaii	0.00
23	New Hampshire	1.06	47	Rhode Island	0.00

District of Columbia   6.36

Source: Morgan Quitno Corporation using data from U.S. Bureau of the Census
    "Government Finances: 1990-1991 (Preliminary Report)" (March 1993)
*Preliminary data.

State and Local Government Expenditures for Judicial and Legal Services in 1991

National Total = $15,377,798,000*

RANK	STATE	EXPENDITURES	%	RANK	STATE	EXPENDITURES	%
1	California	$3,038,440,000	19.76%	26	Alabama	$162,471,000	1.06%
2	New York	1,763,767,000	11.47%	27	Kentucky	152,016,000	0.99%
3	Florida	898,578,000	5.84%	28	Iowa	145,238,000	0.94%
4	Texas	740,142,000	4.81%	29	Kansas	125,306,000	0.81%
5	Ohio	644,621,000	4.19%	30	Hawaii	123,225,000	0.80%
6	Pennsylvania	619,163,000	4.03%	31	Nevada	116,426,000	0.76%
7	New Jersey	583,565,000	3.79%	32	South Carolina	109,528,000	0.71%
8	Michigan	567,440,000	3.69%	33	Oklahoma	104,024,000	0.68%
9	Illinois	562,136,000	3.66%	34	Alaska	100,471,000	0.65%
10	Massachusetts	360,026,000	2.34%	35	Utah	86,538,000	0.56%
11	Arizona	306,736,000	1.99%	36	New Mexico	85,809,000	0.56%
12	Maryland	305,356,000	1.99%	37	Mississippi	69,724,000	0.45%
13	Virginia	286,995,000	1.87%	38	New Hampshire	67,248,000	0.44%
14	Washington	276,154,000	1.80%	39	Rhode Island	66,319,000	0.43%
15	Wisconsin	265,060,000	1.72%	40	West Virginia	61,866,000	0.40%
16	Georgia	260,138,000	1.69%	41	Arkansas	61,503,000	0.40%
17	Minnesota	256,221,000	1.67%	42	Nebraska	57,610,000	0.37%
18	North Carolina	240,229,000	1.56%	43	Delaware	50,917,000	0.33%
19	Connecticut	198,381,000	1.29%	44	Idaho	44,857,000	0.29%
20	Tennessee	192,378,000	1.25%	45	Maine	43,340,000	0.28%
21	Colorado	189,115,000	1.23%	46	Montana	34,290,000	0.22%
22	Louisiana	187,432,000	1.22%	47	Wyoming	28,962,000	0.19%
23	Indiana	183,086,000	1.19%	48	North Dakota	27,566,000	0.18%
24	Missouri	181,248,000	1.18%	49	Vermont	26,436,000	0.17%
25	Oregon	171,518,000	1.12%	50	South Dakota	23,244,000	0.15%
					District of Columbia	124,939,000	0.81%

Source: U.S. Bureau of the Census

"Government Finances: 1990-1991 (Preliminary Report)" (March 1993)

*Direct expenditures. Preliminary data. Includes Courts, Prosecution and Legal Services and Public Defense.

Per Capita State and Local Government Expenditures for Judicial and Legal Services in 1991

National Per Capita = $60.98*

RANK	STATE	PER CAPITA	RANK	STATE	PER CAPITA
1	Alaska	$176.26	26	Kansas	$50.22
2	Hawaii	108.57	27	Utah	48.89
3	California	100.01	28	Illinois	48.70
4	New York	97.67	29	Vermont	46.62
5	Nevada	90.67	30	Virginia	45.66
6	Arizona	81.80	31	Louisiana	44.08
7	New Jersey	75.20	32	North Dakota	43.41
8	Delaware	74.88	33	Idaho	43.17
9	Florida	67.68	34	Texas	42.66
10	Rhode Island	66.05	35	Montana	42.44
11	Wyoming	62.96	36	Kentucky	40.94
12	Maryland	62.83	37	Alabama	39.73
13	New Hampshire	60.86	38	Georgia	39.28
14	Michigan	60.57	39	Tennessee	38.84
15	Connecticut	60.28	40	Nebraska	36.16
16	Massachusetts	60.04	41	North Carolina	35.66
17	Ohio	58.93	42	Missouri	35.14
18	Oregon	58.70	43	Maine	35.09
19	Minnesota	57.81	44	West Virginia	34.35
20	Colorado	56.00	45	South Dakota	33.06
21	New Mexico	55.43	46	Oklahoma	32.76
22	Washington	55.03	47	Indiana	32.64
23	Wisconsin	53.49	48	South Carolina	30.77
24	Iowa	51.96	49	Mississippi	26.90
25	Pennsylvania	51.77	50	Arkansas	25.93

District of Columbia   208.93

Source: Morgan Quitno Corporation using data from U.S. Bureau of the Census
    "Government Finances: 1990–1991 (Preliminary Report)" (March 1993)
*Direct expenditures. Preliminary data. Includes Courts, Prosecution and Legal Services and Public Defense.

State and Local Government Expenditures for Judicial and Legal Services
As a Percent of All Direct Expenditures in 1991
National Percent = 1.45% of Direct Expenditures*

RANK	STATE	PERCENT	RANK	STATE	PERCENT
1	Hawaii	2.13	26	Virginia	1.25
2	California	2.08	27	Kentucky	1.23
3	Nevada	1.99	28	Connecticut	1.21
4	Arizona	1.95	28	Minnesota	1.21
5	New Hampshire	1.76	30	Massachusetts	1.20
6	Florida	1.74	31	Louisiana	1.18
7	Delaware	1.67	32	Missouri	1.16
8	New Jersey	1.61	33	Alabama	1.15
9	Alaska	1.60	34	North Dakota	1.13
10	Ohio	1.53	34	Wyoming	1.13
11	New York	1.50	36	Washington	1.11
12	Maryland	1.49	37	Vermont	1.09
13	Rhode Island	1.47	38	Montana	1.07
14	Michigan	1.45	39	Tennessee	1.06
14	New Mexico	1.45	40	Georgia	1.05
16	Kansas	1.39	41	South Dakota	1.02
16	Oregon	1.39	41	West Virginia	1.02
18	Colorado	1.38	43	Indiana	0.99
18	Iowa	1.38	43	North Carolina	0.99
18	Pennsylvania	1.38	45	Oklahoma	0.98
21	Idaho	1.36	46	Arkansas	0.96
22	Wisconsin	1.32	47	Mississippi	0.89
23	Illinois	1.29	48	Maine	0.87
24	Texas	1.27	49	Nebraska	0.83
25	Utah	1.26	50	South Carolina	0.82

District of Columbia   2.20

Source: Morgan Quitno Corporation using data from U.S. Bureau of the Census
"Government Finances: 1990-1991 (Preliminary Report)" (March 1993)
*Preliminary data. Includes Courts, Prosecution and Legal Services and Public Defense.

State Government Expenditures for Judicial and Legal Services in 1991

National Total = $5,919,570,000*

RANK	STATE	EXPENDITURES	%	RANK	STATE	EXPENDITURES	%
1	New York	$1,047,061,000	17.69%	26	Louisiana	$76,784,000	1.30%
2	Florida	418,309,000	7.07%	27	Tennessee	76,387,000	1.29%
3	Massachusetts	317,106,000	5.36%	28	New Mexico	75,843,000	1.28%
4	California	296,422,000	5.01%	29	Oklahoma	67,460,000	1.14%
5	New Jersey	228,097,000	3.85%	30	Arizona	66,733,000	1.13%
6	North Carolina	213,189,000	3.60%	31	Rhode Island	59,150,000	1.00%
7	Texas	177,826,000	3.00%	32	New Hampshire	57,139,000	0.97%
8	Connecticut	177,040,000	2.99%	33	Utah	56,637,000	0.96%
9	Illinois	175,382,000	2.96%	34	Georgia	56,331,000	0.95%
10	Maryland	169,893,000	2.87%	35	Washington	50,042,000	0.85%
11	Pennsylvania	147,960,000	2.50%	36	Indiana	48,225,000	0.81%
12	Michigan	144,013,000	2.43%	37	Delaware	44,160,000	0.75%
13	Virginia	142,807,000	2.41%	38	West Virginia	41,286,000	0.70%
14	Kentucky	125,415,000	2.12%	39	Maine	36,156,000	0.61%
15	Wisconsin	114,305,000	1.93%	40	South Carolina	31,330,000	0.53%
16	Oregon	110,886,000	1.87%	41	Mississippi	29,584,000	0.50%
17	Alabama	109,448,000	1.85%	42	Nevada	27,835,000	0.47%
18	Iowa	105,387,000	1.78%	43	Nebraska	25,329,000	0.43%
19	Colorado	103,095,000	1.74%	44	Arkansas	25,101,000	0.42%
20	Ohio	102,529,000	1.73%	45	Vermont	25,002,000	0.42%
21	Hawaii	95,022,000	1.61%	46	Idaho	22,135,000	0.37%
22	Missouri	91,724,000	1.55%	47	Wyoming	16,357,000	0.28%
23	Alaska	91,105,000	1.54%	48	North Dakota	15,490,000	0.26%
24	Kansas	82,501,000	1.39%	49	South Dakota	13,521,000	0.23%
25	Minnesota	80,079,000	1.35%	50	Montana	8,952,000	0.15%
					District of Columbia**	N/A	N/A

Source: U.S. Bureau of the Census

"Government Finances: 1990-1991 (Preliminary Report)" (March 1993)

*Direct expenditures. Preliminary data. Includes Courts, Prosecution and Legal Services and Public Defense.

**Not applicable

Per Capita State Government Expenditures for Judicial and Legal Services in 1991

National Per Capita = $23.47*

RANK	STATE	PER CAPITA	RANK	STATE	PER CAPITA
1	Alaska	$159.83	26	West Virginia	$22.92
2	Hawaii	83.72	27	Virginia	22.72
3	Delaware	64.94	28	Nevada	21.68
4	Rhode Island	58.91	29	Idaho	21.30
5	New York	57.98	30	Oklahoma	21.25
6	Connecticut	53.80	31	South Dakota	19.23
7	Massachusetts	52.89	32	Minnesota	18.07
8	New Hampshire	51.71	33	Louisiana	18.06
9	New Mexico	48.99	34	Arizona	17.80
10	Vermont	44.10	35	Missouri	17.78
11	Oregon	37.95	36	Nebraska	15.90
12	Iowa	37.71	37	Tennessee	15.42
13	Wyoming	35.56	38	Michigan	15.37
14	Maryland	34.96	39	Illinois	15.19
15	Kentucky	33.78	40	Pennsylvania	12.37
16	Kansas	33.07	41	Mississippi	11.41
17	Utah	32.00	42	Montana	11.08
18	North Carolina	31.64	43	Arkansas	10.58
19	Florida	31.51	44	Texas	10.25
20	Colorado	30.53	45	Washington	9.97
21	New Jersey	29.39	46	California	9.76
22	Maine	29.28	47	Ohio	9.37
23	Alabama	26.77	48	South Carolina	8.80
24	North Dakota	24.39	49	Indiana	8.60
25	Wisconsin	23.07	50	Georgia	8.51

District of Columbia**   N/A

Source: Morgan Quitno Corporation using data from U.S. Bureau of the Census
    "Government Finances: 1990–1991 (Preliminary Report)" (March 1993)
*Direct expenditures. Preliminary data. Includes Courts, Prosecution and Legal Services and Public Defense.
**Not applicable

State Government Expenditures for Judicial and Legal Services as a Percent of All Direct Expenditures: 1991

National Percent = 1.34% of Direct Expenditures*

RANK	STATE	PERCENT	RANK	STATE	PERCENT
1	New Hampshire	3.04	26	New Jersey	1.33
2	New Mexico	2.55	27	Maine	1.29
3	Florida	2.48	28	Oklahoma	1.26
4	New York	2.39	29	Arizona	1.22
5	Delaware	2.28	30	South Dakota	1.18
6	Alaska	2.27	31	Nevada	1.16
7	Iowa	2.24	32	West Virginia	1.15
8	Kansas	2.22	33	Tennessee	1.13
8	North Carolina	2.22	34	North Dakota	1.10
10	Hawaii	2.16	35	Nebraska	1.07
11	Rhode Island	2.08	36	Minnesota	1.02
12	Colorado	2.05	37	Illinois	0.97
13	Massachusetts	2.00	38	Louisiana	0.95
14	Oregon	1.96	39	Texas	0.84
15	Connecticut	1.94	40	Michigan	0.83
16	Utah	1.86	40	Mississippi	0.83
17	Kentucky	1.84	42	Pennsylvania	0.75
18	Vermont	1.74	43	Arkansas	0.74
19	Maryland	1.72	44	Indiana	0.61
20	Alabama	1.61	45	California	0.60
21	Wisconsin	1.46	46	Georgia	0.59
22	Virginia	1.45	47	Ohio	0.51
23	Missouri	1.39	48	Montana	0.50
24	Wyoming	1.36	49	South Carolina	0.45
25	Idaho	1.35	50	Washington	0.44

District of Columbia**   N/A

Source: Morgan Quitno Corporation using data from U.S. Bureau of the Census
"Government Finances: 1990-1991 (Preliminary Report)" (March 1993)

*Preliminary data. Includes Courts, Prosecution and Legal Services and Public Defense.

**Not applicable

Local Government Expenditures for Judicial and Legal Services in 1991

National Total = $9,458,228,000*

RANK	STATE	EXPENDITURES	%	RANK	STATE	EXPENDITURES	%
1	California	$2,742,018,000	28.99%	26	Massachusetts	$42,920,000	0.45%
2	New York	716,706,000	7.58%	27	Kansas	42,805,000	0.45%
3	Texas	562,316,000	5.95%	28	Mississippi	40,140,000	0.42%
4	Ohio	542,092,000	5.73%	29	Iowa	39,851,000	0.42%
5	Florida	480,269,000	5.08%	30	Oklahoma	36,564,000	0.39%
6	Pennsylvania	471,203,000	4.98%	31	Arkansas	36,402,000	0.38%
7	Michigan	423,427,000	4.48%	32	Nebraska	32,281,000	0.34%
8	Illinois	386,754,000	4.09%	33	Utah	29,901,000	0.32%
9	New Jersey	355,468,000	3.76%	34	Hawaii	28,203,000	0.30%
10	Arizona	240,003,000	2.54%	35	North Carolina	27,040,000	0.29%
11	Washington	226,112,000	2.39%	36	Kentucky	26,601,000	0.28%
12	Georgia	203,807,000	2.15%	37	Montana	25,338,000	0.27%
13	Minnesota	176,142,000	1.86%	38	Idaho	22,722,000	0.24%
14	Wisconsin	150,755,000	1.59%	39	Connecticut	21,341,000	0.23%
15	Virginia	144,188,000	1.52%	40	West Virginia	20,580,000	0.22%
16	Maryland	135,463,000	1.43%	41	Wyoming	12,605,000	0.13%
17	Indiana	134,861,000	1.43%	42	North Dakota	12,076,000	0.13%
18	Tennessee	115,991,000	1.23%	43	New Hampshire	10,109,000	0.11%
19	Louisiana	110,648,000	1.17%	44	New Mexico	9,966,000	0.11%
20	Missouri	89,524,000	0.95%	45	South Dakota	9,723,000	0.10%
21	Nevada	88,591,000	0.94%	46	Alaska	9,366,000	0.10%
22	Colorado	86,020,000	0.91%	47	Maine	7,184,000	0.08%
23	South Carolina	78,198,000	0.83%	48	Rhode Island	7,169,000	0.08%
24	Oregon	60,632,000	0.64%	49	Delaware	6,757,000	0.07%
25	Alabama	53,023,000	0.56%	50	Vermont	1,434,000	0.02%
					District of Columbia	124,939,000	1.32%

Source: U.S. Bureau of the Census

"Government Finances: 1990–1991 (Preliminary Report)" (March 1993)

*Direct expenditures. Preliminary data. Includes Courts, Prosecution and Legal Services and Public Defense.

**Not applicable

Per Capita Local Government Expenditures for Judicial and Legal Services in 1991

National Per Capita = $37.51*

RANK	STATE	PER CAPITA		RANK	STATE	PER CAPITA
1	California	$90.26		26	Idaho	$21.87
2	Nevada	69.00		27	Oregon	20.75
3	Arizona	64.00		28	Nebraska	20.26
4	Ohio	49.56		29	North Dakota	19.02
5	New Jersey	45.81		30	Missouri	17.36
6	Michigan	45.20		31	Kansas	17.16
7	Washington	45.06		32	Utah	16.89
8	Minnesota	39.74		33	Alaska	16.43
9	New York	39.69		34	Mississippi	15.49
10	Pennsylvania	39.39		35	Arkansas	15.35
11	Florida	36.17		36	Iowa	14.26
12	Illinois	33.51		37	South Dakota	13.83
13	Texas	32.41		38	Alabama	12.97
14	Montana	31.36		39	Oklahoma	11.52
15	Georgia	30.77		40	West Virginia	11.43
16	Wisconsin	30.42		41	Delaware	9.94
17	Maryland	27.87		42	New Hampshire	9.15
18	Wyoming	27.40		43	Kentucky	7.16
19	Louisiana	26.02		43	Massachusetts	7.16
20	Colorado	25.47		45	Rhode Island	7.14
21	Hawaii	24.85		46	Connecticut	6.48
22	Indiana	24.04		47	New Mexico	6.44
23	Tennessee	23.42		48	Maine	5.82
24	Virginia	22.94		49	North Carolina	4.01
25	South Carolina	21.97		50	Vermont	2.53

District of Columbia   208.93

Source: Morgan Quitno Corporation using data from U.S. Bureau of the Census
"Government Finances: 1990-1991 (Preliminary Report)" (March 1993)
*Direct expenditures. Preliminary data. Includes Courts, Prosecution and Legal Services and Public Defense.

Local Government Expenditures for Judicial and Legal Services as a Percent of All Direct Expenditures: 1991

National Percent = 1.53% of Direct Expenditures*

RANK	STATE	PERCENT	RANK	STATE	PERCENT
1	California	2.83	26	Colorado	1.00
2	Nevada	2.58	27	Missouri	0.99
3	Ohio	2.46	28	New York	0.97
4	Arizona	2.35	29	Mississippi	0.93
5	Hawaii	2.06	30	Wyoming	0.92
6	Michigan	1.95	31	Oregon	0.91
7	Pennsylvania	1.89	32	South Dakota	0.85
8	New Jersey	1.87	33	West Virginia	0.83
9	Montana	1.81	34	Kansas	0.81
10	Washington	1.68	35	Utah	0.78
11	Texas	1.53	36	Alabama	0.72
12	Illinois	1.51	37	Nebraska	0.70
13	Louisiana	1.41	38	Iowa	0.69
14	Florida	1.38	38	Oklahoma	0.69
15	Idaho	1.37	40	Delaware	0.60
16	Georgia	1.34	41	New Hampshire	0.52
17	Minnesota	1.32	42	Kentucky	0.48
18	Maryland	1.28	43	Rhode Island	0.43
19	Indiana	1.27	44	Alaska	0.41
20	South Carolina	1.24	45	New Mexico	0.34
20	Wisconsin	1.24	46	Maine	0.33
22	Arkansas	1.19	47	Massachusetts	0.30
23	North Dakota	1.16	48	Connecticut	0.29
24	Virginia	1.11	49	North Carolina	0.18
25	Tennessee	1.02	50	Vermont	0.14

District of Columbia   2.20

Source: Morgan Quitno Corporation using data from U.S. Bureau of the Census
    "Government Finances: 1990–1991 (Preliminary Report)" (March 1993)
*Preliminary data. Includes Courts, Prosecution and Legal Services and Public Defense.

Base Salary for Justices of States' Highest Courts in 1993

National Mean = $92,383*

RANK	STATE	SALARY	RANK	STATE	SALARY
1	California	$121,207	26	North Carolina	$91,855
2	New York	117,500	27	Arizona	91,728
3	New Jersey	115,000	28	New Hampshire	91,287
4	Washington	107,200	29	Iowa	90,950
5	Alabama	107,125	30	Massachusetts	90,450
6	Michigan	106,610	31	Arkansas	90,416
7	Connecticut	106,553	32	Utah	89,300
8	Delaware	105,100	33	Nebraska	88,157
9	Pennsylvania	105,000	34	Mississippi	85,800
10	Alaska	104,472	35	Nevada	85,000
11	Illinois	103,097	35	Wyoming	85,000
12	Ohio	101,150	37	Kansas	84,465
13	Florida	100,443	38	Colorado	84,000
14	Virginia	99,709	39	Oklahoma	83,871
15	Maryland	99,000	40	Maine	83,616
16	Tennessee	96,348	41	Indiana	81,000
17	Georgia	96,118	42	Idaho	79,183
18	Rhode Island	95,149	43	Kentucky	78,273
19	Wisconsin	94,906	44	Oregon	76,400
20	Texas	94,685	45	New Mexico	75,000
21	Minnesota	94,395	46	Vermont	73,890
22	Louisiana	94,000	47	South Dakota	72,079
23	Hawaii	93,780	48	West Virginia	72,000
24	South Carolina	92,986	49	North Dakota	71,555
25	Missouri	92,910	50	Montana	64,452

District of Columbia   141,700

Source: National Center for State Courts
"Survey of Judicial Salaries" (July 1993, Volume 19, Number 2)

Base Salary of Judges of Intermediate Appellate Courts in 1993

National Mean = $90,644

RANK	STATE	SALARY		RANK	STATE	SALARY
1	California	$113,632		26	North Carolina	$86,996
2	New Jersey	108,000		27	Missouri	86,755
3	New York	106,625		28	Utah	85,250
4	Alabama	106,125		29	Nebraska	83,749
5	Michigan	102,346		30	Massachusetts	83,708
6	Washington	101,900		31	Kansas	81,451
7	Pennsylvania	101,500		32	Colorado	79,500
8	Connecticut	99,077		33	Oklahoma	78,660
9	Alaska	98,688		34	Idaho	78,183
10	Illinois	97,032		35	Indiana	76,500
11	Georgia	95,509		36	Kentucky	75,078
12	Florida	95,421		37	Oregon	74,600
13	Virginia	94,724		38	New Mexico	71,250
14	Ohio	94,200		–	Delaware*	N/A
15	Maryland	92,500		–	Maine*	N/A
16	Tennessee	91,860		–	Mississippi*	N/A
17	Texas	89,952		–	Montana*	N/A
18	Hawaii	89,780		–	Nevada*	N/A
19	Arizona	89,544		–	New Hampshire*	N/A
20	Wisconsin	89,358		–	North Dakota*	N/A
21	Louisiana	89,000		–	Rhode Island*	N/A
22	Minnesota	88,945		–	South Dakota*	N/A
23	South Carolina	88,338		–	Vermont*	N/A
24	Arkansas	87,563		–	West Virginia*	N/A
25	Iowa	87,450		–	Wyoming*	N/A

District of Columbia*   N/A

Source: National Center for State Courts

"Survey of Judicial Salaries" (July 1993, Volume 19, Number 2)

*No intermediate appellate court.

Base Salaries of Judges of General Trial Courts in 1993

National Mean = $82,357

RANK	STATE	SALARY		RANK	STATE	SALARY
1	New Jersey	$100,000		26	Nebraska	$81,546
2	Delaware	99,900		27	Utah	81,200
3	New York	99,500		28	Massachusetts	80,360
4	California	99,297		29	Missouri	80,356
5	Alaska	96,600		30	Maine	79,073
5	Washington	96,600		31	Nevada	79,000
7	Connecticut	94,647		32	North Carolina	77,289
8	Michigan	94,133		33	Wyoming	77,000
9	Virginia	92,564		34	Mississippi	76,200
10	Florida	90,399		35	Ohio	76,150
11	Pennsylvania	90,000		36	Colorado	75,000
12	Illinois	89,041		37	Idaho	74,214
13	Maryland	89,000		38	Kansas	73,430
14	South Carolina	88,338		39	Georgia	73,344
15	Tennessee	87,900		40	Alabama	72,500
16	Arizona	87,360		41	Kentucky	71,883
17	Hawaii	86,780		42	Oklahoma	71,329
18	Rhode Island	85,666		43	Vermont	70,188
19	New Hampshire	85,564		44	Oregon	69,600
20	Texas	85,217		45	New Mexico	67,500
21	Arkansas	84,706		46	South Dakota	67,314
22	Louisiana	84,000		47	North Dakota	65,970
23	Wisconsin	83,773		48	West Virginia	65,000
24	Minnesota	83,494		49	Montana	63,178
25	Iowa	83,150		50	Indiana	61,740
					District of Columbia	133,600

Source: National Center for State Courts
"Survey of Judicial Salaries" (July 1993, Volume 19, Number 2)

State and Local Government Justice System Payroll in 1990

National Total = $46,467,936,000*

RANK	STATE	PAYROLL	%	RANK	STATE	PAYROLL	%
1	California	$7,541,844,000	16.23%	26	Oregon	$458,124,000	0.99%
2	New York	6,252,576,000	13.46%	27	South Carolina	448,704,000	0.97%
3	Florida	2,820,276,000	6.07%	28	Oklahoma	396,036,000	0.85%
4	Texas	2,576,856,000	5.55%	29	Iowa	379,908,000	0.82%
5	Illinois	2,114,568,000	4.55%	30	Kentucky	373,140,000	0.80%
6	New Jersey	2,034,624,000	4.38%	31	Kansas	360,540,000	0.78%
7	Michigan	1,760,100,000	3.79%	32	Nevada	299,472,000	0.64%
8	Pennsylvania	1,728,096,000	3.72%	33	Hawaii	245,952,000	0.53%
9	Ohio	1,497,084,000	3.22%	34	New Mexico	233,904,000	0.50%
10	Massachusetts	1,179,684,000	2.54%	35	Mississippi	220,824,000	0.48%
11	Maryland	1,116,300,000	2.40%	36	Utah	207,552,000	0.45%
12	Georgia	1,077,120,000	2.32%	37	Arkansas	200,928,000	0.43%
13	Virginia	969,996,000	2.09%	38	Rhode Island	196,548,000	0.42%
14	North Carolina	898,944,000	1.93%	39	Nebraska	193,332,000	0.42%
15	Arizona	810,912,000	1.75%	40	Alaska	181,308,000	0.39%
16	Washington	744,708,000	1.60%	41	New Hampshire	146,364,000	0.31%
17	Missouri	717,300,000	1.54%	42	Maine	141,096,000	0.30%
18	Wisconsin	703,404,000	1.51%	43	Delaware	138,024,000	0.30%
19	Indiana	617,100,000	1.33%	44	Idaho	127,344,000	0.27%
20	Minnesota	603,120,000	1.30%	45	West Virginia	126,924,000	0.27%
21	Connecticut	601,668,000	1.29%	46	Montana	87,540,000	0.19%
22	Tennessee	591,996,000	1.27%	47	Wyoming	75,336,000	0.16%
23	Colorado	575,484,000	1.24%	48	Vermont	72,264,000	0.16%
24	Louisiana	571,392,000	1.23%	49	South Dakota	66,300,000	0.14%
25	Alabama	503,400,000	1.08%	50	North Dakota	59,892,000	0.13%
					District of Columbia	422,028,000	0.91%

Source: Morgan Quitno Corporation using data from U.S. Department of Justice, Bureau of Justice Statistics

"Justice Expenditure and Employment 1990" (NCJ–137754, forthcoming)

*Based on 12 times the October 1990 monthly payroll. Includes payrolls for Police protection, Courts, Prosecution and Legal Services, Public Defense and Corrections.

State and Local Government Payroll for Police Protection in 1990

National Total = $22,421,760,000*

RANK	STATE	PAYROLL	%	RANK	STATE	PAYROLL	%
1	California	$3,480,300,000	15.52%	26	Oregon	$209,688,000	0.94%
2	New York	2,881,056,000	12.85%	27	South Carolina	206,700,000	0.92%
3	Florida	1,355,964,000	6.05%	28	Oklahoma	191,268,000	0.85%
4	Texas	1,249,908,000	5.57%	29	Kansas	173,400,000	0.77%
5	Illinois	1,240,968,000	5.53%	30	Kentucky	172,248,000	0.77%
6	New Jersey	1,011,108,000	4.51%	31	Iowa	163,404,000	0.73%
7	Pennsylvania	904,212,000	4.03%	32	Nevada	127,356,000	0.57%
8	Michigan	766,392,000	3.42%	33	Hawaii	114,504,000	0.51%
9	Ohio	709,644,000	3.16%	34	Mississippi	109,848,000	0.49%
10	Massachusetts	657,756,000	2.93%	35	New Mexico	105,336,000	0.47%
11	Maryland	521,124,000	2.32%	36	Utah	103,104,000	0.46%
12	Virginia	464,592,000	2.07%	37	Rhode Island	101,040,000	0.45%
13	North Carolina	439,824,000	1.96%	38	Nebraska	98,796,000	0.44%
14	Georgia	427,296,000	1.91%	39	Arkansas	98,184,000	0.44%
15	Missouri	388,776,000	1.73%	40	New Hampshire	90,696,000	0.40%
16	Wisconsin	383,772,000	1.71%	41	Maine	78,648,000	0.35%
17	Arizona	373,404,000	1.67%	42	Alaska	68,604,000	0.31%
18	Washington	365,952,000	1.63%	43	Idaho	66,252,000	0.30%
19	Indiana	301,644,000	1.35%	44	West Virginia	65,448,000	0.29%
20	Minnesota	299,268,000	1.33%	45	Delaware	63,792,000	0.28%
21	Connecticut	298,224,000	1.33%	46	Montana	43,092,000	0.19%
22	Colorado	283,512,000	1.26%	47	Wyoming	41,100,000	0.18%
23	Tennessee	280,872,000	1.25%	48	South Dakota	35,640,000	0.16%
24	Louisiana	278,112,000	1.24%	49	Vermont	33,936,000	0.15%
25	Alabama	258,888,000	1.15%	50	North Dakota	31,476,000	0.14%
					District of Columbia	205,656,000	0.92%

Source: Morgan Quitno Corporation using data from U.S. Department of Justice, Bureau of Justice Statistics
"Justice Expenditure and Employment 1990" (NCJ-137754, forthcoming)
*Based on 12 times the October 1990 monthly payroll.

State and Local Government Payroll for Corrections in 1990

National Total = $14,686,692,000*

RANK	STATE	PAYROLL	%
1	California	$2,358,744,000	16.06%
2	New York	2,254,740,000	15.35%
3	Florida	927,156,000	6.31%
4	Texas	809,388,000	5.51%
5	Michigan	681,192,000	4.64%
6	New Jersey	572,304,000	3.90%
7	Illinois	496,728,000	3.38%
8	Georgia	458,148,000	3.12%
9	Pennsylvania	457,800,000	3.12%
10	Ohio	453,000,000	3.08%
11	Maryland	393,096,000	2.68%
12	Virginia	338,760,000	2.31%
13	North Carolina	310,092,000	2.11%
14	Massachusetts	296,820,000	2.02%
15	Arizona	256,020,000	1.74%
16	Washington	221,352,000	1.51%
17	Indiana	197,196,000	1.34%
18	Tennessee	191,100,000	1.30%
19	Connecticut	185,712,000	1.26%
20	Louisiana	183,996,000	1.25%
21	Wisconsin	179,976,000	1.23%
22	Missouri	176,052,000	1.20%
23	South Carolina	174,744,000	1.19%
24	Colorado	168,096,000	1.14%
25	Minnesota	154,188,000	1.05%

RANK	STATE	PAYROLL	%
26	Oregon	$147,636,000	1.01%
27	Alabama	142,944,000	0.97%
28	Iowa	126,552,000	0.86%
29	Oklahoma	126,036,000	0.86%
30	Kansas	118,968,000	0.81%
31	Kentucky	113,124,000	0.77%
32	Nevada	108,120,000	0.74%
33	New Mexico	78,360,000	0.53%
34	Mississippi	68,028,000	0.46%
35	Arkansas	62,808,000	0.43%
36	Rhode Island	59,928,000	0.41%
37	Utah	57,732,000	0.39%
38	Alaska	56,748,000	0.39%
39	Hawaii	55,680,000	0.38%
40	Nebraska	53,532,000	0.36%
41	Maine	42,972,000	0.29%
42	Delaware	37,224,000	0.25%
43	Idaho	30,756,000	0.21%
44	New Hampshire	28,488,000	0.19%
45	West Virginia	26,808,000	0.18%
46	Montana	24,216,000	0.16%
47	Vermont	21,948,000	0.15%
48	Wyoming	18,336,000	0.12%
49	South Dakota	16,608,000	0.11%
50	North Dakota	10,872,000	0.07%

	District of Columbia	155,868,000	1.06%

Source: Morgan Quitno Corporation using data from U.S. Department of Justice, Bureau of Justice Statistics
    "Justice Expenditure and Employment 1990" (NCJ-137754, forthcoming)
*Based on 12 times the October 1990 monthly payroll.

State and Local Government Payroll for Courts in 1990

National Total = $5,628,288,000*

RANK	STATE	PAYROLL	%	RANK	STATE	PAYROLL	%
1	California	$903,240,000	16.05%	26	Iowa	$57,732,000	1.03%
2	New York	677,580,000	12.04%	27	Oregon	53,664,000	0.95%
3	Texas	312,108,000	5.55%	28	Kentucky	51,624,000	0.92%
4	Florida	287,196,000	5.10%	29	South Carolina	49,932,000	0.89%
5	Pennsylvania	262,836,000	4.67%	30	Kansas	46,932,000	0.83%
6	New Jersey	252,828,000	4.49%	31	Oklahoma	39,504,000	0.70%
7	Michigan	228,852,000	4.07%	32	Hawaii	36,432,000	0.65%
8	Illinois	228,516,000	4.06%	33	Nevada	32,916,000	0.58%
9	Ohio	217,992,000	3.87%	34	Utah	29,352,000	0.52%
10	Massachusetts	160,980,000	2.86%	35	Mississippi	28,344,000	0.50%
11	Georgia	136,356,000	2.42%	36	New Mexico	27,204,000	0.48%
12	Maryland	118,116,000	2.10%	37	Delaware	26,700,000	0.47%
13	Virginia	112,752,000	2.00%	38	Arkansas	25,992,000	0.46%
14	Missouri	101,508,000	1.80%	39	Alaska	25,260,000	0.45%
15	North Carolina	100,812,000	1.79%	40	West Virginia	24,612,000	0.44%
16	Arizona	94,644,000	1.68%	41	Nebraska	24,336,000	0.43%
17	Washington	81,456,000	1.45%	42	Rhode Island	22,908,000	0.41%
18	Minnesota	81,252,000	1.44%	43	New Hampshire	20,232,000	0.36%
19	Louisiana	79,908,000	1.42%	44	Idaho	18,108,000	0.32%
20	Tennessee	77,820,000	1.38%	45	North Dakota	12,600,000	0.22%
21	Wisconsin	74,376,000	1.32%	46	Montana	11,652,000	0.21%
22	Indiana	73,944,000	1.31%	47	Maine	11,448,000	0.20%
23	Alabama	72,324,000	1.29%	48	Wyoming	9,816,000	0.17%
24	Colorado	68,388,000	1.22%	49	Vermont	9,132,000	0.16%
25	Connecticut	66,348,000	1.18%	50	South Dakota	8,508,000	0.15%
					District of Columbia	46,884,000	0.83%

Source: Morgan Quitno Corporation using data from U.S. Department of Justice, Bureau of Justice Statistics
   "Justice Expenditure and Employment 1990" (NCJ-137754, forthcoming)
*Based on 12 times the October 1990 monthly payroll.

State and Local Government Payroll for Prosecution and Legal Services in 1990

National Total = $3,017,016,000*

RANK	STATE	PAYROLL	%		RANK	STATE	PAYROLL	%
1	California	$609,048,000	20.19%		26	Tennessee	$32,292,000	1.07%
2	New York	383,880,000	12.72%		27	Kentucky	30,072,000	1.00%
3	Texas	189,444,000	6.28%		28	Louisiana	28,140,000	0.93%
4	Florida	161,628,000	5.36%		29	Iowa	27,744,000	0.92%
5	New Jersey	161,256,000	5.34%		30	Alabama	27,372,000	0.91%
6	Illinois	105,732,000	3.50%		31	Alaska	26,388,000	0.87%
7	Ohio	102,732,000	3.41%		32	Nevada	25,656,000	0.85%
8	Pennsylvania	86,484,000	2.87%		33	New Mexico	18,192,000	0.60%
9	Michigan	78,240,000	2.59%		34	Kansas	17,712,000	0.59%
10	Washington	70,296,000	2.33%		35	Utah	16,620,000	0.55%
11	Arizona	68,448,000	2.27%		36	Nebraska	13,740,000	0.46%
12	Minnesota	55,836,000	1.85%		37	Mississippi	13,356,000	0.44%
13	Maryland	54,840,000	1.82%		38	South Carolina	12,672,000	0.42%
14	Massachusetts	52,116,000	1.73%		39	Arkansas	11,736,000	0.39%
15	Georgia	48,372,000	1.60%		40	Idaho	10,800,000	0.36%
16	Wisconsin	48,336,000	1.60%		41	Rhode Island	10,200,000	0.34%
17	Virginia	45,972,000	1.52%		42	West Virginia	9,612,000	0.32%
18	Colorado	43,140,000	1.43%		43	Maine	7,896,000	0.26%
19	Oregon	42,552,000	1.41%		44	Montana	7,188,000	0.24%
20	Missouri	38,952,000	1.29%		45	New Hampshire	6,900,000	0.23%
21	Oklahoma	36,612,000	1.21%		46	Delaware	6,480,000	0.21%
22	Indiana	36,588,000	1.21%		47	Wyoming	5,160,000	0.17%
23	Connecticut	36,048,000	1.19%		48	South Dakota	5,112,000	0.17%
24	North Carolina	35,148,000	1.16%		49	Vermont	4,992,000	0.17%
25	Hawaii	32,940,000	1.09%		50	North Dakota	4,920,000	0.16%
						District of Columbia	11,436,000	0.38%

Source: Morgan Quitno Corporation using data from U.S. Department of Justice, Bureau of Justice Statistics
    "Justice Expenditure and Employment 1990" (NCJ–137754, forthcoming)
*Based on 12 times the October 1990 monthly payroll.

State and Local Government Payroll for Public Defense in 1990

National Total = $532,116,000*

RANK	STATE	PAYROLL	%	RANK	STATE	PAYROLL	%
1	California	$163,356,000	30.70%	26	Iowa	$4,224,000	0.79%
2	Florida	57,048,000	10.72%	27	Virginia	3,744,000	0.70%
3	New Jersey	36,324,000	6.83%	28	Michigan	3,288,000	0.62%
4	Illinois	33,540,000	6.30%	29	Kansas	3,084,000	0.58%
5	New York	20,676,000	3.89%	30	Delaware	2,880,000	0.54%
6	Maryland	17,052,000	3.20%	31	Texas	2,868,000	0.54%
7	Arizona	15,564,000	2.92%	32	Oklahoma	2,616,000	0.49%
8	Wisconsin	15,516,000	2.92%	33	Nebraska	2,328,000	0.44%
9	Pennsylvania	13,296,000	2.50%	34	Rhode Island	2,280,000	0.43%
10	Ohio	12,264,000	2.30%	35	Vermont	1,992,000	0.37%
11	Minnesota	11,868,000	2.23%	36	South Carolina	1,572,000	0.30%
12	Colorado	11,100,000	2.09%	37	Idaho	1,428,000	0.27%
13	Connecticut	10,572,000	1.99%	38	Arkansas	1,392,000	0.26%
14	Missouri	10,140,000	1.91%	39	Mississippi	1,188,000	0.22%
15	Tennessee	8,700,000	1.63%	40	Oregon	996,000	0.19%
16	Massachusetts	8,088,000	1.52%	41	Wyoming	876,000	0.16%
17	Indiana	6,096,000	1.15%	42	South Dakota	432,000	0.08%
18	North Carolina	5,580,000	1.05%	42	West Virginia	432,000	0.08%
19	Nevada	5,424,000	1.02%	44	Montana	420,000	0.08%
20	Washington	4,944,000	0.93%	45	Louisiana	324,000	0.06%
21	Kentucky	4,824,000	0.91%	46	Alabama	240,000	0.05%
22	Georgia	4,644,000	0.87%	47	Utah	96,000	0.02%
22	Hawaii	4,644,000	0.87%	48	Maine	36,000	0.01%
24	New Mexico	4,464,000	0.84%	49	North Dakota	12,000	0.00%
25	Alaska	4,308,000	0.81%	50	New Hampshire	0	0.00%

| | District of Columbia | 1,176,000 | 0.22% |

Source: Morgan Quitno Corporation using data from U.S. Department of Justice, Bureau of Justice Statistics
"Justice Expenditure and Employment 1990" (NCJ-137754, forthcoming)
*Based on 12 times the October 1990 monthly payroll.

State Victim Compensation Claims Filed in 1989

National Total = 95,234 Claims*

RANK	STATE	CLAIMS	%	RANK	STATE	CLAIMS	%
1	California	33,402	35.07%	26	Nevada	419	0.44%
2	New York	22,445	23.57%	27	Utah	347	0.36%
3	Texas	6,777	7.12%	28	Montana	345	0.36%
4	New Jersey	3,767	3.96%	29	West Virginia	279	0.29%
5	South Carolina	3,261	3.42%	30	Delaware	272	0.29%
6	Florida	3,062	3.22%	31	Alaska	263	0.28%
7	Washington	2,895	3.04%	32	Rhode Island	245	0.26%
8	Michigan	1,951	2.05%	33	Idaho	169	0.18%
9	Pennsylvania	1,702	1.79%	34	New Mexico	138	0.14%
10	Wisconsin	1,369	1.44%	35	North Dakota	93	0.10%
11	Maryland	1,221	1.28%	36	Wyoming	62	0.07%
12	Oregon	1,220	1.28%	–	Arizona*	N/A	N/A
13	Tennessee	1,031	1.08%	–	Arkansas*	N/A	N/A
14	Virginia	889	0.93%	–	Colorado*	N/A	N/A
15	Connecticut	862	0.91%	–	Georgia*	N/A	N/A
16	Missouri	857	0.90%	–	Illinois*	N/A	N/A
17	Indiana	799	0.84%	–	Maine*	N/A	N/A
18	Hawaii	744	0.78%	–	Massachusetts*	N/A	N/A
19	Alabama	740	0.78%	–	Mississippi*	N/A	N/A
20	Oklahoma	712	0.75%	–	Nebraska*	N/A	N/A
21	Iowa	677	0.71%	–	New Hampshire*	N/A	N/A
22	Minnesota	635	0.67%	–	North Carolina*	N/A	N/A
23	Kentucky	592	0.62%	–	Ohio*	N/A	N/A
24	Kansas	534	0.56%	–	South Dakota*	N/A	N/A
25	Louisiana	422	0.44%	–	Vermont*	N/A	N/A
					District of Columbia*	N/A	N/A

Source: U.S. Department of Justice, National Institute of Justice
   "Compensating Crime Victims: A Summary of Policies and Practices" (January 1992, NCJ-136500)
*Not available.

State Victim Compensation Benefits Paid in 1989

National Total = $125,618,237

RANK	STATE	BENEFITS	%	RANK	STATE	BENEFITS	%
1	California	$38,455,000	30.61%	26	Iowa	$716,914	0.57%
2	Texas	17,369,000	13.83%	27	Oklahoma	715,418	0.57%
3	New York	11,196,519	8.91%	28	Louisiana	696,424	0.55%
4	Florida	6,722,529	5.35%	29	Nevada	687,752	0.55%
5	Washington	6,349,918	5.05%	30	Alaska	651,545	0.52%
6	New Jersey	4,893,552	3.90%	31	Utah	639,531	0.51%
7	Tennessee	3,800,000	3.03%	32	Kansas	615,540	0.49%
8	Maryland	2,946,417	2.35%	33	Hawaii	504,687	0.40%
9	Massachusetts	2,647,018	2.11%	34	New Mexico	376,802	0.30%
10	Michigan	2,490,029	1.98%	35	Montana	347,528	0.28%
11	Oregon	2,305,135	1.84%	36	Arizona	303,803	0.24%
12	Pennsylvania	2,256,872	1.80%	37	Idaho	276,005	0.22%
13	Connecticut	1,834,313	1.46%	38	North Dakota	200,196	0.16%
14	Missouri	1,831,167	1.46%	39	Wyoming	69,288	0.06%
15	Virginia	1,690,582	1.35%	40	Nebraska	23,000	0.02%
16	Minnesota	1,586,903	1.26%	–	Arkansas*	N/A	N/A
17	Indiana	1,537,093	1.22%	–	Colorado*	N/A	N/A
18	Alabama	1,488,639	1.19%	–	Georgia*	N/A	N/A
19	Wisconsin	1,300,000	1.03%	–	Illinois*	N/A	N/A
20	South Carolina	1,263,164	1.01%	–	Maine*	N/A	N/A
21	Rhode Island	1,105,833	0.88%	–	Mississippi*	N/A	N/A
22	West Virginia	992,872	0.79%	–	New Hampshire*	N/A	N/A
23	North Carolina	988,924	0.79%	–	Ohio*	N/A	N/A
24	Kentucky	841,350	0.67%	–	South Dakota*	N/A	N/A
25	Delaware	837,967	0.67%	–	Vermont*	N/A	N/A
					District of Columbia*	N/A	N/A

Source: U.S. Department of Justice, National Institute of Justice
   "Compensating Crime Victims: A Summary of Policies and Practices" (January 1992, NCJ–136500)
*Not available.

Average State Victim Compensation Benefit Paid in 1989

National Average = $3,066

RANK	STATE	AVERAGE BENEFIT		RANK	STATE	AVERAGE BENEFIT
1	Rhode Island	$8,800		26	Kansas	$1,948
2	Massachusetts	6,700		27	Minnesota	1,831
3	Nebraska	6,000		28	Wisconsin	1,804
3	West Virginia	6,000		29	Iowa	1,800
5	Maryland	5,000		30	Pennsylvania	1,609
6	Delaware	4,530		31	Oklahoma	1,555
7	Texas	4,422		32	California	1,375
8	New Jersey	4,211		33	North Carolina	1,300
9	Nevada	4,038		34	Montana	1,186
10	Florida	4,000		35	South Carolina	1,128
10	Oregon	4,000		36	Wyoming	1,117
12	Alaska	3,900		37	Hawaii	1,030
13	Connecticut	3,800		38	New York	764
14	Tennessee	3,688		39	Arizona	695
15	New Mexico	3,623		–	Arkansas*	N/A
16	Kentucky	3,535		–	Colorado*	N/A
17	Alabama	3,500		–	Georgia*	N/A
18	Missouri	3,399		–	Illinois*	N/A
19	Idaho	3,388		–	Maine*	N/A
20	Virginia	3,000		–	Mississippi*	N/A
21	Utah	2,600		–	New Hampshire*	N/A
22	Louisiana	2,400		–	Ohio*	N/A
23	Michigan	2,300		–	South Dakota*	N/A
24	Indiana	2,200		–	Vermont*	N/A
25	North Dakota	2,155		–	Washington*	N/A
					District of Columbia*	N/A

Source: U.S. Department of Justice, National Institute of Justice

"Compensating Crime Victims: A Summary of Policies and Practices" (January 1992, NCJ-136500)

*Not available.

V. LAW ENFORCEMENT

Table	Title
219	Law Enforcement Agencies in 1992
220	Population per Law Enforcement Agency in 1992
221	Law Enforcement Agencies per 1,000 Square Miles in 1992
222	Full-Time Sworn Officers in Law Enforcement Agencies in 1992
223	Percent of Full-Time Law Enforcement Agency Employees Who Are Sworn Officers: 1992
224	Full-Time Sworn Officers in Law Enforcement Agencies per 10,000 Population in 1992
225	Full-Time Sworn Law Enforcement Officers per 1,000 Square Miles in 1992
226	Full-Time Employees in Law Enforcement Agencies in 1992
227	Full-Time Employees in Law Enforcement Agencies per 10,000 Population in 1992
228	Full-Time Sworn Officers in State Police Departments in 1992
229	Percent of Full-Time State Police Department Employees Who Are Sworn Officers: 1992
230	Rate of Full-Time Sworn Officers in State Police Departments in 1992
231	Male Officers in State Police Departments in 1990
232	Female Officers in State Police Departments in 1990
233	Female Officers as a Percent of All Officers in State Police Departments in 1990
234	White Officers in State Police Departments in 1990
235	White Officers as a Percent of All Officers in State Police Departments in 1990
236	Black Officers in State Police Departments in 1990
237	Black Officers as a Percent of All Officers in State Police Departments in 1990
238	Hispanic Officers in State Police Departments in 1990
239	Hispanic Officers as a Percent of All Officers in State Police Departments in 1990
240	Full-Time Employees in State Police Departments in 1992
241	Local Police Departments in 1992
242	Full-Time Sworn Officers in Local Police Departments in 1992
243	Percent of Full-Time Local Police Department Employees Who Are Sworn Officers: 1992
244	Rate of Full-Time Sworn Officers in Local Police Departments in 1992
245	Full-Time Employees in Local Police Departments in 1992
246	Sheriffs' Departments in 1992
247	Full-Time Sworn Officers in Sheriffs' Departments in 1992
248	Percent of Full-Time Sheriffs' Departments Employees Who Are Sworn Officers: 1992
249	Rate of Full-Time Sworn Officers in Sheriffs' Departments in 1992
250	Full-Time Employees in Sheriffs' Departments in 1992
251	Special Police Agencies in 1992
252	Full-Time Sworn Officers in Special Police Departments in 1992

V. LAW ENFORCEMENT (continued)

Table	Title
253	Percent of Full-Time Special Police Department Employees Who Are Sworn Officers: 1992
254	Rate of Full-Time Sworn Officers in Special Police Departments in 1992
255	Full-Time Employees in Special Police Departments in 1992
256	Law Enforcement Officers Feloniously Killed in 1992
257	Law Enforcement Officers Feloniously Killed: 1983 to 1992
258	U.S. District Court Judgeships in 1992
259	Criminal Cases Filed in U.S. District Court in 1992
260	Criminal Cases Completed in U.S. District Court in 1992
261	Median Length of Federal Criminal Cases in 1992
262	Federal Prosecutions of Corrupt Public Officials: 1976 to 1990
263	State and Local Justice System Employment in 1990
264	Rate of State and Local Justice System Employment in 1990
265	State Judges of General Jurisdiction in 1990
266	Rate of State Judges of General Jurisdiction in 1990
267	State and Local Courts Employment in 1990
268	State and Local Prosecution Employment in 1990
269	Full-Time State Prosecuting Attorneys in 1990
270	State and Local Public Defense Employment in 1990
271	Public Defenders in 1990
272	Authorized Wiretaps: 1991 and 1992

Law Enforcement Agencies in 1992

National Total = 17,358 Agencies*

RANK	STATE	AGENCIES	%	RANK	STATE	AGENCIES	%
1	Texas	1,712	9.86%	26	Arkansas	277	1.60%
2	Pennsylvania	1,167	6.72%	27	South Carolina	255	1.47%
3	Ohio	908	5.23%	28	Washington	252	1.45%
4	Illinois	894	5.15%	29	Nebraska	247	1.42%
5	Missouri	594	3.42%	30	New Hampshire	228	1.31%
6	Michigan	578	3.33%	30	West Virginia	228	1.31%
6	New York	578	3.33%	32	Colorado	218	1.26%
8	Georgia	540	3.11%	33	Oregon	183	1.05%
9	New Jersey	534	3.08%	34	South Dakota	171	0.99%
10	Wisconsin	506	2.92%	35	Maine	142	0.82%
11	California	493	2.84%	36	North Dakota	134	0.77%
12	North Carolina	458	2.64%	37	Connecticut	133	0.77%
13	Minnesota	456	2.63%	38	Utah	127	0.73%
14	Indiana	448	2.58%	39	Maryland	124	0.71%
15	Iowa	427	2.46%	40	Montana	119	0.69%
16	Oklahoma	410	2.36%	41	New Mexico	115	0.66%
17	Massachusetts	388	2.24%	42	Idaho	112	0.65%
18	Alabama	377	2.17%	43	Arizona	102	0.59%
18	Kentucky	377	2.17%	44	Wyoming	77	0.44%
20	Florida	371	2.14%	45	Vermont	73	0.42%
21	Louisiana	348	2.00%	46	Alaska	48	0.28%
22	Kansas	345	1.99%	46	Rhode Island	48	0.28%
23	Virginia	327	1.88%	48	Delaware	42	0.24%
24	Tennessee	326	1.88%	49	Nevada	35	0.20%
25	Mississippi	297	1.71%	50	Hawaii	6	0.03%
					District of Columbia	3	0.02%

Source: U.S. Department of Justice, Bureau of Justice Statistics

"Census of State and Local Law Enforcement Agencies, 1992" (Bulletin, July 1993, NCJ-142972)

*Includes state and local police, sheriffs' departments and special police agencies.

Population per Law Enforcement Agency in 1992

National Rate = 14,695 Population per Agency*

RANK	STATE	RATE		RANK	STATE	RATE
1	Hawaii	193,333		26	Louisiana	12,319
2	California	62,611		27	Alaska	12,229
3	Maryland	39,581		28	Ohio	12,132
4	Nevada	37,914		29	Alabama	10,971
5	Arizona	37,569		30	Texas	10,313
6	Florida	36,356		31	Pennsylvania	10,290
7	New York	31,348		32	Kentucky	9,960
8	Connecticut	24,669		33	Wisconsin	9,895
9	Rhode Island	20,938		34	Minnesota	9,825
10	Washington	20,381		35	Idaho	9,527
11	Virginia	19,502		36	Mississippi	8,801
12	Delaware	16,405		37	Missouri	8,742
13	Michigan	16,327		38	Maine	8,697
14	Oregon	16,268		39	Arkansas	8,661
15	Colorado	15,917		40	West Virginia	7,947
16	Massachusetts	15,459		41	Oklahoma	7,834
17	Tennessee	15,411		42	Vermont	7,808
18	North Carolina	14,941		43	Kansas	7,313
19	New Jersey	14,586		44	Montana	6,924
20	Utah	14,276		45	Iowa	6,585
21	South Carolina	14,129		46	Nebraska	6,502
22	New Mexico	13,748		47	Wyoming	6,052
23	Illinois	13,010		48	New Hampshire	4,873
24	Indiana	12,638		49	North Dakota	4,746
25	Georgia	12,502		50	South Dakota	4,158

District of Columbia 196,333

Source: Morgan Quitno Corporation using data from U.S. Department of Justice, Bureau of Justice Statistics
"Census of State and Local Law Enforcement Agencies, 1992" (Bulletin, July 1993, NCJ-142972)
*Includes state and local police, sheriffs' departments and special police agencies.

Law Enforcement Agencies per 1,000 Square Miles in 1992

National Rate = 4.58 Agencies per 1,000 Square Miles*

RANK	STATE	RATE	RANK	STATE	RATE
1	New Jersey	61.22	26	Texas	6.37
2	Massachusetts	36.76	27	Mississippi	6.13
3	Rhode Island	31.07	28	Michigan	5.97
4	Pennsylvania	25.34	29	Oklahoma	5.87
5	New Hampshire	24.38	30	Florida	5.64
6	Connecticut	23.99	31	Minnesota	5.24
7	Ohio	20.26	32	Arkansas	5.21
8	Delaware	16.87	33	Kansas	4.19
9	Illinois	15.44	34	Maine	4.01
10	Indiana	12.30	35	Washington	3.53
11	New York	10.61	36	Nebraska	3.19
12	Maryland	9.99	37	California	3.01
13	West Virginia	9.41	38	South Dakota	2.22
14	Kentucky	9.33	39	Colorado	2.09
15	Georgia	9.08	40	North Dakota	1.90
16	Missouri	8.52	41	Oregon	1.86
17	North Carolina	8.51	42	Utah	1.50
18	South Carolina	7.97	43	Idaho	1.34
19	Tennessee	7.74	44	New Mexico	0.95
20	Wisconsin	7.72	45	Arizona	0.89
21	Virginia	7.65	46	Montana	0.81
22	Iowa	7.59	47	Wyoming	0.79
22	Vermont	7.59	48	Hawaii	0.55
24	Alabama	7.19	49	Nevada	0.32
25	Louisiana	6.71	50	Alaska	0.07
				District of Columbia**	N/A

Source: Morgan Quitno Corporation using data from U.S. Department of Justice, Bureau of Justice Statistics
"Census of State and Local Law Enforcement Agencies, 1992" (Bulletin, July 1993, NCJ-142972)
*Includes state and local police, sheriffs' departments and special police agencies.
**The District of Columbia has three agencies for its 68 square miles.

Full-Time Sworn Officers in Law Enforcement Agencies in 1992

National Total = 603,954 Officers*

RANK	STATE	OFFICERS	%	RANK	STATE	OFFICERS	%
1	New York	68,208	11.29%	26	Minnesota	7,365	1.22%
2	California	65,797	10.89%	27	Oklahoma	6,458	1.07%
3	Texas	41,349	6.85%	28	Kentucky	6,085	1.01%
4	Illinois	35,674	5.91%	29	Kansas	5,631	0.93%
5	Florida	32,879	5.44%	30	Oregon	5,495	0.91%
6	New Jersey	26,688	4.42%	31	Iowa	4,703	0.78%
7	Pennsylvania	23,700	3.92%	32	Mississippi	4,675	0.77%
8	Ohio	20,929	3.47%	33	Arkansas	4,475	0.74%
9	Michigan	19,642	3.25%	34	New Mexico	3,420	0.57%
10	Georgia	16,792	2.78%	35	Nebraska	3,084	0.51%
11	Virginia	16,365	2.71%	36	Nevada	3,052	0.51%
12	Massachusetts	16,014	2.65%	37	Utah	2,979	0.49%
13	Louisiana	15,049	2.49%	38	Hawaii	2,783	0.46%
14	North Carolina	14,586	2.42%	39	West Virginia	2,622	0.43%
15	Maryland	12,601	2.09%	40	Rhode Island	2,389	0.40%
16	Wisconsin	11,594	1.92%	41	Maine	2,267	0.38%
17	Missouri	11,266	1.87%	42	Idaho	2,157	0.36%
18	Tennessee	10,379	1.72%	43	New Hampshire	2,139	0.35%
19	Indiana	10,038	1.66%	44	Delaware	1,572	0.26%
20	Alabama	8,771	1.45%	45	Montana	1,410	0.23%
21	Colorado	8,726	1.44%	46	Wyoming	1,210	0.20%
22	Washington	8,192	1.36%	47	South Dakota	1,145	0.19%
23	Arizona	7,900	1.31%	48	North Dakota	1,060	0.18%
24	South Carolina	7,752	1.28%	49	Alaska	1,057	0.18%
25	Connecticut	7,639	1.26%	50	Vermont	978	0.16%
					District of Columbia	5,213	0.86%

Source: U.S. Department of Justice, Bureau of Justice Statistics

"Census of State and Local Law Enforcement Agencies, 1992" (Bulletin, July 1993, NCJ-142972)

*Includes state and local police, sheriffs' departments and special police agencies.

Percent of Full–Time Law Enforcement Agency Employees Who Are Sworn Officers: 1992

National Rate = 71.81% of Employees are Sworn Officers*

RANK	STATE	PERCENT	RANK	STATE	PERCENT
1	Louisiana	86.64	26	South Dakota	71.92
2	Pennsylvania	83.67	27	Kansas	71.90
3	Rhode Island	82.64	28	Ohio	70.43
4	Connecticut	82.35	29	Alabama	70.07
5	New Jersey	81.40	30	Mississippi	69.89
6	New York	80.08	31	Colorado	69.48
7	Hawaii	80.02	32	New Mexico	68.99
8	Delaware	78.36	33	Georgia	68.49
9	Illinois	77.23	34	Maine	68.43
10	South Carolina	76.76	35	Oklahoma	67.59
11	Kentucky	76.55	36	Indiana	67.21
12	Virginia	76.28	37	West Virginia	67.02
13	Wisconsin	75.88	38	Montana	66.48
14	Massachusetts	75.61	39	Oregon	66.13
15	Iowa	75.16	40	Arkansas	65.59
16	Maryland	74.69	41	California	65.42
17	Michigan	74.47	42	Texas	64.36
18	North Carolina	74.29	43	Washington	64.34
19	New Hampshire	73.91	44	Alaska	64.26
20	Idaho	73.82	45	Tennessee	63.48
21	Vermont	73.59	46	Utah	61.64
22	Nebraska	73.53	47	Nevada	61.13
23	Missouri	73.30	48	Florida	60.87
24	North Dakota	73.15	49	Wyoming	60.02
25	Minnesota	72.41	50	Arizona	59.65

District of Columbia   84.43

Source: Morgan Quitno Corporation using data from U.S. Department of Justice, Bureau of Justice Statistics
"Census of State and Local Law Enforcement Agencies, 1992" (Bulletin, July 1993, NCJ-142972)
*Includes state and local police, sheriffs' departments and special police agencies.

Full-Time Sworn Officers in Law Enforcement Agencies per 10,000 Population in 1992

National Rate = 23.68 Officers per 10,000 Population*

RANK	STATE	RATE	RANK	STATE	RATE
1	New York	37.64	26	Michigan	20.81
2	Louisiana	35.10	27	Tennessee	20.66
3	New Jersey	34.26	28	Arizona	20.62
4	Illinois	30.67	29	Idaho	20.22
5	Massachusetts	26.70	30	Oklahoma	20.11
6	Wyoming	25.97	31	Pennsylvania	19.74
7	Maryland	25.67	32	New Hampshire	19.25
8	Virginia	25.66	33	Nebraska	19.20
9	Colorado	25.15	34	Ohio	19.00
10	Georgia	24.87	35	Arkansas	18.65
11	Florida	24.38	36	Oregon	18.46
12	Hawaii	23.99	37	Maine	18.36
13	Rhode Island	23.77	38	Alaska	18.01
14	Texas	23.42	39	Mississippi	17.88
15	Connecticut	23.28	40	Indiana	17.73
16	Wisconsin	23.16	41	Vermont	17.16
17	Nevada	23.00	42	Montana	17.11
18	Delaware	22.82	43	Iowa	16.72
19	Kansas	22.32	44	North Dakota	16.67
20	Missouri	21.69	45	Minnesota	16.44
21	New Mexico	21.63	46	Utah	16.43
22	South Carolina	21.52	47	Kentucky	16.21
23	California	21.32	48	South Dakota	16.10
23	North Carolina	21.32	49	Washington	15.95
25	Alabama	21.21	50	West Virginia	14.47

District of Columbia   88.51

Source: Morgan Quitno Corporation using data from U.S. Department of Justice, Bureau of Justice Statistics
"Census of State and Local Law Enforcement Agencies, 1992" (Bulletin, July 1993, NCJ-142972)
*Includes state and local police, sheriffs' departments and special police agencies.

Full-Time Sworn Law Enforcement Officers per 1,000 Square Miles in 1992

National Rate = 159 Officers per 1,000 Square Miles*

RANK	STATE	RATE	RANK	STATE	RATE
1	New Jersey	3,060	26	Texas	154
2	Rhode Island	1,546	27	Kentucky	151
3	Massachusetts	1,517	28	Washington	115
4	Connecticut	1,378	29	West Virginia	108
5	New York	1,252	30	Vermont	102
6	Maryland	1,016	31	Mississippi	97
7	Delaware	632	32	Oklahoma	92
8	Illinois	616	33	Minnesota	85
9	Pennsylvania	515	34	Arkansas	84
10	Florida	500	34	Colorado	84
11	Ohio	467	34	Iowa	84
12	California	402	37	Arizona	69
13	Virginia	383	38	Kansas	68
14	Louisiana	290	39	Maine	64
15	Georgia	282	40	Oregon	56
16	Indiana	276	41	Nebraska	40
17	North Carolina	271	42	Utah	35
18	Hawaii	255	43	Nevada	28
19	Tennessee	246	43	New Mexico	28
20	South Carolina	242	45	Idaho	26
21	New Hampshire	229	46	North Dakota	15
22	Michigan	203	46	South Dakota	15
23	Wisconsin	177	48	Wyoming	12
24	Alabama	167	49	Montana	10
25	Missouri	162	50	Alaska	2

District of Columbia**   N/A

Source: Morgan Quitno Corporation using data from U.S. Department of Justice, Bureau of Justice Statistics
"Census of State and Local Law Enforcement Agencies, 1992" (Bulletin, July 1993, NCJ-142972)
*Includes state and local police, sheriffs' departments and special police agencies.
**The District of Columbia has 5,213 sworn officers for its 68 square miles.

Full–Time Employees in Law Enforcement Agencies in 1992

National Total = 841,099 Employees*

RANK	STATE	EMPLOYEES	%	RANK	STATE	EMPLOYEES	%
1	California	100,582	11.96%	26	Oklahoma	9,554	1.14%
2	New York	85,177	10.13%	27	Connecticut	9,276	1.10%
3	Texas	64,247	7.64%	28	Oregon	8,310	0.99%
4	Florida	54,011	6.42%	29	Kentucky	7,949	0.95%
5	Illinois	46,189	5.49%	30	Kansas	7,832	0.93%
6	New Jersey	32,785	3.90%	31	Arkansas	6,823	0.81%
7	Ohio	29,718	3.53%	32	Mississippi	6,689	0.80%
8	Pennsylvania	28,326	3.37%	33	Iowa	6,257	0.74%
9	Michigan	26,375	3.14%	34	Nevada	4,993	0.59%
10	Georgia	24,516	2.91%	35	New Mexico	4,957	0.59%
11	Virginia	21,454	2.55%	36	Utah	4,833	0.57%
12	Massachusetts	21,181	2.52%	37	Nebraska	4,194	0.50%
13	North Carolina	19,633	2.33%	38	West Virginia	3,912	0.47%
14	Louisiana	17,370	2.07%	39	Hawaii	3,478	0.41%
15	Maryland	16,871	2.01%	40	Maine	3,313	0.39%
16	Tennessee	16,349	1.94%	41	Idaho	2,922	0.35%
17	Missouri	15,370	1.83%	42	New Hampshire	2,894	0.34%
18	Wisconsin	15,279	1.82%	43	Rhode Island	2,891	0.34%
19	Indiana	14,935	1.78%	44	Montana	2,121	0.25%
20	Arizona	13,243	1.57%	45	Wyoming	2,016	0.24%
21	Washington	12,733	1.51%	46	Delaware	2,006	0.24%
22	Colorado	12,559	1.49%	47	Alaska	1,645	0.20%
23	Alabama	12,517	1.49%	48	South Dakota	1,592	0.19%
24	Minnesota	10,171	1.21%	49	North Dakota	1,449	0.17%
25	South Carolina	10,099	1.20%	50	Vermont	1,329	0.16%
					District of Columbia	6,174	0.73%

Source: U.S. Department of Justice, Bureau of Justice Statistics
   "Census of State and Local Law Enforcement Agencies, 1992" (Bulletin, July 1993, NCJ–142972)
*Includes state and local police, sheriffs' departments and special police agencies.

Full-Time Employees in Law Enforcement Agencies per 10,000 Population in 1992

National Rate = 32.97 Employees per 10,000 Population*

RANK	STATE	RATE	RANK	STATE	RATE
1	New York	47.01	26	North Carolina	28.69
2	Wyoming	43.26	27	Arkansas	28.44
3	New Jersey	42.09	28	Connecticut	28.27
4	Louisiana	40.52	29	South Carolina	28.03
5	Florida	40.04	30	Alaska	28.02
6	Illinois	39.71	31	Michigan	27.95
7	Nevada	37.63	32	Oregon	27.91
8	Texas	36.39	33	Idaho	27.39
9	Georgia	36.31	34	Ohio	26.98
10	Colorado	36.19	35	Maine	26.83
11	Massachusetts	35.31	36	Utah	26.66
12	Arizona	34.56	37	Indiana	26.38
13	Maryland	34.37	38	Nebraska	26.11
14	Virginia	33.64	39	New Hampshire	26.05
15	California	32.59	40	Montana	25.74
16	Tennessee	32.54	41	Mississippi	25.59
17	New Mexico	31.35	42	Washington	24.79
18	Kansas	31.04	43	Pennsylvania	23.59
19	Wisconsin	30.52	44	Vermont	23.32
20	Alabama	30.26	45	North Dakota	22.78
21	Hawaii	29.98	46	Minnesota	22.70
22	Oklahoma	29.74	47	South Dakota	22.39
23	Missouri	29.60	48	Iowa	22.25
24	Delaware	29.11	49	West Virginia	21.59
25	Rhode Island	28.77	50	Kentucky	21.17

District of Columbia   104.82

Source: Morgan Quitno Corporation using data from U.S. Department of Justice, Bureau of Justice Statistics
"Census of State and Local Law Enforcement Agencies, 1992" (Bulletin, July 1993, NCJ-142972)
*Includes state and local police, sheriffs' departments and special police agencies.

Full–Time Sworn Officers in State Police Departments in 1992

National Total = 52,980 Officers

RANK	STATE	OFFICERS	%	RANK	STATE	OFFICERS	%
1	California	6,062	11.44%	26	Alabama	629	1.19%
2	Pennsylvania	4,075	7.69%	27	Kansas	604	1.14%
3	New York	4,013	7.57%	28	Delaware	505	0.95%
4	Texas	2,789	5.26%	29	Nebraska	502	0.95%
5	New Jersey	2,572	4.85%	30	Minnesota	501	0.95%
6	Massachusetts	2,070	3.91%	31	Mississippi	499	0.94%
7	Michigan	2,019	3.81%	32	Wisconsin	498	0.94%
8	Illinois	1,977	3.73%	33	Colorado	493	0.93%
9	Maryland	1,700	3.21%	34	Arkansas	484	0.91%
10	Virginia	1,606	3.03%	35	West Virginia	468	0.88%
11	Florida	1,605	3.03%	36	New Mexico	425	0.80%
12	Ohio	1,292	2.44%	37	Iowa	410	0.77%
13	North Carolina	1,260	2.38%	38	Utah	365	0.69%
14	South Carolina	1,193	2.25%	39	Maine	332	0.63%
15	Arizona	1,100	2.08%	40	Nevada	306	0.58%
16	Indiana	1,097	2.07%	41	Vermont	285	0.54%
17	Washington	1,032	1.95%	42	Alaska	260	0.49%
18	Kentucky	960	1.81%	43	New Hampshire	250	0.47%
19	Connecticut	905	1.71%	44	Montana	200	0.38%
19	Oregon	905	1.71%	45	Idaho	192	0.36%
21	Missouri	883	1.67%	46	Rhode Island	165	0.31%
22	Oklahoma	786	1.48%	47	Wyoming	157	0.30%
23	Tennessee	782	1.48%	48	South Dakota	151	0.29%
24	Georgia	777	1.47%	49	North Dakota	125	0.24%
25	Louisiana	714	1.35%	50	Hawaii	0	0.00%
					District of Columbia	0	0.00%

Source: U.S. Department of Justice, Bureau of Justice Statistics

"Census of State and Local Law Enforcement Agencies, 1992" (Bulletin, July 1993, NCJ–142972)

*All states except Hawaii and the District of Columbia have a state police department.

Percent of Full-Time State Police Department Employees Who Are Sworn Officers: 1992

National Rate = 67.43% of Employees*

RANK	STATE	PERCENT	RANK	STATE	PERCENT
1	South Carolina	100.00	26	Michigan	69.31
2	Utah	92.41	27	Minnesota	69.29
3	South Dakota	89.35	28	Louisiana	68.52
4	Iowa	89.32	29	Connecticut	68.51
5	New York	85.67	30	Arizona	68.28
6	Rhode Island	81.28	31	California	68.16
7	Massachusetts	80.26	32	Vermont	66.90
8	Oregon	79.04	33	Nevada	66.67
9	North Carolina	78.65	34	West Virginia	63.76
10	Nebraska	78.07	35	Indiana	62.87
11	Pennsylvania	77.89	36	North Dakota	62.81
12	New Mexico	76.99	37	Illinois	59.91
13	Montana	76.34	38	Mississippi	59.55
14	Florida	76.21	39	Alaska	59.23
15	Idaho	75.59	40	Kentucky	58.04
16	Wisconsin	74.89	41	Oklahoma	55.90
17	Kansas	73.57	42	Ohio	55.03
18	New Hampshire	73.53	43	Wyoming	50.97
19	Delaware	73.51	44	Tennessee	50.68
20	Virginia	72.80	45	Texas	49.76
21	New Jersey	72.45	45	Washington	49.76
22	Maine	72.17	47	Alabama	49.10
23	Colorado	71.66	48	Missouri	48.17
24	Arkansas	71.28	49	Georgia	40.89
25	Maryland	70.83	–	Hawaii**	N/A

District of Columbia**   N/A

Source: Morgan Quitno Corporation using data from U.S. Department of Justice, Bureau of Justice Statistics
   "Census of State and Local Law Enforcement Agencies, 1992" (Bulletin, July 1993, NCJ-142972)
*All states except Hawaii and the District of Columbia have a state police department.
**Not applicable.

Rate of Full–Time Sworn Officers in State Police Departments in 1992

National Rate = 2.08 Officers per 10,000 Population*

RANK	STATE	RATE	RANK	STATE	RATE
1	Delaware	7.33	26	South Dakota	2.12
2	Vermont	5.00	27	Arkansas	2.02
3	Alaska	4.43	28	Utah	2.01
4	Maryland	3.46	28	Washington	2.01
5	Massachusetts	3.45	30	North Dakota	1.97
6	Pennsylvania	3.39	31	California	1.96
7	Wyoming	3.37	32	Indiana	1.94
8	South Carolina	3.31	33	Mississippi	1.91
9	New Jersey	3.30	34	North Carolina	1.84
10	Nebraska	3.13	35	Idaho	1.80
11	Oregon	3.04	36	Illinois	1.70
12	Arizona	2.87	36	Missouri	1.70
13	Connecticut	2.76	38	Louisiana	1.67
14	Maine	2.69	39	Rhode Island	1.64
14	New Mexico	2.69	40	Texas	1.58
16	West Virginia	2.58	41	Tennessee	1.56
17	Kentucky	2.56	42	Alabama	1.52
18	Virginia	2.52	43	Iowa	1.46
19	Oklahoma	2.45	44	Colorado	1.42
20	Montana	2.43	45	Florida	1.19
21	Kansas	2.39	46	Ohio	1.17
22	Nevada	2.31	47	Georgia	1.15
23	New Hampshire	2.25	48	Minnesota	1.12
24	New York	2.21	49	Wisconsin	0.99
25	Michigan	2.14	50	Hawaii	0.00
				District of Columbia	0.00

Source: Morgan Quitno Corporation using data from U.S. Department of Justice, Bureau of Justice Statistics
"Census of State and Local Law Enforcement Agencies, 1992" (Bulletin, July 1993, NCJ–142972)
*All states except Hawaii and the District of Columbia have a state police department.

Male Officers in State Police Departments in 1990

National Total = 49,974 Male Officers*

RANK	STATE	OFFICERS	%	RANK	STATE	OFFICERS	%
1	California	5,493	10.99%	26	Alabama	669	1.34%
2	Pennsylvania	3,972	7.95%	27	Kansas	552	1.10%
3	New York	3,776	7.56%	28	West Virginia	510	1.02%
4	Texas	2,722	5.45%	29	Mississippi	504	1.01%
5	New Jersey	2,550	5.10%	30	Minnesota	492	0.98%
6	Illinois	2,204	4.41%	31	Delaware	488	0.98%
7	Michigan	2,093	4.19%	32	Colorado	477	0.95%
8	Virginia	1,634	3.27%	33	Arkansas	459	0.92%
9	Maryland	1,538	3.08%	34	Nebraska	449	0.90%
10	Florida	1,524	3.05%	35	Wisconsin	422	0.84%
11	North Carolina	1,238	2.48%	36	Iowa	402	0.80%
12	Ohio	1,191	2.38%	37	New Mexico	361	0.72%
13	Massachusetts	1,066	2.13%	38	Maine	342	0.68%
14	Indiana	1,060	2.12%	39	Utah	309	0.62%
15	South Carolina	973	1.95%	40	Vermont	282	0.56%
16	Arizona	949	1.90%	41	Nevada	257	0.51%
17	Washington	943	1.89%	42	New Hampshire	241	0.48%
18	Connecticut	930	1.86%	43	Alaska	234	0.47%
19	Kentucky	888	1.78%	44	Montana	191	0.38%
20	Missouri	859	1.72%	45	Idaho	187	0.37%
21	Oregon	847	1.69%	46	Rhode Island	173	0.35%
22	Tennessee	821	1.64%	47	Wyoming	147	0.29%
23	Georgia	805	1.61%	48	South Dakota	145	0.29%
24	Oklahoma	790	1.58%	49	North Dakota	114	0.23%
25	Louisiana	701	1.40%	–	Hawaii**	N/A	N/A

Source: Morgan Quitno Corporation using data from U.S. Department of Justice, Bureau of Justice Statistics
   "Law Enforcement Management and Administrative Statistics, 1990" (September 1992, NCJ-134436)
*Full-time sworn officers.
**Hawaii does not have a state police department.

Female Officers in State Police Departments in 1990

National Total = 2,398 Female Officers*

RANK	STATE	OFFICERS	%	RANK	STATE	OFFICERS	%
1	California	465	19.39%	26	Arkansas	17	0.71%
2	New York	237	9.88%	26	New Hampshire	17	0.71%
3	Michigan	185	7.71%	26	Tennessee	17	0.71%
4	Illinois	156	6.51%	29	Nebraska	14	0.58%
5	Florida	125	5.21%	29	New Mexico	14	0.58%
6	Pennsylvania	119	4.96%	31	Iowa	13	0.54%
7	Maryland	118	4.92%	31	Maine	13	0.54%
8	Massachusetts	96	4.00%	31	Utah	13	0.54%
9	Texas	64	2.67%	34	Kentucky	12	0.50%
10	New Jersey	63	2.63%	34	Missouri	12	0.50%
11	Wisconsin	60	2.50%	34	Vermont	12	0.50%
12	Ohio	56	2.34%	37	Oklahoma	11	0.46%
13	Connecticut	52	2.17%	38	West Virginia	10	0.42%
14	Virginia	45	1.88%	39	Montana	9	0.38%
15	Arizona	44	1.83%	40	Alabama	8	0.33%
15	Indiana	44	1.83%	40	Mississippi	8	0.33%
17	Kansas	39	1.63%	40	Nevada	8	0.33%
18	Washington	35	1.46%	43	Louisiana	7	0.29%
19	Delaware	32	1.33%	43	North Carolina	7	0.29%
20	Oregon	28	1.17%	43	Rhode Island	7	0.29%
21	Georgia	27	1.13%	46	Idaho	2	0.08%
22	Alaska	18	0.75%	46	South Dakota	2	0.08%
22	Colorado	18	0.75%	46	Wyoming	2	0.08%
22	Minnesota	18	0.75%	49	North Dakota	1	0.04%
22	South Carolina	18	0.75%	–	Hawaii**	N/A	N/A

Source: Morgan Quitno Corporation using data from U.S. Department of Justice, Bureau of Justice Statistics
    "Law Enforcement Management and Administrative Statistics, 1990" (September 1992, NCJ-134436)
*Full-time sworn officers.
**Hawaii does not have a state police department.

Female Officers as a Percent of All Officers in State Police Departments in 1990

National Percent = 4.6% of Officers*

RANK	STATE	PERCENT		RANK	STATE	PERCENT
1	Wisconsin	12.4		26	Minnesota	3.5
2	Massachusetts	8.3		27	Georgia	3.2
3	Michigan	8.1		27	Oregon	3.2
4	California	7.8		29	Iowa	3.1
5	Florida	7.6		30	Nebraska	3.0
6	Alaska	7.1		30	Nevada	3.0
6	Maryland	7.1		32	Pennsylvania	2.9
8	Illinois	6.6		33	Virginia	2.7
8	Kansas	6.6		34	New Jersey	2.4
8	New Hampshire	6.6		35	Texas	2.3
11	Delaware	6.2		36	Tennessee	2.0
12	New York	5.9		37	West Virginia	1.9
13	Connecticut	5.3		38	South Carolina	1.8
14	Montana	4.5		39	Mississippi	1.6
14	Ohio	4.5		40	Missouri	1.4
16	Arizona	4.4		40	Oklahoma	1.4
17	Vermont	4.1		40	South Dakota	1.4
18	Indiana	4.0		43	Kentucky	1.3
18	Utah	4.0		43	Wyoming	1.3
20	Rhode Island	3.9		45	Alabama	1.2
21	Maine	3.7		46	Idaho	1.1
21	New Mexico	3.7		47	Louisiana	1.0
23	Arkansas	3.6		48	North Dakota	0.9
23	Colorado	3.6		49	North Carolina	0.6
23	Washington	3.6		–	Hawaii**	N/A

Source: U.S. Department of Justice, Bureau of Justice Statistics
   "Law Enforcement Management and Administrative Statistics, 1990" (September 1992, NCJ-134436)

*Full-time sworn officers.

**Hawaii does not have a state police department.

White Officers in State Police Departments in 1990

National Total = 45,586 White Officers*

RANK	STATE	OFFICERS	%	RANK	STATE	OFFICERS	%
1	California	4,903	10.76%	26	Kansas	575	1.26%
2	Pennsylvania	3,666	8.04%	27	West Virginia	510	1.12%
3	New York	3,335	7.32%	28	Minnesota	497	1.09%
4	New Jersey	2,260	4.96%	29	Alabama	464	1.02%
5	Texas	2,140	4.69%	30	Delaware	458	1.00%
6	Michigan	1,993	4.37%	31	Nebraska	453	0.99%
7	Illinois	1,949	4.28%	32	Wisconsin	452	0.99%
8	Virginia	1,561	3.42%	33	Colorado	433	0.95%
9	Maryland	1,366	3.00%	34	Arkansas	421	0.92%
10	Florida	1,346	2.95%	35	Iowa	407	0.89%
11	Ohio	1,129	2.48%	36	Mississippi	397	0.87%
12	Massachusetts	1,073	2.35%	37	Maine	355	0.78%
12	North Carolina	1,073	2.35%	38	Utah	310	0.68%
14	Indiana	1,008	2.21%	39	Vermont	288	0.63%
15	Washington	906	1.99%	40	New Mexico	265	0.58%
16	Connecticut	876	1.92%	41	New Hampshire	256	0.56%
17	Kentucky	867	1.90%	42	Nevada	240	0.53%
18	South Carolina	857	1.88%	43	Alaska	236	0.52%
19	Oregon	846	1.86%	44	Montana	196	0.43%
20	Arizona	823	1.81%	45	Idaho	183	0.40%
21	Missouri	790	1.73%	46	Rhode Island	172	0.38%
22	Tennessee	779	1.71%	47	Wyoming	148	0.32%
23	Georgia	742	1.63%	48	South Dakota	145	0.32%
24	Oklahoma	711	1.56%	49	North Dakota	111	0.24%
25	Louisiana	615	1.35%	–	Hawaii**	N/A	N/A

Source: Morgan Quitno Corporation using data from U.S. Department of Justice, Bureau of Justice Statistics

"Law Enforcement Management and Administrative Statistics, 1990" (September 1992, NCJ-134436)

*Full-time sworn officers.

**Hawaii does not have a state police department.

White Officers as a Percent of All Officers in State Police Departments in 1990

National Percent = 87.0% of Officers*

RANK	STATE	PERCENT	RANK	STATE	PERCENT
1	Maine	100.0	26	Nevada	90.6
2	Wyoming	99.3	27	Ohio	90.5
3	New Hampshire	99.2	28	Pennsylvania	89.6
4	South Dakota	98.6	29	Connecticut	89.2
5	Iowa	98.1	29	Georgia	89.2
5	West Virginia	98.1	31	Oklahoma	88.8
7	Montana	98.0	32	Arkansas	88.4
7	Vermont	98.0	33	Delaware	88.1
9	Nebraska	97.8	34	Colorado	87.5
10	Minnesota	97.5	34	Michigan	87.5
11	Kansas	97.3	36	Louisiana	86.9
12	Idaho	96.8	37	New Jersey	86.5
13	Oregon	96.7	37	South Carolina	86.5
14	North Dakota	96.5	39	North Carolina	86.2
15	Kentucky	96.3	40	New York	83.1
15	Utah	96.3	41	Arizona	82.9
17	Rhode Island	95.6	42	Illinois	82.6
18	Wisconsin	93.8	43	Maryland	82.5
19	Alaska	93.7	44	California	82.3
20	Tennessee	93.0	45	Florida	81.6
20	Virginia	93.0	46	Mississippi	77.5
22	Washington	92.6	47	Texas	76.8
23	Massachusetts	92.3	48	New Mexico	70.7
24	Indiana	91.3	49	Alabama	68.5
25	Missouri	90.7	–	Hawaii**	N/A

Source: U.S. Department of Justice, Bureau of Justice Statistics
   "Law Enforcement Management and Administrative Statistics, 1990" (September 1992, NCJ-134436)
*Full-time sworn officers.
**Hawaii does not have a state police department.

Black Officers in State Police Departments in 1990

National Total = 3,923 Black Officers*

RANK	STATE	OFFICERS	%	RANK	STATE	OFFICERS	%
1	New York	401	10.22%	26	Kentucky	29	0.74%
2	Pennsylvania	340	8.67%	26	Washington	29	0.74%
3	Maryland	277	7.06%	28	Arizona	20	0.51%
4	Illinois	274	6.98%	29	Colorado	10	0.25%
5	California	232	5.91%	29	Wisconsin	10	0.25%
6	Alabama	213	5.43%	31	West Virginia	9	0.23%
7	New Jersey	206	5.25%	32	Kansas	6	0.15%
8	Florida	201	5.12%	32	Nevada	6	0.15%
9	Michigan	198	5.05%	32	Vermont	6	0.15%
10	Texas	164	4.18%	35	Minnesota	5	0.13%
11	North Carolina	156	3.98%	35	Oregon	5	0.13%
12	South Carolina	132	3.36%	37	Alaska	4	0.10%
13	Mississippi	115	2.93%	37	Iowa	4	0.10%
14	Virginia	114	2.91%	37	New Mexico	4	0.10%
15	Ohio	99	2.52%	37	Rhode Island	4	0.10%
16	Indiana	91	2.32%	41	Nebraska	3	0.08%
16	Louisiana	91	2.32%	42	New Hampshire	1	0.03%
18	Georgia	88	2.24%	42	Wyoming	1	0.03%
19	Missouri	64	1.63%	44	Idaho	0	0.00%
20	Massachusetts	63	1.61%	44	Maine	0	0.00%
21	Connecticut	56	1.43%	44	Montana	0	0.00%
22	Tennessee	54	1.38%	44	North Dakota	0	0.00%
23	Delaware	51	1.30%	44	South Dakota	0	0.00%
24	Arkansas	50	1.27%	44	Utah	0	0.00%
25	Oklahoma	37	0.94%	–	Hawaii**	N/A	N/A

Source: Morgan Quitno Corporation using data from U.S. Department of Justice, Bureau of Justice Statistics
"Law Enforcement Management and Administrative Statistics, 1990" (September 1992, NCJ-134436)

*Full-time sworn officers.

**Hawaii does not have a state police department.

Black Officers as a Percent of All Officers in State Police Departments in 1990

National Percent = 7.5% of Officers*

RANK	STATE	PERCENT	RANK	STATE	PERCENT
1	Alabama	31.5	26	Kentucky	3.2
2	Mississippi	22.5	27	Washington	3.0
3	Maryland	16.7	28	Nevada	2.3
4	South Carolina	13.3	29	Rhode Island	2.2
5	Louisiana	12.9	30	Wisconsin	2.1
6	North Carolina	12.5	31	Arizona	2.0
7	Florida	12.2	31	Colorado	2.0
8	Illinois	11.6	31	Vermont	2.0
9	Georgia	10.6	34	West Virginia	1.7
10	Arkansas	10.5	35	Alaska	1.6
11	New York	10.0	36	New Mexico	1.1
12	Delaware	9.8	37	Iowa	1.0
13	Michigan	8.7	37	Kansas	1.0
14	Pennsylvania	8.3	37	Minnesota	1.0
15	Indiana	8.2	40	Wyoming	0.7
16	New Jersey	7.9	41	Nebraska	0.6
16	Ohio	7.9	41	Oregon	0.6
18	Missouri	7.3	43	New Hampshire	0.4
19	Virginia	6.8	44	Idaho	0.0
20	Tennessee	6.4	44	Maine	0.0
21	Texas	5.9	44	Montana	0.0
22	Connecticut	5.7	44	North Dakota	0.0
23	Massachusetts	5.4	44	South Dakota	0.0
24	Oklahoma	4.6	44	Utah	0.0
25	California	3.9	–	Hawaii**	N/A

Source: U.S. Department of Justice, Bureau of Justice Statistics

"Law Enforcement Management and Administrative Statistics, 1990" (September 1992, NCJ-134436)

*Full-time sworn officers.

**Hawaii does not have a state police department.

Hispanic Officers in State Police Departments in 1990

National Total = 2,315 Hispanic Officers*

RANK	STATE	OFFICERS	%	RANK	STATE	OFFICERS	%
1	California	661	28.55%	25	Idaho	5	0.22%
2	Texas	465	20.09%	25	Oklahoma	5	0.22%
3	New York	265	11.45%	28	Rhode Island	4	0.17%
4	Arizona	126	5.44%	29	Iowa	3	0.13%
5	Illinois	113	4.88%	29	Kentucky	3	0.13%
6	New Jersey	110	4.75%	29	Maryland	3	0.13%
7	New Mexico	100	4.32%	29	Tennessee	3	0.13%
8	Florida	96	4.15%	33	Arkansas	2	0.09%
9	Michigan	62	2.68%	33	Louisiana	2	0.09%
10	Pennsylvania	61	2.63%	33	Minnesota	2	0.09%
11	Colorado	46	1.99%	33	South Carolina	2	0.09%
12	Connecticut	45	1.94%	33	Virginia	2	0.09%
13	Massachusetts	21	0.91%	38	Georgia	1	0.04%
14	Washington	15	0.65%	38	West Virginia	1	0.04%
15	Nevada	12	0.52%	40	Alabama	0	0.00%
15	Ohio	12	0.52%	40	Maine	0	0.00%
17	Delaware	11	0.48%	40	Mississippi	0	0.00%
18	Oregon	10	0.43%	40	Montana	0	0.00%
19	Wisconsin	8	0.35%	40	New Hampshire	0	0.00%
20	Kansas	7	0.30%	40	North Carolina	0	0.00%
20	Missouri	7	0.30%	40	North Dakota	0	0.00%
20	Utah	7	0.30%	40	South Dakota	0	0.00%
23	Indiana	6	0.26%	40	Vermont	0	0.00%
23	Nebraska	6	0.26%	40	Wyoming	0	0.00%
25	Alaska	5	0.22%	–	Hawaii**	N/A	N/A

Source: Morgan Quitno Corporation using data from U.S. Department of Justice, Bureau of Justice Statistics
    "Law Enforcement Management and Administrative Statistics, 1990" (September 1992, NCJ-134436)
*Full-time sworn officers.
**Hawaii does not have a state police department.

Hispanic Officers as a Percent of All Officers in State Police Departments in 1990

National Percent = 4.4% of Officers*

RANK	STATE	PERCENT	RANK	STATE	PERCENT
1	New Mexico	26.7	26	Missouri	0.8
2	Texas	16.7	27	Iowa	0.7
3	Arizona	12.7	28	Oklahoma	0.6
4	California	11.1	29	Indiana	0.5
5	Colorado	9.3	30	Arkansas	0.4
6	New York	6.6	30	Minnesota	0.4
7	Florida	5.8	30	Tennessee	0.4
8	Illinois	4.8	33	Kentucky	0.3
9	Connecticut	4.6	33	Louisiana	0.3
10	Nevada	4.5	35	Maryland	0.2
11	New Jersey	4.2	35	South Carolina	0.2
12	Michigan	2.7	35	West Virginia	0.2
13	Idaho	2.6	38	Georgia	0.1
14	Rhode Island	2.2	38	Virginia	0.1
14	Utah	2.2	40	Alabama	0.0
16	Delaware	2.1	40	Maine	0.0
17	Alaska	2.0	40	Mississippi	0.0
18	Massachusetts	1.8	40	Montana	0.0
19	Wisconsin	1.7	40	New Hampshire	0.0
20	Pennsylvania	1.5	40	North Carolina	0.0
20	Washington	1.5	40	North Dakota	0.0
22	Nebraska	1.3	40	South Dakota	0.0
23	Kansas	1.2	40	Vermont	0.0
24	Oregon	1.1	40	Wyoming	0.0
25	Ohio	1.0	–	Hawaii**	N/A

Source: U.S. Department of Justice, Bureau of Justice Statistics

"Law Enforcement Management and Administrative Statistics, 1990" (September 1992, NCJ-134436)

*Full-time sworn officers.

**Hawaii does not have a state police department.

Full-Time Employees in State Police Departments in 1992

National Total = 78,570 Employees*

RANK	STATE	EMPLOYEES	%	RANK	STATE	EMPLOYEES	%
1	California	8,894	11.32%	26	Louisiana	1,042	1.33%
2	Texas	5,605	7.13%	27	Mississippi	838	1.07%
3	Pennsylvania	5,232	6.66%	28	Kansas	821	1.04%
4	New York	4,684	5.96%	29	West Virginia	734	0.93%
5	New Jersey	3,550	4.52%	30	Minnesota	723	0.92%
6	Illinois	3,300	4.20%	31	Colorado	688	0.88%
7	Michigan	2,913	3.71%	32	Delaware	687	0.87%
8	Massachusetts	2,579	3.28%	33	Arkansas	679	0.86%
9	Maryland	2,400	3.05%	34	Wisconsin	665	0.85%
10	Ohio	2,348	2.99%	35	Nebraska	643	0.82%
11	Virginia	2,206	2.81%	36	New Mexico	552	0.70%
12	Florida	2,106	2.68%	37	Maine	460	0.59%
13	Washington	2,074	2.64%	38	Iowa	459	0.58%
14	Georgia	1,900	2.42%	38	Nevada	459	0.58%
15	Missouri	1,833	2.33%	40	Alaska	439	0.56%
16	Indiana	1,745	2.22%	41	Vermont	426	0.54%
17	Kentucky	1,654	2.11%	42	Utah	395	0.50%
18	Arizona	1,611	2.05%	43	New Hampshire	340	0.43%
19	North Carolina	1,602	2.04%	44	Wyoming	308	0.39%
20	Tennessee	1,543	1.96%	45	Montana	262	0.33%
21	Oklahoma	1,406	1.79%	46	Idaho	254	0.32%
22	Connecticut	1,321	1.68%	47	Rhode Island	203	0.26%
23	Alabama	1,281	1.63%	48	North Dakota	199	0.25%
24	South Carolina	1,193	1.52%	49	South Dakota	169	0.22%
25	Oregon	1,145	1.46%	50	Hawaii	0	0.00%

District of Columbia   0   0.00%

Source: U.S. Department of Justice, Bureau of Justice Statistics

"Census of State and Local Law Enforcement Agencies, 1992" (Bulletin, July 1993, NCJ-142972)

*All states except Hawaii and the District of Columbia have a state police department.

Local Police Departments in 1992

National Total = 12,502 Departments*

RANK	STATE	DEPARTMENTS	%	RANK	STATE	DEPARTMENTS	%
1	Pennsylvania	1,049	8.39%	26	Mississippi	189	1.51%
2	Ohio	776	6.21%	27	South Carolina	188	1.50%
3	Illinois	748	5.98%	28	Arkansas	185	1.48%
4	Texas	632	5.06%	29	Virginia	167	1.34%
5	New Jersey	488	3.90%	30	West Virginia	158	1.26%
6	Michigan	474	3.79%	31	Nebraska	149	1.19%
7	Missouri	463	3.70%	32	Colorado	140	1.12%
7	New York	463	3.70%	33	Oregon	137	1.10%
9	Wisconsin	417	3.34%	34	Maine	119	0.95%
10	Minnesota	359	2.87%	35	Connecticut	108	0.86%
11	Georgia	343	2.74%	36	South Dakota	102	0.82%
12	California	341	2.73%	37	Utah	84	0.67%
12	Massachusetts	341	2.73%	38	Maryland	78	0.62%
14	Indiana	336	2.69%	39	North Dakota	76	0.61%
15	North Carolina	332	2.66%	40	Arizona	75	0.60%
16	Iowa	321	2.57%	41	New Mexico	72	0.58%
17	Oklahoma	312	2.50%	42	Idaho	66	0.53%
18	Alabama	285	2.28%	43	Montana	59	0.47%
18	Florida	285	2.28%	44	Vermont	57	0.46%
20	Louisiana	256	2.05%	45	Wyoming	50	0.40%
21	Kentucky	240	1.92%	46	Alaska	43	0.34%
22	Kansas	221	1.77%	47	Rhode Island	39	0.31%
23	New Hampshire	214	1.71%	48	Delaware	33	0.26%
24	Tennessee	211	1.69%	49	Nevada	14	0.11%
25	Washington	202	1.62%	50	Hawaii	4	0.03%
					District of Columbia	1	0.01%

Source: U.S. Department of Justice, Bureau of Justice Statistics
     "Census of State and Local Law Enforcement Agencies, 1992" (Bulletin, July 1993, NCJ-142972)
*Includes consolidated police-sheriffs' departments.

Full-Time Sworn Officers in Local Police Departments in 1992

National Total = 373,061 Officers*

RANK	STATE	OFFICERS	%	RANK	STATE	OFFICERS	%
1	New York	45,822	12.28%	26	Oklahoma	4,529	1.21%
2	California	33,191	8.90%	27	Kentucky	3,804	1.02%
3	Illinois	24,988	6.70%	28	South Carolina	3,481	0.93%
4	Texas	24,576	6.59%	29	Kansas	3,189	0.85%
5	New Jersey	19,221	5.15%	30	Iowa	2,863	0.77%
6	Florida	18,037	4.83%	31	Oregon	2,782	0.75%
7	Pennsylvania	17,256	4.63%	32	Mississippi	2,745	0.74%
8	Ohio	14,668	3.93%	33	Hawaii	2,690	0.72%
9	Michigan	13,027	3.49%	34	Arkansas	2,494	0.67%
10	Massachusetts	12,087	3.24%	35	New Mexico	2,092	0.56%
11	Georgia	9,404	2.52%	36	Rhode Island	2,024	0.54%
12	Maryland	8,273	2.22%	37	Nevada	1,795	0.48%
13	Virginia	8,205	2.20%	38	Nebraska	1,720	0.46%
14	North Carolina	8,023	2.15%	39	New Hampshire	1,717	0.46%
15	Missouri	7,921	2.12%	40	Utah	1,546	0.41%
16	Wisconsin	7,184	1.93%	41	Maine	1,399	0.38%
17	Tennessee	6,214	1.67%	42	West Virginia	1,260	0.34%
18	Connecticut	6,068	1.63%	43	Idaho	921	0.25%
19	Indiana	5,992	1.61%	44	Delaware	887	0.24%
20	Alabama	5,640	1.51%	45	Alaska	677	0.18%
21	Louisiana	5,548	1.49%	46	South Dakota	648	0.17%
22	Arizona	5,209	1.40%	47	Vermont	594	0.16%
23	Colorado	4,787	1.28%	48	Wyoming	584	0.16%
24	Washington	4,704	1.26%	49	Montana	568	0.15%
25	Minnesota	4,580	1.23%	50	North Dakota	538	0.14%
					District of Columbia	4,889	1.31%

Source: U.S. Department of Justice, Bureau of Justice Statistics

"Census of State and Local Law Enforcement Agencies, 1992" (Bulletin, July 1993, NCJ-142972)

*Includes consolidated police-sheriff departments.

Percent of Full–Time Local Police Department Employees Who Are Sworn Officers: 1992

National Rate = 78.33% of Employees*

RANK	STATE	PERCENT		RANK	STATE	PERCENT
1	Pennsylvania	86.68		26	Maine	79.22
2	Massachusetts	85.02		27	Vermont	78.99
3	Delaware	84.72		28	New Hampshire	78.37
4	New Jersey	84.33		29	Virginia	77.93
5	Connecticut	83.86		30	Montana	77.49
6	Michigan	83.31		31	Alabama	77.31
7	Minnesota	83.18		32	Arkansas	76.46
8	West Virginia	82.51		33	Indiana	76.20
9	Rhode Island	82.41		33	Missouri	76.20
10	Iowa	82.36		35	Tennessee	75.74
11	Utah	82.15		36	Kansas	75.66
12	Louisiana	82.07		37	Mississippi	75.56
13	North Carolina	81.83		38	Washington	75.31
14	Ohio	81.78		39	Oklahoma	75.13
15	Wisconsin	81.68		40	Georgia	75.09
16	Maryland	81.46		41	Texas	74.34
17	New York	81.24		42	Colorado	74.27
18	Illinois	80.68		43	Wyoming	73.09
19	South Dakota	80.60		44	Arizona	72.57
20	Kentucky	80.58		45	Oregon	71.65
21	South Carolina	80.52		46	California	70.70
22	Nebraska	80.11		47	Florida	70.46
23	Idaho	80.02		48	New Mexico	69.66
24	North Dakota	79.82		49	Alaska	63.21
25	Hawaii	79.49		50	Nevada	56.54

District of Columbia   85.03

Source: Morgan Quitno Corporation using data from U.S. Department of Justice, Bureau of Justice Statistics
"Census of State and Local Law Enforcement Agencies, 1992" (Bulletin, July 1993, NCJ-142972)
*Includes consolidated police-sheriff departments.

Rate of Full-Time Sworn Officers in Local Police Departments in 1992

National Rate = 14.63 Officers per 10,000 Population*

RANK	STATE	RATE	RANK	STATE	RATE
1	New York	25.29	25	Virginia	12.87
2	New Jersey	24.68	27	Kansas	12.64
3	Hawaii	23.19	28	Wyoming	12.53
4	Illinois	21.48	29	Tennessee	12.37
5	Massachusetts	20.15	30	North Carolina	11.72
6	Rhode Island	20.14	31	Alaska	11.53
7	Connecticut	18.49	32	Maine	11.33
8	Maryland	16.86	33	California	10.75
9	New Hampshire	15.45	34	Nebraska	10.71
10	Missouri	15.25	35	Indiana	10.58
11	Pennsylvania	14.37	36	Mississippi	10.50
12	Wisconsin	14.35	37	Vermont	10.42
13	Oklahoma	14.10	38	Arkansas	10.40
14	Georgia	13.93	39	Minnesota	10.22
15	Texas	13.92	40	Iowa	10.18
16	Colorado	13.80	41	Kentucky	10.13
16	Michigan	13.80	42	South Carolina	9.66
18	Alabama	13.64	43	Oregon	9.34
19	Arizona	13.59	44	Washington	9.16
20	Nevada	13.53	45	South Dakota	9.11
21	Florida	13.37	46	Idaho	8.63
22	Ohio	13.32	47	Utah	8.53
23	New Mexico	13.23	48	North Dakota	8.46
24	Louisiana	12.94	49	West Virginia	6.95
25	Delaware	12.87	50	Montana	6.89

District of Columbia   83.01

Source: Morgan Quitno Corporation using data from U.S. Department of Justice, Bureau of Justice Statistics
"Census of State and Local Law Enforcement Agencies, 1992" (Bulletin, July 1993, NCJ-142972)
*Includes consolidated police-sheriff departments.

Full-Time Employees in Local Police Departments in 1992

National Total = 476,261 Employees

RANK	STATE	EMPLOYEES	%	RANK	STATE	EMPLOYEES	%
1	New York	56,406	11.84%	26	Minnesota	5,506	1.16%
2	California	46,947	9.86%	27	Kentucky	4,721	0.99%
3	Texas	33,059	6.94%	28	South Carolina	4,323	0.91%
4	Illinois	30,971	6.50%	29	Kansas	4,215	0.89%
5	Florida	25,598	5.37%	30	Oregon	3,883	0.82%
6	New Jersey	22,793	4.79%	31	Mississippi	3,633	0.76%
7	Pennsylvania	19,907	4.18%	32	Iowa	3,476	0.73%
8	Ohio	17,936	3.77%	33	Hawaii	3,384	0.71%
9	Michigan	15,636	3.28%	34	Arkansas	3,262	0.68%
10	Massachusetts	14,217	2.99%	35	Nevada	3,175	0.67%
11	Georgia	12,524	2.63%	36	New Mexico	3,003	0.63%
12	Virginia	10,529	2.21%	37	Rhode Island	2,456	0.52%
13	Missouri	10,395	2.18%	38	New Hampshire	2,191	0.46%
14	Maryland	10,156	2.13%	39	Nebraska	2,147	0.45%
15	North Carolina	9,805	2.06%	40	Utah	1,882	0.40%
16	Wisconsin	8,795	1.85%	41	Maine	1,766	0.37%
17	Tennessee	8,204	1.72%	42	West Virginia	1,527	0.32%
18	Indiana	7,864	1.65%	43	Idaho	1,151	0.24%
19	Alabama	7,295	1.53%	44	Alaska	1,071	0.22%
20	Connecticut	7,236	1.52%	45	Delaware	1,047	0.22%
21	Arizona	7,178	1.51%	46	South Dakota	804	0.17%
22	Louisiana	6,760	1.42%	47	Wyoming	799	0.17%
23	Colorado	6,445	1.35%	48	Vermont	752	0.16%
24	Washington	6,246	1.31%	49	Montana	733	0.15%
25	Oklahoma	6,028	1.27%	50	North Dakota	674	0.14%
					District of Columbia	5,750	1.21%

Source: U.S. Department of Justice, Bureau of Justice Statistics
"Census of State and Local Law Enforcement Agencies, 1992" (Bulletin, July 1993, NCJ-142972)
*Includes consolidated police-sheriff departments.

Sheriffs' Departments in 1992

National Total = 3,086 Departments*

RANK	STATE	DEPARTMENTS	%	RANK	STATE	DEPARTMENTS	%
1	Texas	255	8.26%	26	California	58	1.88%
2	Georgia	159	5.15%	27	New York	57	1.85%
3	Virginia	125	4.05%	28	Montana	55	1.78%
4	Kentucky	120	3.89%	28	West Virginia	55	1.78%
5	Missouri	114	3.69%	30	North Dakota	53	1.72%
6	Kansas	105	3.40%	31	South Carolina	46	1.49%
7	Illinois	102	3.31%	32	Idaho	44	1.43%
8	North Carolina	100	3.24%	33	Washington	39	1.26%
9	Iowa	99	3.21%	34	Oregon	36	1.17%
10	Tennessee	95	3.08%	35	New Mexico	33	1.07%
11	Nebraska	93	3.01%	36	Utah	29	0.94%
12	Indiana	91	2.95%	37	Maryland	24	0.78%
13	Ohio	88	2.85%	38	Wyoming	23	0.75%
14	Minnesota	87	2.82%	39	New Jersey	21	0.68%
15	Michigan	83	2.69%	40	Maine	16	0.52%
16	Mississippi	82	2.66%	40	Nevada	16	0.52%
17	Oklahoma	77	2.50%	42	Arizona	15	0.49%
18	Arkansas	75	2.43%	43	Massachusetts	14	0.45%
19	Wisconsin	72	2.33%	43	Vermont	14	0.45%
20	Alabama	67	2.17%	45	New Hampshire	10	0.32%
21	Pennsylvania	66	2.14%	46	Connecticut	8	0.26%
21	South Dakota	66	2.14%	47	Rhode Island	4	0.13%
23	Florida	65	2.11%	48	Delaware	3	0.10%
24	Louisiana	64	2.07%	49	Alaska	0	0.00%
25	Colorado	63	2.04%	49	Hawaii	0	0.00%
					District of Columbia	0	0.00%

Source: U.S. Department of Justice, Bureau of Justice Statistics
    "Census of State and Local Law Enforcement Agencies, 1992" (Bulletin, July 1993, NCJ-142972)
*Sheriffs' departments generally operate at the county level.

Full-Time Sworn Officers in Sheriffs' Departments in 1992

National Total = 136,542 Officers*

RANK	STATE	OFFICERS	%	RANK	STATE	OFFICERS	%
1	California	22,552	16.52%	26	Massachusetts	1,264	0.93%
2	Florida	11,805	8.65%	27	Iowa	1,217	0.89%
3	Texas	9,876	7.23%	28	Mississippi	1,107	0.81%
4	Louisiana	8,217	6.02%	29	Pennsylvania	1,076	0.79%
5	Illinois	7,845	5.75%	30	Arkansas	1,054	0.77%
6	Georgia	5,852	4.29%	31	Kentucky	1,041	0.76%
7	Virginia	5,590	4.09%	32	Idaho	1,032	0.76%
8	New York	5,039	3.69%	33	Oklahoma	842	0.62%
9	North Carolina	4,596	3.37%	34	Utah	818	0.60%
10	Michigan	3,954	2.90%	35	Nevada	808	0.59%
11	Ohio	3,870	2.83%	36	New Mexico	792	0.58%
12	New Jersey	3,833	2.81%	37	Nebraska	769	0.56%
13	Wisconsin	3,309	2.42%	38	West Virginia	651	0.48%
14	Colorado	3,042	2.23%	39	Montana	595	0.44%
15	Tennessee	2,866	2.10%	40	Wyoming	448	0.33%
16	South Carolina	2,494	1.83%	41	Connecticut	418	0.31%
17	Indiana	2,389	1.75%	42	Maine	367	0.27%
18	Washington	2,228	1.63%	43	North Dakota	348	0.25%
19	Missouri	2,071	1.52%	44	South Dakota	338	0.25%
20	Alabama	1,902	1.39%	45	Rhode Island	124	0.09%
21	Minnesota	1,887	1.38%	46	New Hampshire	104	0.08%
22	Oregon	1,691	1.24%	47	Vermont	78	0.06%
23	Kansas	1,546	1.13%	48	Delaware	22	0.02%
24	Arizona	1,427	1.05%	49	Alaska	0	0.00%
25	Maryland	1,348	0.99%	49	Hawaii	0	0.00%
					District of Columbia	0	0.00%

Source: U.S. Department of Justice, Bureau of Justice Statistics
   "Census of State and Local Law Enforcement Agencies, 1992" (Bulletin, July 1993, NCJ-142972)
*Sheriffs' departments generally operate at the county level.

Percent of Full-Time Sheriffs' Departments Employees Who Are Sworn Officers: 1992

National Rate = 60.59% of Employees*

RANK	STATE	PERCENT	RANK	STATE	PERCENT
1	Rhode Island	99.20	26	Nebraska	59.02
2	Connecticut	98.35	27	Michigan	57.63
3	Louisiana	92.44	28	Montana	57.54
4	Kentucky	91.24	29	Arkansas	57.00
5	Virginia	85.34	30	South Dakota	56.05
6	New Jersey	81.45	31	Delaware	55.00
7	Missouri	79.08	32	Washington	54.47
8	Pennsylvania	74.05	33	Minnesota	54.44
9	South Carolina	72.86	34	Oregon	54.43
10	Illinois	72.52	35	New York	54.28
11	Nevada	70.75	36	Maryland	52.95
12	Georgia	69.82	37	Indiana	51.92
13	Wisconsin	69.63	38	Texas	51.77
14	North Dakota	69.18	39	Ohio	51.45
15	Idaho	68.71	40	Wyoming	51.20
16	Colorado	67.41	41	Oklahoma	48.50
17	New Hampshire	65.82	42	Tennessee	48.35
18	Vermont	65.55	43	Florida	48.33
19	North Carolina	64.65	44	Utah	47.86
20	Kansas	64.50	45	West Virginia	47.41
21	New Mexico	63.82	46	Maine	40.96
22	Mississippi	62.61	47	Massachusetts	34.97
23	California	62.22	48	Arizona	34.01
24	Alabama	59.96	–	Alaska**	N/A
25	Iowa	59.14	–	Hawaii**	N/A

	District of Columbia**	N/A

Source: Morgan Quitno Corporation using data from U.S. Department of Justice, Bureau of Justice Statistics
     "Census of State and Local Law Enforcement Agencies, 1992" (Bulletin, July 1993, NCJ-142972)
*Sheriffs' departments generally operate at the county level.
**Not applicable.

Rate of Full–Time Sworn Officers in Sheriffs' Departments in 1992

National Rate = 5.35 Officers per 10,000 Population*

RANK	STATE	RATE	RANK	STATE	RATE
1	Louisiana	19.17	26	Arkansas	4.39
2	Idaho	9.67	27	Washington	4.34
3	Wyoming	9.61	28	Iowa	4.33
4	Colorado	8.77	29	Mississippi	4.23
4	Virginia	8.77	30	Indiana	4.22
6	Florida	8.75	31	Minnesota	4.21
7	Georgia	8.67	32	Michigan	4.19
8	California	7.31	33	Missouri	3.99
9	Montana	7.22	34	Arizona	3.72
10	South Carolina	6.92	35	West Virginia	3.59
11	Illinois	6.74	36	Ohio	3.51
12	North Carolina	6.72	37	Maine	2.97
13	Wisconsin	6.61	38	New York	2.78
14	Kansas	6.13	39	Kentucky	2.77
15	Nevada	6.09	40	Maryland	2.75
16	Tennessee	5.70	41	Oklahoma	2.62
17	Oregon	5.68	42	Massachusetts	2.11
18	Texas	5.59	43	Vermont	1.37
19	North Dakota	5.47	44	Connecticut	1.27
20	New Mexico	5.01	45	Rhode Island	1.23
21	New Jersey	4.92	46	New Hampshire	0.94
22	Nebraska	4.79	47	Pennsylvania	0.90
23	South Dakota	4.75	48	Delaware	0.32
24	Alabama	4.60	49	Alaska	0.00
25	Utah	4.51	49	Hawaii	0.00
				District of Columbia	0.00

Source: Morgan Quitno Corporation using data from U.S. Department of Justice, Bureau of Justice Statistics
   "Census of State and Local Law Enforcement Agencies, 1992" (Bulletin, July 1993, NCJ–142972)
*Sheriffs' departments generally operate at the county level.

Full–Time Employees in Sheriffs' Departments in 1992

National Total = 225,342 Employees*

RANK	STATE	EMPLOYEES	%	RANK	STATE	EMPLOYEES	%
1	California	36,243	16.08%	26	Kansas	2,397	1.06%
2	Florida	24,426	10.84%	27	Iowa	2,058	0.91%
3	Texas	19,077	8.47%	28	Arkansas	1,849	0.82%
4	Illinois	10,817	4.80%	29	Mississippi	1,768	0.78%
5	New York	9,284	4.12%	30	Oklahoma	1,736	0.77%
6	Louisiana	8,889	3.94%	31	Utah	1,709	0.76%
7	Georgia	8,381	3.72%	32	Idaho	1,502	0.67%
8	Ohio	7,522	3.34%	33	Pennsylvania	1,453	0.64%
9	North Carolina	7,109	3.15%	34	West Virginia	1,373	0.61%
10	Michigan	6,861	3.04%	35	Nebraska	1,303	0.58%
11	Virginia	6,550	2.91%	36	New Mexico	1,241	0.55%
12	Tennessee	5,927	2.63%	37	Nevada	1,142	0.51%
13	Wisconsin	4,752	2.11%	38	Kentucky	1,141	0.51%
14	New Jersey	4,706	2.09%	39	Montana	1,034	0.46%
15	Indiana	4,601	2.04%	40	Maine	896	0.40%
16	Colorado	4,513	2.00%	41	Wyoming	875	0.39%
17	Arizona	4,196	1.86%	42	South Dakota	603	0.27%
18	Washington	4,090	1.82%	43	North Dakota	503	0.22%
19	Massachusetts	3,615	1.60%	44	Connecticut	425	0.19%
20	Minnesota	3,466	1.54%	45	New Hampshire	158	0.07%
21	South Carolina	3,423	1.52%	46	Rhode Island	125	0.06%
22	Alabama	3,172	1.41%	47	Vermont	119	0.05%
23	Oregon	3,107	1.38%	48	Delaware	40	0.02%
24	Missouri	2,619	1.16%	49	Alaska	0	0.00%
25	Maryland	2,546	1.13%	49	Hawaii	0	0.00%
					District of Columbia	0	0.00%

Source: U.S. Department of Justice, Bureau of Justice Statistics

"Census of State and Local Law Enforcement Agencies, 1992" (Bulletin, July 1993, NCJ-142972)

*Sheriffs' departments generally operate at the county level.

Special Police Agencies in 1992

National Total = 1,721 Agencies*

RANK	STATE	AGENCIES	%	RANK	STATE	AGENCIES	%
1	Texas	824	47.88%	23	Missouri	16	0.93%
2	California	93	5.40%	23	Wisconsin	16	0.93%
3	New York	57	3.31%	28	Colorado	14	0.81%
4	Pennsylvania	51	2.96%	28	West Virginia	14	0.81%
5	Illinois	43	2.50%	30	Utah	13	0.76%
5	Ohio	43	2.50%	31	Arizona	11	0.64%
7	Georgia	37	2.15%	32	Washington	10	0.58%
8	Virginia	34	1.98%	33	Minnesota	9	0.52%
9	Massachusetts	32	1.86%	33	New Mexico	9	0.52%
10	Louisiana	27	1.57%	33	Oregon	9	0.52%
11	Mississippi	25	1.45%	36	Iowa	6	0.35%
11	North Carolina	25	1.45%	36	Maine	6	0.35%
13	Alabama	24	1.39%	38	Delaware	5	0.29%
13	New Jersey	24	1.39%	39	Alaska	4	0.23%
15	Maryland	21	1.22%	39	Montana	4	0.23%
16	Florida	20	1.16%	39	Nebraska	4	0.23%
16	Indiana	20	1.16%	39	Nevada	4	0.23%
16	Michigan	20	1.16%	39	North Dakota	4	0.23%
16	Oklahoma	20	1.16%	39	Rhode Island	4	0.23%
16	South Carolina	20	1.16%	45	New Hampshire	3	0.17%
21	Tennessee	19	1.10%	45	Wyoming	3	0.17%
22	Kansas	18	1.05%	47	Hawaii	2	0.12%
23	Arkansas	16	0.93%	47	South Dakota	2	0.12%
23	Connecticut	16	0.93%	49	Idaho	1	0.06%
23	Kentucky	16	0.93%	49	Vermont	1	0.06%
					District of Columbia	2	0.12%

Source: U.S. Department of Justice, Bureau of Justice Statistics
"Census of State and Local Law Enforcement Agencies, 1992" (Bulletin, July 1993, NCJ–142972)
*Agencies with special jurisdictions or special enforcement responsibilities. Texas' total includes 751 county constable offices.

Full–Time Sworn Officers in Special Police Departments in 1992

National Total = 41,371 Officers*

RANK	STATE	OFFICERS	%	RANK	STATE	OFFICERS	%
1	New York	13,334	32.23%	26	Oklahoma	301	0.73%
2	Texas	4,108	9.93%	27	Kansas	292	0.71%
3	California	3,992	9.65%	28	Kentucky	280	0.68%
4	Florida	1,432	3.46%	29	Utah	250	0.60%
5	Pennsylvania	1,293	3.13%	30	Connecticut	248	0.60%
6	Maryland	1,280	3.09%	31	West Virginia	243	0.59%
7	Ohio	1,099	2.66%	32	Washington	228	0.55%
8	New Jersey	1,062	2.57%	33	Iowa	213	0.51%
9	Virginia	964	2.33%	34	Maine	169	0.41%
10	Illinois	864	2.09%	35	Arizona	164	0.40%
11	Georgia	759	1.83%	36	Delaware	158	0.38%
12	North Carolina	707	1.71%	37	Nevada	143	0.35%
13	Michigan	642	1.55%	38	Alaska	120	0.29%
14	Wisconsin	603	1.46%	39	Oregon	117	0.28%
15	Alabama	600	1.45%	40	New Mexico	111	0.27%
16	Massachusetts	593	1.43%	41	Hawaii	93	0.22%
17	South Carolina	584	1.41%	41	Nebraska	93	0.22%
18	Louisiana	570	1.38%	43	Rhode Island	76	0.18%
19	Indiana	560	1.35%	44	New Hampshire	68	0.16%
20	Tennessee	517	1.25%	45	North Dakota	49	0.12%
21	Arkansas	443	1.07%	46	Montana	47	0.11%
22	Colorado	404	0.98%	47	Vermont	21	0.05%
23	Minnesota	397	0.96%	47	Wyoming	21	0.05%
24	Missouri	391	0.95%	49	Idaho	12	0.03%
25	Mississippi	324	0.78%	50	South Dakota	8	0.02%
					District of Columbia	324	0.78%

Source: U.S. Department of Justice, Bureau of Justice Statistics

"Census of State and Local Law Enforcement Agencies, 1992" (Bulletin, July 1993, NCJ–142972)

*Agencies with special jurisdictions or special enforcement responsibilities. Texas' total includes 751 county constable offices with 1,723 sworn constable office employees.

Percent of Full–Time Special Police Department Employees Who Are Sworn Officers: 1992

National Rate = 67.90% of Employees*

RANK	STATE	PERCENT	RANK	STATE	PERCENT
1	Hawaii	98.94	26	New Mexico	68.94
2	Nebraska	92.08	27	Delaware	68.10
3	New York	90.08	28	North Dakota	67.12
4	Alaska	88.89	29	Oregon	66.86
5	Maine	88.48	30	Michigan	66.53
6	West Virginia	87.41	31	Nevada	65.90
7	Connecticut	84.35	32	Vermont	65.63
8	Louisiana	83.95	33	Kentucky	64.67
9	Minnesota	83.40	34	Arizona	63.57
10	Iowa	80.68	35	North Carolina	63.29
11	Idaho	80.00	36	Texas	63.14
12	Illinois	78.47	37	Wyoming	61.76
13	Oklahoma	78.39	38	New Jersey	61.18
14	Alabama	78.02	39	Ohio	57.48
15	Indiana	77.24	40	Wisconsin	56.51
16	Massachusetts	77.01	41	Montana	51.09
17	Tennessee	76.59	42	South Carolina	50.34
18	Florida	76.13	43	South Dakota	50.00
19	Missouri	74.76	44	California	46.98
20	Pennsylvania	74.57	45	Virginia	44.44
21	Kansas	73.18	46	Georgia	44.36
22	Maryland	72.36	47	Colorado	44.25
23	Mississippi	72.00	48	Arkansas	42.88
24	Rhode Island	71.03	49	New Hampshire	33.17
25	Washington	70.59	50	Utah	29.52

	District of Columbia	76.42

Source: Morgan Quitno Corporation using data from U.S. Department of Justice, Bureau of Justice Statistics
"Census of State and Local Law Enforcement Agencies, 1992" (Bulletin, July 1993, NCJ-142972)
*Agencies with special jurisdictions or special enforcement responsibilities. Texas' total includes 751 county constable offices with 1,723 sworn constable office employees.

Rate of Full-Time Sworn Officers in Special Police Departments in 1992

National Rate = 1.62 Officers per 10,000 Population*

RANK	STATE	RATE	RANK	STATE	RATE
1	New York	7.36	26	Ohio	1.00
2	Maryland	2.61	27	Indiana	0.99
3	Texas	2.33	27	Massachusetts	0.99
4	Delaware	2.29	29	Oklahoma	0.94
5	Alaska	2.04	30	Minnesota	0.89
6	Arkansas	1.85	31	Hawaii	0.80
7	South Carolina	1.62	32	North Dakota	0.77
8	Virginia	1.51	33	Connecticut	0.76
9	Alabama	1.45	33	Iowa	0.76
10	Utah	1.38	33	Rhode Island	0.76
11	Maine	1.37	36	Kentucky	0.75
12	New Jersey	1.36	36	Missouri	0.75
13	West Virginia	1.34	38	Illinois	0.74
14	Louisiana	1.33	39	New Mexico	0.70
15	California	1.29	40	Michigan	0.68
16	Mississippi	1.24	41	New Hampshire	0.61
17	Wisconsin	1.20	42	Nebraska	0.58
18	Colorado	1.16	43	Montana	0.57
18	Kansas	1.16	44	Wyoming	0.45
20	Georgia	1.12	45	Washington	0.44
21	Nevada	1.08	46	Arizona	0.43
21	Pennsylvania	1.08	47	Oregon	0.39
23	Florida	1.06	48	Vermont	0.37
24	North Carolina	1.03	49	Idaho	0.11
24	Tennessee	1.03	49	South Dakota	0.11

District of Columbia   5.50

Source: Morgan Quitno Corporation using data from U.S. Department of Justice, Bureau of Justice Statistics
    "Census of State and Local Law Enforcement Agencies, 1992" (Bulletin, July 1993, NCJ-142972)
*Agencies with special jurisdictions or special enforcement responsibilities. Texas' total includes 751 county constable offices with 1,723 sworn constable office employees.

Full-Time Employees in Special Police Departments in 1992

National Total = 60,926 Employees*

RANK	STATE	EMPLOYEES	%	RANK	STATE	EMPLOYEES	%
1	New York	14,803	24.30%	26	Mississippi	450	0.74%
2	California	8,498	13.95%	27	Kentucky	433	0.71%
3	Texas	6,506	10.68%	28	Kansas	399	0.65%
4	Virginia	2,169	3.56%	29	Oklahoma	384	0.63%
5	Ohio	1,912	3.14%	30	Washington	323	0.53%
6	Florida	1,881	3.09%	31	Connecticut	294	0.48%
7	Maryland	1,769	2.90%	32	West Virginia	278	0.46%
8	New Jersey	1,736	2.85%	33	Iowa	264	0.43%
9	Pennsylvania	1,734	2.85%	34	Arizona	258	0.42%
10	Georgia	1,711	2.81%	35	Delaware	232	0.38%
11	South Carolina	1,160	1.90%	36	Nevada	217	0.36%
12	North Carolina	1,117	1.83%	37	New Hampshire	205	0.34%
13	Illinois	1,101	1.81%	38	Maine	191	0.31%
14	Wisconsin	1,067	1.75%	39	Oregon	175	0.29%
15	Arkansas	1,033	1.70%	40	New Mexico	161	0.26%
16	Michigan	965	1.58%	41	Alaska	135	0.22%
17	Colorado	913	1.50%	42	Rhode Island	107	0.18%
18	Utah	847	1.39%	43	Nebraska	101	0.17%
19	Massachusetts	770	1.26%	44	Hawaii	94	0.15%
20	Alabama	769	1.26%	45	Montana	92	0.15%
21	Indiana	725	1.19%	46	North Dakota	73	0.12%
22	Louisiana	679	1.11%	47	Wyoming	34	0.06%
23	Tennessee	675	1.11%	48	Vermont	32	0.05%
24	Missouri	523	0.86%	49	South Dakota	16	0.03%
25	Minnesota	476	0.78%	50	Idaho	15	0.02%
					District of Columbia	424	0.70%

Source: U.S. Department of Justice, Bureau of Justice Statistics
"Census of State and Local Law Enforcement Agencies, 1992" (Bulletin, July 1993, NCJ-142972)
*Agencies with special jurisdictions or special enforcement responsibilities. Texas' total includes 751 county constable offices with about 2,000 employees.

Law Enforcement Officers Feloniously Killed in 1992

National Total = 57 Officers*

RANK	STATE	OFFICERS	%	RANK	STATE	OFFICERS	%
1	California	6	10.53%	24	Indiana	0	0.00%
2	Illinois	5	8.77%	24	Iowa	0	0.00%
3	Kentucky	4	7.02%	24	Kansas	0	0.00%
3	New York	4	7.02%	24	Maine	0	0.00%
3	South Carolina	4	7.02%	24	Massachusetts	0	0.00%
6	Florida	3	5.26%	24	Michigan	0	0.00%
6	Louisiana	3	5.26%	24	Montana	0	0.00%
6	North Carolina	3	5.26%	24	Nebraska	0	0.00%
6	Pennsylvania	3	5.26%	24	Nevada	0	0.00%
6	Texas	3	5.26%	24	New Hampshire	0	0.00%
11	Colorado	2	3.51%	24	New Jersey	0	0.00%
11	Georgia	2	3.51%	24	New Mexico	0	0.00%
11	Maryland	2	3.51%	24	North Dakota	0	0.00%
11	Mississippi	2	3.51%	24	Ohio	0	0.00%
11	Oregon	2	3.51%	24	Oklahoma	0	0.00%
16	Alabama	1	1.75%	24	Rhode Island	0	0.00%
16	Alaska	1	1.75%	24	South Dakota	0	0.00%
16	Arizona	1	1.75%	24	Tennessee	0	0.00%
16	Arkansas	1	1.75%	24	Utah	0	0.00%
16	Connecticut	1	1.75%	24	Vermont	0	0.00%
16	Idaho	1	1.75%	24	Virginia	0	0.00%
16	Minnesota	1	1.75%	24	Washington	0	0.00%
16	Missouri	1	1.75%	24	West Virginia	0	0.00%
24	Delaware	0	0.00%	24	Wisconsin	0	0.00%
24	Hawaii	0	0.00%	24	Wyoming	0	0.00%

District of Columbia   1   1.75%

Source: U.S. Department of Justice, Federal Bureau of Investigation
   unpublished data

*Total does not include five officers killed in Puerto Rico in 1992.

Law Enforcement Officers Feloniously Killed: 1983 to 1992

National Total = 664 Officers*

RANK	STATE	OFFICERS	%	RANK	STATE	OFFICERS	%
1	Texas	70	10.54%	26	New Jersey	9	1.36%
2	California	57	8.58%	27	Washington	8	1.20%
3	Florida	51	7.68%	27	Wisconsin	8	1.20%
4	New York	38	5.72%	29	Alaska	7	1.05%
5	Georgia	30	4.52%	29	Minnesota	7	1.05%
6	Illinois	29	4.37%	29	New Mexico	7	1.05%
7	Michigan	28	4.22%	32	Kansas	5	0.75%
8	Mississippi	25	3.77%	32	Montana	5	0.75%
9	Pennsylvania	20	3.01%	34	Hawaii	4	0.60%
10	Arizona	19	2.86%	35	Connecticut	3	0.45%
11	Missouri	18	2.71%	35	Nevada	3	0.45%
11	Virginia	18	2.71%	35	Oregon	3	0.45%
13	Kentucky	17	2.56%	35	West Virginia	3	0.45%
13	Louisiana	17	2.56%	39	Idaho	2	0.30%
13	South Carolina	17	2.56%	39	Iowa	2	0.30%
16	Alabama	15	2.26%	39	Maine	2	0.30%
16	North Carolina	15	2.26%	39	Nebraska	2	0.30%
18	Ohio	14	2.11%	39	North Dakota	2	0.30%
19	Arkansas	13	1.96%	44	South Dakota	1	0.15%
19	Tennessee	13	1.96%	44	Utah	1	0.15%
21	Maryland	12	1.81%	44	Wyoming	1	0.15%
22	Colorado	10	1.51%	47	Delaware	0	0.00%
22	Indiana	10	1.51%	47	New Hampshire	0	0.00%
22	Massachusetts	10	1.51%	47	Rhode Island	0	0.00%
22	Oklahoma	10	1.51%	47	Vermont	0	0.00%
					District of Columbia	3	0.45%

Source: U.S. Department of Justice, Federal Bureau of Investigation
   unpublished data

*Total does not include 49 officers killed in U.S. Territories or abroad. Of this total, 44 officers were killed in Puerto Rico.

U.S. District Court Judgeships in 1992

National Total = 649 Judges*

RANK	STATE	JUDGESHIPS	%	RANK	STATE	JUDGESHIPS	%
1	California	56	8.63%	25	Arkansas	8	1.23%
2	New York	52	8.01%	25	Connecticut	8	1.23%
3	Texas	47	7.24%	25	West Virginia	8	1.23%
4	Pennsylvania	39	6.01%	29	Colorado	7	1.08%
5	Florida	31	4.78%	29	Minnesota	7	1.08%
6	Illinois	30	4.62%	31	Kansas	6	0.92%
7	Louisiana	22	3.39%	31	Oregon	6	0.92%
8	Michigan	20	3.08%	31	Wisconsin	6	0.92%
8	Ohio	20	3.08%	34	Iowa	5	0.77%
10	Georgia	18	2.77%	34	New Mexico	5	0.77%
11	New Jersey	17	2.62%	34	Utah	5	0.77%
12	Alabama	14	2.16%	37	Delaware	4	0.62%
12	Missouri	14	2.16%	37	Hawaii	4	0.62%
12	Tennessee	14	2.16%	37	Nebraska	4	0.62%
12	Virginia	14	2.16%	37	Nevada	4	0.62%
16	Massachusetts	13	2.00%	41	Alaska	3	0.46%
17	North Carolina	11	1.69%	41	Maine	3	0.46%
17	Oklahoma	11	1.69%	41	Montana	3	0.46%
17	Washington	11	1.69%	41	New Hampshire	3	0.46%
20	Indiana	10	1.54%	41	Rhode Island	3	0.46%
20	Maryland	10	1.54%	41	South Dakota	3	0.46%
22	Kentucky	9	1.39%	41	Wyoming	3	0.46%
22	Mississippi	9	1.39%	48	Idaho	2	0.31%
22	South Carolina	9	1.39%	48	North Dakota	2	0.31%
25	Arizona	8	1.23%	48	Vermont	2	0.31%
					District of Columbia	15	2.31%

Source: Administrative Office of the United States Courts
"1992 Federal Court Management Statistics" (March 1993)
*Total includes 11 judgeships in U.S. territories.

Criminal Cases Filed in U.S. District Court in 1992

National Total = 48,366 Criminal Cases*

RANK	STATE	CASES	%	RANK	STATE	CASES	%
1	Texas	4,515	9.34%	26	West Virginia	585	1.21%
2	California	4,316	8.92%	27	Oregon	543	1.12%
3	New York	3,311	6.85%	28	Colorado	495	1.02%
4	Georgia	3,016	6.24%	29	Arkansas	440	0.91%
5	Virginia	2,651	5.48%	30	Nevada	432	0.89%
6	Florida	2,409	4.98%	31	Mississippi	403	0.83%
7	North Carolina	1,985	4.10%	32	Wisconsin	386	0.80%
8	Hawaii	1,658	3.43%	33	Utah	339	0.70%
9	Washington	1,651	3.41%	34	Massachusetts	325	0.67%
10	Arizona	1,556	3.22%	35	Kansas	324	0.67%
11	Illinois	1,299	2.69%	36	Minnesota	296	0.61%
12	Tennessee	1,234	2.55%	37	Alaska	290	0.60%
13	Pennsylvania	1,217	2.52%	38	Montana	243	0.50%
14	Alabama	1,033	2.14%	39	Connecticut	237	0.49%
15	Ohio	988	2.04%	39	Iowa	237	0.49%
16	Michigan	925	1.91%	41	Nebraska	221	0.46%
17	Missouri	879	1.82%	42	South Dakota	193	0.40%
18	New Jersey	804	1.66%	43	North Dakota	158	0.33%
19	Kentucky	736	1.52%	44	Rhode Island	149	0.31%
20	Louisiana	729	1.51%	45	Maine	148	0.31%
21	Oklahoma	682	1.41%	46	Delaware	117	0.24%
22	Maryland	650	1.34%	47	Idaho	108	0.22%
23	South Carolina	648	1.34%	48	Wyoming	107	0.22%
24	New Mexico	639	1.32%	49	Vermont	106	0.22%
25	Indiana	589	1.22%	50	New Hampshire	79	0.16%
					District of Columbia	541	1.12%

Source: Administrative Office of the United States Courts

"Judicial Business of the United States Courts, Annual Report of the Director, 1992"

*Total includes criminal cases filed in U.S. territories.

Criminal Cases Completed in U.S. District Court in 1992

National Total = 44,147 Criminal Cases*

RANK	STATE	CASES	%	RANK	STATE	CASES	%
1	Texas	4,365	9.89%	26	South Carolina	539	1.22%
2	California	3,389	7.68%	27	Oregon	531	1.20%
3	Georgia	2,800	6.34%	28	Arkansas	407	0.92%
4	New York	2,762	6.26%	29	Colorado	399	0.90%
5	Virginia	2,608	5.91%	30	Wisconsin	358	0.81%
6	Florida	2,271	5.14%	31	Mississippi	349	0.79%
7	North Carolina	1,909	4.32%	32	Nevada	333	0.75%
8	Washington	1,434	3.25%	33	Kansas	316	0.72%
9	Hawaii	1,359	3.08%	34	Utah	296	0.67%
10	Arizona	1,298	2.94%	35	Alaska	293	0.66%
11	Tennessee	1,174	2.66%	36	Minnesota	284	0.64%
12	Illinois	1,134	2.57%	37	Connecticut	260	0.59%
13	Pennsylvania	1,118	2.53%	38	Massachusetts	229	0.52%
14	Ohio	986	2.23%	39	Montana	219	0.50%
15	Alabama	966	2.19%	40	Iowa	213	0.48%
16	Missouri	803	1.82%	40	South Dakota	213	0.48%
17	Louisiana	794	1.80%	42	Nebraska	185	0.42%
18	Michigan	789	1.79%	43	North Dakota	152	0.34%
19	Kentucky	751	1.70%	44	Maine	151	0.34%
20	New Jersey	720	1.63%	45	Rhode Island	128	0.29%
21	Oklahoma	709	1.61%	46	Vermont	118	0.27%
22	Maryland	665	1.51%	47	Delaware	117	0.27%
23	New Mexico	595	1.35%	48	Idaho	104	0.24%
24	West Virginia	558	1.26%	49	Wyoming	99	0.22%
25	Indiana	550	1.25%	50	New Hampshire	77	0.17%
					District of Columbia	538	1.22%

Source: Administrative Office of the United States Courts

"Judicial Business of the United States Courts, Annual Report of the Director, 1992"

*Total includes criminal cases completed in U.S. territories.

Median Length of Federal Criminal Cases in 1992

National Median = 5.90 Months*

RANK	STATE	MONTHS	RANK	STATE	MONTHS
1	Vermont	11.90	25	New Mexico	6.20
2	Massachusetts	10.00	27	Maine	6.10
3	South Carolina	8.70	27	Minnesota	6.10
4	Nebraska	8.30	29	Pennsylvania	5.93
5	Nevada	8.00	30	Kansas	5.90
6	New Jersey	7.60	30	Mississippi	5.90
7	New York	7.58	30	Wyoming	5.90
8	Georgia	7.23	33	Indiana	5.85
9	Hawaii	7.20	34	South Dakota	5.60
9	Kentucky	7.20	35	Utah	5.50
9	Maryland	7.20	36	Virginia	5.45
12	New Hampshire	7.10	37	Rhode Island	5.40
13	Illinois	6.83	37	West Virginia	5.40
14	Iowa	6.70	39	Montana	5.20
15	North Carolina	6.60	40	Alaska	5.00
16	California	6.58	40	Delaware	5.00
17	Michigan	6.55	40	Wisconsin	5.00
17	Ohio	6.55	43	Arkansas	4.80
19	Florida	6.50	43	Texas	4.80
20	Tennessee	6.37	45	Louisiana	4.63
21	Arizona	6.30	46	Colorado	4.60
21	Connecticut	6.30	47	Washington	4.40
21	Oregon	6.30	48	Oklahoma	4.03
24	Missouri	6.25	49	Alabama	3.93
25	Idaho	6.20	50	North Dakota	3.90

District of Columbia		5.70

Source: Administrative Office of the United States Courts
    "1992 Federal Court Management Statistics" (March 1993)
*Felony cases from filing to final disposition in U.S. District Courts.

Federal Prosecutions of Corrupt Public Officials: 1976 to 1990

National Total = 9,470 Officials

RANK	STATE	OFFICIALS	%	RANK	STATE	OFFICIALS	%
1	New York	1,077	11.37%	26	West Virginia	92	0.97%
2	California	707	7.47%	27	Arizona	76	0.80%
3	Illinois	669	7.06%	27	Kansas	76	0.80%
4	Pennsylvania	613	6.47%	29	Colorado	75	0.79%
5	Ohio	420	4.44%	30	Minnesota	73	0.77%
6	Tennessee	417	4.40%	31	Arkansas	70	0.74%
7	Texas	405	4.28%	32	New Mexico	64	0.68%
8	Florida	373	3.94%	33	Iowa	61	0.64%
9	Georgia	340	3.59%	34	Alaska	53	0.56%
10	Alabama	264	2.79%	35	South Dakota	52	0.55%
11	Louisiana	253	2.67%	36	Montana	47	0.50%
12	Oklahoma	252	2.66%	37	Nebraska	45	0.48%
13	Michigan	248	2.62%	38	Utah	34	0.36%
14	Virginia	240	2.53%	39	Washington	33	0.35%
15	South Carolina	228	2.41%	40	Oregon	32	0.34%
16	New Jersey	208	2.20%	41	Rhode Island	31	0.33%
17	Massachusetts	204	2.15%	42	Nevada	30	0.32%
18	Mississippi	189	2.00%	43	Hawaii	27	0.29%
19	Maryland	178	1.88%	43	Maine	27	0.29%
20	Indiana	168	1.77%	45	New Hampshire	21	0.22%
21	North Carolina	156	1.65%	45	North Dakota	21	0.22%
22	Kentucky	139	1.47%	47	Idaho	19	0.20%
23	Missouri	135	1.43%	48	Delaware	17	0.18%
24	Wisconsin	110	1.16%	49	Wyoming	14	0.15%
25	Connecticut	105	1.11%	50	Vermont	3	0.03%
					District of Columbia	279	2.95%

Source: U.S. Department of Justice, Public Integrity Section
"Report to Congress on the Activities and Operations of the Public Integrity Section for 1990" (September 1991)

State and Local Justice System Employment in 1990

National Total = 1,522,411 Employees*

RANK	STATE	EMPLOYEES	%	RANK	STATE	EMPLOYEES	%
1	California	188,018	12.35%	26	Connecticut	17,319	1.14%
2	New York	167,193	10.98%	27	Oklahoma	16,940	1.11%
3	Texas	103,808	6.82%	28	Kentucky	16,851	1.11%
4	Florida	99,485	6.53%	29	Oregon	15,177	1.00%
5	Illinois	68,906	4.53%	30	Kansas	14,207	0.93%
6	New Jersey	61,721	4.05%	31	Iowa	12,559	0.82%
7	Pennsylvania	58,748	3.86%	32	Mississippi	11,400	0.75%
8	Ohio	53,736	3.53%	33	Arkansas	10,249	0.67%
9	Michigan	51,754	3.40%	34	New Mexico	9,792	0.64%
10	Georgia	43,031	2.83%	35	Nevada	9,330	0.61%
11	North Carolina	36,881	2.42%	36	Nebraska	8,224	0.54%
12	Virginia	36,561	2.40%	37	Utah	7,857	0.52%
13	Massachusetts	34,573	2.27%	38	Hawaii	7,351	0.48%
14	Maryland	32,932	2.16%	39	West Virginia	6,452	0.42%
15	Missouri	28,874	1.90%	40	Rhode Island	6,018	0.40%
16	Louisiana	27,408	1.80%	41	Maine	5,438	0.36%
17	Arizona	26,872	1.77%	42	Idaho	5,332	0.35%
18	Indiana	26,832	1.76%	43	New Hampshire	5,197	0.34%
19	Tennessee	25,993	1.71%	44	Alaska	4,875	0.32%
20	Washington	23,893	1.57%	45	Delaware	4,810	0.32%
21	Wisconsin	23,810	1.56%	46	Montana	3,865	0.25%
22	Alabama	21,328	1.40%	47	Wyoming	3,153	0.21%
23	South Carolina	20,577	1.35%	48	South Dakota	3,063	0.20%
24	Colorado	18,824	1.24%	49	North Dakota	2,533	0.17%
25	Minnesota	18,360	1.21%	50	Vermont	2,509	0.16%
					District of Columbia	11,792	0.77%

Source: U.S. Department of Justice, Bureau of Justice Statistics
   "Justice Expenditure and Employment in 1990" (Bulletin, September 1992, NCJ-135777)
*Full-time equivalent. Includes police, courts, prosecution, public defense, corrections and other activities.

Rate of State and Local Justice System Employment in 1990

National Rate = 61.21 Employees per 10,000 Population*

RANK	STATE	RATE		RANK	STATE	RATE
1	New York	92.93		26	Oklahoma	53.85
2	Alaska	88.63		27	Oregon	53.40
3	New Jersey	79.84		28	Tennessee	53.30
4	Nevada	77.63		29	Idaho	52.96
5	Florida	76.89		30	Alabama	52.78
6	Arizona	73.32		31	Connecticut	52.69
7	Delaware	72.20		32	Nebraska	52.10
8	Wyoming	69.51		33	Ohio	49.54
9	Maryland	68.87		34	Pennsylvania	49.44
10	Georgia	66.42		35	Washington	49.09
11	Hawaii	66.33		36	Wisconsin	48.67
12	Louisiana	64.95		37	Indiana	48.40
13	New Mexico	64.63		38	Montana	48.37
14	California	63.18		39	New Hampshire	46.85
15	Texas	61.11		40	Kentucky	45.72
16	Illinois	60.28		41	Utah	45.60
17	Rhode Island	59.97		42	Iowa	45.23
18	Virginia	59.09		43	Vermont	44.58
19	South Carolina	59.02		44	Mississippi	44.30
20	Massachusetts	57.46		45	Maine	44.29
21	Kansas	57.34		46	South Dakota	44.01
22	Colorado	57.14		47	Arkansas	43.60
23	Missouri	56.43		48	Minnesota	41.96
24	Michigan	55.68		49	North Dakota	39.65
25	North Carolina	55.64		50	West Virginia	35.97

District of Columbia   194.30

Source: U.S. Department of Justice, Bureau of Justice Statistics
"Justice Expenditure and Employment in 1990" (Bulletin, September 1992, NCJ-135777)
*Full-time equivalent. Includes police, courts, prosecution, public defense, corrections and other activities.

State Judges of General Jurisdiction in 1990

National Total = 8,468 Judges

RANK	STATE	JUDGES	%	RANK	STATE	JUDGES	%
1	Illinois	810	9.57%	26	Colorado	110	1.30%
2	California	789	9.32%	27	Tennessee	105	1.24%
3	New York	568	6.71%	28	Arkansas	98	1.16%
4	Florida	421	4.97%	29	Kentucky	91	1.07%
5	Texas	384	4.53%	30	Oregon	90	1.06%
6	New Jersey	359	4.24%	31	Mississippi	79	0.93%
7	Ohio	344	4.06%	32	North Carolina	77	0.91%
8	Pennsylvania	342	4.04%	33	West Virginia	60	0.71%
9	Massachusetts	320	3.78%	34	New Mexico	59	0.70%
10	Missouri	303	3.58%	35	Nebraska	48	0.57%
11	Minnesota	241	2.85%	36	Montana	41	0.48%
12	Indiana	229	2.70%	37	Nevada	37	0.44%
13	Oklahoma	210	2.48%	38	South Dakota	36	0.43%
13	Wisconsin	210	2.48%	39	Idaho	33	0.39%
15	Michigan	200	2.36%	40	South Carolina	31	0.37%
16	Louisiana	194	2.29%	41	Alaska	30	0.35%
17	Iowa	176	2.08%	42	Utah	29	0.34%
18	Connecticut	150	1.77%	42	Vermont	29	0.34%
19	Georgia	148	1.75%	44	North Dakota	27	0.32%
19	Kansas	148	1.75%	45	New Hampshire	26	0.31%
21	Washington	147	1.74%	46	Hawaii	24	0.28%
22	Virginia	131	1.55%	47	Rhode Island	21	0.25%
23	Alabama	124	1.46%	48	Wyoming	17	0.20%
24	Arizona	116	1.37%	49	Maine	16	0.19%
24	Maryland	116	1.37%	50	Delaware	15	0.18%
					District of Columbia	59	0.70%

Source: U.S. Department of Justice, Bureau of Justice Statistics
"State Justice Sourcebook of Statistics and Research" (September 1992, NCJ-137991)

Rate of State Judges of General Jurisdiction in 1990

National Rate = 3.40 Judges per 100,000 Population*

RANK	STATE	RATE	RANK	STATE	RATE
1	Illinois	7.09	25	Oregon	3.17
2	Oklahoma	6.68	27	Arizona	3.16
3	Iowa	6.34	27	New York	3.16
4	Kansas	5.97	29	Nevada	3.08
5	Missouri	5.92	30	Alabama	3.07
6	Minnesota	5.51	30	Mississippi	3.07
7	Alaska	5.45	32	Nebraska	3.04
8	Massachusetts	5.32	33	Washington	3.02
9	South Dakota	5.17	34	Pennsylvania	2.88
10	Vermont	5.15	35	California	2.65
11	Montana	5.13	36	Kentucky	2.47
12	New Jersey	4.64	37	Maryland	2.43
13	Louisiana	4.60	38	New Hampshire	2.34
14	Connecticut	4.56	39	Georgia	2.28
15	Wisconsin	4.29	40	Texas	2.26
16	North Dakota	4.23	41	Delaware	2.25
17	Arkansas	4.17	42	Hawaii	2.17
18	Indiana	4.13	43	Michigan	2.15
19	New Mexico	3.89	43	Tennessee	2.15
20	Wyoming	3.75	45	Virginia	2.12
21	West Virginia	3.35	46	Rhode Island	2.09
22	Colorado	3.34	47	Utah	1.68
23	Idaho	3.28	48	Maine	1.30
24	Florida	3.25	49	North Carolina	1.16
25	Ohio	3.17	50	South Carolina	0.89
				District of Columbia	9.72

Source: Morgan Quitno Corporation using data from U.S. Department of Justice, Bureau of Justice Statistics
"State Justice Sourcebook of Statistics and Research" (September 1992, NCJ-137991)

State and Local Courts Employment in 1990

National Total = 190,142 Employees*

RANK	STATE	EMPLOYEES	%	RANK	STATE	EMPLOYEES	%
1	California	23,752	12.49%	26	South Carolina	2,166	1.14%
2	New York	16,097	8.47%	27	Oregon	1,909	1.00%
3	Texas	12,873	6.77%	28	Connecticut	1,865	0.98%
4	Florida	10,711	5.63%	29	Kansas	1,754	0.92%
5	Pennsylvania	10,605	5.58%	30	Iowa	1,643	0.86%
6	Ohio	9,294	4.89%	31	Oklahoma	1,597	0.84%
7	New Jersey	8,854	4.66%	32	Mississippi	1,324	0.70%
8	Illinois	8,615	4.53%	33	Arkansas	1,237	0.65%
9	Michigan	7,591	3.99%	34	Hawaii	1,225	0.64%
10	Georgia	5,214	2.74%	35	West Virginia	1,186	0.62%
11	Massachusetts	4,929	2.59%	36	Nevada	1,052	0.55%
12	Maryland	4,329	2.28%	36	Utah	1,052	0.55%
13	Virginia	4,012	2.11%	38	Delaware	999	0.53%
14	Missouri	3,982	2.09%	39	New Mexico	992	0.52%
15	Indiana	3,581	1.88%	40	Nebraska	949	0.50%
16	North Carolina	3,451	1.81%	41	Idaho	755	0.40%
17	Arizona	3,368	1.77%	42	Rhode Island	744	0.39%
18	Tennessee	3,186	1.68%	43	New Hampshire	686	0.36%
19	Louisiana	3,119	1.64%	44	Alaska	666	0.35%
20	Alabama	2,779	1.46%	45	Montana	531	0.28%
21	Washington	2,686	1.41%	46	North Dakota	489	0.26%
22	Wisconsin	2,527	1.33%	47	Maine	437	0.23%
23	Minnesota	2,421	1.27%	48	Wyoming	383	0.20%
24	Kentucky	2,382	1.25%	49	South Dakota	320	0.17%
25	Colorado	2,274	1.20%	50	Vermont	293	0.15%
					District of Columbia	1,256	0.66%

Source: U.S. Department of Justice, Bureau of Justice Statistics
"Justice Expenditure and Employment in 1990" (Bulletin, September 1992, NCJ-135777)
*Full-time equivalent.

State and Local Prosecution Employment in 1990

National Total = 87,454 Employees*

RANK	STATE	EMPLOYEES	%	RANK	STATE	EMPLOYEES	%
1	California	13,648	15.61%	26	Alabama	1,005	1.15%
2	New York	9,864	11.28%	27	Hawaii	994	1.14%
3	Texas	6,403	7.32%	28	North Carolina	958	1.10%
4	Florida	5,252	6.01%	29	Iowa	864	0.99%
5	New Jersey	4,216	4.82%	30	Connecticut	853	0.98%
6	Ohio	3,750	4.29%	31	Nevada	685	0.78%
7	Illinois	3,534	4.04%	32	Kansas	677	0.77%
8	Pennsylvania	2,765	3.16%	33	New Mexico	601	0.69%
9	Washington	2,111	2.41%	34	Alaska	588	0.67%
10	Michigan	1,992	2.28%	35	Nebraska	492	0.56%
11	Arizona	1,900	2.17%	36	Arkansas	481	0.55%
12	Indiana	1,717	1.96%	37	Utah	476	0.54%
13	Massachusetts	1,587	1.81%	38	South Carolina	470	0.54%
14	Minnesota	1,499	1.71%	39	West Virginia	421	0.48%
15	Maryland	1,497	1.71%	40	Mississippi	420	0.48%
16	Wisconsin	1,482	1.69%	41	Idaho	414	0.47%
17	Oregon	1,464	1.67%	42	Rhode Island	333	0.38%
18	Georgia	1,461	1.67%	43	Maine	271	0.31%
19	Missouri	1,334	1.53%	44	Montana	265	0.30%
20	Colorado	1,329	1.52%	45	Delaware	211	0.24%
21	Virginia	1,291	1.48%	46	New Hampshire	207	0.24%
22	Oklahoma	1,273	1.46%	47	South Dakota	206	0.24%
23	Kentucky	1,184	1.35%	48	Wyoming	174	0.20%
24	Tennessee	1,134	1.30%	49	North Dakota	173	0.20%
25	Louisiana	1,104	1.26%	50	Vermont	156	0.18%
					District of Columbia	268	0.31%

Source: U.S. Department of Justice, Bureau of Justice Statistics

"Justice Expenditure and Employment in 1990" (Bulletin, September 1992, NCJ-135777)

*Full-time equivalent. Includes employees of attorneys general, district attorneys, state's attorneys and their affiliated offices.

Full-Time State Prosecuting Attorneys in 1990

National Total = 17,396 Prosecuting Attorneys*

RANK	STATE	PROSECUTORS	%	RANK	STATE	PROSECUTORS	%
1	California	3,340	19.20%	26	Utah	106	0.61%
2	New York	2,500	14.37%	27	North Dakota	94	0.54%
3	Florida	1,338	7.69%	28	Alaska	77	0.44%
4	Illinois	1,227	7.05%	28	Rhode Island	77	0.44%
5	Washington	1,042	5.99%	30	Mississippi	75	0.43%
6	New Jersey	817	4.70%	31	Arkansas	68	0.39%
7	Oklahoma	609	3.50%	32	Michigan	60	0.34%
8	Arizona	533	3.06%	33	Vermont	57	0.33%
9	Louisiana	527	3.03%	34	West Virginia	55	0.32%
10	Georgia	464	2.67%	35	Delaware	52	0.30%
11	Colorado	452	2.60%	36	South Dakota	32	0.18%
12	Wisconsin	435	2.50%	37	Montana	29	0.17%
13	Maryland	409	2.35%	38	Nebraska	16	0.09%
14	Alabama	325	1.87%	39	Kentucky	11	0.06%
15	Virginia	318	1.83%	–	Idaho**	N/A	N/A
16	Oregon	310	1.78%	–	Kansas**	N/A	N/A
17	North Carolina	304	1.75%	–	Maine**	N/A	N/A
18	Iowa	235	1.35%	–	Massachusetts**	N/A	N/A
19	Connecticut	196	1.13%	–	Minnesota**	N/A	N/A
20	New Hampshire	177	1.02%	–	Missouri**	N/A	N/A
21	New Mexico	176	1.01%	–	Ohio**	N/A	N/A
22	Nevada	167	0.96%	–	Pennsylvania**	N/A	N/A
23	Hawaii	152	0.87%	–	Tennessee**	N/A	N/A
24	South Carolina	141	0.81%	–	Texas**	N/A	N/A
25	Indiana	118	0.68%	–	Wyoming**	N/A	N/A

District of Columbia 275 1.58%

Source: U.S. Department of Justice, Bureau of Justice Statistics
"State Justice Sourcebook of Statistics and Research" (September 1992, NCJ-137991)

*Total is only for those states reporting.

**Not available.

State and Local Public Defense Employment in 1990

National Total = 14,618 Employees*

RANK	STATE	EMPLOYEES	%	RANK	STATE	EMPLOYEES	%
1	California	3,203	21.91%	25	Texas	120	0.82%
2	Florida	1,838	12.57%	27	Iowa	105	0.72%
3	Illinois	1,150	7.87%	28	Kansas	95	0.65%
4	New Jersey	895	6.12%	29	Alaska	92	0.63%
5	Pennsylvania	589	4.03%	30	Delaware	90	0.62%
6	New York	586	4.01%	31	Michigan	86	0.59%
7	Maryland	486	3.32%	32	Oklahoma	83	0.57%
8	Ohio	481	3.29%	33	Nebraska	81	0.55%
9	Arizona	457	3.13%	34	Arkansas	65	0.44%
10	Wisconsin	417	2.85%	34	Rhode Island	65	0.44%
11	Missouri	405	2.77%	36	Vermont	62	0.42%
12	Minnesota	307	2.10%	37	South Carolina	58	0.40%
13	Colorado	285	1.95%	38	Idaho	57	0.39%
14	Tennessee	278	1.90%	39	Mississippi	44	0.30%
15	Indiana	267	1.83%	40	Oregon	34	0.23%
16	Connecticut	248	1.70%	41	Wyoming	31	0.21%
17	Massachusetts	238	1.63%	42	West Virginia	17	0.12%
18	Washington	192	1.31%	43	Montana	15	0.10%
19	Kentucky	186	1.27%	44	Louisiana	14	0.10%
20	North Carolina	163	1.12%	45	South Dakota	13	0.09%
21	New Mexico	155	1.06%	46	Alabama	6	0.04%
22	Georgia	144	0.99%	47	Utah	4	0.03%
23	Virginia	135	0.92%	48	Maine	1	0.01%
24	Nevada	124	0.85%	49	New Hampshire	0	0.00%
25	Hawaii	120	0.82%	49	North Dakota	0	0.00%
					District of Columbia	31	0.21%

Source: U.S. Department of Justice, Bureau of Justice Statistics
"Justice Expenditure and Employment in 1990" (Bulletin, September 1992, NCJ-135777)
*Full-time equivalent.

Public Defenders in 1990

National Total = 13,319 Public Defenders*

RANK	STATE	DEFENDERS	%	RANK	STATE	DEFENDERS	%
1	New York	5,000	37.54%	26	Nevada	78	0.59%
2	California	1,997	14.99%	26	New Mexico	78	0.59%
3	Florida	855	6.42%	28	Utah	66	0.50%
4	Illinois	789	5.92%	29	New Hampshire	57	0.43%
5	Washington	550	4.13%	30	Alaska	54	0.41%
6	Ohio	324	2.43%	31	Kansas	46	0.35%
7	Indiana	300	2.25%	32	Delaware	40	0.30%
8	Wisconsin	285	2.14%	33	Wyoming	38	0.29%
9	New Jersey	251	1.88%	34	Arkansas	36	0.27%
10	Maryland	244	1.83%	35	Rhode Island	32	0.24%
11	Tennessee	243	1.82%	35	West Virginia	32	0.24%
12	Missouri	232	1.74%	37	Vermont	30	0.23%
13	Minnesota	158	1.19%	38	Nebraska	25	0.19%
14	Colorado	155	1.16%	39	South Dakota	15	0.11%
15	Oregon	148	1.11%	40	Alabama	3	0.02%
16	Connecticut	130	0.98%	41	Arizona	0	0.00%
17	Virginia	126	0.95%	41	Maine	0	0.00%
18	Louisiana	125	0.94%	41	Michigan	0	0.00%
19	Massachusetts	117	0.88%	–	Idaho**	N/A	N/A
20	South Carolina	116	0.87%	–	Kentucky**	N/A	N/A
21	Georgia	101	0.76%	–	Montana**	N/A	N/A
22	Mississippi	100	0.75%	–	North Dakota**	N/A	N/A
23	Iowa	91	0.68%	–	Oklahoma**	N/A	N/A
24	Hawaii	88	0.66%	–	Pennsylvania**	N/A	N/A
25	North Carolina	87	0.65%	–	Texas**	N/A	N/A
					District of Columbia	77	0.58%

Source: U.S. Department of Justice, Bureau of Justice Statistics

"State Justice Sourcebook of Statistics and Research" (September 1992, NCJ-137991)

Total is only for those states reporting.

**Not available.*

Authorized Wiretaps: 1991 and 1992

National Total = 1,078 Authorized Wiretaps*

RANK	STATE	WIRETAPS	%	RANK	STATE	WIRETAPS	%
1	New York	333	30.89%	26	Delaware	0	0.00%
2	New Jersey	209	19.39%	26	Hawaii	0	0.00%
3	Florida	159	14.75%	26	Idaho	0	0.00%
4	Pennsylvania	153	14.19%	26	Illinois	0	0.00%
5	Maryland	41	3.80%	26	Iowa	0	0.00%
6	Georgia	26	2.41%	26	Louisiana	0	0.00%
7	Connecticut	23	2.13%	26	Mississippi	0	0.00%
8	Massachusetts	19	1.76%	26	Missouri	0	0.00%
9	Arizona	18	1.67%	26	North Dakota	0	0.00%
10	Texas	14	1.30%	26	Ohio	0	0.00%
11	Nevada	11	1.02%	26	Oregon	0	0.00%
11	Utah	11	1.02%	26	South Dakota	0	0.00%
13	Kansas	10	0.93%	–	Alabama**	N/A	N/A
14	New Mexico	8	0.74%	–	Alaska**	N/A	N/A
15	Colorado	7	0.65%	–	Arkansas**	N/A	N/A
15	Nebraska	7	0.65%	–	Kentucky**	N/A	N/A
17	Minnesota	6	0.56%	–	Maine**	N/A	N/A
17	Rhode Island	6	0.56%	–	Michigan**	N/A	N/A
19	Virginia	4	0.37%	–	Montana**	N/A	N/A
20	California	3	0.28%	–	North Carolina**	N/A	N/A
20	Indiana	3	0.28%	–	South Carolina**	N/A	N/A
20	Wisconsin	3	0.28%	–	Tennessee**	N/A	N/A
23	New Hampshire	2	0.19%	–	Vermont**	N/A	N/A
23	Oklahoma	2	0.19%	–	Washington**	N/A	N/A
25	Wyoming	1	0.09%	–	West Virginia**	N/A	N/A

District of Columbia   0   0.00%

Source: Administrative Office of the United States Courts
   "Wiretap Report 1991 and 1992"

*Total does not include 696 wiretaps authorized under federal statute.

**No statute authorizing wiretaps.

VI. OFFENSES

Table	Title
273	Crimes in 1992
274	Average Time Between Crimes in 1992
275	Crimes per Square Mile in 1992
276	Percent Change in Number of Crimes: 1991 to 1992
277	Crime Rate in 1992
278	Percent Change in Crime Rate: 1991 to 1992
279	Violent Crimes in 1992
280	Average Time Between Violent Crimes in 1992
281	Violent Crimes per Square Mile in 1992
282	Percent Change in Number of Violent Crimes: 1991 to 1992
283	Violent Crime Rate in 1992
284	Percent Change in Violent Crime Rate: 1991 to 1992
285	Violent Crime Rate with Firearms in 1992
286	Murders in 1992
287	Average Time Between Murders in 1992
288	Percent Change in Number of Murders: 1991 to 1992
289	Murder Rate in 1992
290	Percent Change in Murder Rate: 1991 to 1992
291	Murders with Firearms in 1992
292	Murder Rate with Firearms in 1992
293	Percent of Murders Involving Firearms in 1992
294	Murders with Handguns in 1992
295	Murder Rate with Handguns in 1992
296	Percent of Murders Involving Handguns in 1992
297	Murders with Rifles in 1992
298	Percent of Murders Involving Rifles in 1992
299	Murders with Shotguns in 1992
300	Percent of Murders Involving Shotguns in 1992
301	Murders with Knives or Cutting Instruments in 1992
302	Percent of Murders Involving Knives or Cutting Instruments in 1992
303	Murders by Hands, Fists or Feet in 1992
304	Percent of Murders Involving Hands, Fists or Feet in 1992
305	Rapes in 1992
306	Average Time Between Rapes in 1992

VI. OFFENSES (continued)

Table	Title
307	Percent Change in Number of Rapes: 1991 to 1992
308	Rape Rate in 1992
309	Percent Change in Rape Rate: 1991 to 1992
310	Rape Rate per 100,000 Female Population in 1992
311	Robberies in 1992
312	Average Time Between Robberies in 1992
313	Percent Change in Number of Robberies: 1991 to 1992
314	Robbery Rate in 1992
315	Percent Change in Robbery Rate: 1991 to 1992
316	Robberies with Firearms in 1992
317	Robbery Rate with Firearms in 1992
318	Percent of Robberies Involving Firearms in 1992
319	Robberies with Knives or Cutting Instruments in 1992
320	Percent of Robberies Involving Knives or Cutting Instruments in 1992
321	Robberies with Blunt Objects and Other Dangerous Weapons in 1992
322	Percent of Robberies Involving Blunt Objects and Other Dangerous Objects in 1992
323	Robberies Using Hands, Fists or Feet in 1992
324	Percent of Robberies Using Hands, Fists or Feet in 1992
325	Aggravated Assaults in 1992
326	Average Time Between Aggravated Assaults in 1992
327	Percent Change in Number of Aggravated Assaults: 1991 to 1992
328	Aggravated Assault Rate in 1992
329	Percent Change in Rate of Aggravated Assaults: 1991 to 1992
330	Aggravated Assaults with Firearms in 1992
331	Aggravated Assault Rate with Firearms in 1992
332	Percent of Aggravated Assaults Involving Firearms in 1992
333	Aggravated Assaults with Knives or Cutting Instruments in 1992
334	Percent of Aggravated Assaults Involving Knives or Cutting Instruments in 1992
335	Aggravated Assaults with Blunt Objects and Other Dangerous Weapons in 1992
336	Percent of Aggravated Assaults Involving Blunt Objects and Other Dangerous Objects in 1992
337	Aggravated Assaults Using Hands, Fists or Feet in 1992
338	Percent of Aggravated Assaults Involving Hands, Fists or Feet in 1992

VI. OFFENSES (continued)

Table	Title
339	Property Crimes in 1992
340	Average Time Between Property Crimes in 1992
341	Property Crimes per Square Mile in 1992
342	Percent Change in Number of Property Crimes: 1991 to 1992
343	Property Crime Rate in 1992
344	Percent Change in Rate of Property Crime: 1991 to 1992
345	Burglaries in 1992
346	Average Time Between Burglaries in 1992
347	Percent Change in Number of Burglaries: 1991 to 1992
348	Burglary Rate in 1992
349	Percent Change in Rate of Burglaries: 1991 to 1992
350	Larceny and Theft in 1992
351	Average Time Between Larcenies-Thefts in 1992
352	Percent Change in Number of Larcenies and Thefts: 1991 to 1992
353	Larceny and Theft Rate in 1992
354	Percent Change in Rate of Larceny and Theft: 1991 to 1992
355	Motor Vehicle Thefts in 1992
356	Average Time Between Motor Vehicle Thefts in 1992
357	Percent Change in Number of Motor Vehicle Thefts: 1991 to 1992
358	Motor Vehicle Theft Rate in 1992
359	Percent Change in Rate of Motor Vehicle Thefts: 1991 to 1992
360	Crime in Urban Areas in 1992
361	Urban Crime Rate in 1992
362	Percent of Crime Occurring in Urban Areas in 1992
363	Crime in Rural Areas in 1992
364	Rural Crime Rate in 1992
365	Percent of Crime Occurring in Rural Areas in 1992
366	Violent Crime in Urban Areas in 1992
367	Percent of Violent Crime Occurring in Urban Areas in 1992
368	Violent Crime in Rural Areas in 1992
369	Percent of Violent Crime Occurring in Rural Areas in 1992
370	Murder in Urban Areas in 1992

VI. OFFENSES (continued)

Table	Title
371	Percent of Murders Occurring in Urban Areas in 1992
372	Murder in Rural Areas in 1992
373	Percent of Murders Occurring in Rural Areas in 1992
374	Rape in Urban Areas in 1992
375	Percent of Rapes Occurring in Urban Areas in 1992
376	Rape in Rural Areas in 1992
377	Percent of Rapes Occurring in Rural Areas in 1992
378	Robbery in Urban Areas in 1992
379	Percent of Robberies Occurring in Urban Areas in 1992
380	Robbery in Rural Areas in 1992
381	Percent of Robberies Occurring in Rural Areas in 1992
382	Aggravated Assault in Urban Areas in 1992
383	Percent of Aggravated Assaults Occurring in Urban Areas in 1992
384	Aggravated Assault in Rural Areas in 1992
385	Percent of Aggravated Assaults Occurring in Rural Areas in 1992
386	Property Crime in Urban Areas in 1992
387	Percent of Property Crime Occurring in Urban Areas in 1992
388	Property Crime in Rural Areas in 1992
389	Percent of Property Crime Occurring in Rural Areas in 1992
390	Burglary in Urban Areas in 1992
391	Percent of Burglaries Occurring in Urban Areas in 1992
392	Burglary in Rural Areas in 1992
393	Percent of Burglaries Occurring in Rural Areas in 1992
394	Larceny and Theft in Urban Areas in 1992
395	Percent of Larcenies and Thefts Occurring in Urban Areas in 1992
396	Larceny and Theft in Rural Areas in 1992
397	Percent of Larcenies and Thefts Occurring in Rural Areas in 1992
398	Motor Vehicle Theft in Urban Areas in 1992
399	Percent of Motor Vehicle Thefts Occurring in Urban Areas in 1992
400	Motor Vehicle Thefts in Rural Areas in 1992
401	Percent of Motor Vehicle Thefts Occurring in Rural Areas in 1992
402	Crimes Reported at Universities and Colleges in 1992

VI. OFFENSES (continued)

Table	Title
403	Crimes Reported at Universities and Colleges as a Percent of All Crimes in 1992
404	Violent Crimes Reported at Universities and Colleges in 1992
405	Violent Crimes Reported at Universities and Colleges as a Percent of All Violent Crimes in 1992
406	Property Crimes Reported at Universities and Colleges in 1992
407	Property Crimes Reported at Universities and Colleges as a Percent of All Property Crimes in 1992
408	Bank Robberies in 1992
409	Bombings in 1992
410	Crimes in 1988
411	Crime Rate in 1988
412	Percent Change in Number of Crimes: 1988 to 1992
413	Percent Change in Crime Rate: 1988 to 1992
414	Violent Crimes in 1988
415	Violent Crime Rate in 1988
416	Percent Change in Number of Violent Crimes: 1988 to 1992
417	Percent Change in Violent Crime Rate: 1988 to 1992
418	Murders in 1988
419	Murder Rate in 1988
420	Percent Change in Number of Murders: 1988 to 1992
421	Percent Change in Murder Rate: 1988 to 1992
422	Rapes in 1988
423	Rape Rate in 1988
424	Percent Change in Number of Rapes: 1988 to 1992
425	Percent Change in Rape Rate: 1988 to 1992
426	Aggravated Assaults in 1988
427	Aggravated Assault Rate in 1988
428	Percent Change in Number of Aggravated Assaults: 1988 to 1992
429	Percent Change in Rate of Aggravated Assaults: 1988 to 1992
430	Robberies in 1988
431	Robbery Rate in 1988
432	Percent Change in Number of Robberies: 1988 to 1992
433	Percent Change in Robbery Rate: 1988 to 1992
434	Property Crimes in 1988

VI. OFFENSES (continued)

Table	Title
435	Property Crime Rate in 1988
436	Percent Change in Number of Property Crimes: 1988 to 1992
437	Percent Change in Rate of Property Crime: 1988 to 1992
438	Burglaries in 1988
439	Burglary Rate in 1988
440	Percent Change in Number of Burglaries: 1988 to 1992
441	Percent Change in Rate of Burglaries: 1988 to 1992
442	Larceny and Theft in 1988
443	Larceny and Theft Rate in 1988
444	Percent Change in Number of Larcenies and Thefts: 1988 to 1992
445	Percent Change in Rate of Larcenies and Thefts: 1988 to 1992
446	Motor Vehicle Thefts in 1988
447	Motor Vehicle Theft Rate in 1988
448	Percent Change in Number of Motor Vehicle Thefts: 1988 to 1992
449	Percent Change in Rate of Motor Vehicle Thefts: 1988 to 1992
450	Percent of Crimes Cleared in 1991
451	Percent of Violent Crimes Cleared in 1991
452	Percent of Murders Cleared in 1991
453	Percent of Rapes Cleared in 1991
454	Percent of Robberies Cleared in 1991
455	Percent of Aggravated Assaults Cleared in 1991
456	Percent of Property Crimes Cleared in 1991
457	Percent of Burglaries Cleared in 1991
458	Percent of Larcenies and Thefts Cleared in 1991
459	Percent of Motor Vehicle Thefts Cleared in 1991

Crimes in 1992

National Total = 14,438,191 Crimes

RANK	STATE	CRIMES	%	RANK	STATE	CRIMES	%
1	California	2,061,761	14.28%	26	Oklahoma	174,464	1.21%
2	Texas	1,246,148	8.63%	27	Oregon	173,289	1.20%
3	Florida	1,127,360	7.81%	28	Connecticut	165,787	1.15%
4	New York	1,061,489	7.35%	29	Kansas	134,222	0.93%
5	Illinois	670,564	4.64%	30	Kentucky	124,799	0.86%
6	Michigan	529,472	3.67%	31	Arkansas	114,233	0.79%
7	Ohio	513,952	3.56%	32	Mississippi	111,944	0.78%
8	Georgia	432,430	3.00%	33	Iowa	111,275	0.77%
9	Pennsylvania	407,431	2.82%	34	Utah	102,589	0.71%
10	North Carolina	397,047	2.75%	35	New Mexico	101,723	0.70%
11	New Jersey	394,463	2.73%	36	Nevada	82,324	0.57%
12	Washington	317,035	2.20%	37	Hawaii	70,899	0.49%
13	Maryland	305,503	2.12%	38	Nebraska	69,444	0.48%
14	Massachusetts	300,071	2.08%	39	West Virginia	47,288	0.33%
15	Louisiana	280,647	1.94%	40	Rhode Island	46,009	0.32%
16	Virginia	274,118	1.90%	41	Maine	43,516	0.30%
17	Arizona	269,335	1.87%	42	Idaho	42,639	0.30%
18	Indiana	265,375	1.84%	43	Montana	37,872	0.26%
19	Missouri	264,694	1.83%	44	New Hampshire	34,225	0.24%
20	Tennessee	258,021	1.79%	45	Delaware	33,406	0.23%
21	Alabama	217,889	1.51%	46	Alaska	32,693	0.23%
22	Wisconsin	216,254	1.50%	47	South Dakota	21,322	0.15%
23	South Carolina	212,327	1.47%	48	Wyoming	21,320	0.15%
24	Colorado	206,770	1.43%	49	Vermont	19,437	0.13%
25	Minnesota	205,664	1.42%	50	North Dakota	18,465	0.13%
					District of Columbia	67,187	0.47%

Source: U.S. Department of Justice, Federal Bureau of Investigation

"Crime in the United States 1992" (Uniform Crime Reports, October 3, 1993)

*Includes murder, rape, robbery, aggravated assault, burglary, larceny-theft, motor vehicle theft and arson.

Average Time Between Crimes in 1992

National Rate = A Crime Occurs Every 2 Seconds*

RANK	STATE	MINUTES.SECONDS	RANK	STATE	MINUTES.SECONDS
1	North Dakota	28.32	26	Minnesota	2.34
2	Vermont	27.07	27	Colorado	2.33
3	South Dakota	24.43	28	South Carolina	2.29
3	Wyoming	24.43	29	Wisconsin	2.26
5	Alaska	16.07	30	Alabama	2.25
6	Delaware	15.47	31	Tennessee	2.02
7	New Hampshire	15.24	32	Indiana	1.59
8	Montana	13.55	32	Missouri	1.59
9	Idaho	12.22	34	Arizona	1.58
10	Maine	12.07	35	Virginia	1.55
11	Rhode Island	11.28	36	Louisiana	1.53
12	West Virginia	11.09	37	Massachusetts	1.46
13	Nebraska	7.35	38	Maryland	1.44
14	Hawaii	7.26	39	Washington	1.40
15	Nevada	6.24	40	New Jersey	1.20
16	New Mexico	5.11	40	North Carolina	1.20
17	Utah	5.08	42	Pennsylvania	1.17
18	Iowa	4.44	43	Georgia	1.13
19	Mississippi	4.43	44	Ohio	1.02
20	Arkansas	4.37	45	Michigan	1.00
21	Kentucky	4.13	46	Illinois	0.47
22	Kansas	3.56	47	New York	0.30
23	Connecticut	3.11	48	Florida	0.28
24	Oregon	3.02	49	Texas	0.25
25	Oklahoma	3.01	50	California	0.16

District of Columbia   7.50

Source: Morgan Quitno Corporation using data from U.S. Department of Justice, Federal Bureau of Investigation
"Crime in the United States 1992" (Uniform Crime Reports, October 3, 1993)

*Includes murder, rape, robbery, aggravated assault, burglary, larceny-theft, motor vehicle theft and arson.

Crimes per Square Mile in 1992

National Rate = 3.81 Crimes per Square Mile*

RANK	STATE	RATE	RANK	STATE	RATE
1	New Jersey	45.23	26	New Hampshire	3.66
2	Connecticut	29.90	27	Wisconsin	3.30
3	Rhode Island	29.78	28	Kentucky	3.09
4	Massachusetts	28.43	29	Oklahoma	2.50
5	Maryland	24.62	30	Minnesota	2.37
6	New York	19.49	31	Arizona	2.36
7	Florida	17.14	32	Mississippi	2.31
8	Delaware	13.42	33	Arkansas	2.15
9	California	12.59	34	Vermont	2.02
10	Illinois	11.58	35	Colorado	1.99
11	Ohio	11.46	36	Iowa	1.98
12	Pennsylvania	8.85	37	West Virginia	1.95
13	North Carolina	7.38	38	Oregon	1.76
14	Indiana	7.29	39	Kansas	1.63
15	Georgia	7.27	40	Maine	1.23
16	South Carolina	6.63	41	Utah	1.21
17	Hawaii	6.49	42	Nebraska	0.90
18	Virginia	6.41	43	New Mexico	0.84
19	Tennessee	6.12	44	Nevada	0.74
20	Michigan	5.47	45	Idaho	0.51
21	Louisiana	5.41	46	South Dakota	0.28
22	Texas	4.64	47	Montana	0.26
23	Washington	4.45	47	North Dakota	0.26
24	Alabama	4.16	49	Wyoming	0.22
25	Missouri	3.80	50	Alaska	0.05

District of Columbia   988.04

Source: Morgan Quitno Corporation using data from U.S. Department of Justice, Federal Bureau of Investigation
"Crime in the United States 1992" (Uniform Crime Reports, October 3, 1993)
*Includes murder, rape, robbery, aggravated assault, burglary, larceny-theft, motor vehicle theft and arson.

Percent Change in Number of Crimes: 1991 to 1992

National Percent Change = 2.9% Decrease*

RANK	STATE	PERCENT CHANGE	RANK	STATE	PERCENT CHANGE
1	Montana	28.5	26	Idaho	(2.2)
2	Wyoming	5.6	27	Wisconsin	(2.3)
3	Hawaii	4.6	28	Kansas	(2.8)
4	North Dakota	4.1	29	Tennessee	(2.9)
5	Utah	3.4	30	Arizona	(3.0)
6	Minnesota	3.2	31	Oklahoma	(3.1)
7	Oregon	3.0	32	South Carolina	(3.5)
8	Louisiana	2.7	33	Iowa	(3.7)
9	Mississippi	2.3	34	Pennsylvania	(4.3)
10	Nevada	1.8	35	Missouri	(5.2)
11	Maryland	1.2	36	Illinois	(5.3)
12	Colorado	0.8	37	Virginia	(5.4)
13	Alaska	0.6	38	New York	(5.9)
13	Georgia	0.6	39	Massachusetts	(6.0)
15	California	0.2	40	Connecticut	(6.1)
15	Washington	0.2	41	New Jersey	(6.4)
17	Kentucky	0.1	42	Maine	(6.5)
17	Nebraska	0.1	43	Ohio	(6.6)
17	North Carolina	0.1	44	Arkansas	(6.9)
20	Alabama	(0.7)	45	Michigan	(7.9)
20	Florida	(0.7)	46	Texas	(8.1)
22	West Virginia	(1.4)	47	Rhode Island	(9.1)
23	South Dakota	(1.5)	48	New Hampshire	(10.2)
24	New Mexico	(1.6)	49	Vermont	(13.3)
25	Indiana	(1.8)	50	Delaware	(16.3)

District of Columbia   4.3

Source: U.S. Department of Justice, Federal Bureau of Investigation
"Crime in the United States 1992" (Uniform Crime Reports, October 3, 1993))
*Includes murder, rape, robbery, aggravated assault, burglary, larceny-theft, motor vehicle theft and arson.

Crime Rate in 1992

National Rate = 5,660.2 Crimes per 100,000 Population*

RANK	STATE	RATE	RANK	STATE	RATE
1	Florida	8,358.2	26	New Jersey	5,064.4
2	Texas	7,057.9	27	Connecticut	5,052.9
3	Arizona	7,028.6	28	Massachusetts	5,002.9
4	California	6,679.5	29	Delaware	4,848.5
5	Louisiana	6,546.5	30	Arkansas	4,761.7
6	New Mexico	6,434.1	31	Indiana	4,686.9
7	Georgia	6,405.4	32	Ohio	4,665.5
8	Maryland	6,224.6	33	Montana	4,596.1
9	Nevada	6,203.8	34	Minnesota	4,590.7
10	Washington	6,172.8	35	Rhode Island	4,578.0
11	Hawaii	6,112.0	36	Wyoming	4,575.1
12	Colorado	5,958.8	37	Nebraska	4,324.0
13	South Carolina	5,893.1	38	Wisconsin	4,319.0
14	New York	5,858.4	39	Virginia	4,298.5
15	Oregon	5,820.9	40	Mississippi	4,282.5
16	North Carolina	5,802.2	41	Idaho	3,996.2
17	Illinois	5,765.3	42	Iowa	3,957.1
18	Utah	5,658.5	43	Maine	3,523.6
19	Michigan	5,610.6	44	Vermont	3,410.0
20	Alaska	5,569.5	45	Pennsylvania	3,392.7
21	Oklahoma	5,431.6	46	Kentucky	3,323.5
22	Kansas	5,319.9	47	New Hampshire	3,080.6
23	Alabama	5,268.1	48	South Dakota	2,998.9
24	Tennessee	5,135.8	49	North Dakota	2,903.3
25	Missouri	5,097.1	50	West Virginia	2,609.7
				District of Columbia	11,407.0

Source: U.S. Department of Justice, Federal Bureau of Investigation
"Crime in the United States 1992" (Uniform Crime Reports, October 3, 1993)
*Includes murder, rape, robbery, aggravated assault, burglary, larceny-theft, motor vehicle theft and arson.

Percent Change in Crime Rate: 1991 to 1992

National Percent Change = 4.0% Decrease*

RANK	STATE	PERCENT CHANGE		RANK	STATE	PERCENT CHANGE
1	Montana	26.0		26	New Mexico	(3.7)
2	Wyoming	4.2		27	Kansas	(3.9)
3	North Dakota	3.9		28	Oklahoma	(4.2)
4	Hawaii	2.4		29	Iowa	(4.3)
5	Minnesota	2.1		29	Tennessee	(4.3)
6	Louisiana	1.9		31	South Carolina	(4.6)
7	Mississippi	1.5		32	Pennsylvania	(4.7)
8	Oregon	1.1		33	Idaho	(4.8)
9	Utah	0.9		34	Arizona	(5.1)
10	Maryland	0.2		35	Connecticut	(5.8)
11	Nebraska	(0.7)		36	Missouri	(5.9)
12	Kentucky	(1.0)		37	Illinois	(6.0)
13	California	(1.4)		37	Massachusetts	(6.0)
13	Georgia	(1.4)		39	New York	(6.2)
15	Nevada	(1.5)		40	Maine	(6.5)
15	North Carolina	(1.5)		41	Virginia	(6.7)
17	Alabama	(1.8)		42	New Jersey	(6.8)
18	Colorado	(1.9)		43	Ohio	(7.3)
19	West Virginia	(2.0)		44	Arkansas	(8.0)
20	Washington	(2.1)		45	Michigan	(8.6)
21	Florida	(2.2)		46	Rhode Island	(9.2)
22	Alaska	(2.3)		47	Texas	(9.7)
23	South Dakota	(2.6)		48	New Hampshire	(10.7)
24	Indiana	(2.7)		49	Vermont	(13.8)
25	Wisconsin	(3.3)		50	Delaware	(17.4)

District of Columbia   5.9

Source: U.S. Department of Justice, Federal Bureau of Investigation

"Crime in the United States 1992" (Uniform Crime Reports, October 3, 1993)

*Includes murder, rape, robbery, aggravated assault, burglary, larceny-theft, motor vehicle theft and arson.

Violent Crimes in 1992

National Total = 1,932,274 Violent Crimes*

RANK	STATE	CRIMES	%		RANK	STATE	CRIMES	%
1	California	345,624	17.89%		26	Connecticut	16,252	0.84%
2	New York	203,311	10.52%		27	Oregon	15,189	0.79%
3	Florida	162,827	8.43%		28	Minnesota	15,144	0.78%
4	Texas	142,369	7.37%		29	New Mexico	14,781	0.76%
5	Illinois	113,664	5.88%		30	Arkansas	13,831	0.72%
6	Michigan	72,672	3.76%		31	Wisconsin	13,806	0.71%
7	Ohio	57,935	3.00%		32	Kansas	12,888	0.67%
8	Pennsylvania	51,276	2.65%		33	Mississippi	10,763	0.56%
9	Georgia	49,496	2.56%		34	Nevada	9,247	0.48%
10	Maryland	49,085	2.54%		35	Iowa	7,816	0.40%
11	New Jersey	48,745	2.52%		36	Nebraska	5,598	0.29%
12	Massachusetts	46,727	2.42%		37	Utah	5,267	0.27%
13	North Carolina	46,600	2.41%		38	Delaware	4,280	0.22%
14	Louisiana	42,209	2.18%		39	Rhode Island	3,965	0.21%
15	Missouri	38,448	1.99%		40	Alaska	3,877	0.20%
16	Tennessee	37,487	1.94%		41	West Virginia	3,833	0.20%
17	Alabama	36,052	1.87%		42	Idaho	3,003	0.16%
18	South Carolina	34,029	1.76%		43	Hawaii	2,998	0.16%
19	Indiana	28,791	1.49%		44	Maine	1,616	0.08%
20	Washington	27,454	1.42%		45	Wyoming	1,489	0.08%
21	Arizona	25,706	1.33%		46	Montana	1,400	0.07%
22	Virginia	23,907	1.24%		47	New Hampshire	1,397	0.07%
23	Kentucky	20,107	1.04%		48	South Dakota	1,383	0.07%
24	Colorado	20,086	1.04%		49	Vermont	624	0.03%
25	Oklahoma	20,005	1.04%		50	North Dakota	530	0.03%
						District of Columbia	16,685	0.86%

Source: U.S. Department of Justice, Federal Bureau of Investigation
    "Crime in the United States 1992" (Uniform Crime Reports, October 3, 1993)
*Violent crimes are offenses of murder, forcible rape, robbery and aggravated assault.

Average Time Between Violent Crimes in 1992

National Rate = A Violent Crime Occurs Every 16 Seconds*

RANK	STATE	MINUTES.SECONDS	RANK	STATE	MINUTES.SECONDS
1	North Dakota	994.25	26	Oklahoma	26.21
2	Vermont	844.37	27	Colorado	26.14
3	South Dakota	381.05	28	Kentucky	26.13
4	New Hampshire	377.16	29	Virginia	22.03
5	Montana	376.28	30	Arizona	20.30
6	Wyoming	353.58	31	Washington	19.12
7	Maine	326.08	32	Indiana	18.19
8	Hawaii	175.48	33	South Carolina	15.29
9	Idaho	175.30	34	Alabama	14.37
10	West Virginia	137.30	35	Tennessee	14.04
11	Alaska	135.56	36	Missouri	13.43
12	Rhode Island	132.55	37	Louisiana	12.29
13	Delaware	123.08	38	North Carolina	11.19
14	Utah	100.04	39	Massachusetts	11.17
15	Nebraska	94.09	40	New Jersey	10.49
16	Iowa	67.26	41	Maryland	10.44
17	Nevada	57.00	42	Georgia	10.39
18	Mississippi	48.58	43	Pennsylvania	10.17
19	Kansas	40.53	44	Ohio	9.06
20	Wisconsin	38.10	45	Michigan	7.15
21	Arkansas	38.07	46	Illinois	4.38
22	New Mexico	35.40	47	Texas	3.42
23	Minnesota	34.48	48	Florida	3.14
24	Oregon	34.42	49	New York	2.35
25	Connecticut	32.26	50	California	1.31
				District of Columbia	31.35

Source: Morgan Quitno Corporation using data from U.S. Department of Justice, Federal Bureau of Investigation

"Crime in the United States 1992" (Uniform Crime Reports, October 3, 1993)

*Violent crimes are offenses of murder, forcible rape, robbery and aggravated assault.

Violent Crimes per Square Mile in 1992

National Rate = 0.51 Violent Crimes per Square Mile*

RANK	STATE	RATE	RANK	STATE	RATE
1	New Jersey	5.59	26	Oklahoma	0.29
2	Massachusetts	4.43	27	Hawaii	0.27
3	Maryland	3.96	28	Arkansas	0.26
4	New York	3.73	29	Arizona	0.23
5	Connecticut	2.93	30	Mississippi	0.22
6	Rhode Island	2.57	31	Wisconsin	0.21
7	Florida	2.48	32	Colorado	0.19
8	California	2.11	33	Minnesota	0.17
9	Illinois	1.96	34	Kansas	0.16
10	Delaware	1.72	34	West Virginia	0.16
11	Ohio	1.29	36	New Hampshire	0.15
12	Pennsylvania	1.11	36	Oregon	0.15
13	South Carolina	1.06	38	Iowa	0.14
14	Tennessee	0.89	39	New Mexico	0.12
15	North Carolina	0.87	40	Nevada	0.08
16	Georgia	0.83	41	Nebraska	0.07
17	Louisiana	0.81	42	Utah	0.06
18	Indiana	0.79	42	Vermont	0.06
19	Michigan	0.75	44	Maine	0.05
20	Alabama	0.69	45	Idaho	0.04
21	Virginia	0.56	46	South Dakota	0.02
22	Missouri	0.55	46	Wyoming	0.02
23	Texas	0.53	48	Alaska	0.01
24	Kentucky	0.50	48	Montana	0.01
25	Washington	0.39	48	North Dakota	0.01

District of Columbia   245.37

Source: Morgan Quitno Corporation using data from U.S. Department of Justice, Federal Bureau of Investigation

"Crime in the United States 1992" (Uniform Crime Reports, October 3, 1993)

*Violent crimes are offenses of murder, forcible rape, robbery and aggravated assault.

Percent Change in Number of Violent Crimes: 1991 to 1992

National Percent Change = 1.1% Increase*

RANK	STATE	PERCENT CHANGE	RANK	STATE	PERCENT CHANGE
1	North Dakota	27.7	26	Florida	3.6
2	Montana	23.9	27	Kansas	3.4
3	Kentucky	23.6	28	Oregon	2.7
4	New Mexico	14.4	29	Arizona	2.2
5	West Virginia	11.4	30	Virginia	1.9
6	Alaska	10.8	31	Indiana	1.6
7	Hawaii	9.3	32	Georgia	1.2
8	Minnesota	8.1	33	Wisconsin	0.6
9	South Dakota	8.0	34	Idaho	(0.4)
10	Oklahoma	7.9	35	Maine	(0.9)
11	Mississippi	6.7	36	New Jersey	(1.0)
12	Nevada	6.4	37	Arkansas	(1.7)
13	Colorado	6.3	37	South Carolina	(1.7)
14	New Hampshire	6.0	39	Missouri	(2.3)
15	Massachusetts	5.9	39	Texas	(2.3)
16	Maryland	5.6	41	New York	(3.3)
17	North Carolina	5.1	42	Michigan	(3.4)
18	Nebraska	5.0	43	Pennsylvania	(4.7)
19	Washington	4.7	44	Illinois	(5.2)
20	Alabama	4.4	45	Ohio	(5.7)
20	California	4.4	45	Vermont	(5.7)
20	Louisiana	4.4	47	Iowa	(7.8)
23	Tennessee	4.3	48	Connecticut	(8.5)
23	Wyoming	4.3	49	Delaware	(11.9)
25	Utah	3.7	50	Rhode Island	(14.5)

District of Columbia   13.7

Source: U.S. Department of Justice, Federal Bureau of Investigation

"Crime in the United States 1992" (Uniform Crime Reports, October 3, 1993)

*Violent crimes are offenses of murder, forcible rape, robbery and aggravated assault.

Violent Crime Rate in 1992

National Rate = 757.5 Violent Crimes per 100,000 Population*

RANK	STATE	RATE	RANK	STATE	RATE
1	Florida	1,207.2	26	Washington	534.5
2	New York	1,122.1	27	Ohio	525.9
3	California	1,119.7	28	Kansas	510.8
4	Maryland	1,000.1	29	Oregon	510.2
5	Louisiana	984.6	30	Indiana	508.5
6	Illinois	977.3	31	Connecticut	495.3
7	South Carolina	944.5	32	Pennsylvania	427.0
8	New Mexico	934.9	33	Mississippi	411.7
9	Alabama	871.7	34	Rhode Island	394.5
10	Texas	806.3	35	Virginia	374.9
11	Massachusetts	779.0	36	Nebraska	348.6
12	Michigan	770.1	37	Minnesota	338.0
13	Tennessee	746.2	38	Wyoming	319.5
14	Missouri	740.4	39	Utah	290.5
15	Georgia	733.2	40	Idaho	281.4
16	Nevada	696.8	41	Iowa	278.0
17	North Carolina	681.0	42	Wisconsin	275.7
18	Arizona	670.8	43	Hawaii	258.4
19	Alaska	660.5	44	West Virginia	211.5
20	New Jersey	625.8	45	South Dakota	194.5
21	Oklahoma	622.8	46	Montana	169.9
22	Delaware	621.2	47	Maine	130.9
23	Colorado	578.8	48	New Hampshire	125.7
24	Arkansas	576.5	49	Vermont	109.5
25	Kentucky	535.5	50	North Dakota	83.3

District of Columbia   2,832.8

Source: U.S. Department of Justice, Federal Bureau of Investigation
    "Crime in the United States 1992" (Uniform Crime Reports, October 3, 1993)
*Violent crimes are offenses of murder, forcible rape, robbery and aggravated assault.

Percent Change in Violent Crime Rate: 1991 to 1992

National Percent Change = 0.1% Decrease*

RANK	STATE	PERCENT CHANGE	RANK	STATE	PERCENT CHANGE
1	North Dakota	27.4	26	Florida	1.9
2	Kentucky	22.3	27	Utah	1.3
3	Montana	21.4	28	Oregon	0.8
4	New Mexico	12.0	29	Indiana	0.6
5	West Virginia	10.7	30	Virginia	0.5
6	Alaska	7.6	31	Arizona	0.0
7	Minnesota	7.0	32	Wisconsin	(0.5)
8	Hawaii	6.9	33	Georgia	(0.7)
9	South Dakota	6.8	34	Maine	(0.9)
10	Oklahoma	6.7	35	New Jersey	(1.4)
11	Massachusetts	5.8	36	Arkansas	(2.8)
11	Mississippi	5.8	37	South Carolina	(2.9)
13	New Hampshire	5.4	38	Missouri	(3.0)
14	Maryland	4.6	39	Idaho	(3.1)
15	Nebraska	4.2	40	New York	(3.6)
16	Colorado	3.5	41	Texas	(4.0)
16	Louisiana	3.5	42	Michigan	(4.1)
18	North Carolina	3.4	43	Pennsylvania	(5.1)
19	Alabama	3.3	44	Illinois	(6.0)
20	Wyoming	3.0	45	Vermont	(6.3)
21	Nevada	2.9	46	Ohio	(6.4)
22	Tennessee	2.8	47	Connecticut	(8.2)
23	California	2.7	48	Iowa	(8.3)
24	Washington	2.3	49	Delaware	(13.0)
25	Kansas	2.2	50	Rhode Island	(14.6)

District of Columbia   15.5

Source: U.S. Department of Justice, Federal Bureau of Investigation

"Crime in the United States 1992" (Uniform Crime Reports, October 3, 1993)

*Violent crimes are offenses of murder, forcible rape, robbery and aggravated assault.

Violent Crime Rate with Firearms in 1992

National Rate = 206.8 Violent Crimes per 100,000 Population*

RANK	STATE	RATE	RANK	STATE	RATE
1	Maryland	368.8	26	Oregon	116.8
2	Illinois	350.2	27	Virginia	110.0
3	Louisiana	345.5	28	Pennsylvania	103.4
4	Florida	324.1	29	Mississippi	101.0
5	New York	320.0	30	Wisconsin	92.1
6	California	312.9	31	Indiana	92.0
7	Missouri	262.8	32	Massachusetts	79.4
8	Texas	260.0	33	Minnesota	70.7
9	Michigan	237.9	34	Rhode Island	56.4
10	Georgia	231.2	35	Utah	50.0
11	South Carolina	226.3	36	West Virginia	45.8
12	Tennessee	225.0	37	Wyoming	45.5
13	North Carolina	208.8	38	Idaho	41.1
14	Arizona	207.4	39	Montana	30.9
15	Nevada	198.1	40	Hawaii	29.4
16	Arkansas	181.1	41	Delaware	27.7
17	New Mexico	175.1	42	South Dakota	27.1
18	Oklahoma	169.8	43	Nebraska	18.2
19	Kansas	165.9	44	Vermont	17.4
20	Colorado	151.9	45	Iowa	16.6
21	Alaska	142.1	46	New Hampshire	15.0
22	New Jersey	140.7	47	North Dakota	6.0
23	Ohio	135.9	–	Alabama**	N/A
24	Washington	122.9	–	Kentucky**	N/A
25	Connecticut	119.4	–	Maine**	N/A

District of Columbia   1,003.2

Source: Morgan Quitno Corporation using data from U.S. Department of Justice, Federal Bureau of Investigation

   "Crime in the United States 1992" (Uniform Crime Reports, October 3, 1993)

*Includes murder, robbery and aggravated assault. Rate reflects only those violent crimes for which the type of weapon was known.

**Data not available for all three crimes.

Murders in 1992

National Total = 23,760 Murders*

RANK	STATE	MURDERS	%
1	California	3,921	16.50%
2	New York	2,397	10.09%
3	Texas	2,239	9.42%
4	Illinois	1,322	5.56%
5	Florida	1,208	5.08%
6	Michigan	938	3.95%
7	Louisiana	747	3.14%
8	Pennsylvania	746	3.14%
9	Georgia	741	3.12%
10	Ohio	724	3.05%
11	North Carolina	723	3.04%
12	Maryland	596	2.51%
13	Virginia	564	2.37%
14	Missouri	547	2.30%
15	Tennessee	520	2.19%
16	Indiana	464	1.95%
17	Alabama	455	1.91%
18	New Jersey	397	1.67%
19	South Carolina	373	1.57%
20	Mississippi	320	1.35%
21	Arizona	312	1.31%
22	Arkansas	259	1.09%
23	Washington	258	1.09%
24	Wisconsin	218	0.92%
25	Colorado	216	0.91%

RANK	STATE	MURDERS	%
25	Kentucky	216	0.91%
27	Massachusetts	214	0.90%
28	Oklahoma	210	0.88%
29	Connecticut	166	0.70%
30	Kansas	151	0.64%
31	Minnesota	150	0.63%
32	Nevada	145	0.61%
33	New Mexico	141	0.59%
34	Oregon	139	0.59%
35	West Virginia	115	0.48%
36	Nebraska	68	0.29%
37	Utah	54	0.23%
38	Alaska	44	0.19%
38	Iowa	44	0.19%
40	Hawaii	42	0.18%
41	Idaho	37	0.16%
42	Rhode Island	36	0.15%
43	Delaware	32	0.13%
44	Montana	24	0.10%
45	Maine	21	0.09%
46	New Hampshire	18	0.08%
47	Wyoming	17	0.07%
48	North Dakota	12	0.05%
48	Vermont	12	0.05%
50	South Dakota	4	0.02%

	District of Columbia	443	1.86%

Source: U.S. Department of Justice, Federal Bureau of Investigation

"Crime in the United States 1992" (Uniform Crime Reports, October 3, 1993)

*Includes nonnegligent manslaughter.

Average Time Between Murders in 1992

National Rate = A Murder Occurs Every 22 Minutes*

RANK	STATE	HOURS.MINUTES	RANK	STATE	HOURS.MINUTES
1	South Dakota	2,196.00	25	Kentucky	40.40
2	North Dakota	732.00	27	Wisconsin	40.17
2	Vermont	732.00	28	Washington	34.03
4	Wyoming	516.43	29	Arkansas	33.55
5	New Hampshire	488.00	30	Arizona	28.09
6	Maine	418.17	31	Mississippi	27.27
7	Montana	366.00	32	South Carolina	23.33
8	Delaware	274.30	33	New Jersey	22.08
9	Rhode Island	244.00	34	Alabama	19.19
10	Idaho	237.25	35	Indiana	18.56
11	Hawaii	209.08	36	Tennessee	16.53
12	Alaska	199.38	37	Missouri	16.04
12	Iowa	199.38	38	Virginia	15.34
14	Utah	162.40	39	Maryland	14.44
15	Nebraska	129.11	40	North Carolina	12.09
16	West Virginia	76.23	41	Ohio	12.08
17	Oregon	63.11	42	Georgia	11.51
18	New Mexico	62.18	43	Louisiana	11.46
19	Nevada	60.35	43	Pennsylvania	11.46
20	Minnesota	58.34	45	Michigan	9.22
21	Kansas	58.10	46	Florida	7.16
22	Connecticut	52.55	47	Illinois	6.38
23	Oklahoma	41.50	48	Texas	3.55
24	Massachusetts	41.03	49	New York	3.40
25	Colorado	40.40	50	California	2.14
				District of Columbia	19.50

Source: Morgan Quitno Corporation using data from U.S. Department of Justice, Federal Bureau of Investigation
  "Crime in the United States 1992" (Uniform Crime Reports, October 3, 1993)
*Includes nonnegligent manslaughter.

Percent Change in Number of Murders: 1991 to 1992

National Percent Change = 3.8% Decrease*

RANK	STATE	PERCENT CHANGE	RANK	STATE	PERCENT CHANGE
1	Idaho	94.7	26	Rhode Island	(2.7)
2	North Dakota	71.4	27	Alabama	(3.0)
3	Maine	40.0	28	Florida	(3.2)
4	Nebraska	30.8	29	Virginia	(3.3)
5	Washington	22.3	30	Mississippi	(3.6)
6	Minnesota	14.5	31	Nevada	(4.6)
7	Montana	14.3	32	Tennessee	(4.9)
8	Wyoming	13.3	33	North Carolina	(6.0)
9	Indiana	9.7	34	Hawaii	(6.7)
10	Colorado	8.5	35	New York	(6.8)
11	Arizona	7.2	36	Michigan	(7.0)
12	Alaska	4.8	37	South Carolina	(7.2)
13	Maryland	4.7	38	Ohio	(7.5)
14	Oregon	4.5	39	Oklahoma	(8.7)
15	Louisiana	3.8	40	Wisconsin	(8.8)
15	Utah	3.8	41	Connecticut	(11.2)
17	West Virginia	3.6	42	Georgia	(12.7)
18	Illinois	1.7	43	Delaware	(13.5)
19	California	1.6	43	New Mexico	(13.5)
20	Missouri	0.7	45	Massachusetts	(14.1)
21	Vermont	0.0	46	Kentucky	(14.6)
22	Kansas	(1.3)	47	Texas	(15.6)
23	Pennsylvania	(1.6)	48	Iowa	(22.8)
24	Arkansas	(1.9)	49	New Hampshire	(55.0)
25	New Jersey	(2.2)	50	South Dakota	(66.7)

District of Columbia   (8.1)

Source: U.S. Department of Justice, Federal Bureau of Investigation

"Crime in the United States 1992" (Uniform Crime Reports, October 3, 1993)

*Includes nonnegligent manslaughter.

Murder Rate in 1992

National Rate = 9.3 Murders per 100,000 Population*

RANK	STATE	RATE		RANK	STATE	RATE
1	Louisiana	17.4		26	Colorado	6.2
2	New York	13.2		26	Pennsylvania	6.2
3	California	12.7		28	Kansas	6.0
3	Texas	12.7		29	Kentucky	5.8
5	Mississippi	12.2		30	Connecticut	5.1
6	Maryland	12.1		30	New Jersey	5.1
7	Illinois	11.4		32	Washington	5.0
8	Alabama	11.0		33	Oregon	4.7
8	Georgia	11.0		34	Delaware	4.6
10	Nevada	10.9		35	Wisconsin	4.4
11	Arkansas	10.8		36	Nebraska	4.2
12	North Carolina	10.6		37	Hawaii	3.6
13	Missouri	10.5		37	Massachusetts	3.6
14	South Carolina	10.4		37	Rhode Island	3.6
14	Tennessee	10.4		37	Wyoming	3.6
16	Michigan	9.9		41	Idaho	3.5
17	Florida	9.0		42	Minnesota	3.3
18	New Mexico	8.9		43	Utah	3.0
19	Virginia	8.8		44	Montana	2.9
20	Indiana	8.2		45	Vermont	2.1
21	Arizona	8.1		46	North Dakota	1.9
22	Alaska	7.5		47	Maine	1.7
23	Ohio	6.6		48	Iowa	1.6
24	Oklahoma	6.5		48	New Hampshire	1.6
25	West Virginia	6.3		50	South Dakota	0.6

District of Columbia   75.2

Source: U.S. Department of Justice, Federal Bureau of Investigation
   "Crime in the United States 1992" (Uniform Crime Reports, October 3, 1993)
*Includes nonnegligent manslaughter.

Percent Change in Murder Rate: 1991 to 1992

National Percent Change = 5.1% Decrease*

RANK	STATE	PERCENT CHANGE		RANK	STATE	PERCENT CHANGE
1	Idaho	94.4		25	Rhode Island	(2.7)
2	North Dakota	72.7		27	Alabama	(4.3)
3	Maine	41.7		27	Florida	(4.3)
4	Nebraska	27.3		29	Mississippi	(4.7)
5	Washington	19.0		30	Virginia	(5.4)
6	Montana	11.5		31	Tennessee	(5.5)
7	Minnesota	10.0		32	New York	(7.0)
8	Indiana	9.3		32	North Carolina	(7.0)
9	Wyoming	9.1		34	Nevada	(7.6)
10	Colorado	5.1		35	South Carolina	(8.0)
11	Arizona	3.8		36	Michigan	(8.3)
12	Maryland	3.4		36	Ohio	(8.3)
12	Utah	3.4		36	Wisconsin	(8.3)
14	Louisiana	3.0		39	Oklahoma	(9.7)
15	Oregon	2.2		40	Hawaii	(10.0)
16	West Virginia	1.6		41	Connecticut	(10.5)
17	Alaska	1.4		42	Georgia	(14.1)
18	Illinois	0.9		43	Massachusetts	(14.3)
19	California	0.0		44	Kentucky	(14.7)
19	Missouri	0.0		45	Delaware	(14.8)
19	Vermont	0.0		46	New Mexico	(15.2)
22	Kansas	(1.6)		47	Texas	(17.0)
22	Pennsylvania	(1.6)		48	Iowa	(20.0)
24	New Jersey	(1.9)		49	New Hampshire	(55.6)
25	Arkansas	(2.7)		50	South Dakota	(64.7)

District of Columbia   (6.7)

Source: U.S. Department of Justice, Federal Bureau of Investigation
    "Crime in the United States 1992" (Uniform Crime Reports, October 3, 1993)
*Includes nonnegligent manslaughter.

Murders with Firearms in 1992

National Total = 15,377 Murders with Firearms*

RANK	STATE	MURDERS	%	RANK	STATE	MURDERS	%
1	California	2,851	18.54%	26	Colorado	119	0.77%
2	New York	1,760	11.45%	27	Connecticut	114	0.74%
3	Texas	1,627	10.58%	28	Wisconsin	113	0.73%
4	Illinois	832	5.41%	29	Massachusetts	89	0.58%
5	Florida	712	4.63%	30	West Virginia	82	0.53%
6	Michigan	655	4.26%	31	Kansas	73	0.47%
7	Louisiana	507	3.30%	32	Minnesota	72	0.47%
8	North Carolina	450	2.93%	33	Nevada	70	0.46%
8	Pennsylvania	450	2.93%	34	Oregon	60	0.39%
10	Georgia	443	2.88%	35	New Mexico	53	0.34%
11	Maryland	428	2.78%	36	Nebraska	26	0.17%
11	Ohio	428	2.78%	37	Alaska	24	0.16%
13	Virginia	407	2.65%	38	Utah	23	0.15%
14	Tennessee	301	1.96%	39	Idaho	21	0.14%
15	Missouri	296	1.92%	40	Rhode Island	17	0.11%
16	South Carolina	251	1.63%	41	Hawaii	15	0.10%
17	Indiana	239	1.55%	42	Montana	12	0.08%
18	Alabama	230	1.50%	42	New Hampshire	12	0.08%
19	Arizona	210	1.37%	44	Iowa	9	0.06%
20	New Jersey	190	1.24%	45	Delaware	8	0.05%
21	Arkansas	185	1.20%	45	North Dakota	8	0.05%
22	Washington	137	0.89%	47	Wyoming	7	0.05%
23	Mississippi	133	0.86%	48	Vermont	6	0.04%
24	Kentucky	128	0.83%	49	South Dakota	0	0.00%
25	Oklahoma	126	0.82%	–	Maine**	N/A	N/A

District of Columbia		368	2.39%

Source: U.S. Department of Justice, Federal Bureau of Investigation

"Crime in the United States 1992" (Uniform Crime Reports, October 3, 1993)

*Of the 22,507 murders in 1992 for which supplemental data were received by the F.B.I. There were an additional 1,253 murders for which the type of murder weapon was not reported to the F.B.I. Includes nonnegligent manslaughter.

**Not available.

Murder Rate with Firearms in 1992

National Rate = 6.03 Murders per 100,000 Population*

RANK	STATE	RATE	RANK	STATE	RATE
1	Louisiana	11.83	26	Connecticut	3.47
2	New York	9.71	27	Colorado	3.43
3	California	9.24	28	Kentucky	3.41
4	Texas	9.21	29	New Mexico	3.35
5	Maryland	8.72	30	Kansas	2.89
6	Arkansas	7.71	31	Washington	2.67
7	Illinois	7.15	32	New Jersey	2.44
8	South Carolina	6.97	33	Wisconsin	2.26
9	Michigan	6.94	34	Oregon	2.02
10	North Carolina	6.58	35	Idaho	1.97
11	Georgia	6.56	36	Rhode Island	1.69
12	Virginia	6.38	37	Nebraska	1.62
13	Tennessee	5.99	38	Minnesota	1.61
14	Missouri	5.70	39	Wyoming	1.50
15	Alabama	5.56	40	Massachusetts	1.48
16	Arizona	5.48	41	Montana	1.46
17	Florida	5.28	42	Hawaii	1.29
17	Nevada	5.28	43	Utah	1.27
19	Mississippi	5.09	44	North Dakota	1.26
20	West Virginia	4.53	45	Delaware	1.16
21	Indiana	4.22	46	New Hampshire	1.08
22	Alaska	4.09	47	Vermont	1.05
23	Oklahoma	3.92	48	Iowa	0.32
24	Ohio	3.89	49	South Dakota	0.00
25	Pennsylvania	3.75	–	Maine**	N/A

	District of Columbia	62.48

Source: Morgan Quitno Corporation using data from U.S. Department of Justice, Federal Bureau of Investigation

"Crime in the United States 1992" (Uniform Crime Reports, October 3, 1993)

*Of the 22,507 murders in 1992 for which supplemental data were received by the F.B.I. There were an additional 1,253 murders for which the type of murder weapon was not reported to the F.B.I. Includes nonnegligent manslaughter.

**Not available.

Percent of Murders Involving Firearms in 1992

National Percent = 68.32% of Murders*

RANK	STATE	PERCENT		RANK	STATE	PERCENT
1	Louisiana	76.93		26	Wisconsin	61.41
2	Arkansas	74.30		27	Oklahoma	61.17
3	New York	74.01		28	Kentucky	60.66
4	California	72.71		29	Florida	60.54
5	Texas	72.67		30	Idaho	60.00
6	Virginia	72.29		30	Vermont	60.00
7	West Virginia	71.93		32	New Mexico	59.55
8	Maryland	71.81		33	Alabama	58.82
9	Michigan	70.13		34	Alaska	55.81
10	South Carolina	69.53		35	Colorado	55.61
11	Tennessee	69.35		36	Kansas	54.89
12	Arizona	69.08		37	Minnesota	54.14
13	Connecticut	68.67		38	Nevada	53.85
14	Illinois	68.36		39	Washington	53.73
15	Indiana	67.32		40	Massachusetts	50.00
16	Montana	66.67		41	Rhode Island	48.57
16	New Hampshire	66.67		42	New Jersey	47.86
16	North Dakota	66.67		43	Utah	45.10
19	Ohio	66.15		44	Oregon	43.80
20	Georgia	66.02		45	Wyoming	41.18
21	Pennsylvania	65.79		46	Delaware	40.00
22	Mississippi	65.52		47	Iowa	39.13
23	Missouri	64.63		48	Hawaii	35.71
24	North Carolina	63.56		49	South Dakota	0.00
25	Nebraska	61.90		–	Maine**	N/A

District of Columbia   83.26

Source: Morgan Quitno Corporation using data from U.S. Department of Justice, Federal Bureau of Investigation
    "Crime in the United States 1992" (Uniform Crime Reports, October 3, 1993)
*Of the 22,507 murders in 1992 for which supplemental data were received by the F.B.I. There were an additional 1,253 murders for which the type of murder weapon was not reported to the F.B.I. Includes nonnegligent manslaughter.
**Not available.

Murders with Handguns in 1992

National Total = 12,489 Murders with Handguns*

RANK	STATE	MURDERS	%		RANK	STATE	MURDERS	%
1	California	2,442	19.55%		26	Oklahoma	98	0.78%
2	New York	1,643	13.16%		27	Colorado	88	0.70%
3	Texas	1,164	9.32%		28	Wisconsin	84	0.67%
4	Illinois	689	5.52%		29	Massachusetts	71	0.57%
5	Florida	507	4.06%		30	Kansas	63	0.50%
6	Louisiana	445	3.56%		31	Nevada	61	0.49%
7	Maryland	392	3.14%		32	West Virginia	57	0.46%
8	Michigan	388	3.11%		33	Minnesota	54	0.43%
9	Georgia	373	2.99%		34	New Mexico	42	0.34%
10	Pennsylvania	371	2.97%		35	Oregon	36	0.29%
11	Ohio	367	2.94%		36	Utah	19	0.15%
12	North Carolina	340	2.72%		37	Nebraska	18	0.14%
13	Virginia	336	2.69%		38	Alaska	15	0.12%
14	Tennessee	250	2.00%		39	Idaho	12	0.10%
15	Alabama	196	1.57%		40	Montana	11	0.09%
16	Indiana	190	1.52%		40	Rhode Island	11	0.09%
17	Missouri	189	1.51%		42	Hawaii	10	0.08%
18	South Carolina	180	1.44%		42	New Hampshire	10	0.08%
19	Arizona	165	1.32%		44	Iowa	7	0.06%
20	New Jersey	151	1.21%		45	Wyoming	5	0.04%
21	Arkansas	137	1.10%		46	Delaware	4	0.03%
22	Washington	115	0.92%		47	North Dakota	2	0.02%
23	Mississippi	113	0.90%		47	Vermont	2	0.02%
24	Connecticut	99	0.79%		49	South Dakota	0	0.00%
24	Kentucky	99	0.79%		–	Maine**	N/A	N/A

District of Columbia 368 2.95%

Source: U.S. Department of Justice, Federal Bureau of Investigation

"Crime in the United States 1992" (Uniform Crime Reports, October 3, 1993)

*Of the 22,507 murders in 1992 for which supplemental data were received by the F.B.I. There were an additional 1,253 murders for which the type of murder weapon was not reported to the F.B.I. Includes nonnegligent manslaughter.

**Not available.

Murder Rate with Handguns in 1992

National Rate = 4.90 Murders per 100,000 Population*

RANK	STATE	RATE	RANK	STATE	RATE
1	Louisiana	10.38	26	New Mexico	2.66
2	New York	9.07	27	Kentucky	2.64
3	Maryland	7.99	28	Alaska	2.56
4	California	7.91	29	Colorado	2.54
5	Texas	6.59	30	Kansas	2.50
6	Illinois	5.92	31	Washington	2.24
7	Arkansas	5.71	32	New Jersey	1.94
8	Georgia	5.53	33	Wisconsin	1.68
9	Virginia	5.27	34	Montana	1.33
10	South Carolina	5.00	35	Minnesota	1.21
11	Tennessee	4.98	35	Oregon	1.21
12	North Carolina	4.97	37	Massachusetts	1.18
13	Alabama	4.74	38	Idaho	1.12
14	Nevada	4.60	38	Nebraska	1.12
15	Mississippi	4.32	40	Rhode Island	1.09
16	Arizona	4.31	41	Wyoming	1.07
17	Michigan	4.11	42	Utah	1.05
18	Florida	3.76	43	New Hampshire	0.90
19	Missouri	3.64	44	Hawaii	0.86
20	Indiana	3.36	45	Delaware	0.58
21	Ohio	3.33	46	Vermont	0.35
22	West Virginia	3.15	47	North Dakota	0.31
23	Pennsylvania	3.09	48	Iowa	0.25
24	Oklahoma	3.05	49	South Dakota	0.00
25	Connecticut	3.02	–	Maine**	N/A

District of Columbia   62.48

Source: Morgan Quitno Corporation using data from U.S. Department of Justice, Federal Bureau of Investigation

"Crime in the United States 1992" (Uniform Crime Reports, October 3, 1993)

*Of the 22,507 murders in 1992 for which supplemental data were received by the F.B.I. There were an additional 1,253 murders for which the type of murder weapon was not reported to the F.B.I. Includes nonnegligent manslaughter.

**Not available.

Percent of Murders Involving Handguns in 1992

National Percent = 55.49% of Murders*

RANK	STATE	PERCENT		RANK	STATE	PERCENT
1	New York	69.09		26	Kentucky	46.92
2	Louisiana	67.53		26	Nevada	46.92
3	Maryland	65.77		28	Wisconsin	45.65
4	California	62.28		29	Washington	45.10
5	Montana	61.11		30	Florida	43.11
6	Virginia	59.68		31	Nebraska	42.86
7	Connecticut	59.64		32	Michigan	41.54
8	Tennessee	57.60		33	Missouri	41.27
9	Ohio	56.72		34	Colorado	41.12
10	Illinois	56.61		35	Minnesota	40.60
11	Mississippi	55.67		36	Massachusetts	39.89
12	Georgia	55.59		37	New Jersey	38.04
13	New Hampshire	55.56		38	Utah	37.25
14	Arkansas	55.02		39	Alaska	34.88
15	Arizona	54.28		40	Idaho	34.29
16	Pennsylvania	54.24		41	Rhode Island	31.43
17	Indiana	53.52		42	Iowa	30.43
18	Texas	51.99		43	Wyoming	29.41
19	Alabama	50.13		44	Oregon	26.28
20	West Virginia	50.00		45	Hawaii	23.81
21	South Carolina	49.86		46	Delaware	20.00
22	North Carolina	48.02		46	Vermont	20.00
23	Oklahoma	47.57		48	North Dakota	16.67
24	Kansas	47.37		49	South Dakota	0.00
25	New Mexico	47.19		–	Maine**	N/A

District of Columbia   83.26

Source: Morgan Quitno Corporation using data from U.S. Department of Justice, Federal Bureau of Investigation
        "Crime in the United States 1992" (Uniform Crime Reports, October 3, 1993)
*Of the 22,507 murders in 1992 for which supplemental data were received by the F.B.I. There were an additional 1,253 murders for which the type of murder weapon was not reported to the F.B.I. Includes nonnegligent manslaughter.
**Not available.

Murders with Rifles in 1992

National Total = 698 Murders with Rifles*

RANK	STATE	MURDERS	%	RANK	STATE	MURDERS	%
1	California	163	23.35%	26	Idaho	7	1.00%
2	Texas	73	10.46%	26	Minnesota	7	1.00%
3	Michigan	45	6.45%	28	Kansas	6	0.86%
4	North Carolina	36	5.16%	29	Alaska	5	0.72%
5	Georgia	21	3.01%	29	Maryland	5	0.72%
6	Florida	20	2.87%	29	Massachusetts	5	0.72%
6	New York	20	2.87%	29	New Mexico	5	0.72%
6	South Carolina	20	2.87%	29	West Virginia	5	0.72%
6	Virginia	20	2.87%	34	Connecticut	4	0.57%
10	Louisiana	18	2.58%	34	Mississippi	4	0.57%
11	Illinois	17	2.44%	34	North Dakota	4	0.57%
11	Pennsylvania	17	2.44%	37	Hawaii	3	0.43%
13	Indiana	16	2.29%	37	Nevada	3	0.43%
13	Tennessee	16	2.29%	37	New Jersey	3	0.43%
15	Alabama	13	1.86%	40	Nebraska	2	0.29%
15	Oklahoma	13	1.86%	40	Rhode Island	2	0.29%
15	Oregon	13	1.86%	40	Utah	2	0.29%
18	Arkansas	12	1.72%	40	Vermont	2	0.29%
19	Ohio	11	1.58%	40	Wyoming	2	0.29%
19	Washington	11	1.58%	45	Delaware	1	0.14%
21	Colorado	10	1.43%	45	Iowa	1	0.14%
22	Missouri	9	1.29%	45	Montana	1	0.14%
22	Wisconsin	9	1.29%	48	New Hampshire	0	0.00%
24	Arizona	8	1.15%	48	South Dakota	0	0.00%
24	Kentucky	8	1.15%	–	Maine**	N/A	N/A
					District of Columbia	0	0.00%

Source: U.S. Department of Justice, Federal Bureau of Investigation
    "Crime in the United States 1992" (Uniform Crime Reports, October 3, 1993)
*Of the 22,507 murders in 1992 for which supplemental data were received by the F.B.I. There were an additional 1,253 murders for which the type of murder weapon was not reported to the F.B.I. Includes nonnegligent manslaughter.
**Not available.

Percent of Murders Involving Rifles in 1992

National Percent = 3.10% of Murders*

RANK	STATE	PERCENT	RANK	STATE	PERCENT
1	North Dakota	33.33	26	California	4.16
2	Idaho	20.00	27	Utah	3.92
2	Vermont	20.00	28	Kentucky	3.79
4	Wyoming	11.76	29	Tennessee	3.69
5	Alaska	11.63	30	Virginia	3.55
6	Oregon	9.49	31	Alabama	3.32
7	Hawaii	7.14	32	Texas	3.26
8	Oklahoma	6.31	33	Georgia	3.13
9	Rhode Island	5.71	34	Massachusetts	2.81
10	New Mexico	5.62	35	Louisiana	2.73
11	Montana	5.56	36	Arizona	2.63
12	South Carolina	5.54	37	Pennsylvania	2.49
13	Minnesota	5.26	38	Connecticut	2.41
14	North Carolina	5.08	39	Nevada	2.31
15	Delaware	5.00	40	Mississippi	1.97
16	Wisconsin	4.89	40	Missouri	1.97
17	Arkansas	4.82	42	Florida	1.70
17	Michigan	4.82	42	Ohio	1.70
19	Nebraska	4.76	44	Illinois	1.40
20	Colorado	4.67	45	Maryland	0.84
21	Indiana	4.51	45	New York	0.84
21	Kansas	4.51	47	New Jersey	0.76
23	West Virginia	4.39	48	New Hampshire	0.00
24	Iowa	4.35	48	South Dakota	0.00
25	Washington	4.31	–	Maine**	N/A

District of Columbia   0.00

Source: Morgan Quitno Corporation using data from U.S. Department of Justice, Federal Bureau of Investigation
    "Crime in the United States 1992" (Uniform Crime Reports, October 3, 1993)
*Of the 22,507 murders in 1992 for which supplemental data were received by the F.B.I. There were an additional 1,253 murders for which the type of murder weapon was not reported to the F.B.I. Includes nonnegligent manslaughter.
**Not available.

Murders with Shotguns in 1992

National Total = 1,104 Murders with Shotguns*

RANK	STATE	MURDERS	%	RANK	STATE	MURDERS	%
1	California	173	15.67%	24	Wisconsin	13	1.18%
2	Texas	144	13.04%	27	Colorado	10	0.91%
3	North Carolina	74	6.70%	28	Washington	7	0.63%
4	Michigan	67	6.07%	29	Nebraska	6	0.54%
5	New York	59	5.34%	29	Nevada	6	0.54%
6	Virginia	41	3.71%	31	Connecticut	5	0.45%
7	South Carolina	39	3.53%	31	Oregon	5	0.45%
8	Florida	38	3.44%	33	Alaska	4	0.36%
8	Georgia	38	3.44%	33	Kansas	4	0.36%
10	Illinois	35	3.17%	33	Minnesota	4	0.36%
11	Ohio	32	2.90%	33	New Mexico	4	0.36%
11	Tennessee	32	2.90%	37	Massachusetts	3	0.27%
13	Pennsylvania	27	2.45%	38	Hawaii	2	0.18%
14	Arkansas	26	2.36%	38	New Hampshire	2	0.18%
15	Maryland	25	2.26%	40	Delaware	1	0.09%
16	Indiana	23	2.08%	40	North Dakota	1	0.09%
17	Louisiana	22	1.99%	40	Rhode Island	1	0.09%
17	Missouri	22	1.99%	40	Utah	1	0.09%
19	Alabama	21	1.90%	44	Idaho	0	0.00%
20	West Virginia	18	1.63%	44	Iowa	0	0.00%
21	New Jersey	15	1.36%	44	Montana	0	0.00%
22	Arizona	14	1.27%	44	South Dakota	0	0.00%
22	Oklahoma	14	1.27%	44	Vermont	0	0.00%
24	Kentucky	13	1.18%	44	Wyoming	0	0.00%
24	Mississippi	13	1.18%	–	Maine**	N/A	N/A
					District of Columbia	0	0.00%

Source: U.S. Department of Justice, Federal Bureau of Investigation
    "Crime in the United States 1992" (Uniform Crime Reports, October 3, 1993)
*Of the 22,507 murders in 1992 for which supplemental data were received by the F.B.I. There were an additional 1,253 murders for which the type of murder weapon was not reported to the F.B.I. Includes nonnegligent manslaughter.
**Not available.

Percent of Murders Involving Shotguns in 1992

National Percent = 4.91% of Murders*

RANK	STATE	PERCENT		RANK	STATE	PERCENT
1	West Virginia	15.79		26	Arizona	4.61
2	Nebraska	14.29		27	New Mexico	4.49
3	New Hampshire	11.11		28	California	4.41
4	South Carolina	10.80		29	Maryland	4.19
5	North Carolina	10.45		30	Pennsylvania	3.95
6	Arkansas	10.44		31	New Jersey	3.78
7	Alaska	9.30		32	Oregon	3.65
8	North Dakota	8.33		33	Louisiana	3.34
9	Tennessee	7.37		34	Florida	3.23
10	Virginia	7.28		35	Connecticut	3.01
11	Michigan	7.17		35	Kansas	3.01
12	Wisconsin	7.07		35	Minnesota	3.01
13	Oklahoma	6.80		38	Illinois	2.88
14	Indiana	6.48		39	Rhode Island	2.86
15	Texas	6.43		40	Washington	2.75
16	Mississippi	6.40		41	New York	2.48
17	Kentucky	6.16		42	Utah	1.96
18	Georgia	5.66		43	Massachusetts	1.69
19	Alabama	5.37		44	Idaho	0.00
20	Delaware	5.00		44	Iowa	0.00
21	Ohio	4.95		44	Montana	0.00
22	Missouri	4.80		44	South Dakota	0.00
23	Hawaii	4.76		44	Vermont	0.00
24	Colorado	4.67		44	Wyoming	0.00
25	Nevada	4.62		–	Maine**	N/A

District of Columbia   0.00

Source: Morgan Quitno Corporation using data from U.S. Department of Justice, Federal Bureau of Investigation
"Crime in the United States 1992" (Uniform Crime Reports, October 3, 1993)
*Of the 22,507 murders in 1992 for which supplemental data were received by the F.B.I. There were an additional 1,253 murders for which the type of murder weapon was not reported to the F.B.I. Includes nonnegligent manslaughter.
**Not available.

Murders with Knives or Cutting Instruments in 1992

National Total = 3,265 Murders with Knives or Cutting Instruments*

RANK	STATE	MURDERS	%	RANK	STATE	MURDERS	%
1	California	544	16.66%	26	Wisconsin	34	1.04%
2	Texas	299	9.16%	27	Kentucky	33	1.01%
3	New York	297	9.10%	27	Minnesota	33	1.01%
4	Illinois	196	6.00%	29	Arizona	31	0.95%
5	Michigan	133	4.07%	29	Connecticut	31	0.95%
6	Florida	131	4.01%	31	Nevada	27	0.83%
7	North Carolina	114	3.49%	32	Oregon	19	0.58%
8	Pennsylvania	105	3.22%	33	New Mexico	17	0.52%
9	Georgia	104	3.19%	34	West Virginia	16	0.49%
10	New Jersey	99	3.03%	35	Kansas	15	0.46%
11	Ohio	92	2.82%	36	Alaska	10	0.31%
12	Maryland	90	2.76%	37	Utah	9	0.28%
13	Louisiana	80	2.45%	38	Hawaii	8	0.25%
14	Virginia	69	2.11%	39	Idaho	5	0.15%
15	Tennessee	66	2.02%	39	Rhode Island	5	0.15%
16	Alabama	64	1.96%	41	Delaware	4	0.12%
17	Missouri	57	1.75%	41	Nebraska	4	0.12%
17	Washington	57	1.75%	41	South Dakota	4	0.12%
19	Indiana	56	1.72%	41	Wyoming	4	0.12%
19	South Carolina	56	1.72%	45	Iowa	3	0.09%
21	Colorado	46	1.41%	46	Vermont	2	0.06%
22	Oklahoma	44	1.35%	47	New Hampshire	1	0.03%
23	Massachusetts	41	1.26%	47	North Dakota	1	0.03%
24	Arkansas	38	1.16%	49	Montana	0	0.00%
25	Mississippi	35	1.07%	–	Maine**	N/A	N/A
					District of Columbia	36	1.10%

Source: U.S. Department of Justice, Federal Bureau of Investigation

"Crime in the United States 1992" (Uniform Crime Reports, October 3, 1993)

*Of the 22,507 murders in 1992 for which supplemental data were received by the F.B.I. There were an additional 1,253 murders for which the type of murder weapon was not reported to the F.B.I. Includes nonnegligent manslaughter.

**Not available.

Percent of Murders Involving Knives or Cutting Instruments in 1992

National Percent = 14.51% of Murders*

RANK	STATE	PERCENT		RANK	STATE	PERCENT
1	South Dakota	100.00		26	Pennsylvania	15.35
2	New Jersey	24.94		27	Arkansas	15.26
3	Minnesota	24.81		28	Tennessee	15.21
4	Wyoming	23.53		29	Maryland	15.10
5	Alaska	23.26		30	Idaho	14.29
6	Massachusetts	23.03		30	Rhode Island	14.29
7	Washington	22.35		32	Michigan	14.24
8	Colorado	21.50		33	Ohio	14.22
9	Oklahoma	21.36		34	West Virginia	14.04
10	Nevada	20.77		35	California	13.87
11	Delaware	20.00		35	Oregon	13.87
11	Vermont	20.00		37	Texas	13.35
13	New Mexico	19.10		38	Iowa	13.04
14	Hawaii	19.05		39	New York	12.49
15	Connecticut	18.67		40	Missouri	12.45
16	Wisconsin	18.48		41	Virginia	12.26
17	Utah	17.65		42	Louisiana	12.14
18	Mississippi	17.24		43	Kansas	11.28
19	Alabama	16.37		44	Florida	11.14
20	Illinois	16.11		45	Arizona	10.20
21	North Carolina	16.10		46	Nebraska	9.52
22	Indiana	15.77		47	North Dakota	8.33
23	Kentucky	15.64		48	New Hampshire	5.56
24	South Carolina	15.51		49	Montana	0.00
25	Georgia	15.50		–	Maine**	N/A

District of Columbia   8.14

Source: Morgan Quitno Corporation using data from U.S. Department of Justice, Federal Bureau of Investigation
     "Crime in the United States 1992" (Uniform Crime Reports, October 3, 1993)
*Of the 22,507 murders in 1992 for which supplemental data were received by the F.B.I. There were an additional 1,253 murders for which the type of murder weapon was not reported to the F.B.I. Includes nonnegligent manslaughter.
**Not available.

Murders by Hands, Fists or Feet in 1992

National Total = 1,121 Murders by Hands, Fists or Feet*

RANK	STATE	MURDERS	%	RANK	STATE	MURDERS	%
1	California	173	15.43%	26	Colorado	12	1.07%
2	New York	122	10.88%	26	Minnesota	12	1.07%
3	Texas	83	7.40%	26	Tennessee	12	1.07%
4	Florida	68	6.07%	29	Arkansas	11	0.98%
5	Illinois	58	5.17%	29	Hawaii	11	0.98%
6	New Jersey	43	3.84%	29	Missouri	11	0.98%
6	Ohio	43	3.84%	32	Mississippi	10	0.89%
8	Pennsylvania	41	3.66%	33	Nevada	9	0.80%
9	Georgia	36	3.21%	34	Utah	7	0.62%
9	North Carolina	36	3.21%	34	West Virginia	7	0.62%
11	Virginia	33	2.94%	36	Iowa	5	0.45%
12	Michigan	29	2.59%	36	New Mexico	5	0.45%
13	Washington	22	1.96%	38	Wyoming	4	0.36%
14	Massachusetts	20	1.78%	39	Idaho	3	0.27%
15	South Carolina	19	1.69%	39	Montana	3	0.27%
16	Maryland	18	1.61%	41	Alaska	2	0.18%
16	Wisconsin	18	1.61%	41	Connecticut	2	0.18%
18	Alabama	17	1.52%	41	Delaware	2	0.18%
18	Kansas	17	1.52%	41	Nebraska	2	0.18%
18	Oklahoma	17	1.52%	41	New Hampshire	2	0.18%
21	Arizona	16	1.43%	46	North Dakota	0	0.00%
21	Oregon	16	1.43%	46	Rhode Island	0	0.00%
23	Kentucky	15	1.34%	46	South Dakota	0	0.00%
23	Louisiana	15	1.34%	46	Vermont	0	0.00%
25	Indiana	14	1.25%	–	Maine**	N/A	N/A
					District of Columbia	0	0.00%

Source: U.S. Department of Justice, Federal Bureau of Investigation

"Crime in the United States 1992" (Uniform Crime Reports, October 3, 1993)

*Of the 22,507 murders in 1992 for which supplemental data were received by the F.B.I. There were an additional 1,253 murders for which the type of murder weapon was not reported to the F.B.I. Includes nonnegligent manslaughter.

**Not available.

Percent of Murders Involving Hands, Fists or Feet in 1992

National Percent = 4.98% of Murders*

RANK	STATE	PERCENT	RANK	STATE	PERCENT
1	Hawaii	26.19	26	Georgia	5.37
2	Wyoming	23.53	27	Arizona	5.26
3	Iowa	21.74	27	South Carolina	5.26
4	Montana	16.67	29	New York	5.13
5	Utah	13.73	30	North Carolina	5.08
6	Kansas	12.78	31	Mississippi	4.93
7	Oregon	11.68	32	Illinois	4.77
8	Massachusetts	11.24	33	Nebraska	4.76
9	New Hampshire	11.11	34	Alaska	4.65
10	New Jersey	10.83	35	Arkansas	4.42
11	Delaware	10.00	36	California	4.41
12	Wisconsin	9.78	37	Alabama	4.35
13	Minnesota	9.02	38	Indiana	3.94
14	Washington	8.63	39	Texas	3.71
15	Idaho	8.57	40	Michigan	3.10
16	Oklahoma	8.25	41	Maryland	3.02
17	Kentucky	7.11	42	Tennessee	2.76
18	Nevada	6.92	43	Missouri	2.40
19	Ohio	6.65	44	Louisiana	2.28
20	West Virginia	6.14	45	Connecticut	1.20
21	Pennsylvania	5.99	46	North Dakota	0.00
22	Virginia	5.86	46	Rhode Island	0.00
23	Florida	5.78	46	South Dakota	0.00
24	New Mexico	5.62	46	Vermont	0.00
25	Colorado	5.61	–	Maine**	N/A

District of Columbia   0.00

Source: Morgan Quitno Corporation using data from U.S. Department of Justice, Federal Bureau of Investigation
    "Crime in the United States 1992" (Uniform Crime Reports, October 3, 1993)
*Of the 22,507 murders in 1992 for which supplemental data were received by the F.B.I. There were an additional 1,253 murders for which the type of murder weapon was not reported to the F.B.I. Includes nonnegligent manslaughter.
**Not available.

Rapes in 1992

National Total = 109,062 Rapes*

RANK	STATE	RAPES	%	RANK	STATE	RAPES	%
1	California	12,761	11.70%	26	Oklahoma	1,556	1.43%
2	Texas	9,437	8.65%	27	Wisconsin	1,315	1.21%
3	Michigan	7,550	6.92%	28	Kentucky	1,209	1.11%
4	Florida	7,310	6.70%	29	Mississippi	1,166	1.07%
5	Ohio	5,739	5.26%	30	Kansas	1,042	0.96%
6	New York	5,152	4.72%	31	Arkansas	990	0.91%
7	Illinois	4,312	3.95%	31	New Mexico	990	0.91%
8	Washington	3,697	3.39%	33	Connecticut	884	0.81%
9	Pennsylvania	3,324	3.05%	34	Nevada	833	0.76%
10	Georgia	3,057	2.80%	35	Utah	823	0.75%
11	North Carolina	2,455	2.25%	36	Delaware	591	0.54%
12	Indiana	2,398	2.20%	37	Alaska	579	0.53%
13	New Jersey	2,392	2.19%	38	Iowa	528	0.48%
14	Tennessee	2,377	2.18%	39	Nebraska	504	0.46%
15	Maryland	2,278	2.09%	40	Hawaii	440	0.40%
16	Massachusetts	2,166	1.99%	41	New Hampshire	424	0.39%
17	South Carolina	2,072	1.90%	42	West Virginia	393	0.36%
18	Virginia	2,008	1.84%	43	South Dakota	368	0.34%
19	Missouri	1,895	1.74%	44	Idaho	339	0.31%
20	Minnesota	1,840	1.69%	45	Rhode Island	311	0.29%
21	Louisiana	1,813	1.66%	46	Maine	294	0.27%
22	Alabama	1,704	1.56%	47	Montana	210	0.19%
23	Arizona	1,647	1.51%	48	Wyoming	163	0.15%
24	Colorado	1,641	1.50%	49	North Dakota	148	0.14%
25	Oregon	1,580	1.45%	50	Vermont	142	0.13%
					District of Columbia	215	0.20%

Source: U.S. Department of Justice, Federal Bureau of Investigation
    "Crime in the United States 1992" (Uniform Crime Reports, October 3, 1993)
*Forcible rape is the carnal knowledge of a female forcibly and against her will. Assaults or attempts to commit rape by force or threat of force are included. However, statutory rape without force and other sex offenses are excluded.

Average Time Between Rapes in 1992

National Rate = A Rape Occurs Every 4 Minutes, 49 Seconds*

RANK	STATE	HOURS.MINUTES		RANK	STATE	HOURS.MINUTES
1	Vermont	61.52		26	Oregon	5.34
2	North Dakota	59.21		27	Colorado	5.21
3	Wyoming	53.53		28	Arizona	5.20
4	Montana	41.50		29	Alabama	5.10
5	Maine	29.53		30	Louisiana	4.51
6	Rhode Island	28.14		31	Minnesota	4.46
7	Idaho	25.55		32	Missouri	4.38
8	South Dakota	23.52		33	Virginia	4.22
9	West Virginia	22.21		34	South Carolina	4.14
10	New Hampshire	20.43		35	Massachusetts	4.04
11	Hawaii	19.58		36	Maryland	3.52
12	Nebraska	17.26		37	Tennessee	3.42
13	Iowa	16.38		38	Indiana	3.40
14	Alaska	15.10		38	New Jersey	3.40
15	Delaware	14.52		40	North Carolina	3.35
16	Utah	10.40		41	Georgia	2.52
17	Nevada	10.33		42	Pennsylvania	2.38
18	Connecticut	9.56		43	Washington	2.23
19	Arkansas	8.52		44	Illinois	2.02
19	New Mexico	8.52		45	New York	1.42
21	Kansas	8.26		46	Ohio	1.32
22	Mississippi	7.32		47	Florida	1.12
23	Kentucky	7.16		48	Michigan	1.10
24	Wisconsin	6.41		49	Texas	0.56
25	Oklahoma	5.39		50	California	0.41

District of Columbia   40.52

Source: Morgan Quitno Corporation using data from U.S. Department of Justice, Federal Bureau of Investigation

"Crime in the United States 1992" (Uniform Crime Reports, October 3, 1993)

*Forcible rape is the carnal knowledge of a female forcibly and against her will. Assaults or attempts to commit rape by force or threat of force are included. However, statutory rape without force and other sex offenses are excluded.

Percent Change in Number of Rapes: 1991 to 1992

National Percent Change = 2.3% Increase*

RANK	STATE	PERCENT CHANGE	RANK	STATE	PERCENT CHANGE
1	Wyoming	37.0	26	Tennessee	3.4
2	South Dakota	31.9	27	Colorado	3.3
3	Montana	31.3	28	Michigan	2.4
4	New Hampshire	28.5	29	Maryland	2.2
5	North Dakota	27.6	30	Utah	1.9
6	New Mexico	22.1	31	Texas	1.8
7	Hawaii	17.3	32	New York	1.3
8	Alabama	17.1	33	Oregon	1.2
9	Idaho	13.0	34	Delaware	0.5
10	Nebraska	12.8	35	Rhode Island	0.3
11	Massachusetts	12.5	36	Ohio	(0.2)
12	Alaska	10.7	37	California	(1.0)
13	Georgia	9.2	38	South Carolina	(1.2)
14	Maine	8.9	39	Nevada	(1.8)
15	Missouri	7.9	40	Mississippi	(2.8)
16	Virginia	6.9	41	Pennsylvania	(3.2)
17	Florida	6.5	42	Oklahoma	(3.7)
18	New Jersey	5.9	43	West Virginia	(5.3)
19	North Carolina	5.3	44	Arkansas	(6.4)
20	Washington	4.8	45	Illinois	(6.6)
21	Minnesota	4.4	46	Kansas	(6.8)
21	Wisconsin	4.4	47	Connecticut	(7.9)
23	Louisiana	4.3	48	Kentucky	(8.1)
24	Arizona	3.6	49	Iowa	(9.4)
25	Indiana	3.5	50	Vermont	(17.9)
				District of Columbia	0.5

Source: U.S. Department of Justice, Federal Bureau of Investigation

"Crime in the United States 1992" (Uniform Crime Reports, October 3, 1993)

*Forcible rape is the carnal knowledge of a female forcibly and against her will. Assaults or attempts to commit rape by force or threat of force are included. However, statutory rape without force and other sex offenses are excluded.

Rape Rate in 1992

National Rate = 42.8 Rapes per 100,000 Population*

RANK	STATE	RATE	RANK	STATE	RATE
1	Alaska	98.6	26	Alabama	41.2
2	Delaware	85.8	27	Minnesota	41.1
3	Michigan	80.0	28	New Hampshire	38.2
4	Washington	72.0	29	Hawaii	37.9
5	Nevada	62.8	30	Illinois	37.1
6	New Mexico	62.6	31	Missouri	36.5
7	South Carolina	57.5	32	Massachusetts	36.1
8	Florida	54.2	33	North Carolina	35.9
9	Texas	53.4	34	Wyoming	35.0
10	Oregon	53.1	35	Kentucky	32.2
11	Ohio	52.1	36	Idaho	31.8
12	South Dakota	51.8	37	Virginia	31.5
13	Oklahoma	48.4	38	Nebraska	31.4
14	Colorado	47.3	39	Rhode Island	30.9
14	Tennessee	47.3	40	New Jersey	30.7
16	Maryland	46.4	41	New York	28.4
17	Utah	45.4	42	Pennsylvania	27.7
18	Georgia	45.3	43	Connecticut	26.9
19	Mississippi	44.6	44	Wisconsin	26.3
20	Arizona	43.0	45	Montana	25.5
21	Indiana	42.4	46	Vermont	24.9
22	Louisiana	42.3	47	Maine	23.8
23	Arkansas	41.3	48	North Dakota	23.3
23	California	41.3	49	West Virginia	21.7
23	Kansas	41.3	50	Iowa	18.8

District of Columbia   36.5

Source: U.S. Department of Justice, Federal Bureau of Investigation

"Crime in the United States 1992" (Uniform Crime Reports, October 3, 1993)

*Forcible rape is the carnal knowledge of a female forcibly and against her will. Assaults or attempts to commit rape by force or threat of force are included. However, statutory rape without force and other sex offenses are excluded.

Percent Change in Rape Rate: 1991 to 1992

National Percent Change = 1.2% Increase*

RANK	STATE	PERCENT CHANGE	RANK	STATE	PERCENT CHANGE
1	Wyoming	35.1	26	Michigan	1.7
2	South Dakota	30.5	27	Arizona	1.4
3	Montana	28.8	28	Maryland	1.1
4	New Hampshire	27.8	29	New York	0.7
5	North Dakota	27.3	30	Colorado	0.6
6	New Mexico	19.5	31	Rhode Island	0.0
7	Alabama	15.7	31	Texas	0.0
8	Hawaii	14.8	33	Utah	(0.4)
9	Massachusetts	12.5	34	Oregon	(0.6)
10	Nebraska	11.7	35	Delaware	(0.8)
11	Idaho	10.0	35	Ohio	(0.8)
12	Maine	8.7	37	South Carolina	(2.4)
13	Alaska	7.4	38	California	(2.6)
13	Missouri	7.4	39	Pennsylvania	(3.5)
15	Georgia	7.1	40	Mississippi	(3.7)
16	New Jersey	5.5	41	Nevada	(4.8)
17	Virginia	5.4	42	Oklahoma	(4.9)
18	Florida	4.8	43	West Virginia	(5.7)
19	North Carolina	3.8	44	Illinois	(7.3)
20	Wisconsin	3.5	45	Arkansas	(7.4)
21	Louisiana	3.4	46	Kansas	(7.8)
22	Minnesota	3.3	47	Connecticut	(7.9)
23	Indiana	2.7	48	Kentucky	(9.0)
24	Washington	2.4	49	Iowa	(10.0)
25	Tennessee	1.9	50	Vermont	(18.4)

District of Columbia   2.0

Source: U.S. Department of Justice, Federal Bureau of Investigation
    "Crime in the United States 1992" (Uniform Crime Reports, October 3, 1993)
*Forcible rape is the carnal knowledge of a female forcibly and against her will. Assaults or attempts to commit rape by force or threat of force are included. However, statutory rape without force and other sex offenses are excluded.

Rape Rate per 100,000 Female Population in 1992

National Rate = 84.41 Rapes per 100,000 Females*

RANK	STATE	RATE	RANK	STATE	RATE
1	Alaska	214.44	26	Arkansas	80.62
2	Delaware	168.86	27	Alabama	80.00
3	Michigan	156.70	28	Hawaii	78.85
4	Washington	146.13	29	New Hampshire	75.18
5	Nevada	132.22	30	Illinois	72.68
6	New Mexico	125.95	31	Wyoming	71.18
7	South Carolina	112.92	32	Missouri	70.92
8	Texas	107.18	33	North Carolina	70.79
9	Florida	106.72	34	Massachusetts	69.53
10	Oregon	106.40	35	Idaho	64.94
11	South Dakota	103.08	36	Kentucky	63.13
12	Ohio	101.29	37	Virginia	62.67
13	Colorado	96.30	38	Nebraska	61.76
14	Oklahoma	95.52	39	New Jersey	59.65
15	Tennessee	92.56	40	Rhode Island	59.58
16	Utah	92.37	41	New York	54.84
17	Maryland	91.05	42	Pennsylvania	53.39
18	Georgia	89.73	43	Connecticut	52.12
19	Arizona	86.78	44	Wisconsin	52.00
20	Mississippi	86.24	45	Montana	51.47
21	California	84.11	46	Vermont	49.13
22	Indiana	83.00	47	North Dakota	46.54
23	Louisiana	82.26	48	Maine	46.45
24	Kansas	82.05	49	West Virginia	42.03
25	Minnesota	81.52	50	Iowa	36.67

District of Columbia   67.40

Source: Morgan Quitno Corporation using data from U.S. Department of Justice, Federal Bureau of Investigation
"Crime in the United States 1992" (Uniform Crime Reports, October 3, 1993)
Rate was determined using 1991 female population figures. Forcible rape is the carnal knowledge of a female forcibly and against her will. Assaults or attempts to commit rape by force or threat of force are included. However, statutory rape without force and other sex offenses are excluded.

Robberies in 1992

National Total = 672,478 Robberies*

RANK	STATE	ROBBERIES	%
1	California	130,897	19.46%
2	New York	108,154	16.08%
3	Florida	49,482	7.36%
4	Illinois	47,973	7.13%
5	Texas	44,588	6.63%
6	New Jersey	22,216	3.30%
7	Ohio	21,925	3.26%
8	Pennsylvania	21,701	3.23%
9	Maryland	21,054	3.13%
10	Michigan	20,902	3.11%
11	Georgia	16,863	2.51%
12	North Carolina	12,784	1.90%
13	Missouri	11,783	1.75%
14	Louisiana	11,636	1.73%
15	Massachusetts	11,059	1.64%
16	Tennessee	10,964	1.63%
17	Virginia	8,787	1.31%
18	Washington	7,178	1.07%
19	Indiana	6,921	1.03%
20	Connecticut	6,918	1.03%
21	Alabama	6,819	1.01%
22	South Carolina	6,148	0.91%
23	Wisconsin	5,997	0.89%
24	Arizona	5,867	0.87%
25	Minnesota	4,906	0.73%

RANK	STATE	ROBBERIES	%
26	Oregon	4,507	0.67%
27	Nevada	4,397	0.65%
28	Oklahoma	4,376	0.65%
29	Colorado	4,180	0.62%
30	Kansas	3,277	0.49%
31	Kentucky	3,273	0.49%
32	Mississippi	3,254	0.48%
33	Arkansas	3,011	0.45%
34	New Mexico	2,202	0.33%
35	Hawaii	1,151	0.17%
36	Iowa	1,113	0.17%
37	Delaware	1,042	0.15%
38	Utah	1,014	0.15%
39	Rhode Island	950	0.14%
40	Nebraska	911	0.14%
41	West Virginia	788	0.12%
42	Alaska	640	0.10%
43	New Hampshire	367	0.05%
44	Maine	288	0.04%
45	Idaho	229	0.03%
46	Montana	222	0.03%
47	South Dakota	120	0.02%
48	Wyoming	84	0.01%
49	Vermont	51	0.01%
50	North Dakota	50	0.01%
	District of Columbia	7,459	1.11%

Source: U.S. Department of Justice, Federal Bureau of Investigation
    "Crime in the United States 1992" (Uniform Crime Reports, October 3, 1993)
*Robbery is the taking of anything of value by force or threat of force. Attempts are included.

Average Time Between Robberies in 1992

National Rate = A Robbery Occurs Every 47 Seconds*

RANK	STATE	HOURS.MINUTES
1	North Dakota	175.41
2	Vermont	172.14
3	Wyoming	104.34
4	South Dakota	73.12
5	Montana	39.34
6	Idaho	38.22
7	Maine	30.30
8	New Hampshire	23.56
9	Alaska	13.44
10	West Virginia	11.09
11	Nebraska	9.38
12	Rhode Island	9.15
13	Utah	8.40
14	Delaware	8.26
15	Iowa	7.53
16	Hawaii	7.38
17	New Mexico	3.59
18	Arkansas	2.55
19	Mississippi	2.42
20	Kansas	2.41
20	Kentucky	2.41
22	Colorado	2.06
23	Oklahoma	2.01
24	Nevada	2.00
25	Oregon	1.57

RANK	STATE	HOURS.MINUTES
26	Minnesota	1.47
27	Arizona	1.30
28	Wisconsin	1.28
29	South Carolina	1.26
30	Alabama	1.17
31	Connecticut	1.16
31	Indiana	1.16
33	Washington	1.13
34	Virginia	1.00
35	Tennessee	0.48
36	Massachusetts	0.47
37	Louisiana	0.45
37	Missouri	0.45
39	North Carolina	0.41
40	Georgia	0.31
41	Maryland	0.25
41	Michigan	0.25
43	New Jersey	0.24
43	Ohio	0.24
43	Pennsylvania	0.24
46	Texas	0.12
47	Florida	0.11
47	Illinois	0.11
49	New York	0.05
50	California	0.04

District of Columbia   1.11

Source: Morgan Quitno Corporation using data from U.S. Department of Justice, Federal Bureau of Investigation
"Crime in the United States 1992" (Uniform Crime Reports, October 3, 1993)
*Robbery is the taking of anything of value by force or threat of force. Attempts are included.

Percent Change in Number of Robberies: 1991 to 1992

National Percent Change = 2.2% Decrease*

RANK	STATE	PERCENT CHANGE	RANK	STATE	PERCENT CHANGE
1	Montana	48.0	26	New Hampshire	0.5
2	New Mexico	18.3	27	Alaska	(0.8)
3	Hawaii	16.7	28	Washington	(1.7)
4	Colorado	15.2	29	Louisiana	(1.9)
5	Minnesota	12.9	30	North Dakota	(2.0)
6	Nevada	9.6	31	New Jersey	(2.3)
7	Alabama	9.2	32	New York	(3.7)
8	Mississippi	7.9	33	Georgia	(5.1)
9	Oklahoma	6.9	33	Kansas	(5.1)
10	North Carolina	6.6	35	Massachusetts	(5.2)
11	Idaho	6.5	36	Arizona	(5.6)
12	Indiana	6.4	37	Connecticut	(6.3)
12	Maryland	6.4	38	Arkansas	(6.4)
14	Wyoming	6.3	38	Pennsylvania	(6.4)
15	Kentucky	6.1	40	Florida	(6.8)
16	Nebraska	5.8	40	Ohio	(6.8)
17	California	4.8	42	Michigan	(8.3)
18	Tennessee	4.0	43	Illinois	(8.9)
19	Utah	3.9	44	Missouri	(9.0)
20	Maine	2.9	45	South Dakota	(9.1)
21	Oregon	2.7	46	Texas	(10.3)
22	Wisconsin	1.7	47	Iowa	(11.5)
23	Virginia	1.6	48	Rhode Island	(23.0)
24	West Virginia	1.2	49	Vermont	(23.9)
25	South Carolina	0.9	50	Delaware	(28.6)
				District of Columbia	2.6

Source: U.S. Department of Justice, Federal Bureau of Investigation
"Crime in the United States 1992" (Uniform Crime Reports, October 3, 1993)
*Robbery is the taking of anything of value by force or threat of force. Attempts are included.

Robbery Rate in 1992

National Rate = 263.6 Robberies per 100,000 Population*

RANK	STATE	RATE	RANK	STATE	RATE
1	New York	596.9	26	Virginia	137.8
2	Maryland	429.0	27	Oklahoma	136.2
3	California	424.1	28	Kansas	129.9
4	Illinois	412.5	29	Arkansas	125.5
5	Florida	366.9	30	Mississippi	124.5
6	Nevada	331.3	31	Indiana	122.2
7	New Jersey	285.2	32	Colorado	120.5
8	Louisiana	271.4	33	Wisconsin	119.8
9	Texas	252.5	34	Minnesota	109.5
10	Georgia	249.8	35	Alaska	109.0
11	Missouri	226.9	36	Hawaii	99.2
12	Michigan	221.5	37	Rhode Island	94.5
13	Tennessee	218.2	38	Kentucky	87.2
14	Connecticut	210.9	39	Nebraska	56.7
15	Ohio	199.0	40	Utah	55.9
16	North Carolina	186.8	41	West Virginia	43.5
17	Massachusetts	184.4	42	Iowa	39.6
18	Pennsylvania	180.7	43	New Hampshire	33.0
19	South Carolina	170.6	44	Montana	26.9
20	Alabama	164.9	45	Maine	23.3
21	Arizona	153.1	46	Idaho	21.5
22	Oregon	151.4	47	Wyoming	18.0
23	Delaware	151.2	48	South Dakota	16.9
24	Washington	139.8	49	Vermont	8.9
25	New Mexico	139.3	50	North Dakota	7.9

District of Columbia   1,266.4

Source: U.S. Department of Justice, Federal Bureau of Investigation
     "Crime in the United States 1992" (Uniform Crime Reports, October 3, 1993)
*Robbery is the taking of anything of value by force or threat of force. Attempts are included.

Percent Change in Robbery Rate: 1991 to 1992

National Percent Change = 3.3% Decrease*

RANK	STATE	PERCENT CHANGE	RANK	STATE	PERCENT CHANGE
1	Montana	44.6	26	South Carolina	(0.3)
2	New Mexico	15.8	27	North Dakota	(1.3)
3	Hawaii	14.2	28	Louisiana	(2.7)
4	Colorado	12.2	28	New Jersey	(2.7)
5	Minnesota	11.7	30	Alaska	(3.7)
6	Alabama	7.9	31	Washington	(3.9)
7	Mississippi	7.1	32	New York	(4.1)
8	Nevada	6.0	33	Massachusetts	(5.2)
9	Oklahoma	5.7	34	Connecticut	(6.0)
10	Maryland	5.4	35	Kansas	(6.1)
11	Indiana	5.3	36	Pennsylvania	(6.8)
12	Nebraska	5.0	37	Georgia	(6.9)
13	Kentucky	4.9	38	Arkansas	(7.4)
13	North Carolina	4.9	39	Ohio	(7.5)
15	Wyoming	4.7	40	Arizona	(7.6)
16	Idaho	3.9	41	Florida	(8.2)
17	California	3.1	42	Michigan	(9.0)
18	Maine	2.6	43	Illinois	(9.6)
19	Tennessee	2.5	43	Missouri	(9.6)
20	Utah	1.5	45	South Dakota	(10.1)
21	Oregon	0.9	46	Texas	(11.9)
22	Wisconsin	0.7	47	Iowa	(12.0)
23	West Virginia	0.5	48	Rhode Island	(23.1)
24	Virginia	0.1	49	Vermont	(24.6)
25	New Hampshire	0.0	50	Delaware	(29.6)

District of Columbia   4.2

Source: U.S. Department of Justice, Federal Bureau of Investigation
   "Crime in the United States 1992" (Uniform Crime Reports, October 3, 1993)
*Robbery is the taking of anything of value by force or threat of force. Attempts are included.

Robberies with Firearms in 1992

National Total = 260,289 Robberies with Firearms*

RANK	STATE	ROBBERIES	%	RANK	STATE	ROBBERIES	%
1	California	50,119	19.26%	26	Oregon	1,405	0.54%
2	New York	39,276	15.09%	27	Kansas	1,379	0.53%
3	Texas	20,068	7.71%	28	Arkansas	1,365	0.52%
4	Illinois	19,881	7.64%	29	Colorado	1,271	0.49%
5	Florida	17,986	6.91%	30	Mississippi	1,140	0.44%
6	Maryland	11,620	4.46%	31	Minnesota	1,136	0.44%
7	Michigan	9,767	3.75%	32	New Mexico	880	0.34%
8	Pennsylvania	8,127	3.12%	33	West Virginia	307	0.12%
9	Georgia	7,927	3.05%	34	Utah	289	0.11%
10	Ohio	7,881	3.03%	35	Rhode Island	234	0.09%
11	New Jersey	6,935	2.66%	36	Alaska	211	0.08%
12	Louisiana	6,580	2.53%	37	Hawaii	115	0.04%
13	Tennessee	5,574	2.14%	38	Iowa	111	0.04%
14	Missouri	5,246	2.02%	39	Nebraska	90	0.03%
15	North Carolina	5,075	1.95%	40	New Hampshire	79	0.03%
16	Virginia	4,002	1.54%	41	Maine	59	0.02%
17	Wisconsin	3,142	1.21%	42	Idaho	57	0.02%
18	Connecticut	2,743	1.05%	43	Delaware	50	0.02%
19	Massachusetts	2,377	0.91%	44	Montana	38	0.01%
20	Washington	2,262	0.87%	45	South Dakota	31	0.01%
21	Indiana	2,229	0.86%	46	Wyoming	25	0.01%
22	Arizona	2,063	0.79%	47	Vermont	12	0.00%
23	South Carolina	2,048	0.79%	48	North Dakota	9	0.00%
24	Nevada	1,898	0.73%	–	Alabama**	N/A	N/A
25	Oklahoma	1,737	0.67%	–	Kentucky**	N/A	N/A

District of Columbia 3,433 1.32%

Source: U.S. Department of Justice, Federal Bureau of Investigation

"Crime in the United States 1992" (Uniform Crime Reports, October 3, 1993)

*Of the 643,431 robberies in 1992 for which supplemental data were received by the F.B.I. There were an additional 29,047 robberies for which the type of weapon was not reported to the F.B.I. Robbery is the taking or attempting to take anything of value by force or threat of force.

**Not available.

Robbery Rate with Firearms in 1992

National Rate = 102.0 Robberies per 100,000 Population*

RANK	STATE	RATE		RANK	STATE	RATE
1	Maryland	236.8		26	Oregon	47.2
2	New York	216.8		27	Washington	44.0
3	Illinois	170.9		28	Mississippi	43.6
4	California	162.4		29	Massachusetts	39.6
5	Louisiana	153.5		30	Indiana	39.4
6	Nevada	143.0		31	Colorado	36.6
7	Florida	133.3		32	Alaska	35.9
8	Georgia	117.4		33	Minnesota	25.4
9	Texas	113.7		34	Rhode Island	23.3
10	Tennessee	110.9		35	West Virginia	16.9
11	Michigan	103.5		36	Utah	15.9
12	Missouri	101.0		37	Hawaii	9.9
13	New Jersey	89.0		38	Delaware	7.3
14	Connecticut	83.6		39	New Hampshire	7.1
15	North Carolina	74.2		40	Nebraska	5.6
16	Ohio	71.5		41	Wyoming	5.4
17	Pennsylvania	67.7		42	Idaho	5.3
18	Virginia	62.8		43	Maine	4.8
18	Wisconsin	62.8		44	Montana	4.6
20	Arkansas	56.9		45	South Dakota	4.4
21	South Carolina	56.8		46	Iowa	3.9
22	New Mexico	55.7		47	Vermont	2.1
23	Kansas	54.7		48	North Dakota	1.4
24	Oklahoma	54.1		–	Alabama**	N/A
25	Arizona	53.8		–	Kentucky**	N/A

District of Columbia   582.9

Source: Morgan Quitno Corporation using data from U.S. Department of Justice, Federal Bureau of Investigation
   "Crime in the United States 1992" (Uniform Crime Reports, October 3, 1993)
*Of the 643,431 robberies in 1992 for which supplemental data were received by the F.B.I. There were an additional 29,047 robberies for which the type of weapon was not reported to the F.B.I. Robbery is the taking or attempting to take anything of value by force or threat of force.
**Not available.

Percent of Robberies Involving Firearms in 1992

National Rate = 40.45% of Robberies*

RANK	STATE	PERCENT		RANK	STATE	PERCENT
1	Louisiana	60.62		26	South Carolina	36.30
2	Maryland	55.24		27	Arizona	35.92
3	Tennessee	52.98		28	Alaska	33.92
4	Wisconsin	52.91		29	Nebraska	33.33
5	Mississippi	51.75		30	Vermont	32.43
6	Georgia	49.44		31	Washington	31.85
7	New Mexico	47.77		32	Colorado	31.48
8	Michigan	47.40		33	Oregon	31.44
9	Missouri	46.26		34	New Jersey	31.22
10	Virginia	45.54		35	Wyoming	30.49
11	Arkansas	45.45		36	Utah	29.31
12	Texas	45.02		37	Idaho	28.64
13	Nevada	44.33		38	South Dakota	27.43
14	Illinois	42.65		39	Montana	25.33
15	Kansas	42.37		40	Delaware	24.63
16	Indiana	40.59		40	Rhode Island	24.63
17	North Carolina	40.40		42	Massachusetts	24.28
18	Oklahoma	39.76		43	Minnesota	23.19
19	Connecticut	39.65		44	New Hampshire	22.57
19	Pennsylvania	39.65		45	Maine	21.69
21	West Virginia	39.01		46	North Dakota	19.57
22	Ohio	39.00		47	Iowa	19.10
23	California	38.30		48	Hawaii	9.99
24	Florida	37.34		–	Alabama**	N/A
25	New York	37.29		–	Kentucky**	N/A

District of Columbia   46.02

Source: Morgan Quitno Corporation using data from U.S. Department of Justice, Federal Bureau of Investigation
    "Crime in the United States 1992" (Uniform Crime Reports, October 3, 1993)
*Of the 643,431 robberies in 1992 for which supplemental data were received by the F.B.I. There were an additional 29,047 robberies for which the type of weapon was not reported to the F.B.I. Robbery is the taking or attempting to take anything of value by force or threat of force.
**Not available.

Robberies with Knives or Cutting Instruments in 1992

National Total = 67,373 Robberies with Knives or Cutting Instruments*

RANK	STATE	ROBBERIES	%	RANK	STATE	ROBBERIES	%
1	New York	16,014	23.77%	26	Minnesota	468	0.69%
2	California	14,120	20.96%	27	Nevada	379	0.56%
3	Texas	4,752	7.05%	28	Oklahoma	376	0.56%
4	Illinois	4,366	6.48%	29	Kansas	280	0.42%
5	Florida	3,395	5.04%	30	Arkansas	267	0.40%
6	New Jersey	2,510	3.73%	31	New Mexico	219	0.33%
7	Massachusetts	2,133	3.17%	32	Mississippi	160	0.24%
8	Pennsylvania	1,884	2.80%	33	Rhode Island	153	0.23%
9	Michigan	1,595	2.37%	34	Utah	94	0.14%
10	Maryland	1,499	2.22%	35	Alaska	72	0.11%
11	Ohio	1,335	1.98%	36	Hawaii	69	0.10%
12	North Carolina	1,136	1.69%	37	West Virginia	59	0.09%
13	Georgia	1,090	1.62%	38	Iowa	53	0.08%
14	Missouri	851	1.26%	39	New Hampshire	48	0.07%
15	Tennessee	835	1.24%	40	Idaho	32	0.05%
16	Virginia	768	1.14%	41	Nebraska	27	0.04%
17	Connecticut	762	1.13%	42	Maine	25	0.04%
18	Washington	743	1.10%	43	South Dakota	24	0.04%
19	Louisiana	721	1.07%	44	Delaware	23	0.03%
20	Arizona	616	0.91%	45	Montana	14	0.02%
21	South Carolina	613	0.91%	46	Wyoming	10	0.01%
22	Oregon	589	0.87%	47	North Dakota	8	0.01%
23	Indiana	520	0.77%	48	Vermont	6	0.01%
24	Colorado	484	0.72%	–	Alabama**	N/A	N/A
25	Wisconsin	481	0.71%	–	Kentucky**	N/A	N/A

District of Columbia   695   1.03%

Source: U.S. Department of Justice, Federal Bureau of Investigation

    "Crime in the United States 1992" (Uniform Crime Reports, October 3, 1993)

*Of the 643,431 robberies in 1992 for which supplemental data were received by the F.B.I. There were an additional 29,047 robberies for which the type of weapon was not reported to the F.B.I. Robbery is the taking or attempting to take anything of value by force or threat of force. **Not available.

Percent of Robberies Involving Knives or Cutting Instruments in 1992

National Rate = 10.47% of Robberies*

RANK	STATE	PERCENT		RANK	STATE	PERCENT
1	Massachusetts	21.79		26	Illinois	9.37
2	South Dakota	21.24		27	Montana	9.33
3	North Dakota	17.39		28	Maine	9.19
4	Vermont	16.22		28	Pennsylvania	9.19
5	Rhode Island	16.11		30	Iowa	9.12
6	Idaho	16.08		31	North Carolina	9.04
7	New York	15.20		32	Arkansas	8.89
8	New Hampshire	13.71		33	Nevada	8.85
9	Oregon	13.18		34	Virginia	8.74
10	Wyoming	12.20		35	Oklahoma	8.61
11	Colorado	11.99		36	Kansas	8.60
12	New Mexico	11.89		37	Wisconsin	8.10
13	Alaska	11.58		38	Tennessee	7.94
14	Delaware	11.33		39	Michigan	7.74
15	New Jersey	11.30		40	Missouri	7.50
16	Connecticut	11.01		40	West Virginia	7.50
17	South Carolina	10.86		42	Mississippi	7.26
18	California	10.79		43	Maryland	7.13
19	Arizona	10.72		44	Florida	7.05
20	Texas	10.66		45	Georgia	6.80
21	Washington	10.46		46	Louisiana	6.64
22	Nebraska	10.00		47	Ohio	6.61
23	Minnesota	9.55		48	Hawaii	5.99
24	Utah	9.53		–	Alabama**	N/A
25	Indiana	9.47		–	Kentucky**	N/A

District of Columbia   9.32

Source: Morgan Quitno Corporation using data from U.S. Department of Justice, Federal Bureau of Investigation
    "Crime in the United States 1992" (Uniform Crime Reports, October 3, 1993)
*Of the 643,431 robberies in 1992 for which supplemental data were received by the F.B.I. There were an additional 29,047 robberies for which the type of weapon was not reported to the F.B.I. Robbery is the taking or attempting to take anything of value by force or threat of force.
**Not available.

Robberies with Blunt Objects and Other Dangerous Weapons in 1992

National Total = 60,870 Robberies with Blunt Objects and Other Dangerous Weapons*

RANK	STATE	ROBBERIES	%	RANK	STATE	ROBBERIES	%
1	California	15,899	26.12%	26	Indiana	323	0.53%
2	New York	9,846	16.18%	27	Oklahoma	277	0.46%
3	Texas	4,386	7.21%	28	Wisconsin	267	0.44%
4	Florida	3,601	5.92%	29	Arkansas	243	0.40%
5	Illinois	3,387	5.56%	30	Nevada	180	0.30%
6	Michigan	3,329	5.47%	31	New Mexico	172	0.28%
7	Georgia	2,291	3.76%	32	Utah	141	0.23%
8	Ohio	2,044	3.36%	33	Mississippi	135	0.22%
9	New Jersey	1,790	2.94%	34	Iowa	77	0.13%
10	Pennsylvania	1,275	2.09%	35	Rhode Island	54	0.09%
11	Maryland	1,230	2.02%	36	West Virginia	47	0.08%
12	North Carolina	1,194	1.96%	37	Alaska	39	0.06%
13	Massachusetts	973	1.60%	38	Hawaii	26	0.04%
14	Missouri	880	1.45%	39	Nebraska	25	0.04%
15	Louisiana	861	1.41%	40	New Hampshire	23	0.04%
16	Virginia	662	1.09%	40	North Dakota	23	0.04%
17	Tennessee	639	1.05%	42	Idaho	20	0.03%
18	South Carolina	604	0.99%	42	Montana	20	0.03%
19	Washington	560	0.92%	44	Maine	17	0.03%
20	Arizona	556	0.91%	45	South Dakota	9	0.01%
21	Colorado	506	0.83%	46	Delaware	6	0.01%
22	Connecticut	491	0.81%	47	Wyoming	5	0.01%
23	Kansas	482	0.79%	48	Vermont	0	0.00%
24	Minnesota	411	0.68%	–	Alabama**	N/A	N/A
25	Oregon	371	0.61%	–	Kentucky**	N/A	N/A

District of Columbia 473 0.78%

Source: U.S. Department of Justice, Federal Bureau of Investigation
    "Crime in the United States 1992" (Uniform Crime Reports, October 3, 1993)
*Of the 643,431 robberies in 1992 for which supplemental data were received by the F.B.I. There were an additional 29,047 robberies for which the type of weapon was not reported to the F.B.I. Robbery is the taking or attempting to take anything of value by force or threat of force.
**Not available.

Percent of Robberies Involving Blunt Objects and Other Dangerous Objects in 1992

National Rate = 9.46% of Robberies*

RANK	STATE	PERCENT		RANK	STATE	PERCENT
1	North Dakota	50.00		26	Washington	7.88
2	Michigan	16.16		27	Missouri	7.76
3	Kansas	14.81		28	Virginia	7.53
4	Utah	14.30		29	Florida	7.48
5	Georgia	14.29		30	Illinois	7.27
6	Montana	13.33		31	Connecticut	7.10
7	Iowa	13.25		32	New Hampshire	6.57
8	Colorado	12.53		33	Oklahoma	6.34
9	California	12.15		34	Alaska	6.27
10	South Carolina	10.71		35	Maine	6.25
11	Ohio	10.11		36	Pennsylvania	6.22
12	Idaho	10.05		37	Mississippi	6.13
13	Massachusetts	9.94		38	Wyoming	6.10
14	Texas	9.84		39	Tennessee	6.07
15	Arizona	9.68		40	West Virginia	5.97
16	North Carolina	9.50		41	Indiana	5.88
17	New York	9.35		42	Maryland	5.85
18	New Mexico	9.34		43	Rhode Island	5.68
19	Nebraska	9.26		44	Wisconsin	4.50
20	Minnesota	8.39		45	Nevada	4.20
21	Oregon	8.30		46	Delaware	2.96
22	Arkansas	8.09		47	Hawaii	2.26
23	New Jersey	8.06		48	Vermont	0.00
24	South Dakota	7.96		–	Alabama**	N/A
25	Louisiana	7.93		–	Kentucky**	N/A

District of Columbia   6.34

Source: Morgan Quitno Corporation using data from U.S. Department of Justice, Federal Bureau of Investigation
     "Crime in the United States 1992" (Uniform Crime Reports, October 3, 1993)
*Of the 643,431 robberies in 1992 for which supplemental data were received by the F.B.I. There were an additional 29,047 robberies for which the type of weapon was not reported to the F.B.I. Robbery is the taking or attempting to take anything of value by force or threat of force.
**Not available.

Robberies Using Hands, Fists or Feet in 1992

National Total = 254,899 Robberies Using Hands, Fists or Feet*

RANK	STATE	ROBBERIES	%	RANK	STATE	ROBBERIES	%
1	California	50,704	19.89%	26	Oklahoma	1,979	0.78%
2	New York	40,187	15.77%	27	Nevada	1,825	0.72%
3	Florida	23,187	9.10%	28	Colorado	1,776	0.70%
4	Illinois	18,985	7.45%	29	Arkansas	1,128	0.44%
5	Texas	15,372	6.03%	30	Kansas	1,114	0.44%
6	New Jersey	10,980	4.31%	31	Hawaii	941	0.37%
7	Pennsylvania	9,210	3.61%	32	Mississippi	768	0.30%
8	Ohio	8,950	3.51%	33	New Mexico	571	0.22%
9	Maryland	6,686	2.62%	34	Rhode Island	509	0.20%
10	Michigan	5,914	2.32%	35	Utah	462	0.18%
11	North Carolina	5,158	2.02%	36	West Virginia	374	0.15%
12	Georgia	4,725	1.85%	37	Iowa	340	0.13%
13	Missouri	4,363	1.71%	38	Alaska	300	0.12%
14	Massachusetts	4,306	1.69%	39	New Hampshire	200	0.08%
15	Washington	3,538	1.39%	40	Maine	171	0.07%
16	Tennessee	3,472	1.36%	41	Nebraska	128	0.05%
17	Virginia	3,355	1.32%	42	Delaware	124	0.05%
18	Connecticut	2,922	1.15%	43	Idaho	90	0.04%
19	Minnesota	2,883	1.13%	44	Montana	78	0.03%
20	Louisiana	2,692	1.06%	45	South Dakota	49	0.02%
21	Arizona	2,509	0.98%	46	Wyoming	42	0.02%
22	Indiana	2,420	0.95%	47	Vermont	19	0.01%
23	South Carolina	2,377	0.93%	48	North Dakota	6	0.00%
24	Oregon	2,104	0.83%	–	Alabama**	N/A	N/A
25	Wisconsin	2,048	0.80%	–	Kentucky**	N/A	N/A

	District of Columbia	2,858	1.12%

Source: U.S. Department of Justice, Federal Bureau of Investigation
   "Crime in the United States 1992" (Uniform Crime Reports, October 3, 1993)

*Of the 643,431 robberies in 1992 for which supplemental data were received by the F.B.I. There were an additional 29,047 robberies for which the type of weapon was not reported to the F.B.I. Robbery is the taking or attempting to take anything of value by force or threat of force.

**Not available.

Percent of Robberies Using Hands, Fists or Feet in 1992

National Rate = 39.62% of Robberies*

RANK	STATE	PERCENT	RANK	STATE	PERCENT
1	Hawaii	81.75	26	Arizona	43.68
2	Maine	62.87	27	South Dakota	43.36
3	Delaware	61.08	28	Nevada	42.62
4	Minnesota	58.86	29	Connecticut	42.24
5	Iowa	58.52	30	South Carolina	42.13
6	New Hampshire	57.14	31	North Carolina	41.06
7	Rhode Island	53.58	32	Illinois	40.72
8	Montana	52.00	33	California	38.75
9	Vermont	51.35	34	Missouri	38.47
10	Wyoming	51.22	35	Virginia	38.18
11	Washington	49.81	36	New York	38.16
12	New Jersey	49.43	37	Arkansas	37.56
13	Alaska	48.23	38	Mississippi	34.86
14	Florida	48.14	39	Wisconsin	34.49
15	West Virginia	47.52	40	Texas	34.48
16	Nebraska	47.41	41	Kansas	34.22
17	Oregon	47.08	42	Tennessee	33.00
18	Utah	46.86	43	Maryland	31.79
19	Oklahoma	45.30	44	New Mexico	31.00
20	Idaho	45.23	45	Georgia	29.47
21	Pennsylvania	44.94	46	Michigan	28.70
22	Ohio	44.29	47	Louisiana	24.80
23	Indiana	44.06	48	North Dakota	13.04
24	Colorado	43.99	–	Alabama**	N/A
24	Massachusetts	43.99	–	Kentucky**	N/A

District of Columbia   38.32

Source: Morgan Quitno Corporation using data from U.S. Department of Justice, Federal Bureau of Investigation
"Crime in the United States 1992" (Uniform Crime Reports, October 3, 1993)
*Of the 643,431 robberies in 1992 for which supplemental data were received by the F.B.I. There were an additional 29,047 robberies for which the type of weapon was not reported to the F.B.I. Robbery is the taking or attempting to take anything of value by force or threat of force.
**Not available.

Aggravated Assaults in 1992

National Total = 1,126,974 Aggravated Assaults*

RANK	STATE	ASSAULTS	%	RANK	STATE	ASSAULTS	%
1	California	198,045	17.57%	26	New Mexico	11,448	1.02%
2	Florida	104,827	9.30%	27	Arkansas	9,571	0.85%
3	New York	87,608	7.77%	28	Oregon	8,963	0.80%
4	Texas	86,105	7.64%	29	Kansas	8,418	0.75%
5	Illinois	60,057	5.33%	30	Connecticut	8,284	0.74%
6	Michigan	43,282	3.84%	31	Minnesota	8,248	0.73%
7	Massachusetts	33,288	2.95%	32	Wisconsin	6,276	0.56%
8	North Carolina	30,638	2.72%	33	Iowa	6,131	0.54%
9	Ohio	29,547	2.62%	34	Mississippi	6,023	0.53%
10	Georgia	28,835	2.56%	35	Nebraska	4,115	0.37%
11	Louisiana	28,013	2.49%	36	Nevada	3,872	0.34%
12	Alabama	27,074	2.40%	37	Utah	3,376	0.30%
13	Pennsylvania	25,505	2.26%	38	Rhode Island	2,668	0.24%
14	South Carolina	25,436	2.26%	39	Delaware	2,615	0.23%
15	Maryland	25,157	2.23%	40	Alaska	2,614	0.23%
16	Missouri	24,223	2.15%	41	West Virginia	2,537	0.23%
17	New Jersey	23,740	2.11%	42	Idaho	2,398	0.21%
18	Tennessee	23,626	2.10%	43	Hawaii	1,365	0.12%
19	Indiana	19,008	1.69%	44	Wyoming	1,225	0.11%
20	Arizona	17,880	1.59%	45	Maine	1,013	0.09%
21	Washington	16,321	1.45%	46	Montana	944	0.08%
22	Kentucky	15,409	1.37%	47	South Dakota	891	0.08%
23	Colorado	14,049	1.25%	48	New Hampshire	588	0.05%
24	Oklahoma	13,863	1.23%	49	Vermont	419	0.04%
25	Virginia	12,548	1.11%	50	North Dakota	320	0.03%
					District of Columbia	8,568	0.76%

Source: U.S. Department of Justice, Federal Bureau of Investigation
  "Crime in the United States 1992" (Uniform Crime Reports, October 3, 1993)
*Aggravated assault is an attack for the purpose of inflicting severe bodily injury.

Average Time Between Aggravated Assaults in 1992

National Rate = An Aggravated Assault Occurs Every 28 Seconds*

RANK	STATE	MINUTES.SECONDS	RANK	STATE	MINUTES.SECONDS
1	North Dakota	1,647.00	26	Virginia	42.00
2	Vermont	1,257.51	27	Oklahoma	38.01
3	New Hampshire	896.20	28	Colorado	37.31
4	South Dakota	591.31	29	Kentucky	34.12
5	Montana	558.19	30	Washington	32.17
6	Maine	520.17	31	Arizona	29.29
7	Wyoming	430.14	32	Indiana	27.44
8	Hawaii	386.07	33	Tennessee	22.19
9	Idaho	219.47	34	New Jersey	22.12
10	West Virginia	207.44	35	Missouri	21.46
11	Alaska	201.37	36	Maryland	20.57
12	Delaware	201.33	37	South Carolina	20.43
13	Rhode Island	197.32	38	Pennsylvania	20.40
14	Utah	156.07	39	Alabama	19.28
15	Nevada	136.07	40	Louisiana	18.49
16	Nebraska	128.05	41	Georgia	18.17
17	Mississippi	87.30	42	Ohio	17.50
18	Iowa	85.58	43	North Carolina	17.12
19	Wisconsin	83.59	44	Massachusetts	15.50
20	Minnesota	63.54	45	Michigan	12.11
21	Connecticut	63.37	46	Illinois	8.47
22	Kansas	62.37	47	Texas	6.07
23	Oregon	58.48	48	New York	6.01
24	Arkansas	55.04	49	Florida	5.02
25	New Mexico	46.02	50	California	2.40

District of Columbia   61.31

Source: Morgan Quitno Corporation using data from U.S. Department of Justice, Federal Bureau of Investigation
"Crime in the United States 1992" (Uniform Crime Reports, October 3, 1993)
*Aggravated assault is an attack for the purpose of inflicting severe bodily injury.

Percent Change in Number of Aggravated Assaults: 1991 to 1992

National Percent Change = 3.1% Increase*

RANK	STATE	PERCENT CHANGE	RANK	STATE	PERCENT CHANGE
1	North Dakota	32.8	26	Oregon	2.9
2	Kentucky	32.7	27	Alabama	2.8
3	West Virginia	18.8	28	Texas	2.4
4	Montana	18.1	29	Vermont	2.2
5	Alaska	14.2	30	Hawaii	2.0
6	New Mexico	13.5	31	Virginia	1.6
7	Oklahoma	10.1	32	New Hampshire	0.9
8	Massachusetts	9.9	32	Wyoming	0.9
9	Florida	9.1	34	Missouri	0.5
10	Kansas	8.7	35	Arkansas	0.4
10	Mississippi	8.7	36	Indiana	(0.5)
12	Washington	7.5	36	New Jersey	(0.5)
13	Louisiana	7.2	38	Wisconsin	(0.9)
14	Minnesota	6.2	39	Michigan	(1.8)
15	Maryland	5.3	40	Illinois	(2.2)
16	Nevada	5.2	41	South Carolina	(2.3)
17	Georgia	4.9	42	New York	(2.9)
18	Arizona	4.8	43	Idaho	(3.4)
19	North Carolina	4.7	44	Pennsylvania	(3.5)
19	Tennessee	4.7	45	Maine	(5.0)
21	California	4.5	46	Delaware	(5.7)
22	Colorado	4.3	47	Ohio	(5.9)
23	Utah	4.2	48	Iowa	(6.8)
24	South Dakota	3.8	49	Connecticut	(10.2)
25	Nebraska	3.7	50	Rhode Island	(12.7)
				District of Columbia	27.8

Source: U.S. Department of Justice, Federal Bureau of Investigation
"Crime in the United States 1992" (Uniform Crime Reports, October 3, 1993)
*Aggravated assault is an attack for the purpose of inflicting severe bodily injury.

Aggravated Assault Rate in 1992

National Rate = 441.8 Aggravated Assaults per 100,000 Population*

RANK	STATE	RATE		RANK	STATE	RATE
1	Florida	777.2		26	Washington	317.8
2	New Mexico	724.1		27	New Jersey	304.8
3	South Carolina	706.0		28	Oregon	301.1
4	Alabama	654.6		29	Nevada	291.8
5	Louisiana	653.4		30	Ohio	268.2
6	California	641.6		31	Rhode Island	265.5
7	Massachusetts	555.0		32	Wyoming	262.9
8	Illinois	516.4		33	Nebraska	256.2
9	Maryland	512.6		34	Connecticut	252.5
10	Texas	487.7		35	Mississippi	230.4
11	New York	483.5		36	Idaho	224.7
12	Tennessee	470.3		37	Iowa	218.0
13	Arizona	466.6		38	Pennsylvania	212.4
14	Missouri	466.5		39	Virginia	196.8
15	Michigan	458.6		40	Utah	186.2
16	North Carolina	447.7		41	Minnesota	184.1
17	Alaska	445.3		42	West Virginia	140.0
18	Oklahoma	431.6		43	South Dakota	125.3
19	Georgia	427.1		43	Wisconsin	125.3
20	Kentucky	410.4		45	Hawaii	117.7
21	Colorado	404.9		46	Montana	114.6
22	Arkansas	399.0		47	Maine	82.0
23	Delaware	379.5		48	Vermont	73.5
24	Indiana	335.7		49	New Hampshire	52.9
25	Kansas	333.7		50	North Dakota	50.3

District of Columbia   1,454.7

Source: U.S. Department of Justice, Federal Bureau of Investigation
  "Crime in the United States 1992" (Uniform Crime Reports, October 3, 1993)
*Aggravated assault is an attack for the purpose of inflicting severe bodily injury.

Percent Change in Rate of Aggravated Assaults: 1991 to 1992

National Percent Change = 2.0% Increase*

RANK	STATE	PERCENT CHANGE	RANK	STATE	PERCENT CHANGE
1	North Dakota	32.4	26	Alabama	1.6
2	Kentucky	31.2	27	Colorado	1.5
3	West Virginia	18.1	28	Oregon	1.0
4	Montana	15.9	29	Texas	0.6
5	New Mexico	11.1	30	New Hampshire	0.2
6	Alaska	10.9	30	Virginia	0.2
7	Massachusetts	9.9	32	Hawaii	(0.2)
8	Oklahoma	8.8	32	Missouri	(0.2)
9	Mississippi	7.8	34	Wyoming	(0.4)
10	Kansas	7.5	35	Arkansas	(0.7)
11	Florida	7.4	36	New Jersey	(0.8)
12	Louisiana	6.4	37	Indiana	(1.4)
13	Washington	5.1	38	Wisconsin	(1.9)
14	Minnesota	5.0	39	Michigan	(2.5)
15	Maryland	4.3	40	Illinois	(2.9)
16	Tennessee	3.2	41	New York	(3.2)
17	North Carolina	3.1	42	South Carolina	(3.4)
18	California	2.9	43	Pennsylvania	(3.9)
18	Georgia	2.9	44	Maine	(5.0)
20	Nebraska	2.8	45	Idaho	(5.9)
21	South Dakota	2.7	46	Ohio	(6.6)
22	Arizona	2.6	47	Delaware	(6.9)
23	Nevada	1.8	48	Iowa	(7.4)
24	Utah	1.7	49	Connecticut	(10.0)
24	Vermont	1.7	50	Rhode Island	(12.8)

District of Columbia   29.7

Source: U.S. Department of Justice, Federal Bureau of Investigation
   "Crime in the United States 1992" (Uniform Crime Reports, October 3, 1993)
*Aggravated assault is an attack for the purpose of inflicting severe bodily injury.

Aggravated Assaults with Firearms in 1992

National Total = 251,883 Aggravated Assaults with Firearms*

RANK	STATE	ASSAULTS	%		RANK	STATE	ASSAULTS	%
1	California	43,617	17.32%		26	Oregon	2,013	0.80%
2	Florida	25,011	9.93%		27	Minnesota	1,961	0.78%
3	Texas	24,213	9.61%		28	New Mexico	1,836	0.73%
4	Illinois	20,020	7.95%		29	Mississippi	1,367	0.54%
5	New York	16,941	6.73%		30	Wisconsin	1,355	0.54%
6	Michigan	12,030	4.78%		31	Connecticut	1,060	0.42%
7	North Carolina	8,763	3.48%		32	Nevada	661	0.26%
8	Missouri	8,105	3.22%		33	Alaska	599	0.24%
9	Louisiana	7,723	3.07%		34	Utah	594	0.24%
10	Georgia	7,241	2.87%		35	West Virginia	441	0.18%
11	Ohio	6,665	2.65%		36	Idaho	361	0.14%
12	Maryland	6,054	2.40%		37	Iowa	346	0.14%
13	South Carolina	5,854	2.32%		38	Rhode Island	316	0.13%
14	Arizona	5,675	2.25%		39	Hawaii	211	0.08%
15	Tennessee	5,429	2.16%		40	Montana	205	0.08%
16	Washington	3,912	1.55%		41	Wyoming	180	0.07%
17	Colorado	3,880	1.54%		42	Nebraska	177	0.07%
18	Pennsylvania	3,840	1.52%		43	South Dakota	162	0.06%
19	New Jersey	3,836	1.52%		44	Delaware	133	0.05%
20	Oklahoma	3,592	1.43%		45	Vermont	81	0.03%
21	Arkansas	2,795	1.11%		46	New Hampshire	76	0.03%
22	Indiana	2,739	1.09%		47	Maine	52	0.02%
23	Kansas	2,733	1.09%		48	North Dakota	21	0.01%
24	Virginia	2,604	1.03%		–	Alabama**	N/A	N/A
25	Massachusetts	2,295	0.91%		–	Kentucky**	N/A	N/A

District of Columbia	2,108	0.84%

Source: U.S. Department of Justice, Federal Bureau of Investigation

"Crime in the United States 1992" (Uniform Crime Reports, October 3, 1993)

*Of the 1,015,976 aggravated assaults in 1992 for which supplemental data were received by the F.B.I. There were an additional 110,998 aggravated assaults for which the type of weapon was not reported to the F.B.I. Aggravated assault is an attack for the purpose of inflicting severe bodily injury.

**Not available.

Aggravated Assault Rate with Firearms in 1992

National Rate = 98.7 Aggravated Assaults per 100,000 Population*

RANK	STATE	RATE	RANK	STATE	RATE
1	Florida	185.4	26	New Jersey	49.2
2	Louisiana	180.1	27	Indiana	48.4
3	Illinois	172.1	28	Minnesota	43.8
4	South Carolina	162.5	29	Virginia	40.8
5	Missouri	156.1	30	Wyoming	38.6
6	Arizona	148.1	31	Massachusetts	38.3
7	California	141.3	32	Idaho	33.8
8	Texas	137.1	33	Utah	32.8
9	North Carolina	128.1	34	Connecticut	32.3
10	Michigan	127.5	35	Pennsylvania	32.0
11	Maryland	123.3	36	Rhode Island	31.4
12	Arkansas	116.5	37	Wisconsin	27.1
13	New Mexico	116.1	38	Montana	24.9
14	Colorado	111.8	39	West Virginia	24.3
14	Oklahoma	111.8	40	South Dakota	22.8
16	Kansas	108.3	41	Delaware	19.3
17	Tennessee	108.1	42	Hawaii	18.2
18	Georgia	107.3	43	Vermont	14.2
19	Alaska	102.0	44	Iowa	12.3
20	New York	93.5	45	Nebraska	11.0
21	Washington	76.2	46	New Hampshire	6.8
22	Oregon	67.6	47	Maine	4.2
23	Ohio	60.5	48	North Dakota	3.3
24	Mississippi	52.3	–	Alabama**	N/A
25	Nevada	49.8	–	Kentucky**	N/A

District of Columbia   357.9

Source: Morgan Quitno Corporation using data from U.S. Department of Justice, Federal Bureau of Investigation
   "Crime in the United States 1992" (Uniform Crime Reports, October 3, 1993)
*Of the 1,015,976 aggravated assaults in 1992 for which supplemental data were received by the F.B.I. There were an additional 110,998 aggravated assaults for which the type of weapon was not reported to the F.B.I. Aggravated assault is an attack for the purpose of inflicting severe bodily injury.
**Not available.

Percent of Aggravated Assaults Involving Firearms in 1992

National Rate = 24.79% of Aggravated Assaults*

RANK	STATE	PERCENT	RANK	STATE	PERCENT
1	Mississippi	40.18	26	Wisconsin	22.09
2	Missouri	37.17	27	California	22.05
3	Illinois	34.88	28	Virginia	20.75
4	Louisiana	34.40	29	New York	20.15
5	Kansas	33.04	30	Nevada	19.89
6	Arizona	32.92	31	Idaho	19.76
7	Montana	29.97	32	South Dakota	19.68
8	North Carolina	29.37	33	Indiana	19.17
9	Arkansas	29.27	34	Pennsylvania	18.66
10	Colorado	29.06	35	Utah	18.51
11	Georgia	28.78	36	West Virginia	17.40
12	Michigan	28.45	37	Delaware	16.50
13	Tennessee	28.31	38	New Jersey	16.16
14	Texas	28.14	39	Hawaii	15.46
15	Ohio	26.76	40	Wyoming	15.10
16	Oklahoma	26.34	41	New Hampshire	14.31
17	South Carolina	26.15	42	Iowa	13.09
18	Florida	24.61	43	Connecticut	12.80
19	Washington	24.26	44	Rhode Island	11.84
20	Maryland	24.08	45	Nebraska	10.55
21	Alaska	24.01	46	Massachusetts	8.28
22	Minnesota	23.84	47	North Dakota	7.17
23	Vermont	23.41	48	Maine	5.53
24	New Mexico	23.01	–	Alabama**	N/A
25	Oregon	22.76	–	Kentucky**	N/A

District of Columbia   24.60

Source: Morgan Quitno Corporation using data from U.S. Department of Justice, Federal Bureau of Investigation
        "Crime in the United States 1992" (Uniform Crime Reports, October 3, 1993)
*Of the 1,015,976 aggravated assaults in 1992 for which supplemental data were received by the F.B.I. There were an additional 110,998 aggravated assaults for which the type of weapon was not reported to the F.B.I. Aggravated assault is an attack for the purpose of inflicting severe bodily injury.
**Not available.

Aggravated Assaults with Knives or Cutting Instruments in 1992

National Total = 184,844 Aggravated Assaults with Knives or Cutting Instruments*

RANK	STATE	ASSAULTS	%	RANK	STATE	ASSAULTS	%
1	California	24,926	13.48%	26	Arkansas	1,465	0.79%
2	New York	20,353	11.01%	27	Connecticut	1,429	0.77%
3	Florida	19,888	10.76%	28	Kansas	1,333	0.72%
4	Texas	16,897	9.14%	29	New Mexico	1,314	0.71%
5	Illinois	12,886	6.97%	30	Wisconsin	876	0.47%
6	Michigan	7,441	4.03%	31	Nevada	636	0.34%
7	North Carolina	5,752	3.11%	32	Mississippi	633	0.34%
8	New Jersey	5,724	3.10%	33	Utah	601	0.33%
9	Georgia	5,572	3.01%	34	Alaska	583	0.32%
10	South Carolina	5,141	2.78%	35	West Virginia	533	0.29%
11	Maryland	5,088	2.75%	36	Iowa	459	0.25%
12	Massachusetts	4,834	2.62%	37	Rhode Island	431	0.23%
13	Ohio	4,426	2.39%	38	Idaho	338	0.18%
14	Louisiana	3,717	2.01%	39	Nebraska	303	0.16%
15	Missouri	3,478	1.88%	40	Delaware	233	0.13%
16	Tennessee	3,456	1.87%	41	South Dakota	178	0.10%
17	Pennsylvania	3,234	1.75%	42	Wyoming	162	0.09%
18	Virginia	2,898	1.57%	43	Maine	139	0.08%
19	Washington	2,713	1.47%	44	Montana	130	0.07%
20	Arizona	2,644	1.43%	45	Hawaii	123	0.07%
21	Colorado	2,331	1.26%	46	New Hampshire	99	0.05%
22	Oklahoma	2,013	1.09%	47	Vermont	49	0.03%
23	Minnesota	1,954	1.06%	48	North Dakota	43	0.02%
24	Indiana	1,823	0.99%	–	Alabama**	N/A	N/A
25	Oregon	1,537	0.83%	–	Kentucky**	N/A	N/A

District of Columbia   2,028   1.10%

Source: U.S. Department of Justice, Federal Bureau of Investigation
   "Crime in the United States 1992" (Uniform Crime Reports, October 3, 1993)
*Of the 1,015,976 aggravated assaults in 1992 for which supplemental data were received by the F.B.I. There were an additional 110,998 aggravated assaults for which the type of weapon was not reported to the F.B.I. Aggravated assault is an attack for the purpose of inflicting severe bodily injury.
**Not available.

Percent of Aggravated Assaults Involving Knives or Cutting Instruments in 1992

National Rate = 18.19% of Aggravated Assaults*

RANK	STATE	PERCENT	RANK	STATE	PERCENT
1	Delaware	28.91	26	Colorado	17.46
2	New York	24.21	27	Massachusetts	17.43
3	New Jersey	24.11	28	Oregon	17.38
4	Minnesota	23.76	29	Iowa	17.37
5	Alaska	23.37	30	Connecticut	17.25
6	Virginia	23.10	31	Washington	16.82
7	South Carolina	22.97	32	Louisiana	16.56
8	Illinois	22.45	33	New Mexico	16.47
9	Georgia	22.15	34	Rhode Island	16.15
10	South Dakota	21.63	35	Kansas	16.11
11	West Virginia	21.03	36	Missouri	15.95
12	Maryland	20.24	37	Pennsylvania	15.72
13	Texas	19.64	38	Arizona	15.34
14	Florida	19.57	38	Arkansas	15.34
15	North Carolina	19.28	40	Maine	14.79
16	Nevada	19.13	41	Oklahoma	14.76
17	Montana	19.01	42	North Dakota	14.68
18	Utah	18.73	43	Wisconsin	14.28
19	New Hampshire	18.64	44	Vermont	14.16
20	Mississippi	18.61	45	Wyoming	13.59
21	Idaho	18.50	46	Indiana	12.76
22	Nebraska	18.06	47	California	12.60
23	Tennessee	18.02	48	Hawaii	9.01
24	Ohio	17.77	–	Alabama**	N/A
25	Michigan	17.60	–	Kentucky**	N/A

District of Columbia   23.67

Source: Morgan Quitno Corporation using data from U.S. Department of Justice, Federal Bureau of Investigation
   "Crime in the United States 1992" (Uniform Crime Reports, October 3, 1993)
*Of the 1,015,976 aggravated assaults in 1992 for which supplemental data were received by the F.B.I. There were an additional 110,998 aggravated assaults for which the type of weapon was not reported to the F.B.I. Aggravated assault is an attack for the purpose of inflicting severe bodily injury.
**Not available.

Aggravated Assaults with Blunt Objects and Other Dangerous Weapons in 1992

National Total = 319,083 Aggravated Assaults with Blunt Objects and Other Dangerous Weapons*

RANK	STATE	ASSAULTS	%	RANK	STATE	ASSAULTS	%
1	California	55,722	17.46%	26	New Mexico	2,779	0.87%
2	Florida	41,218	12.92%	27	Kansas	2,741	0.86%
3	New York	27,367	8.58%	28	Minnesota	2,408	0.75%
4	Texas	21,698	6.80%	29	Arkansas	2,267	0.71%
5	Illinois	20,607	6.46%	30	Wisconsin	1,203	0.38%
6	Michigan	17,311	5.43%	31	Utah	1,103	0.35%
7	Maryland	9,914	3.11%	32	Nevada	1,098	0.34%
8	Massachusetts	9,093	2.85%	33	Iowa	960	0.30%
9	South Carolina	8,346	2.62%	34	Rhode Island	863	0.27%
10	North Carolina	7,712	2.42%	35	Nebraska	690	0.22%
11	Georgia	7,630	2.39%	36	Mississippi	661	0.21%
12	New Jersey	7,405	2.32%	37	West Virginia	637	0.20%
13	Ohio	7,249	2.27%	38	Alaska	589	0.18%
14	Missouri	6,915	2.17%	39	Idaho	554	0.17%
15	Tennessee	6,151	1.93%	40	Delaware	306	0.10%
16	Louisiana	5,873	1.84%	41	Wyoming	281	0.09%
17	Arizona	4,917	1.54%	42	Hawaii	233	0.07%
18	Washington	4,883	1.53%	43	Maine	230	0.07%
19	Pennsylvania	4,555	1.43%	44	South Dakota	223	0.07%
20	Colorado	4,255	1.33%	45	New Hampshire	126	0.04%
21	Oklahoma	3,951	1.24%	46	Montana	115	0.04%
22	Indiana	3,632	1.14%	47	Vermont	90	0.03%
23	Virginia	3,080	0.97%	48	North Dakota	83	0.03%
24	Connecticut	2,988	0.94%	–	Alabama**	N/A	N/A
25	Oregon	2,889	0.91%	–	Kentucky**	N/A	N/A

District of Columbia   3,482   1.09%

Source: U.S. Department of Justice, Federal Bureau of Investigation

"Crime in the United States 1992" (Uniform Crime Reports, October 3, 1993)

*Of the 1,015,976 aggravated assaults in 1992 for which supplemental data were received by the F.B.I. There were an additional 110,998 aggravated assaults for which the type of weapon was not reported to the F.B.I. Aggravated assault is an attack for the purpose of inflicting severe bodily injury.

**Not available.

Percent of Aggravated Assaults Involving Blunt Objects and Other Dangerous Objects in 1992

National Rate = 31.41% of Aggravated Assaults*

RANK	STATE	PERCENT	RANK	STATE	PERCENT
1	Nebraska	41.12	26	Ohio	29.11
2	Michigan	40.94	27	Oklahoma	28.97
3	Florida	40.55	28	Arizona	28.52
4	Maryland	39.44	29	North Dakota	28.33
5	Delaware	37.97	30	California	28.16
6	South Carolina	37.29	31	South Dakota	27.10
7	Iowa	36.32	32	Louisiana	26.16
8	Connecticut	36.07	33	Vermont	26.01
9	Illinois	35.90	34	North Carolina	25.85
10	New Mexico	34.83	35	Indiana	25.42
11	Utah	34.37	36	Texas	25.22
12	Kansas	33.13	37	West Virginia	25.13
13	Nevada	33.03	38	Virginia	24.55
14	Massachusetts	32.80	39	Maine	24.47
15	Oregon	32.66	40	Arkansas	23.74
16	New York	32.55	41	New Hampshire	23.73
17	Rhode Island	32.35	42	Alaska	23.61
18	Tennessee	32.08	43	Wyoming	23.57
19	Colorado	31.87	44	Pennsylvania	22.14
20	Missouri	31.71	45	Wisconsin	19.61
21	New Jersey	31.19	46	Mississippi	19.43
22	Georgia	30.33	47	Hawaii	17.07
23	Idaho	30.32	48	Montana	16.81
24	Washington	30.28	–	Alabama**	N/A
25	Minnesota	29.28	–	Kentucky**	N/A

District of Columbia   40.64

Source: Morgan Quitno Corporation using data from U.S. Department of Justice, Federal Bureau of Investigation
      "Crime in the United States 1992" (Uniform Crime Reports, October 3, 1993)
*Of the 1,015,976 aggravated assaults in 1992 for which supplemental data were received by the F.B.I. There were an additional 110,998 aggravated assaults for which the type of weapon was not reported to the F.B.I. Aggravated assault is an attack for the purpose of inflicting severe bodily injury.
**Not available.

Aggravated Assaults Using Hands, Fists or Feet in 1992

National Total = 260,166 Aggravated Assaults Using Hands, Fists or Feet*

RANK	STATE	ASSAULTS	%	RANK	STATE	ASSAULTS	%
1	California	73,587	28.28%	26	Wisconsin	2,701	1.04%
2	Texas	23,224	8.93%	27	Oregon	2,406	0.92%
3	New York	19,414	7.46%	28	New Mexico	2,049	0.79%
4	Florida	15,524	5.97%	29	Minnesota	1,901	0.73%
5	Massachusetts	11,504	4.42%	30	Kansas	1,466	0.56%
6	Pennsylvania	8,947	3.44%	31	Rhode Island	1,058	0.41%
7	North Carolina	7,611	2.93%	32	Nevada	929	0.36%
8	New Jersey	6,773	2.60%	33	West Virginia	924	0.36%
9	Ohio	6,564	2.52%	34	Utah	911	0.35%
10	Indiana	6,096	2.34%	35	Iowa	878	0.34%
11	Michigan	5,499	2.11%	36	Hawaii	798	0.31%
12	Louisiana	5,137	1.97%	37	Mississippi	741	0.28%
13	Georgia	4,716	1.81%	38	Alaska	724	0.28%
14	Washington	4,617	1.77%	39	Idaho	574	0.22%
15	Tennessee	4,138	1.59%	40	Wyoming	569	0.22%
16	Maryland	4,083	1.57%	41	Maine	519	0.20%
17	Oklahoma	4,080	1.57%	42	Nebraska	508	0.20%
18	Arizona	4,004	1.54%	43	South Dakota	260	0.10%
19	Virginia	3,966	1.52%	44	Montana	234	0.09%
20	Illinois	3,882	1.49%	45	New Hampshire	230	0.09%
21	Missouri	3,306	1.27%	46	North Dakota	146	0.06%
22	South Carolina	3,043	1.17%	47	Delaware	134	0.05%
23	Arkansas	3,021	1.16%	48	Vermont	126	0.05%
24	Colorado	2,887	1.11%	–	Alabama**	N/A	N/A
25	Connecticut	2,807	1.08%	–	Kentucky**	N/A	N/A
					District of Columbia	950	0.37%

Source: U.S. Department of Justice, Federal Bureau of Investigation

"Crime in the United States 1992" (Uniform Crime Reports, October 3, 1993)

*Of the 1,015,976 aggravated assaults in 1992 for which supplemental data were received by the F.B.I. There were an additional 110,998 aggravated assaults for which the type of weapon was not reported to the F.B.I. Aggravated assault is an attack for the purpose of inflicting severe bodily injury.

**Not available.

Percent of Aggravated Assaults Involving Hands, Fists or Feet in 1992

National Rate = 25.61% of Aggravated Assaults*

RANK	STATE	PERCENT	RANK	STATE	PERCENT
1	Hawaii	58.46	26	Utah	28.39
2	Maine	55.21	27	Nevada	27.95
3	North Dakota	49.83	28	Oregon	27.20
4	Wyoming	47.73	29	Texas	26.99
5	Wisconsin	44.03	30	Ohio	26.36
6	Pennsylvania	43.48	31	New Mexico	25.68
7	New Hampshire	43.31	32	North Carolina	25.51
8	Indiana	42.66	33	Arizona	23.23
9	Massachusetts	41.49	34	Minnesota	23.12
10	Rhode Island	39.66	35	New York	23.09
11	California	37.19	36	Louisiana	22.88
12	West Virginia	36.45	37	Mississippi	21.78
13	Vermont	36.42	38	Colorado	21.62
14	Montana	34.21	39	Tennessee	21.58
15	Connecticut	33.88	40	Georgia	18.74
16	Iowa	33.22	41	Kansas	17.72
17	Arkansas	31.64	42	Delaware	16.63
18	Virginia	31.61	43	Maryland	16.24
19	South Dakota	31.59	44	Florida	15.27
20	Idaho	31.42	45	Missouri	15.16
21	Nebraska	30.27	46	South Carolina	13.59
22	Oklahoma	29.92	47	Michigan	13.01
23	Alaska	29.02	48	Illinois	6.76
24	Washington	28.63	–	Alabama**	N/A
25	New Jersey	28.53	–	Kentucky**	N/A

District of Columbia   11.09

Source: Morgan Quitno Corporation using data from U.S. Department of Justice, Federal Bureau of Investigation
"Crime in the United States 1992" (Uniform Crime Reports, October 3, 1993)

*Of the 1,015,976 aggravated assaults in 1992 for which supplemental data were received by the F.B.I. There were an additional 110,998 aggravated assaults for which the type of weapon was not reported to the F.B.I. Aggravated assault is an attack for the purpose of inflicting severe bodily injury.
**Not available.

Property Crimes in 1992

National Total = 12,505,917 Property Crimes*

RANK	STATE	CRIMES	%	RANK	STATE	CRIMES	%
1	California	1,716,137	13.72%	26	Oregon	158,100	1.26%
2	Texas	1,103,779	8.83%	27	Oklahoma	154,459	1.24%
3	Florida	964,533	7.71%	28	Connecticut	149,535	1.20%
4	New York	858,178	6.86%	29	Kansas	121,334	0.97%
5	Illinois	556,900	4.45%	30	Kentucky	104,692	0.84%
6	Michigan	456,800	3.65%	31	Iowa	103,459	0.83%
7	Ohio	456,017	3.65%	32	Mississippi	101,181	0.81%
8	Georgia	382,934	3.06%	33	Arkansas	100,402	0.80%
9	Pennsylvania	356,155	2.85%	34	Utah	97,322	0.78%
10	North Carolina	350,447	2.80%	35	New Mexico	86,942	0.70%
11	New Jersey	345,718	2.76%	36	Nevada	73,077	0.58%
12	Washington	289,581	2.32%	37	Hawaii	67,901	0.54%
13	Maryland	256,418	2.05%	38	Nebraska	63,846	0.51%
14	Massachusetts	253,344	2.03%	39	West Virginia	43,455	0.35%
15	Virginia	250,211	2.00%	40	Rhode Island	42,044	0.34%
16	Arizona	243,629	1.95%	41	Maine	41,900	0.34%
17	Louisiana	238,438	1.91%	42	Idaho	39,636	0.32%
18	Indiana	236,584	1.89%	43	Montana	36,472	0.29%
19	Missouri	226,246	1.81%	44	New Hampshire	32,828	0.26%
20	Tennessee	220,534	1.76%	45	Delaware	29,126	0.23%
21	Wisconsin	202,448	1.62%	46	Alaska	28,816	0.23%
22	Minnesota	190,520	1.52%	47	South Dakota	19,939	0.16%
23	Colorado	186,684	1.49%	48	Wyoming	19,831	0.16%
24	Alabama	181,837	1.45%	49	Vermont	18,813	0.15%
25	South Carolina	178,298	1.43%	50	North Dakota	17,935	0.14%
					District of Columbia	50,502	0.40%

Source: U.S. Department of Justice, Federal Bureau of Investigation
   "Crime in the United States 1992" (Uniform Crime Reports, October 3, 1993)
*Property crimes are offenses of burglary, larceny-theft and motor vehicle theft. Attempts are included.

Average Time Between Property Crimes in 1992

National Rate = A Property Crime Occurs Every 2.5 Seconds*

RANK	STATE	MINUTES.SECONDS	RANK	STATE	MINUTES.SECONDS
1	North Dakota	29.23	26	South Carolina	2.58
2	Vermont	28.01	27	Alabama	2.54
3	Wyoming	26.35	28	Colorado	2.49
4	South Dakota	26.26	29	Minnesota	2.46
5	Alaska	18.17	30	Wisconsin	2.36
6	Delaware	18.06	31	Tennessee	2.23
7	New Hampshire	16.03	32	Missouri	2.20
8	Montana	14.27	33	Indiana	2.14
9	Idaho	13.18	34	Louisiana	2.13
10	Maine	12.35	35	Arizona	2.10
11	Rhode Island	12.32	36	Virginia	2.07
12	West Virginia	12.08	37	Massachusetts	2.05
13	Nebraska	8.15	38	Maryland	2.04
14	Hawaii	7.46	39	Washington	1.49
15	Nevada	7.13	40	New Jersey	1.31
16	New Mexico	6.04	41	North Carolina	1.30
17	Utah	5.25	42	Pennsylvania	1.29
18	Arkansas	5.15	43	Georgia	1.23
19	Mississippi	5.13	44	Ohio	1.10
20	Iowa	5.05	45	Michigan	1.09
21	Kentucky	5.02	46	Illinois	0.57
22	Kansas	4.20	47	New York	0.37
23	Connecticut	3.31	48	Florida	0.33
24	Oklahoma	3.25	49	Texas	0.29
25	Oregon	3.20	50	California	0.18

District of Columbia 10.26

Source: Morgan Quitno Corporation using data from U.S. Department of Justice, Federal Bureau of Investigation
"Crime in the United States 1992" (Uniform Crime Reports, October 3, 1993)
*Property crimes are offenses of burglary, larceny-theft and motor vehicle theft. Attempts are included.

Property Crimes per Square Mile in 1992

National Rate = 3.30 Property Crimes per Square Mile

RANK	STATE	RATE	RANK	STATE	RATE
1	New Jersey	39.64	26	Missouri	3.25
2	Rhode Island	27.21	27	Wisconsin	3.09
3	Connecticut	26.97	28	Kentucky	2.59
4	Massachusetts	24.00	29	Oklahoma	2.21
5	Maryland	20.67	30	Minnesota	2.19
6	New York	15.75	31	Arizona	2.14
7	Florida	14.67	32	Mississippi	2.09
8	Delaware	11.70	33	Vermont	1.96
9	California	10.48	34	Arkansas	1.89
10	Ohio	10.17	35	Iowa	1.84
11	Illinois	9.62	36	Colorado	1.79
12	Pennsylvania	7.73	36	West Virginia	1.79
13	North Carolina	6.51	38	Oregon	1.61
14	Indiana	6.50	39	Kansas	1.47
15	Georgia	6.44	40	Maine	1.18
16	Hawaii	6.21	41	Utah	1.15
17	Virginia	5.85	42	Nebraska	0.83
18	South Carolina	5.57	43	New Mexico	0.71
19	Tennessee	5.23	44	Nevada	0.66
20	Michigan	4.72	45	Idaho	0.47
21	Louisiana	4.60	46	South Dakota	0.26
22	Texas	4.11	47	Montana	0.25
23	Washington	4.06	47	North Dakota	0.25
24	New Hampshire	3.51	49	Wyoming	0.20
25	Alabama	3.47	50	Alaska	0.04

District of Columbia   742.68

Source: Morgan Quitno Corporation using data from U.S. Department of Justice, Federal Bureau of Investigation
   "Crime in the United States 1992" (Uniform Crime Reports, October 3, 1993)
*Property crimes are offenses of burglary, larceny-theft and motor vehicle theft. Attempts are included.

Percent Change in Number of Property Crimes: 1991 to 1992

National Percent Change = 3.5% Decrease*

RANK	STATE	PERCENT CHANGE	RANK	STATE	PERCENT CHANGE
1	Montana	28.7	26	Iowa	(3.4)
2	Wyoming	5.7	26	Kansas	(3.4)
3	Hawaii	4.4	26	Kentucky	(3.4)
4	North Dakota	3.5	29	Arizona	(3.5)
5	Utah	3.3	30	South Carolina	(3.8)
6	Oregon	3.1	31	New Mexico	(3.9)
7	Minnesota	2.8	32	Tennessee	(4.1)
8	Louisiana	2.5	33	Pennsylvania	(4.2)
9	Mississippi	1.9	34	Oklahoma	(4.3)
10	Nevada	1.2	35	Illinois	(5.3)
11	Georgia	0.5	36	Missouri	(5.7)
12	Maryland	0.4	37	Connecticut	(5.8)
13	Colorado	0.2	38	Virginia	(6.0)
14	Washington	(0.2)	39	New York	(6.5)
15	Nebraska	(0.3)	40	Maine	(6.7)
16	North Carolina	(0.5)	41	Ohio	(6.8)
17	Alaska	(0.6)	42	New Jersey	(7.1)
17	California	(0.6)	43	Arkansas	(7.6)
19	Florida	(1.3)	44	Massachusetts	(7.9)
20	Alabama	(1.6)	45	Rhode Island	(8.5)
21	South Dakota	(2.1)	46	Michigan	(8.6)
22	Indiana	(2.2)	47	Texas	(8.8)
23	Idaho	(2.3)	48	New Hampshire	(10.7)
24	West Virginia	(2.4)	49	Vermont	(13.6)
25	Wisconsin	(2.5)	50	Delaware	(16.9)

District of Columbia   1.6

Source: U.S. Department of Justice, Federal Bureau of Investigation

"Crime in the United States 1992" (Uniform Crime Reports, October 3, 1993)

*Property crimes are offenses of burglary, larceny-theft and motor vehicle theft. Attempts are included.

Property Crime Rate in 1992

National Rate = 4,902.7 Property Crimes per 100,000 Population*

RANK	STATE	RATE	RANK	STATE	RATE
1	Florida	7,151.0	26	Alabama	4,396.4
2	Arizona	6,357.8	27	Tennessee	4,389.6
3	Texas	6,251.6	28	Missouri	4,356.7
4	Hawaii	5,853.5	29	Wyoming	4,255.6
5	Georgia	5,672.3	30	Minnesota	4,252.7
6	Washington	5,638.3	31	Delaware	4,227.3
7	Louisiana	5,561.9	32	Massachusetts	4,223.8
8	California	5,559.8	33	Arkansas	4,185.2
9	Nevada	5,506.9	34	Rhode Island	4,183.5
10	New Mexico	5,499.2	35	Indiana	4,178.5
11	Colorado	5,379.9	36	Ohio	4,139.6
12	Utah	5,368.0	37	Wisconsin	4,043.3
13	Oregon	5,310.7	38	Nebraska	3,975.5
14	Maryland	5,224.5	39	Virginia	3,923.6
15	North Carolina	5,121.2	40	Mississippi	3,870.7
16	South Carolina	4,948.6	41	Idaho	3,714.7
17	Alaska	4,909.0	42	Iowa	3,679.2
18	Michigan	4,840.5	43	Maine	3,392.7
19	Kansas	4,809.1	44	Vermont	3,300.5
20	Oklahoma	4,808.8	45	Pennsylvania	2,965.7
21	Illinois	4,788.1	46	New Hampshire	2,954.8
22	New York	4,736.3	47	North Dakota	2,820.0
23	Connecticut	4,557.6	48	South Dakota	2,804.4
24	New Jersey	4,438.5	49	Kentucky	2,788.1
25	Montana	4,426.2	50	West Virginia	2,398.2
				District of Columbia	8,574.2

Source: U.S. Department of Justice, Federal Bureau of Investigation
"Crime in the United States 1992" (Uniform Crime Reports, October 3, 1993)
*Property crimes are offenses of burglary, larceny-theft and motor vehicle theft. Attempts are included.

Percent Change in Rate of Property Crime: 1991 to 1992

National Percent Change = 4.6% Decrease*

RANK	STATE	PERCENT CHANGE	RANK	STATE	PERCENT CHANGE
1	Montana	26.2	26	Kansas	(4.5)
2	Wyoming	4.3	26	Kentucky	(4.5)
3	North Dakota	3.4	28	Pennsylvania	(4.6)
4	Hawaii	2.2	29	Idaho	(4.9)
5	Minnesota	1.7	30	South Carolina	(5.0)
6	Louisiana	1.6	31	Oklahoma	(5.4)
7	Oregon	1.2	31	Tennessee	(5.4)
8	Mississippi	1.0	33	Connecticut	(5.5)
9	Utah	0.9	34	Arizona	(5.6)
10	Maryland	(0.5)	35	New Mexico	(5.9)
11	Nebraska	(1.1)	36	Illinois	(6.0)
12	Georgia	(1.4)	37	Missouri	(6.4)
13	Nevada	(2.0)	38	Maine	(6.7)
14	North Carolina	(2.1)	39	New York	(6.8)
15	California	(2.2)	40	Virginia	(7.3)
16	Colorado	(2.4)	41	Ohio	(7.4)
17	Washington	(2.5)	42	New Jersey	(7.5)
18	Alabama	(2.8)	43	Massachusetts	(7.9)
19	Florida	(2.9)	44	Rhode Island	(8.6)
20	West Virginia	(3.0)	45	Arkansas	(8.7)
21	Indiana	(3.1)	46	Michigan	(9.3)
22	South Dakota	(3.2)	47	Texas	(10.4)
23	Alaska	(3.5)	48	New Hampshire	(11.2)
23	Wisconsin	(3.5)	49	Vermont	(14.0)
25	Iowa	(4.0)	50	Delaware	(18.0)

District of Columbia   3.1

Source: U.S. Department of Justice, Federal Bureau of Investigation
"Crime in the United States 1992" (Uniform Crime Reports, October 3, 1993)
*Property crimes are offenses of burglary, larceny-theft and motor vehicle theft. Attempts are included.

Burglaries in 1992

National Total = 2,979,884 Burglaries*

RANK	STATE	BURGLARIES	%		RANK	STATE	BURGLARIES	%
1	California	427,491	14.35%		26	Connecticut	36,372	1.22%
2	Texas	268,928	9.02%		27	Wisconsin	34,645	1.16%
3	Florida	254,755	8.55%		28	Mississippi	33,533	1.13%
4	New York	193,548	6.50%		29	Oregon	32,945	1.11%
5	Illinois	125,306	4.21%		30	Kansas	32,639	1.10%
6	North Carolina	113,117	3.80%		31	Kentucky	27,378	0.92%
7	Ohio	104,357	3.50%		32	Arkansas	26,214	0.88%
8	Michigan	98,257	3.30%		33	New Mexico	23,896	0.80%
9	Georgia	97,402	3.27%		34	Iowa	21,197	0.71%
10	Pennsylvania	75,834	2.54%		35	Nevada	17,108	0.57%
11	New Jersey	75,508	2.53%		36	Utah	16,045	0.54%
12	Massachusetts	64,318	2.16%		37	Hawaii	13,006	0.44%
13	Tennessee	63,665	2.14%		38	Nebraska	11,477	0.39%
14	Louisiana	58,574	1.97%		39	West Virginia	11,287	0.38%
15	Washington	57,612	1.93%		40	Rhode Island	10,529	0.35%
16	Missouri	57,127	1.92%		41	Maine	10,156	0.34%
17	Maryland	55,520	1.86%		42	Idaho	7,934	0.27%
18	Arizona	54,095	1.82%		43	New Hampshire	6,909	0.23%
19	Indiana	53,907	1.81%		44	Delaware	6,598	0.22%
20	South Carolina	49,669	1.67%		45	Montana	5,306	0.18%
21	Alabama	49,053	1.65%		46	Alaska	5,170	0.17%
22	Virginia	45,217	1.52%		47	Vermont	4,706	0.16%
23	Oklahoma	43,678	1.47%		48	South Dakota	3,849	0.13%
24	Minnesota	39,859	1.34%		49	Wyoming	3,127	0.10%
25	Colorado	37,853	1.27%		50	North Dakota	2,487	0.08%
						District of Columbia	10,721	0.36%

Source: U.S. Department of Justice, Federal Bureau of Investigation
    "Crime in the United States 1992" (Uniform Crime Reports, October 3, 1993)
*Burglary is the unlawful entry of a structure to commit a felony or theft. Attempts are included.

Average Time Between Burglaries in 1992

National Rate = A Burglary Occurs Every 11 Seconds*

RANK	STATE	MINUTES.SECONDS	RANK	STATE	MINUTES.SECONDS
1	North Dakota	211.55	26	Colorado	13.55
2	Wyoming	168.33	27	Minnesota	13.13
3	South Dakota	136.56	28	Oklahoma	12.04
4	Vermont	111.59	29	Virginia	11.40
5	Alaska	101.56	30	Alabama	10.44
6	Montana	99.20	31	South Carolina	10.37
7	Delaware	79.53	32	Indiana	9.47
8	New Hampshire	76.17	33	Arizona	9.44
9	Idaho	66.26	34	Maryland	9.29
10	Maine	51.53	35	Missouri	9.14
11	Rhode Island	50.04	36	Washington	9.09
12	West Virginia	46.41	37	Louisiana	9.00
13	Nebraska	45.55	38	Tennessee	8.17
14	Hawaii	40.31	39	Massachusetts	8.11
15	Utah	32.51	40	New Jersey	6.59
16	Nevada	30.49	41	Pennsylvania	6.57
17	Iowa	24.52	42	Georgia	5.25
18	New Mexico	22.04	43	Michigan	5.22
19	Arkansas	20.07	44	Ohio	5.03
20	Kentucky	19.15	45	North Carolina	4.40
21	Kansas	16.09	46	Illinois	4.13
22	Oregon	16.00	47	New York	2.43
23	Mississippi	15.43	48	Florida	2.04
24	Wisconsin	15.13	49	Texas	1.58
25	Connecticut	14.29	50	California	1.14

District of Columbia   49.10

Source: Morgan Quitno Corporation using data from U.S. Department of Justice, Federal Bureau of Investigation
"Crime in the United States 1992" (Uniform Crime Reports, October 3, 1993)
*Burglary is the unlawful entry of a structure to commit a felony or theft. Attempts are included.

Percent Change in Number of Burglaries: 1991 to 1992

National Percent Change = 5.6% Decrease*

RANK	STATE	PERCENT CHANGE	RANK	STATE	PERCENT CHANGE
1	Montana	25.4	26	Oklahoma	(6.9)
2	Utah	7.9	27	Rhode Island	(7.0)
3	Minnesota	5.4	27	Wisconsin	(7.0)
4	North Dakota	5.1	29	Washington	(7.1)
5	California	0.7	30	Connecticut	(7.2)
6	Kansas	0.1	30	Hawaii	(7.2)
7	Nebraska	(0.8)	30	South Dakota	(7.2)
7	North Carolina	(0.8)	33	Alaska	(7.4)
9	Maryland	(1.3)	33	Kentucky	(7.4)
10	Indiana	(1.7)	35	Idaho	(7.6)
11	Wyoming	(1.8)	36	Massachusetts	(8.1)
12	Louisiana	(2.4)	36	Virginia	(8.1)
13	Georgia	(2.9)	38	Iowa	(8.9)
13	Mississippi	(2.9)	38	Maine	(8.9)
15	Illinois	(3.1)	40	Ohio	(9.6)
16	Colorado	(3.2)	41	Arkansas	(9.9)
17	Oregon	(4.1)	42	Arizona	(10.3)
17	South Carolina	(4.1)	43	New Mexico	(10.4)
19	New Jersey	(4.2)	44	Michigan	(11.6)
20	Florida	(4.3)	44	Missouri	(11.6)
21	Nevada	(5.1)	46	Pennsylvania	(11.9)
22	Alabama	(5.4)	47	Delaware	(14.0)
22	New York	(5.4)	47	Texas	(14.0)
24	Tennessee	(5.8)	49	New Hampshire	(15.0)
25	West Virginia	(6.0)	50	Vermont	(18.6)

District of Columbia   (13.6)

Source: U.S. Department of Justice, Federal Bureau of Investigation

"Crime in the United States 1992" (Uniform Crime Reports, October 3, 1993)

*Burglary is the unlawful entry of a structure to commit a felony or theft. Attempts are included.

Burglary Rate in 1992

National Rate = 1,168.2 Burglaries per 100,000 Population*

RANK	STATE	RATE	RANK	STATE	RATE
1	Florida	1,888.8	26	New York	1,068.2
2	North Carolina	1,653.0	27	Rhode Island	1,047.7
3	Texas	1,523.2	28	Michigan	1,041.2
4	New Mexico	1,511.4	29	New Jersey	969.4
5	Georgia	1,442.8	30	Delaware	957.6
6	Arizona	1,411.7	31	Indiana	952.1
7	California	1,384.9	32	Ohio	947.3
8	South Carolina	1,378.5	33	Minnesota	889.7
9	Louisiana	1,366.3	34	Utah	885.0
10	Oklahoma	1,359.8	35	Alaska	880.7
11	Kansas	1,293.7	36	Vermont	825.6
12	Nevada	1,289.2	37	Maine	822.3
13	Mississippi	1,282.8	38	Iowa	753.8
14	Tennessee	1,267.2	39	Idaho	743.6
15	Alabama	1,186.0	40	Kentucky	729.1
16	Maryland	1,131.2	41	Nebraska	714.6
17	Washington	1,121.7	42	Virginia	709.1
18	Hawaii	1,121.2	43	Wisconsin	691.9
19	Connecticut	1,108.6	44	Wyoming	671.0
20	Oregon	1,106.7	45	Montana	643.9
21	Missouri	1,100.1	46	Pennsylvania	631.5
22	Arkansas	1,092.7	47	West Virginia	622.9
23	Colorado	1,090.9	48	New Hampshire	621.9
24	Illinois	1,077.3	49	South Dakota	541.4
25	Massachusetts	1,072.3	50	North Dakota	391.0

District of Columbia   1,820.2

Source: U.S. Department of Justice, Federal Bureau of Investigation

"Crime in the United States 1992" (Uniform Crime Reports, October 3, 1993)

*Burglary is the unlawful entry of a structure to commit a felony or theft. Attempts are included.

Percent Change in Rate of Burglaries: 1991 to 1992

National Percent Change = 6.7% Decrease

RANK	STATE	PERCENT CHANGE	RANK	STATE	PERCENT CHANGE
1	Montana	23.0	26	Tennessee	(7.2)
2	Utah	5.3	27	Wisconsin	(7.9)
3	North Dakota	4.9	28	Oklahoma	(8.0)
4	Minnesota	4.2	29	Massachusetts	(8.1)
5	California	(0.9)	30	Nevada	(8.2)
6	Kansas	(1.0)	30	South Dakota	(8.2)
7	Nebraska	(1.7)	32	Kentucky	(8.5)
8	Maryland	(2.3)	33	Maine	(8.9)
8	North Carolina	(2.3)	34	Hawaii	(9.2)
10	Indiana	(2.6)	34	Washington	(9.2)
11	Wyoming	(3.1)	36	Virginia	(9.4)
12	Louisiana	(3.2)	37	Iowa	(9.5)
13	Mississippi	(3.7)	38	Idaho	(10.0)
14	Illinois	(3.8)	39	Alaska	(10.1)
15	New Jersey	(4.6)	40	Ohio	(10.2)
16	Georgia	(4.7)	41	Arkansas	(10.9)
17	South Carolina	(5.3)	42	Arizona	(12.2)
18	New York	(5.7)	42	Michigan	(12.2)
19	Colorado	(5.8)	42	Missouri	(12.2)
19	Florida	(5.8)	42	Pennsylvania	(12.2)
21	Oregon	(5.9)	46	New Mexico	(12.3)
22	Alabama	(6.5)	47	Delaware	(15.1)
23	West Virginia	(6.6)	48	New Hampshire	(15.4)
24	Connecticut	(6.9)	49	Texas	(15.5)
25	Rhode Island	(7.1)	50	Vermont	(19.1)

District of Columbia   (12.3)

Source: U.S. Department of Justice, Federal Bureau of Investigation
"Crime in the United States 1992" (Uniform Crime Reports, October 3, 1993)
*Burglary is the unlawful entry of a structure to commit a felony or theft. Attempts are included.

Larceny and Theft in 1992

National Total = 7,915,199 Larcenies and Thefts*

RANK	STATE	LARCENIES	%	RANK	STATE	LARCENIES	%
1	California	968,534	12.24%	26	Oregon	109,274	1.38%
2	Texas	689,780	8.71%	27	Oklahoma	94,180	1.19%
3	Florida	598,093	7.56%	28	Connecticut	89,463	1.13%
4	New York	495,708	6.26%	29	Kansas	80,526	1.02%
5	Illinois	359,618	4.54%	30	Iowa	77,788	0.98%
6	Ohio	299,774	3.79%	31	Utah	76,964	0.97%
7	Michigan	299,486	3.78%	32	Kentucky	69,186	0.87%
8	Georgia	246,619	3.12%	33	Arkansas	66,288	0.84%
9	Pennsylvania	224,150	2.83%	34	Mississippi	58,851	0.74%
10	North Carolina	217,717	2.75%	35	New Mexico	57,072	0.72%
11	Washington	207,755	2.62%	36	Hawaii	50,544	0.64%
12	New Jersey	206,686	2.61%	37	Nebraska	49,144	0.62%
13	Virginia	185,506	2.34%	38	Nevada	46,714	0.59%
14	Maryland	165,244	2.09%	39	Idaho	30,023	0.38%
15	Arizona	158,053	2.00%	40	Maine	29,966	0.38%
16	Indiana	157,181	1.99%	41	Montana	29,243	0.37%
17	Louisiana	152,938	1.93%	42	West Virginia	29,200	0.37%
18	Wisconsin	146,198	1.85%	43	Rhode Island	24,052	0.30%
19	Missouri	143,288	1.81%	44	New Hampshire	23,754	0.30%
20	Massachusetts	141,610	1.79%	45	Alaska	20,728	0.26%
21	Minnesota	134,750	1.70%	46	Delaware	20,419	0.26%
22	Colorado	131,169	1.66%	47	Wyoming	16,003	0.20%
23	Tennessee	127,934	1.62%	48	South Dakota	15,371	0.19%
24	Alabama	117,801	1.49%	49	North Dakota	14,498	0.18%
25	South Carolina	116,186	1.47%	50	Vermont	13,507	0.17%

District of Columbia   30,663   0.39%

Source: U.S. Department of Justice, Federal Bureau of Investigation

"Crime in the United States 1992" (Uniform Crime Reports, October 3, 1993)

*Larceny and theft is the unlawful taking of property. Attempts are included.

Average Time Between Larcenies-Thefts in 1992

National Rate = A Larceny-Theft Occurs Every 3.9 Seconds*

RANK	STATE	MINUTES.SECONDS	RANK	STATE	MINUTES.SECONDS
1	Vermont	39.01	26	South Carolina	4.32
2	North Dakota	36.21	27	Alabama	4.28
3	South Dakota	34.17	28	Tennessee	4.07
4	Wyoming	32.56	29	Colorado	4.01
5	Delaware	25.49	30	Minnesota	3.55
6	Alaska	25.26	31	Massachusetts	3.43
7	New Hampshire	22.11	32	Missouri	3.41
8	Rhode Island	21.55	33	Wisconsin	3.37
9	West Virginia	18.03	34	Louisiana	3.27
10	Montana	18.01	35	Indiana	3.21
11	Maine	17.35	36	Arizona	3.20
12	Idaho	17.33	37	Maryland	3.11
13	Nevada	11.17	38	Virginia	2.50
14	Nebraska	10.43	39	New Jersey	2.33
15	Hawaii	10.26	40	Washington	2.32
16	New Mexico	9.14	41	North Carolina	2.25
17	Mississippi	8.58	42	Pennsylvania	2.21
18	Arkansas	7.57	43	Georgia	2.08
19	Kentucky	7.37	44	Michigan	1.46
20	Utah	6.51	44	Ohio	1.46
21	Iowa	6.47	46	Illinois	1.28
22	Kansas	6.33	47	New York	1.04
23	Connecticut	5.53	48	Florida	0.53
24	Oklahoma	5.36	49	Texas	0.46
25	Oregon	4.49	50	California	0.33

District of Columbia 17.11

Source: Morgan Quitno Corporation using data from U.S. Department of Justice, Federal Bureau of Investigation
"Crime in the United States 1992" (Uniform Crime Reports, October 3, 1993)
*Larceny and theft is the unlawful taking of property. Attempts are included.

Percent Change in Number of Larcenies and Thefts: 1991 to 1992

National Percent Change = 2.8% Decrease*

RANK	STATE	PERCENT CHANGE	RANK	STATE	PERCENT CHANGE
1	Montana	30.3	25	Wisconsin	(1.7)
2	Wyoming	7.6	27	California	(1.8)
3	Hawaii	7.1	28	Missouri	(2.2)
4	Oregon	3.9	29	New Mexico	(2.3)
5	Louisiana	3.1	30	Indiana	(2.4)
6	Georgia	2.6	30	Kentucky	(2.4)
6	Minnesota	2.6	32	Oklahoma	(2.7)
6	Mississippi	2.6	33	South Carolina	(3.0)
6	Utah	2.6	33	Tennessee	(3.0)
10	North Dakota	2.4	35	Connecticut	(4.2)
11	Nevada	2.0	36	Kansas	(4.4)
12	Alaska	1.7	37	Virginia	(5.2)
13	Maryland	1.1	38	Massachusetts	(5.5)
14	Washington	0.9	39	Maine	(5.6)
15	Nebraska	0.1	40	Ohio	(6.0)
16	North Carolina	(0.2)	41	Illinois	(6.1)
17	Alabama	(0.3)	41	Texas	(6.1)
17	South Dakota	(0.3)	43	New Jersey	(6.7)
19	Idaho	(0.4)	44	New York	(6.8)
20	West Virginia	(0.6)	45	Arkansas	(7.3)
21	Arizona	(1.2)	46	Michigan	(7.8)
21	Colorado	(1.2)	47	New Hampshire	(9.4)
23	Florida	(1.5)	48	Rhode Island	(9.8)
24	Iowa	(1.6)	49	Vermont	(10.9)
25	Pennsylvania	(1.7)	50	Delaware	(17.8)

District of Columbia   5.1

Source: U.S. Department of Justice, Federal Bureau of Investigation
    "Crime in the United States 1992" (Uniform Crime Reports, October 3, 1993)
*Larceny and theft is the unlawful taking of property. Attempts are included.

Larceny and Theft Rate in 1992

National Rate = 3,103.0 Larcenies and Thefts per 100,000 Population*

RANK	STATE	RATE	RANK	STATE	RATE
1	Florida	4,434.3	26	Oklahoma	2,932.1
2	Hawaii	4,357.2	27	Wisconsin	2,919.9
3	Utah	4,245.1	28	Virginia	2,909.0
4	Arizona	4,124.6	29	Alabama	2,848.2
5	Washington	4,045.1	30	Idaho	2,813.8
6	Texas	3,906.8	31	Indiana	2,776.1
7	Colorado	3,780.1	32	Iowa	2,766.3
8	Oregon	3,670.6	33	Arkansas	2,763.2
9	Georgia	3,653.1	34	Missouri	2,759.3
10	New Mexico	3,609.9	35	New York	2,735.8
11	Louisiana	3,567.5	36	Connecticut	2,726.7
12	Montana	3,548.9	37	Ohio	2,721.3
13	Alaska	3,531.2	38	New Jersey	2,653.6
14	Nevada	3,520.3	39	Tennessee	2,546.5
15	Wyoming	3,434.1	40	Maine	2,426.4
16	Maryland	3,366.8	41	Rhode Island	2,393.2
17	South Carolina	3,224.7	42	Vermont	2,369.6
18	Kansas	3,191.7	43	Massachusetts	2,361.0
19	North Carolina	3,181.6	44	North Dakota	2,279.6
20	Michigan	3,173.5	45	Mississippi	2,251.4
21	California	3,137.8	46	South Dakota	2,161.9
22	Illinois	3,091.9	47	New Hampshire	2,138.1
23	Nebraska	3,060.0	48	Pennsylvania	1,866.5
24	Minnesota	3,007.8	49	Kentucky	1,842.5
25	Delaware	2,963.6	50	West Virginia	1,611.5

District of Columbia   5,205.9

Source: U.S. Department of Justice, Federal Bureau of Investigation
   "Crime in the United States 1992" (Uniform Crime Reports, October 3, 1993)
*Larceny and theft is the unlawful taking of property. Attempts are included.

Percent Change in Rate of Larceny and Theft: 1991 to 1992

National Percent Change = 3.9% Decrease*

RANK	STATE	PERCENT CHANGE	RANK	STATE	PERCENT CHANGE
1	Montana	27.7	26	Arizona	(3.3)
2	Wyoming	6.3	26	California	(3.3)
3	Hawaii	4.8	26	Indiana	(3.3)
4	Louisiana	2.3	29	Kentucky	(3.5)
4	North Dakota	2.3	30	Colorado	(3.8)
6	Oregon	2.0	31	Connecticut	(3.9)
7	Mississippi	1.7	31	Oklahoma	(3.9)
8	Minnesota	1.5	33	South Carolina	(4.2)
9	Georgia	0.7	34	Tennessee	(4.3)
10	Maryland	0.1	35	New Mexico	(4.4)
10	Utah	0.1	36	Kansas	(5.5)
12	Nebraska	(0.7)	37	Maine	(5.6)
13	Alaska	(1.2)	37	Massachusetts	(5.6)
13	West Virginia	(1.2)	39	Virginia	(6.5)
15	Nevada	(1.3)	40	Ohio	(6.7)
16	Alabama	(1.4)	41	Illinois	(6.8)
16	South Dakota	(1.4)	42	New Jersey	(7.1)
16	Washington	(1.4)	42	New York	(7.1)
19	North Carolina	(1.8)	44	Texas	(7.7)
20	Pennsylvania	(2.1)	45	Arkansas	(8.3)
21	Iowa	(2.2)	46	Michigan	(8.5)
22	Wisconsin	(2.7)	47	New Hampshire	(9.9)
23	Missouri	(2.9)	47	Rhode Island	(9.9)
24	Florida	(3.0)	49	Vermont	(11.4)
24	Idaho	(3.0)	50	Delaware	(18.9)

District of Columbia   6.7

Source: U.S. Department of Justice, Federal Bureau of Investigation
"Crime in the United States 1992" (Uniform Crime Reports, October 3, 1993)
*Larceny and theft is the unlawful taking of property. Attempts are included.

Motor Vehicle Thefts in 1992

National Total = 1,610,834 Motor Vehicle Thefts*

RANK	STATE	VEHICLE THEFTS	%	RANK	STATE	VEHICLE THEFTS	%
1	California	320,112	19.87%	26	Oregon	15,881	0.99%
2	New York	168,922	10.49%	27	Alabama	14,983	0.93%
3	Texas	145,071	9.01%	28	South Carolina	12,443	0.77%
4	Florida	111,685	6.93%	29	Nevada	9,255	0.57%
5	Illinois	71,976	4.47%	30	Mississippi	8,797	0.55%
6	New Jersey	63,524	3.94%	31	Kansas	8,169	0.51%
7	Michigan	59,057	3.67%	32	Kentucky	8,128	0.50%
8	Pennsylvania	56,171	3.49%	33	Arkansas	7,900	0.49%
9	Ohio	51,886	3.22%	34	Rhode Island	7,463	0.46%
10	Massachusetts	47,416	2.94%	35	New Mexico	5,974	0.37%
11	Georgia	38,913	2.42%	36	Iowa	4,474	0.28%
12	Maryland	35,654	2.21%	37	Hawaii	4,351	0.27%
13	Arizona	31,481	1.95%	38	Utah	4,313	0.27%
14	Tennessee	28,935	1.80%	39	Nebraska	3,225	0.20%
15	Louisiana	26,926	1.67%	40	West Virginia	2,968	0.18%
16	Missouri	25,831	1.60%	41	Alaska	2,918	0.18%
17	Indiana	25,496	1.58%	42	New Hampshire	2,165	0.13%
18	Washington	24,214	1.50%	43	Delaware	2,109	0.13%
19	Connecticut	23,700	1.47%	44	Montana	1,923	0.12%
20	Wisconsin	21,605	1.34%	45	Maine	1,778	0.11%
21	North Carolina	19,613	1.22%	46	Idaho	1,679	0.10%
22	Virginia	19,488	1.21%	47	North Dakota	950	0.06%
23	Colorado	17,662	1.10%	48	South Dakota	719	0.04%
24	Oklahoma	16,601	1.03%	49	Wyoming	701	0.04%
25	Minnesota	15,911	0.99%	50	Vermont	600	0.04%
					District of Columbia	9,118	0.57%

Source: U.S. Department of Justice, Federal Bureau of Investigation
"Crime in the United States 1992" (Uniform Crime Reports, October 3, 1993)
*Includes the theft or attempted theft of a self-propelled vehicle. Excludes motorboats, construction equipment, airplanes, and farming equipment.

Average Time Between Motor Vehicle Thefts in 1992

National Rate = A Motor Vehicle Theft Occurs Every 19.6 Seconds*

RANK	STATE	MINUTES.SECONDS	RANK	STATE	MINUTES.SECONDS
1	Vermont	878.24	26	Minnesota	33.07
2	Wyoming	751.50	27	Oklahoma	31.45
3	South Dakota	733.01	28	Colorado	29.50
4	North Dakota	554.47	29	Virginia	27.02
5	Idaho	313.54	30	North Carolina	26.52
6	Maine	296.25	31	Wisconsin	24.23
7	Montana	274.04	32	Connecticut	22.14
8	Delaware	249.54	33	Washington	21.46
9	New Hampshire	243.26	34	Indiana	20.40
10	Alaska	180.37	35	Missouri	20.24
11	West Virginia	177.34	36	Louisiana	19.34
12	Nebraska	163.25	37	Tennessee	18.13
13	Utah	122.12	38	Arizona	16.44
14	Hawaii	121.08	39	Maryland	14.47
15	Iowa	117.48	40	Georgia	13.32
16	New Mexico	88.13	41	Massachusetts	11.07
17	Rhode Island	70.37	42	Ohio	10.10
18	Arkansas	66.43	43	Pennsylvania	9.23
19	Kentucky	64.50	44	Michigan	8.55
20	Kansas	64.31	45	New Jersey	8.18
21	Mississippi	59.55	46	Illinois	7.19
22	Nevada	56.57	47	Florida	4.43
23	South Carolina	42.22	48	Texas	3.38
24	Alabama	35.11	49	New York	3.07
25	Oregon	33.11	50	California	1.39

District of Columbia 57.48

Source: Morgan Quitno Corporation using data from U.S. Department of Justice, Federal Bureau of Investigation
"Crime in the United States 1988" (Uniform Crime Reports, 1988)
*Includes the theft or attempted theft of a self-propelled vehicle. Excludes motorboats, construction equipment, airplanes, and farming equipment.

Percent Change in Number of Motor Vehicle Thefts: 1991 to 1992

National Percent Change = 3.1% Decrease*

RANK	STATE	PERCENT CHANGE	RANK	STATE	PERCENT CHANGE
1	Colorado	22.6	26	Alaska	(4.1)
2	Mississippi	18.6	27	Illinois	(4.8)
3	North Dakota	18.0	27	Nebraska	(4.8)
4	Montana	15.4	27	Tennessee	(4.8)
5	Oregon	14.6	30	Ohio	(5.2)
6	Hawaii	14.1	31	West Virginia	(5.8)
7	New Mexico	11.4	32	Oklahoma	(6.1)
8	Nevada	10.5	33	Iowa	(6.2)
9	Louisiana	10.4	34	Rhode Island	(6.4)
10	Washington	8.6	35	Kansas	(6.7)
11	Florida	7.4	36	New York	(6.8)
12	Kentucky	2.0	37	Michigan	(7.2)
13	California	1.4	38	Virginia	(8.4)
14	Minnesota	1.2	39	Idaho	(9.4)
15	Utah	1.1	40	Connecticut	(9.5)
16	Alabama	0.8	41	South Carolina	(9.7)
17	Maryland	0.4	42	Missouri	(10.3)
18	Wisconsin	(0.1)	43	South Dakota	(11.0)
19	Wyoming	(1.4)	44	New Hampshire	(11.1)
20	Indiana	(2.2)	45	Texas	(11.5)
21	Arkansas	(2.4)	46	New Jersey	(11.6)
22	Arizona	(2.5)	47	Maine	(11.8)
22	Pennsylvania	(2.5)	48	Massachusetts	(13.9)
24	North Carolina	(2.7)	49	Delaware	(17.3)
25	Georgia	(3.9)	50	Vermont	(26.7)
				District of Columbia	12.1

Source: U.S. Department of Justice, Federal Bureau of Investigation

"Crime in the United States 1992" (Uniform Crime Reports, October 3, 1993)

*Includes the theft or attempted theft of a self-propelled vehicle. Excludes motorboats, construction equipment, airplanes, and farming equipment.

Motor Vehicle Theft Rate in 1992

National Rate = 631.5 Motor Vehicle Thefts per 100,000 Population*

RANK	STATE	RATE	RANK	STATE	RATE
1	California	1,037.1	26	Wisconsin	431.5
2	New York	932.3	27	New Mexico	377.9
3	Florida	828.0	28	Hawaii	375.1
4	Texas	821.7	29	Alabama	362.3
5	Arizona	821.5	30	Minnesota	355.2
6	New Jersey	815.6	31	South Carolina	345.4
7	Massachusetts	790.5	32	Mississippi	336.5
8	Rhode Island	742.6	33	Arkansas	329.3
9	Maryland	726.4	34	Kansas	323.8
10	Connecticut	722.3	35	Delaware	306.1
11	Nevada	697.4	36	Virginia	305.6
12	Louisiana	628.1	37	North Carolina	286.6
13	Michigan	625.8	38	Utah	237.9
14	Illinois	618.8	39	Montana	233.4
15	Georgia	576.4	40	Kentucky	216.5
16	Tennessee	575.9	41	Nebraska	200.8
17	Oregon	533.5	42	New Hampshire	194.9
18	Oklahoma	516.8	43	West Virginia	163.8
19	Colorado	509.0	44	Iowa	159.1
20	Missouri	497.4	45	Idaho	157.4
21	Alaska	497.1	46	Wyoming	150.4
22	Washington	471.5	47	North Dakota	149.4
23	Ohio	471.0	48	Maine	144.0
24	Pennsylvania	467.7	49	Vermont	105.3
25	Indiana	450.3	50	South Dakota	101.1

District of Columbia   1,548.0

Source: U.S. Department of Justice, Federal Bureau of Investigation

"Crime in the United States 1992" (Uniform Crime Reports, October 3, 1993)

*Includes the theft or attempted theft of a self-propelled vehicle. Excludes motorboats, construction equipment, airplanes, and farming equipment.

Percent Change in Rate of Motor Vehicle Thefts: 1991 to 1992

National Percent Change = 4.2% Decrease*

RANK	STATE	PERCENT CHANGE	RANK	STATE	PERCENT CHANGE
1	Colorado	19.4	25	Nebraska	(5.6)
2	North Dakota	17.8	27	Georgia	(5.7)
3	Mississippi	17.5	28	Ohio	(5.9)
4	Montana	13.1	29	Tennessee	(6.1)
5	Oregon	12.5	30	West Virginia	(6.3)
6	Hawaii	11.6	31	Rhode Island	(6.5)
7	Louisiana	9.5	32	Iowa	(6.8)
8	New Mexico	9.1	33	Alaska	(6.9)
9	Nevada	6.9	34	New York	(7.1)
10	Washington	6.1	35	Oklahoma	(7.2)
11	Florida	5.7	36	Kansas	(7.7)
12	Kentucky	0.9	37	Michigan	(7.9)
13	California	(0.2)	38	Connecticut	(9.2)
14	Alabama	(0.3)	39	Virginia	(9.7)
15	Maryland	(0.6)	40	South Carolina	(10.8)
16	Wisconsin	(1.1)	41	Missouri	(10.9)
17	Utah	(1.3)	42	New Hampshire	(11.5)
18	Minnesota	(2.3)	43	Idaho	(11.7)
19	Wyoming	(2.7)	44	Maine	(11.8)
20	Pennsylvania	(2.9)	45	New Jersey	(11.9)
21	Indiana	(3.1)	46	South Dakota	(12.0)
22	Arkansas	(3.5)	47	Texas	(13.0)
23	North Carolina	(4.2)	48	Massachusetts	(14.0)
24	Arizona	(4.6)	49	Delaware	(18.4)
25	Illinois	(5.6)	50	Vermont	(27.1)

District of Columbia   13.8

Source: U.S. Department of Justice, Federal Bureau of Investigation
   "Crime in the United States 1992" (Uniform Crime Reports, October 3, 1993)
*Includes the theft or attempted theft of a self-propelled vehicle. Excludes motorboats, construction equipment, airplanes, and farming equipment.

Crime in Urban Areas in 1992

National Total = 13,131,945 Crimes*

RANK	STATE	CRIMES	%	RANK	STATE	CRIMES	%
1	California	2,040,645	15.54%	26	Connecticut	162,254	1.24%
2	Texas	1,213,471	9.24%	27	Oregon	160,822	1.22%
3	Florida	1,094,075	8.33%	28	Kansas	125,671	0.96%
4	New York	1,041,197	7.93%	29	Kentucky	105,224	0.80%
5	Michigan	501,167	3.82%	30	Arkansas	102,223	0.78%
6	Ohio	495,284	3.77%	31	Mississippi	100,838	0.77%
7	Georgia	396,924	3.02%	32	Iowa	100,125	0.76%
8	New Jersey	394,463	3.00%	33	Utah	98,161	0.75%
9	Pennsylvania	391,267	2.98%	34	New Mexico	92,202	0.70%
10	North Carolina	355,910	2.71%	35	Nevada	77,302	0.59%
11	Washington	302,617	2.30%	36	Nebraska	63,094	0.48%
12	Massachusetts	299,954	2.28%	37	Hawaii	56,315	0.43%
13	Maryland	298,553	2.27%	38	Rhode Island	45,983	0.35%
14	Arizona	264,472	2.01%	39	Maine	37,122	0.28%
15	Louisiana	263,094	2.00%	40	West Virginia	35,979	0.27%
16	Virginia	257,492	1.96%	41	Idaho	35,070	0.27%
17	Missouri	251,620	1.92%	42	New Hampshire	33,355	0.25%
18	Indiana	245,689	1.87%	43	Delaware	30,306	0.23%
19	Tennessee	240,115	1.83%	44	Montana	26,395	0.20%
20	Alabama	207,519	1.58%	45	Alaska	25,414	0.19%
21	Wisconsin	199,108	1.52%	46	Wyoming	18,642	0.14%
22	Colorado	196,758	1.50%	47	South Dakota	17,846	0.14%
23	Minnesota	187,512	1.43%	48	North Dakota	16,180	0.12%
24	South Carolina	181,280	1.38%	49	Vermont	14,024	0.11%
25	Oklahoma	164,025	1.25%	–	Illinois**	N/A	N/A

District of Columbia 67,187 0.51%

Source: Morgan Quitno Corporation using data from U.S. Department of Justice, Federal Bureau of Investigation
"Crime in the United States 1992" (Uniform Crime Reports, October 3, 1993)

*The F.B.I. defines urban areas as Metropolitan Statistical Areas and other cities outside such areas. Includes murder, rape, robbery, aggravated assault, burglary, larceny-theft, motor vehicle theft and arson.

**Not available.

Urban Crime Rate in 1992

National Rate = 7,020 Crimes per 100,000 Urban Population*

RANK	STATE	RATE		RANK	STATE	RATE
1	North Carolina	10,663		26	Indiana	6,828
2	Florida	9,976		27	Maine	6,776
3	Georgia	9,687		28	Utah	6,548
4	South Carolina	9,514		29	Wyoming	6,327
5	Louisiana	9,161		30	Montana	6,287
6	Texas	8,900		31	Connecticut	6,237
7	Alabama	8,506		32	Delaware	6,229
8	New Mexico	8,339		33	Wisconsin	6,199
9	Mississippi	8,329		34	Ohio	6,161
10	Arizona	8,247		35	Minnesota	6,135
11	Washington	8,139		36	Idaho	6,065
12	Arkansas	8,126		37	Nebraska	6,044
13	Tennessee	8,085		38	Virginia	5,997
14	Oregon	8,028		39	Iowa	5,949
15	Vermont	7,742		40	Massachusetts	5,917
16	Oklahoma	7,700		41	New Hampshire	5,897
17	Maryland	7,678		42	Hawaii	5,710
18	Michigan	7,645		43	New Jersey	5,708
19	California	7,401		44	West Virginia	5,551
20	Kansas	7,338		45	Kentucky	5,508
21	Nevada	7,283		46	Rhode Island	5,326
22	Colorado	7,246		47	South Dakota	5,130
23	Missouri	7,156		48	Pennsylvania	4,778
24	New York	6,866		49	North Dakota	4,754
25	Alaska	6,846		–	Illinois**	N/A

District of Columbia   11,071

Source: Morgan Quitno Corporation using data from U.S. Department of Justice, Federal Bureau of Investigation
    "Crime in the United States 1992" (Uniform Crime Reports, October 3, 1993)

*The F.B.I. defines urban areas as Metropolitan Statistical Areas and other cities outside such areas. Rates determined using 1990 urban population figures. Includes murder, rape, robbery, aggravated assault, burglary, larceny-theft, motor vehicle theft and arson.

**Not available.

Percent of Crime Occurring in Urban Areas in 1992

National Percent = 95.38% of Crimes*

RANK	STATE	PERCENT	RANK	STATE	PERCENT
1	New Jersey	100.00	26	Oregon	92.81
2	Massachusetts	99.96	27	Indiana	92.58
3	Rhode Island	99.94	28	Wisconsin	92.07
4	California	98.98	29	Georgia	91.79
5	Arizona	98.19	30	Minnesota	91.17
6	New York	98.09	31	Nebraska	90.86
7	Connecticut	97.87	32	Delaware	90.72
8	Maryland	97.73	33	New Mexico	90.64
9	New Hampshire	97.46	34	Mississippi	90.08
10	Texas	97.38	35	Iowa	89.98
11	Florida	97.05	36	North Carolina	89.64
12	Ohio	96.37	37	Arkansas	89.49
13	Pennsylvania	96.03	38	North Dakota	87.63
14	Utah	95.68	39	Wyoming	87.44
15	Washington	95.45	40	South Carolina	85.38
16	Alabama	95.24	41	Maine	85.31
17	Colorado	95.16	42	Kentucky	84.31
18	Missouri	95.06	43	South Dakota	83.70
19	Michigan	94.65	44	Idaho	82.25
20	Oklahoma	94.02	45	Hawaii	79.43
21	Virginia	93.93	46	Alaska	77.74
22	Nevada	93.90	47	West Virginia	76.08
23	Louisiana	93.75	48	Vermont	72.15
24	Kansas	93.63	49	Montana	69.70
25	Tennessee	93.06	–	Illinois**	N/A

District of Columbia   100.00

Source: Morgan Quitno Corporation using data from U.S. Department of Justice, Federal Bureau of Investigation
    "Crime in the United States 1992" (Uniform Crime Reports, October 3, 1993)
*The F.B.I. defines urban areas as Metropolitan Statistical Areas and other cities outside such areas. Includes murder, rape, robbery, aggravated assault, burglary, larceny-theft, motor vehicle theft and arson.
**Not available.

Crime in Rural Areas in 1992

National Total = 635,682 Crimes*

RANK	STATE	CRIMES	%	RANK	STATE	CRIMES	%
1	North Carolina	41,137	6.47%	26	Mississippi	11,106	1.75%
2	Georgia	35,506	5.59%	27	Oklahoma	10,439	1.64%
3	Florida	33,285	5.24%	28	Alabama	10,370	1.63%
4	Texas	32,677	5.14%	29	Colorado	10,012	1.58%
5	South Carolina	31,047	4.88%	30	New Mexico	9,521	1.50%
6	Michigan	28,305	4.45%	31	Kansas	8,551	1.35%
7	California	21,116	3.32%	32	Idaho	7,569	1.19%
8	New York	20,292	3.19%	33	Alaska	7,279	1.15%
9	Indiana	19,686	3.10%	34	Maryland	6,950	1.09%
10	Kentucky	19,575	3.08%	35	Maine	6,394	1.01%
11	Ohio	18,668	2.94%	36	Nebraska	6,350	1.00%
12	Minnesota	18,152	2.86%	37	Vermont	5,413	0.85%
13	Tennessee	17,906	2.82%	38	Nevada	5,022	0.79%
14	Louisiana	17,553	2.76%	39	Arizona	4,863	0.77%
15	Wisconsin	17,146	2.70%	40	Utah	4,428	0.70%
16	Virginia	16,626	2.62%	41	Connecticut	3,533	0.56%
17	Pennsylvania	16,164	2.54%	42	South Dakota	3,476	0.55%
18	Hawaii	14,584	2.29%	43	Delaware	3,100	0.49%
19	Washington	14,418	2.27%	44	Wyoming	2,678	0.42%
20	Missouri	13,074	2.06%	45	North Dakota	2,285	0.36%
21	Oregon	12,467	1.96%	46	New Hampshire	870	0.14%
22	Arkansas	12,010	1.89%	47	Massachusetts	117	0.02%
23	Montana	11,477	1.81%	48	Rhode Island	26	0.00%
24	West Virginia	11,309	1.78%	49	New Jersey	0	0.00%
25	Iowa	11,150	1.75%	–	Illinois**	N/A	N/A

District of Columbia   0   0.00%

Source: U.S. Department of Justice, Federal Bureau of Investigation

"Crime in the United States 1992" (Uniform Crime Reports, October 3, 1993)

*The F.B.I. defines rural areas as those other than Metropolitan Statistical Areas and other cities outside such areas. Includes murder, rape, robbery, aggravated assault, burglary, larceny-theft, motor vehicle theft and arson.

**Not available.

Rural Crime Rate in 1992

National Rate = 1,031 Crimes per 100,000 Rural Population*

RANK	STATE	RATE		RANK	STATE	RATE
1	Hawaii	11,948		26	Oklahoma	1,028
2	Alaska	4,071		27	Wisconsin	1,021
3	Nevada	3,577		28	Iowa	1,019
4	Montana	3,026		29	Indiana	1,012
5	New Mexico	2,325		30	South Dakota	999
6	Utah	1,979		31	West Virginia	987
7	South Carolina	1,963		32	Texas	975
8	Idaho	1,766		33	California	965
9	Colorado	1,730		34	Maine	940
10	Delaware	1,725		35	Tennessee	939
11	Florida	1,689		36	Virginia	878
12	Wyoming	1,685		37	Missouri	817
13	Georgia	1,491		38	Mississippi	815
14	Oregon	1,486		39	Maryland	778
15	Vermont	1,418		40	North Dakota	766
16	Minnesota	1,377		41	New York	718
17	Louisiana	1,302		42	Ohio	665
18	Washington	1,255		43	Alabama	648
19	North Carolina	1,250		44	Connecticut	515
20	Nebraska	1,188		45	Pennsylvania	438
21	Kansas	1,118		46	New Hampshire	160
22	Kentucky	1,103		47	Rhode Island	19
23	Arkansas	1,099		48	Massachusetts	12
24	Arizona	1,061		49	New Jersey	0
25	Michigan	1,033		–	Illinois**	N/A

District of Columbia   0

Source: Morgan Quitno Corporation using data from U.S. Department of Justice, Federal Bureau of Investigation
   "Crime in the United States 1992" (Uniform Crime Reports, October 3, 1993)
*The F.B.I. defines rural areas as other than Metropolitan Statistical Areas and other cities. Rates determined using 1990 Census rural population figures. Includes murder, rape, robbery, aggravated assault, burglary, larceny-theft, motor vehicle theft and arson.
**Not available.

Percent of Crime Occurring in Rural Areas in 1992

National Percent = 4.62% of Crimes*

RANK	STATE	PERCENT	RANK	STATE	PERCENT
1	Montana	30.30	26	Kansas	6.37
2	Vermont	27.85	27	Louisiana	6.25
3	West Virginia	23.92	28	Nevada	6.10
4	Alaska	22.26	29	Virginia	6.07
5	Hawaii	20.57	30	Oklahoma	5.98
6	Idaho	17.75	31	Michigan	5.35
7	South Dakota	16.30	32	Missouri	4.94
8	Kentucky	15.69	33	Colorado	4.84
9	Maine	14.69	34	Alabama	4.76
10	South Carolina	14.62	35	Washington	4.55
11	Wyoming	12.56	36	Utah	4.32
12	North Dakota	12.37	37	Pennsylvania	3.97
13	Arkansas	10.51	38	Ohio	3.63
14	North Carolina	10.36	39	Florida	2.95
15	Iowa	10.02	40	Texas	2.62
16	Mississippi	9.92	41	New Hampshire	2.54
17	New Mexico	9.36	42	Maryland	2.27
18	Delaware	9.28	43	Connecticut	2.13
19	Nebraska	9.14	44	New York	1.91
20	Minnesota	8.83	45	Arizona	1.81
21	Georgia	8.21	46	California	1.02
22	Wisconsin	7.93	47	Rhode Island	0.06
23	Indiana	7.42	48	Massachusetts	0.04
24	Oregon	7.19	49	New Jersey	0.00
25	Tennessee	6.94	–	Illinois**	N/A

District of Columbia   0.00

Source: Morgan Quitno Corporation using data from U.S. Department of Justice, Federal Bureau of Investigation

"Crime in the United States 1992" (Uniform Crime Reports, October 3, 1993)

*The F.B.I. defines rural areas as those other than Metropolitan Statistical Areas and other cities outside such areas. Includes murder, rape, robbery, aggravated assault, burglary, larceny-theft, motor vehicle theft and arson.

**Not available.

Violent Crime in Urban Areas in 1992

National Total = 1,748,883 Violent Crimes*

RANK	STATE	CRIMES	%	RANK	STATE	CRIMES	%
1	California	342,907	19.61%	26	Oregon	14,304	0.82%
2	New York	201,338	11.51%	27	Minnesota	14,260	0.82%
3	Florida	157,914	9.03%	28	New Mexico	12,897	0.74%
4	Texas	138,704	7.93%	29	Wisconsin	12,831	0.73%
5	Michigan	70,008	4.00%	30	Arkansas	12,722	0.73%
6	Ohio	56,572	3.23%	31	Kansas	12,113	0.69%
7	Pennsylvania	50,126	2.87%	32	Mississippi	9,210	0.53%
8	New Jersey	48,745	2.79%	33	Nevada	8,473	0.48%
9	Maryland	47,969	2.74%	34	Iowa	7,283	0.42%
10	Massachusetts	46,697	2.67%	35	Nebraska	5,324	0.30%
11	Georgia	45,084	2.58%	36	Utah	4,948	0.28%
12	North Carolina	42,675	2.44%	37	Rhode Island	3,959	0.23%
13	Louisiana	38,784	2.22%	38	Delaware	3,716	0.21%
14	Missouri	36,901	2.11%	39	Alaska	2,987	0.17%
15	Tennessee	35,513	2.03%	40	West Virginia	2,791	0.16%
16	Alabama	34,455	1.97%	41	Hawaii	2,491	0.14%
17	South Carolina	28,834	1.65%	42	Idaho	2,349	0.13%
18	Washington	26,347	1.51%	43	Maine	1,327	0.08%
19	Indiana	26,277	1.50%	44	New Hampshire	1,301	0.07%
20	Arizona	24,979	1.43%	45	Wyoming	1,211	0.07%
21	Virginia	22,260	1.27%	46	South Dakota	1,143	0.07%
22	Colorado	19,399	1.11%	47	Montana	798	0.05%
23	Oklahoma	19,078	1.09%	48	North Dakota	480	0.03%
24	Connecticut	15,749	0.90%	49	Vermont	399	0.02%
25	Kentucky	15,566	0.89%	–	Illinois**	N/A	N/A

	District of Columbia	16,685	0.95%

Source: Morgan Quitno Corporation using data from U.S. Department of Justice, Federal Bureau of Investigation
   "Crime in the United States 1992" (Uniform Crime Reports, October 3, 1993)
*The F.B.I. defines urban areas as Metropolitan Statistical Areas and other cities outside such areas. Violent crimes are offenses of murder, forcible rape, robbery and aggravated assault.
**Not available.

Percent of Violent Crime Occurring in Urban Areas in 1992

National Percent = 96.17% of Violent Crimes*

RANK	STATE	PERCENT	RANK	STATE	PERCENT
1	New Jersey	100.00	26	New Hampshire	93.13
2	Massachusetts	99.94	27	Virginia	93.11
3	Rhode Island	99.85	28	Wisconsin	92.94
4	California	99.21	29	Arkansas	91.98
5	New York	99.03	30	Louisiana	91.89
6	Pennsylvania	97.76	31	Nevada	91.63
7	Maryland	97.73	32	North Carolina	91.58
8	Ohio	97.65	33	Indiana	91.27
9	Texas	97.43	34	Georgia	91.09
10	Arizona	97.17	35	North Dakota	90.57
11	Florida	96.98	36	New Mexico	87.25
12	Connecticut	96.90	37	Delaware	86.82
13	Colorado	96.58	38	Mississippi	85.57
14	Michigan	96.33	39	South Carolina	84.73
15	Missouri	95.98	40	Hawaii	83.09
16	Washington	95.97	41	South Dakota	82.65
17	Alabama	95.57	42	Maine	82.12
18	Oklahoma	95.37	43	Wyoming	81.33
19	Nebraska	95.11	44	Idaho	78.22
20	Tennessee	94.73	45	Kentucky	77.42
21	Oregon	94.17	46	Alaska	77.04
22	Minnesota	94.16	47	West Virginia	72.82
23	Kansas	93.99	48	Vermont	63.94
24	Utah	93.94	49	Montana	57.00
25	Iowa	93.18	–	Illinois**	N/A

District of Columbia   100.00

Source: Morgan Quitno Corporation using data from U.S. Department of Justice, Federal Bureau of Investigation
   "Crime in the United States 1992" (Uniform Crime Reports, October 3, 1993)
*The F.B.I. defines urban areas as Metropolitan Statistical Areas and other cities outside such areas. Violent crimes are offenses of murder, forcible rape, robbery and aggravated assault.
**Not available.

Violent Crime in Rural Areas in 1992

National Total = 69,727 Violent Crimes*

RANK	STATE	CRIMES	%	RANK	STATE	CRIMES	%
1	South Carolina	5,195	7.45%	26	Alaska	890	1.28%
2	Florida	4,913	7.05%	27	Oregon	885	1.27%
3	Kentucky	4,541	6.51%	28	Minnesota	884	1.27%
4	Georgia	4,412	6.33%	29	Kansas	775	1.11%
5	North Carolina	3,925	5.63%	30	Nevada	774	1.11%
6	Texas	3,665	5.26%	31	Arizona	727	1.04%
7	Louisiana	3,425	4.91%	32	Colorado	687	0.99%
8	California	2,717	3.90%	33	Idaho	654	0.94%
9	Michigan	2,664	3.82%	34	Montana	602	0.86%
10	Indiana	2,514	3.61%	35	Delaware	564	0.81%
11	Tennessee	1,974	2.83%	36	Iowa	533	0.76%
12	New York	1,973	2.83%	37	Hawaii	507	0.73%
13	New Mexico	1,884	2.70%	38	Connecticut	503	0.72%
14	Virginia	1,647	2.36%	39	Utah	319	0.46%
15	Alabama	1,597	2.29%	40	Maine	289	0.41%
16	Mississippi	1,553	2.23%	41	Wyoming	278	0.40%
17	Missouri	1,547	2.22%	42	Nebraska	274	0.39%
18	Ohio	1,363	1.95%	43	South Dakota	240	0.34%
19	Pennsylvania	1,150	1.65%	44	Vermont	225	0.32%
20	Maryland	1,116	1.60%	45	New Hampshire	96	0.14%
21	Arkansas	1,109	1.59%	46	North Dakota	50	0.07%
22	Washington	1,107	1.59%	47	Massachusetts	30	0.04%
23	West Virginia	1,042	1.49%	48	Rhode Island	6	0.01%
24	Wisconsin	975	1.40%	49	New Jersey	0	0.00%
25	Oklahoma	927	1.33%	–	Illinois**	N/A	N/A
					District of Columbia	0	0.00%

Source: U.S. Department of Justice, Federal Bureau of Investigation
   "Crime in the United States 1992" (Uniform Crime Reports, October 3, 1993)
*The F.B.I. defines rural areas as those other than Metropolitan Statistical Areas and other cities outside such areas. Violent crimes are offenses of murder, forcible rape, robbery and aggravated assault.
**Not available.

Percent of Violent Crime Occurring in Rural Areas in 1992

National Percent = 3.83% of Violent Crimes*

RANK	STATE	PERCENT	RANK	STATE	PERCENT
1	Montana	43.00	26	Utah	6.06
2	Vermont	36.06	27	Kansas	6.01
3	West Virginia	27.18	28	Minnesota	5.84
4	Alaska	22.96	29	Oregon	5.83
5	Kentucky	22.58	30	Tennessee	5.27
6	Idaho	21.78	31	Nebraska	4.89
7	Wyoming	18.67	32	Oklahoma	4.63
8	Maine	17.88	33	Alabama	4.43
9	South Dakota	17.35	34	Washington	4.03
10	Hawaii	16.91	35	Missouri	4.02
11	South Carolina	15.27	36	Michigan	3.67
12	Mississippi	14.43	37	Colorado	3.42
13	Delaware	13.18	38	Connecticut	3.10
14	New Mexico	12.75	39	Florida	3.02
15	North Dakota	9.43	40	Arizona	2.83
16	Georgia	8.91	41	Texas	2.57
17	Indiana	8.73	42	Ohio	2.35
18	North Carolina	8.42	43	Maryland	2.27
19	Nevada	8.37	44	Pennsylvania	2.24
20	Louisiana	8.11	45	New York	0.97
21	Arkansas	8.02	46	California	0.79
22	Wisconsin	7.06	47	Rhode Island	0.15
23	Virginia	6.89	48	Massachusetts	0.06
24	New Hampshire	6.87	49	New Jersey	0.00
25	Iowa	6.82	–	Illinois**	N/A

District of Columbia   0.00

Source: Morgan Quitno Corporation using data from U.S. Department of Justice, Federal Bureau of Investigation
  "Crime in the United States 1992" (Uniform Crime Reports, October 3, 1993)
*The F.B.I. defines rural areas as those other than Metropolitan Statistical Areas and other cities outside such areas. Violent crimes are offenses of murder, forcible rape, robbery and aggravated assault.
**Not available.

Murder in Urban Areas in 1992

National Total = 22,090 Murders*

RANK	STATE	MURDERS	%	RANK	STATE	MURDERS	%
1	California	3,881	17.57%	26	Arkansas	188	0.85%
2	New York	2,371	10.73%	27	Oklahoma	175	0.79%
3	Texas	2,115	9.57%	28	Connecticut	163	0.74%
4	Illinois	1,303	5.90%	29	Kansas	144	0.65%
5	Florida	1,158	5.24%	30	Nevada	139	0.63%
6	Michigan	908	4.11%	31	Minnesota	131	0.59%
7	Pennsylvania	702	3.18%	32	Kentucky	122	0.55%
8	Ohio	697	3.16%	33	Oregon	121	0.55%
9	Louisiana	681	3.08%	34	New Mexico	100	0.45%
10	Georgia	640	2.90%	35	West Virginia	74	0.33%
11	Maryland	587	2.66%	36	Nebraska	63	0.29%
12	North Carolina	570	2.58%	37	Utah	44	0.20%
13	Missouri	511	2.31%	38	Rhode Island	36	0.16%
14	Virginia	492	2.23%	39	Iowa	33	0.15%
15	Tennessee	457	2.07%	40	Hawaii	32	0.14%
16	Alabama	418	1.89%	41	Delaware	30	0.14%
17	New Jersey	397	1.80%	42	Alaska	26	0.12%
18	Indiana	366	1.66%	43	Idaho	23	0.10%
19	Arizona	299	1.35%	44	New Hampshire	17	0.08%
20	South Carolina	287	1.30%	45	Maine	15	0.07%
21	Mississippi	254	1.15%	46	Wyoming	12	0.05%
22	Washington	234	1.06%	47	North Dakota	10	0.05%
23	Massachusetts	213	0.96%	48	Montana	6	0.03%
24	Wisconsin	199	0.90%	48	Vermont	6	0.03%
25	Colorado	197	0.89%	50	South Dakota	0	0.00%

District of Columbia   443   2.01%

Source: Morgan Quitno Corporation using data from U.S. Department of Justice, Federal Bureau of Investigation
"Crime in the United States 1992" (Uniform Crime Reports, October 3, 1993)
*The F.B.I. defines urban areas as Metropolitan Statistical Areas and other cities outside such areas. Includes nonnegligent manslaughter.

Percent of Murders Occurring in Urban Areas in 1992

National Percent = 92.97% of Murders*

RANK	STATE	PERCENT	RANK	STATE	PERCENT
1	New Jersey	100.00	26	Tennessee	87.88
1	Rhode Island	100.00	27	Minnesota	87.33
3	Massachusetts	99.53	28	Virginia	87.23
4	California	98.98	29	Oregon	87.05
5	New York	98.92	30	Georgia	86.37
6	Illinois	98.56	31	North Dakota	83.33
7	Maryland	98.49	31	Oklahoma	83.33
8	Connecticut	98.19	33	Utah	81.48
9	Michigan	96.80	34	Mississippi	79.38
10	Ohio	96.27	35	Indiana	78.88
11	Florida	95.86	36	North Carolina	78.84
11	Nevada	95.86	37	South Carolina	76.94
13	Arizona	95.83	38	Hawaii	76.19
14	Kansas	95.36	39	Iowa	75.00
15	Texas	94.46	40	Arkansas	72.59
16	New Hampshire	94.44	41	Maine	71.43
17	Pennsylvania	94.10	42	New Mexico	70.92
18	Delaware	93.75	43	Wyoming	70.59
19	Missouri	93.42	44	West Virginia	64.35
20	Nebraska	92.65	45	Idaho	62.16
21	Alabama	91.87	46	Alaska	59.09
22	Wisconsin	91.28	47	Kentucky	56.48
23	Colorado	91.20	48	Vermont	50.00
24	Louisiana	91.16	49	Montana	25.00
25	Washington	90.70	50	South Dakota	0.00
				District of Columbia	100.00

Source: Morgan Quitno Corporation using data from U.S. Department of Justice, Federal Bureau of Investigation
    "Crime in the United States 1992" (Uniform Crime Reports, October 3, 1993)
*The F.B.I. defines urban areas as Metropolitan Statistical Areas and other cities outside such areas. Includes nonnegligent manslaughter.

Murder in Rural Areas in 1992

National Total = 1,670 Murders*

RANK	STATE	MURDERS	%	RANK	STATE	MURDERS	%
1	North Carolina	153	9.16%	24	Minnesota	19	1.14%
2	Texas	124	7.43%	24	Wisconsin	19	1.14%
3	Georgia	101	6.05%	28	Alaska	18	1.08%
4	Indiana	98	5.87%	28	Montana	18	1.08%
5	Kentucky	94	5.63%	28	Oregon	18	1.08%
6	South Carolina	86	5.15%	31	Idaho	14	0.84%
7	Virginia	72	4.31%	32	Arizona	13	0.78%
8	Arkansas	71	4.25%	33	Iowa	11	0.66%
9	Louisiana	66	3.95%	34	Hawaii	10	0.60%
9	Mississippi	66	3.95%	34	Utah	10	0.60%
11	Tennessee	63	3.77%	36	Maryland	9	0.54%
12	Florida	50	2.99%	37	Kansas	7	0.42%
13	Pennsylvania	44	2.63%	38	Maine	6	0.36%
14	New Mexico	41	2.46%	38	Nevada	6	0.36%
14	West Virginia	41	2.46%	38	Vermont	6	0.36%
16	California	40	2.40%	41	Nebraska	5	0.30%
17	Alabama	37	2.22%	41	Wyoming	5	0.30%
18	Missouri	36	2.16%	43	South Dakota	4	0.24%
19	Oklahoma	35	2.10%	44	Connecticut	3	0.18%
20	Michigan	30	1.80%	45	Delaware	2	0.12%
21	Ohio	27	1.62%	45	North Dakota	2	0.12%
22	New York	26	1.56%	47	Massachusetts	1	0.06%
23	Washington	24	1.44%	47	New Hampshire	1	0.06%
24	Colorado	19	1.14%	49	New Jersey	0	0.00%
24	Illinois	19	1.14%	49	Rhode Island	0	0.00%
					District of Columbia	0	0.00%

Source: Morgan Quitno Corporation using data from U.S. Department of Justice, Federal Bureau of Investigation
    "Crime in the United States 1992" (Uniform Crime Reports, October 3, 1993)
*The F.B.I. defines rural areas as those other than Metropolitan Statistical Areas and other cities outside such areas. Includes nonnegligent manslaughter.

Percent of Murders Occurring in Rural Areas in 1992

National Percent = 7.03% of Murders*

RANK	STATE	PERCENT	RANK	STATE	PERCENT
1	South Dakota	100.00	26	Washington	9.30
2	Montana	75.00	27	Louisiana	8.84
3	Vermont	50.00	28	Colorado	8.80
4	Kentucky	43.52	29	Wisconsin	8.72
5	Alaska	40.91	30	Alabama	8.13
6	Idaho	37.84	31	Nebraska	7.35
7	West Virginia	35.65	32	Missouri	6.58
8	Wyoming	29.41	33	Delaware	6.25
9	New Mexico	29.08	34	Pennsylvania	5.90
10	Maine	28.57	35	New Hampshire	5.56
11	Arkansas	27.41	36	Texas	5.54
12	Iowa	25.00	37	Kansas	4.64
13	Hawaii	23.81	38	Arizona	4.17
14	South Carolina	23.06	39	Florida	4.14
15	North Carolina	21.16	39	Nevada	4.14
16	Indiana	21.12	41	Ohio	3.73
17	Mississippi	20.63	42	Michigan	3.20
18	Utah	18.52	43	Connecticut	1.81
19	North Dakota	16.67	44	Maryland	1.51
19	Oklahoma	16.67	45	Illinois	1.44
21	Georgia	13.63	46	New York	1.08
22	Oregon	12.95	47	California	1.02
23	Virginia	12.77	48	Massachusetts	0.47
24	Minnesota	12.67	49	New Jersey	0.00
25	Tennessee	12.12	49	Rhode Island	0.00

District of Columbia   0.00

Source: Morgan Quitno Corporation using data from U.S. Department of Justice, Federal Bureau of Investigation
   "Crime in the United States 1992" (Uniform Crime Reports, October 3, 1993)
*The F.B.I. defines rural areas as those other than Metropolitan Statistical Areas and other cities outside such areas. Includes nonnegligent manslaughter.

Rape in Urban Areas in 1992

National Total = 96,853 Rapes*

RANK	STATE	RAPES	%	RANK	STATE	RAPES	%
1	California	12,548	12.96%	26	Wisconsin	1,206	1.25%
2	Texas	9,098	9.39%	27	Mississippi	965	1.00%
3	Florida	6,894	7.12%	28	Kansas	964	1.00%
4	Michigan	6,457	6.67%	29	Arkansas	847	0.87%
5	Ohio	5,535	5.71%	30	Connecticut	846	0.87%
6	New York	4,978	5.14%	31	Nevada	794	0.82%
7	Washington	3,414	3.52%	32	Kentucky	792	0.82%
8	Pennsylvania	3,074	3.17%	33	New Mexico	776	0.80%
9	Georgia	2,769	2.86%	34	Utah	758	0.78%
10	New Jersey	2,392	2.47%	35	Delaware	481	0.50%
11	Tennessee	2,248	2.32%	36	Iowa	459	0.47%
12	Indiana	2,183	2.25%	37	Nebraska	445	0.46%
12	North Carolina	2,183	2.25%	38	Alaska	393	0.41%
14	Maryland	2,181	2.25%	39	New Hampshire	390	0.40%
15	Massachusetts	2,164	2.23%	40	Hawaii	344	0.36%
16	Virginia	1,809	1.87%	41	Rhode Island	311	0.32%
17	Missouri	1,737	1.79%	42	West Virginia	289	0.30%
18	South Carolina	1,705	1.76%	43	South Dakota	282	0.29%
19	Minnesota	1,686	1.74%	44	Idaho	259	0.27%
20	Louisiana	1,625	1.68%	45	Maine	223	0.23%
21	Colorado	1,612	1.66%	46	Wyoming	138	0.14%
22	Arizona	1,601	1.65%	47	Montana	133	0.14%
23	Alabama	1,567	1.62%	48	North Dakota	128	0.13%
24	Oklahoma	1,476	1.52%	49	Vermont	96	0.10%
25	Oregon	1,383	1.43%	–	Illinois**	N/A	N/A

District of Columbia 215 0.22%

Source: Morgan Quitno Corporation using data from U.S. Department of Justice, Federal Bureau of Investigation
      "Crime in the United States 1992" (Uniform Crime Reports, October 3, 1993)

*The F.B.I. defines urban areas as Metropolitan Statistical Areas and other cities outside such areas. Forcible rape is the carnal knowledge of a female forcibly and against her will. Assaults or attempts to commit rape by force or threat of force are included. However, statutory rape without force and other sex offenses are excluded.

**Not available.

Percent of Rapes Occurring in Urban Areas in 1992

National Percent = 92.46% of Rapes*

RANK	STATE	PERCENT	RANK	STATE	PERCENT
1	New Jersey	100.00	26	Georgia	90.58
1	Rhode Island	100.00	27	Virginia	90.09
3	Massachusetts	99.91	28	Louisiana	89.63
4	California	98.33	29	North Carolina	88.92
5	Colorado	98.23	30	Nebraska	88.29
6	Arizona	97.21	31	Oregon	87.53
7	New York	96.62	32	Iowa	86.93
8	Ohio	96.45	33	North Dakota	86.49
9	Texas	96.41	34	Arkansas	85.56
10	Maryland	95.74	35	Michigan	85.52
11	Connecticut	95.70	36	Wyoming	84.66
12	Nevada	95.32	37	Mississippi	82.76
13	Oklahoma	94.86	38	South Carolina	82.29
14	Tennessee	94.57	39	Delaware	81.39
15	Florida	94.31	40	New Mexico	78.38
16	Kansas	92.51	41	Hawaii	78.18
17	Pennsylvania	92.48	42	South Dakota	76.63
18	Washington	92.35	43	Idaho	76.40
19	Utah	92.10	44	Maine	75.85
20	New Hampshire	91.98	45	West Virginia	73.54
21	Alabama	91.96	46	Alaska	67.88
22	Wisconsin	91.71	47	Vermont	67.61
23	Missouri	91.66	48	Kentucky	65.51
24	Minnesota	91.63	49	Montana	63.33
25	Indiana	91.03	–	Illinois**	N/A

District of Columbia 100.00

Source: Morgan Quitno Corporation using data from U.S. Department of Justice, Federal Bureau of Investigation
"Crime in the United States 1992" (Uniform Crime Reports, October 3, 1993)

*The F.B.I. defines urban areas as Metropolitan Statistical Areas and other cities outside such areas. Forcible rape is the carnal knowledge of a female forcibly and against her will. Assaults or attempts to commit rape by force or threat of force are included. However, statutory rape without force and other sex offenses are excluded.

**Not available.

Rape in Rural Areas in 1992

National Total = 7,897 Rapes*

RANK	STATE	RAPES	%	RANK	STATE	RAPES	%
1	Michigan	1,093	13.84%	26	Wisconsin	109	1.38%
2	Kentucky	417	5.28%	27	West Virginia	104	1.32%
3	Florida	416	5.27%	28	Maryland	97	1.23%
4	South Carolina	367	4.65%	29	Hawaii	96	1.22%
5	Texas	339	4.29%	30	South Dakota	86	1.09%
6	Georgia	288	3.65%	31	Idaho	80	1.01%
7	Washington	283	3.58%	31	Oklahoma	80	1.01%
8	North Carolina	272	3.44%	33	Kansas	78	0.99%
9	Pennsylvania	250	3.17%	34	Montana	77	0.98%
10	Indiana	215	2.72%	35	Maine	71	0.90%
11	New Mexico	214	2.71%	36	Iowa	69	0.87%
12	California	213	2.70%	37	Utah	65	0.82%
13	Ohio	204	2.58%	38	Nebraska	59	0.75%
14	Mississippi	201	2.55%	39	Arizona	46	0.58%
15	Virginia	199	2.52%	39	Vermont	46	0.58%
16	Oregon	197	2.49%	41	Nevada	39	0.49%
17	Louisiana	188	2.38%	42	Connecticut	38	0.48%
18	Alaska	186	2.36%	43	New Hampshire	34	0.43%
19	New York	174	2.20%	44	Colorado	29	0.37%
20	Missouri	158	2.00%	45	Wyoming	25	0.32%
21	Minnesota	154	1.95%	46	North Dakota	20	0.25%
22	Arkansas	143	1.81%	47	Massachusetts	2	0.03%
23	Alabama	137	1.73%	48	New Jersey	0	0.00%
24	Tennessee	129	1.63%	48	Rhode Island	0	0.00%
25	Delaware	110	1.39%	–	Illinois**	N/A	N/A

District of Columbia　　　　0　　0.00%

Source: U.S. Department of Justice, Federal Bureau of Investigation

"Crime in the United States 1992" (Uniform Crime Reports, October 3, 1993)

*The F.B.I. defines rural areas as those other than Metropolitan Statistical Areas and other cities outside such areas. Forcible rape is the carnal knowledge of a female forcibly and against her will. Assaults or attempts to commit rape by force or threat of force are included. However, statutory rape without force and other sex offenses are excluded.

**Not available.

376

Percent of Rapes Occurring in Rural Areas in 1992

National Percent = 7.54% of Rapes*

RANK	STATE	PERCENT	RANK	STATE	PERCENT
1	Montana	36.67	26	Minnesota	8.37
2	Kentucky	34.49	27	Missouri	8.34
3	Vermont	32.39	28	Wisconsin	8.29
4	Alaska	32.12	29	Alabama	8.04
5	West Virginia	26.46	30	New Hampshire	8.02
6	Maine	24.15	31	Utah	7.90
7	Idaho	23.60	32	Washington	7.65
8	South Dakota	23.37	33	Pennsylvania	7.52
9	Hawaii	21.82	34	Kansas	7.49
10	New Mexico	21.62	35	Florida	5.69
11	Delaware	18.61	36	Tennessee	5.43
12	South Carolina	17.71	37	Oklahoma	5.14
13	Mississippi	17.24	38	Nevada	4.68
14	Wyoming	15.34	39	Connecticut	4.30
15	Michigan	14.48	40	Maryland	4.26
16	Arkansas	14.44	41	Texas	3.59
17	North Dakota	13.51	42	Ohio	3.55
18	Iowa	13.07	43	New York	3.38
19	Oregon	12.47	44	Arizona	2.79
20	Nebraska	11.71	45	Colorado	1.77
21	North Carolina	11.08	46	California	1.67
22	Louisiana	10.37	47	Massachusetts	0.09
23	Virginia	9.91	48	New Jersey	0.00
24	Georgia	9.42	48	Rhode Island	0.00
25	Indiana	8.97	–	Illinois**	N/A

District of Columbia   0.00

Source: Morgan Quitno Corporation using data from U.S. Department of Justice, Federal Bureau of Investigation
     "Crime in the United States 1992" (Uniform Crime Reports, October 3, 1993)
*The F.B.I. defines rural areas as those other than Metropolitan Statistical Areas and other cities outside such areas. Forcible rape is the carnal knowledge of a female forcibly and against her will. Assaults or attempts to commit rape by force or threat of force are included. However, statutory rape without force and other sex offenses are excluded.
**Not available.

Robbery in Urban Areas in 1992

National Total = 667,268 Robberies*

RANK	STATE	ROBBERIES	%	RANK	STATE	ROBBERIES	%
1	California	130,707	19.59%	26	Oregon	4,429	0.66%
2	New York	108,057	16.19%	27	Nevada	4,352	0.65%
3	Florida	48,899	7.33%	28	Oklahoma	4,326	0.65%
4	Illinois	47,910	7.18%	29	Colorado	4,141	0.62%
5	Texas	44,369	6.65%	30	Kansas	3,237	0.49%
6	New Jersey	22,216	3.33%	31	Kentucky	3,121	0.47%
7	Ohio	21,815	3.27%	32	Mississippi	3,059	0.46%
8	Pennsylvania	21,583	3.23%	33	Arkansas	2,919	0.44%
9	Maryland	20,946	3.14%	34	New Mexico	2,063	0.31%
10	Michigan	20,808	3.12%	35	Iowa	1,094	0.16%
11	Georgia	16,411	2.46%	36	Hawaii	1,036	0.16%
12	North Carolina	12,359	1.85%	37	Delaware	1,004	0.15%
13	Missouri	11,716	1.76%	38	Utah	998	0.15%
14	Louisiana	11,506	1.72%	39	Rhode Island	950	0.14%
15	Massachusetts	11,057	1.66%	40	Nebraska	899	0.13%
16	Tennessee	10,854	1.63%	41	West Virginia	705	0.11%
17	Virginia	8,635	1.29%	42	Alaska	597	0.09%
18	Washington	7,112	1.07%	43	New Hampshire	362	0.05%
19	Connecticut	6,877	1.03%	44	Maine	256	0.04%
20	Indiana	6,799	1.02%	45	Idaho	199	0.03%
21	Alabama	6,713	1.01%	46	Montana	191	0.03%
22	Wisconsin	5,969	0.89%	47	South Dakota	104	0.02%
23	Arizona	5,850	0.88%	48	Wyoming	73	0.01%
24	South Carolina	5,554	0.83%	49	North Dakota	48	0.01%
25	Minnesota	4,882	0.73%	50	Vermont	42	0.01%
					District of Columbia	7,459	1.12%

Source: Morgan Quitno Corporation using data from U.S. Department of Justice, Federal Bureau of Investigation
    "Crime in the United States 1992" (Uniform Crime Reports, October 3, 1993)
*The F.B.I. defines urban areas as Metropolitan Statistical Areas and other cities outside such areas. Robbery is the taking of anything of value by force or threat of force. Attempts are included.

Percent of Robberies Occurring in Urban Areas in 1992

National Percent = 99.23% of Robberies*

RANK	STATE	PERCENT		RANK	STATE	PERCENT
1	New Jersey	100.00		26	New Hampshire	98.64
1	Rhode Island	100.00		27	Alabama	98.45
3	Massachusetts	99.98		28	Utah	98.42
4	New York	99.91		29	Iowa	98.29
5	Illinois	99.87		30	Oregon	98.27
6	California	99.85		30	Virginia	98.27
7	Arizona	99.71		32	Indiana	98.24
8	Michigan	99.55		33	Georgia	97.32
9	Wisconsin	99.53		34	Arkansas	96.94
10	Minnesota	99.51		35	North Carolina	96.68
10	Texas	99.51		36	Delaware	96.35
12	Ohio	99.50		37	North Dakota	96.00
13	Maryland	99.49		38	Kentucky	95.36
14	Pennsylvania	99.46		39	Mississippi	94.01
15	Missouri	99.43		40	New Mexico	93.69
16	Connecticut	99.41		41	Alaska	93.28
17	Washington	99.08		42	South Carolina	90.34
18	Colorado	99.07		43	Hawaii	90.01
19	Tennessee	99.00		44	West Virginia	89.47
20	Nevada	98.98		45	Maine	88.89
21	Louisiana	98.88		46	Idaho	86.90
22	Oklahoma	98.86		46	Wyoming	86.90
23	Florida	98.82		48	South Dakota	86.67
24	Kansas	98.78		49	Montana	86.04
25	Nebraska	98.68		50	Vermont	82.35

District of Columbia   100.00

Source: Morgan Quitno Corporation using data from U.S. Department of Justice, Federal Bureau of Investigation

"Crime in the United States 1992" (Uniform Crime Reports, October 3, 1993)

*The F.B.I. defines urban areas as Metropolitan Statistical Areas and other cities outside such areas. Robbery is the taking of anything of value by force or threat of force. Attempts are included.

Robbery in Rural Areas in 1992

National Total = 5,210 Robberies*

RANK	STATE	ROBBERIES	%	RANK	STATE	ROBBERIES	%
1	South Carolina	594	11.40%	26	Illinois	63	1.21%
2	Florida	583	11.19%	27	Oklahoma	50	0.96%
3	Georgia	452	8.68%	28	Nevada	45	0.86%
4	North Carolina	425	8.16%	29	Alaska	43	0.83%
5	Texas	219	4.20%	30	Connecticut	41	0.79%
6	Mississippi	195	3.74%	31	Kansas	40	0.77%
7	California	190	3.65%	32	Colorado	39	0.75%
8	Kentucky	152	2.92%	33	Delaware	38	0.73%
8	Virginia	152	2.92%	34	Maine	32	0.61%
10	New Mexico	139	2.67%	35	Montana	31	0.60%
11	Louisiana	130	2.50%	36	Idaho	30	0.58%
12	Indiana	122	2.34%	37	Wisconsin	28	0.54%
13	Pennsylvania	118	2.26%	38	Minnesota	24	0.46%
14	Hawaii	115	2.21%	39	Iowa	19	0.36%
15	Ohio	110	2.11%	40	Arizona	17	0.33%
15	Tennessee	110	2.11%	41	South Dakota	16	0.31%
17	Maryland	108	2.07%	41	Utah	16	0.31%
18	Alabama	106	2.03%	43	Nebraska	12	0.23%
19	New York	97	1.86%	44	Wyoming	11	0.21%
20	Michigan	94	1.80%	45	Vermont	9	0.17%
21	Arkansas	92	1.77%	46	New Hampshire	5	0.10%
22	West Virginia	83	1.59%	47	Massachusetts	2	0.04%
23	Oregon	78	1.50%	47	North Dakota	2	0.04%
24	Missouri	67	1.29%	49	New Jersey	0	0.00%
25	Washington	66	1.27%	49	Rhode Island	0	0.00%
					District of Columbia	0	0.00%

Source: U.S. Department of Justice, Federal Bureau of Investigation
   "Crime in the United States 1992" (Uniform Crime Reports, October 3, 1993)
*The F.B.I. defines rural areas as those other than Metropolitan Statistical Areas and other cities outside such areas. Robbery is the taking of anything
of value by force or threat of force. Attempts are included.

Percent of Robberies Occurring in Rural Areas in 1992

National Percent = 0.77% of Robberies*

RANK	STATE	PERCENT
1	Vermont	17.65
2	Montana	13.96
3	South Dakota	13.33
4	Idaho	13.10
4	Wyoming	13.10
6	Maine	11.11
7	West Virginia	10.53
8	Hawaii	9.99
9	South Carolina	9.66
10	Alaska	6.72
11	New Mexico	6.31
12	Mississippi	5.99
13	Kentucky	4.64
14	North Dakota	4.00
15	Delaware	3.65
16	North Carolina	3.32
17	Arkansas	3.06
18	Georgia	2.68
19	Indiana	1.76
20	Oregon	1.73
20	Virginia	1.73
22	Iowa	1.71
23	Utah	1.58
24	Alabama	1.55
25	New Hampshire	1.36

RANK	STATE	PERCENT
26	Nebraska	1.32
27	Kansas	1.22
28	Florida	1.18
29	Oklahoma	1.14
30	Louisiana	1.12
31	Nevada	1.02
32	Tennessee	1.00
33	Colorado	0.93
34	Washington	0.92
35	Connecticut	0.59
36	Missouri	0.57
37	Pennsylvania	0.54
38	Maryland	0.51
39	Ohio	0.50
40	Minnesota	0.49
40	Texas	0.49
42	Wisconsin	0.47
43	Michigan	0.45
44	Arizona	0.29
45	California	0.15
46	Illinois	0.13
47	New York	0.09
48	Massachusetts	0.02
49	New Jersey	0.00
49	Rhode Island	0.00
	District of Columbia	0.00

Source: Morgan Quitno Corporation using data from U.S. Department of Justice, Federal Bureau of Investigation
    "Crime in the United States 1992" (Uniform Crime Reports, October 3, 1993)
*The F.B.I. defines rural areas as those other than Metropolitan Statistical Areas and other cities outside such areas. Robbery is the taking of anything
of value by force or threat of force. Attempts are included.

Aggravated Assault in Urban Areas in 1992

National Total = 1,071,467 Aggravated Assaults*

RANK	STATE	ASSAULTS	%	RANK	STATE	ASSAULTS	%
1	California	195,771	18.27%	26	New Mexico	9,958	0.93%
2	Florida	100,963	9.42%	27	Arkansas	8,768	0.82%
3	New York	85,932	8.02%	28	Oregon	8,371	0.78%
4	Texas	83,122	7.76%	29	Connecticut	7,863	0.73%
5	Illinois	59,582	5.56%	30	Kansas	7,768	0.72%
6	Michigan	41,835	3.90%	31	Minnesota	7,561	0.71%
7	Massachusetts	33,263	3.10%	32	Iowa	5,697	0.53%
8	Ohio	28,525	2.66%	33	Wisconsin	5,457	0.51%
9	North Carolina	27,563	2.57%	34	Mississippi	4,932	0.46%
10	Alabama	25,757	2.40%	35	Nebraska	3,917	0.37%
11	Georgia	25,264	2.36%	36	Nevada	3,188	0.30%
12	Louisiana	24,972	2.33%	37	Utah	3,148	0.29%
13	Pennsylvania	24,767	2.31%	38	Rhode Island	2,662	0.25%
14	Maryland	24,255	2.26%	39	Delaware	2,201	0.21%
15	New Jersey	23,740	2.22%	40	Alaska	1,971	0.18%
16	Missouri	22,937	2.14%	41	Idaho	1,868	0.17%
17	Tennessee	21,954	2.05%	42	West Virginia	1,723	0.16%
18	South Carolina	21,288	1.99%	43	Hawaii	1,079	0.10%
19	Arizona	17,229	1.61%	44	Wyoming	988	0.09%
20	Indiana	16,929	1.58%	45	Maine	833	0.08%
21	Washington	15,587	1.45%	46	South Dakota	757	0.07%
22	Colorado	13,449	1.26%	47	New Hampshire	532	0.05%
23	Oklahoma	13,101	1.22%	48	Montana	468	0.04%
24	Kentucky	11,531	1.08%	49	North Dakota	294	0.03%
25	Virginia	11,324	1.06%	50	Vermont	255	0.02%
					District of Columbia	8,568	0.80%

Source: Morgan Quitno Corporation using data from U.S. Department of Justice, Federal Bureau of Investigation
"Crime in the United States 1992" (Uniform Crime Reports, October 3, 1993)
*The F.B.I. defines urban areas as Metropolitan Statistical Areas and other cities outside such areas. Aggravated assault is an attack for the purpose of inflicting severe bodily injury.

Percent of Aggravated Assaults Occurring in Urban Areas in 1992

National Percent = 95.07% of Aggravated Assaults*

RANK	STATE	PERCENT	RANK	STATE	PERCENT
1	New Jersey	100.00	26	Kansas	92.28
2	Massachusetts	99.92	27	North Dakota	91.88
3	Rhode Island	99.78	28	Minnesota	91.67
4	Illinois	99.21	29	Arkansas	91.61
5	California	98.85	30	New Hampshire	90.48
6	New York	98.09	31	Virginia	90.25
7	Wyoming	97.34	32	North Carolina	89.96
8	Pennsylvania	97.11	33	Louisiana	89.14
9	Michigan	96.66	34	Indiana	89.06
10	Ohio	96.54	35	Georgia	87.62
10	Texas	96.54	36	New Mexico	86.98
12	Maryland	96.41	37	Wisconsin	86.95
13	Arizona	96.36	38	South Dakota	84.96
14	Florida	96.31	39	Delaware	84.17
15	Colorado	95.73	40	South Carolina	83.69
16	Washington	95.50	41	Nevada	82.33
17	Nebraska	95.19	42	Maine	82.23
18	Alabama	95.14	43	Mississippi	81.89
19	Connecticut	94.92	44	Hawaii	79.05
20	Missouri	94.69	45	Idaho	77.90
21	Oklahoma	94.50	46	Alaska	75.40
22	Oregon	93.40	47	Kentucky	74.83
23	Utah	93.25	48	West Virginia	67.91
24	Iowa	92.92	49	Vermont	60.86
24	Tennessee	92.92	50	Montana	49.58

District of Columbia 100.00

Source: Morgan Quitno Corporation using data from U.S. Department of Justice, Federal Bureau of Investigation
    "Crime in the United States 1992" (Uniform Crime Reports, October 3, 1993)
*The F.B.I. defines urban areas as Metropolitan Statistical Areas and other cities outside such areas. Aggravated assault is an attack for the purpose
of inflicting severe bodily injury.

Aggravated Assault in Rural Areas in 1992

National Total = 55,507 Aggravated Assaults*

RANK	STATE	ASSAULTS	%	RANK	STATE	ASSAULTS	%
1	South Carolina	4,148	7.47%	26	Minnesota	687	1.24%
2	Kentucky	3,878	6.99%	27	Nevada	684	1.23%
3	Florida	3,864	6.96%	28	Arizona	651	1.17%
4	Georgia	3,571	6.43%	29	Kansas	650	1.17%
5	North Carolina	3,075	5.54%	30	Alaska	643	1.16%
6	Louisiana	3,041	5.48%	31	Colorado	600	1.08%
7	Texas	2,983	5.37%	32	Oregon	592	1.07%
8	California	2,274	4.10%	33	Idaho	530	0.95%
9	Indiana	2,079	3.75%	34	Montana	476	0.86%
10	New York	1,676	3.02%	35	Illinois	475	0.86%
11	Tennessee	1,672	3.01%	36	Iowa	434	0.78%
12	New Mexico	1,490	2.68%	37	Connecticut	421	0.76%
13	Michigan	1,447	2.61%	38	Delaware	414	0.75%
14	Alabama	1,317	2.37%	39	Hawaii	286	0.52%
15	Missouri	1,286	2.32%	40	Wyoming	237	0.43%
16	Virginia	1,224	2.21%	41	Utah	228	0.41%
17	Mississippi	1,091	1.97%	42	Nebraska	198	0.36%
18	Ohio	1,022	1.84%	43	Maine	180	0.32%
19	Maryland	902	1.63%	44	Vermont	164	0.30%
20	Wisconsin	819	1.48%	45	South Dakota	134	0.24%
21	West Virginia	814	1.47%	46	New Hampshire	56	0.10%
22	Arkansas	803	1.45%	47	North Dakota	26	0.05%
23	Oklahoma	762	1.37%	48	Massachusetts	25	0.05%
24	Pennsylvania	738	1.33%	49	Rhode Island	6	0.01%
25	Washington	734	1.32%	50	New Jersey	0	0.00%
					District of Columbia	0	0.00%

Source: U.S. Department of Justice, Federal Bureau of Investigation

"Crime in the United States 1992" (Uniform Crime Reports, October 3, 1993)

*The F.B.I. defines rural areas as those other than Metropolitan Statistical Areas and other cities outside such areas. Aggravated assault is an attack for the purpose of inflicting severe bodily injury.

Percent of Aggravated Assaults Occurring in Rural Areas in 1992

National Percent = 4.93% of Aggravated Assaults*

RANK	STATE	PERCENT	RANK	STATE	PERCENT
1	Montana	50.42	26	Kansas	7.72
2	Vermont	39.14	27	Iowa	7.08
3	West Virginia	32.09	27	Tennessee	7.08
4	Kentucky	25.17	29	Utah	6.75
5	Alaska	24.60	30	Oregon	6.60
6	Idaho	22.10	31	Oklahoma	5.50
7	Hawaii	20.95	32	Missouri	5.31
8	Wyoming	19.35	33	Connecticut	5.08
9	Mississippi	18.11	34	Alabama	4.86
10	Maine	17.77	35	Nebraska	4.81
11	Nevada	17.67	36	Washington	4.50
12	South Carolina	16.31	37	Colorado	4.27
13	Delaware	15.83	38	Florida	3.69
14	South Dakota	15.04	39	Arizona	3.64
15	Wisconsin	13.05	40	Maryland	3.59
16	New Mexico	13.02	41	Ohio	3.46
17	Georgia	12.38	41	Texas	3.46
18	Indiana	10.94	43	Michigan	3.34
19	Louisiana	10.86	44	Pennsylvania	2.89
20	North Carolina	10.04	45	New York	1.91
21	Virginia	9.75	46	California	1.15
22	New Hampshire	9.52	47	Illinois	0.79
23	Arkansas	8.39	48	Rhode Island	0.22
24	Minnesota	8.33	49	Massachusetts	0.08
25	North Dakota	8.13	50	New Jersey	0.00
				District of Columbia	0.00

Source: Morgan Quitno Corporation using data from U.S. Department of Justice, Federal Bureau of Investigation
    "Crime in the United States 1992" (Uniform Crime Reports, October 3, 1993)
*The F.B.I. defines rural areas as those other than Metropolitan Statistical Areas and other cities outside such areas. Aggravated assault is an attack
for the purpose of inflicting severe bodily injury.

Property Crime in Urban Areas in 1992

National Total = 11,928,462 Property Crimes*

RANK	STATE	CRIMES	%	RANK	STATE	CRIMES	%
1	California	1,697,738	14.23%	26	Oregon	146,518	1.23%
2	Texas	1,074,767	9.01%	27	Connecticut	146,505	1.23%
3	Florida	936,161	7.85%	28	Oklahoma	144,947	1.22%
4	New York	839,859	7.04%	29	Kansas	113,558	0.95%
5	Illinois	545,400	4.57%	30	Utah	93,213	0.78%
6	Ohio	438,712	3.68%	31	Iowa	92,842	0.78%
7	Michigan	431,159	3.61%	32	Mississippi	91,628	0.77%
8	Georgia	351,840	2.95%	33	Kentucky	89,658	0.75%
9	New Jersey	345,718	2.90%	34	Arkansas	89,501	0.75%
10	Pennsylvania	341,141	2.86%	35	New Mexico	79,305	0.66%
11	North Carolina	313,235	2.63%	36	Nevada	68,829	0.58%
12	Washington	276,270	2.32%	37	Nebraska	57,770	0.48%
13	Massachusetts	253,257	2.12%	38	Hawaii	53,824	0.45%
14	Maryland	250,584	2.10%	39	Rhode Island	42,024	0.35%
15	Arizona	239,493	2.01%	40	Maine	35,795	0.30%
16	Virginia	235,232	1.97%	41	West Virginia	33,188	0.28%
17	Louisiana	224,310	1.88%	42	Idaho	32,721	0.27%
18	Indiana	219,412	1.84%	43	New Hampshire	32,054	0.27%
19	Missouri	214,719	1.80%	44	Delaware	26,590	0.22%
20	Tennessee	204,602	1.72%	45	Montana	25,597	0.21%
21	Wisconsin	186,277	1.56%	46	Alaska	22,427	0.19%
22	Colorado	177,359	1.49%	47	Wyoming	17,431	0.15%
23	Minnesota	173,252	1.45%	48	South Dakota	16,703	0.14%
24	Alabama	173,064	1.45%	49	North Dakota	15,700	0.13%
25	South Carolina	152,446	1.28%	50	Vermont	13,625	0.11%
					District of Columbia	50,502	0.42%

Source: Morgan Quitno Corporation using data from U.S. Department of Justice, Federal Bureau of Investigation
"Crime in the United States 1992" (Uniform Crime Reports, October 3, 1993)
*The F.B.I. defines urban areas as Metropolitan Statistical Areas and other cities outside such areas. Property crimes are offenses of burglary, larceny-theft and motor vehicle theft. Attempts are included.

Percent of Property Crime Occurring in Urban Areas in 1992

National Percent = 95.38% of Property Crimes*

RANK	STATE	PERCENT	RANK	STATE	PERCENT
1	New Jersey	100.00	26	Tennessee	92.78
2	Massachusetts	99.97	27	Indiana	92.74
3	Rhode Island	99.95	28	Oregon	92.67
4	California	98.93	29	Wisconsin	92.01
5	Arizona	98.30	30	Georgia	91.88
6	Connecticut	97.97	31	Delaware	91.29
7	Illinois	97.93	32	New Mexico	91.22
8	New York	97.87	33	Minnesota	90.94
9	Maryland	97.72	34	Mississippi	90.56
10	New Hampshire	97.64	35	Nebraska	90.48
11	Texas	97.37	36	Iowa	89.74
12	Florida	97.06	37	North Carolina	89.38
13	Ohio	96.21	38	Arkansas	89.14
14	Pennsylvania	95.78	39	Wyoming	87.90
14	Utah	95.78	40	North Dakota	87.54
16	Washington	95.40	41	Kentucky	85.64
17	Alabama	95.18	42	South Carolina	85.50
18	Colorado	95.00	43	Maine	85.43
19	Missouri	94.91	44	South Dakota	83.77
20	Michigan	94.39	45	Idaho	82.55
21	Nevada	94.19	46	Hawaii	79.27
22	Louisiana	94.07	47	Alaska	77.83
23	Virginia	94.01	48	West Virginia	76.37
24	Oklahoma	93.84	49	Vermont	72.42
25	Kansas	93.59	50	Montana	70.18

District of Columbia   100.00

Source: Morgan Quitno Corporation using data from U.S. Department of Justice, Federal Bureau of Investigation
    "Crime in the United States 1992" (Uniform Crime Reports, October 3, 1993)
*The F.B.I. defines urban areas as Metropolitan Statistical Areas and other cities outside such areas. Property crimes are offenses of burglary, larceny-theft and motor vehicle theft. Attempts are included.

Property Crime in Rural Areas in 1992

National Total = 577,455 Property Crimes*

RANK	STATE	CRIMES	%	RANK	STATE	CRIMES	%
1	North Carolina	37,212	6.44%	26	West Virginia	10,267	1.78%
2	Georgia	31,094	5.38%	27	Mississippi	9,553	1.65%
3	Texas	29,012	5.02%	28	Oklahoma	9,512	1.65%
4	Florida	28,372	4.91%	29	Colorado	9,325	1.61%
5	South Carolina	25,852	4.48%	30	Alabama	8,773	1.52%
6	Michigan	25,641	4.44%	31	Kansas	7,776	1.35%
7	California	18,399	3.19%	32	New Mexico	7,637	1.32%
8	New York	18,319	3.17%	33	Idaho	6,915	1.20%
9	Ohio	17,305	3.00%	34	Alaska	6,389	1.11%
10	Minnesota	17,268	2.99%	35	Maine	6,105	1.06%
11	Indiana	17,172	2.97%	36	Nebraska	6,076	1.05%
12	Wisconsin	16,171	2.80%	37	Maryland	5,834	1.01%
13	Tennessee	15,932	2.76%	38	Vermont	5,188	0.90%
14	Kentucky	15,034	2.60%	39	Nevada	4,248	0.74%
15	Pennsylvania	15,014	2.60%	40	Arizona	4,136	0.72%
16	Virginia	14,979	2.59%	41	Utah	4,109	0.71%
17	Louisiana	14,128	2.45%	42	South Dakota	3,236	0.56%
18	Hawaii	14,077	2.44%	43	Connecticut	3,030	0.52%
19	Washington	13,311	2.31%	44	Delaware	2,536	0.44%
20	Oregon	11,582	2.01%	45	Wyoming	2,400	0.42%
21	Missouri	11,527	2.00%	46	North Dakota	2,235	0.39%
22	Illinois	11,500	1.99%	47	New Hampshire	774	0.13%
23	Arkansas	10,901	1.89%	48	Massachusetts	87	0.02%
24	Montana	10,875	1.88%	49	Rhode Island	20	0.00%
25	Iowa	10,617	1.84%	50	New Jersey	0	0.00%
					District of Columbia	0	0.00%

Source: U.S. Department of Justice, Federal Bureau of Investigation
"Crime in the United States 1992" (Uniform Crime Reports, October 3, 1993)
*The F.B.I. defines rural areas as those other than Metropolitan Statistical Areas and other cities outside such areas. Property crimes are offenses of burglary, larceny-theft and motor vehicle theft. Attempts are included.

Percent of Property Crime Occurring in Rural Areas in 1992

National Percent = 4.62% of Property Crimes*

RANK	STATE	PERCENT		RANK	STATE	PERCENT
1	Montana	29.82		26	Kansas	6.41
2	Vermont	27.58		27	Oklahoma	6.16
3	West Virginia	23.63		28	Virginia	5.99
4	Alaska	22.17		29	Louisiana	5.93
5	Hawaii	20.73		30	Nevada	5.81
6	Idaho	17.45		31	Michigan	5.61
7	South Dakota	16.23		32	Missouri	5.09
8	Maine	14.57		33	Colorado	5.00
9	South Carolina	14.50		34	Alabama	4.82
10	Kentucky	14.36		35	Washington	4.60
11	North Dakota	12.46		36	Pennsylvania	4.22
12	Wyoming	12.10		36	Utah	4.22
13	Arkansas	10.86		38	Ohio	3.79
14	North Carolina	10.62		39	Florida	2.94
15	Iowa	10.26		40	Texas	2.63
16	Nebraska	9.52		41	New Hampshire	2.36
17	Mississippi	9.44		42	Maryland	2.28
18	Minnesota	9.06		43	New York	2.13
19	New Mexico	8.78		44	Illinois	2.07
20	Delaware	8.71		45	Connecticut	2.03
21	Georgia	8.12		46	Arizona	1.70
22	Wisconsin	7.99		47	California	1.07
23	Oregon	7.33		48	Rhode Island	0.05
24	Indiana	7.26		49	Massachusetts	0.03
25	Tennessee	7.22		50	New Jersey	0.00
					District of Columbia	0.00

Source: U.S. Department of Justice, Federal Bureau of Investigation
   "Crime in the United States 1992" (Uniform Crime Reports, October 3, 1993)
*The F.B.I. defines rural areas as those other than Metropolitan Statistical Areas and other cities outside such areas. Property crimes are offenses of burglary, larceny-theft and motor vehicle theft. Attempts are included.

Burglary in Urban Areas in 1992

National Total = 2,768,597 Burglaries*

RANK	STATE	BURGLARIES	%	RANK	STATE	BURGLARIES	%
1	California	420,511	15.19%	26	Minnesota	34,053	1.23%
2	Texas	256,520	9.27%	27	Kansas	29,597	1.07%
3	Florida	244,857	8.84%	28	Oregon	29,164	1.05%
4	New York	186,905	6.75%	29	Wisconsin	28,914	1.04%
5	Illinois	121,025	4.37%	30	Mississippi	28,903	1.04%
6	Ohio	98,811	3.57%	31	Arkansas	22,181	0.80%
7	North Carolina	95,449	3.45%	32	Kentucky	21,471	0.78%
8	Michigan	88,474	3.20%	33	New Mexico	20,832	0.75%
9	Georgia	85,966	3.11%	34	Iowa	17,943	0.65%
10	New Jersey	75,508	2.73%	35	Nevada	15,907	0.57%
11	Pennsylvania	69,292	2.50%	36	Utah	14,992	0.54%
12	Massachusetts	64,290	2.32%	37	Rhode Island	10,525	0.38%
13	Tennessee	56,548	2.04%	38	Nebraska	9,835	0.36%
14	Louisiana	54,415	1.97%	39	Hawaii	9,675	0.35%
15	Maryland	53,604	1.94%	40	West Virginia	7,549	0.27%
16	Washington	53,145	1.92%	41	Maine	7,492	0.27%
17	Arizona	52,591	1.90%	42	New Hampshire	6,572	0.24%
18	Missouri	51,957	1.88%	43	Idaho	5,846	0.21%
19	Indiana	47,967	1.73%	44	Delaware	5,616	0.20%
20	Alabama	45,034	1.63%	45	Alaska	3,503	0.13%
21	Virginia	40,571	1.47%	46	Montana	3,109	0.11%
22	South Carolina	40,384	1.46%	47	South Dakota	2,817	0.10%
23	Oklahoma	39,560	1.43%	48	Vermont	2,551	0.09%
24	Colorado	35,766	1.29%	49	Wyoming	2,472	0.09%
25	Connecticut	35,346	1.28%	50	North Dakota	1,861	0.07%

District of Columbia   10,721   0.39%

Source: Morgan Quitno Corporation using data from U.S. Department of Justice, Federal Bureau of Investigation

"Crime in the United States 1992" (Uniform Crime Reports, October 3, 1993)

*The F.B.I. defines urban areas as Metropolitan Statistical Areas and other cities outside such areas. Burglary is the unlawful entry of a structure to commit a felony or theft. Attempts are included.

Percent of Burglaries Occurring in Urban Areas in 1992

National Percent = 92.91% of Burglaries*

RANK	STATE	PERCENT	RANK	STATE	PERCENT
1	New Jersey	100.00	26	Indiana	88.98
2	Massachusetts	99.96	27	Tennessee	88.82
2	Rhode Island	99.96	28	Oregon	88.52
4	California	98.37	29	Georgia	88.26
5	Arizona	97.22	30	New Mexico	87.18
6	Connecticut	97.18	31	Mississippi	86.19
7	Illinois	96.58	32	Nebraska	85.69
8	New York	96.57	33	Minnesota	85.43
9	Maryland	96.55	34	Delaware	85.12
10	Florida	96.11	35	Iowa	84.65
11	Texas	95.39	36	Arkansas	84.62
12	New Hampshire	95.12	37	North Carolina	84.38
13	Ohio	94.69	38	Wisconsin	83.46
14	Colorado	94.49	39	South Carolina	81.31
15	Utah	93.44	40	Wyoming	79.05
16	Nevada	92.98	41	Kentucky	78.42
17	Louisiana	92.90	42	North Dakota	74.83
18	Washington	92.25	43	Hawaii	74.39
19	Alabama	91.81	44	Maine	73.77
20	Pennsylvania	91.37	45	Idaho	73.68
21	Missouri	90.95	46	South Dakota	73.19
22	Kansas	90.68	47	Alaska	67.76
23	Oklahoma	90.57	48	West Virginia	66.88
24	Michigan	90.04	49	Montana	58.59
25	Virginia	89.73	50	Vermont	54.21

District of Columbia   100.00

Source: Morgan Quitno Corporation using data from U.S. Department of Justice, Federal Bureau of Investigation
"Crime in the United States 1992" (Uniform Crime Reports, October 3, 1993)
*The F.B.I. defines urban areas as Metropolitan Statistical Areas and other cities outside such areas. Burglary is the unlawful entry of a structure to commit a felony or theft. Attempts are included.

Burglary in Rural Areas in 1992

National Total = 211,287 Burglaries*

RANK	STATE	BURGLARIES	%
1	North Carolina	17,668	8.36%
2	Texas	12,408	5.87%
3	Georgia	11,436	5.41%
4	Florida	9,898	4.68%
5	Michigan	9,783	4.63%
6	South Carolina	9,285	4.39%
7	Tennessee	7,117	3.37%
8	California	6,980	3.30%
9	New York	6,643	3.14%
10	Pennsylvania	6,542	3.10%
11	Indiana	5,940	2.81%
12	Kentucky	5,907	2.80%
13	Minnesota	5,806	2.75%
14	Wisconsin	5,731	2.71%
15	Ohio	5,546	2.62%
16	Missouri	5,170	2.45%
17	Virginia	4,646	2.20%
18	Mississippi	4,630	2.19%
19	Washington	4,467	2.11%
20	Illinois	4,281	2.03%
21	Louisiana	4,159	1.97%
22	Oklahoma	4,118	1.95%
23	Arkansas	4,033	1.91%
24	Alabama	4,019	1.90%
25	Oregon	3,781	1.79%

RANK	STATE	BURGLARIES	%
26	West Virginia	3,738	1.77%
27	Hawaii	3,331	1.58%
28	Iowa	3,254	1.54%
29	New Mexico	3,064	1.45%
30	Kansas	3,042	1.44%
31	Maine	2,664	1.26%
32	Montana	2,197	1.04%
33	Vermont	2,155	1.02%
34	Idaho	2,088	0.99%
35	Colorado	2,087	0.99%
36	Maryland	1,916	0.91%
37	Alaska	1,667	0.79%
38	Nebraska	1,642	0.78%
39	Arizona	1,504	0.71%
40	Nevada	1,201	0.57%
41	Utah	1,053	0.50%
42	South Dakota	1,032	0.49%
43	Connecticut	1,026	0.49%
44	Delaware	982	0.46%
45	Wyoming	655	0.31%
46	North Dakota	626	0.30%
47	New Hampshire	337	0.16%
48	Massachusetts	28	0.01%
49	Rhode Island	4	0.00%
50	New Jersey	0	0.00%

| | District of Columbia | 0 | 0.00% |

Source: U.S. Department of Justice, Federal Bureau of Investigation
   "Crime in the United States 1992" (Uniform Crime Reports, October 3, 1993)
*The F.B.I. defines rural areas as those other than Metropolitan Statistical Areas and other cities outside such areas. Burglary is the unlawful entry of a structure to commit a felony or theft. Attempts are included.

Percent of Burglaries Occurring in Rural Areas in 1992

National Percent = 7.09% of Burglaries*

RANK	STATE	PERCENT	RANK	STATE	PERCENT
1	Vermont	45.79	26	Virginia	10.27
2	Montana	41.41	27	Michigan	9.96
3	West Virginia	33.12	28	Oklahoma	9.43
4	Alaska	32.24	29	Kansas	9.32
5	South Dakota	26.81	30	Missouri	9.05
6	Idaho	26.32	31	Pennsylvania	8.63
7	Maine	26.23	32	Alabama	8.19
8	Hawaii	25.61	33	Washington	7.75
9	North Dakota	25.17	34	Louisiana	7.10
10	Kentucky	21.58	35	Nevada	7.02
11	Wyoming	20.95	36	Utah	6.56
12	South Carolina	18.69	37	Colorado	5.51
13	Wisconsin	16.54	38	Ohio	5.31
14	North Carolina	15.62	39	New Hampshire	4.88
15	Arkansas	15.38	40	Texas	4.61
16	Iowa	15.35	41	Florida	3.89
17	Delaware	14.88	42	Maryland	3.45
18	Minnesota	14.57	43	New York	3.43
19	Nebraska	14.31	44	Illinois	3.42
20	Mississippi	13.81	45	Connecticut	2.82
21	New Mexico	12.82	46	Arizona	2.78
22	Georgia	11.74	47	California	1.63
23	Oregon	11.48	48	Massachusetts	0.04
24	Tennessee	11.18	48	Rhode Island	0.04
25	Indiana	11.02	50	New Jersey	0.00
				District of Columbia	0.00

Source: Morgan Quitno Corporation using data from U.S. Department of Justice, Federal Bureau of Investigation

"Crime in the United States 1992" (Uniform Crime Reports, October 3, 1993)

*The F.B.I. defines rural areas as those other than Metropolitan Statistical Areas and other cities outside such areas. Burglary is the unlawful entry of a structure to commit a felony or theft. Attempts are included.

Larceny and Theft in Urban Areas in 1992

National Total = 7,583,919 Larcenies and Thefts*

RANK	STATE	LARCENIES	%	RANK	STATE	LARCENIES	%
1	California	958,166	12.63%	26	South Carolina	101,221	1.33%
2	Texas	674,716	8.90%	27	Oklahoma	89,388	1.18%
3	Florida	581,490	7.67%	28	Connecticut	87,756	1.16%
4	New York	484,569	6.39%	29	Kansas	76,121	1.00%
5	Illinois	352,902	4.65%	30	Utah	74,121	0.98%
6	Ohio	289,009	3.81%	31	Iowa	70,945	0.94%
7	Michigan	284,683	3.75%	32	Kentucky	61,327	0.81%
8	Georgia	229,190	3.02%	33	Arkansas	60,159	0.79%
9	Pennsylvania	216,851	2.86%	34	Mississippi	54,581	0.72%
10	New Jersey	206,686	2.73%	35	New Mexico	53,110	0.70%
11	North Carolina	200,581	2.64%	36	Nebraska	44,976	0.59%
12	Washington	199,646	2.63%	37	Nevada	43,865	0.58%
13	Virginia	176,028	2.32%	38	Hawaii	40,523	0.53%
14	Maryland	161,650	2.13%	39	Maine	26,822	0.35%
15	Arizona	155,731	2.05%	40	Idaho	25,543	0.34%
16	Indiana	147,068	1.94%	41	Rhode Island	24,037	0.32%
17	Louisiana	143,581	1.89%	42	West Virginia	23,703	0.31%
18	Massachusetts	141,571	1.87%	43	New Hampshire	23,346	0.31%
19	Missouri	137,470	1.81%	44	Montana	21,283	0.28%
20	Wisconsin	136,585	1.80%	45	Delaware	18,935	0.25%
21	Minnesota	124,516	1.64%	46	Alaska	16,602	0.22%
22	Colorado	124,330	1.64%	47	Wyoming	14,361	0.19%
23	Tennessee	120,594	1.59%	48	South Dakota	13,310	0.18%
24	Alabama	113,632	1.50%	49	North Dakota	13,048	0.17%
25	Oregon	102,288	1.35%	50	Vermont	10,640	0.14%
					District of Columbia	30,663	0.40%

Source: Morgan Quitno Corporation using data from U.S. Department of Justice, Federal Bureau of Investigation

   "Crime in the United States 1992" (Uniform Crime Reports, October 3, 1993)

*The F.B.I. defines urban areas as Metropolitan Statistical Areas and other cities outside such areas. Larceny and theft is the unlawful taking of property. Attempts are included.

Percent of Larcenies and Thefts Occurring in Urban Areas in 1992

National Percent = 95.81% of Larcenies and Thefts*

RANK	STATE	PERCENT	RANK	STATE	PERCENT
1	New Jersey	100.00	26	Louisiana	93.88
2	Massachusetts	99.97	27	Oregon	93.61
3	Rhode Island	99.94	28	Indiana	93.57
4	California	98.93	29	Wisconsin	93.42
5	Arizona	98.53	30	New Mexico	93.06
6	New Hampshire	98.28	31	Georgia	92.93
7	Illinois	98.13	32	Mississippi	92.74
8	Connecticut	98.09	33	Delaware	92.73
9	Maryland	97.83	34	Minnesota	92.41
10	Texas	97.82	35	North Carolina	92.13
11	New York	97.75	36	Nebraska	91.52
12	Florida	97.22	37	Iowa	91.20
13	Pennsylvania	96.74	38	Arkansas	90.75
14	Alabama	96.46	39	North Dakota	90.00
15	Ohio	96.41	40	Wyoming	89.74
16	Utah	96.31	41	Maine	89.51
17	Washington	96.10	42	Kentucky	88.64
18	Missouri	95.94	43	South Carolina	87.12
19	Michigan	95.06	44	South Dakota	86.59
20	Oklahoma	94.91	45	Idaho	85.08
21	Virginia	94.89	46	West Virginia	81.17
22	Colorado	94.79	47	Hawaii	80.17
23	Kansas	94.53	48	Alaska	80.09
24	Tennessee	94.26	49	Vermont	78.77
25	Nevada	93.90	50	Montana	72.78

District of Columbia 100.00

Source: Morgan Quitno Corporation using data from U.S. Department of Justice, Federal Bureau of Investigation
    "Crime in the United States 1992" (Uniform Crime Reports, October 3, 1993)
*The F.B.I. defines urban areas as Metropolitan Statistical Areas and other cities outside such areas. Larceny and theft is the unlawful taking of property. Attempts are included.

Larceny and Theft in Rural Areas in 1992

National Total = 331,280 Larcenies and Thefts*

RANK	STATE	LARCENIES	%	RANK	STATE	LARCENIES	%
1	Georgia	17,429	5.26%	26	Missouri	5,818	1.76%
2	North Carolina	17,136	5.17%	27	West Virginia	5,497	1.66%
3	Florida	16,603	5.01%	28	Oklahoma	4,792	1.45%
4	Texas	15,064	4.55%	29	Idaho	4,480	1.35%
5	South Carolina	14,965	4.52%	30	Kansas	4,405	1.33%
6	Michigan	14,803	4.47%	31	Mississippi	4,270	1.29%
7	New York	11,139	3.36%	32	Alabama	4,169	1.26%
8	Ohio	10,765	3.25%	33	Nebraska	4,168	1.26%
9	California	10,368	3.13%	34	Alaska	4,126	1.25%
10	Minnesota	10,234	3.09%	35	New Mexico	3,962	1.20%
11	Indiana	10,113	3.05%	36	Maryland	3,594	1.08%
12	Hawaii	10,021	3.02%	37	Maine	3,144	0.95%
13	Wisconsin	9,613	2.90%	38	Vermont	2,867	0.87%
14	Virginia	9,478	2.86%	39	Nevada	2,849	0.86%
15	Louisiana	9,357	2.82%	40	Utah	2,843	0.86%
16	Washington	8,109	2.45%	41	Arizona	2,322	0.70%
17	Montana	7,960	2.40%	42	South Dakota	2,061	0.62%
18	Kentucky	7,859	2.37%	43	Connecticut	1,707	0.52%
19	Tennessee	7,340	2.22%	44	Wyoming	1,642	0.50%
20	Pennsylvania	7,299	2.20%	45	Delaware	1,484	0.45%
21	Oregon	6,986	2.11%	46	North Dakota	1,450	0.44%
22	Iowa	6,843	2.07%	47	New Hampshire	408	0.12%
23	Colorado	6,839	2.06%	48	Massachusetts	39	0.01%
24	Illinois	6,716	2.03%	49	Rhode Island	15	0.00%
25	Arkansas	6,129	1.85%	50	New Jersey	0	0.00%
					District of Columbia	0	0.00%

Source: U.S. Department of Justice, Federal Bureau of Investigation
   "Crime in the United States 1992" (Uniform Crime Reports, October 3, 1993)
*The F.B.I. defines rural areas as those other than Metropolitan Statistical Areas and other cities outside such areas. Larceny and theft is the unlawful taking of property. Attempts are included.

Percent of Larcenies and Thefts Occurring in Rural Areas in 1992

National Percent = 4.19% of Larcenies and Thefts*

RANK	STATE	PERCENT	RANK	STATE	PERCENT
1	Montana	27.22	26	Nevada	6.10
2	Vermont	21.23	27	Tennessee	5.74
3	Alaska	19.91	28	Kansas	5.47
4	Hawaii	19.83	29	Colorado	5.21
5	West Virginia	18.83	30	Virginia	5.11
6	Idaho	14.92	31	Oklahoma	5.09
7	South Dakota	13.41	32	Michigan	4.94
8	South Carolina	12.88	33	Missouri	4.06
9	Kentucky	11.36	34	Washington	3.90
10	Maine	10.49	35	Utah	3.69
11	Wyoming	10.26	36	Ohio	3.59
12	North Dakota	10.00	37	Alabama	3.54
13	Arkansas	9.25	38	Pennsylvania	3.26
14	Iowa	8.80	39	Florida	2.78
15	Nebraska	8.48	40	New York	2.25
16	North Carolina	7.87	41	Texas	2.18
17	Minnesota	7.59	42	Maryland	2.17
18	Delaware	7.27	43	Connecticut	1.91
19	Mississippi	7.26	44	Illinois	1.87
20	Georgia	7.07	45	New Hampshire	1.72
21	New Mexico	6.94	46	Arizona	1.47
22	Wisconsin	6.58	47	California	1.07
23	Indiana	6.43	48	Rhode Island	0.06
24	Oregon	6.39	49	Massachusetts	0.03
25	Louisiana	6.12	50	New Jersey	0.00

District of Columbia   0.00

Source: Morgan Quitno Corporation using data from U.S. Department of Justice, Federal Bureau of Investigation
 "Crime in the United States 1992" (Uniform Crime Reports, October 3, 1993)
*The F.B.I. defines rural areas as those other than Metropolitan Statistical Areas and other cities outside such areas. Larceny and theft is the unlawful taking of property. Attempts are included.

Motor Vehicle Theft in Urban Areas in 1992

National Total = 1,575,946 Motor Vehicle Thefts*

RANK	STATE	VEHICLE THEFTS	%	RANK	STATE	VEHICLE THEFTS	%
1	California	319,061	20.25%	26	Minnesota	14,683	0.93%
2	New York	168,385	10.68%	27	Alabama	14,398	0.91%
3	Texas	143,531	9.11%	28	South Carolina	10,841	0.69%
4	Florida	109,814	6.97%	29	Nevada	9,057	0.57%
5	Illinois	71,473	4.54%	30	Mississippi	8,144	0.52%
6	New Jersey	63,524	4.03%	31	Kansas	7,840	0.50%
7	Michigan	58,002	3.68%	32	Rhode Island	7,462	0.47%
8	Pennsylvania	54,998	3.49%	33	Arkansas	7,161	0.45%
9	Ohio	50,892	3.23%	34	Kentucky	6,860	0.44%
10	Massachusetts	47,396	3.01%	35	New Mexico	5,363	0.34%
11	Georgia	36,684	2.33%	36	Utah	4,100	0.26%
12	Maryland	35,330	2.24%	37	Iowa	3,954	0.25%
13	Arizona	31,171	1.98%	38	Hawaii	3,626	0.23%
14	Tennessee	27,460	1.74%	39	Nebraska	2,959	0.19%
15	Louisiana	26,314	1.67%	40	Alaska	2,322	0.15%
16	Missouri	25,292	1.60%	41	New Hampshire	2,136	0.14%
17	Indiana	24,377	1.55%	42	Delaware	2,039	0.13%
18	Washington	23,479	1.49%	43	West Virginia	1,936	0.12%
19	Connecticut	23,403	1.49%	44	Maine	1,481	0.09%
20	Wisconsin	20,778	1.32%	45	Idaho	1,332	0.08%
21	Virginia	18,633	1.18%	46	Montana	1,205	0.08%
22	Colorado	17,263	1.10%	47	North Dakota	791	0.05%
23	North Carolina	17,205	1.09%	48	Wyoming	598	0.04%
24	Oklahoma	15,999	1.02%	49	South Dakota	576	0.04%
25	Oregon	15,066	0.96%	50	Vermont	434	0.03%
					District of Columbia	9,118	0.58%

Source: Morgan Quitno Corporation using data from U.S. Department of Justice, Federal Bureau of Investigation
"Crime in the United States 1992" (Uniform Crime Reports, October 3, 1993)
*The F.B.I. defines urban areas as Metropolitan Statistical Areas and other cities outside such areas. Motor vehicle theft includes the theft or attempted theft of a self-propelled vehicle. Excludes motorboats, construction equipment, airplanes, and farming equipment.

Percent of Motor Vehicle Thefts Occurring in Urban Areas in 1992

National Percent = 97.83% of Motor Vehicle Thefts*

RANK	STATE	PERCENT	RANK	STATE	PERCENT
1	New Jersey	100.00	26	Indiana	95.61
2	Rhode Island	99.99	26	Virginia	95.61
3	Massachusetts	99.96	28	Utah	95.06
4	New York	99.68	29	Tennessee	94.90
5	California	99.67	30	Oregon	94.87
6	Illinois	99.30	31	Georgia	94.27
7	Maryland	99.09	32	Mississippi	92.58
8	Arizona	99.02	33	Minnesota	92.28
9	Texas	98.94	34	Nebraska	91.75
10	Connecticut	98.75	35	Arkansas	90.65
11	New Hampshire	98.66	36	New Mexico	89.77
12	Florida	98.32	37	Iowa	88.38
13	Michigan	98.21	38	North Carolina	87.72
14	Ohio	98.08	39	South Carolina	87.13
15	Missouri	97.91	40	Wyoming	85.31
15	Pennsylvania	97.91	41	Kentucky	84.40
17	Nevada	97.86	42	Hawaii	83.34
18	Colorado	97.74	43	Maine	83.30
19	Louisiana	97.73	44	North Dakota	83.26
20	Washington	96.96	45	South Dakota	80.11
21	Delaware	96.68	46	Alaska	79.58
22	Oklahoma	96.37	47	Idaho	79.33
23	Wisconsin	96.17	48	Vermont	72.33
24	Alabama	96.10	49	West Virginia	65.23
25	Kansas	95.97	50	Montana	62.66

District of Columbia   100.00

Source: Morgan Quitno Corporation using data from U.S. Department of Justice, Federal Bureau of Investigation
    "Crime in the United States 1992" (Uniform Crime Reports, October 3, 1993)
*The F.B.I. defines urban areas as Metropolitan Statistical Areas and other cities outside such areas. Motor vehicle theft includes the theft or attempted theft of a self-propelled vehicle. Excludes motorboats, construction equipment, airplanes, and farming equipment.

Motor Vehicle Thefts in Rural Areas in 1992

National Total = 34,888 Motor Vehicle Thefts*

RANK	STATE	VEHICLE THEFTS	%	RANK	STATE	VEHICLE THEFTS	%
1	North Carolina	2,408	6.90%	26	Alaska	596	1.71%
2	Georgia	2,229	6.39%	27	Alabama	585	1.68%
3	Florida	1,871	5.36%	28	Missouri	539	1.54%
4	South Carolina	1,602	4.59%	29	New York	537	1.54%
5	Texas	1,540	4.41%	30	Iowa	520	1.49%
6	Tennessee	1,475	4.23%	31	Illinois	503	1.44%
7	Kentucky	1,268	3.63%	32	Colorado	399	1.14%
8	Minnesota	1,228	3.52%	33	Idaho	347	0.99%
9	Pennsylvania	1,173	3.36%	34	Kansas	329	0.94%
10	Indiana	1,119	3.21%	35	Maryland	324	0.93%
11	Michigan	1,055	3.02%	36	Arizona	310	0.89%
12	California	1,051	3.01%	37	Connecticut	297	0.85%
13	West Virginia	1,032	2.96%	37	Maine	297	0.85%
14	Ohio	994	2.85%	39	Nebraska	266	0.76%
15	Virginia	855	2.45%	40	Utah	213	0.61%
16	Wisconsin	827	2.37%	41	Nevada	198	0.57%
17	Oregon	815	2.34%	42	Vermont	166	0.48%
18	Arkansas	739	2.12%	43	North Dakota	159	0.46%
19	Washington	735	2.11%	44	South Dakota	143	0.41%
20	Hawaii	725	2.08%	45	Wyoming	103	0.30%
21	Montana	718	2.06%	46	Delaware	70	0.20%
22	Mississippi	653	1.87%	47	New Hampshire	29	0.08%
23	Louisiana	612	1.75%	48	Massachusetts	20	0.06%
24	New Mexico	611	1.75%	49	Rhode Island	1	0.00%
25	Oklahoma	602	1.73%	50	New Jersey	0	0.00%
					District of Columbia	0	0.00%

Source: U.S. Department of Justice, Federal Bureau of Investigation

"Crime in the United States 1992" (Uniform Crime Reports, October 3, 1993)

*The F.B.I. defines rural areas as those other than Metropolitan Statistical Areas and other cities outside such areas. Motor vehicle theft includes the theft or attempted theft of a self-propelled vehicle. Excludes motorboats, construction equipment, airplanes, and farming equipment.

Percent of Motor Vehicle Thefts Occurring in Rural Areas in 1992

National Percent = 2.17% of Motor Vehicle Thefts*

RANK	STATE	PERCENT	RANK	STATE	PERCENT
1	Montana	37.34	26	Kansas	4.03
2	West Virginia	34.77	27	Alabama	3.90
3	Vermont	27.67	28	Wisconsin	3.83
4	Idaho	20.67	29	Oklahoma	3.63
5	Alaska	20.42	30	Delaware	3.32
6	South Dakota	19.89	31	Washington	3.04
7	North Dakota	16.74	32	Louisiana	2.27
8	Maine	16.70	33	Colorado	2.26
9	Hawaii	16.66	34	Nevada	2.14
10	Kentucky	15.60	35	Missouri	2.09
11	Wyoming	14.69	35	Pennsylvania	2.09
12	South Carolina	12.87	37	Ohio	1.92
13	North Carolina	12.28	38	Michigan	1.79
14	Iowa	11.62	39	Florida	1.68
15	New Mexico	10.23	40	New Hampshire	1.34
16	Arkansas	9.35	41	Connecticut	1.25
17	Nebraska	8.25	42	Texas	1.06
18	Minnesota	7.72	43	Arizona	0.98
19	Mississippi	7.42	44	Maryland	0.91
20	Georgia	5.73	45	Illinois	0.70
21	Oregon	5.13	46	California	0.33
22	Tennessee	5.10	47	New York	0.32
23	Utah	4.94	48	Massachusetts	0.04
24	Indiana	4.39	49	Rhode Island	0.01
24	Virginia	4.39	50	New Jersey	0.00
				District of Columbia	0.00

Source: Morgan Quitno Corporation using data from U.S. Department of Justice, Federal Bureau of Investigation
    "Crime in the United States 1992" (Uniform Crime Reports, October 3, 1993)
*The F.B.I. defines rural areas as those other than Metropolitan Statistical Areas and other cities outside such areas. Motor vehicle theft includes the theft or attempted theft of a self-propelled vehicle. Excludes motorboats, construction equipment, airplanes, and farming equipment.

Crimes Reported at Universities and Colleges in 1992

National Reported Total = 134,287 Crimes*

RANK	STATE	CRIMES	%	RANK	STATE	CRIMES	%
1	California	19,585	14.58%	26	New Mexico	1,780	1.33%
2	Texas	11,823	8.80%	27	Oklahoma	1,674	1.25%
3	Michigan	7,419	5.52%	28	Tennessee	1,670	1.24%
4	New York	6,785	5.05%	29	Minnesota	1,372	1.02%
5	Ohio	6,187	4.61%	30	Missouri	1,263	0.94%
6	North Carolina	5,423	4.04%	31	Alabama	1,256	0.94%
7	Illinois	5,235	3.90%	32	Nebraska	1,056	0.79%
8	Virginia	4,935	3.67%	33	Arkansas	963	0.72%
9	Indiana	4,572	3.40%	34	Nevada	845	0.63%
10	Florida	4,361	3.25%	35	West Virginia	739	0.55%
11	New Jersey	4,243	3.16%	36	Iowa	664	0.49%
12	Maryland	3,993	2.97%	37	Mississippi	476	0.35%
13	Georgia	3,658	2.72%	38	Maine	443	0.33%
14	Arizona	3,465	2.58%	39	Vermont	419	0.31%
15	Massachusetts	3,084	2.30%	40	Wyoming	408	0.30%
16	Colorado	2,823	2.10%	41	New Hampshire	360	0.27%
17	Wisconsin	2,739	2.04%	42	North Dakota	289	0.22%
18	Kentucky	2,531	1.88%	43	Rhode Island	273	0.20%
19	Pennsylvania	2,376	1.77%	44	South Dakota	221	0.16%
20	South Carolina	2,282	1.70%	–	Alaska**	N/A	N/A
21	Washington	2,227	1.66%	–	Delaware**	N/A	N/A
22	Louisiana	2,206	1.64%	–	Hawaii**	N/A	N/A
23	Connecticut	2,152	1.60%	–	Idaho**	N/A	N/A
24	Utah	2,100	1.56%	–	Montana**	N/A	N/A
25	Kansas	1,914	1.43%	–	Oregon**	N/A	N/A

District of Columbia**   N/A   N/A

Source: U.S. Department of Justice, Federal Bureau of Investigation

"Crime in the United States 1992" (Uniform Crime Reports, October 3, 1993)

*Total is only for states shown separately.

**Not available.

Crimes Reported at Universities and Colleges as a Percent of All Crimes in 1992

National Percent = 0.93% of Crimes*

RANK	STATE	PERCENT	RANK	STATE	PERCENT
1	Arizona	10.60	26	Maine	1.02
2	Vermont	2.16	27	Oklahoma	0.96
3	Utah	2.05	28	California	0.95
4	Kentucky	2.03	28	Texas	0.95
5	Wyoming	1.91	30	Georgia	0.85
6	Virginia	1.80	31	Arkansas	0.84
7	New Mexico	1.75	32	Louisiana	0.79
8	Indiana	1.72	33	Illinois	0.78
9	North Dakota	1.57	34	Washington	0.70
10	West Virginia	1.56	35	Minnesota	0.67
11	Nebraska	1.52	36	Tennessee	0.65
12	Kansas	1.43	37	New York	0.64
13	Michigan	1.40	38	Iowa	0.60
14	Colorado	1.37	39	Rhode Island	0.59
14	North Carolina	1.37	40	Alabama	0.58
16	Maryland	1.31	40	Pennsylvania	0.58
17	Connecticut	1.30	42	Missouri	0.48
18	Wisconsin	1.27	43	Mississippi	0.43
19	Ohio	1.20	44	Florida	0.39
20	New Jersey	1.08	–	Alaska**	N/A
21	South Carolina	1.07	–	Delaware**	N/A
22	New Hampshire	1.05	–	Hawaii**	N/A
23	South Dakota	1.04	–	Idaho**	N/A
24	Massachusetts	1.03	–	Montana**	N/A
24	Nevada	1.03	–	Oregon**	N/A
				District of Columbia**	N/A

Source: Morgan Quitno Corporation using data from U.S. Department of Justice, Federal Bureau of Investigation "Crime in the United States 1992" (Uniform Crime Reports, October 3, 1993)

*National percent is only for states shown separately.

**Not available.

Violent Crimes Reported at Universities and Colleges in 1992

National Reported Total = 3,243 Violent Crimes*

RANK	STATE	VIOLENT CRIMES	%
1	California	375	11.56%
2	Texas	276	8.51%
3	North Carolina	240	7.40%
4	Virginia	191	5.89%
5	Michigan	186	5.74%
6	New Jersey	167	5.15%
7	Indiana	159	4.90%
8	Ohio	157	4.84%
9	Florida	130	4.01%
9	Maryland	130	4.01%
11	New York	121	3.73%
12	Massachusetts	111	3.42%
13	Kentucky	97	2.99%
14	Louisiana	88	2.71%
15	Georgia	86	2.65%
16	South Carolina	69	2.13%
17	Colorado	65	2.00%
18	Pennsylvania	58	1.79%
19	Arizona	57	1.76%
20	New Mexico	48	1.48%
21	Oklahoma	39	1.20%
22	Arkansas	38	1.17%
22	Kansas	38	1.17%
24	Connecticut	34	1.05%
25	Washington	33	1.02%

RANK	STATE	VIOLENT CRIMES	%
26	Utah	31	0.96%
27	Nevada	27	0.83%
27	Tennessee	27	0.83%
29	Alabama	24	0.74%
30	Wisconsin	21	0.65%
31	Missouri	20	0.62%
32	Minnesota	16	0.49%
32	West Virginia	16	0.49%
34	Iowa	14	0.43%
35	Nebraska	11	0.34%
36	North Dakota	10	0.31%
37	Rhode Island	7	0.22%
37	Wyoming	7	0.22%
39	Mississippi	6	0.19%
40	New Hampshire	5	0.15%
40	Vermont	5	0.15%
42	Maine	3	0.09%
43	South Dakota	2	0.06%
–	Alaska**	N/A	N/A
–	Delaware**	N/A	N/A
–	Hawaii**	N/A	N/A
–	Idaho**	N/A	N/A
–	Illinois**	N/A	N/A
–	Montana**	N/A	N/A
–	Oregon**	N/A	N/A
	District of Columbia**	N/A	N/A

Source: U.S. Department of Justice, Federal Bureau of Investigation
   "Crime in the United States 1992" (Uniform Crime Reports, October 3, 1993)

*Total is only for states shown separately. Violent crimes are offenses of murder, forcible rape, robbery and aggravated assault.

**Not available.

Violent Crimes Reported at Universities and Colleges as a Percent of All Violent Crimes in 1992

National Percent = 0.17% of Violent Crimes*

RANK	STATE	PERCENT		RANK	STATE	PERCENT
1	North Dakota	1.89		26	Maine	0.19
2	Arizona	1.47		26	Oklahoma	0.19
3	Vermont	0.80		26	Texas	0.19
3	Virginia	0.80		29	Iowa	0.18
5	Utah	0.59		29	Rhode Island	0.18
6	Indiana	0.55		31	Georgia	0.17
7	North Carolina	0.52		32	Wisconsin	0.15
8	Kentucky	0.48		33	South Dakota	0.14
9	Wyoming	0.47		34	Washington	0.12
10	West Virginia	0.42		35	California	0.11
11	New Hampshire	0.36		35	Minnesota	0.11
12	New Jersey	0.34		35	Pennsylvania	0.11
13	Colorado	0.32		38	Florida	0.08
13	New Mexico	0.32		39	Alabama	0.07
15	Kansas	0.29		39	Tennessee	0.07
15	Nevada	0.29		41	Mississippi	0.06
17	Arkansas	0.27		41	New York	0.06
17	Ohio	0.27		43	Missouri	0.05
19	Maryland	0.26		–	Alaska**	N/A
19	Michigan	0.26		–	Delaware**	N/A
21	Massachusetts	0.24		–	Hawaii**	N/A
22	Connecticut	0.21		–	Idaho**	N/A
22	Louisiana	0.21		–	Illinois**	N/A
24	Nebraska	0.20		–	Montana**	N/A
24	South Carolina	0.20		–	Oregon**	N/A

District of Columbia**   N/A

Source: Morgan Quitno Corporation using data from U.S. Department of Justice, Federal Bureau of Investigation
   "Crime in the United States 1992" (Uniform Crime Reports, October 3, 1993)
*National percent is only for states shown separately. Violent crimes are offenses of murder, forcible rape, robbery and aggravated assault.
**Not available.

Property Crimes Reported at Universities and Colleges in 1992

National Reported Total = 131,044 Property Crimes*

RANK	STATE	CRIMES	%	RANK	STATE	CRIMES	%
1	California	19,210	14.66%	26	New Mexico	1,732	1.32%
2	Texas	11,547	8.81%	27	Tennessee	1,643	1.25%
3	Michigan	7,233	5.52%	28	Oklahoma	1,635	1.25%
4	New York	6,664	5.09%	29	Minnesota	1,356	1.03%
5	Ohio	6,030	4.60%	30	Missouri	1,243	0.95%
6	Illinois	5,236	4.00%	31	Alabama	1,232	0.94%
7	North Carolina	5,183	3.96%	32	Nebraska	1,045	0.80%
8	Virginia	4,744	3.62%	33	Arkansas	925	0.71%
9	Indiana	4,413	3.37%	34	Nevada	818	0.62%
10	Florida	4,231	3.23%	35	West Virginia	723	0.55%
11	New Jersey	4,076	3.11%	36	Iowa	650	0.50%
12	Maryland	3,863	2.95%	37	Mississippi	470	0.36%
13	Georgia	3,572	2.73%	38	Maine	440	0.34%
14	Arizona	3,408	2.60%	39	Vermont	414	0.32%
15	Massachusetts	2,973	2.27%	40	Wyoming	401	0.31%
16	Colorado	2,758	2.10%	41	New Hampshire	355	0.27%
17	Wisconsin	2,718	2.07%	42	North Dakota	279	0.21%
18	Kentucky	2,434	1.86%	43	Rhode Island	266	0.20%
19	Pennsylvania	2,318	1.77%	44	South Dakota	219	0.17%
20	South Carolina	2,213	1.69%	–	Alaska**	N/A	N/A
21	Washington	2,194	1.67%	–	Delaware**	N/A	N/A
22	Connecticut	2,118	1.62%	–	Hawaii**	N/A	N/A
22	Louisiana	2,118	1.62%	–	Idaho**	N/A	N/A
24	Utah	2,069	1.58%	–	Montana**	N/A	N/A
25	Kansas	1,876	1.43%	–	Oregon**	N/A	N/A
					District of Columbia**	N/A	N/A

Source: U.S. Department of Justice, Federal Bureau of Investigation
"Crime in the United States 1992" (Uniform Crime Reports, October 3, 1993)

*Total is only for states shown separately. Property crimes are offenses of burglary, larceny-theft, motor vehicle theft and arson.

**Not available.

Property Crimes Reported at Universities and Colleges as a Percent of All Property Crimes in 1992

National Percent = 1.05% of Property Crimes*

RANK	STATE	PERCENT	RANK	STATE	PERCENT
1	Arizona	11.83	26	New Hampshire	1.08
2	Kentucky	2.32	27	Oklahoma	1.06
3	Vermont	2.20	28	Maine	1.05
4	Utah	2.13	28	Texas	1.05
5	Wyoming	2.02	30	Illinois	0.94
6	New Mexico	1.99	31	Georgia	0.93
7	Virginia	1.90	32	Arkansas	0.92
8	Indiana	1.87	33	Louisiana	0.89
9	West Virginia	1.66	34	New York	0.78
10	Nebraska	1.64	35	Washington	0.76
11	Michigan	1.58	36	Tennessee	0.75
12	North Dakota	1.56	37	Minnesota	0.71
13	Kansas	1.55	38	Alabama	0.68
14	Maryland	1.51	39	Pennsylvania	0.65
15	Colorado	1.48	40	Iowa	0.63
15	North Carolina	1.48	40	Rhode Island	0.63
17	Connecticut	1.42	42	Missouri	0.55
18	Wisconsin	1.34	43	Mississippi	0.46
19	Ohio	1.32	44	Florida	0.44
20	South Carolina	1.24	–	Alaska**	N/A
21	New Jersey	1.18	–	Delaware**	N/A
22	Massachusetts	1.17	–	Hawaii**	N/A
23	California	1.12	–	Idaho**	N/A
23	Nevada	1.12	–	Montana**	N/A
25	South Dakota	1.10	–	Oregon**	N/A
				District of Columbia**	N/A

Source: Morgan Quitno Corporation using data from U.S. Department of Justice, Federal Bureau of Investigation
"Crime in the United States 1992" (Uniform Crime Reports, October 3, 1993)
*National percent is only for states shown separately. Property crimes are offenses of burglary, larceny-theft, motor vehicle theft and arson.
**Not available.

Bank Robberies in 1992

National Total = 9,014 Robberies*

RANK	STATE	ROBBERIES	%	RANK	STATE	ROBBERIES	%
1	California	3,401	37.73%	26	Colorado	69	0.77%
2	New York	598	6.63%	27	Kansas	56	0.62%
3	Florida	518	5.75%	28	Minnesota	45	0.50%
4	North Carolina	322	3.57%	29	Louisiana	39	0.43%
5	Michigan	305	3.38%	30	Arkansas	36	0.40%
6	Washington	302	3.35%	31	Kentucky	35	0.39%
7	Ohio	287	3.18%	32	New Mexico	33	0.37%
8	Pennsylvania	271	3.01%	33	Oklahoma	30	0.33%
9	Oregon	257	2.85%	34	Mississippi	25	0.28%
10	Arizona	250	2.77%	35	Hawaii	24	0.27%
11	Massachusetts	235	2.61%	36	Nebraska	18	0.20%
12	Texas	211	2.34%	37	Utah	17	0.19%
13	Maryland	209	2.32%	38	Alaska	13	0.14%
14	Virginia	162	1.80%	39	Idaho	12	0.13%
15	Tennessee	158	1.75%	39	Iowa	12	0.13%
16	Georgia	138	1.53%	41	Delaware	10	0.11%
17	Nevada	122	1.35%	42	West Virginia	8	0.09%
18	New Jersey	113	1.25%	43	New Hampshire	6	0.07%
19	Illinois	108	1.20%	44	Maine	5	0.06%
20	Indiana	99	1.10%	45	Rhode Island	4	0.04%
21	Wisconsin	86	0.95%	45	South Dakota	4	0.04%
22	Missouri	85	0.94%	47	Vermont	3	0.03%
23	Connecticut	79	0.88%	48	Wyoming	2	0.02%
23	South Carolina	79	0.88%	49	Montana	1	0.01%
25	Alabama	74	0.82%	49	North Dakota	1	0.01%
					District of Columbia	37	0.41%

Source: U.S. Department of Justice, Federal Bureau of Investigation

"Bank Crime Statistics, Federally Insured Financial Institutions, January 1, 1992 – December 31, 1992"

*Does not include 48 robberies in Puerto Rico and 1 in Guam. In addition, there were 361 bank burglaries, 88 bank larcenies and 48 extortions. Of these 9,512 bank crimes, loot valued at $68,123,601 was taken in 8,797 cases. Of this, $10,127,233 was recovered.

Bombings in 1992

National Total = 2,471 Bombings*

RANK	STATE	BOMBINGS	%	RANK	STATE	BOMBINGS	%
1	California	396	16.03%	25	New Jersey	26	1.05%
2	Illinois	306	12.38%	25	Utah	26	1.05%
3	Arizona	186	7.53%	28	Nevada	22	0.89%
4	Florida	177	7.16%	28	New Mexico	22	0.89%
5	Texas	106	4.29%	30	Kansas	21	0.85%
6	Michigan	104	4.21%	31	Oklahoma	20	0.81%
7	Ohio	103	4.17%	32	Massachusetts	17	0.69%
8	New York	93	3.76%	33	Kentucky	16	0.65%
9	Colorado	77	3.12%	34	Alabama	13	0.53%
10	Iowa	63	2.55%	34	Nebraska	13	0.53%
11	Pennsylvania	56	2.27%	36	Mississippi	9	0.36%
12	Tennessee	52	2.10%	37	Vermont	7	0.28%
12	Washington	52	2.10%	38	West Virginia	6	0.24%
14	Maryland	51	2.06%	39	Delaware	5	0.20%
14	Missouri	51	2.06%	39	Idaho	5	0.20%
16	Indiana	43	1.74%	39	Montana	5	0.20%
17	Louisiana	40	1.62%	39	Rhode Island	5	0.20%
18	Oregon	39	1.58%	39	South Carolina	5	0.20%
19	North Carolina	34	1.38%	44	Maine	4	0.16%
20	Virginia	33	1.34%	45	Wyoming	3	0.12%
21	Minnesota	32	1.30%	46	Hawaii	2	0.08%
21	Wisconsin	32	1.30%	46	North Dakota	2	0.08%
23	Georgia	28	1.13%	48	Alaska	1	0.04%
24	Connecticut	27	1.09%	48	New Hampshire	1	0.04%
25	Arkansas	26	1.05%	48	South Dakota	1	0.04%
					District of Columbia	7	0.28%

Source: U.S. Department of Justice, Federal Bureau of Investigation, Bomb Data Center
"Bomb Summary 1992"

*Includes explosive and incendiary bombings and excludes bombing attempts. Total does not include 21 bombings in Puerto Rico and 1 in Guam.
There were 126 deaths and 349 injuries from bombings in 1992.

Crimes in 1988

National Total = 13,923,086 Crimes*

RANK	STATE	CRIMES	%	RANK	STATE	CRIMES	%
1	California	1,869,092	13.42%	26	Minnesota	185,792	1.33%
2	Texas	1,345,369	9.66%	27	Oklahoma	182,373	1.31%
3	New York	1,129,241	8.11%	28	Connecticut	165,214	1.19%
4	Florida	1,106,212	7.95%	29	Kansas	121,363	0.87%
5	Illinois	648,873	4.66%	30	Kentucky	116,646	0.84%
6	Michigan	565,847	4.06%	31	Iowa	115,533	0.83%
7	Ohio	505,034	3.63%	32	Arkansas	102,199	0.73%
8	New Jersey	408,800	2.94%	33	New Mexico	99,755	0.72%
9	Georgia	404,965	2.91%	34	Mississippi	94,384	0.68%
10	Pennsylvania	382,020	2.74%	35	Utah	94,333	0.68%
11	Washington	328,551	2.36%	36	Nevada	68,403	0.49%
12	North Carolina	317,310	2.28%	37	Nebraska	66,282	0.48%
13	Massachusetts	293,015	2.10%	38	Hawaii	65,460	0.47%
14	Maryland	264,923	1.90%	39	Rhode Island	51,784	0.37%
15	Arizona	258,955	1.86%	40	Maine	43,147	0.31%
16	Louisiana	254,624	1.83%	41	West Virginia	42,179	0.30%
17	Virginia	250,436	1.80%	42	Idaho	39,690	0.29%
18	Missouri	248,971	1.79%	43	New Hampshire	36,573	0.26%
19	Indiana	231,364	1.66%	44	Montana	34,307	0.25%
20	Tennessee	219,852	1.58%	45	Delaware	31,674	0.23%
21	Colorado	203,267	1.46%	46	Alaska	25,248	0.18%
22	Oregon	193,479	1.39%	47	Vermont	23,577	0.17%
23	Wisconsin	192,959	1.39%	48	Wyoming	18,685	0.13%
24	South Carolina	189,053	1.36%	49	South Dakota	18,454	0.13%
25	Alabama	188,261	1.35%	50	North Dakota	18,087	0.13%
					District of Columbia	61,471	0.44%

Source: U.S. Department of Justice, Federal Bureau of Investigation
"Crime in the United States 1988" (Uniform Crime Reports, 1988)
*Includes murder, rape, robbery, aggravated assault, burglary, larceny-theft, motor vehicle theft and arson.

Crime Rate in 1988

National Rate = 5,664 Crimes per 100,000 Population*

RANK	STATE	RATE		RANK	STATE	RATE
1	Florida	8,938		26	North Carolina	4,862
2	Texas	8,018		27	Missouri	4,845
3	Arizona	7,471		28	Delaware	4,799
4	Washington	7,113		29	Ohio	4,645
5	Oregon	7,059		30	Alabama	4,562
6	California	6,636		31	Tennessee	4,469
7	New Mexico	6,606		32	Minnesota	4,315
8	Nevada	6,453		33	Montana	4,267
9	Georgia	6,327		34	Vermont	4,240
10	New York	6,310		35	Arkansas	4,220
11	Colorado	6,178		36	Virginia	4,177
12	Michigan	6,084		37	Indiana	4,150
13	Hawaii	5,989		38	Nebraska	4,140
14	Louisiana	5,761		39	Iowa	4,077
15	Maryland	5,705		40	Idaho	3,973
16	Illinois	5,621		41	Wisconsin	3,972
17	Oklahoma	5,589		42	Wyoming	3,967
18	Utah	5,579		43	Mississippi	3,593
19	South Carolina	5,412		44	Maine	3,578
20	New Jersey	5,295		45	New Hampshire	3,334
21	Rhode Island	5,204		46	Pennsylvania	3,176
22	Connecticut	5,098		47	Kentucky	3,135
23	Massachusetts	4,991		48	North Dakota	2,728
24	Alaska	4,922		49	South Dakota	2,581
25	Kansas	4,880		50	West Virginia	2,239
					District of Columbia	9,915

Source: U.S. Department of Justice, Federal Bureau of Investigation
   "Crime in the United States 1988" (Uniform Crime Reports, 1988)
*Includes murder, rape, robbery, aggravated assault, burglary, larceny-theft, motor vehicle theft and arson.

Percent Change in Number of Crimes: 1988 to 1992

National Percent Change = 3.70% Increase*

RANK	STATE	PERCENT CHANGE	RANK	STATE	PERCENT CHANGE
1	Alaska	29.49	26	Pennsylvania	6.65
2	North Carolina	25.13	27	Missouri	6.32
3	Nevada	20.35	28	Delaware	5.47
4	Mississippi	18.60	29	Nebraska	4.77
5	Tennessee	17.36	30	Arizona	4.01
6	Alabama	15.74	31	Illinois	3.34
7	South Dakota	15.54	32	Massachusetts	2.41
8	Maryland	15.32	33	North Dakota	2.09
9	Indiana	14.70	34	New Mexico	1.97
10	Wyoming	14.10	35	Florida	1.91
11	South Carolina	12.31	36	Ohio	1.77
12	West Virginia	12.11	37	Colorado	1.72
13	Wisconsin	12.07	38	Maine	0.86
14	Arkansas	11.78	39	Connecticut	0.35
15	Minnesota	10.70	40	New Jersey	(3.51)
16	Kansas	10.60	40	Washington	(3.51)
17	Montana	10.39	42	Iowa	(3.69)
18	California	10.31	43	Oklahoma	(4.34)
19	Louisiana	10.22	44	New York	(6.00)
20	Virginia	9.46	45	New Hampshire	(6.42)
21	Utah	8.75	46	Michigan	(6.43)
22	Hawaii	8.31	47	Texas	(7.38)
23	Idaho	7.43	48	Oregon	(10.44)
24	Kentucky	6.99	49	Rhode Island	(11.15)
25	Georgia	6.78	50	Vermont	(17.56)

District of Columbia   9.30

Source: Morgan Quitno Corporation using data from U.S. Department of Justice, Federal Bureau of Investigation
"Crime in the United States" (Uniform Crime Reports, 1988 and 1992 editions)
*Includes murder, rape, robbery, aggravated assault, burglary, larceny-theft, motor vehicle theft and arson.

Percent Change in Crime Rate: 1988 to 1992

National Percent Change = 0.07% Decrease*

RANK	STATE	PERCENT CHANGE		RANK	STATE	PERCENT CHANGE
1	North Carolina	19.34		26	Utah	1.42
2	Mississippi	19.19		27	Georgia	1.24
3	West Virginia	16.56		28	Delaware	1.03
4	South Dakota	16.19		29	California	0.66
5	Alabama	15.48		30	Idaho	0.58
6	Wyoming	15.33		31	Ohio	0.44
7	Tennessee	14.92		32	Massachusetts	0.24
8	Louisiana	13.63		33	Connecticut	(0.88)
9	Alaska	13.16		34	Maine	(1.52)
10	Indiana	12.94		35	New Mexico	(2.60)
11	Arkansas	12.84		36	Oklahoma	(2.82)
12	Maryland	9.11		37	Iowa	(2.94)
13	Kansas	9.01		38	Colorado	(3.55)
14	South Carolina	8.89		39	Nevada	(3.86)
15	Wisconsin	8.74		40	New Jersey	(4.36)
16	Montana	7.71		41	Arizona	(5.92)
17	Pennsylvania	6.82		42	Florida	(6.49)
18	North Dakota	6.43		43	New York	(7.16)
19	Minnesota	6.39		44	New Hampshire	(7.60)
20	Kentucky	6.01		45	Michigan	(7.78)
21	Missouri	5.20		46	Texas	(11.97)
22	Nebraska	4.44		47	Rhode Island	(12.03)
23	Virginia	2.91		48	Washington	(13.22)
24	Illinois	2.57		49	Oregon	(17.54)
25	Hawaii	2.05		50	Vermont	(19.58)

District of Columbia   15.05

Source: Morgan Quitno Corporation using data from U.S. Department of Justice, Federal Bureau of Investigation
"Crime in the United States" (Uniform Crime Reports, 1988 and 1992 editions)
*Includes murder, rape, robbery, aggravated assault, burglary, larceny-theft, motor vehicle theft and arson.

Violent Crimes in 1988

National Total = 1,566,221 Violent Crimes*

RANK	STATE	CRIMES	%	RANK	STATE	CRIMES	%
1	California	261,912	16.72%	26	Oklahoma	14,179	0.91%
2	New York	196,396	12.54%	27	Minnesota	12,490	0.80%
3	Florida	138,343	8.83%	28	Kentucky	12,284	0.78%
4	Texas	109,499	6.99%	29	Wisconsin	10,414	0.66%
5	Illinois	93,557	5.97%	30	Arkansas	10,237	0.65%
6	Michigan	68,980	4.40%	31	New Mexico	9,938	0.63%
7	Ohio	49,144	3.14%	32	Kansas	9,083	0.58%
8	New Jersey	44,993	2.87%	33	Mississippi	8,544	0.55%
9	Pennsylvania	43,534	2.78%	34	Nevada	8,275	0.53%
10	Georgia	42,589	2.72%	35	Iowa	7,279	0.46%
11	Maryland	37,466	2.39%	36	Nebraska	4,374	0.28%
12	Massachusetts	36,376	2.32%	37	Utah	4,110	0.26%
13	North Carolina	32,753	2.09%	38	Rhode Island	3,947	0.25%
14	Louisiana	31,711	2.02%	39	Delaware	2,981	0.19%
15	Missouri	28,393	1.81%	40	Hawaii	2,810	0.18%
16	Tennessee	26,205	1.67%	41	Alaska	2,682	0.17%
17	South Carolina	25,889	1.65%	42	West Virginia	2,476	0.16%
18	Alabama	23,052	1.47%	43	Idaho	2,345	0.15%
19	Washington	21,543	1.38%	44	Maine	1,898	0.12%
20	Indiana	21,187	1.35%	45	New Hampshire	1,622	0.10%
21	Arizona	21,147	1.35%	46	Wyoming	1,479	0.09%
22	Virginia	17,940	1.15%	47	Montana	989	0.06%
23	Colorado	15,548	0.99%	48	South Dakota	813	0.05%
24	Oregon	14,959	0.96%	49	Vermont	791	0.05%
25	Connecticut	14,759	0.94%	50	North Dakota	392	0.03%
					District of Columbia	11,914	0.76%

Source: U.S. Department of Justice, Federal Bureau of Investigation

"Crime in the United States 1988" (Uniform Crime Reports, 1988)

*Violent crimes are offenses of murder, forcible rape, robbery and aggravated assault. Includes rape and robbery attempts.

Violent Crime Rate in 1988

National Rate = 637 Violent Crimes per 100,000 Population*

RANK	STATE	RATE	RANK	STATE	RATE
1	Florida	1,118	25	Ohio	452
2	New York	1,097	27	Oklahoma	435
3	California	930	28	Arkansas	423
4	Illinois	810	29	Rhode Island	397
5	Maryland	807	30	Indiana	380
6	Nevada	781	31	Kansas	365
7	Michigan	742	32	Pennsylvania	362
8	South Carolina	741	33	Kentucky	330
9	Louisiana	717	34	Mississippi	325
10	Georgia	665	35	Wyoming	314
11	New Mexico	658	36	Virginia	299
12	Texas	653	37	Minnesota	290
13	Massachusetts	620	38	Nebraska	273
14	Arizona	610	39	Hawaii	257
15	New Jersey	583	39	Iowa	257
16	Alabama	559	41	Utah	243
17	Missouri	553	42	Idaho	235
18	Oregon	546	43	Wisconsin	214
19	Tennessee	533	44	Maine	157
20	Alaska	523	45	New Hampshire	148
21	North Carolina	502	46	Vermont	142
22	Colorado	473	47	West Virginia	131
23	Washington	466	48	Montana	123
24	Connecticut	455	49	South Dakota	114
25	Delaware	452	50	North Dakota	59

District of Columbia   1,922

Source: U.S. Department of Justice, Federal Bureau of Investigation
*Crime in the United States 1988" (Uniform Crime Reports, 1988)

*Violent crimes are offenses of murder, forcible rape, robbery and aggravated assault. Includes rape and robbery attempts.

Percent Change in Number of Violent Crimes: 1988 to 1992

National Percent Change = 23.37% Increase*

RANK	STATE	PERCENT CHANGE	RANK	STATE	PERCENT CHANGE
1	South Dakota	70.11	26	Utah	28.15
2	Kentucky	63.68	27	Idaho	28.06
3	Alabama	56.39	28	Nebraska	27.98
4	West Virginia	54.81	29	Washington	27.44
5	New Mexico	48.73	30	Mississippi	25.97
6	Alaska	44.56	31	Arizona	21.56
7	Delaware	43.58	32	Illinois	21.49
8	Tennessee	43.05	33	Minnesota	21.25
9	North Carolina	42.28	34	Ohio	17.89
10	Kansas	41.89	35	Pennsylvania	17.78
11	Montana	41.56	36	Florida	17.70
12	Oklahoma	41.09	37	Georgia	16.22
13	Indiana	35.89	38	Nevada	11.75
14	Missouri	35.41	39	Connecticut	10.12
15	North Dakota	35.20	40	New Jersey	8.34
16	Arkansas	35.11	41	Iowa	7.38
17	Virginia	33.26	42	Hawaii	6.69
18	Louisiana	33.11	43	Michigan	5.35
19	Wisconsin	32.57	44	New York	3.52
20	California	31.96	45	Oregon	1.54
21	South Carolina	31.44	46	Wyoming	0.68
22	Maryland	31.01	47	Rhode Island	0.46
23	Texas	30.02	48	New Hampshire	(13.87)
24	Colorado	29.19	49	Maine	(14.86)
25	Massachusetts	28.46	50	Vermont	(21.11)

District of Columbia   40.05

Source: Morgan Quitno Corporation using data from U.S. Department of Justice, Federal Bureau of Investigation
"Crime in the United States" (Uniform Crime Reports, 1988 and 1992 editions)
*Violent crimes are offenses of murder, forcible rape, robbery and aggravated assault. Includes rape and robbery attempts.

Percent Change in Violent Crime Rate: 1988 to 1992

National Percent Change = 18.92% Increase*

RANK	STATE	PERCENT CHANGE		RANK	STATE	PERCENT CHANGE
1	South Dakota	70.61		26	Colorado	22.37
2	Kentucky	62.27		27	Illinois	20.65
3	West Virginia	61.45		28	California	20.40
4	Alabama	55.94		29	Idaho	19.74
5	Oklahoma	43.17		30	Utah	19.55
6	New Mexico	42.08		31	Pennsylvania	17.96
7	North Dakota	41.19		32	Minnesota	16.55
8	Tennessee	40.00		33	Ohio	16.35
9	Kansas	39.95		34	Washington	14.70
10	Montana	38.13		35	Georgia	10.26
11	Delaware	37.43		36	Arizona	9.97
12	Louisiana	37.32		37	Connecticut	8.86
13	Arkansas	36.29		38	Iowa	8.17
14	North Carolina	35.66		39	Florida	7.98
15	Missouri	33.89		40	New Jersey	7.34
16	Indiana	33.82		41	Michigan	3.79
17	Wisconsin	28.83		42	New York	2.29
18	Nebraska	27.69		43	Wyoming	1.75
19	South Carolina	27.46		44	Hawaii	0.54
20	Mississippi	26.68		45	Rhode Island	(0.63)
21	Alaska	26.29		46	Oregon	(6.56)
22	Massachusetts	25.65		47	Nevada	(10.78)
23	Virginia	25.38		48	New Hampshire	(15.07)
24	Maryland	23.93		49	Maine	(16.62)
25	Texas	23.48		50	Vermont	(22.89)

District of Columbia   47.39

Source: Morgan Quitno Corporation using data from U.S. Department of Justice, Federal Bureau of Investigation
"Crime in the United States" (Uniform Crime Reports, 1988 and 1992 editions)
*Violent crimes are offenses of murder, forcible rape, robbery and aggravated assault. Includes rape and robbery attempts.

Murders in 1988

National Total = 20,675 Murders*

RANK	STATE	MURDERS	%
1	California	2,936	14.20%
2	New York	2,244	10.85%
3	Texas	2,022	9.78%
4	Florida	1,416	6.85%
5	Michigan	1,009	4.88%
6	Illinois	991	4.79%
7	Georgia	748	3.62%
8	Pennsylvania	660	3.19%
9	Ohio	585	2.83%
10	Louisiana	512	2.48%
11	North Carolina	510	2.47%
12	Virginia	468	2.26%
13	Tennessee	461	2.23%
14	Maryland	449	2.17%
15	Missouri	413	2.00%
16	New Jersey	411	1.99%
17	Alabama	408	1.97%
18	Indiana	358	1.73%
19	South Carolina	325	1.57%
20	Arizona	294	1.42%
21	Washington	264	1.28%
22	Oklahoma	243	1.18%
23	Kentucky	229	1.11%
24	Mississippi	225	1.09%
25	Arkansas	211	1.02%

RANK	STATE	MURDERS	%
26	Massachusetts	208	1.01%
27	Colorado	187	0.90%
28	Connecticut	174	0.84%
29	New Mexico	173	0.84%
30	Wisconsin	144	0.70%
31	Oregon	139	0.67%
32	Minnesota	124	0.60%
33	Nevada	111	0.54%
34	West Virginia	93	0.45%
35	Kansas	85	0.41%
36	Nebraska	58	0.28%
37	Iowa	47	0.23%
37	Utah	47	0.23%
39	Hawaii	44	0.21%
40	Rhode Island	41	0.20%
41	Maine	37	0.18%
42	Idaho	36	0.17%
43	Delaware	34	0.16%
44	Alaska	29	0.14%
45	New Hampshire	25	0.12%
46	South Dakota	22	0.11%
47	Montana	21	0.10%
48	North Dakota	12	0.06%
48	Wyoming	12	0.06%
50	Vermont	11	0.05%

| | District of Columbia | 369 | 1.78% |

Source: U.S. Department of Justice, Federal Bureau of Investigation
   "Crime in the United States 1988" (Uniform Crime Reports, 1988)
*Includes nonnegligent manslaughter.

Murder Rate in 1988

National Rate = 8.4 Murders per 100,000 Population*

RANK	STATE	RATE	RANK	STATE	RATE
1	New York	12.5	24	Washington	5.7
2	Texas	12.1	27	Pennsylvania	5.5
3	Georgia	11.7	28	Connecticut	5.4
4	Louisiana	11.6	28	Ohio	5.4
5	New Mexico	11.5	30	New Jersey	5.3
6	Florida	11.4	31	Delaware	5.2
7	Michigan	10.8	32	Oregon	5.1
8	Nevada	10.5	33	West Virginia	4.9
9	California	10.4	34	Rhode Island	4.1
10	Alabama	9.9	35	Hawaii	4.0
11	Maryland	9.7	36	Idaho	3.6
12	Tennessee	9.4	36	Nebraska	3.6
13	South Carolina	9.3	38	Massachusetts	3.5
14	Arkansas	8.7	39	Kansas	3.4
15	Illinois	8.6	40	Maine	3.1
15	Mississippi	8.6	40	South Dakota	3.1
17	Arizona	8.5	42	Wisconsin	3.0
18	Missouri	8.0	43	Minnesota	2.9
19	North Carolina	7.8	44	Utah	2.8
19	Virginia	7.8	45	Montana	2.6
21	Oklahoma	7.4	46	Wyoming	2.5
22	Indiana	6.4	47	New Hampshire	2.3
23	Kentucky	6.2	48	Vermont	2.0
24	Alaska	5.7	49	North Dakota	1.8
24	Colorado	5.7	50	Iowa	1.7

District of Columbia   59.5

Source: Morgan Quitno Corporation using data from U.S. Department of Justice, Federal Bureau of Investigation
"Crime in the United States 1988" (Uniform Crime Reports, 1988)
*Includes nonnegligent manslaughter.

Percent Change in Number of Murders: 1988 to 1992

National Percent Change = 14.92% Increase*

RANK	STATE	PERCENT CHANGE	RANK	STATE	PERCENT CHANGE
1	Kansas	77.65	26	Alabama	11.52
2	Alaska	51.72	27	Texas	10.73
3	Wisconsin	51.39	28	Vermont	9.09
4	Louisiana	45.90	29	New York	6.82
5	Mississippi	42.22	30	Arizona	6.12
6	North Carolina	41.76	31	Massachusetts	2.88
7	Wyoming	41.67	32	Idaho	2.78
8	California	33.55	33	North Dakota	0.00
9	Illinois	33.40	33	Oregon	0.00
10	Maryland	32.74	35	Georgia	(0.94)
11	Missouri	32.45	36	Washington	(2.27)
12	Nevada	30.63	37	New Jersey	(3.41)
13	Indiana	29.61	38	Hawaii	(4.55)
14	Ohio	23.76	39	Connecticut	(4.60)
15	West Virginia	23.66	40	Kentucky	(5.68)
16	Arkansas	22.75	41	Delaware	(5.88)
17	Minnesota	20.97	42	Iowa	(6.38)
18	Virginia	20.51	43	Michigan	(7.04)
19	Nebraska	17.24	44	Rhode Island	(12.20)
20	Colorado	15.51	45	Oklahoma	(13.58)
21	Utah	14.89	46	Florida	(14.69)
22	South Carolina	14.77	47	New Mexico	(18.50)
23	Montana	14.29	48	New Hampshire	(28.00)
24	Pennsylvania	13.03	49	Maine	(43.24)
25	Tennessee	12.80	50	South Dakota	(81.82)

District of Columbia   20.05

Source: Morgan Quitno Corporation using data from U.S. Department of Justice, Federal Bureau of Investigation
   "Crime in the United States" (Uniform Crime Reports, 1988 and 1992 editions)
*Includes nonnegligent manslaughter.

Percent Change in Murder Rate: 1988 to 1992

National Percent Change = 10.71% Increase*

RANK	STATE	PERCENT CHANGE	RANK	STATE	PERCENT CHANGE
1	Kansas	76.47	26	New York	5.60
2	Louisiana	50.00	27	North Dakota	5.56
3	Wisconsin	46.67	28	Vermont	5.00
4	Wyoming	44.00	29	Texas	4.96
5	Mississippi	41.86	30	Nevada	3.81
6	North Carolina	35.90	31	Massachusetts	2.86
7	Illinois	32.56	32	Idaho	(2.78)
8	Alaska	31.58	33	New Jersey	(3.77)
9	Missouri	31.25	34	Arizona	(4.71)
10	West Virginia	28.57	35	Connecticut	(5.56)
11	Indiana	28.12	36	Iowa	(5.88)
12	Maryland	24.74	37	Georgia	(5.98)
13	Arkansas	24.14	38	Kentucky	(6.45)
14	Ohio	22.22	39	Oregon	(7.84)
15	California	22.12	40	Michigan	(8.33)
16	Nebraska	16.67	41	Hawaii	(10.00)
17	Minnesota	13.79	42	Delaware	(11.54)
18	Virginia	12.82	43	Oklahoma	(12.16)
19	Pennsylvania	12.73	44	Rhode Island	(12.20)
20	South Carolina	11.83	45	Washington	(12.28)
21	Montana	11.54	46	Florida	(21.05)
22	Alabama	11.11	47	New Mexico	(22.61)
23	Tennessee	10.64	48	New Hampshire	(30.43)
24	Colorado	8.77	49	Maine	(45.16)
25	Utah	7.14	50	South Dakota	(80.65)

District of Columbia   26.39

Source: Morgan Quitno Corporation using data from U.S. Department of Justice, Federal Bureau of Investigation
   "Crime in the United States" (Uniform Crime Reports)
*Includes nonnegligent manslaughter.

Rapes in 1988

National Total = 92,486 Rapes*

RANK	STATE	RAPES	%
1	California	11,780	12.74%
2	Texas	8,119	8.78%
3	Michigan	6,462	6.99%
4	Florida	6,154	6.65%
5	New York	5,479	5.92%
6	Ohio	4,632	5.01%
7	Illinois	4,449	4.81%
8	Pennsylvania	2,992	3.24%
9	Georgia	2,970	3.21%
10	Washington	2,611	2.82%
11	New Jersey	2,600	2.81%
12	Tennessee	2,201	2.38%
13	Massachusetts	1,876	2.03%
14	North Carolina	1,833	1.98%
15	Indiana	1,731	1.87%
16	Maryland	1,721	1.86%
17	Louisiana	1,702	1.84%
18	Virginia	1,622	1.75%
19	Missouri	1,505	1.63%
20	South Carolina	1,493	1.61%
21	Arizona	1,345	1.45%
22	Minnesota	1,337	1.45%
23	Colorado	1,269	1.37%
24	Oklahoma	1,229	1.33%
25	Alabama	1,228	1.33%

RANK	STATE	RAPES	%
26	Oregon	1,111	1.20%
27	Wisconsin	965	1.04%
28	Mississippi	951	1.03%
29	Connecticut	849	0.92%
30	Kentucky	835	0.90%
31	Nevada	782	0.85%
32	Arkansas	780	0.84%
33	Kansas	779	0.84%
34	New Mexico	580	0.63%
35	Delaware	491	0.53%
36	Iowa	446	0.48%
37	Utah	399	0.43%
38	Nebraska	385	0.42%
39	Hawaii	355	0.38%
40	West Virginia	353	0.38%
41	Rhode Island	303	0.33%
42	Alaska	296	0.32%
43	New Hampshire	276	0.30%
44	Maine	224	0.24%
45	South Dakota	192	0.21%
46	Idaho	179	0.19%
47	Montana	135	0.15%
48	Vermont	128	0.14%
49	Wyoming	113	0.12%
50	North Dakota	74	0.08%

District of Columbia   165   0.18%

Source: U.S. Department of Justice, Federal Bureau of Investigation
"Crime in the United States 1988" (Uniform Crime Reports, 1988)

*Forcible rape is the carnal knowledge of a female forcibly and against her will. Assaults or attempts to commit rape by force or threat of force are included. However, statutory rape without force and other sex offenses are excluded.

Rape Rate in 1988

National Rate = 38 Rapes per 100,000 Population*

RANK	STATE	RATE
1	Delaware	74
1	Nevada	74
3	Michigan	69
4	Alaska	58
5	Washington	57
6	Florida	50
7	Texas	48
8	Georgia	46
9	Tennessee	45
10	Ohio	43
10	South Carolina	43
12	California	42
13	Oregon	41
14	Arizona	39
14	Colorado	39
14	Illinois	39
14	Louisiana	39
18	New Mexico	38
18	Oklahoma	38
20	Maryland	37
21	Mississippi	36
22	New Jersey	34
23	Arkansas	32
23	Hawaii	32
23	Massachusetts	32

RANK	STATE	RATE
26	Indiana	31
26	Kansas	31
26	Minnesota	31
26	New York	31
30	Alabama	30
30	Rhode Island	30
32	Missouri	29
33	North Carolina	28
34	South Dakota	27
34	Virginia	27
36	Connecticut	26
37	New Hampshire	25
37	Pennsylvania	25
39	Nebraska	24
39	Utah	24
39	Wyoming	24
42	Vermont	23
43	Kentucky	22
44	Wisconsin	20
45	Maine	19
45	West Virginia	19
47	Idaho	18
48	Montana	17
49	Iowa	16
50	North Dakota	11

District of Columbia   27

Source: U.S. Department of Justice, Federal Bureau of Investigation
     "Crime in the United States 1988" (Uniform Crime Reports, 1988)
*Forcible rape is the carnal knowledge of a female forcibly and against her will. Assaults or attempts to commit rape by force or threat of force are included. However, statutory rape without force and other sex offenses are excluded.

Percent Change in Number of Rapes: 1988 to 1992

National Percent Change = 17.92% Increase*

RANK	STATE	PERCENT CHANGE		RANK	STATE	PERCENT CHANGE
1	Utah	106.27		26	Missouri	25.91
2	North Dakota	100.00		27	Hawaii	23.94
3	Alaska	95.61		28	Ohio	23.90
4	South Dakota	91.67		29	Virginia	23.80
5	Idaho	89.39		30	Mississippi	22.61
6	New Mexico	70.69		31	Arizona	22.45
7	Montana	55.56		32	Delaware	20.37
8	New Hampshire	53.62		33	Florida	18.78
9	Kentucky	44.79		34	Iowa	18.39
10	Wyoming	44.25		35	Michigan	16.84
11	Oregon	42.21		36	Texas	16.23
12	Washington	41.59		37	Massachusetts	15.46
13	South Carolina	38.78		38	West Virginia	11.33
14	Alabama	38.76		39	Pennsylvania	11.10
15	Indiana	38.53		40	Vermont	10.94
16	Minnesota	37.62		41	California	8.33
17	Wisconsin	36.27		42	Tennessee	8.00
18	North Carolina	33.93		43	Louisiana	6.52
19	Kansas	33.76		43	Nevada	6.52
20	Maryland	32.36		45	Connecticut	4.12
21	Maine	31.25		46	Georgia	2.93
22	Nebraska	30.91		47	Rhode Island	2.64
23	Colorado	29.31		48	Illinois	(3.08)
24	Arkansas	26.92		49	New York	(5.97)
25	Oklahoma	26.61		50	New Jersey	(8.00)

District of Columbia   30.30

Source: Morgan Quitno Corporation using data from U.S. Department of Justice, Federal Bureau of Investigation
   "Crime in the United States" (Uniform Crime Reports, 1988 and 1992 editions)
*Forcible rape is the carnal knowledge of a female forcibly and against her will. Assaults or attempts to commit rape by force or threat of force are included. However, statutory rape without force and other sex offenses are excluded.

Percent Change in Rape Rate: 1988 to 1992

National Percent Change = 12.63% Increase*

RANK	STATE	PERCENT CHANGE	RANK	STATE	PERCENT CHANGE
1	North Dakota	111.82	26	Mississippi	23.89
2	South Dakota	91.85	27	Colorado	21.28
3	Utah	89.17	28	Ohio	21.16
4	Idaho	76.67	29	Hawaii	18.44
5	Alaska	70.00	30	Iowa	17.50
6	New Mexico	64.74	31	Virginia	16.67
7	New Hampshire	52.80	32	Delaware	15.95
8	Montana	50.00	33	Michigan	15.94
9	Kentucky	46.36	34	West Virginia	14.21
10	Wyoming	45.83	35	Massachusetts	12.81
11	Alabama	37.33	36	Texas	11.25
12	Indiana	36.77	37	Pennsylvania	10.80
13	South Carolina	33.72	38	Arizona	10.26
14	Kansas	33.23	39	Louisiana	8.46
15	Minnesota	32.58	40	Florida	8.40
16	Wisconsin	31.50	41	Vermont	8.26
17	Nebraska	30.83	42	Tennessee	5.11
18	Oregon	29.51	43	Connecticut	3.46
19	Arkansas	29.06	44	Rhode Island	3.00
20	North Carolina	28.21	45	Georgia	(1.52)
21	Oklahoma	27.37	46	California	(1.67)
22	Washington	26.32	47	Illinois	(4.87)
23	Missouri	25.86	48	New York	(8.39)
24	Maryland	25.41	49	New Jersey	(9.71)
25	Maine	25.26	50	Nevada	(15.14)

District of Columbia   35.19

Source: Morgan Quitno Corporation using data from U.S. Department of Justice, Federal Bureau of Investigation
   "Crime in the United States" (Uniform Crime Reports, 1988 and 1992 editions)
*Forcible rape is the carnal knowledge of a female forcibly and against her will. Assaults or attempts to commit rape by force or threat of force are included. However, statutory rape without force and other sex offenses are excluded.

Aggravated Assaults in 1988

National Total = 910,092 Aggravated Assaults*

RANK	STATE	ASSAULTS	%	RANK	STATE	ASSAULTS	%
1	California	161,055	17.70%	26	Oregon	8,420	0.93%
2	New York	91,239	10.03%	27	Connecticut	7,656	0.84%
3	Florida	80,857	8.88%	28	New Mexico	7,628	0.84%
4	Texas	60,057	6.60%	29	Arkansas	7,209	0.79%
5	Illinois	52,020	5.72%	30	Minnesota	6,950	0.76%
6	Michigan	39,085	4.29%	31	Kansas	6,083	0.67%
7	Ohio	26,381	2.90%	32	Wisconsin	6,047	0.66%
8	Massachusetts	23,940	2.63%	33	Iowa	5,654	0.62%
9	North Carolina	23,325	2.56%	34	Mississippi	5,340	0.59%
10	Georgia	23,278	2.56%	35	Nevada	4,295	0.47%
11	Pennsylvania	23,275	2.56%	36	Nebraska	3,033	0.33%
12	New Jersey	23,055	2.53%	37	Utah	2,749	0.30%
13	Maryland	21,302	2.34%	38	Rhode Island	2,457	0.27%
14	Louisiana	20,259	2.23%	39	Alaska	1,983	0.22%
15	South Carolina	19,714	2.17%	40	Idaho	1,928	0.21%
16	Missouri	17,837	1.96%	41	Delaware	1,672	0.18%
17	Alabama	16,556	1.82%	42	Hawaii	1,492	0.16%
18	Tennessee	15,006	1.65%	43	West Virginia	1,386	0.15%
19	Arizona	14,758	1.62%	44	Maine	1,326	0.15%
20	Indiana	14,135	1.55%	45	Wyoming	1,283	0.14%
21	Washington	11,930	1.31%	46	New Hampshire	1,090	0.12%
22	Colorado	10,842	1.19%	47	Montana	651	0.07%
23	Oklahoma	9,279	1.02%	48	Vermont	563	0.06%
24	Virginia	9,102	1.00%	49	South Dakota	512	0.06%
25	Kentucky	8,456	0.93%	50	North Dakota	252	0.03%
					District of Columbia	5,690	0.63%

Source: U.S. Department of Justice, Federal Bureau of Investigation
    "Crime in the United States 1988" (Uniform Crime Reports, 1988)
*Aggravated assault is an attack for the purpose of inflicting severe bodily injury.

Aggravated Assault Rate in 1988

National Rate = 370 Aggravated Assaults per 100,000 Population*

RANK	STATE	RATE	RANK	STATE	RATE
1	Florida	653	26	Washington	258
2	California	572	27	Indiana	254
3	South Carolina	564	28	Delaware	253
4	New York	510	29	Rhode Island	247
5	New Mexico	505	30	Kansas	245
6	Maryland	459	31	Ohio	243
7	Louisiana	458	32	Connecticut	236
8	Illinois	451	33	Kentucky	227
9	Arizona	426	34	Mississippi	203
10	Michigan	420	35	Iowa	200
11	Massachusetts	408	36	Pennsylvania	194
12	Nevada	405	37	Idaho	193
13	Alabama	401	38	Nebraska	189
14	Alaska	387	39	Utah	163
15	Georgia	364	40	Minnesota	161
16	Texas	358	41	Virginia	152
17	North Carolina	357	42	Hawaii	137
18	Missouri	347	43	Wisconsin	124
19	Colorado	330	44	Maine	110
20	Oregon	307	45	Vermont	101
21	Tennessee	305	46	New Hampshire	99
22	New Jersey	299	47	Montana	81
23	Arkansas	298	48	West Virginia	74
24	Oklahoma	284	49	South Dakota	72
25	Wyoming	272	50	North Dakota	38

District of Columbia 918

Source: U.S. Department of Justice, Federal Bureau of Investigation
  "Crime in the United States 1988" (Uniform Crime Reports, 1988)
Aggravated assault is an attack for the purpose of inflicting severe bodily injury.

Percent Change in Number of Aggravated Assaults: 1988 to 1992

National Percent Change = 23.83% Increase*

RANK	STATE	PERCENT CHANGE		RANK	STATE	PERCENT CHANGE
1	West Virginia	83.04		26	Idaho	24.38
2	Kentucky	82.23		27	Georgia	23.87
3	South Dakota	74.02		28	California	22.97
4	Alabama	63.53		29	Utah	22.81
5	Tennessee	57.44		30	Arizona	21.15
6	Delaware	56.40		31	Minnesota	18.68
7	New Mexico	50.08		32	Maryland	18.10
8	Oklahoma	49.40		33	Illinois	15.45
9	Montana	45.01		34	Mississippi	12.79
10	Texas	43.37		35	Ohio	12.00
11	Massachusetts	39.05		36	Michigan	10.74
12	Kansas	38.39		37	Pennsylvania	9.58
13	Louisiana	38.27		38	Rhode Island	8.59
14	Virginia	37.86		39	Iowa	8.44
15	Washington	36.81		40	Connecticut	8.20
16	Missouri	35.80		41	Oregon	6.45
17	Nebraska	35.67		42	Wisconsin	3.79
18	Indiana	34.47		43	New Jersey	2.97
19	Arkansas	32.76		44	New York	(3.98)
20	Alaska	31.82		45	Wyoming	(4.52)
21	North Carolina	31.35		46	Hawaii	(8.51)
22	Florida	29.64		47	Nevada	(9.85)
23	Colorado	29.58		48	Maine	(23.60)
24	South Carolina	29.03		49	Vermont	(25.58)
25	North Dakota	26.98		50	New Hampshire	(46.06)

District of Columbia   50.58

Source: Morgan Quitno Corporation using data from U.S. Department of Justice, Federal Bureau of Investigation
"Crime in the United States" (Uniform Crime Reports, 1988 and 1992 editions)
*Aggravated assault is an attack for the purpose of inflicting severe bodily injury.

Percent Change in Rate of Aggravated Assaults: 1988 to 1992

National Percent Change = 19.41% Increase*

RANK	STATE	PERCENT CHANGE	RANK	STATE	PERCENT CHANGE
1	West Virginia	89.19	26	Idaho	16.42
2	Kentucky	80.79	27	Alaska	15.06
3	South Dakota	74.03	28	Illinois	14.50
4	Alabama	63.24	29	Minnesota	14.35
5	Tennessee	54.20	30	Utah	14.23
6	Oklahoma	51.97	31	Mississippi	13.50
7	Delaware	50.00	32	California	12.17
8	New Mexico	43.39	33	Maryland	11.68
9	Louisiana	42.66	34	Ohio	10.37
10	Montana	41.48	35	Arizona	9.53
11	Texas	36.23	36	Pennsylvania	9.48
12	Kansas	36.20	37	Michigan	9.19
13	Massachusetts	36.03	38	Iowa	9.00
14	Nebraska	35.56	39	Rhode Island	7.49
15	Missouri	34.44	40	Connecticut	6.99
16	Arkansas	33.89	41	New Jersey	1.94
17	North Dakota	32.37	42	Wisconsin	1.05
18	Indiana	32.17	43	Oregon	(1.92)
19	Virginia	29.47	44	Wyoming	(3.35)
20	North Carolina	25.41	45	New York	(5.20)
21	South Carolina	25.18	46	Hawaii	(14.09)
22	Washington	23.18	47	Maine	(25.45)
23	Colorado	22.70	48	Vermont	(27.23)
24	Florida	19.02	49	Nevada	(27.95)
25	Georgia	17.34	50	New Hampshire	(46.57)

District of Columbia   58.46

Source: Morgan Quitno Corporation using data from U.S. Department of Justice, Federal Bureau of Investigation
"Crime in the United States" (Uniform Crime Reports, 1988 and 1992 editions)
*Aggravated assault is an attack for the purpose of inflicting severe bodily injury.

Robberies in 1988

National Total = 542,968 Robberies*

RANK	STATE	ROBBERIES	%	RANK	STATE	ROBBERIES	%
1	New York	97,434	17.94%	26	Oklahoma	3,428	0.63%
2	California	86,141	15.86%	27	Wisconsin	3,258	0.60%
3	Florida	49,916	9.19%	28	Colorado	3,250	0.60%
4	Texas	39,301	7.24%	29	Nevada	3,087	0.57%
5	Illinois	36,097	6.65%	30	Kentucky	2,764	0.51%
6	Michigan	22,424	4.13%	31	Kansas	2,136	0.39%
7	New Jersey	18,927	3.49%	32	Arkansas	2,037	0.38%
8	Ohio	17,546	3.23%	33	Mississippi	2,028	0.37%
9	Pennsylvania	16,607	3.06%	34	New Mexico	1,557	0.29%
10	Georgia	15,593	2.87%	35	Rhode Island	1,146	0.21%
11	Maryland	13,994	2.58%	36	Iowa	1,132	0.21%
12	Massachusetts	10,352	1.91%	37	Hawaii	919	0.17%
13	Louisiana	9,238	1.70%	38	Utah	915	0.17%
14	Missouri	8,638	1.59%	39	Nebraska	898	0.17%
15	Tennessee	8,537	1.57%	40	Delaware	784	0.14%
16	North Carolina	7,085	1.30%	41	West Virginia	644	0.12%
17	Virginia	6,748	1.24%	42	Alaska	374	0.07%
18	Washington	6,738	1.24%	43	Maine	311	0.06%
19	Connecticut	6,080	1.12%	44	New Hampshire	231	0.04%
20	Oregon	5,289	0.97%	45	Idaho	202	0.04%
21	Indiana	4,963	0.91%	46	Montana	182	0.03%
22	Alabama	4,860	0.90%	47	Vermont	89	0.02%
23	Arizona	4,750	0.87%	48	South Dakota	87	0.02%
24	South Carolina	4,357	0.80%	49	Wyoming	71	0.01%
25	Minnesota	4,079	0.75%	50	North Dakota	54	0.01%
					District of Columbia	5,690	1.05%

Source: U.S. Department of Justice, Federal Bureau of Investigation
    "Crime in the United States 1988" (Uniform Crime Reports, 1988)
*Robbery is the taking of anything of value by force or threat of force. Attempts are included.

Robbery Rate in 1988

National Rate = 221 Robberies per 100,000 Population*

RANK	STATE	RATE		RANK	STATE	RATE
1	New York	544		26	North Carolina	109
2	Florida	403		27	Oklahoma	105
3	Illinois	313		28	New Mexico	103
4	California	306		29	Colorado	99
5	Maryland	301		30	Minnesota	95
6	Nevada	291		31	Indiana	89
7	New Jersey	245		32	Kansas	86
8	Georgia	244		33	Arkansas	84
9	Michigan	241		33	Hawaii	84
10	Texas	234		35	Mississippi	77
11	Louisiana	209		36	Kentucky	74
12	Oregon	193		37	Alaska	73
13	Connecticut	188		38	Wisconsin	67
14	Massachusetts	176		39	Nebraska	56
15	Tennessee	174		40	Utah	54
16	Missouri	168		41	Iowa	40
17	Ohio	161		42	West Virginia	34
18	Washington	146		43	Maine	26
19	Pennsylvania	138		44	Montana	23
20	Arizona	137		45	New Hampshire	21
21	South Carolina	125		46	Idaho	20
22	Delaware	119		47	Vermont	16
23	Alabama	118		48	Wyoming	15
24	Rhode Island	115		49	South Dakota	12
25	Virginia	113		50	North Dakota	8

District of Columbia   918

Source: U.S. Department of Justice, Federal Bureau of Investigation
  "Crime in the United States 1988" (Uniform Crime Reports, 1988)
*Robbery is the taking of anything of value by force or threat of force. Attempts are included.

Percent Change in Number of Robberies: 1988 to 1992

National Percent Change = 23.85% Increase*

RANK	STATE	PERCENT CHANGE	RANK	STATE	PERCENT CHANGE
1	Wisconsin	84.07	26	Ohio	24.96
2	North Carolina	80.44	27	Arizona	23.52
3	Alaska	71.12	28	West Virginia	22.36
4	Mississippi	60.45	29	Montana	21.98
5	New Hampshire	58.87	30	Minnesota	20.27
6	Kansas	53.42	31	Kentucky	18.42
7	California	51.96	32	Wyoming	18.31
8	Maryland	50.45	33	New Jersey	17.38
9	Arkansas	47.82	34	Connecticut	13.78
10	Nevada	42.44	35	Texas	13.45
11	New Mexico	41.43	36	Idaho	13.37
12	South Carolina	41.11	37	New York	11.00
13	Alabama	40.31	38	Utah	10.82
14	Indiana	39.45	39	Georgia	8.14
15	South Dakota	37.93	40	Massachusetts	6.83
16	Missouri	36.41	41	Washington	6.53
17	Delaware	32.91	42	Nebraska	1.45
18	Illinois	32.90	43	Florida	(0.87)
19	Pennsylvania	30.67	44	Iowa	(1.68)
20	Virginia	30.22	45	Michigan	(6.79)
21	Colorado	28.62	46	Maine	(7.40)
22	Tennessee	28.43	47	North Dakota	(7.41)
23	Oklahoma	27.65	48	Oregon	(14.79)
24	Louisiana	25.96	49	Rhode Island	(17.10)
25	Hawaii	25.24	50	Vermont	(42.70)

District of Columbia   31.09

Source: Morgan Quitno Corporation using data from U.S. Department of Justice, Federal Bureau of Investigation
"Crime in the United States" (Uniform Crime Reports, 1988 and 1992 editions)
*Robbery is the taking of anything of value by force or threat of force. Attempts are included.

Percent Change in Robbery Rate: 1988 to 1992

National Percent Change = 19.28% Increase*

RANK	STATE	PERCENT CHANGE	RANK	STATE	PERCENT CHANGE
1	Wisconsin	78.81	26	Wyoming	20.00
2	North Carolina	71.38	27	Hawaii	18.10
3	Mississippi	61.69	28	Kentucky	17.84
4	New Hampshire	57.14	29	Montana	16.96
5	Kansas	51.05	30	New Jersey	16.41
6	Arkansas	49.40	31	Minnesota	15.26
7	Alaska	49.32	32	Nevada	13.85
8	Maryland	42.52	33	Connecticut	12.18
9	South Dakota	40.83	34	Arizona	11.75
10	Alabama	39.75	35	New York	9.72
11	California	38.59	36	Texas	7.91
12	Indiana	37.30	37	Idaho	7.50
13	South Carolina	36.48	38	Massachusetts	4.77
14	New Mexico	35.24	39	Utah	3.52
15	Missouri	35.06	40	Georgia	2.38
16	Illinois	31.79	41	Nebraska	1.25
17	Pennsylvania	30.94	42	Iowa	(1.00)
18	Louisiana	29.86	43	North Dakota	(1.25)
19	Oklahoma	29.71	44	Washington	(4.25)
20	West Virginia	27.94	45	Michigan	(8.09)
21	Delaware	27.06	46	Florida	(8.96)
22	Tennessee	25.40	47	Maine	(10.38)
23	Ohio	23.60	48	Rhode Island	(17.83)
24	Virginia	21.95	49	Oregon	(21.55)
25	Colorado	21.72	50	Vermont	(44.38)

District of Columbia   37.95

Source: Morgan Quitno Corporation using data from U.S. Department of Justice, Federal Bureau of Investigation
"Crime in the United States" (Uniform Crime Reports, 1988 and 1992 editions)
*Robbery is the taking of anything of value by force or threat of force. Attempts are included.

Property Crimes in 1988

National Total = 12,356,865 Property Crimes*

RANK	STATE	CRIMES	%	RANK	STATE	CRIMES	%
1	California	1,607,180	13.01%	26	Alabama	165,209	1.34%
2	Texas	1,235,870	10.00%	27	South Carolina	163,164	1.32%
3	Florida	967,869	7.83%	28	Connecticut	150,455	1.22%
4	New York	932,845	7.55%	29	Kansas	112,280	0.91%
5	Illinois	555,316	4.49%	30	Iowa	108,254	0.88%
6	Michigan	496,867	4.02%	31	Kentucky	104,362	0.84%
7	Ohio	455,890	3.69%	32	Arkansas	91,962	0.74%
8	New Jersey	363,807	2.94%	33	Utah	90,223	0.73%
9	Georgia	362,376	2.93%	34	New Mexico	89,817	0.73%
10	Pennsylvania	338,486	2.74%	35	Mississippi	85,840	0.69%
11	Washington	307,008	2.48%	36	Hawaii	62,650	0.51%
12	North Carolina	284,557	2.30%	37	Nebraska	61,908	0.50%
13	Massachusetts	256,639	2.08%	38	Nevada	60,128	0.49%
14	Arizona	237,808	1.92%	39	Rhode Island	47,837	0.39%
15	Virginia	232,496	1.88%	40	Maine	41,249	0.33%
16	Maryland	227,457	1.84%	41	West Virginia	39,703	0.32%
17	Louisiana	222,913	1.80%	42	Idaho	37,345	0.30%
18	Missouri	220,578	1.79%	43	New Hampshire	34,951	0.28%
19	Indiana	210,177	1.70%	44	Montana	33,318	0.27%
20	Tennessee	193,647	1.57%	45	Delaware	28,693	0.23%
21	Colorado	187,719	1.52%	46	Vermont	22,786	0.18%
22	Wisconsin	182,545	1.48%	47	Alaska	22,566	0.18%
23	Oregon	178,520	1.44%	48	North Dakota	17,695	0.14%
24	Minnesota	173,302	1.40%	49	South Dakota	17,641	0.14%
25	Oklahoma	168,194	1.36%	50	Wyoming	17,206	0.14%
					District of Columbia	49,557	0.40%

Source: U.S. Department of Justice, Federal Bureau of Investigation
        "Crime in the United States 1988" (Uniform Crime Reports, 1988)
*Property crimes are offenses of burglary, larceny-theft and motor vehicle theft. Attempts are included.

Property Crime Rate in 1988

National Rate = 5,027 Property Crimes per 100,000 Population*

RANK	STATE	RATE	RANK	STATE	RATE
1	Florida	7,820	26	North Carolina	4,360
2	Texas	7,365	27	Delaware	4,347
3	Arizona	6,861	28	Missouri	4,292
4	Washington	6,647	29	Ohio	4,193
5	Oregon	6,513	30	Montana	4,144
6	New Mexico	5,948	31	Vermont	4,098
7	Hawaii	5,732	32	Minnesota	4,025
8	California	5,706	33	Alabama	4,003
8	Colorado	5,706	34	Tennessee	3,937
10	Nevada	5,672	35	Virginia	3,878
11	Georgia	5,661	36	Nebraska	3,867
12	Michigan	5,343	37	Iowa	3,820
13	Utah	5,335	38	Arkansas	3,797
14	New York	5,212	39	Indiana	3,770
15	Oklahoma	5,155	40	Wisconsin	3,758
16	Louisiana	5,043	41	Idaho	3,738
17	Maryland	4,898	42	Wyoming	3,653
18	Illinois	4,810	43	Maine	3,420
19	Rhode Island	4,808	44	Mississippi	3,268
20	New Jersey	4,713	45	New Hampshire	3,186
21	South Carolina	4,671	46	Pennsylvania	2,814
22	Connecticut	4,642	47	Kentucky	2,805
23	Kansas	4,515	48	North Dakota	2,669
24	Alaska	4,399	49	South Dakota	2,467
25	Massachusetts	4,371	50	West Virginia	2,107

District of Columbia   7,993

Source: U.S. Department of Justice, Federal Bureau of Investigation

"Crime in the United States 1988" (Uniform Crime Reports, 1988)

*Property crimes are offenses of burglary, larceny-theft and motor vehicle theft. Attempts are included.

Percent Change in Number of Property Crimes: 1988 to 1992

National Percent Change = 1.21% Increase*

RANK	STATE	PERCENT CHANGE	RANK	STATE	PERCENT CHANGE
1	Alaska	27.70	26	Nebraska	3.13
2	North Carolina	23.16	27	Missouri	2.57
3	Nevada	21.54	28	Arizona	2.45
4	Mississippi	17.87	29	Maine	1.58
5	Wyoming	15.26	30	Delaware	1.51
6	Tennessee	13.88	31	North Dakota	1.36
7	South Dakota	13.03	32	Kentucky	0.32
8	Maryland	12.73	33	Illinois	0.29
9	Indiana	12.56	34	Ohio	0.03
10	Wisconsin	10.90	35	Florida	(0.34)
11	Alabama	10.06	36	Colorado	(0.55)
12	Minnesota	9.94	37	Connecticut	(0.61)
13	Montana	9.47	38	Massachusetts	(1.28)
14	West Virginia	9.45	39	New Mexico	(3.20)
15	South Carolina	9.28	40	Iowa	(4.43)
16	Arkansas	9.18	41	New Jersey	(4.97)
17	Hawaii	8.38	42	Washington	(5.68)
18	Kansas	8.06	43	New Hampshire	(6.07)
19	Utah	7.87	44	New York	(8.00)
20	Virginia	7.62	45	Michigan	(8.06)
21	Louisiana	6.96	46	Oklahoma	(8.17)
22	California	6.78	47	Texas	(10.69)
23	Idaho	6.13	48	Oregon	(11.44)
24	Georgia	5.67	49	Rhode Island	(12.11)
25	Pennsylvania	5.22	50	Vermont	(17.44)

District of Columbia   1.91

Source: Morgan Quitno Corporation using data from U.S. Department of Justice, Federal Bureau of Investigation
    "Crime in the United States" (Uniform Crime Reports, 1988 and 1992 editions)
*Property crimes are offenses of burglary, larceny-theft and motor vehicle theft. Attempts are included.

Percent Change in Rate of Property Crime: 1988 to 1992

National Percent Change = 2.47% Decrease*

RANK	STATE	PERCENT CHANGE	RANK	STATE	PERCENT CHANGE
1	Mississippi	18.44	26	Illinois	(0.46)
2	North Carolina	17.46	27	Kentucky	(0.60)
3	Wyoming	16.50	28	Idaho	(0.62)
4	West Virginia	13.82	29	Maine	(0.80)
5	South Dakota	13.68	30	Ohio	(1.27)
6	Alaska	11.59	31	Connecticut	(1.82)
7	Tennessee	11.50	32	California	(2.56)
8	Indiana	10.84	33	Delaware	(2.75)
9	Louisiana	10.29	34	Nevada	(2.91)
10	Arkansas	10.22	35	Massachusetts	(3.37)
11	Alabama	9.83	36	Iowa	(3.69)
12	Wisconsin	7.59	37	Colorado	(5.72)
13	Montana	6.81	38	New Jersey	(5.82)
14	Maryland	6.67	39	Oklahoma	(6.72)
15	Kansas	6.51	40	New Hampshire	(7.26)
16	South Carolina	5.94	41	Arizona	(7.33)
17	Minnesota	5.66	42	New Mexico	(7.55)
17	North Dakota	5.66	43	Florida	(8.55)
19	Pennsylvania	5.39	44	New York	(9.13)
20	Nebraska	2.81	45	Michigan	(9.40)
21	Hawaii	2.12	46	Rhode Island	(12.99)
22	Missouri	1.51	47	Texas	(15.12)
23	Virginia	1.18	48	Washington	(15.18)
24	Utah	0.62	49	Oregon	(18.46)
25	Georgia	0.20	50	Vermont	(19.46)

District of Columbia 7.27

Source: Morgan Quitno Corporation using data from U.S. Department of Justice, Federal Bureau of Investigation
"Crime in the United States" (Uniform Crime Reports, 1988 and 1992 editions)
*Property crimes are offenses of burglary, larceny-theft and motor vehicle theft. Attempts are included.

Burglaries in 1988

National Total = 3,218,077 Burglaries*

RANK	STATE	BURGLARIES	%	RANK	STATE	BURGLARIES	%
1	California	407,631	12.67%	26	Connecticut	39,477	1.23%
2	Texas	361,972	11.25%	27	Minnesota	39,167	1.22%
3	Florida	283,960	8.82%	28	Wisconsin	35,423	1.10%
4	New York	218,060	6.78%	29	Mississippi	33,651	1.05%
5	Illinois	130,292	4.05%	30	Kentucky	30,747	0.96%
6	Michigan	122,254	3.80%	31	Kansas	29,321	0.91%
7	Ohio	112,130	3.48%	32	New Mexico	27,737	0.86%
8	Georgia	103,106	3.20%	33	Arkansas	26,443	0.82%
9	North Carolina	90,791	2.82%	34	Iowa	24,211	0.75%
10	Washington	85,711	2.66%	35	Nevada	16,376	0.51%
11	Pennsylvania	83,791	2.60%	36	Utah	14,898	0.46%
12	New Jersey	75,675	2.35%	37	Hawaii	13,726	0.43%
13	Louisiana	63,843	1.98%	38	Rhode Island	12,550	0.39%
14	Massachusetts	62,307	1.94%	39	Nebraska	12,251	0.38%
15	Tennessee	60,894	1.89%	40	West Virginia	11,510	0.36%
16	Missouri	58,605	1.82%	41	Maine	9,852	0.31%
17	Arizona	54,773	1.70%	42	Idaho	8,691	0.27%
18	Maryland	54,735	1.70%	43	New Hampshire	7,489	0.23%
19	Oklahoma	53,624	1.67%	44	Delaware	6,868	0.21%
20	Indiana	52,137	1.62%	45	Vermont	6,098	0.19%
21	Alabama	50,920	1.58%	46	Montana	5,657	0.18%
22	South Carolina	49,467	1.54%	47	Alaska	4,321	0.13%
23	Virginia	49,069	1.52%	48	South Dakota	3,703	0.12%
24	Oregon	48,355	1.50%	49	Wyoming	3,103	0.10%
25	Colorado	45,503	1.41%	50	North Dakota	2,902	0.09%
					District of Columbia	12,300	0.38%

Source: U.S. Department of Justice, Federal Bureau of Investigation
"Crime in the United States 1988" (Uniform Crime Reports, 1988)
*Burglary is the unlawful entry of a structure to commit a felony or theft. Attempts are included.

Burglary Rate in 1988

National Rate = 1,309 Burglaries per 100,000 Population*

RANK	STATE	RATE		RANK	STATE	RATE
1	Florida	2,294		26	Illinois	1,129
2	Texas	2,157		27	Vermont	1,097
3	Washington	1,856		28	Arkansas	1,092
4	New Mexico	1,837		29	Massachusetts	1,061
5	Oregon	1,764		30	Delaware	1,041
6	Oklahoma	1,643		31	Ohio	1,031
7	Georgia	1,611		32	New Jersey	980
8	Arizona	1,580		33	Indiana	935
9	Nevada	1,545		34	Minnesota	910
10	California	1,447		35	Utah	881
11	Louisiana	1,444		36	Idaho	870
12	South Carolina	1,416		37	Iowa	854
13	North Carolina	1,391		38	Alaska	842
14	Colorado	1,383		39	Kentucky	826
15	Michigan	1,315		40	Virginia	818
16	Mississippi	1,281		41	Maine	817
17	Rhode Island	1,261		42	Nebraska	765
18	Hawaii	1,256		43	Wisconsin	729
19	Tennessee	1,238		44	Montana	704
20	Alabama	1,234		45	Pennsylvania	697
21	Connecticut	1,218		46	New Hampshire	683
21	New York	1,218		47	Wyoming	659
23	Kansas	1,179		48	West Virginia	611
23	Maryland	1,179		49	South Dakota	518
25	Missouri	1,140		50	North Dakota	438

District of Columbia 1,984

Source: U.S. Department of Justice, Federal Bureau of Investigation
    "Crime in the United States 1988" (Uniform Crime Reports, 1988)
*Burglary is the unlawful entry of a structure to commit a felony or theft. Attempts are included.

Percent Change in Number of Burglaries: 1988 to 1992

National Percent Change = 7.40% Decrease*

RANK	STATE	PERCENT CHANGE	RANK	STATE	PERCENT CHANGE
1	North Carolina	24.59	26	Hawaii	(5.25)
2	Alaska	19.65	27	Georgia	(5.53)
3	Kansas	11.32	28	Montana	(6.20)
4	Utah	7.70	29	Nebraska	(6.32)
5	California	4.87	30	Ohio	(6.93)
6	Tennessee	4.55	31	New Hampshire	(7.74)
7	Nevada	4.47	32	Virginia	(7.85)
8	South Dakota	3.94	33	Connecticut	(7.87)
9	Indiana	3.39	34	Louisiana	(8.25)
10	Massachusetts	3.23	35	Idaho	(8.71)
11	Maine	3.09	36	Pennsylvania	(9.50)
12	Minnesota	1.77	37	Florida	(10.28)
13	Maryland	1.43	38	Kentucky	(10.96)
14	Wyoming	0.77	39	New York	(11.24)
15	South Carolina	0.41	40	Iowa	(12.45)
16	New Jersey	(0.22)	41	New Mexico	(13.85)
17	Mississippi	(0.35)	42	North Dakota	(14.30)
18	Arkansas	(0.87)	43	Rhode Island	(16.10)
19	Arizona	(1.24)	44	Colorado	(16.81)
20	West Virginia	(1.94)	45	Oklahoma	(18.55)
21	Wisconsin	(2.20)	46	Michigan	(19.63)
22	Missouri	(2.52)	47	Vermont	(22.83)
23	Alabama	(3.67)	48	Texas	(25.70)
24	Illinois	(3.83)	49	Oregon	(31.87)
25	Delaware	(3.93)	50	Washington	(32.78)

District of Columbia   (12.84)

Source: Morgan Quitno Corporation using data from U.S. Department of Justice, Federal Bureau of Investigation
    "Crime in the United States" (Uniform Crime Reports, 1988 and 1992 editions)
*Burglary is the unlawful entry of a structure to commit a felony or theft. Attempts are included.

Percent Change in Rate of Burglaries: 1988 to 1992

National Percent Change = 10.76% Decrease*

RANK	STATE	PERCENT CHANGE	RANK	STATE	PERCENT CHANGE
1	North Carolina	18.84	26	Ohio	(8.12)
2	Kansas	9.73	27	Montana	(8.54)
3	Alaska	4.60	28	New Hampshire	(8.95)
4	South Dakota	4.52	29	Connecticut	(8.98)
5	Tennessee	2.36	30	Pennsylvania	(9.40)
6	West Virginia	1.95	31	Georgia	(10.44)
7	Indiana	1.83	32	Arizona	(10.65)
8	Wyoming	1.82	33	Hawaii	(10.73)
9	Massachusetts	1.07	33	North Dakota	(10.73)
10	Maine	0.65	35	Iowa	(11.73)
11	Utah	0.45	35	Kentucky	(11.73)
12	Mississippi	0.14	37	New York	(12.30)
13	Arkansas	0.06	38	Virginia	(13.31)
14	New Jersey	(1.08)	39	Idaho	(14.53)
15	Minnesota	(2.23)	40	Nevada	(16.56)
16	South Carolina	(2.65)	41	Rhode Island	(16.92)
17	Missouri	(3.50)	42	Oklahoma	(17.24)
18	Alabama	(3.89)	43	Florida	(17.66)
19	Maryland	(4.05)	44	New Mexico	(17.72)
20	California	(4.29)	45	Michigan	(20.82)
21	Illinois	(4.58)	46	Colorado	(21.12)
22	Wisconsin	(5.09)	47	Vermont	(24.74)
23	Louisiana	(5.38)	48	Texas	(29.38)
24	Nebraska	(6.59)	49	Oregon	(37.26)
25	Delaware	(8.01)	50	Washington	(39.56)

District of Columbia   (8.26)

Source: Morgan Quitno Corporation using data from U.S. Department of Justice, Federal Bureau of Investigation
"Crime in the United States" (Uniform Crime Reports, 1988 and 1992 editions)
*Burglary is the unlawful entry of a structure to commit a felony or theft. Attempts are included.

Larceny and Theft in 1988

National Total = 7,705,872 Larcenies and Thefts*

RANK	STATE	LARCENIES	%		RANK	STATE	LARCENIES	%
1	California	933,636	12.12%		26	South Carolina	103,055	1.34%
2	Texas	739,642	9.60%		27	Oklahoma	96,418	1.25%
3	Florida	589,215	7.65%		28	Connecticut	91,079	1.18%
4	New York	560,887	7.28%		29	Iowa	79,447	1.03%
5	Illinois	355,148	4.61%		30	Kansas	76,927	1.00%
6	Michigan	305,693	3.97%		31	Utah	71,677	0.93%
7	Ohio	300,355	3.90%		32	Kentucky	66,711	0.87%
8	Georgia	223,768	2.90%		33	Arkansas	60,363	0.78%
9	New Jersey	219,086	2.84%		34	New Mexico	56,192	0.73%
10	Pennsylvania	203,362	2.64%		35	Mississippi	47,818	0.62%
11	Washington	201,301	2.61%		36	Nebraska	46,634	0.61%
12	North Carolina	177,426	2.30%		37	Hawaii	44,946	0.58%
13	Arizona	167,121	2.17%		38	Nevada	37,401	0.49%
14	Virginia	165,343	2.15%		39	Maine	28,928	0.38%
15	Massachusetts	141,933	1.84%		40	Rhode Island	27,049	0.35%
16	Maryland	141,509	1.84%		41	Idaho	26,893	0.35%
17	Missouri	139,648	1.81%		42	Montana	25,921	0.34%
18	Louisiana	139,141	1.81%		43	West Virginia	25,147	0.33%
19	Indiana	138,335	1.80%		44	New Hampshire	24,964	0.32%
20	Wisconsin	134,046	1.74%		45	Delaware	19,824	0.26%
21	Colorado	128,331	1.67%		46	Alaska	15,911	0.21%
22	Minnesota	119,526	1.55%		47	Vermont	15,591	0.20%
23	Oregon	113,872	1.48%		48	North Dakota	14,007	0.18%
24	Tennessee	106,052	1.38%		49	Wyoming	13,432	0.17%
25	Alabama	103,282	1.34%		50	South Dakota	13,255	0.17%

	District of Columbia	28,624	0.37%

Source: U.S. Department of Justice, Federal Bureau of Investigation
    "Crime in the United States 1988" (Uniform Crime Reports, 1988)
*Larceny and theft is the unlawful taking of property. Attempts are included.

Larceny and Theft Rate in 1988

National Rate = 3,135 Larcenies and Thefts per 100,000 Population*

RANK	STATE	RATE
1	Arizona	4,822
2	Florida	4,761
3	Texas	4,408
4	Washington	4,358
5	Utah	4,239
6	Oregon	4,154
7	Hawaii	4,112
8	Colorado	3,901
9	New Mexico	3,721
10	Nevada	3,528
11	Georgia	3,496
12	California	3,315
13	Michigan	3,287
14	Montana	3,224
15	Louisiana	3,148
16	New York	3,134
17	Alaska	3,102
18	Kansas	3,093
19	Illinois	3,076
20	Maryland	3,047
21	Delaware	3,004
22	Oklahoma	2,955
23	South Carolina	2,950
24	Nebraska	2,913
25	Wyoming	2,852

RANK	STATE	RATE
26	New Jersey	2,838
27	Connecticut	2,810
28	Vermont	2,804
29	Iowa	2,803
30	Minnesota	2,776
31	Ohio	2,763
32	Wisconsin	2,759
33	Virginia	2,758
34	North Carolina	2,719
35	Rhode Island	2,718
36	Missouri	2,717
37	Idaho	2,692
38	Alabama	2,503
39	Arkansas	2,492
40	Indiana	2,481
41	Massachusetts	2,418
42	Maine	2,399
43	New Hampshire	2,276
44	Tennessee	2,156
45	North Dakota	2,113
46	South Dakota	1,854
47	Mississippi	1,820
48	Kentucky	1,793
49	Pennsylvania	1,691
50	West Virginia	1,335

District of Columbia   4,617

Source: U.S. Department of Justice, Federal Bureau of Investigation
    "Crime in the United States 1988" (Uniform Crime Reports, 1988)
*Larceny and theft is the unlawful taking of property. Attempts are included.

Percent Change in Number of Larcenies and Thefts: 1988 to 1992

National Percent Change = 2.72% Increase*

RANK	STATE	PERCENT CHANGE	RANK	STATE	PERCENT CHANGE
1	Alaska	30.27	26	California	3.74
2	Nevada	24.90	27	Kentucky	3.71
3	Mississippi	23.07	28	Maine	3.59
4	North Carolina	22.71	29	North Dakota	3.51
5	Tennessee	20.63	30	Washington	3.21
6	Wyoming	19.14	31	Delaware	3.00
7	Maryland	16.77	32	Missouri	2.61
8	West Virginia	16.12	33	Colorado	2.21
9	South Dakota	15.96	34	New Mexico	1.57
10	Alabama	14.06	35	Florida	1.51
11	Indiana	13.62	36	Illinois	1.26
12	Montana	12.82	37	Ohio	(0.19)
13	Minnesota	12.74	38	Massachusetts	(0.23)
13	South Carolina	12.74	39	Connecticut	(1.77)
15	Hawaii	12.45	40	Michigan	(2.03)
16	Virginia	12.19	41	Iowa	(2.09)
17	Idaho	11.64	42	Oklahoma	(2.32)
18	Pennsylvania	10.22	43	Oregon	(4.04)
19	Georgia	10.21	44	New Hampshire	(4.85)
20	Louisiana	9.92	45	Arizona	(5.43)
21	Arkansas	9.82	46	New Jersey	(5.66)
22	Wisconsin	9.07	47	Texas	(6.74)
23	Utah	7.38	48	Rhode Island	(11.08)
24	Nebraska	5.38	49	New York	(11.62)
25	Kansas	4.68	50	Vermont	(13.37)

District of Columbia   7.12

Source: Morgan Quitno Corporation using data from U.S. Department of Justice, Federal Bureau of Investigation
   "Crime in the United States" (Uniform Crime Reports, 1988 and 1992 editions)
*Larceny and theft is the unlawful taking of property. Attempts are included.

Percent Change in Rate of Larcenies and Thefts: 1988 to 1992

National Percent Change = 1.02% Decrease*

RANK	STATE	PERCENT CHANGE	RANK	STATE	PERCENT CHANGE
1	Mississippi	23.70	26	Missouri	1.56
2	West Virginia	20.71	27	Maine	1.14
3	Wyoming	20.41	28	Illinois	0.52
4	Tennessee	18.11	29	Utah	0.14
5	North Carolina	17.01	30	Nevada	(0.22)
6	South Dakota	16.61	31	Oklahoma	(0.77)
7	Alaska	13.84	32	Iowa	(1.31)
8	Alabama	13.79	33	Delaware	(1.34)
9	Louisiana	13.33	34	Ohio	(1.51)
10	Indiana	11.89	35	Massachusetts	(2.36)
11	Arkansas	10.88	36	Connecticut	(2.96)
12	Maryland	10.50	37	New Mexico	(2.99)
13	Pennsylvania	10.38	38	Colorado	(3.10)
14	Montana	10.08	39	Michigan	(3.45)
15	South Carolina	9.31	40	California	(5.35)
16	Minnesota	8.35	41	New Hampshire	(6.06)
17	North Dakota	7.88	42	New Jersey	(6.50)
18	Hawaii	5.96	43	Florida	(6.86)
19	Wisconsin	5.83	44	Washington	(7.18)
20	Virginia	5.47	45	Texas	(11.37)
21	Nebraska	5.05	46	Oregon	(11.64)
22	Idaho	4.52	47	Rhode Island	(11.95)
23	Georgia	4.49	48	New York	(12.71)
24	Kansas	3.19	49	Arizona	(14.46)
25	Kentucky	2.76	50	Vermont	(15.49)

District of Columbia   12.76

Source: Morgan Quitno Corporation using data from U.S. Department of Justice, Federal Bureau of Investigation
   "Crime in the United States" (Uniform Crime Reports, 1988 and 1992 editions)
*Larceny and theft is the unlawful taking of property. Attempts are included.

Motor Vehicle Thefts in 1988

National Total = 1,432,916 Motor Vehicle Thefts*

RANK	STATE	VEHICLE THEFTS	%	RANK	STATE	VEHICLE THEFTS	%
1	California	265,913	18.56%	26	Wisconsin	13,076	0.91%
2	New York	153,898	10.74%	27	Alabama	11,007	0.77%
3	Texas	134,256	9.37%	28	South Carolina	10,642	0.74%
4	Florida	94,694	6.61%	29	Rhode Island	8,238	0.57%
5	Illinois	69,876	4.88%	30	Kentucky	6,904	0.48%
6	New Jersey	69,046	4.82%	31	Nevada	6,351	0.44%
7	Michigan	68,920	4.81%	32	Kansas	6,032	0.42%
8	Massachusetts	52,399	3.66%	33	New Mexico	5,888	0.41%
9	Pennsylvania	51,333	3.58%	34	Arkansas	5,156	0.36%
10	Ohio	43,405	3.03%	35	Iowa	4,596	0.32%
11	Georgia	35,502	2.48%	36	Mississippi	4,371	0.31%
12	Maryland	31,213	2.18%	37	Hawaii	3,978	0.28%
13	Tennessee	26,701	1.86%	38	Utah	3,648	0.25%
14	Missouri	22,325	1.56%	39	West Virginia	3,046	0.21%
15	Washington	19,996	1.40%	40	Nebraska	3,023	0.21%
16	Louisiana	19,929	1.39%	41	New Hampshire	2,498	0.17%
17	Connecticut	19,899	1.39%	42	Maine	2,469	0.17%
18	Indiana	19,705	1.38%	43	Alaska	2,334	0.16%
19	Oklahoma	18,152	1.27%	44	Delaware	2,001	0.14%
20	Virginia	18,084	1.26%	45	Idaho	1,761	0.12%
21	North Carolina	16,340	1.14%	46	Montana	1,740	0.12%
22	Oregon	16,293	1.14%	47	Vermont	1,097	0.08%
23	Arizona	15,914	1.11%	48	North Dakota	786	0.05%
24	Minnesota	14,609	1.02%	49	South Dakota	683	0.05%
25	Colorado	13,885	0.97%	50	Wyoming	671	0.05%
					District of Columbia	8,633	0.60%

Source: U.S. Department of Justice, Federal Bureau of Investigation

"Crime in the United States 1988" (Uniform Crime Reports, 1988)

*The theft or attempted theft of a self-propelled vehicle. Excludes motorboats, construction equipment, airplanes, and farming equipment.

Motor Vehicle Theft Rate in 1988

National Rate = 583 Motor Vehicle Thefts per 100,000 Population*

RANK	STATE	RATE	RANK	STATE	RATE
1	California	944	26	Hawaii	364
2	New Jersey	894	27	Indiana	353
3	Massachusetts	893	28	Minnesota	339
4	New York	860	29	South Carolina	305
5	Rhode Island	828	30	Delaware	303
6	Texas	800	31	Virginia	302
7	Florida	765	32	Wisconsin	269
8	Michigan	741	33	Alabama	267
9	Maryland	672	34	North Carolina	250
10	Connecticut	614	35	Kansas	243
11	Illinois	605	36	New Hampshire	228
12	Nevada	599	37	Montana	216
13	Oregon	594	37	Utah	216
14	Oklahoma	556	39	Arkansas	213
15	Georgia	555	40	Maine	205
16	Tennessee	543	41	Vermont	197
17	Arizona	459	42	Nebraska	189
18	Alaska	455	43	Kentucky	186
19	Louisiana	451	44	Idaho	176
20	Missouri	434	45	Mississippi	166
21	Washington	433	46	Iowa	162
22	Pennsylvania	427	46	West Virginia	162
23	Colorado	422	48	Wyoming	142
24	Ohio	399	49	North Dakota	119
25	New Mexico	390	50	South Dakota	96

District of Columbia   1,392

Source: U.S. Department of Justice, Federal Bureau of Investigation

"Crime in the United States 1988" (Uniform Crime Reports, 1988)

*The theft or attempted theft of a self-propelled vehicle. Excludes motorboats, construction equipment, airplanes, and farming equipment.

Percent Change in Number of Motor Vehicle Thefts: 1988 to 1992

National Percent Change = 12.42% Increase*

RANK	STATE	PERCENT CHANGE	RANK	STATE	PERCENT CHANGE
1	Mississippi	101.26	26	Georgia	9.61
2	Arizona	97.82	27	Pennsylvania	9.42
3	Wisconsin	65.23	28	Hawaii	9.38
4	Arkansas	53.22	29	Minnesota	8.91
5	Nevada	45.73	30	Tennessee	8.37
6	Alabama	36.12	31	Texas	8.06
7	Kansas	35.43	32	Virginia	7.76
8	Louisiana	35.11	33	Nebraska	6.68
9	Indiana	29.39	34	Delaware	5.40
10	Colorado	27.20	35	South Dakota	5.27
11	Alaska	25.02	36	Wyoming	4.47
12	Washington	21.09	37	Illinois	3.01
13	North Dakota	20.87	38	New Mexico	1.46
14	California	20.38	39	Oregon	(2.53)
15	North Carolina	20.03	40	West Virginia	(2.56)
16	Ohio	19.54	41	Iowa	(2.65)
17	Connecticut	19.10	42	Idaho	(4.66)
18	Utah	18.23	43	New Jersey	(8.00)
19	Florida	17.94	44	Oklahoma	(8.54)
20	Kentucky	17.73	45	Rhode Island	(9.41)
21	South Carolina	16.92	46	Massachusetts	(9.51)
22	Missouri	15.70	47	New Hampshire	(13.33)
23	Maryland	14.23	48	Michigan	(14.31)
24	Montana	10.52	49	Maine	(27.99)
25	New York	9.76	50	Vermont	(45.31)

District of Columbia   5.62

Source: Morgan Quitno Corporation using data from U.S. Department of Justice, Federal Bureau of Investigation
    "Crime in the United States" (Uniform Crime Reports, 1988 and 1992 editions)
*The theft or attempted theft of a self-propelled vehicle. Excludes motorboats, construction equipment, airplanes, and farming equipment.

Percent Change in Rate of Motor Vehicle Thefts: 1988 to 1992

National Percent Change = 8.32% Increase*

RANK	STATE	PERCENT CHANGE	RANK	STATE	PERCENT CHANGE
1	Mississippi	102.71	26	Montana	8.06
2	Arizona	78.98	27	Nebraska	6.24
3	Wisconsin	60.41	28	Tennessee	6.06
4	Arkansas	54.60	29	Wyoming	5.92
5	Louisiana	39.27	30	South Dakota	5.31
6	Alabama	35.69	31	Minnesota	4.78
7	Kansas	33.25	32	Georgia	3.86
8	Indiana	27.56	33	Hawaii	3.05
9	North Dakota	25.55	34	Texas	2.71
10	Colorado	20.62	35	Illinois	2.28
11	Ohio	18.05	36	Virginia	1.19
12	Connecticut	17.64	37	West Virginia	1.11
13	Nevada	16.43	38	Delaware	1.02
14	Kentucky	16.40	39	Iowa	(1.79)
15	North Carolina	14.64	40	New Mexico	(3.10)
16	Missouri	14.61	41	Oklahoma	(7.05)
17	South Carolina	13.25	42	New Jersey	(8.77)
18	Utah	10.14	43	Oregon	(10.19)
19	California	9.86	44	Rhode Island	(10.31)
20	Pennsylvania	9.53	45	Idaho	(10.57)
21	Alaska	9.25	46	Massachusetts	(11.48)
22	Washington	8.89	47	New Hampshire	(14.52)
23	New York	8.41	48	Michigan	(15.55)
24	Florida	8.24	49	Maine	(29.76)
25	Maryland	8.10	50	Vermont	(46.55)
				District of Columbia	11.21

Source: Morgan Quitno Corporation using data from U.S. Department of Justice, Federal Bureau of Investigation
   "Crime in the United States" (Uniform Crime Reports, 1988 and 1992 editions)
*The theft or attempted theft of a self-propelled vehicle. Excludes motorboats, construction equipment, airplanes, and farming equipment.

Percent of Crimes Cleared in 1991

National Percent = 21.2% of Crimes*

RANK	STATE	PERCENT	RANK	STATE	PERCENT
1	North Dakota	34.5	26	Mississippi	22.3
2	Maine	30.6	27	Tennessee	22.2
3	Vermont	30.2	28	Washington	22.0
4	Wyoming	29.4	29	Arizona	21.8
5	South Dakota	29.3	30	Florida	21.7
6	Idaho	29.2	31	California	21.3
7	Utah	28.5	32	Illinois	21.2
8	Nebraska	28.3	33	Connecticut	21.1
9	Alaska	27.8	33	Ohio	21.1
10	Kentucky	26.6	35	Hawaii	21.0
11	Virginia	26.2	36	Louisiana	20.6
12	Delaware	25.7	37	Georgia	20.5
13	Pennsylvania	25.0	38	Indiana	20.4
14	Colorado	24.7	38	Oklahoma	20.4
15	Arkansas	24.4	40	Texas	20.1
16	Wisconsin	24.1	41	Nevada	19.6
17	Oregon	23.6	42	New Jersey	19.3
18	Missouri	23.3	43	Minnesota	17.7
18	North Carolina	23.3	43	New York	17.7
20	New Mexico	23.1	45	Rhode Island	16.7
21	West Virginia	22.9	46	New Hampshire	16.6
22	Montana	22.8	47	Kansas	16.0
23	Maryland	22.6	48	Michigan	15.2
24	Massachusetts	22.5	–	Iowa**	N/A
25	Alabama	22.4	–	South Carolina**	N/A

District of Columbia   16.4

Source: U.S. Department of Justice, Federal Bureau of Investigation
        unpublished data

*Includes murder, rape, robbery, aggravated assault, burglary, larceny-theft, motor vehicle theft and arson. A crime is considered cleared when at least one person is arrested, charged and turned over to the court for prosecution. Clearances recorded in 1991 may be for crimes which occurred in prior years. Several crimes may be cleared by the arrest of one person while the arrest of many persons may clear only one crime.

**Not available.

Percent of Violent Crimes Cleared in 1991

National Percent = 44.7% Cleared*

RANK	STATE	PERCENT	RANK	STATE	PERCENT
1	Wyoming	75.5	26	Florida	47.2
2	North Dakota	70.0	26	Illinois	47.2
3	Idaho	67.5	28	California	47.0
4	Nebraska	66.7	28	Texas	47.0
5	Maine	64.7	30	Mississippi	46.9
6	South Dakota	63.9	31	Maryland	46.8
7	Virginia	60.5	32	Tennessee	46.6
8	Colorado	60.1	33	Washington	45.9
9	Delaware	55.9	34	Rhode Island	45.1
10	New Mexico	54.9	35	Connecticut	45.0
11	North Carolina	54.2	36	Missouri	44.4
12	Vermont	53.7	37	New Jersey	44.2
13	Wisconsin	53.5	38	Alabama	43.8
14	Kentucky	53.3	38	Oregon	43.8
15	Oklahoma	53.2	40	Georgia	42.9
16	Indiana	52.1	41	Ohio	40.6
17	Arkansas	51.9	42	Alaska	40.5
18	Utah	51.8	43	Louisiana	38.6
19	Montana	51.6	44	Kansas	37.6
20	Arizona	51.3	45	New York	33.7
21	West Virginia	51.1	46	Michigan	29.6
22	Massachusetts	50.3	47	Minnesota	26.5
23	Pennsylvania	49.1	48	Nevada	24.3
24	Hawaii	47.7	–	Iowa**	N/A
25	New Hampshire	47.6	–	South Carolina**	N/A

District of Columbia   37.2

Source: U.S. Department of Justice, Federal Bureau of Investigation
        unpublished data

*Includes murder, rape, robbery and aggravated assault. A crime is considered cleared when at least one person is arrested, charged and turned over to the court for prosecution. Clearances recorded in 1991 may be for crimes which occurred in prior years. Several crimes may be cleared by the arrest of one person while the arrest of many persons may clear only one crime.

**Not available.

451

Percent of Murders Cleared in 1991

National Percent = 67.2% Cleared*

RANK	STATE	PERCENT
1	North Dakota	125.0
2	Wyoming	106.7
3	Idaho	105.3
4	South Dakota	100.0
5	Maine	92.9
6	West Virginia	92.8
7	Nebraska	92.3
8	Vermont	90.0
9	New Hampshire	87.9
10	Oklahoma	86.5
11	Mississippi	85.7
12	Wisconsin	84.5
13	Connecticut	82.8
14	North Carolina	82.4
15	Arkansas	81.4
16	Pennsylvania	80.7
17	Kentucky	80.2
18	Hawaii	80.0
19	Virginia	77.9
20	Missouri	76.1
20	Tennessee	76.1
22	New Mexico	74.8
23	New Jersey	73.8
24	Washington	73.4
25	Alabama	73.1

RANK	STATE	PERCENT
26	Arizona	73.0
26	Rhode Island	73.0
28	Indiana	69.5
29	Texas	69.2
30	Maryland	68.7
31	Ohio	66.5
32	Florida	64.8
33	Utah	64.7
34	Georgia	64.4
35	Kansas	63.6
36	Delaware	63.2
37	Oregon	62.9
38	Louisiana	62.0
39	California	61.9
40	Colorado	61.5
41	Michigan	60.1
42	Illinois	58.6
43	Massachusetts	57.8
44	New York	55.9
45	Montana	53.8
46	Nevada	51.8
47	Minnesota	45.8
48	Alaska	41.4
–	Iowa**	N/A
–	South Carolina**	N/A

District of Columbia   59.7

Source: U.S. Department of Justice, Federal Bureau of Investigation
   unpublished data

*Includes nonnegligent manslaughter. A crime is considered cleared when at least one person is arrested, charged and turned over to the court for prosecution. Clearances recorded in 1991 may be for crimes which occurred in prior years. Several crimes may be cleared by the arrest of one person while the arrest of many persons may clear only one crime.

**Not available.

Percent of Rapes Cleared in 1991

National Percent = 51.8% Cleared*

RANK	STATE	PERCENT	RANK	STATE	PERCENT
1	Hawaii	77.3	26	California	53.2
2	Virginia	73.0	27	Maine	53.0
3	North Dakota	69.6	28	Alabama	51.8
4	Nebraska	68.9	29	Connecticut	50.8
5	Pennsylvania	65.9	29	Louisiana	50.8
6	Wyoming	64.7	31	New Mexico	49.4
7	Idaho	62.7	31	Utah	49.4
8	Delaware	62.2	33	Georgia	47.7
9	Wisconsin	60.8	34	Ohio	47.2
10	Maryland	59.5	35	South Dakota	46.3
11	Texas	58.5	36	Oregon	45.6
12	Kentucky	58.2	37	Washington	44.3
13	Massachusetts	58.0	38	Montana	44.2
14	Florida	57.9	39	Vermont	43.4
14	North Carolina	57.9	40	Arizona	41.7
16	Missouri	57.6	41	Rhode Island	41.6
17	New Jersey	57.4	42	New Hampshire	41.2
18	Colorado	57.3	43	Kansas	35.3
18	West Virginia	57.3	44	Michigan	27.8
20	Arkansas	56.4	45	Minnesota	26.7
20	Oklahoma	56.4	46	Nevada	26.4
22	Mississippi	54.3	47	Alaska	17.4
23	New York	54.2	–	Illinois**	N/A
24	Tennessee	53.9	–	Iowa**	N/A
25	Indiana	53.3	–	South Carolina**	N/A

District of Columbia   73.8

Source: U.S. Department of Justice, Federal Bureau of Investigation
    unpublished data

*Forcible rape including attempts. However, statutory rape without force and other sex offenses are excluded. A crime is considered cleared when at least one person is arrested, charged and turned over to the court for prosecution. Clearances recorded in 1991 may be for crimes which occurred in prior years. Several crimes may be cleared by the arrest of one person while the arrest of many persons may clear only one crime.

**Not available.

453

Percent of Robberies Cleared in 1991

National Percent = 24.3% Cleared*

RANK	STATE	PERCENT
1	Idaho	49.1
2	South Dakota	43.7
3	Maine	41.5
4	Nebraska	40.7
5	Wyoming	40.5
6	Oklahoma	37.4
7	Virginia	36.9
8	North Carolina	34.5
9	Colorado	33.4
10	Kentucky	33.2
11	Utah	32.2
12	Pennsylvania	31.0
13	Arkansas	30.8
13	Wisconsin	30.8
15	New Hampshire	30.7
16	Delaware	30.6
17	Hawaii	29.3
17	Oregon	29.3
19	Alabama	28.8
20	Massachusetts	28.5
21	Arizona	27.9
22	Mississippi	27.5
23	Georgia	27.1
23	Texas	27.1
25	West Virginia	26.7

RANK	STATE	PERCENT
26	Tennessee	25.7
27	Ohio	25.4
28	North Dakota	25.0
29	Washington	24.9
30	New Jersey	24.8
31	California	24.7
32	Connecticut	24.2
33	Illinois	23.9
33	Missouri	23.9
35	Florida	23.4
36	Indiana	23.0
37	Maryland	22.1
38	Vermont	21.4
39	New York	21.1
40	Montana	21.0
41	New Mexico	20.9
42	Rhode Island	19.0
43	Kansas	16.4
44	Louisiana	15.8
45	Alaska	15.7
46	Nevada	13.4
47	Michigan	12.9
48	Minnesota	8.2
–	Iowa**	N/A
–	South Carolina**	N/A

District of Columbia   19.7

Source: U.S. Department of Justice, Federal Bureau of Investigation
    unpublished data

*Robbery is the taking of anything of value by force or threat of force. Attempts are included. A crime is considered cleared when at least one person is arrested, charged and turned over to the court for prosecution. Clearances recorded in 1991 may be for crimes which occurred in prior years. Several crimes may be cleared by the arrest of one person while the arrest of many persons may clear only one crime.

**Not available.

Percent of Aggravated Assaults Cleared in 1991

National Percent = 56.5% Cleared*

RANK	STATE	PERCENT	RANK	STATE	PERCENT
1	Wyoming	78.5	26	Arkansas	57.8
2	Virginia	74.4	26	Illinois	57.8
3	Maine	73.5	28	Oklahoma	57.3
4	North Dakota	73.3	29	Mississippi	56.9
5	South Dakota	72.5	30	Texas	56.7
6	Wisconsin	72.1	30	West Virginia	56.7
7	Nebraska	71.8	32	Tennessee	56.5
8	Idaho	69.4	33	Washington	56.1
9	Delaware	67.8	34	Alaska	55.7
10	Colorado	67.6	34	Kentucky	55.7
11	Maryland	65.5	36	Rhode Island	55.6
12	New Mexico	62.6	37	Missouri	54.1
12	Pennsylvania	62.6	38	Hawaii	51.9
14	Indiana	62.2	39	Georgia	51.6
15	Vermont	61.8	40	Ohio	51.0
16	North Carolina	61.3	41	Oregon	50.6
17	California	60.9	42	Louisiana	49.4
17	New Jersey	60.9	43	New York	47.6
19	Connecticut	60.5	44	Kansas	47.1
20	Arizona	60.2	45	Alabama	46.4
21	Florida	59.7	46	Michigan	37.8
22	New Hampshire	59.4	47	Minnesota	36.3
23	Massachusetts	59.0	48	Nevada	35.5
24	Montana	58.7	–	Iowa**	N/A
25	Utah	58.3	–	South Carolina**	N/A

District of Columbia   53.4

Source: U.S. Department of Justice, Federal Bureau of Investigation
        unpublished data

*Aggravated assault is an attack for the purpose of inflicting severe bodily injury. A crime is considered cleared when at least one person is arrested, charged and turned over to the court for prosecution. Clearances recorded in 1991 may be for crimes which occurred in prior years. Several crimes may be cleared by the arrest of one person while the arrest of many persons may clear only one crime.

**Not available.

Percent of Property Crimes Cleared in 1991

National Percent = 17.8% Cleared*

RANK	STATE	PERCENT	RANK	STATE	PERCENT
1	North Dakota	33.6	26	Nevada	19.0
2	Vermont	29.4	27	Arizona	18.9
3	Maine	29.3	28	New Mexico	18.5
4	Utah	27.2	28	Ohio	18.5
5	South Dakota	27.1	30	Connecticut	18.4
6	Idaho	26.3	31	Georgia	18.2
7	Alaska	26.2	31	Maryland	18.2
8	Wyoming	25.9	31	Tennessee	18.2
9	Nebraska	25.1	34	Alabama	18.1
10	Virginia	23.2	35	Massachusetts	17.7
11	Wisconsin	22.2	36	Florida	17.6
12	Oregon	21.7	37	Louisiana	17.5
13	Montana	21.6	38	Minnesota	17.0
14	Delaware	21.5	39	Texas	16.9
14	Pennsylvania	21.5	40	Indiana	16.8
16	Colorado	21.1	41	Oklahoma	16.7
17	Arkansas	20.8	42	California	16.3
18	West Virginia	20.7	43	New Jersey	16.0
19	Kentucky	20.5	44	New Hampshire	15.5
20	Mississippi	19.9	45	New York	14.0
21	Hawaii	19.8	46	Kansas	13.9
21	Washington	19.8	46	Rhode Island	13.9
23	Missouri	19.7	48	Michigan	13.0
24	North Carolina	19.4	–	Iowa**	N/A
25	Illinois	19.1	–	South Carolina**	N/A

District of Columbia   10.3

Source: U.S. Department of Justice, Federal Bureau of Investigation
     unpublished data

*Includes burglary, larceny-theft, motor vehicle theft and arson. A crime is considered cleared when at least one person is arrested, charged and turned over to the court for prosecution. Clearances recorded in 1991 may be for crimes which occurred in prior years. Several crimes may be cleared by the arrest of one person while the arrest of many persons may clear only one crime.

**Not available.

Percent of Burglaries Cleared in 1991

National Percent = 13.5% Cleared*

RANK	STATE	PERCENT		RANK	STATE	PERCENT
1	Maine	24.1		25	Montana	14.2
2	Virginia	23.3		27	New Jersey	13.9
3	Wyoming	20.8		28	Texas	13.8
4	Vermont	20.7		29	Oklahoma	13.4
5	South Dakota	20.5		30	Alabama	13.3
6	North Dakota	18.9		31	Mississippi	13.2
7	Idaho	18.3		32	Georgia	13.1
8	Delaware	18.0		33	California	12.9
9	Maryland	17.7		34	Ohio	12.4
10	Kentucky	16.9		35	Washington	11.9
11	Massachusetts	16.6		36	Alaska	11.6
12	Pennsylvania	16.3		36	Connecticut	11.6
13	Nebraska	16.2		38	New York	11.4
13	Utah	16.2		39	Louisiana	11.3
15	Hawaii	16.0		40	Indiana	11.2
16	Wisconsin	15.6		41	Arizona	11.1
17	North Carolina	15.5		42	Illinois	11.0
18	Missouri	15.3		43	New Mexico	9.1
19	Arkansas	15.1		44	Nevada	8.8
20	Florida	14.8		44	New Hampshire	8.8
21	Oregon	14.5		46	Minnesota	8.6
21	West Virginia	14.5		47	Kansas	8.4
23	Rhode Island	14.3		48	Michigan	7.7
23	Tennessee	14.3		–	Iowa**	N/A
25	Colorado	14.2		–	South Carolina**	N/A

District of Columbia   11.9

Source: U.S. Department of Justice, Federal Bureau of Investigation
    unpublished data

*Burglary is the unlawful entry of a structure to commit a felony or theft. Attempts are included. A crime is considered cleared when at least one person is arrested, charged and turned over to the court for prosecution. Clearances recorded in 1991 may be for crimes which occurred in prior years. Several crimes may be cleared by the arrest of one person while the arrest of many persons may clear only one crime.

**Not available.

Percent of Larcenies and Thefts Cleared in 1991

National Percent = 20.3% Cleared*

RANK	STATE	PERCENT	RANK	STATE	PERCENT
1	North Dakota	34.1	26	Missouri	22.3
2	Vermont	32.9	27	Kentucky	21.6
3	Alaska	30.9	28	Tennessee	21.3
4	Maine	30.2	29	Louisiana	21.1
5	Utah	29.0	30	Hawaii	21.0
6	Idaho	28.1	31	Alabama	20.9
6	South Dakota	28.1	32	Ohio	20.7
8	Nebraska	26.4	33	New Jersey	20.4
9	Wyoming	26.3	34	North Carolina	20.3
10	Pennsylvania	24.9	35	California	19.5
11	Oregon	24.5	35	Georgia	19.5
12	Wisconsin	24.4	35	Minnesota	19.5
13	Nevada	24.3	38	Florida	19.1
14	Connecticut	23.3	39	Texas	18.8
14	Delaware	23.3	40	Indiana	18.7
14	Mississippi	23.3	41	Maryland	18.6
17	West Virginia	23.2	42	Oklahoma	18.2
18	Colorado	23.0	43	Massachusetts	18.1
19	Arizona	22.9	44	New Hampshire	18.0
19	New Mexico	22.9	45	New York	17.0
21	Virginia	22.7	46	Kansas	16.2
22	Montana	22.6	47	Rhode Island	15.9
23	Arkansas	22.5	48	Michigan	15.3
23	Washington	22.5	–	Iowa**	N/A
25	Illinois	22.4	–	South Carolina**	N/A

District of Columbia   9.1

Source: U.S. Department of Justice, Federal Bureau of Investigation
    unpublished data

*Larceny and theft is the unlawful taking of property. Attempts are included. A crime is considered cleared when at least one person is arrested, charged and turned over to the court for prosecution. Clearances recorded in 1991 may be for crimes which occurred in prior years. Several crimes may be cleared by the arrest of one person while the arrest of many persons may clear only one crime.

**Not available.

Percent of Motor Vehicle Thefts Cleared in 1991

National Percent = 13.9% Cleared*

RANK	STATE	PERCENT		RANK	STATE	PERCENT
1	North Dakota	64.9		25	Minnesota	16.9
2	Maine	44.6		25	Oklahoma	16.9
3	Wyoming	41.5		28	Florida	16.1
4	South Dakota	41.3		28	Pennsylvania	16.1
5	Nebraska	36.5		30	Indiana	15.9
6	Utah	35.1		31	New Mexico	15.6
7	Vermont	34.1		32	Missouri	15.0
8	Idaho	33.5		33	Delaware	14.3
9	North Carolina	31.9		34	Texas	14.2
10	Montana	28.5		35	Alabama	13.7
11	Virginia	27.9		36	Arizona	13.6
12	Arkansas	26.5		37	Tennessee	13.5
13	Kentucky	24.0		38	Nevada	12.2
14	Georgia	23.5		39	Illinois	12.1
14	Mississippi	23.5		39	Kansas	12.1
16	Colorado	22.1		41	Louisiana	11.2
17	West Virginia	20.2		42	California	11.1
18	Hawaii	19.7		43	New Hampshire	11.0
19	Ohio	19.2		44	Connecticut	10.8
20	Wisconsin	18.6		45	Michigan	10.6
21	Oregon	18.3		46	New York	8.2
22	Massachusetts	18.2		47	Rhode Island	6.4
23	Alaska	18.0		48	New Jersey	4.7
24	Washington	17.6		–	Iowa**	N/A
25	Maryland	16.9		–	South Carolina**	N/A

District of Columbia   12.0

Source: U.S. Department of Justice, Federal Bureau of Investigation
    unpublished data

*Motor vehicle theft includes the theft or attempted theft of a self-propelled vehicle. A crime is considered cleared when at least one person is arrested, charged and turned over to the court for prosecution. Clearances recorded in 1991 may be for crimes which occurred in prior years. Several crimes may be cleared by the arrest of one person while the arrest of many persons may clear only one crime.

**Not available.

VII. APPENDIX

Table	Title
A-1	Resident State Population in 1992
A-2	Resident State Population in 1991
A-3	Resident State Population in 1990
A-4	Urban Population in 1990
A-5	Rural Population in 1990

Resident State Population in 1992

National Total = 255,082,000*

RANK	STATE	POPULATION	%	RANK	STATE	POPULATION	%
1	California	30,867,000	12.10%	26	Colorado	3,470,000	1.36%
2	New York	18,119,000	7.10%	27	Connecticut	3,281,000	1.29%
3	Texas	17,656,000	6.92%	28	Oklahoma	3,212,000	1.26%
4	Florida	13,488,000	5.29%	29	Oregon	2,977,000	1.17%
5	Pennsylvania	12,009,000	4.71%	30	Iowa	2,812,000	1.10%
6	Illinois	11,631,000	4.56%	31	Mississippi	2,614,000	1.02%
7	Ohio	11,016,000	4.32%	32	Kansas	2,523,000	0.99%
8	Michigan	9,437,000	3.70%	33	Arkansas	2,399,000	0.94%
9	New Jersey	7,789,000	3.05%	34	Utah	1,813,000	0.71%
10	North Carolina	6,843,000	2.68%	35	West Virginia	1,812,000	0.71%
11	Georgia	6,751,000	2.65%	36	Nebraska	1,606,000	0.63%
12	Virginia	6,377,000	2.50%	37	New Mexico	1,581,000	0.62%
13	Massachusetts	5,998,000	2.35%	38	Nevada	1,327,000	0.52%
14	Indiana	5,662,000	2.22%	39	Maine	1,235,000	0.48%
15	Missouri	5,193,000	2.04%	40	Hawaii	1,160,000	0.45%
16	Washington	5,136,000	2.01%	41	New Hampshire	1,111,000	0.44%
17	Tennessee	5,024,000	1.97%	42	Idaho	1,067,000	0.42%
18	Wisconsin	5,007,000	1.96%	43	Rhode Island	1,005,000	0.39%
19	Maryland	4,908,000	1.92%	44	Montana	824,000	0.32%
20	Minnesota	4,480,000	1.76%	45	South Dakota	711,000	0.28%
21	Louisiana	4,287,000	1.68%	46	Delaware	689,000	0.27%
22	Alabama	4,136,000	1.62%	47	North Dakota	636,000	0.25%
23	Arizona	3,832,000	1.50%	48	Alaska	587,000	0.23%
24	Kentucky	3,755,000	1.47%	49	Vermont	570,000	0.22%
25	South Carolina	3,603,000	1.41%	50	Wyoming	466,000	0.18%
					District of Columbia	589,000	0.23%

Source: U.S. Bureau of the Census
     Press Release CB92-276 (December 30, 1992)
*Estimate as of July 1, 1992.

Resident State Population in 1991

National Total = 252,177,000*

RANK	STATE	POPULATION	%	RANK	STATE	POPULATION	%
1	California	30,380,000	12.05%	26	Colorado	3,377,000	1.34%
2	New York	18,058,000	7.16%	27	Connecticut	3,291,000	1.31%
3	Texas	17,349,000	6.88%	28	Oklahoma	3,175,000	1.26%
4	Florida	13,277,000	5.26%	29	Oregon	2,922,000	1.16%
5	Pennsylvania	11,961,000	4.74%	30	Iowa	2,795,000	1.11%
6	Illinois	11,543,000	4.58%	31	Mississippi	2,592,000	1.03%
7	Ohio	10,939,000	4.34%	32	Kansas	2,495,000	0.99%
8	Michigan	9,368,000	3.71%	33	Arkansas	2,372,000	0.94%
9	New Jersey	7,760,000	3.08%	34	West Virginia	1,801,000	0.71%
10	North Carolina	6,737,000	2.67%	35	Utah	1,770,000	0.70%
11	Georgia	6,623,000	2.63%	36	Nebraska	1,593,000	0.63%
12	Virginia	6,286,000	2.49%	37	New Mexico	1,548,000	0.61%
13	Massachusetts	5,996,000	2.38%	38	Nevada	1,284,000	0.51%
14	Indiana	5,610,000	2.22%	39	Maine	1,235,000	0.49%
15	Missouri	5,158,000	2.05%	40	Hawaii	1,135,000	0.45%
16	Washington	5,018,000	1.99%	41	New Hampshire	1,105,000	0.44%
17	Wisconsin	4,955,000	1.96%	42	Idaho	1,039,000	0.41%
18	Tennessee	4,953,000	1.96%	43	Rhode Island	1,004,000	0.40%
19	Maryland	4,860,000	1.93%	44	Montana	808,000	0.32%
20	Minnesota	4,432,000	1.76%	45	South Dakota	703,000	0.28%
21	Louisiana	4,252,000	1.69%	46	Delaware	680,000	0.27%
22	Alabama	4,089,000	1.62%	47	North Dakota	635,000	0.25%
23	Arizona	3,750,000	1.49%	48	Alaska	570,000	0.23%
24	Kentucky	3,713,000	1.47%	49	Vermont	567,000	0.22%
25	South Carolina	3,560,000	1.41%	50	Wyoming	460,000	0.18%
					District of Columbia	598,000	0.24%

Source: U.S. Bureau of the Census
   Press Release CB 91-346 (December 30, 1991)
*Estimate as of July 1, 1991.

Resident State Population in 1990

National Total = 248,709,873

RANK	STATE	POPULATION	%	RANK	STATE	POPULATION	%
1	California	29,760,021	11.97%	26	Colorado	3,294,394	1.32%
2	New York	17,990,455	7.23%	27	Connecticut	3,287,116	1.32%
3	Texas	16,986,510	6.83%	28	Oklahoma	3,145,585	1.26%
4	Florida	12,937,926	5.20%	29	Oregon	2,842,321	1.14%
5	Pennsylvania	11,881,632	4.78%	30	Iowa	2,776,755	1.12%
6	Illinois	11,430,602	4.60%	31	Mississippi	2,573,216	1.03%
7	Ohio	10,847,115	4.36%	32	Kansas	2,477,574	1.00%
8	Michigan	9,295,297	3.74%	33	Arkansas	2,350,725	0.95%
9	New Jersey	7,730,188	3.11%	34	West Virginia	1,793,477	0.72%
10	North Carolina	6,628,637	2.67%	35	Utah	1,722,850	0.69%
11	Georgia	6,478,216	2.60%	36	Nebraska	1,578,385	0.63%
12	Virginia	6,187,358	2.49%	37	New Mexico	1,515,069	0.61%
13	Massachusetts	6,016,425	2.42%	38	Maine	1,227,928	0.49%
14	Indiana	5,544,159	2.23%	39	Nevada	1,201,833	0.48%
15	Missouri	5,117,073	2.06%	40	New Hampshire	1,109,252	0.45%
16	Wisconsin	4,891,769	1.97%	41	Hawaii	1,108,229	0.45%
17	Tennessee	4,877,185	1.96%	42	Idaho	1,006,749	0.40%
18	Washington	4,866,692	1.96%	43	Rhode Island	1,003,464	0.40%
19	Maryland	4,781,468	1.92%	44	Montana	799,065	0.32%
20	Minnesota	4,375,099	1.76%	45	South Dakota	696,004	0.28%
21	Louisiana	4,219,973	1.70%	46	Delaware	666,168	0.27%
22	Alabama	4,040,587	1.62%	47	North Dakota	638,800	0.26%
23	Kentucky	3,685,296	1.48%	48	Vermont	562,758	0.23%
24	Arizona	3,665,228	1.47%	49	Alaska	550,043	0.22%
25	South Carolina	3,486,703	1.40%	50	Wyoming	453,588	0.18%
					District of Columbia	606,900	0.24%

Source: U.S. Bureau of the Census
Press Release CB 91-100 (March 11, 1991)

Urban Population in 1990

National Total = 187,053,487 Urban Population*

RANK	STATE	POPULATION	%	RANK	STATE	POPULATION	%
1	California	27,571,321	14.74%	26	Oklahoma	2,130,139	1.14%
2	New York	15,164,047	8.11%	27	Oregon	2,003,271	1.07%
3	Texas	13,634,517	7.29%	28	Kentucky	1,910,325	1.02%
4	Florida	10,967,328	5.86%	29	South Carolina	1,905,378	1.02%
5	Illinois	9,668,552	5.17%	30	Kansas	1,712,564	0.92%
6	Pennsylvania	8,188,295	4.38%	31	Iowa	1,683,065	0.90%
7	Ohio	8,039,409	4.30%	32	Utah	1,499,081	0.80%
8	New Jersey	6,910,220	3.69%	33	Arkansas	1,258,021	0.67%
9	Michigan	6,555,842	3.50%	34	Mississippi	1,210,729	0.65%
10	Massachusetts	5,069,603	2.71%	35	New Mexico	1,105,651	0.59%
11	Virginia	4,293,443	2.30%	36	Nevada	1,061,444	0.57%
12	Georgia	4,097,339	2.19%	37	Nebraska	1,043,984	0.56%
13	Maryland	3,888,429	2.08%	38	Hawaii	986,171	0.53%
14	Washington	3,717,948	1.99%	39	Rhode Island	863,381	0.46%
15	Indiana	3,598,099	1.92%	40	West Virginia	648,184	0.35%
16	Missouri	3,516,009	1.88%	41	Idaho	578,214	0.31%
17	North Carolina	3,337,778	1.78%	42	New Hampshire	565,670	0.30%
18	Wisconsin	3,211,956	1.72%	43	Maine	547,824	0.29%
19	Arizona	3,206,973	1.71%	44	Delaware	486,501	0.26%
20	Minnesota	3,056,474	1.63%	45	Montana	419,826	0.22%
21	Tennessee	2,969,948	1.59%	46	Alaska	371,235	0.20%
22	Louisiana	2,871,759	1.54%	47	South Dakota	347,903	0.19%
23	Colorado	2,715,517	1.45%	48	North Dakota	340,339	0.18%
24	Connecticut	2,601,548	1.39%	49	Wyoming	294,635	0.16%
25	Alabama	2,439,549	1.30%	50	Vermont	181,149	0.10%
					District of Columbia	606,900	0.32%

Source: U.S. Bureau of the Census
Press Release CB 91-334 (December 18, 1991)
*Urban population is composed of persons living in densely populated areas and in places of 2,500 or more outside urbanized areas.

Rural Population in 1990

National Total = 61,656,386 Rural Population*

RANK	STATE	POPULATION	%	RANK	STATE	POPULATION	%
1	Pennsylvania	3,693,348	5.99%	26	Oklahoma	1,015,446	1.65%
2	Texas	3,351,993	5.44%	27	Massachusetts	946,822	1.54%
3	North Carolina	3,290,859	5.34%	28	Maryland	893,039	1.45%
4	New York	2,826,408	4.58%	29	Oregon	839,050	1.36%
5	Ohio	2,807,706	4.55%	30	New Jersey	819,968	1.33%
6	Michigan	2,739,455	4.44%	31	Kansas	765,010	1.24%
7	Georgia	2,380,877	3.86%	32	Connecticut	685,568	1.11%
8	California	2,188,700	3.55%	33	Maine	680,104	1.10%
9	Florida	1,970,598	3.20%	34	Colorado	578,877	0.94%
10	Indiana	1,946,060	3.16%	35	New Hampshire	543,582	0.88%
11	Tennessee	1,907,237	3.09%	36	Nebraska	534,401	0.87%
12	Virginia	1,893,915	3.07%	37	Arizona	458,255	0.74%
13	Kentucky	1,774,971	2.88%	38	Idaho	428,535	0.70%
14	Illinois	1,762,050	2.86%	39	New Mexico	409,418	0.66%
15	Wisconsin	1,679,813	2.72%	40	Vermont	381,609	0.62%
16	Missouri	1,601,064	2.60%	41	Montana	379,239	0.62%
17	Alabama	1,601,038	2.60%	42	South Dakota	348,101	0.56%
18	South Carolina	1,581,325	2.56%	43	North Dakota	298,461	0.48%
19	Mississippi	1,362,487	2.21%	44	Utah	223,769	0.36%
20	Louisiana	1,348,214	2.19%	45	Delaware	179,667	0.29%
21	Minnesota	1,318,625	2.14%	46	Alaska	178,808	0.29%
22	Washington	1,148,744	1.86%	47	Wyoming	158,953	0.26%
23	West Virginia	1,145,293	1.86%	48	Nevada	140,389	0.23%
24	Iowa	1,093,690	1.77%	49	Rhode Island	140,083	0.23%
25	Arkansas	1,092,704	1.77%	50	Hawaii	122,058	0.20%
					District of Columbia	0	0.00%

Source: U.S. Bureau of the Census
Press Release CB 91-334 (December 18, 1991)

*Rural population is composed of persons living outside urbanized areas and places of less than 2,500 or in the open countryside.

VIII. SOURCES

Administrative Office of the U.S. Courts
Statistics Division
One Columbus Circle
Washington, DC   20544
202-273-2290

American Correctional Association
8025 Laurel Lakes Court
Laurel, MD   20707
301-206-5100

Bureau of the Census
3 Silver Hill & Suitlands Roads
Suitland, MD   20746
301-763-4040

Bureau of Justice Statistics & Clearinghouse
Box 6000
Rockville, MD   20850
800-732-3277

Corrections Compendium
CEGA Publishing
P.O. Box 81826
Lincoln, NE   68501
402-464-0602

Drugs and Crime Data Center & Clearinghouse
1600 Research Boulevard
Rockville, MD   20850
800-666-3332

Drug Enforcement Administration
700 Army Navy Drive
Arlington, VA   22202
202-307-7977

Federal Bureau of Investigation
J. Edgar Hoover FBI Building
10th Street and Pennsylvania Avenue, NW
Washington, DC   20535
202-324-3000

National Archive of Criminal Justice Data
P.O. Box 1248
Ann Arbor, MI   48106
800-999-0960

National Association of State Alcohol and Drug Abuse Directors, Inc.
444 North Capitol Street, NW
Washington, DC   20001
202-783-6868

National Center for State Courts
300 Newport Avenue
Williamsburg, VA   23187-8798
804-253-2000

National Institute of Justice
U.S. Department of Justice
633 Indiana Avenue, NW
Washington, DC   20530
202-307-2966

Public Integrity Section
Criminal Division
U.S. Department of Justice
1400 New York Avenue, NW
Washington, DC   20005
202-514-1412

Substance Abuse and Mental Health Services Administration
U.S. Department of Health
  and Human Services
5600 Fishers Lane
Rockville, MD   20857
301-443-4795

IX. INDEX

Admissions to prisons 96-99
Agencies, law enforcement 219-221
Aggravated assault, 1988: 426-429
Aggravated assault, arrests for 11-12
Aggravated assault, by weapon used 330-338
Aggravated assault, clearances 455
Aggravated assault, in rural areas 384-385
Aggravated assault, in urban areas 382-383
Aggravated assault, juvenile arrests for 45-46
Aggravated assault, rate 12,328-329,331,383,385, 427,429
Aggravated assault, time between 326
Aggravated assault 11-12,45-46,325-338,382-385, 426-429,455
AIDS, deaths in prison 113-114
AIDS, prisoners with 115-116
Alcohol & drug treatment, expenditures for 164-169
Alcohol & drug treatment, clients by age 162-163
Alcohol & drug treatment, clients by race 156-161
Alcohol & drug treatment, clients by sex 152-155
Alcohol & drug treatment, clients in 150-163
Alcohol & drug treatment, juveniles in 162-163
Alcohol & drug treatment 150-170
Appeal or bond, prisoners released on 108
Arrest, crime clearances 450-459
Arrest rates, violent crime 4,6,8,10,12
Arrest rates 2,4,6,8,10,12,14,16,18,20,22,24,26, 28,30,32,34
Arrests, aggravated assault 11-12,45-46
Arrests, arson 21-22,55-56
Arrests, burglary 15-16,49-50
Arrests, drug abuse violations 27-28,61-62
Arrests, larceny and theft 17-18,51-52
Arrests, motor vehicle theft 19-20,53-54
Arrests, murder 5-6,39-40
Arrests, offenses against families and children 33-34,67-68
Arrests, property crime 13-22,47-56
Arrests, prostitution & commercialized vice 31-32,65-66

Arrests, rape 7-8,41-42
Arrests, robbery 9-10,43-44
Arrests, sex offenses 29-30,63-64
Arrests, violent crime 3-12
Arrests, weapons violations 23-24,57-58
Arrests 1-68
Arrests for driving under influence 25-26,59-60
Arrests of juveniles 35-68
Arson, arrests for 21-22
Arson, juvenile arrests for 55-56
Attorneys, prosecuting 269
Bank robberies 408
Black jail inmates 138-139
Black law enforcement officers 236-237
Black state prisoners 78,89-90
Blacks under sentence of death 89-90
Bombings 409
Bond or appeal, prisoners released on 108
Boot camps, participants 147
Burglary, 1988: 438-441
Burglary, arrests for 15-16
Burglary, time between 346
Burglary, clearances 457
Burglary, in rural areas 392-393
Burglary, in urban areas 390-391
Burglary, juvenile arrests for 49-50
Burglary, rate 16,348-349,439,441
Burglary 15-16,49-50,345-349,390-393,438-441,457
Capacities, prisons 74
Capital punishment 83-95
Car theft, 1988: 446-449
Car theft, arrests 19-20,53-54
Car theft, clearances 459
Car theft, in rural areas 400-401
Car theft, in urban areas 398-399
Car theft, rate 20,358-359,447,449
Car theft, time between 356
Car theft 19-20, 53-54,355-359,398-401,446-449, 459
Cases, federal criminal 259-261

Children and families, arrests for offenses against 33-34,67-68
Children and families, juvenile arrests for offenses against 67-68
Clearances, crime 450-459
Cocaine removals 149
College and university crime 402-407
Commercialized vice and prostitution, arrests for 31-32,65-66
Commercialized vice and prostitution, juvenile arrests for 65-66
Commuted death sentences 94-95
Compensation, victim 216-218
Conditional prison releases 101-102
Correctional institutions, prisoners in 69-82
Correctional officer, inmates per 130
Correctional officers, by sex 128-129
Correctional officers, salaries 132
Correctional officers, turnover rates 131
Correctional officers 127-132
Corrections, expenditures for 189-197
Corrections, payroll 212
Court commitments, admissions to prison through 97
Courts, employment in 267
Courts, payroll 213
Crime, clearances 450-459
Crime, in 1988: 410-449
Crime, property 13-22,47-56,339,359,386-401, 406-407,434-449,456-459
Crime, time between 274,280,287,306,312, 326, 340,346,351,356
Crime, universities and colleges 402-407
Crime, violent 3-12,37-46,279-338,366-385, 404-405,414-429,451-455
Crime rates, rural 364
Crime rates, urban 361
Crime rates 277,283,285,289,292,295,308, 310,314,328,331,343,348,353,358,361,364, 411, 413,415,417,419,421,423,425,427,429, 431,433,435,437,439,441,443,445,447,449

IX. INDEX (continued)

Criminal cases, federal 259-261
Death penalty 83-95
Death sentences, by race 87-90
Death sentences, by sex 84-86
Death sentences 83-95
Death sentences overturned 94-95
Deaths, law enforcement officers 256-257
Deaths, prisoners 110-114,117-118
Defenders, public 271
Driving under influence, arrests for 25-26
Driving under influence, juvenile arrests 59-60
Drug abuse violations, arrests for 27-28
Drug abuse violations, juvenile arrests 61-62
Drug & alcohol abuse services, expenditures for 164-169
Drug & alcohol treatment, clients by age 162-163
Drug & alcohol treatment, clients by race 156-161
Drug & alcohol treatment, clients by sex 152-155
Drug & alcohol treatment, clients in 150-163
Drug & alcohol treatment, juveniles in 162-163
Drug & alcohol treatment, units 170
Drug & alcohol treatment 150-170
DUI, arrests 25-26
DUI, juvenile arrests 59-60
Employees, correctional institutions 122-123
Employees, probation, pardon, parole 124-125
Employment, justice system 263-271
Employment, law enforcement agencies 222-240, 242-245,247-250,252-255
Employment, local police dept 242-245
Employment, sheriffs' dept 247-250
Employment, special police agencies 252-255
Employment, state police dept 228-240
Escaped prisoners 109
Escapees returned 99
Executions 91-92
Expenditures, per inmate 80
Facilities, juvenile 146
Facilities, juveniles held in 142-144

Families and children, arrests for offenses against 33-34
Families and children, juvenile arrests for offenses against 67-68
Female correctional officers 129
Female jail inmates 135
Female law enforcement officers 232-233
Female prisoners 75-77,85-86
Females, in drug and alcohol treatment 154-155
Females under sentence of death 85-86
Guns, crimes involving 285,291-300,316-318, 330-332
Handguns, murders involving 294-296
Hispanic jail inmates 140-141
Hispanic law enforcement officers 238-239
HIV/AIDS, prisoners testing positive for 115-116
Incarceration rate 73
Inmate expenditures 80
Inmates, jail 133-141
Inmates, juvenile 142-146
Inmates, prison 69-79,81-118
Jail inmates, by race 136-141
Jail inmates, by sex 134-135
Jail inmates 133-141
Judges, salaries of 207-209
Judges, state 265-266
Judgeships, U.S. district court 258
Judicial and legal services, expenditures for 198-206
Justice activities, expenditures for 171-206
Justice system, payroll 210-215
Juvenile arrests, aggravated assault 45-46
Juvenile arrests, arson 55-56
Juvenile arrests, burglary 49-50
Juvenile arrests, driving under influence 59-60
Juvenile arrests, drug abuse violations 61-62
Juvenile arrests, larceny and theft 51-52
Juvenile arrests, motor vehicle theft 53-54
Juvenile arrests, murder 39-40
Juvenile arrests, offenses against families and children 67-68

Juvenile arrests, percent of 36,38,40,42,44,46, 48,50,52,54,56,58,60,62,64,66,68
Juvenile arrests, property crime 47-56
Juvenile arrests, prostitution and commercialized vice 65-66
Juvenile arrests, rape 41-42
Juvenile arrests, robbery 43-44
Juvenile arrests, sex offenses 63-64
Juvenile arrests, violent crime 37-46
Juvenile arrests, weapons violations 57-58
Juvenile arrests 35-68
Juvenile custody rate 143
Juvenile facilities, discharges from 145
Juvenile facilities 146
Juveniles, alcohol and drug treatment 162-163
Juveniles, in custody 142-144
Knives, crimes involving 301-302,319-320, 333-334
Larcenies and thefts, time between 351
Larceny and theft, 1988: 442-445
Larceny and theft, arrests for 17-18,51-52
Larceny and theft, clearances 458
Larceny and theft, in rural areas 396-397
Larceny and theft, in urban areas 394-395
Larceny and theft, juvenile arrests for 51,52
Larceny and theft, rate 18,353,443,445
Larceny and theft 17-18,51-52,350-354,394-397, 442-445,458
Law enforcement agencies 219-221,241,246,251
Law enforcement officers, by race 234-239
Law enforcement officers, by sex 231-233
Law enforcement officers, rate of 224-225,227, 230,244,249,254
Law enforcement officers 222-25,228-239,242-244,247-249,252-254
Legal and judicial services, expenditures for 198-206
Life sentences, prisoners serving 81-82
Local and state government expenditures, corrections 189-197

IX. INDEX (continued)

Local and state government expenditures, judicial and legal services 198-206

Local and state government expenditures, justice activities 171-206

Local and state government expenditures, police protection 180-188

Local police department employment 242-245

Male correctional officers 128

Male jail inmates 134

Male law enforcement officers 231

Male prisoners 84

Males, in drug and alcohol treatment 152-153

Males under sentence of death 84

Marijuana seizures 148

Motor vehicle theft, 1988: 446-449

Motor vehicle theft, arrests for 19-20

Motor vehicle theft, clearances 459

Motor vehicle theft, in rural areas 400-401

Motor vehicle theft, in urban areas 398-399

Motor vehicle theft, juvenile arrests for 53-54

Motor vehicle theft, rate 358-359,447,449

Motor vehicle theft, time between 356

Motor vehicle thefts 19-20,53-54,355-359,446-449,459

Murder, 1988: 418-421

Murder, arrests for 5,6

Murder, clearances 452

Murder, in rural areas 372-373

Murder, in urban areas 370-371

Murder, juvenile arrests for 39-40

Murder, rate 289-290,292,295,419,421

Murder, time between 287

Murder, weapon used 291-304

Murder 5-6,39-40,286-304,370-373,418-421,452

Offenses 273-459

Officers, by race 234-239

Officers, by sex 128-129,231-233

Officers, correctional 127-129

Officers, deaths of 256-257

Officers, law enforcement 222-225,228,230-239, 242-244,247-249,252-254

Officers, local police 242-244

Officers, sherrifs' dept 247-249

Officers, special police 252-254

Officers, state police 228-239

Overturned death sentences 94-95

Parole, employees 124-125

Parole, prisoners released on 103

Parole, violators returned to prison 98

Payroll, corrections 212

Payroll, courts 213

Payroll, justice system 210-215

Payroll, police 211

Payroll, prosecution and legal services 214

Personal weapons, crimes involving 303-304,323-324,337-338

Police, government expenditures for 180-188

Police, payroll 211

Police, special 251-255

Prison capacities 74

Prison employees 122-123

Prisoner deaths, by AIDS 113-114

Prisoner deaths, by illness 111-112

Prisoner deaths, by suicide 117-118

Prisoner deaths 110-117

Prisoner releases, conditional 101,102

Prisoner releases, on appeal or bond 108

Prisoner releases, parole 103

Prisoner releases, probation 104

Prisoner releases, supervised mandatory release 105

Prisoner releases, unconditional 106-107

Prisoner releases 100-108

Prisoners, by race 78-79,87-90

Prisoners, by sex 75-76,84-86

Prisoners, change in number 71

Prisoners, escaped 109

Prisoners, executed 91-92

Prisoners, female 75-77,85-86

Prisoners, male 84

Prisoners, serving life sentences 81-82

Prisoners, under death sentence 83-90

Prisoners 69-79,81-118

Probation, adults on 119-120

Probation, pardon, parole, employees in 124-125

Probation, prisoners released on 104

Property crime, 1988: 434-449

Property crime, arrests for 13-22,47-56

Property crime, average time between 340

Property crime, clearances 456-459

Property crime, juvenile arrests for 47-56

Property crime, per square mile 341

Property crime, rate 14,343-344,435,437

Property crime,rural 388-389,392-393, 396-397,400-401

Property crime, universities and colleges 406-407

Property crime, urban 386-387,390-391,394-395, 398-399

Property crime 13-22,47-56,339-359,386-401, 406-407, 434-449, 456-459

Prosecuting attorneys 269

Prosecution, employment in 268

Prosecution and legal services, payroll 214

Prostitution, arrests for 31-32,65-66

Prostitution, juvenile arrests for 65-66

Public defense, employment in 270-271

Public officials, prosecution of 262

Rape, 1988: 422-425

Rape, arrests for 7-8,41-42

Rape, clearances 453

Rape, in rural areas 376-377

Rape, in urban areas 374-375

Rape, juvenile arrests for 41-42

Rape, rate 8,308-310,423,425

Rape, time between 306

Rape 7-8,41-42,305-310,374-377,422,425,453

Releases, from juvenile facilities 145

Releases, from prisons 100-108

Rifles, murders involving 297-298

Robbery, 1988: 430-433

Robbery, arrests for 9-10

Robbery, bank 408

Robbery, by weapon used 316-324

Robbery, clearances 454

IX. INDEX (continued)

Robbery, in rural areas 380-381
Robbery, in urban areas 378-379
Robbery, juvenile arrests for 43-44
Robbery, rate 10,314-315,317,431,433
Robbery, time between 312
Robbery 9-10,43-44,311-324,378-381,430-433,
    454
Rural crime 363-365,368-369,372-373,376-377,
    380- 381,384-385,388-389,392-393,396-397,
    400-401
Salaries, correctional officers 132
Salaries, judges 207-209
Sentenced prisoners 72-73
Sex offenses, arrests for 29-30,63-64
Sex offenses, juvenile arrests for 63-64
Sheriffs' department employees 247-250
Sheriffs' departments 246-250
Shotguns, murders involving 299-300
Special police 251-255
State & local government expenditures,
    corrections 189-197
State & local government expenditures, judicial
    and legal services 198-206
State & local government expenditures, justice
    activities 171-206
State and local government expenditures, police
    protection 180-188
State law enforcement officers, by race 234-239
State law enforcement officers, by sex 231-233
State police, department employment 240
Suicides, prisoner 117-118
Supervised mandatory releases 105
Theft and larceny, 1988: 442-445
Theft and larceny, clearances 458
Theft and larceny, in rural areas 396-397
Theft and larceny, in urban areas 394-395
Theft and larceny, rate 18,353,443,445
Theft and larceny 17-18,51-52,350-354,394-397,
    442-445,458
Thefts and larceny, time between 351
Unconditional prison releases 106-107

University and college crime 402-407
Urban crime 360-362,366-367,370-371,374-375,
    378-379,382-383,386-387,390-391,394-395, 398-399
Vice and prostitution, arrests 31-32,65-66
Vice and prostitution, juvenile arrests 65-66
Victim compensation 216-218
Violent crime, 1988: 414-429
Violent crime, arrests for 3-12,37-46
Violent crime, clearances 451-455
Violent crime, juvenile arrests 37-46
Violent crime, per square mile 281
Violent crime, rates 4,283,285,415,417
Violent crime, rural 368-369,372-373,376-377,
    380-381,384-385
Violent crime, universities and colleges 404-405
Violent crime, urban 366-367,370-371,374-375,
    378-379,382-383
Violent crime, weapon used 285,291-304,316-324,
    330-338
Violent crime 3-12,37-46,279-338,366-385,404-
    405,414-429,451-455
Weapons, and violent crime 285,291-304,316-324,
    330-338
Weapons violations, arrests for 23-24,57-58
Weapons violations, juvenile arrests for 57-58
White jail inmates 136-137
White law enforcement officers 234-235
White state prisoners 79,87-88
Whites under sentence of death 87-88
Wiretaps 272

Arrests

Corrections

Drugs and Alcohol

Finance

Law Enforcement

Offenses

CHAPTER INDEX

HOW TO USE THIS INDEX

Place left thumb on the outer edge of this page. To locate the desired entry, fold back the remaining page edges and align the index edge mark with the appropriate page edge mark.